READINGS
IN ART HISTORY
Third Edition

VOLUME I

Readings

in Art History
Third Edition

VOLUME I • ANCIENT EGYPT

THROUGH THE MIDDLE AGES

Edited by Harold Spencer

Charles Scribner's Sons, New York

Copyright © 1982, 1976, 1969 Charles Scribner's Sons

Library of Congress Cataloging in Publication Data
Main entry under title:

Readings in art history.

Includes bibliographical references and indexes.
Contents: v.   1. Ancient Egypt through the
Middle Ages.
1. Art—History—Addresses, essays, lectures.
I. Spencer, Harold, 1920-
N5300.R38   1982   709   82-5521
ISBN 0-684-17619-X (v. 1)   AACR2

1 3 5 7 9 11 13 15 17 19   F/P   20 18 16 14 12 10 8 6 4 2

Printed in the United States of America

Contents

INTRODUCTION   3

1. *Egyptian Art*   7
   WILLIAM STEVENSON SMITH

2. *Dramatic and Scenic Coherence in Assyrian Art*   21
   HENRIETTE A. GROENEWEGEN-FRANKFORT

3. *The General Characteristics of Greek Sculpture*   35
   GISELA M. A. RICHTER

4. *Art and Experience in Ancient Greece*   51
   J. J. POLLITT

5. *The Parthenon*   85
   BERNARD ASHMOLE

6. *The Aesthetics of Greek Architecture*   111
   RHYS CARPENTER

7. *Hellenistic Art*   129
   GEORGE M. A. HANFMANN

8. *Roman Architecture*   149
   WILLIAM L. MAC DONALD

9. *The Great Frieze in the Villa of the Mysteries*   173
   OTTO J. BRENDEL

CONTENTS

10. *Origins of Christian Iconography*   213
    ANDRÉ GRABAR

11. *Byzantine Mosaics*   235
    OTTO DEMUS

12. *The Origins of the Bay System*   255
    WALTER HORN

13. *The Romanesque Church and Romanesque Decoration*   289
    HENRI FOCILLON

14. *The Iconography of a Romanesque Tympanum at Vézelay*   313
    ADOLF KATZENELLENBOGEN

15. *Medieval Iconography*   327
    EMILE MÂLE

16. *The Byzantine Contribution to Western Art of the*   355
    Twelfth and Thirteenth Centuries
    ERNST KITZINGER

17. *The General Problems of the Gothic Style*   387
    PAUL FRANKL

18. *The Classical Tradition in the Middle Ages*   415
    ERWIN PANOFSKY

19. *Duccio and Giotto*   443
    JOHN WHITE

20. *Painting in Florence and Siena after the Black Death*   463
    MILLARD MEISS

    INDEX   493

*READINGS
IN ART HISTORY*
Third Edition

VOLUME I

INTRODUCTION

The aim of this anthology is to assemble in convenient form a useful series of modern writings on several aspects of the history of art in the Western world. It is intended primarily, but not exclusively, as a supplement to the texts usually assigned in introductory courses in the history of Western art. To this extent it is a practical measure: the problem of providing multiple copies of supplementary readings on library reserve shelves has, at one time or another, haunted all who teach such courses. The paperbound anthology seems a reasonable answer, however partial the solution it offers. But this anthology's usefulness is not limited to introductory surveys of Western art. Advanced students in the history of art may also consult it with profit, and students of Western civilization and the history of ideas will find it a valuable resource.

The selections in this anthology range from problems of style, technique, iconography, and theories of art to the relevant historical and socioeconomic contexts within which a work of art acquires its form and performs its function. The sequence of the selections approximates customary chronology, so that the readings correlate with traditional periods. Some selections, however, reach beyond the limits of a single period or movement, calling attention to wide and deep perspectives of space and time.

This first volume of the anthology covers the long period from ancient Egypt to the beginnings of the Renaissance and attempts to achieve a reasonable balance between the ancient and medieval worlds while giving proportionate attention to sculpture, architecture, and painting. If the emphasis with respect to ancient art has been lavished on Greece and Rome, it is not to imply for them a greater artistic accomplishment than the older civilizations of the Near East, but simply to recognize the preeminent role that classical antiquity has played in the subsequent history of Western art. If the art of the classical world can no longer exercise the claims it once made on the heart and mind of the West, its survival as an exemplar of beauty or grandeur for many periods of art can scarcely be denied. Variations on antique themes have sprung up again and again in generations grown aware of their inheritance or self-consciously seeking identity through the authority of their ancient roots. Other traditions, stemming from the institution of Christianity and the cultures of the barbarian north, but not untouched by the classical heritage, are the predominant ones in the selections from the latter half of this volume and complete the major lines of influence that have lent their force to the shape and substance of Western art before the age of political and industrial revolutions.

A few examples will serve to mark the variety of approaches encountered among the selections comprising this anthology. Otto J. Brendel's analysis of the frieze in the Villa of the Mysteries at Pompeii is a model of the thorough step-by-step process of deciphering an enigma. In this selection the breadth of scholarship is matched by the concentrated focus and sensitivity of the scholar's visual perceptions, a complementary relationship that should be noted by the student of art history. An integrative thrust is also apparent in the selection by Millard Meiss, which examines with fine discrimination the correlations between art and the religious and socioeconomic contexts of late medieval Italy.

The selections by Henriette Groenewegen-Frankfort and Otto Demus, on Assyrian and Byzantine art, respectively, not only define the essential features of these traditions but emphasize the vital bond between form and content. Of special interest in the selection by Demus is the commentary on the relationship between the Byzantine image and its beholder. John White's remarks on Duccio and his contemporaries, while stressing the mutuality of form and content, also provide substance for reflection on such matters as attribution, conservation practices, and late medieval workshops.

While the selection from J. J. Pollitt's study of art and experience in Classical Greece is an excellent integrative overview of a vital era in the art of the ancient world, Bernard Ashmole's discussion on the Parthenon focuses on a single monument, its construction, form, and sculptural decoration.

The excerpts from Emile Mâle's classic work on Gothic art deal with iconographical interpretations, as do those from Adolf Katzenellenbogen's fine study of the meaning of the tympanum at Vézelay,

Introduction

whereas the selection by Rhys Carpenter on Greek architecture emphasizes aesthetic and formal considerations.

There is yet another aspect to the variety encountered in this anthology. The editor has selected writings that vary in the degree of difficulty they present to the reader, thereby increasing the flexibility of the anthology in meeting the diverse needs it addresses in fulfilling its functions.

In many instances the footnotes that accompanied the original publication have been reduced or eliminated, sacrifices to the requirements of available space. In such cases, the function of this anthology as a series of supplementary readings in undergraduate courses of a generalized nature has been the guiding principle, but many footnotes leading to specialized study have been retained.

Although illustrations were limited by necessity, the editor has included as many as possible in an effort to enhance the usefulness of the anthology. They have been placed wherever possible adjacent to the relevant portions of the text. In some instances an illustration from one selection will be found to relate directly or peripherally to another reading. The choice of illustrations also permits comparisons and suggests problems of art history that lie outside the subject matter of the selections they illustrate.

The headnotes accompanying individual selections or groups of selections serve chiefly as bibliographical devices and have been kept somewhat lean so as not to impinge on space better served by the selected readings than by the editor's intrusions. Furthermore, each instructor who uses this anthology will have personal devices for presenting problems in art history. The anthologist would, therefore, defer to the reader by allowing the selections to speak for themselves. The bibliographical references cited in the headnotes are limited to works in English since this anthology is intended primarily for the undergraduate.

Decisions as to what should or could be included were often difficult to make. Important and attractive material was sometimes excluded when it appeared well-nigh impossible to pare it down to the scale imposed by the limitations of space without destroying the sense, unity, and flow of the writer's arguments. Wherever a selection has been edited, the deletions are indicated by ellipses, and when it was necessary to omit some of the illustrations and footnotes, the remaining ones have been renumbered.

INTRODUCTION

No anthology can hope to serve fully the needs of every situation in which it might be used. There is a peculiar inevitability about this condition, manifest in the dilemma of the anthologist and in the refrain of his critics.

It would be ungracious to end this introduction without acknowledging my debt to the scholarship of others too numerous to mention here, and to the contributions of my own teachers, colleagues, and students over the years; to Helen McInnis, Edith Poor, Mary Ward, and Shelley Weinberger at Scribners for their devotion to this project; and to my wife, Editha Spencer, whose perceptions have contributed so much to the shaping of my own.

HAROLD SPENCER

1. EGYPTIAN ART

William Stevenson Smith

INTRODUCTION

From the edge of the eastern plateau that overlooks the modern city of Cairo the panorama that stretches far to the north and south and westward across the Nile to the desert can be read as a symbolic triad: the river which of old gave life to the valley, the great city affirming the continuity of that life, and far to the west on the edge of the desert, the eternal geometry of the Old Kingdom's pyramids. This heraldic confrontation of past and present to the axis of the Nile is a reminder that permanence was a basic dimension of ancient Egypt and the art it produced. So much of this art comes from the ancient tombs that the impulse is strong to view it as an art obsessed with death. But the statues of the dead do not close their eyes, servant statues administer to their needs, and the walls of the tombs celebrate the activities of life—the hunt, the harvest, and the feast. The life in the world of the tombs goes on like the unending cycle of the river's seasons.

The selection that follows, by an eminent Egyptologist, is an excellent introduction to both the forms and content of Egyptian art; but, more than that, the selection joins this art to the wider context of the eastern Mediterranean world, a direction the author explored in detail in a later work, *Interconnections in the Ancient Near East* (1965).

For a general survey of the Egyptian civilization the best work is John A. Wilson, *The Burden of Egypt* (1951), available in a paperbound edition as *The Culture of Ancient Egypt*. An excellent brief survey of Egyptian art is Cyril Aldred, *Development of Ancient Egyptian Art 3200–1315* B.C., 3 vols. (1949–1962). Other works are W. Stevenson Smith, *A History of Egyptian Sculpture and Painting in the Old Kingdom*, 2nd ed. (1949); Alexander Badawy, *Ancient Egyptian Architectural Design: A Study of the Harmonic System* (1965); by the same author, the important comprehensive work, A *History of Egyptian Architecture*, Vol. I (1954), Vol. II (1966), Vol. III (1968), of which the first volume traces the period from the earliest times to the end of the Old Kingdom, the second volume spans the First Intermediate Period, the Middle Kingdom, and the Second Intermediate Period, and the third volume covers the Empire or New Kingdom; Ibrahim Noshy, *The Arts in Ptolemaic Egypt* (1937); William C. Hayes, *The Scepter of Egypt*, 2 vols. (1953–59); E. Baldwin Smith, *Egyptian Architecture as Cultural Expression* (1938); Irmgard Woldering, *The Art of Egypt* (1967); Kazimierz Michalowski, *Art of Ancient Egypt* (1969), a well-illustrated work; Erik Iversen and Yoshiaki Shibata, *Proportions in Egyptian Art* (1976); Ahmed Fakhry, *The Pyramids* (1962); Henri Frankfort (ed.), *The Mural Painting of El-'Amarneh* (1929); Arpag Mekhitarian, *Egyptian Painting*, translated by Stuart Gilbert (1956), a popular text especially useful for its colorplates; Henri Frankfort, *Kingship and the Gods* (1948); and H. A. Groenewegen-Frankfort, *Arrest and Movement* (1951). K. Lange and M. Hirmer, *Egypt* (1968), is a handsomely illustrated picture book, and W. Westendorf, *Painting, Sculpture, and Architecture of Ancient Egypt* (1968), is a small picture book with numerous color illustrations. Heinrich Schäfer's 1919 classic is now translated and revised as *Principles of Egyptian Art* (1974).

Ancient Egypt was protected by formidable desert barriers and confined to a narrow river valley. It was less subject to outside influences than the other great early civilization in Mesopotamia, and its culture presents, as one of its salient characteristics, a long, virtually unbroken continuity. In an almost rainless country the regular rise of the Nile every year provided the striking example of a renewal of life with each annual flood and gave the Egyptian a cheerful assurance of the permanence of established things, suggesting the acceptance that life would somehow continue after death in the same way. The peculiarly Egyptian concern with the continuity of life after death in a form similar to that which had been experienced upon earth provided an element in the development of the arts which was not present to such an extent in other countries. Thus, while architecture, painting, and sculpture ordinarily appeared in the service of the cult of a god or to glorify the wealth and power of a ruler, in Egypt we find emphasis laid upon providing a lasting dwelling-place for the dead, the re-creation of life magically in pictures to serve him, and lastly the provision of a substitute in stone for his perishable body.

This striving of the literal-minded and keenly observant Egyptian towards the re-creation of life for the dead man would seem to be intimately connected with the naturalistic elements in Egyptian art, and is primarily responsible for the impulse to produce portraiture which is a feature of the best of Egyptian sculpture (Fig. 1). This worked against the formalizing tendencies which, particularly in Mesopotamia, led more towards the stylization of forms and the employment of geometric shapes. Its naturalistic elements lend a familiar quality to Egyptian art which never seems a wholly oriental creation, although it displays the same approach to representation which is common to all other ancient peoples before Greek times. All pre-Greek peoples give us a kind of diagram of a thing as man knew it to be, not as it appears to the eye under transitory circumstances. In spite of this attitude towards visual impressions, the Egyptian had an instinct to imitate closely what he saw about him. His natural disposition towards balance and proportion, combined

9

1. Ka-aper, called "Sheikh-el-Beled," Wood, 3'7" High, Dynasty V, 2565–2420 B.C. (Egyptian Museum, Cairo)

2. Limestone statue of Zoser, Dynasty III, 2780–2680 B.C., Old Kingdom, 55" High (Egyptian Museum, Cairo)

with a long-maintained tradition of orderly craftsmanship, strikes a sympathetic note for the Westerner.

The availability of working materials is an influential factor which must be taken into consideration. The abundance of good stone was an advantage the Egyptian had over his contemporaries in southern Mesopotamia, who had to import their stone. The shape and small size of the slabs and boulders available to the Sumerian conditioned the rounded forms and somewhat uneven quality of his sculpture. The Egyptian early learned to cut blocks for building-stone, and the sculptor had a plentiful supply of rectangular blocks from the quarry for his work. This may well be a practical reason for his predisposition towards cubical form (Fig. 2) in contrast to the rounded, conical shapes preferred by the Mesopotamian. It certainly allowed for the largeness of scale which is another outstanding feature of Egyptian work both in sculpture and architecture.

Egyptian Art

One is always conscious that the Egyptian has hewed his forms from the stone block and not modelled them from softer materials, as in Crete, where the only large-scale work that has survived is in plaster relief which assumes a plastic form in contrast to the stone-cutter's technique. This has a modelled projection from the surface which is opposed to the Egyptian tendency to maintain a flat plane in reliefs. In contrast to the timeless, static permanence of Egyptian statues, the instinct of the Cretan, who excelled in the fashioning of delicate small figures of ivory, metal, and faience, was to catch an impression of movement and lively action. The Cretan might be said to see things with a painter's eye. The modelling of his reliefs produces the same impressionistic results as does his painting.

The Mesopotamian, on the other hand, tends away from natural forms in his sculpture and towards formal patterns. There is nothing in Egypt like the way in which the surfaces of the human face of one of the great Assyrian bulls are enlivened by unrealistic but superbly decorative undercuttings and contrasts in planes. It is as though the craftsman's preoccupation with seal engraving impelled him to approach larger works with the formal equipment developed in that craft as well as in textile-making and metal-work. Metal seems to have been a particularly congenial medium, and it is probably no accident that one of the Mesopotamian's finest early creations in sculpture is the magnificent Akkadian copper head from Nineveh.[1]

The marvellous facility with which huge stones were handled became one of the outstanding characteristics of Egyptian architecture. Enduring stone forms were chiefly reserved for the building of temples and tombs, while secular architecture continued to employ sun-dried bricks and wood. This lighter construction has largely disappeared with the destruction of the cities in the Nile valley and the gradual accumulation of silt from the river's annual flood. More has survived of the domestic architecture of the New Kingdom than of other periods, particularly in the Palace of Amenhotep III and at Tell el Amarna. This material, much of which is not well known, helps to balance the impression gained from the overwhelming mass of evidence which is derived from tombs. The excellent preservation of so much which represents the peculiarly Egyptian emphasis upon tomb architecture might have produced a distorted picture if it were not for the beliefs which caused so many personal possessions to be buried in the tombs and so much of the daily life to be represented on the walls of the tomb chapel. A great deal is reflected of what must once have existed in the cities and on the country estates. In the stone buildings, as well as in the pictures, there is evident a particularly happy facility for the adaptation of plant-forms to conventionalized design, especially in the shapes of columnar support. The palaces of the New Kingdom have preserved also something of a purely decorative use of naturalistically represented plant and animal life in ceiling- and floor-paintings, as well as on minor wall-spaces. Something of this sort must have occurred earlier in house decoration.

The covering of wall-surfaces with scenes representing the ruler's relationship with the gods of the temple of the glorification of his acts on earth seems to have been common to all ancient peoples. However, the Egyptian's impulse to re-create life for the dead man, which caused him to make statues for the tomb, also suggested that he cover the walls of the chapel with representations of life on earth (Fig. 3). A desire for permanence early led to the use of low relief carvings on the stone-lined walls of a tomb chapel or temple. Like the statues, these were painted to complete their life-like aspect. In praising the beauty of these carvings there has been a tendency to overlook the fine quality of the painted detail or the work in paint alone which sometimes takes the place of these reliefs. The usual Egyptian practice, which combined the skills of the sculptor and the painter in creating one unified whole in painted relief, has to a certain extent obscured the Egyptian's very real contribution purely as a painter. In early times he was rivalled in this respect only by the Cretan. Egypt has provided us with an amazingly preserved series of examples in the field of wall-painting which range over the whole long period of Egyptian history. The finest examples of Cretan work are limited to a fairly short range of time at the beginning of the Egyptian New Kingdom, while accidents of preservation have confined our knowledge of the painting of Western Asia to a few examples widely separated in time. Thus Egypt provides by far the largest body of evidence for the development of early painting. Moreover, the Egyptian, with his naturalistic approach and meticulous interest in recording the details of what he saw about him, developed an extraordinary dexterity of brushwork and a manipulation of a wide range of color which is hard to match in ancient times. This is most evident in the breaking up of flat surfaces of color by fine brush-strokes of different hues to suggest the fur of an animal or the feathering of a bird. The success achieved in indicating texture is immediately clear if one examines a rare example of such an attempt outside Egypt in the bull's head from the wall-paintings of the palace of Mari in northern Syria[2] or another head of a bull from the Cretan palace of Knossos.[3] In these the detail is indicated summarily by rather coarse dark lines. The emphasis on the thick outlines of the Mesopotamian example is even more apparent in the paintings of the early Assyrian palace[4] of Tukulti-Ninurta, where the strongly marked bordering of the different parts of the composition has been compared to the isolation of the various elements in the design of an oriental carpet. In contrast to this tendency to reduce forms to a decorative pattern, the Egyptian was interested in the outward look of living and inanimate things, and consequently endeavored to perfect his skill in indicating their surface details. He never loses, however, his sense of the clarity of their form or the use that can be made of line for this purpose. The Cretan, on the other hand, seems impatient with such detailed rendering of an animal or a plant form. He presents us with a creature instinct with life and movement, but his lively, instantaneous, impressionistic treatment will not bear too close analysis as to the accuracy of its details.

Thus, within certain limits of his conventions, the Egyptian approaches his subject with careful, painstaking attention to detail. He has a matter-of-fact rather than an imaginative attitude to the world about him, and when he deals with supernatural things manages with a kind of cheerful assurance to give them a familiar, everyday look. Even the most remarkable monsters are rather dryly conceived, and one of his most surprising achievements was the convincing naturalness with which were combined human and animal parts in composite form for the representation of his gods. The Egyptian mind did not run riot in imagining such strange and frightening spirits as appear on the seal designs of Mesopotamia or Crete. Instead there is an almost complacent acceptance of the orderliness and continuity of existence in a mild climate which was spared a good many of the more frightening caprices of nature. There is no expression of that anxiety with which the Mesopotamian regarded the harshness of nature, nor did the Egyptian's surroundings provide him with the broken mountain crags and seascapes that stirred the imagination of the inhabitants of the Aegean.

The rationalized approach to visual impressions developed by the Greeks was foreign to earlier peoples. The Greeks first contrived a consistent way of drawing figures so that their different parts were related to one another in the manner in which they appear to the eye. They then began to experiment with the placing of these figures against a background in which the lines correspond to a series of receding planes which appear natural to the observer. They ended by developing a system of aerial perspective. The absence of a desire on the part of the Egyptian to suggest depth and volume in his painting and reliefs is only one aspect of an attitude towards representation which prevailed throughout the ancient world. It tends to generalization according to the characteristics of the people who employ it, whether this takes the form of avoiding movement, as in Egypt, or crystallizes a typical aspect of lively action, as in Crete.

Specific historical events, if represented at all, are treated as the symbolical memorial of a victory or some other action of the ruler. Often when a battle is actually represented it is given a form which might be considered an enlarged hieroglyph signifying the idea. This is perfectly illustrated by the complementary use of early word-signs and figure representation on the Narmer palette at the beginning of Dynasty I, but the intimate connection between writing and drawing continues throughout all Egyptian monuments. The beautifully made hieroglyphs are small drawings in themselves and form an integral part of larger compositions, while the wall-scenes are really an extension of the written signs. Inscriptions are also a necessary part of the statues. They provided the essential identity of the owner by giving his titles and name, although the portrayal of his outward appearance is usually generalized without individual characteristics, except in certain outstanding works that we shall see appear throughout Egyptian history at periods of remarkable creative effort. Similarly, the subject-matter of the wall-scenes is restricted to typical aspects of Egyptian life which ordinarily lack the narrative element in the sense that they seldom refer to specific happenings. Backgrounds are summarized, with a few trees, a vineyard, the selected parts of a building, or the upright stems of a papyrus thicket to suggest the setting of a scene. At first there is little attempt to deal with the spatial relationship between these simple stage-props and the men and animals which they accompany. Emotion or individual feeling, and the dramatic relationship

14

3. Harvest scene, Tomb of Mene-na (No. 69), Thebes, Egyptian, Dynasty XVIII, *c.* 1412–1402 B.C. (Photography by Egyptian Expedition, The Metropolitan Museum of Art)

4. Fragment of head of King Sesostris III (Se'n Wosret III), 1878–1842 B.C., Quartzite, 6½" High (The Metropolitan Museum of Art, New York, Carnarvon Collection, Gift of Edward S. Harkness, 1926)

between the figures which this might engender, had little place, although we may find certain typified exceptions such as the mourners at a funeral or the dying forms of animals.

However, within this general framework we shall find a constant enlivening of the whole by freshly observed detail and an increasing interest in the treatment of landscape and architectural backgrounds with experiments in the more complicated grouping of figures and their relationships in space. This reached its most advanced stage in the huge compositions of the Ramesside temple reliefs, where topographical and even historical elements, which had first made their appearance in the Eighteenth Dynasty, are handled in a fashion paralleled only by the later Assyrian reliefs. The royal sculpture of the Twelfth Dynasty also shows a first attempt to portray something of man's inner feeling in the somber, careworn faces of Sesostris III (Fig. 4) and Amenemhat III. At the same time the painter brought an advanced technique and a more subtle color sense to the treatment of textures which had already interested the artists of the Old Kingdom. This was to be carried to a most sophisticated stage in the very extensive work of the Eighteenth-Dynasty painters.

Of course it is the significant changes which appear against the background of the long continuity of Egyptian civilization that quicken our interest. One of the fascinations of the study of Egyptian art is in learning to distinguish the variations in a style which is easily recognizable as belonging to that country over a vast length of time from the fourth millennium down to 332 B.C., when the conquest of Alexander the Great brought Dynastic Egypt to an end. Initially one may have the impression of an endless repetition of forms, but closer examination reveals definite characteristics of the Old, Middle, and New Kingdoms. Then we begin to realize the special qualities of the formative stages which led up to these great periods of achievement. First came that brilliant Archaic Period in Dynasties I–III, when civilization was developing out of the primitive conditions of Predynastic times towards a culmination in the Old Kingdom. This so-called Pyramid Age of Dynasties IV–VI began about 2680 B.C. and lasted for some four hundred years. The freshness of a new beginning appears again about 2100 B.C. in Dynasty XI, and shortly after 1600 B.C. in early Dynasty XVIII, when the Middle and New Kingdoms respectively emerged from the darkness of those times of political disintegration

16

known as the First and Second Intermediate Periods. Once again, towards the end of the eighth century B.C. and after a long period of decline, we find new life poured into the old forms. This renewal was stimulated by the invasion of the Kushite kings of the Sudan (which the Greeks called Ethiopia and the Romans Nubia). It strikes us as a more conscious, archaizing effort, lacking in the spontaneity of earlier national revivals. . . .

In looking back over the tremendous span of Egyptian civilization, it should be remembered that from the beginning of historic times the king was always referred to as a god. He was sometimes simply termed the Good God. As Horus he was considered the earthly embodiment of an ancient deity of the sky whose worship was preeminent at the time of the establishment of united rule over the two lands of Upper and Lower Egypt in Dynasty I. As Son of Ra the king represented the direct descent of royalty from the creator sun god. Finally in his assimilation with Osiris he would continue to reign over the realm of the dead; for he was repeating the cycle of the god who was thought to be an ancient king who had passed through death to resurrection. Such a drastic simplification of the Egyptian conception of divine kingship presents ideas which were developed in succeeding periods, but which had been accepted by the end of Dynasty V when the earliest preserved body of religious literature, known as the Pyramid Texts, appears first on the walls of the burial-chambers of King Unas. These potent spells were compiled in order to assist in the king's translation from his earthly body into the world of the gods, and imply the recognition of his human qualities which must undergo transformation after death.

The manifold nature of Egyptian religious beliefs defies summary treatment.[5] We are accustomed to the attempt to resolve opposing views, but we must expect instead a many-sided approach to a phenomenon, with the result that unrelated explanations are accepted side by side. Formidable difficulties are presented by the accumulation of beliefs over the centuries through an additive process which was reluctant to replace one idea wholly with another or to discard the old. There is both continuity and extraordinary fluidity in this. Two gods may be assimilated with one another without losing their separate entities. Likewise there may be various manifestations of the same god, as in the case of Horus, who as avenger of his father Osiris, or the infant son of Isis, is quite a different being from the sky god whose wings span the heavens and whose eyes are the sun and the moon.

We find a mixture of popular beliefs and the attempts of learned men to explain the emergence out of chaos of that order which was personified by the Goddess Maat, who stood for justice, truth, and right. From the beginning the Egyptian felt that he was surrounded not only by friendly but also by hostile spirits which had to be propitiated. He also sensed the more remote and impersonal quality of the great forces of nature whose personifications were revered as well as the gods of each locality. The local deities had at first appeared in the shape of animals, or more rarely were represented by a plant or inanimate object. Later, when they assumed human form, the animal head was frequently retained, or else the original animal, plant, or object was borne as a symbol on the head. The Goddess Nekhbet wore a vulture headdress, and Hathor was shown with the horns of a cow, although she might still manifest herself in the form of that animal. There were a number of different Hathors, although these were generally associated with the idea of a mother goddess. Her worship was accompanied by dancing and sistra-playing, and she came to be thought of as the goddess of love and joy. As Mistress of the Sycamore she was identified with a tree-spirit in an old sanctuary near the Giza Pyramids and became the patroness of the royal family of Dynasty IV. In similar guise she is later found dispensing food and cool drink to the dead. Through an interchange of functions with the sky goddess Nut and the Goddess of the West she was associated with the western mountain at Thebes, where she received the sun at its setting.

In historic times the term "city god" describes what must have been an early conception of a local deity who presided over a community. Generally he formed the head of a family triad, such as we have in the case of Ptah of Memphis with his consort the lioness Sekhmet and their son Nefertem, whose symbol was a lotus flower. As one of the primitive villages assumed leadership over neighboring communities, its local god acquired supremacy in that district. Later political fluctuations might replace the god of such a district by another, or they might bring about his rise to national importance. In this process one god might take on the attributes of his predecessor or, if his worship spread throughout the country, he might assume the qualities of one of the great cosmic deities. In the latter case he was still associated with a particular place, of which he was considered the lord and in which lay his principal sanctuary. Something of this process can be learned from the sacred emblems on the standards of the Nomes or provinces which evidently reflect the independent districts of prehistoric times. Thus in Hermopolis the ibis-headed Thoth, the god of wisdom, had long supplanted Wenut, but her symbol, the hare, continued to be used on the standard of this Fifteenth Nome of Upper Egypt. Neith, on the other hand, always remained mistress of Sais, the capital of the Fifth Nome of Lower Egypt, whose standard bore her arms, a shield and crossed arrows.

The assimilation of one divine being with another is easier to understand if we can grasp something of the Egyptian's conception of a vital force which was present to a varying degree in all things animate and even inanimate. When, in the creation according to the doctrine of Heliopolis, the sun, Atum-Ra, brought into being Shu (air) and Tefnut (moisture), he spread his arms about them and his Ka entered into them. Here is suggested the transmission of a life-force which remained in continuous operation from the beginning of the world. It was thus that divine nature was imparted to the king, although its full potentialities could not be realized until after death. Lesser mortals were able to share some part of this force.

The Ka was one of three emanations of the spirit. It was related to, but separate from, the Akh and the Ba. These had all originally belonged only to the gods. They approximate to what we think of as the soul and were all associated with the personality of the individual. One could only become an Akh, a transfigured spirit, after death. Its place was in the heavens remote from the body. The Ba, on the other hand, was an animated aspect of the soul which could move back and forth from the dead body. From the Eighteenth Dynasty onward it is pictured as a human-headed bird, drinking cool water from a pool, perched in the branches of a tree, or fluttering down to join the body in the tomb chamber. The Ka is best viewed as a person's vital force which accompanied him both in life and in death. Certain of its qualities were intensified in the person of the king and they were fully possessed only by supreme beings. The Ka had a separate existence and in one sense can be thought of as a double or as a protective genius. It was closely associated with the tomb statue and with nourishment. Through it the dead man was able to avail himself of the food and drink that he had contracted with his funerary priest to present on stipulated occasions at the false-door of his tomb chapel, and which could be supplemented by the offerings pictured on the walls of this chapel.

NOTES

[1] H. Frankfort, *The Art and Architecture of the Ancient Orient,* Pelican History of Art (Harmondsworth, 1954), plates 42 and 43.

[2] Frankfort, *op. cit.,* plate 69A.

[3] Sir Arthur Evans, *The Palace of Minos,* 1 (London, 1921), 529, Figure 385.

[4] Frankfort, *op. cit.,* plate 74.

[5] See H. Frankfort, *Kingship and the Gods* (Chicago, 1948); *Ancient Egyptian Religion* (New York, 1948); J. Vandier, *La Religion égyptienne,* 2nd ed. (Paris, 1949).

2. DRAMATIC AND SCENIC COHERENCE IN ASSYRIAN ART

Henriette A. Groenewegen-Frankfort

INTRODUCTION

When we extract from the long history of representational art the question of how mankind's experience of the space in which it exists has been interpreted, implied, or to what degree ignored in works of art down through the centuries, we are confronted with many answers. One of these has proved particularly persuasive for the past five hundred years. It has conditioned the Western world to a view through space from a fixed point-of-sight, either through the projection of a perspective system developed in the Renaissance, or, more recently, through the optics of a camera lens. The cubist break with this tradition early in the twentieth century, its various offspring, and the mobility of the motion-picture camera notwithstanding, the post-Renaissance fixed point-of-view persists as a norm. That other modes of representation have achieved efficient ends in harmony with the ritual, commemorative, symbolic, or narrative purposes of representational art is, however, confirmed by the example of ancient Near Eastern art and the art of the Middle Ages.

A desire to account for "the eccentricities of spatial rendering" in the art of the ancient Near East was cited by Henriette A. Groenewegen-Frankfort as the stimulus for the study that resulted in the publication of her book, *Arrest and Movement: An Essay on Space and Time in the Representational Art of the Ancient Near East* (1951). The bulk of the text deals with Egyptian art, followed by two shorter sections on Mesopotamian and Cretan art. Apart from analysis of spatial devices in relief sculpture and painting, this study is a particularly fine presentation of ideas concerning the interrelationship of form and content in ancient art, and it bears significantly on the related subject of visual narrative. This latter aspect of ancient art was the theme of a symposium in 1955, papers from which were published in *American Journal of Archaeology,* LXI, 2 (1957). For the student of art history, these works provide, collectively, an excellent introduction to the genesis of narrative composition. The selection from *Arrest and Movement* that follows analyzes the

Assyrian modes of depicting human and animal images in dramatic and scenic contexts.

On the general field of art in the Asian Near East the reader should consult the convenient survey by Seton Lloyd, *The Art of the Ancient Near East* (1961). More detailed information can be found in Henri Frankfort, *The Art and Architecture of the Ancient Orient* (1970); Eva Strommenger and Max Hirmer, *5000 Years of the Art of Mesopotamia*, exceptionally well-illustrated (1964); André Parrot, *Sumer: The Dawn of Art* (1961), and by the same author, *The Arts of Assyria* (1961); Samuel N. Kramer, *The Sumerians: Their History, Culture, and Character* (1963); James Mellaart, *Çatal Hüyük: A Neolithic Town in Anatolia* (1967); Kathleen Kenyon, *Digging Up Jericho* (1974); Pierre Amiet, *Art of the Ancient Near East* (1980); Ekrem Akurgal, *Art of the Hittites* (1962); and for the Persian region, Edith Porada and R. H. Dyson, *The Art of Ancient Iran* (1965).

A good survey of the general subject of spatiality in Western representational art is provided by the following works, in addition to the book by H. A. Groenewegen-Frankfort: G. M. A. Richter, *Perspective in Greek and Roman Art* (1971); Miriam Bunim, *Space in Medieval Painting and the Forerunners of Perspective* (1929); Ingvar Bergström, *Revival of Antique Illusionistic Wall Painting in Renaissance Art* (1957); John White, *The Birth and Rebirth of Pictorial Space*, rev. ed. (1967); and two articles, Beaumont Newhall, "Photography and the Development of Kinetic Visualization," *Journal of the Warburg and Courtauld Institutes,* VII (1944), 40–45; and Winthrop Judkins, "Toward a Reinterpretation of Cubism," *The Art Bulletin,* XXX (1948), 270–278.

In addition, there are a number of works that can profitably be consulted on the subject of visual perception, namely: J. J. Gibson, *The Perception of the Visual World* (1950); Ernst Kris (with E. H. Gombrich), *Psychoanalytical Explorations in Art* (1952); W. H. Ittelson, *The Ames Demonstrations in Perception* (1952); E. H. Gombrich, *Art and Illusion* (1960, 1961); and Rudolf Arnheim, *Art and Visual Perception* (1954). In connection with the latter one should read Gombrich, *Art and Illusion*, pp. 26–27, and Arnheim's review of this book in *The Art Bulletin,* XLIV (1962).

The selection that follows is reprinted from H. A. Groenewegen-Frankfort, *Arrest and Movement: An Essay on Space and Time in the Representational Art of the Ancient Near East* (1950), with the permission of the publisher, Faber and Faber Ltd., London.

ssyrian art, baffling and full of contradictions like so much that pertains to Assyrian culture, brings one most striking innovation: the commemorative reliefs of the royal palaces are entirely secular and narrative. To see this fact in its true perspective more than a mere sketch of historical events and cultural changes would be needed. The shift of power to a northern centre after a period in which Syrian, Indo-European, and other north-eastern influences prevailed in Mesopotamia under Kassite and Mitannian rule, presents a historical problem that bristles with unanswered and perhaps unanswerable questions. Moreover, the archaeological material from the Middle Assyrian period is so fragmentary that we cannot trace even a formal development which would lead up to the reliefs of Assurnasirpal and the surprising boldness of this new artistic venture. All we can do at present is to point out some significant changes in the few extant reliefs and the glyptic of the Middle Assyrian period which appear to have cultural implications and then to see if these new trends can be tentatively correlated with a changed attitude where the rendering of event in space and time is concerned.

Both Frankfort and Moortgat have discussed the degenerate glyptic of Kassite and Mitannian origin and stressed the remarkable freshness of the Assyrian seals which mark a new beginning.[1] The main points of interest for our problem are a new delight in dynamic scenes such as animals on the move or hunters attacking quarry—actual or mythical—and a vigorous naturalism which even affects the traditional antithetical groups of animals, so that their attitudes appear contingent rather than heraldic. Most remarkable is that this interest in animals and hunting develops at the expense of religious subjects. Presentation scenes are altogether absent, such adoration scenes as occur have least pronounced Assyrian characteristics and are stylistically close to Babylonian ones, while the few reliefs of the period which we possess seem to avoid likewise the well-worn scheme of divine and human confrontation. On the earliest one known, an 'obelisk' showing a number of captives being brought before the king, the epiphany of the god Assur consists of a pair of hands emerging from a cloud and handing down a bow as symbol of the king's power.[2] Here divinity was for the first time shown quite literally transcending the realm of man. In the faïence tile of Tukulti Ninurta we find the same god in a more emblematic form—a winged disk containing his feathered figure—in the act of shooting a bow, floating above the royal figure in a battle scene.[3] On two roughly contemporaneous altar stones we see in the one instance the king flanked by the symbols of the sun—not facing its image—and on the other two royal figures, one kneeling, one standing before an altar which again only supports a symbol.[4]

All the available material of the Middle Assyrian period would therefore confirm Frankfort's observation, which he based mainly on later Assyrian glyptic, that: 'the higher power has become inaccessible and direct contact apparently ceased.'[5]

It would be rash to draw the conclusion that the presence of historical scenes on palace walls and a remarkable absence of religious scenes in the temples could be entirely explained by a changing concept of divinity and a different relation between a more transcendent god and man. The part the god Assur played in fertility rites and his connection with the sacred tree[6] are too obvious and at the same time too obscure than that the transcendence of this lord of hosts could be taken for granted. There does indeed appear to be a curious hesitancy in confronting god and man. There is also, as we shall find, cleavage between secular and non-secular—that is mostly ritual—representation, even within the scope of the palace reliefs. For the secular scenes delight in rendering concrete detail, the religious ones shun actuality—if we may use this term to denote a type of religious imagery in which gods appear and act in human form and in situations analogous to actual life. This same cleavage finds expression in yet another way: the textual recording of the king's achievement on building inscriptions loses its character of a religious dedication, which it had had throughout Mesopotamian history and becomes a purely historical record. We find therefore that at a moment when secular art on a large scale makes its first appearance in history, significant changes had already occurred both in religious pictorial idiom and in texts, and that these seem symptomatic of a widening gulf between the world of man and of the divine.

But before we turn to the battle and hunting scenes on the palace reliefs we must discuss yet another innovation which accentuates the distance between secular and non-secular art: a host of winged monsters in various beneficial functions invades the ritual scenes. Now we cannot discuss here the problem of monsters in Meso- potamia nor speculate on the reasons why these should have appeared throughout such remarkably convincing entities, whether they were composite animals, bullmen or merely fantastic creatures. It is a fact that they occur mostly in semi-decorative context and especially in popular glyptic art, so that we may assume that they were at home in the realm of folk religion. The Assyrian winged creatures which appear on the seals have been fully discussed by Frankfort,[7] those on the reliefs are either in human form or animal headed, for the human-headed bull which in gigantic form guarded the palace entrance occurs only once in an actual scene sporting among fishes in a naval battle.[8] These monsters apparently filled a gap produced by a less concrete religious imagination, yet they failed to inspire the artists of the reliefs. Whether or not they emerged from remoter layers of religious awareness, they gained in the hands of subtle and sophisticated craftsmen an—for monstrous form—almost absurd concreteness in muscular detail. Yet, arranged in stereotyped postures on either side of a formalized tree in a ritual act they lose whatever demonic life they may have had originally and are impressive only through sheer size and workmanship. We shall in our discussion of the late Assyrian reliefs ignore all ritual scenes because they are entirely formal and have no bearing on our problem.

The palace reliefs of Assurnasirpal (885–860) present the first narrative art we possess in Mesopotamia.[9] It has been suggested that they might have been inspired by either first or second-hand knowl- edge of the Egyptian New Kingdom reliefs;[10] this is at least a possibility, but even so the differences between the two would be more significant than any hypothetical plagiarism and we shall only refer to the Egyptian ones in order to throw into relief the peculiar and consistent character of the Assyrian work. It is, for instance, very striking that nowhere in the actual battle reliefs the king should dominate the scene either by his size or by his action; the king looks and acts like any of his soldiers. Fighting is throughout at close quarters and slain victims are strewn about the scene; but the defeat of the enemy is not a foregone conclusion: enemy soldiers striding away from the royal chariot turn back and shoot at the king and repeatedly one of them grabs at a horse's mouth in an effort to halt them. The enemy, moreover, never shows abject terror; the fight is fierce and virile. It is also entirely episodic, not a single battle scene contains a clue to its outcome; consequently, the spectator is held in suspense till he moves on to the next episode, where rows of prisoners or a city in flames complete the story. Such scenes lack entirely the symbolical character which made the Egyptian ones a timeless assertion of inevitable royal victory; they show ephemeral events changing before the spectator's eyes from one phase to another. There are no clear breaks in this pictorial epic, nor is action ever suspended; the movement of figures in one direction always seems purposeful even if no explicit aim is indicated; rows of prisoners seem on the march towards their destination, not displayed in a formal aimless stride. Movement is rarely met by counter-movement except in the case of a siege where the town formed the centre of action (in the reliefs of Seti I at Karnak this was never the case) and the attackers were arranged antithetically. In chariot scenes the galloping horses are not tilted diagonally, although the extended forefeet are off the ground. In fact, all horizontals are usually stressed in this case, the reins, the arrows, the prostrate figures under the horse's belly, so that the level movement is unchecked.

The drawing of the horses, in a surprising variety of gait and posture, is throughout superb. The draughtsmen must have known and lived with them as no Egyptian artist ever did, and with a delicate observation—completely absent in their human figures—could render shades of mood and temperament in sensitive horses' heads, beautifully coordinated movement of neck and body in horses starting to pull up, horses swimming, horses straining up a mountain slope when the rider slackens his rein. These creatures move in a scenic space which, if the register groundline is adhered to, will lack all suggestion of topographical recession, but the register acts as horizon so that the scenes appear as real as life. Frequently, however, the horizon line is ignored and figures superimposed without apparent concern about their spatial relation. The effect may vary but the action is usually so closely knit that such 'floating' figures seem part of a coherent group in space. . . . We have one interesting example of true scenic background, though not yet of stage space (Fig. 5), where the royal cortege is seen passing below the city walls. Figures do not yet always appear in pure profile, there is frequently an awkward twist in the shoulder region, though the burly rather amorphous bodies, almost entirely hidden in long garments, do not

5. King Assurnasirpal II's Chariots Passing a Fortified City, relief from Nimrud, Assyrian, 9th Century B.C., 3'4½" by 7'1" (The British Museum, London)

make the non-functional drawing so obvious that it interferes with the impression of organic corporeality which they convey.

Apart from these details of spatial rendering the following facts stand out: the narrative scheme of consecutive scenes in fairly narrow strips has nowhere been abandoned in favour of one which would allow for a dramatic climax, a summing-up of complex event in one pregnant situation; nor can we observe anywhere a tendency to transcend actuality in the manner of monumental art. The story told remains discursive. This may explain the limitations of the experiments made in the rendering of space: scenic space was intended throughout but it merely depended on the choice of episode whether the horizon line of the register sufficed or whether—especially when the action took place on or near water or was spread out over a large terrain—the problem of the disposition of figures in space had to be faced. Topographical coherence then began to form a new preoccupation for the artist.

Under the reign of Assurnasirpal's successor Shalmaneser an important innovation was made which enhanced the character of scenic space: from now on human figures nearly always appear in pure profile, that is, in a definite relation to the spectator's viewpoint. The remains of this period consist mostly of bronze reliefs which covered the palace gates at Balawat.[11] They are narrow scenes arranged in double strips in such a way that the movement of the figures in the upper row is in opposite direction to that of the lower one. This work, obviously decorative in intention, is strictly narrative in character, but though technically bold it is artistically rather dull. The monotony of the depicted horrors, the records of a series of campaigns, is practically unrelieved and the work is on too small a scale to allow for much experiment. In one instance when a non-military event was depicted topographical scenery was ventured on and the attempt made to represent the head of a valley surrounded by mountains on both sides with a subterranean stream visible through 'windows' in the mountainside. Here some kind of recession has been aimed at in rendering the mountains on the far side of the valley; usually, however, all scenes run parallel to the surface.

The rather fragmentary remains from the reign of Tiglathpilesar III, and the reliefs of Sargon show a continuation and further development of earlier trends. Profile rendering is maintained and the superposition of figures in the now slightly wider registers is more frequent. Groups without groundline are put in at different levels . . . so that the general impression is that of a coherent scene in space although the figures are not yet topographically related. . . .

The reliefs of Sennacherib,[12] less subtle, less dramatic than those of his successor Assurbanipal, are full of experiment in the rendering of scenic space and especially in the disposition of figures in depth. The interest is largely focused on complicated activities involving large groups of people and the relation between these and their local setting. It is interesting to see how persistent efforts were made to emphasize spatial coherence as well as unity of action. In a mountain assault, for instance, soldiers are scattered among trees over a wide area marked with the conventional [scaly] pattern of a mountain side, which can only be conceived as receding. One might be tempted to use the term cavalier perspective here, but strictly speaking both it and 'bird's eye view' presuppose a definite, if unusual, spatial relation between observer and things observed, which is totally absent here. It is true that the receding surface of the mountain side has been made more or less concrete by the conventional pattern and that thereby the scattered human figures and trees could be definitely fixed in relation to it and to each other. Yet they give no clue to the observer's viewpoint, because from a high viewpoint which might reveal their disposition as clearly as the picture shows, the trees could not appear in plain front view. It is, however, undeniable that some sort of spatial coherence of figures and objects, and some illusion of recession has been achieved. How important this coherence of receding space was considered can be gauged by the almost absurd insistence on a patterned background which the reliefs show; trees stuck into such a background must of necessity be conceived as spatially related, and if they are super-imposed this can only mean also related in depth.

The same holds good for the marsh scene [in a relief of Sennacherib] where the superimposed islands are so carefully joined by well-drawn strips of water that there is no loophole for spatial ambiguity, each figure, each object is definitely fixed in relation to every other and yet the viewpoint has not been clarified. Again the illusion of a bird's eye view strengthened by the centrifugal arrangement of some of the reed bushes, is destroyed by the front view rendering of others. But nowhere . . . has any of the surface been left blank. The full consequences of illusionistic scenic render-ing, with its challenge of complete spatial coherence, had been accepted.

More ambitious if rather less successful are the attempts to picture the transport of colossi or the making of artificial mounds for Sennacherib's palace. We are far removed indeed from the first Egyptian effort at such a scene. Here the action is very lively and in each of the different versions we possess a definite moment, a definite place has been chosen to mark the actual phase of the event. The most remarkable is that where the colossus has to cross a dip in the ground near a strip of water. While in some other renderings the rows of figures straining at the ropes have the support of a ground-line; here they are merely spread out on an amorphous plain from which the hillock rises where the king in his chariot overlooks the scene. Here again the river in the foreground with its narrow dams and shadufs at work (all given in straight elevation) are incompatible with a high viewpoint which part of the scene would suggest; and the relation between plain and hill on the right is not clear.

Yet the same passionate interest in receding space leads to another curious experiment. The sieges of hill towns or mountain strongholds had already become livelier and livelier, they were now frequently offset against a mountain background which in some cases rose above the town or castle walls. Diagonal scaling ladders had often lent a dramatic touch to the event,[13] now however it became a matter of ambition to render the actual approach of the attacking army on the mountain side. Such an approach is of necessity in a diagonal line and so we suddenly see, instead of ladders, solid paved diagonal paths leading up to the strongholds, and that means, at any rate conceptually, away from the spectator. The effect is weird in the extreme, the more so because in a misguided effort at realism the angle of ninety degrees between these paths and the climbing figures has been maintained so that the soldiers appear to be falling backward. The wild pattern of diagonals nowhere achieves the illusion of recession or of topographical coherence, but the boldness of this attempted short cut at landscape perspective on a vast scale is astounding and unsurpassed till Hellenistic times.

Sennacherib's innovations must have been considered aesthetically barbarous by those who planned the Assurbanipal reliefs, for they did not venture any further in the direction of illusionistic recession. With the restraint of true and very great artists they did not pursue a naturalism already run wild along topographical lines. The most gifted of them either brought their figures back to the relief surface in fairly narrow parallel scenes or bound them by subtle means in a dramatic situation that could dispense with locality altogether. It is true that some of the motifs survived, but it is interesting to note that when an artist indulges in topographical scenes, as when an aqueduct in its setting is rendered and the strange diagonal rivers are obviously inspired by the diagonal paths, the scene is empty of figures and is therefore much more plausible. In [one example][14] the fleeing Elamites are arranged in parallel registers as of old, but the deserted town walls looming above them tier upon tier, reminders of the threat they must have held, make the implicit victory appear an even more formidable achievement than if a lively siege were given. The new restraint is thus dramatically most effective. One other motif in which an attempt at rendering recession had been made before, namely, that of fugitives or looting soldiers leaving a town, has been developed further. Already on a remarkable relief of Sennacherib two superimposed town walls and a vertical row of soldiers leaving the buildings suggest recession. On another fragment[15] fugitives appear to be walking on a mountain contour line. This motif is repeated more plausibly in an Assurbanipal relief.[16] In Fig. 6, however, the looting soldiers are leaving the gate on a road, clearly indicated by a double line, which widens toward the spectator. The figures, it is true, are clinging rather timidly to the boundary line, not walking in the middle of the road, but the effect of their marching downhill and *toward* the spectator

6. Sack of the City of Hamanu in Elam, relief from Nineveh (Kuyunjik), Assyrian, *c.* 650 B.C., Gypseous alabaster, 36″ by 25″ (The British Museum, London)

has been unmistakably achieved by what is virtually true perspective.

However, as we said before, the greatest artists of the period merely arranged their scenes parallel with the observer; they also were great innovators in the matter of rendering space but not recession; dramatic space was what they aimed at and paradoxically this aim was not achieved with human figures in action, but with animals. There is only one extremely 'human' scene of the king on his couch and a queen or concubine sitting upright on a chair at his feet, which also has an odd if restrained dramatic quality. The head of a slain enemy hanging in a tree near the musicians destroys the illusion of domestic bliss and gives to the festivity an overtone of cruel sensuousness.[17]

Otherwise it would appear as if commemoration of the same human, if unhumane, pursuits, the same patterns of warfare, repeated and elaborated now for centuries, must have wearied at least one artist whom we must consider the greatest of all. The historical epic was, as we saw, discursive and though astonishingly inventive in

31

matters of detail, it lacked the very quality of all great art; being time-bound and space-bound, it never transcended the purely episodic. Throughout a period in which the violence of one small nation brought a staggering amount of suffering on countless peoples, pictorial art recorded battle after battle in a scenic display unhampered by metaphysical considerations with a brutal secularity which, for all its freshness and vigour, had something shallow and naïve. Victory was a man-made thing, it was devoid of the symbolical quality which it had had before both in Egyptian and Mesopotamian art, and which it was to gain later on in Greece in a mythical form. And since victory was man-made and ephemeral, defeat also was a contingency; it lacked that touch of the tragic which gave to the Seti reliefs their peculiar dignity. The artist of the hunting scenes took up a motif as old as mankind and as unchanging; in doing so he not only displayed an astounding virtuosity in the handling of animal form, but showed that he possessed the emotional depth which could convey the tragedy of suffering and defeat, of desperate courage and broken pride.

There is nothing in these scenes to detract from the actual or imminent disaster that befalls those who provide sport for the powerful. There is no indication of looalty or background for these groups of hunted horses and gazelles, yet they form a coherent unit in a space we must conceive as a receding plain. The very emptiness makes them appear more vulnerable, more exposed. The gazelles grazing restlessly, warily, appear under the threat of imminent danger; the backward glance of the male leader gives a peculiar tenseness to their movement. In the group of wild horses the possible escape heightens the tension and lends a horrible poignancy to the mare looking back at her young. In the lion hunt disaster is inevitable; here the group on the right has no dramatic unity, each dying creature is alone in his agony, and this lack of spatial as well as emotional coherence is emphasized by the separate groundlines of the superimposed figures. The greatest dramatic intensity is reached not in the group where the royal chariot is attacked with mad fury, but on the right, where the battle is as yet undecided (Fig. 7); a crouching lion and the terrified horse and his rider are separated by the most dramatic of 'significant voids' ever achieved in Near Eastern Art.

It is strange to consider that shortly before the disastrous finale of the Assyrian Empire, the same people under whose dominion the

7. Lion Facing Horseman, relief from Nineveh (Kuyunjik), Assyrian, 7th Century B.C., 5′3″ by 8′9″ (The British Museum, London)

world had shuddered brought forth an artist who revealed the depth of his fear and pity for these doomed creatures and raised his scenes to the stature of tragedy.

Assyrian art, flowering on the periphery of Mesopotamia proper, occurred on the very brink of a new era. Alien to the predominantly religious character of older Mesopotamian work, and bound, as no other form of art, to the secular power of single monarchs whose achievements it recorded, it vanished when this power was exterminated. One may well ask if not a vestige of its influence could be traced in westerly direction, toward the Greek world. So far this question can only be answered in the negative.

N O T E S

[1] H. Frankfort, *Cylinder Seals*, 186–191; A. Moortgat, 'Assyrische Glyptik des dreizehnten Jahrhundert's', in *Zeitschrift für Assyriologie*, XLVII.
[2] Sidney Smith, *Early History of Assyria*, Pl. XVII.
[3] W. Andrae, *Farbige Keramik von Assur*, Pls. 7, 8.
[4] W. Andrae, *Die Jungeren Ischtartempel in Assur*, Pl. 29–30.
[5] H. Frankfort, *loc. cit.*, 196.

[6] Sidney Smith in *Bulletin of the School of Oriental Studies,* IV (London, 1926–1928), 69–76.

[7] H. Frankfort, *loc. cit.,* p. 198, also *Archiv für Orientforschung,* XII (1937–1939), 128–135.

[8] *Encyclopédie photographique de l'art,* Tome II, Pl. 2, 3.

[9] E. A. Wallis Budge, *Assyrian Sculpture in the British Museum. Reign of Assurnasirpal* (London, 1914).

[10] J. H. Breasted in *Studies Presented to E. Ll. Griffith,* pp. 267–271.

[11] L. W. King, *Bronze reliefs from the Gates of Shalmaneser* (London, 1915).

[12] 705–681 B.C. See A. Paterson, *Assyrian Sculpture in the Palace of Sinacherib* (The Hague, 1915).

[13] Paterson, *loc. cit.,* Pl. 15.

[14] H. R. Hall, *Babylonian and Assyrian Sculpture in the British Museum* (Brussels, 1928), Pl. XLII.

[15] Paterson, *loc. cit.,* Pl. 39.

[16] H. R. Hall, *op. cit.,* Pl. XL.

[17] H. R. Hall, *loc. cit.,* Pl. XLI.

$\mathcal{3}$. THE GENERAL CHARACTERISTICS OF GREEK SCULPTURE

Gisela M. A. Richter

INTRODUCTION

Gisela Richter's *The Sculpture and Sculptors of the Greeks* has been one of the most useful studies of Greek sculpture since its initial publication in 1929. For years, students of Greek art have benefited from her research, published in such works as *Red-Figured Athenian Vases* (1936), *Kouroi, Archaic Greek Youths*, 3rd ed. (1971), *Archaic Greek Art Against its Historical Background* (1949), *Three Critical Periods in Greek Sculpture* (1951), *Ancient Italy* (1955), and *A Handbook of Greek Art*, 4th rev. ed. (1965), which contains a fine selected bibliography on all phases of Greek art, and *Korai, Archaic Greek Maidens* (1968).

Miss Richter was one of those scholars who did not recoil from the risks of generalization. The selection in this anthology accepts such risks, and the result is surely one of the best introductory essays on the nature of Greek sculpture.

Other recommended readings on the sculpture would include Rhys Carpenter, *Greek Sculpture* (1960), which is not strictly speaking a history of Greek sculpture but a study of the techniques in their relationship to style; portions of his *The Esthetic Basis of Greek Art*, rev. ed. (1959), especially Chapter III; the well-illustrated volume by Rein-hard Lulliès with photographs by Max Hirmer, *Greek Sculpture* (1960); J. Charbonneaux, *Greek Bronzes* (1962); E. Langlotz and M. Hirmer, *Ancient Greek Sculpture of South Italy and Sicily* (1965); and Humfry Payne and G. M. Young, *Archaic Marble Sculpture from the Acropolis* (1936). For material on the techniques of sculpture one should mention, in addition to the above works, Stanley Casson, *The Technique of Early Greek Sculpture* (1933); C. Bluemel, *Greek Sculptors at Work* (1955); and, for a discussion of Graeco-Roman copies, Miss Richter's *Ancient Italy* (1955). A series of important works on Greek sculpture has been written by Brunilde S. Ridgway: *The Severe Style in Greek Sculpture* (1970); *The Archaic Style in Greek Sculpture* (1977); and *Fifth Century Styles in Greek Sculpture* (1981). A handy recent publication is John Boardman, *Greek Sculpture: The Archaic Period. A Handbook* (1978). Since Roman copies of Greek sculpture have played such an important role in the history of art, sometimes providing us with our only images of Greek works renowned in antiquity, a recent publication relating to this subject is of exceptional merit: Margarete Bieber, *Ancient Copies: Contributions to the History of Greek and Roman Art* (1977). Other works of interest are Cornelius C. Vermeule III, *Greek Sculpture and Roman Taste: The Purpose and Setting of Graeco-Roman Art in Italy and the Greek Imperial East* (1977); and a fine contribution to the literature pertaining to the history of taste, Francis Haskell and Nicholas Penny, *Taste and the Antique: The Lure of Classical Sculpture 1500–1900* (1981). An earlier work on the attractions of the Graeco-Roman era held for later generations is Cornelius C. Vermeule III, *European Art and the Classical Past* (1964).

W	e must remember that when the Greeks of classical times
	began their career civilization was still young. Everything
	that has happened in the last three thousand years was
to them nonexistent. It is difficult to realize at once what this
implies. It means that their artistic background was confined to the
products of Egypt, Western Asia, and, in part, of Crete; and even
of these their knowledge was limited, especially in literature, for
what existed of Eastern writings was not easily accessible. Their
own past was dimly remembered in the form of myths and legends.
So practically the only literature they knew was Homer; the only
history they were cognizant of was the Trojan war. In religion they
had come in contact in the East with beliefs in heterogeneous gods
and monsters, and from this they had developed the anthropomorphic religion found in Homer and Hesiod. In other words, most of
the influences—artistic, intellectual, and religious—which act upon
the modern man were as yet unformed. The background was simpler
and the human mind had the freshness of youth.

In the centuries in which the classical Greek civilization was
developed great changes happened. From its primitive beginning
it passed through many stages to a more complicated outlook, and
during this time it created a large part of what constitutes our
Western culture. Nevertheless, it is possible to view the Greek mind
as a whole. We will endeavor to do so and to see how its quality
determined the character of Greek sculpture.

The three outstanding characteristics which strike us when we
analyze the Greek mentality applied to art are directness, agility,
and a feeling for beauty.

The directness was no doubt largely the result of a simpler
outlook. It is a quality which we with our more complicated natures
have lost; and when we come in contact with it, it affects us like
a fresh breeze on a sultry day. It enabled the Greeks to keep their
eyes on the essentials without the distraction of superfluous details.
In literature this shows itself in their vivid similes, their keen
observation, and also in a bald sincerity in stating facts.[1] Take such
a description as Aeschylus': . . . ταχύπτεροι πνοαί, . . . ποντίων τε

37

GISELA M. A. RICHTER

κυμάτων ἀνήριθμον γέλασμα, παμμῆτόρ τε γῆ,[2] "Swift winged winds
. . . , and numberless laughter of waves, and earth the mother of
all." Could there be a truer and more beautiful description of the
much-besung wind and sea and earth? It reaches out to the chief
quality of each, transforms it into poetry, and creates thereby
something fundamental and permanent. Or take Clytaemnestra's
analysis of her emotions (in Sophocles' Electra[3]) when she hears of
the death of her son Orestes, whose vengeance she dreaded: "Are
these glad tidings? Rather would I say sad but of profit." It is a
simple statement of the case, without pretense or blinking of facts;
and perfectly concise. Greek literature is full of these pregnant,
clear-eyed sayings. The much-quoted epitaph, "His father Philip
laid here to rest his twelve-year-old son Nicoteles, his high hope,"[4]
is another example of this combination of sincerity and conciseness.
What could be added to the essential facts conveyed in "laid to
rest," "twelve-year-old," and "high hope" which would not be a
superfluity? And let us remember Aristotle's definition of superfluities, "That which makes no perceptible difference by its presence
or its absence is no real part of the whole."[5]

It is this feeling for the whole unencumbered by superfluities
which gives Greek art its peculiar greatness. At the very beginning
of his career the Greek sculptor went straight to the essentials. In
the early "Apollo" statues why is it that in spite of their stiffness
and faulty construction they are full of life? Because the important
functional parts of the body are properly accented, the details are
omitted, and each and every part passes into and connects with
the adjoining part. . . . The rendering is simplified; the important
parts are made to stand out and there are no incidents, no superfluities. The result is that we have the impression of an organic
whole which can function and live (Fig. 8). And this is true of all
Greek sculpture during its best periods.

The second outstanding characteristic of the Greeks we may take
to be their agility. It was stimulated doubtless by the geography
of the country. For the combination of mountains and sea tended
both to separate the Greek peoples from one another and to stimulate emigration. The mountains acted as barriers and the sea invited
adventures. Hence the formation of a number of separate communities distributed over a large area including Greece, western Asia
Minor, the Aegean Islands, southern Italy, and a few outlying places
in Spain and France. This double circumstance insured on the one

8. Kouros of Sounion, Archaic Greek, *c.* 600 B.C. (Marburg-Art Reference Bureau)

hand compact community life in small city states, on the other the variety of stimulus derived from heterogeneous peoples; all of which made for lively activity, because individual responsibility in a small state and rivalry with other states are apt to invite energy. This striving for adventure and for knowledge led the Greeks into many untried paths. It is responsible for the amazing number of their discoveries in almost every field of intellectual activity. "To be learning something is the greatest of pleasures, not only to the philosopher but also to the rest of mankind, however small their capacity for it," is Aristotle's definition of happiness[6] of which Plato's more imaginative rendering is, "He whose heart has been set on the love of learning and on true wisdom and has chiefly exercised this part of himself, this man must without fail have thoughts that are immortal and divine."[7]

In sculpture this agility of mind and this love of knowledge are likewise responsible for a great deal. They meant progress and development. Without them Greek sculpture might have remained stationary, never surpassing the attainments of Oriental artists. The Egyptian sculptor, for instance, with all his wonderful feeling for the value of essentials, practiced his art for thousands of years

39

without solving some of its difficulties. He followed throughout the old law of frontality,[8] his knowledge of anatomy remained primitive, and in his reliefs proper perspective was never attained. The agile mind of the Greek determined to wrestle with these problems. Not content with what had been accomplished before him, he was eager to solve new problems, and so he started out on his adventure of representing a human body in all manner of postures, constructed according to nature, with its parts in proper relation and perspective, both in the round and in relief. To a pioneer in the field it was a formidable task. But with remarkable perseverance the Greek artist accomplished it, and his solution of these problems was like the removal of shackles which had hampered the free development of art for generations. The human figure, by its movements and gestures, could henceforth express action and emotion. . . .

A love of truth and of knowledge could easily have made realists of the Greeks; but their realism was transformed into idealism by their third great characteristic—their feeling for beauty. Beauty to them was not something apart from daily life but interwoven into every phase of it. The beauty of their own landscape undoubtedly quickened their sensibilities in this direction. Its grandeur and suavity, its rich colors and fine contours, its elusive, subtle quality would inevitably influence a young, impressionable people. It would incline them to regard beauty as an integral part of their lives and to find their happiness in the loveliness of their immediate surroundings. And their sense for beauty grew so strong that it became the underlying principle in their lives. For they made a great discovery—one that we have lost since, perhaps through Puritan interpretations, but are beginning to realize again—that goodness and beauty are identical, not only figuratively but actually. "Virtue it appears will be a kind of health and beauty and good habit of the soul; and vice will be a disease and deformity and sickness of it," says Plato in his Republic;[9] and with the Greeks it was a generally accepted principle. "Then good language and good harmony and grace and good rhythm all depend upon a good nature, by which I mean a mind that is really well and nobly constituted in its moral character," Plato says again in his Republic;[10] and in his Symposion:[11] "From the love of the beautiful has sprung every good in heaven and earth." Most eloquent of all is the current Greek expression for a "gentleman"—καλός κἀγαθός, "beautiful and good." Greek and especially Athenian education was planned directly with this end in view; and athletics and music were given the most prominent places, one to foster the beauty of the body, the other of the mind. That exercise develops the body is easily accepted by us today; but that art and music make men good is not so generally believed. Yet the Athenians practised this creed with good results; at least they won a reputation, Plato tells us, "throughout Europe and Asia" "for the beauties of their bodies and the various virtues of their souls."[12] Let us learn from Plato how this can be accomplished. In dealing with the education of his guardians in his Republic,[13] he gives us a specific account. Socrates asks: "Ought we not to seek out artists who by the power of genius can trace out the nature of the fair and the graceful, that our young men, dwelling as it were in a healthful region, may drink in good from every quarter, whence any emanation from noble works may strike upon their eye or their ear, like a gale wafting health from salubrious lands, and win them imperceptibly from their earliest childhood into resemblance, love, and harmony with the true beauty of reason?" And when Glaucon assents Socrates continues: "Is it then on these accounts that we attach such supreme importance to a musical education, because rhythm and harmony sink most deeply into the recesses of the soul, and take most powerful hold of it, bringing gracefulness in their train, and making a man graceful if he be rightly nurtured?" And finally he sums up, "There can be no fairer spectacle than that of a man who combines the possession of moral beauty in his soul with outward beauty of form, corresponding and harmonizing with the former, because the same great pattern enters into both." Translated into conduct this aesthetic ideal became a reverence for sobriety and temperance. As an imaginative, southern people the Greeks no doubt had strong feelings difficult to control; but they recognized that temperance was a kind of harmony, and therefore desirable. So μηδέν ἄγαν, "nothing too much," became their motto, and ὕβρις "insolence," their abomination.

Naturally in the art of sculpture the Greek sense of beauty found a fruitful field. It is directly responsible for the most characteristic quality, idealism. The creation of beauty was the sculptor's chief interest and his types are selected with this end in view. "But when you want to represent beautiful figures," says Socrates to the artist Parrhasius, "since it is not easy to find everything without a flaw in a single human being, do you not then collect from a number what is beautiful in each, so that the whole body may appear beautiful?" And Parrhasius admits that such is their practice. This sums up very simply the Greek point of view. It is not realism and truth to nature but perfection of form that the Greeks consciously strove for. And this beauty of form was further enhanced by their feeling for design, which gave to their work a highly decorative quality. It is particularly strong in the archaic period when stylization took the place of correctness of modeling, but it was not lost even in the more naturalistic periods, and always gives style to the whole—the style which distinguishes art from nature. Indeed it is this sense of composition which the Greek regarded as perhaps the most important element in a work of art. It is clearly brought out in the definition of beauty quoted by Plotinus (as the opinion of some):[14]

> What is it that impresses you when you look at something, attracts you, captivates you, and fills you with joy?
> The general opinion, I may say, is that it is the interrelation of parts toward one another and toward the whole, with the added element of good color, which constitutes beauty as perceived by the eye; in other words, that beauty in visible things as in everything else consists of symmetry and proportion. In their eyes, nothing simple and devoid of parts can be beautiful, only a composite.

This joy in "symmetry and proportion" can be clearly detected in all Greek art.

Another important factor in the "idealism" of Greek sculpture is its simplification. The Greek sculptor felt that to translate the human body into a work of art he must harmonize the multiformity and restlessness of nature and create a unity. We have spoken of his subordination of parts to the whole, his elimination of superfluous details, his restriction to the essentials. Equally important was his simplification of the design. His statue was contained in a unified space,[15] that is, a space with restricted depth. . . . It is important to understand and realize this characteristic of Greek sculpture; for it is very largely through this conception of space that a Greek statue acquires its dignity and grandeur. A figure thus carved can be taken in by the human eye without distraction, and thereby attains that sense of quiet and detachment which makes art a refreshment to the spirit.

This "relief conception," as it has been called by Hildebrand, was inherited by the Greeks from the Egyptians; it was stimulated

by the universal practice of stone carving, in which both the figure
and the space surrounding it were potentially enclosed in the block,
by the demand for architectural sculpture with its uniform depths
of pediments and metopes. That the Greeks recognized its importance from an artistic point of view is shown by their practice of
it even when working in bronze or with figures in which no back
ground had to be considered. It is not until the very latest period,
in such creations as the Dirke monument, that this conception is
given up, and the result is, we feel immediately, a certain restlessness.

Still another determining element in the idealistic impression of
Greek sculpture is beauty of contour. So much of Greek sculpture
was out in the open to be viewed from a distance that the outline
counted for much; and it is the lovely undulating outline of a Greek
statue which impresses us from the first. Indeed this feeling for
contour was so strong in the Greek artist that it shows itself in all
his work, not only in the design of the whole figure, but in every
part of it—the oval of the face, the swing of the eyelids, the curve
of the lips, the drawing of the muscles and of the folds of the
drapery. It is an extraordinarily strong sensitivity for rhythmic
line—which found expression also in the shapes of vases and in vase
painting.

It is, then, sense of structure, simplification of form and design,
harmonious proportion, and rhythmic contour that stand out as the
salient features of Greek sculpture. By them it acquires the grandeur
which we feel in its presence. They give it its spiritual quality. And
since art is a spiritualization of nature it is this spiritualizing quality
which is fundamental, and without which representation is not art.
And so Greek sculpture, throughout its development, has the distinguishing trait of great art.

From our analysis of the Greek mind and its influence on Greek
sculpture we must pass to the chief uses of sculpture in Greece;
for the nature of the demand of course affects the character of the
supply.

Sculpture in Greece was largely religious. Its chief use was for
the decoration of temples either as pediment groups, friezes, or
acroteria, for the cult statues of deities placed in the cella, and for
votive statues and reliefs dedicated in sanctuaries. A large proportion of the sculpture that has survived is therefore architectural.
This demand early developed the technique of relief as well as the

composition of large groups. We should never have had the superb creations of the western pediment of the Olympia temple or the Parthenon frieze but for the long history which preceded them and which gave the sculptor ample opportunities of development. But these pediments and friezes could not vie in importance with the cult statues placed in the interiors of temples. It was round them that the popular worship centered and it was by them that the people obtained a concrete realization of their gods. And so to embody his vision of the deity in a great temple statue was the highest task of a Greek sculptor. Unfortunately hardly any of these statues have survived. We have only descriptions and small reproductions by which to visualize the colossal chryselephantine statues by Phidias, Polyclitus, and Alcamenes. In every estimate of Greek sculpture, therefore, we must remember that its finest creations have been irretrievably lost.

Another important demand for sculpture in Greek times was created by the custom of erecting statues of the victors in the athletic contests given in honor of Zeus, Poseidon, Hera, etc. The statues stood in the public places and in the sacred enclosures in which the games had taken place, and the young athletes were mostly represented nude, for that is how they had engaged in their contests. This practice and the athletic ideal which prompted it led to the development of the nude male type as a favorite form. Not only athletes but gods and heroes were so represented. In this series of nude male figures the ideal human form was gradually worked out and became one of the greatest achievements of Greek sculpture (Fig. 9).

Commemorative sculptures which are so popular today also played an important part in Greece. A significant victory would be celebrated by the erection of a statue or group, like the Nike of Paionios at Olympia, or the bronze Athena of Phidias on the Acropolis which was an offering "from the spoils of the Persians who landed at Marathon." The group of the Tyrannicides set up on the marketplace would remind Athenians every day of their liberation from the tyrants and of the value of their democratic institutions. We hear also of large groups of several figures, e.g., statues of Athena, Apollo, Miltiades, Erechtheus, Cecrops, Pandion, Aegeus, and five other heroes, another offering "from the spoils of Marathon" by Phidias. Such groups in the round must have been remarkable achievements, and it is a grievous loss that they have

9. Poseidon, Greek, Early Classical, *c.* 460–450 B.C., Bronze, 82" High (National Museum, Athens; Alison Frantz)

disappeared. The erection of portraits of distinguished men became increasingly popular as time went on.

Besides these more or less public uses of sculpture there was a large private demand for grave monuments. The chief forms adopted in Athens were slabs with reliefs representing the departed, either alone or with sorrowing relatives, statues in the round, slabs crowned by finials, and vases decorated with reliefs. They supply us with some of the most touching and most "personal" representations we have in Greek art. These sculptured grave monuments remained in vogue until the end of the fourth century B.C. when the "anti-luxury" decree of Demetrius put a sudden stop to this artistic expression. Their constant use during three centuries greatly furthered the development of relief technique.

It is important to become familiar also with the subjects represented in Greek sculpture; for the Greek artist had an entirely different repertoire from our own. Early Christian, medieval, and Renaissance art are from this point of view much nearer to us, since they need little explanation; but when we enter the Greek field we are stepping into an unknown land; and we must be careful to leave behind us any preconceptions we may have.

We have seen how the athletic ideal helped to concentrate interest in the human figure. It accustomed people to seeing the human body in all manner of postures and to appreciating its beauty. Moreover, the Greek with his love of the normal had a tendency

45

to humanize everything. His gods and goddesses are no longer monsters, as often in Eastern art, but assume human form; so do the Nymphs, Satyrs, Centaurs, Tritons, and the other personifications of nature. Even when these start with hybrid shapes they soon lose their animal characteristics and gradually become more and more human. And so Greek sculpture consists largely of figures of human beings representing divinities, heroes, and athletes. Animals and decorative motives find a place and an important one, but they are nevertheless secondary. The human figure is the theme par excellence.

Joined to this humanizing tendency the Greeks had a love for storytelling. Much of Greek religion consists of stories about gods and goddesses and heroes; and these manifold imaginative tales would naturally make a great appeal to the artist. They supplied him with the most varied material, which he used so constantly that definite standardized types soon emerged. Plato's words about literature apply also to sculpture and painting—that art must eschew novelty and be framed after the pattern of those foundation myths which the poets have made familiar. So we must become conversant with these foundation myths. And a delightful process it is; for these stories have the freshness and imaginative quality of a poetic people. In entering this world of Greek fiction with its contests of Lapiths and Centaurs and Amazons, its wonderful deeds of heroes, and its manifold adventures of gods and goddesses, we feel very near the beginning of civilization. We sense the vivaciousness and naïveté of youth. No doubt some of the myths have a historical background; some are certainly rooted in actual experience; but the poet when he took his material transformed fact into fancy and then the artist translated this fancy into a beautiful picture. And so in our interpretation of Greek mythology in Greek art let us endeavor to catch the lovely simplicity of these spirited stories directly and concretely told. It is easy for us with our modern, complicated minds to read our own thoughts into these representations and endow them with farfetched symbolic significance. But thereby we lose the early Greek flavor and become more like the late Latin commentators. . . . To the Greek artist the hero was always Heracles with his lion's skin and club or Theseus with his little chiton and his sword or Perseus with his distinctive paraphernalia, tackling in various ways these dangerous creatures. The whole interest lies in the contest, in the story, and in its artistic rendering. Its subjective significance was outside the artist's scope.

In this connection we may again quote Plato; [16] for in his analytical time a few learned people were beginning to lose the childlikeness of earlier days and search for farfetched interpretations. When Socrates is asked by young Phaedrus whether he believes in the story that Boreas carried off Orithyia he gives an illuminating answer, which it may be well to quote at length, for it states the case admirably: "If I disbelieved," Socrates says, "as the wise men do, I should not be extraordinary; then I might give a rational explanation, that a blast of Boreas, the north wind, pushed her off the neighboring rocks as she was playing with Pharmaceia, and that when she had died in this manner she was said to have been carried off by Boreas. I think, however, such explanations are very pretty in general, but are the inventions of a very clever and laborious and not altogether enviable man, for no other reason than because after this he must explain the forms of the Centaurs, and then that of the Chimaera, and there presses in upon him a whole crowd of such creatures, Gorgons, Pegasoi, and multitudes of strange, inconceivable, portentous natures. If anyone disbelieves in these, and with a rustic sort of wisdom, undertakes to explain each in accordance with probability, he will need a great deal of leisure. Now I have no leisure for them at all. . . . And so I dismiss these matters and accept the customary belief about them."

Surely our interest also lies in these customary beliefs of the people who produced and enjoyed the art which we are endeavoring to understand. So we cannot do better than follow Socrates' advice and not spoil a fairy tale with a laborious mind. We must remember, then, that the only symbolism we shall find in Greek art is the concrete one by which pebbles suggest the beach, a fish the sea, a growing plant the meadow, a pine tree the mountain, a reed the river bank, and a column the house. This practical symbolism was freely used, for such shorthand methods were useful and easily understood, and were thoroughly in line with the Greek tendency to simplification.

The large mass of architectural sculptures—the pediments of the temples, the continuous friezes, the metopes—have almost invariably mythological representations—either legends directly associated with the deity to whom the temple was dedicated (e.g., the birth of Athena and her strife with Poseidon in the pediments of the Parthenon), or the familiar contest scenes of Heracles, Theseus, Lapiths, etc. Only occasionally is there a scene from actual life, for instance, the Panathenaic procession in the Parthenon frieze;

47

though here too the subject is lifted to a higher plane by the actual presence of the gods on the eastern side. The almost total absence of historical representations is striking. Even in single sculptures erected to celebrate a specific victory such subjects are rare; when Miltiades is introduced in Phidias' group commemorative of the battle of Marathon[17] he is associated with Athena, Apollo, and various heroes; the representation of Greeks and Persians on the frieze of the temple of Athena Nike is exceptional. We have not a single representation of the battles of Thermopylae or Salamis, of the Peloponnesian war, of the great plague, of the Sicilian expedition; in short, of the outstanding events which formed the chief preoccupation of the Greeks of the fifth century. How different the Romans or the Egyptians and Assyrians with their endless friezes recording their triumphs over their enemies; how different we ourselves with some of our war monuments and realistic pictures of contemporary battles! The Greeks, in order to convey the strife and stress of their time, had recourse to mythological contests, or to the semi-legendary events of the Trojan war.[18] These were far enough removed to admit of safe treatment, which with the constantly changing alignment of the Greek states was probably an important point. At all events, the Greeks knew that history with the strong partisan and bitter feeling it arouses is not an appropriate subject for sculpture. The same is true of contemporary political events. The Greek was distinctly a "political animal." Of all his contributions to mankind he prided himself most on his civic ideal. Every Athenian citizen was a representative in Congress and a legislator in the law courts. But that part of his life was passed over by the artist. And probably for the same reason for which contemporary wars were omitted—that controversial subjects do not belong to the realm of art.

There were some other aspects of daily life, however, which found a place in Greek sculpture. Not only single statues of athletes but chariot groups were popular dedications; and occasionally even in the fifth century we hear of such "genre" subjects as the statue by Styppax of "a slave roasting entrails and kindling a fire with a blast from his swollen cheeks."[19] In the Hellenistic period such themes greatly gained in vogue, especially in bronze and terracotta statuettes. But the most frequent representations of daily life occur on the grave monuments where the departed were shown in their favorite occupations, as their families liked to remember them. To us these pictures of Greek life are singularly precious; for they are contemporary illustrations of familiar happenings and as such eloquent and trustworthy. We see here men represented as warriors or athletes; women busy with their spinning or putting on their jewelry; children playing ball or caressing their pet animals; and in the family groups we gain a realization of a happy and affectionate family life. And, always, these renderings are simple and direct—with no trace of sentimentality or exaggeration, but with the Greek note of serenity which makes of them something typical and permanent. We are reminded of Nietzsche's famous saying: "Die Griechen sind, wie das Genie, einfach: deshalb sind sie die unsterblichen Lehrer."

NOTES

[1] For an excellent discussion of this subject, cf. Livingstone, *The Greek Genius and Its Meaning to Us.*

[2] *Prometheus Bound* 88 ff.

[3] 766.

[4] Callimachus, *Epigr.* 19.

[5] *Poetics* 8. 4.

[6] *Poetics* IV 4.

[7] *Timaius* 90 A.

[8] Frontality I take to mean a perfect symmetry in the two sides of the body, i.e., the equal distribution of weight on the two legs. This admits of the torsion of the body which we find adequately rendered in some Egyptian sculptures.

[9] IV. 444.

[10] III. 400.

[11] 197.

[12] *Timaius* 21 A–25 D.

[13] III. 401–402.

[14] *Ennead* I. VI. i. Though Plotinus lived in the third century A.D. his teachings are often borrowed from Plato and other philosophers of the fifth and fourth centuries B.C.

[15] Cf. on this subject Hildebrand's remarks in his illuminating book, *Das Problem der Form.*

[16] *Phaidrus* 229 D.

[17] Pausanias X. 10. 1. In Mikon's famous painting of the battle of Marathon, Athena and some popular heroes (Theseus, Heracles, and Echetlus) are likewise introduced (Pausanias I. 16).

[18] We have a few exceptions to this general rule in Greek paintings, for instance in the representation of the battle of Oinoe in the Poikile (Pausanias I. 15).

[19] Pliny, *N. H.* XXXIV. 81.

4. ART AND EXPERIENCE

IN ANCIENT GREECE

J. J. Pollitt

INTRODUCTION

This selection—from a book designed for the general reader and student—is particularly useful for the emphasis it accords the expressive side of Greek art, so often treated essentially in terms of formal developments; but Pollitt's work has other salutary features as well: while its focus is chiefly on the Classical Period (ca. 480 to 323 B.C.), its range is actually much wider, providing the reader with an evocative panorama of Greek art as psychological manifestation and cultural expression from Archaic to Hellenistic times. By placing the visual arts of the Hellenic world in the context of literary, philosophical, social, and political currents, the author effectively amends the image of Greek art as a chronicle of ebb and flow between "the real" and "the ideal."

Cited by Pollitt in his bibliography is a group of four works by a single author that should be noted here: T. B. L. Webster, *Greek Art and Literature, 700–530 B.C.* (1960); *Greek Art and Literature, 530–400 B.C.* (1939); *Art and Literature in Fourth-Century Athens* (1956); and *Hellenistic Poetry and Art* (1964). Two anthologies, J. J. Pollitt, ed., *The Art of Greece, 1400–31 B.C. Sources and Documents* (1965) and Milton C. Nahm, *Selections From Early Greek Philosophy* (1962), will also prove useful to the student. For further exploration of the subject addressed by this selection, see C. M. Bowra, *The Greek Experience* (1958); Bernard Ashmole, *The Classical Ideal in Greek Sculpture* (1964); J. J. Pollitt, "Professional Art Criticism in Ancient Greece," *Gazette des Beaux-Arts*, LXIV (1964), 317–30; J. E. Raven,

"Polyclitus and Pythagoreanism," *Classical Quarterly*, XLV (1951), 147–52; H. D. F. Kitto, *Greek Tragedy* (1939); two works by M. P. Nilsson, *A History of Greek Religion* (1949) and *Greek Popular Religion* (1940); A. J. Festugière, *Personal Religion Among the Greeks* (1954); E. R. Dodds, *The Greeks and the Irrational* (1951); A. R. Burn, *Pericles and Athens* (1948, 1960); C. A. Robinson, Jr., *Athens in the Age of Pericles* (1959); A. Zimmern, *The Greek Commonwealth: Politics and Economics in Fifth-century Athens* (1931); A. H. M. Jones, *Athenian Democracy* (1957); and W. R. Connor, *The New Politicians of Fifth-century Athens* (1971). There is also the Oxford (Clarendon Press) series of monographs under the general title *Greece and Rome*. The best comprehensive history is Martin Robertson, *A History of Greek Art*, 2 vols. (1975).

The selection that follows is reprinted from J. J. Pollitt, *Art and Experience in Classical Greece* (1972), with the permission of the publisher, Cambridge University Press. Copyright © Cambridge University Press, 1972.

ANTECEDENTS AND FIRST PRINCIPLES

ORDER AND CHAOS

A deep-seated need to discover an order in, or superimpose an order on, the flux of physical and psychological experience is a continuing feature of all Greek artistic and philosophical expression. While it is true that every conscious creature feels this need to some extent, the intensity with which the quest for order was carried on by the Greeks was exceptional. Whether as a result of some mysterious tendency in the national psyche or as a spontaneous reaction to their turbulent historical experience after the break-up of the Mycenaean world, the Greeks felt that to live with changing, undefined, unmeasured, seemingly random impressions—to live, in short, with what was expressed by the Greek word *chaos*—was to live in a state of constant anxiety.

An awareness of this anxiety which often haunts Greek thought and expression is of crucial importance in understanding and evaluating Greek art. Looking at Greek sculpture out of its original context or at some of the ribald scenes on Greek painted vases, or recollecting in a general way the spirit of Aristophanic comedy, it is easy to be lured into thinking of the Greeks, especially in the Archaic period, as living in an unneurotic, innocent, emotionally uncomplicated world where there were few restraints on natural impulses. Yet even in a casual survey of the extant fragments of the Archaic lyric poets, this picture of the happy springtime of western civilization quickly vanishes. The lyrics are filled with expressions of a profound anxiety provoked by the irrational uncertainty and mutability of life. Archilochos of Paros, for example, experiences an eclipse of the sun and reacts:

> . . . gloom-filled fear has come upon mankind.
> From now on anything may be believed, anything expected
> among men. No longer should anyone marvel at what he sees,
> not even if the beasts of the field make an exchange with dolphins

for their watery pasture, and the echoing waves of the sea
become dearer than dry land to those who once found the hillside
sweet.

Solon of Athens tries to reconcile the wisdom of Zeus with in-
justice in the world and is bewildered . . . Semonides of Amorgos
despairs at the vanity of human endeavors; Mimnermos of Kolo-
phon shudders at the prospect of old age; and Simonides of Keos
beautifully expresses the fundamental anxiety which underlies all
these specific fears when he says that reversal (*metastasis*) of the
human condition comes more quickly than the overturning of a
dragonfly's wing.[1] True, the lyric poets also give us vigorous
drinking songs and love poems. The youthful vigor of Archaic
Greece is not an illusion, but it finds expression as often under a
cloud of worry as in a clear sky of optimism.

If the apparent mutability of the physical world and of the
human condition was a source of pain and bewilderment to the
Greeks, the discovery of a permanent pattern or an unchanging
substratum by which apparently chaotic experience could be
measured and explained was a source of satisfaction, even joy,
which had something of a religious nature. For the recognition
of order and measure in phenomena did more than simply satisfy
their intellectual curiosity or gratify a desire for tidiness; it also
served as the basis of a spiritual ideal. 'Measure and commensurability are everywhere identified with beauty and excellence' was
Plato's way of putting it in a dialogue in which measure is identified as a primary characteristic of the ultimate good (*Philebus*
64E). Rational definability and spirituality were never mutually
exclusive categories in Greek thought. If the quest for order and
clarity was in essence the search for a kind of spiritual ideal, it
was not an ideal to be perceived in rapturous emotional mysticism
but rather one to be arrived at by patient analysis. When the
Greek saw a mystical light, he was inclined to break it down into
its component wavelengths and, to the extent that such things are
possible, give it rational definition.

We see this process at work especially in Greek philosophy,
which in various ways was aimed at alleviating the anxiety which
is inherent in the more spontaneous expression of lyric poetry.
The Milesian philosophers of the sixth century were interested
above all in discovering a primary substance from which, by an

orderly process of derivation, all other phenomena could be explained. Whether it was water, air in various states of condensation, or some other 'element,' the Milesians used their primal substance as the basis for a cosmology (*kosmos* = order) in which the world was seen as a perfectly functioning machine. Neat, clear, and sublimely undisturbed by the social world of man, who took shape and dissolved within the natural order of things, it was an austere ideal, an astringent antidote to the apparent senselessness of life; but at least it made some kind of sense. The man who contemplated it deeply could feel that he was part of a great system which was impersonal but predictable, and, like Lucretius, who revived the Milesian attitude in a later age, he could derive a peculiar kind of peace from it. As time passed and Greek philosophy developed, the urge to find order in experience was shifted from physics to the realm of mathematical abstraction by the Pythagoreans, and to the world of human behavior by various thinkers of the later fifth century; and, finally, Plato and Aristotle attempted to weave all these foci of interest into comprehensive pictures of the relationship between human life and the world as a whole. But in all these epochs the basic quest—the search for a *kosmos*—remained the same.

These two fundamental forces in Greek thought and expression —anxiety prompted by the apparent irrationality of experience and the drive to allay this anxiety by finding an order which explains experience—had a profound effect upon Greek art and are at the root of its two most essential aesthetic principles:

(1) *The analysis of forms into their component parts.* This is one aspect of the process, also inherent in physical science, which brings unity to the multiplicity of things by finding common bases for all of them. . . . The Greek artist . . . chose to stand aside from nature, to analyze what its constituent elements were, and then to reshape it according to his conception of what it should be. Over the centuries, this process became increasingly subtle, but it was never forgotten, as the great importance which was attached to such concepts as *symmetria* 'commensurability,' and *rhythmos* 'pattern,' in Classical art and art criticism, indicates.

(2) *Representation of the specific in the light of the generic.* Greek artists tended to look for the typical and essential forms which expressed the essential nature of classes of phenomena in the same way that Platonic 'forms' or 'ideas' expressed essential

realities underlying the multiplicity of sense perception. . . . This principle helps to explain why the range of building-types in Greek architecture and the range of subjects in Greek sculpture and painting is so deliberately limited. When one is trying to define essence within multiplicity, whimsical innovations, fantasies, and vagrant moods have no place. Consistency and limit are characteristics of order; diversity is more often a characteristic of chaos.

These two aesthetic principles are best understood not as inflexible edicts but rather as statutes of an artistic common law, subject to reinterpretation in every period. According to changing historical circumstances, their application differed. Perhaps the single greatest difference between the Archaic and Classical periods, for example, was a new attitude in the latter toward the 'specific in the light of the generic principle' insofar as it concerned the representation of emotions and changing states of consciousness. Greek artists in general and Archaic artists in particular were normally reluctant to represent the more obvious expressions of emotional variability—howls of laughter, shrieks of anguish, sneers of disdain and the like. Emotions are most often expressions of reaction to the mutability and uncertainty of human circumstances. Archaic art, like contemporary Milesian philosophy, on the whole chose to transcend the overt expression of emotion and changing states of mind and to rely on purely formal qualities of design to express the orderly world which it envisioned. . . .

One of the distinguishing features of the art of the Classical period was that it broke away from this emotional impassivity in Archaic art. . . .

Greek society, as it had developed in the seven centuries which had followed the breakup of the Mycenaean world after 1200 B.C., consisted of relatively small independent communities or *poleis*[2] as the Greeks themselves called them, in which the sources of power and policy were immediate, familiar, and of personal concern even to those who did not directly wield that power. Because the Orient was also undergoing a period of disruption and readjustment in these centuries and because Greece was on the periphery of the oriental world, the Greek cities were able to evolve their peculiar social forms without the threat of interference from the larger eastern powers. In each of the *poleis* authority, political and moral, ultimately rested in an enfranchized group of citizens. . . .

Perhaps the most overriding characteristic of the Greek cities was the pressure which they exerted upon the individual citizen to merge his life and interests in those of the group. It has sometimes been claimed that the outstanding characteristic of the ancient Greeks was their high esteem for individualism, and it is certainly undeniable that Greece did produce many brilliant, talented, and ambitious individuals, who, if their gifts were used in the service of the *polis*, became prominent men. But if one means by individualism a tolerance of those who reject the group's norms and pursue their own interests in disregard of the dominant values of their society, the *poleis* hardly qualify as hospitable ground. The unconventional individualists of Classical Greece— Themistokles and Socrates, for example—often suffered for their individualism and not infrequently came to a tragic end; and yet even they were essentially what a sociologist would now call 'group-oriented.' In the *Apology*, for example, Plato's Socrates emphasizes that his persistent and at times annoying quest for truth was in the best interest of his fellow citizens, even if they were unable to realize it.

The pressures which the Greek *polis* put upon the individual to merge his interests in those of his society may account for the great emphasis put on the ideas of moderation, restraint, and avoidance of excess in Greek religious and moral thinking. All Greeks were subject to and respected the maxims of the Delphic oracle: 'know thyself' (i.e., 'know your limitations') and 'nothing in excess.' These pleas for restraint and measure, which were summed up in the virtue of *sōphrosynē* ('discretion, temperance, self-control'), were not, it should be emphasized, a purely negative prescription. From Hesiod through Solon to the Classical dramatists and philosophers, such virtues were presented as the key to right living, to a happiness which was in keeping with man's nature and was divinely sanctioned. Men whose desires and ambitions knew no restraint, who defied the accepted measure and order, courted chaos and disaster for themselves and those around them. For the Greeks an irrational overturning of the natural order of things was always fraught with deep anxiety.

CONSCIOUSNESS AND CONSCIENCE

THE EARLY CLASSICAL PERIOD, CA. 480–450 B.C.

The New Range of Expression

The art of the Early Classical period differs from that of the Archaic in its interest in exploring emotions and changing states of mind, particularly in a dramatic context. Archaic statues tend to be iconic, that is, to be unchanging 'presences,' in tune with a higher reality and unaffected by the changing conditions of the world. Early Classical statues tend to be dramatic, and to carry with them the impression that they represent one distinct stage in a series of events. They are more often qualified by association with particular times and circumstances. To illustrate this point most simply we can look at two statues which are not far from one another in date and in function but which make totally different impressions. The 'Strangford Apollo' (Fig. 10), a small (about 3′ 4″ high) *kouros* in Parian marble now in the British Museum, must date from 490 or 485 B.C. and is a good example of the outward humanization which characterizes much late Archaic sculpture. Its scale is strictly human rather than superhuman, and, although the sculptor who made it clearly employed a conventional 'canon' of proportion and composition, the individual elements within that canon more closely approximate a natural mean. Yet although the Strangford *kouros* may impress us as humanized when compared with the 'heroic,' greater than life, atmosphere which surrounds many of the earlier *kouroi* (see Fig. 8, p. 39), it is still fundamentally like them in conception. Its traditional *kouros* stance and impassive face seem to ignore the ordinary human condition. As you look at it, or at any *kouros* in a museum, it will seem to look past you.

By contrast, the 'Kritios Boy' (Fig. 11) in the Acropolis Museum in Athens seems as if he might turn and ask you a question. This figure was found on the Acropolis in Athens in the nineteenth century but is apparently not part of the debris left by the Persian sack of Athens since it was broken and repaired in Antiquity, whereas the figures smashed by the Persians were not. It therefore probably dates from just after 480 B.C. and stands at the very beginning of the Early Classical period. The sculptor (the ascrip-

10. Strangford Apollo, perhaps from Lemnos, *c.* 490 B.C., Marble, Height approximately 3′4″ (The British Museum, London)

tion to Kritios is based on analogies with the Tyrannicides group) broke with the 150-year-old *kouros* stance by shifting the seeming stress of the weight to the left leg while leaving the right leg, with the knee slightly bent, free to balance or propel. The displacement of the weight to the left leg raises the left hip and causes a slight unevenness of the axes of the torso. The head turns to the right, to complete the break with the rigidly frontal *kouroi*. The effect of these technical devices is to create a figure which seems to hesitate and to be uncertain about what it is doing and where it will go. It seems conscious of its surroundings and faced with alternatives which ask for judgement and decision. In short, it seems to live and think.

In the case of the Kritios Boy we intuitively sense a kind of dramatic context for the statue, even though we cannot specify precisely what it is. If we turn to architectural sculptures, which normally represent known mythological episodes and hence have a specific narrative context inherent in them, we none the less still find that a distinct difference in atmosphere separates the products of the Classical period from their Archaic predecessors. One of the most vivid illustrations of the gap in feeling and expression between the two periods occurs in the pedimental sculptures, both apparently depicting combats of Greeks and Trojans, from the temple of Aphaia on the island of Aegina. The west pedimental group of this temple seems to have been completed, along with the temple itself, around 490 B.C. An east pedimental group, also completed at this time, was damaged by an unknown agent and replaced by a new set of sculptures somewhere shortly before or after 480 B.C. While most of the figures from both the west pediment and the new east pediment are fragmentary, there are extant two largely complete figures of fallen, wounded warriors, one from each pediment, which had similar narrative functions in

11. Kritios Boy, found on the Athenian Acropolis, *c.* 480–475 B.C., Marble, Height approximately 2′9″ (Acropolis Museum, Athens; Deutsches Archäologisches Institut)

their respective scenes and invite comparisons.³ The warrior from the west pediment (Fig. 12) has been struck in the chest with a spear (of bronze or wood, now missing) which he grasps with his right hand while he props himself up on his left elbow. His expressionless face, sprucely set off by the beaded bonnet of his hair, stares out at the viewer. His right leg is arched over the left, giving a clear, almost delicate silhouette, evocative of the crisp figures of early Attic red-figure vase paintings. Rather than suffering from an excruciatingly painful wound, he seems to be posing for a dignified court *tableau.*

The fallen warrior from the east pediment is another matter (Fig. 13). As life ebbs away and he sinks toward the earth, he tries futilely, sword (now missing) in hand, to raise himself. His eyes narrow as his consciousness fades; his mouth is slightly open as his breathing grows difficult; he stares at the earth. His enfeebled movements contrast poignantly with his massive physical frame in which, for practically the first time, the individual details of the musculature are fused and unified by a softening of the lines of division between them, and by increasingly subtle modulation of the surface from which one senses the presence of a unified physical force emanating from within the body. The sculptor who conceived the figure had obviously thought carefully about exactly what it meant. He must have asked himself what it must really be like when a powerful warrior is wounded and falls. . . . The warrior from the west pediment seems more like a recumbent *kouros*; his companion from the east pediment is a character in a drama.

Confidence and Doubt

What factors were there which might be said to have brought into being this new analysis of consciousness in Early Classical art? It seems something more than a natural evolution from what had gone on in the Archaic period and should perhaps be ascribed to both a *new self-confidence* and a *new uneasiness* which arose among many thoughtful Greeks in the wake of the Persian Wars.

Confidence and optimism arose, of course, simply from the fact that the Greeks had won. Triumph in the face of such overwhelming odds suggested that perhaps Greek culture, with its restrained, group-conscious, way of life, had received divine sanction and justification. Aeschylus, and following him, Herodotus and others,

12. Fallen Warrior, from the west pediment of the Temple of Aphaia on Aegina, Archaic Greek, Late, *c.* 490 B.C., Length approximately 4′2″ (Staatliche Antikensammlung und Glyptothek, Munich; Hirmer Fotoarchiv)

13. Fallen Warrior, from the east pediment of the Temple of Aphaia on Aegina, Archaic Greek, Late, *c.* 490 B.C., Parian marble, Length 72″ (Staatliche Antikensammlung und Glyptothek, Munich; Hirmer Fotoarchiv)

begin to ponder the question of how *hybris*, 'arrogance, unbridled ambition without restraint,' brings in its wake *atē*, 'folly,' and finally *nemesis*, 'retribution.' There can be no doubt that in Greek eyes the Persians, embodied by the wild figure of Xerxes flogging the sea, had gone through just such a cycle. In the end 'Zeus' (the name covered a multitude of religious and moral conceptions) had punished them. . . . The belief that the Persians had suffered punishment for their *hybris* also made it necessary to believe that there was some kind of order in the immediate world—arrogance was punished, moderation was rewarded. This involved a departure from the thought of the Archaic period, which, unable to discover any rational order in the world of immediate experience had reacted by conceiving of orders which were beyond it. In the Early Classical period, this budding belief that the world as it was might 'make sense' must have provoked a new interest in the nature of its changing conditions. Changing states of consciousness could be understood as aspects of a universal moral order, and it may have been this realization which led the artists of the period to begin exploring them. . . .

But if a new confidence led the Early Classical artists to begin experimenting with the representation of conscious inner life, it was another motive which led them to dwell most often on its sombre, meditative, even haunted aspects. That motive was a new uneasiness of mind produced by the growing belief that men were responsible for their own fortunes, good or bad, and by the implications which this belief had for the course of Greek domestic politics after the Persian Wars.

Art and Drama

The confident yet self-questioning atmosphere which developed in the wake of the victory over the Persians also served to bring to maturity the dominant and most characteristic literary form of the fifth century B.C.—Athenian tragic drama. The dramas were public rites, performed at religious festivals by actors who were, in most cases at least, the fellow citizens of those who witnessed them. They were above all reflections of group-experience. The dramatic poet, whether reflecting the mentality of his time or seeking to shape it (or both), spoke to, and often for, society as a whole. It is therefore not surprising that the best dramas bring into focus simultaneously most of the intellectual and emotional preoccupations of the Early Classical period—the willingness to believe that there is a meaningful moral order in the world, the consequent uneasiness over the human tendency to pursue self-interest through violence, the possible implications of such violence within the moral order, the new significance attached to individual human consciousness and thought, and finally a new conception of what constitutes nobility in human character. When the proud and strong characters of Greek drama are pitted against hostile forces, sometimes circumstantial and sometimes within themselves, which threaten to destroy them, one often feels that the fate of Athens and Greece as a whole in the fifth century is being enacted, either historically or speculatively.

We have already seen how a dramatic quality pervaded the earliest works of Early Classical art. Sculptors and painters seem, in fact, actually to have borrowed some of the technical devices which had been developed in dramatic performances to convey character and narrative action—for example, the formal gestures of actors, the masks which were designed to express at once an individual character and a basic human type, and perhaps also a sense of dramatic timing. Nowhere is the attempt to adapt the themes, spirit, expressive power, and technical components of the great dramatic cycles like the *Oresteia* of Aeschylus to the medium of the visual arts more successfully and grandly carried out than in the sculptures of the temple of Zeus at Olympia. A comparison of the Aeschylus trilogy with these sculptures is instructive.

The *Oresteia* was produced in 458 B.C., a year or so before the pediments of the temple of Zeus at Olympia were completed, and is our most vivid example of how personal, civic, and cosmic themes were woven into one artistic form in Greek drama. In the first two plays of the cycle, the *Agamemnon* and the *Choëphoroi*, we are confronted with a group of strong characters caught in an obscure web of suffering, of mutual and self-destruction, which defies rational explanation. Inheriting the curse of the terrible crimes of his father, Agamemnon commits violence and suffers violence. Divine demands, the pressure of circumstances, and his own arrogant and ambitious nature drive him to sacrifice his own daughter and bring suffering on all who follow him. Clytemnestra, driven by the pain of her daughter's death and by her husband's infidelity, but also by the pressures of her intrigue with Aegisthus and her own will for power, assassinates her husband. Orestes, both protected and spurned by his titanic mother, is then compelled by the dark force of his father's ghost, by a divine command, but also by his own desire to regain his kingdom, to avenge by matricide his father's death, and for this he is pursued by the Furies, the force of an ancient tradition demanding that blood guilt must inevitably be avenged. The forces which sustain and perpetuate this chain of suffering seem to stem both from the characters themselves and from a primeval, chaotic, and brutal world of values which confounds human comprehension. Even Zeus, who overthrew his own father, seems to be involved in, rather than in control of, the avenging destructive forces, and the chorus, speaking from both within and without the dramatic action, is forced to invoke him in bewilderment . . . But in the *Eumenides*, the final drama of the trilogy, Aeschylus brings us out of the earlier dark irrationality into what seems an enlightened world of order and reason. Orestes, defended principally by Athena, the goddess most closely bound up with thought and progress, is tried before a court of Athenian citizens on the Areopagus in Athens, and is acquitted. Athena turns to the Furies, without hostility, . . . and reason and compromise win them over. . . .

The temple of Zeus at Olympia, which was the most important architectural project in Greece proper during the Early Classical period, was completed between 470 and 456 B.C. Although actually financed and built by the people of Elis with the booty which they had won in a war with neighboring towns for control of the Olympic sanctuary, the temple was nevertheless a monument for all Greeks. Not only was it dedicated to their supreme god, but it stood in the most panhellenic of their sanctuaries. Its chief architect was Libon, a local man, but workmen, particularly stone carvers, from many parts of Greece must have been employed on it. The great sculptural groups in the pediments (over eighty feet long and ten feet high in the center) were of Parian marble. . . .

The east pediment group, which faced into the sanctuary of Olympia and toward the starting line from which the Olympic chariot races began, represented the story of the chariot race between King Oinomaos of Pisa and the young, wandering adventurer Pelops. Oinomaos had a daughter, Hippodameia, whom he coveted, some sources say incestuously, and did not want to lose.

Whenever a suitor appeared for her hand, Oinomaos would challenge him to a chariot race from Olympia to the isthmus of Corinth. If the suitor, who took Hippodameia on his chariot and was given a head-start, won the race, he also won the bride, but if he was overtaken by Oinomaos, he was killed. Since Oinomaos had special arms and horses given to him by the god Ares, a number of suitors had met their end in this way. When Pelops arrived in Pisa Hippodameia fell in love with him and persuaded the charioteer Myrtilos, who was also in love with her, to sabotage her father's chariot by replacing its metal linchpins with pins made of wax. In the ensuing race Oinomaos' chariot collapsed and he was killed. Later Myrtilos, either in expectation of a promised reward or urged on by his own inclinations, made amorous advances toward Hippodameia, whereupon he was thrown into the sea by Pelops and drowned; but not, however, before he was able to call down a curse on the line of Pelops.[4]

The designer of the east pediment captures the elements of this story by showing us the moment just prior to the start of the race, when the participants are offering sacrifice, and presumably swearing an oath of fair-play, before the altar of Zeus. The god himself[5] stands in the center. . . .

Taken as a whole the east pediment seems like an episode in a great dramatic cycle. As in drama, the violent action is to take place off-stage. We are confronted with a scene in which the implications of that action are to be pondered. There is a tension in the air. Conflicting motives drive on the characters to their fate. They exist at various states of anxiety and knowledge. There is a moral and religious problem in the scene which they contemplate according to their understanding and which we are forced to contemplate too. The pediment embodies not action, but thought.

The scene in the west pediment of the temple of Zeus formed a marked and, probably, deliberate contrast to the east. It is full of violent action and an almost elemental pitting of right against wrong. The scene represents the battle of the Lapiths (early Thessalian Greeks) and Centaurs, which broke out at the wedding of the hero Peirithoös and his bride Deidameia. The Centaurs were wild creatures, half man and half horse, who lived in the mountains of Thessaly. Wine, to which they had very low resistance, brought out their animal side, and when they had consumed too much of it at Peirithoös' wedding party they attacked his bride and her handmaidens. The party broke up in a wild brawl in which Peirithoös and his comrade Theseus eventually subdued their savage opponents. The designer of the west pediment in all likelihood selected this story to express the triumph of human civilization—with the discipline and adherence to order which it required—over unthinking barbarism. In the center of the pediment stands the towering figure of a young god, who must be Apollo.[6] He can be understood either as a statue within the scene, i.e., a statue representing a statue, or as an invisible spiritual presence. With a gesture of his right arm, without directly participating in the battle, the god who was the guardian of religious law and a patron of civilized institutions, the god who was also present with Athena at the trial in the *Eumenides*, seems to be decreeing order out of chaos. . . .

The west pediment, like the *Eumenides*, celebrates a triumph of rationality. It is another expression of what I have called the 'new confidence' of the Early Classical period and is a meaningful companion piece to the east pediment, which captures the underlying uneasiness of the period.

The New Severity

The new spirit of Early Classical sculpture was accompanied . . . by new ways of rendering details, by new systems of proportion, and by new patterns of composition—in short, by a new style. Modern critics often apply the term 'severe' to this style, and appropriately so. It is a style with few frills, with few ornaments which could be looked upon as delights 'for their own sake.' As the expressive intention is serious, so is the external form austere. . . .

Perhaps the most consistent element in 'severe style' sculpture and painting, the feature which gives it its definitive stamp, is its characteristically 'moody' facial type which is already well-developed around 480 B.C. . . .

If we try to sum up in a general way the motivating forces behind the 'new severity' of Early Classical art, we can point to two factors. One is an anti-traditional feeling, which in this period means to some extent an anti-oriental feeling. Archaic Greek art had never lost touch with the artistic traditions of the ancient Near East from which it had borrowed certain schemes of composition and a good many decorative details (e.g., the *kouros* stance, formal ways of rendering the hair, animal friezes, etc.). After 480/479 B.C. the Orient was increasingly viewed as barbarous and contemptible; and Archaic art, which had been fostered in many cases by Greek tyrants who had been on good terms with the oriental monarchs and had set themselves up in power somewhat on the oriental model, was tainted by these associations. In renouncing strict patterns like the *kouros* stance and abandoning the aristocratic love of jewel-like detail in favor of a new repertoire of austerely unornate but flexible forms which could be used to express a sombre thoughtfulness, the Greeks finally achieved an artistic identity which was completely their own.

The other basic motivating force behind the style was the new emphasis on personal and group responsibility which we have already examined. In a world where it suddenly appeared that men had the power to create and preserve or destroy the conditions in which they lived, it was wise to present an appearance which was severe and seemingly undeluded by the external trappings of power.

Ethos and Pathos

Ancient Greek psychology recognized two forces at the root of human emotional expression—*ēthos*, a man's 'character' as formed by inheritance, habit, and self-discipline, and *pathos*, his spontaneous reaction to experiences in the external world. In the fourth century B.C. and later, . . . both writers and artists began to display and articulate an active interest in just what role these two aspects of human expression should play in the arts. . . .

Movement and Pictorial Space

Just as the confidence of the Early Classical world, its growing belief that meaning and order could be found in the world of immediate experience, had led to an expanded range of emotional expressions, so also it seems to have given rise to an interest in the creation of a broader spatial environment in which figures could be seen to move, as well as to think and react. Along with this quest for a wider 'stage' went a desire to make figures in motion seem more 'real' without sacrificing the rational, definable order which was felt to be essential for a successful artistic composition. . . .

It was perhaps the new significance attached to human action in the Early Classical period which inspired a reassessment of how motion could be represented. Motion was the concomitant, the physical expression, of action. As with emotion, there seems to have been a feeling that the representation of it should become more vivid and immediate and yet not become so fleeting that it began to defy rational analysis. The concept around which new order for the representation of motion was organized was *rhythmos*. The basic meaning of this word was 'shape' or 'pattern.' It seems to have become associated with music (as has its modern descendant 'rhythm') because of its connection with dancing. A dancer, moving in time with music, performed specific 'steps' in time with the 'beat' of the music. Between each step there were momentary 'stops' (called *erēmiai*) in which the body was held for an instant in characteristic positions. The positions were *rhythmoi*, 'patterns' isolated within continual movement. A single, well-chosen *rhythmos* could, in fact, convey the whole nature of a movement. One might give the analogy of a painting of a pendulum-clock. If the artist depicts the pendulum in a diagonal position, in the process of swinging to either the right or left, the viewer instinctively understands that the pendulum is moving; whereas if it is depicted in a vertical position, he is uncertain as to whether it is moving or not.

. . . The most vivid example of a particular *rhythmos* used to define an entire movement in Greek sculpture is the *Diskobolos* ('Discus thrower') of Myron. The original *Diskobolos*, a bronze produced around 460 B.C., has not survived, but its appearance can be reconstructed with reasonable accuracy from a literary description (Quintilian II. 13. 8–10) and from a number of Roman copies, mainly in marble. . . . The discus thrower is represented at the high point of his backswing, the point where, like a pendulum, his motion is arrested for a split second before he lunges forward. The viewer cannot mistake what the motion is; a single *rhythmos* has captured the whole action. Just as *symmetria* . . . gave rational order to form, *rhythmos* gave rational order to motion.

THE WORLD UNDER CONTROL

THE CLASSICAL MOMENT, CA. 450–430 B.C.

The two opposing poles, confidence and doubt, around which the thought and expression of the Early Classical period gravitated, were by nature in conflict. In Athens during the first two decades after the middle of the fifth century, the scale seems to have tipped in favor of confidence, the belief that men could shape their world in accordance with their own vision of it. . . .

A number of forces helped to create this atmosphere of self-belief in the High Classical period: the psychological legacy of the victory over the Persians was still active; there was an anthropocentric drift in Greek philosophy away from concern with the physical world and toward a preoccupation with human society; and the prosperity and power which accrued to Athens from her Aegean confederacy undoubtedly gave some Athenians at least a new sense of well-being. But none of these factors, individually or in concert, can completely explain the new frame of mind. The heady effects of the victory over the Persians were dimming; the anthropocentric drift in philosophy was as much a result as a cause of the new era; and Athens' rise to power was beset with as many set-backs and frustrations as triumphs. What was needed to make all these forces effective and reap their fruit was a will to believe and spokesmen to articulate that will. The Great Believers and also the spokesmen were Pericles the son of Xanthippos and the artists like Pheidias and Sophocles who helped to make the Periclean vision real by giving it witnessable form.

Periclean Athens

Not all Classical art is Athenian nor are all the characteristics of Classical Athens attributable to Pericles, but without Athens Greek art would not have become what it did and without Pericles Athens would not have been what it was. . . .

One of the products of the formal end of hostilities with Persia was the Periclean building program. As a result of an oath sworn by the Greeks before the battle of Plataea not to rebuild the monuments burned by the Persians but rather to leave them in their ruined state as a reminder of the impiety of the barbarian,[7] there

was little building activity in Athens between 479 and 450 B.C.
But peace with Persia made this oath seem less binding, and
Pericles now decided to rebuild the temples and public buildings
of Athens both as monuments to Greece's victory over 'barbarism'
but also, and perhaps even more important in Pericles' mind, as
visible expressions of Athens' new status in Greece. The program
was financed in part by Athens' own resources but also in part by
the treasury which legally was to be used only for the coordinated
actions of the Delian League. The distribution of this money to
what must have been thousands of workmen, traders, and con-
tractors meant prosperity as well as glorification for Athens.
Pericles justified it to the allies at first by maintaining that as long
as Athens gave them protection and security there was no need
for them to worry about how their money was spent. . . .

As the usurpation of the treasury of the Delian League might
suggest, the political events of the period between the signing of
the peace with Persia and the outbreak of the Peloponnesian War
in 431 B.C. contrast in an almost dismal way with Pericles' vision
of Athens and the great buildings which were created to express
it. . . . The complex and wasting Peloponnesian War, . . . with
periodic truces, was to last a generation and alter drastically the
Greek cultural psyche. . . .

At the end of the first year of the war Pericles was selected to
make a public funeral oration in honor of the Athenian soldiers
who had fallen in the first campaigns. This famous speech, as
Thucydides (II. 34–46) presents it, captures better than any other
document the ideals of Periclean Athens and the spirit which
pervades its art. Athens is depicted as the one society where
justice applies equally to all and where social restrictions do not
prevent a man from becoming as great in public life as his natural
capacity permits; submission to law and authority and acceptance
of the dangers of war are maintained voluntarily, without force
and without complaint; power and discipline are balanced by a
free intellectual life and a buoyant spirit; the functioning of the
society is open for all to see; neither secretiveness nor suspicion
exist. Such a society was a paradigm, Pericles felt, for all societies,
the 'school of Hellas.' If it controlled others, it did so by virtue of
innate merit, and its subjects therefore could have no cause for
complaint.

The Funeral Oration is the high water mark in that tide of humanistic optimism which had been growing in Greece since the Persian War. . . .

Man and the Measure of All Things

The confident belief in the value of human thought and action which is expressed in Pericles' Funeral Oration was part of a broad intellectual current in the second half of the fifth century B.C. and extends beyond the confines of Athens. In Greek philosophy it is most clearly articulated in the Sophist movement. The Sophists were a diverse group of itinerant teachers, scholars, and eccentrics who differed widely from one another in the details of their doctrines and activity, but were unified as a group by a common emphasis on the importance of *human perception* and *human institutions* in interpreting experience and establishing values. The tendency of Greek philosophy in the Archaic period, as we have said, was to search for a rational order, a *kosmos*, which was beyond the fallibility of human perception and the mutability of the human condition. The willingness of the thinkers of the Classical period to reverse this trend and bring the *kosmos* 'down to earth' seems to be a reflection of the humanistic confidence of the age.

The most influential of the Sophists was Protagoras of Abdera (*c.* 480–410 B.C.) whose well-known dictum 'man is the measure of all things' has sometimes been expanded beyond its original context to serve as the motto of the Classical period as a whole. What Protagoras actually seems to have meant by this phrase was that all knowledge is subjective, that is, dependent upon the mind and sense organs of the individual, and that objective knowledge which discounted the perceiver is impossible. Each man's personal subjective experience became the standard by which judgements about the nature of existence, knowledge, and ethics were to be made. From this point of view a 'thing' was what it 'seemed' to be; the 'real' nature of an 'object' became a matter for subjective determination; man, and not an absolute standard outside of him, was the measure of it. This attitude, though it might at first seem to be a purely technical point of epistemology, has broad implications which can be extended not only into politics and morality (cf. Plato's critique of the idea in *Theaetetus* 151e–179b) but also into the history of art. Whether by direct influence or by a more general association 'in spirit,' Greek sculpture in the Classical period, and the Parthenon sculptures in particular, show a tendency toward subjectivism in the design of sculptural form, that is, a tendency to think of sculptures not only as hard, 'real' objects known by touch and by measurement but also as impressions, as something which is in the process of change, a part of the flux of experience, bounded not by solidity and 'hard edges' but by flickering shadows and almost undiscernible transitions. . . .

The doctrine of man as the measure of all things, however, can be, and was, also taken to imply a kind of general anthropocentrism, somewhat similar to that of Italy in the fifteenth and sixteenth centuries, in which human institutions, human endeavors, and human achievements are of more consuming interest than cosmological abstractions. One of the fruits of the anthropocentric attitude was the rise of a belief in human progress and the consequent belief in the possibility of a 'golden age.' A doctrine of cultural evolution which saw mankind as progressing, with the help of *technē* (usually translated as 'art' but meaning, more precisely, the orderly application of knowledge for the purpose of producing a specific, predetermined product), . . . passed beyond purely philosophical circles and became one of the general topics of discussion among thoughtful men in the fifth century. It occurs in poetic form in the *Prometheus Bound* of Aeschylus (lines 476–506). . . .

The Parthenon and the Classic Moment

In Archaic Greek art the genre of particular things had outweighed their specific, individual qualities in artistic representation. Hence abstraction, expressed through the geometricization of natural forms, dominated Archaic art. In the fourth century, . . . it is possible to detect the first indications of a taste, which would mature in the Hellenistic period, for the representation of specifics without any emphatic suggestion of the genre or form (in the Platonic sense) from which they were derived. Realism, in short, began to undermine the long-standing role of abstraction in Greek art. In the art of the High Classical period, and particularly in the art of the Parthenon, these two poles of artistic thinking—the absolute and the relative—seem to have been magically balanced. The relativity of sense experience (e.g., optical refinements) coexists, as we have seen, with absolute concepts like 'number.' The mutability of nature, unformed and unreflective, represented by the mountains and the sea which ring the Acropolis are pitted against the formal perfection, seemingly symbolic of the human mind's capacity for abstract thought, of architectural order. The mortal natures of the processionists of the frieze are infused with the traits of undying divinity. Historical time in the west pediment was given equal weight with what seems to have been a symbol of timeless cosmic order in the east.

Besides being an outgrowth of a new anthropocentric drift in Greek philosophy, which we have already discussed, the Classical moment also seems to reflect, in fact to be a projection of, the sense of group solidarity which Pericles' eloquence, combined with prosperity and a degree of luck, had forged in Athens. A Greek *polis*, when understood as a particular pattern of life and not just a geographical grouping of people and their belongings, was essentially an abstract conception just as a 'nation' is today. Personal life, on the other hand, is basically a succession of particular, concrete interests and experiences. In Periclean Athens, if we may believe the picture presented to us in the Funeral Oration, the latter, for many citizens at least, came to be merged without friction into the former. What an individual wanted for himself and what he owed to the ideal were in harmony. . . . Belief in the group, in society raised to the level of an abstraction and revered as a quasi-deity, seems to have been an essential ingredient in the atmosphere of the High Classical period and its art. When the belief was shaken . . . the artistic style which it sustained lost its cohesion.

THE WORLD BEYOND CONTROL

THE LATER FIFTH CENTURY, CA. 430–400 B.C.

The Resurgence of the Irrational

. . . The psychological upheaval in Greece during the Peloponnesian War which is implicit in Thucydides becomes explicit in the greatest of the Athenian dramas of the time. Sophocles' *Oedipus Tyrannus*, produced in 429 B.C., almost at the beginning of the war, portrays a masterful ruler who enters the scene as a great riddle-solver, ferociously intellectual, flushed with confidence from previous success, optimistic, seemingly in firm control of his world but, significantly enough, faced with an inscrutable plague in his city. At the end of the play he is blinded and power-less, comprehending too late the nature of great forces of which he was not the master. Sophocles, religiously inclined and a tradi-tionalist by nature, seems bothered in the *Oedipus* not by the blindness or irrationality of fate but by the blindness and inherent arrogance of the 'man is the measure' philosophy. The pride of the 'hymn to man' in the *Antigone*, written in the 440s, had turned to anxiety by the early 420s.

What appears as anxiety in Sophocles seems to become in the later dramas of Euripides a despairing recognition of the triumph of the irrational, which breaks through the orderly façade of the human intellect like an animal shattering a flimsy cage. Euripides had already sensed this at the beginning of the war when he contrasted the speciously logical and civilized figure of Jason against his demonic and unpredictable wife in the *Medea* (431 B.C.). In *The Trojan Women*, produced in 415 B.C. after the massacre at Melos, he voiced a shocked cry of despair at the conscienceless brutality which was infecting all Greeks; and finally, in the *Bacchae*, written toward the end of his life while in self-imposed exile in Macedonia (408–406 B.C.), he created a frightening picture of the total dominance of savage forces in man and nature. Pentheus, the hero of this last play, is superficially intellectual, skeptical, and confident; his adversary is Dionysos, the god *par excellence* of frenzy and self-abandonment. It is no contest. In the end Pentheus' severed head is carried onto the scene by his mother, who along with the other women of Thebes has torn him apart in a fit of madness inspired by the god.

Drama seems to relive in myth, as we have observed earlier, what Greece itself lived in fact. If the Greeks entered the Pelopon-nesian War with the confidence and power of Oedipus, they extricated themselves from it with only the sundered head of Pentheus.

Refuge in Gesture

What kind of art would one expect to see produced during such an era? By analogy with other troubled periods, the late Roman Empire, for example, or Italy after the sack of Rome in 1527, one might naturally predict that there would be at least some traces of an agonized, tortured, insecure art, expressing the anxieties of the age. But the late fifth century confounds one's expectations. What actually appeared was a style which increasingly stressed grace, softness, the elegant flourish, the mastery of manner. In the period from 430–400 B.C. sculptors in particular devoted a great part of their attention to exploiting the decorative potentialities of the 'wind-blown' style of rendering drapery which had been developed by the sculptors of the Parthenon pediments (see Fig. 16, p. 98).

The most conspicuous example of the new style is found in the reliefs of the parapet which surrounded the graceful little Ionic temple of Athena *Nikē* on the Acropolis (Fig. 14). . . . In these sculptures ornamental beauty has become an end in itself and to a great degree has usurped the role of meaning or 'content' in the specific narrative sense. It is true that they do have a general overall theme—victory, and that the Nikai may be thought of as engaged in a very casual processional movement toward Athena, but compared to the Parthenon frieze where each group of figures was planned so as to contribute through both its form and meaning to a single great design and subject, the parapet seems almost aimless. The very fact that Athena appears thrice, like an ornamental motif, seems to say that the subject is just for show and that it is the ornamental function which counts. The Nikai perform a beautiful ballet, but the choreography seems designed to divert one from giving too much thought to the question of just what the dance is about.

. . . On the surface it is all elegance, but underneath it may reflect a despairing desire to retreat from the difficult intellectual and political realities of the age and to take refuge in gesture. Escapist wish-fulfillment is perhaps just as common a reaction to troubled times as overt agonizing. In the great depression of the 1930s the most popular motion pictures often centered on a stylish and carefree hero and heroine who tap-danced their way with unfailing elegance through a series of soothing, inconsequential episodes to an inevitably happy, if never very believable conclusion. The Nikai of 430–400 B.C. may seem to be swirling their way toward a similar goal, yet one can never quite forget what they are trying to leave behind.

14. Nike adjusting her sandal, from the south side of the parapet of the Temple of Athena Nike, Acropolis, Athens, *c.* 420 B.C., Marble, Height approximately 42" (Acropolis Museum, Athens; Hirmer Fotoarchiv)

Ancient Cults in New Shrines

Another effect of the psychological shocks which the Greeks experienced during the Peloponnesian War seems to have been a new direction in Greek religion. Many indications are discernible of a shift in attention away from the group-oriented state religion, in which the individual was important only insofar as he was a participant in the *polis*, toward cults which involved a personal and emotional relationship with the deity. The former reaches its supreme manifestation in the Parthenon, while the latter is perhaps epitomized by the importation from Epidauros to Athens in 420 B.C. of the cult of Asklepios, the god whose miraculous intervention soothed and healed the afflicted. An unusual religious fervor, with strange mystical and personal elements, marked the god's arrival. His sacred serpent was paraded through Athens in a great procession, and the cult seems to have been temporarily

77

housed in the residence of the poet Sophocles, who was said to have had a vision of the god.

The emotional and mystical tendencies which appeared at this time and which were to become the central focus of Greek religion in the Hellenistic period not only eventually produced new mystery cults, like that of Serapis, which offered the hope of personal salvation, but also spurred a revival of interest in ancient cults whose irrational and mysterious elements only enhanced their attraction. A mystical tradition, having its roots in the Bronze Age and represented in later times principally by the Eleusinian Mysteries and the cult of Dionysos, had always had a place in Greek religion, but the confident rationalism of the period between 480 and 430 B.C. had forced it into the background. That it began to surge to the foreground again in a period in which disillusionment was tinged with an urge to escapism is not surprising.

THE WORLD OF THE INDIVIDUAL

THE FOURTH CENTURY AND ITS HELLENISTIC LEGACY

In the conventional terminology used to describe the significant phases in the development of Greek art, the phrase 'the fourth century' normally refers only to the period from about 400 B.C. to the death of Alexander in 323 B.C. The 'fourth century' is usually seen as the last phase of Classical Greek art, and is distinguished from subsequent 'Hellenistic' art, the art produced during the period from 323 to 31 B.C., when the Mediterranean world was at first dominated by the Macedonian royal dynasties founded by Alexander's successors and later by the growing power of Rome.

In many ways the conventional distinction between the fourth century and the Hellenistic period is justified. The general types of monuments which fourth-century artists were called on to execute tended to be similar to those of the fifth century as were the sources which commissioned them. And many stylistic mannerisms—patterns of composition, methods of rendering hair, musculature, etc.—represent logical extensions of fifth-century practices. But if one approaches the art of the fourth century from the standpoint of *what it expresses*, rather than from the standpoint of formal stylistic analysis, it is possible to make a case for its having more in common with the art of the succeeding Hellenistic Age than with its High Classical precedents. In fact, one might view the period from the early fourth century B.C. to the late first century B.C. as a continuum, with the major break between 'Classical' and whatever one chose to call the succeeding era occurring around the end of the Peloponnesian War.

High Classical Greek art, as represented by the Parthenon frieze, had taken group experience and a faith in the attainments of an entire culture as its principal theme. It was the product of an age which was inclined to believe that human beings through their own rational thought and action could perfect their environment. It was an art, one might say, which seemed to be trying to apotheosize the community and its values.

The Peloponnesian War, as we have seen, shattered this state of mind, and a feeling of disillusionment and withdrawal followed. In line with this new state of mind, art in the succeeding centuries tended increasingly to reflect the experiences and values of man as an individual rather than man as a participant in the community.

Personal Experience and the *Polis*

. . . The Hellenistic Age too was a period of psychological readjustment in which community life and the ideals of a circumscribed, familiar society lost much of their force. Cities like Alexandria and Antioch were in some ways like modern cities in which the 'community' has become so large that it has become impersonal. And in an impersonal urban environment each man is thrown back by necessity upon the world of his private experience. He dwells either on those experiences which are intensely personal or on those which are universal and general— that is, those which can be comprehended by all men without their having to be 'conditioned' by a particular culture.

There are clear examples of this attitude in early Hellenistic literature. The *Characters* of Theophrastus, for example, sketches general types of human personalities—e.g., the boor, the snob, the man who talks too much. . . . Likewise Menander's 'comedies,' more often actually taking the form of what we would call 'melodramas,' presented stock types of characters . . . in plots which involved variations upon a limited repertoire of very general human situations—frustrated love, mistaken identity, false accusations, and, inevitably, reconciliation. . . . The 'New Comedy' exemplified by Menander, in fact, enjoyed great popularity in Italy during the Hellenistic period and served as the basis for the development of Latin comedy by Plautus and Terence.

Thus voluntary withdrawal in the fourth century and a far-reaching change in social conditions in the Hellenistic period brought both eras to the same point—a preoccupation with *personal* and *general* experiences rather than with *communal* experience. . . .

The Exploration of Personal Experience: Human Emotion

The most obvious result of this trend toward personal experience as a subject for artistic exploration was a revival of the interest in representing specific human emotions, particularly basic human feelings like anguish, tenderness, and humor which are universal products of personal experience. In dealing with such subjects the art of the fourth century can be seen as continuing a tendency which had begun in the Early Classical period and had been interrupted by the dominant Olympian calm of the High Classical style, but the earlier trend was not resumed without a new shift in emphasis. *Pathos*, immediate personal reaction to experience, now receives more attention than *ēthos*, perhaps because conceptions of 'character' are inevitably bound up with the morals and ideals of a specific social group and the artists of the period preferred to avoid involvement in such questions. . . .

Although the expression of personal emotions like anguish and tenderness may have been most vividly formulated in the works of the great sculptors of the age, it can also be seen in more modest, or at least more commonplace, anonymous monuments, like Attic grave stelae, and its presence in such works may be taken as an indication of its general appeal. . . .

The Exploration of Personal Experience:
Sensuousness and Sense Perception

Delight in the experience of the senses and the pleasure which results from it are also, like pain and other basic emotional reactions, personal and at the same time universal phenomena (in the sense that they apply to all men regardless of cultural conditions); and it seems to be again for this reason that sensuousness, often bordering on eroticism, becomes an increasingly important factor in the art of the fourth century.

In the cultivation of sensuous appeal no artist played a greater and more decisive role than Praxiteles. A languid, soft grace, which gives the impression of being deliberately anti-Polykleitan, and a dreamy atmosphere pervade most of the works which can be ascribed to him. . . .

The Exploration of Personal Experience: Religious Emotion

. . . A trend toward thinking of religious experience in more personal terms can also be detected in some of the important cult images of the period, particularly those of Asklepios, whose compassionate aspect calls to mind later images of the bearded Christ and may conceivably even have served as a prototype for such images. . . .

Idealism and Abstraction

. . . At the beginning it was suggested that Greek art habitually attempts to represent the specific in the light of the generic and hence to favor the representation of ideal types, rather than random aberrant examples, of men and things. It should be emphasized that the fourth century, in spite of its interest in personal experience, is not really an unqualified exception to this principle. The emotions depicted in most fourth-century sculpture are obviously personal, but they are not idiosyncratic; on the contrary, they are universal experiences, and they are presented as universal types. . . .

But while the tendency toward idealism and abstraction remains strong in the art of the fourth century, it now often appears in a new, consciously intellectual, even scholarly form, which must owe something to the philosophical climate of the period and at times seems rather forced when compared to the spontaneous fusion of abstraction and observation of the High Classical period. The formal divorce of the apparent and the ideal in Platonic thought and the consequent exaltation of ideas (in both the transcendental and everyday sense) at the expense of 'objects' of the physical world, for example, perhaps accounts to an extent for the increasingly frequent appearance of personifications and allegory in the art of the fourth century. It is not unlikely that the artists of the time, eager as ever to demonstrate that they too were intellectuals, able to cope with new currents of thought, and not simply manual laborers, saw in personificatory statues a way of demonstrating their own capacity to comprehend and formulate abstractions. If Plato in the *Crito* was willing to turn an essentially abstract concept like 'the laws' into embodied beings capable of arguing with Socrates, artists like Kephisodotos and Skopas could feel a certain dignity in giving physical form to such ideas as 'peace and wealth' or 'yearning.' Personifications of this sort became increasingly common as the century progressed and once again seem to be the ancestors of a long line of such figures in Hellenistic and Roman art.[8]

Another aspect of this intellectualistic trend in fourth-century idealism is the beginning of what might be called 'classicism'— the conscious repetition of features which were characteristic of the High Classical style of the fifth century—at the very least, its Olympian calm and balanced patterns of composition—as if they now constituted formal, established, and approved types. As we have suggested earlier, there has probably been no single, more influential artistic style in the history of art than that of fifth-century Greece. Since then—often in the Hellenistic and Roman periods, at times even in the Middle Ages, and, of course, with an almost continuous passion between about 1400 and 1900— European art has been marked by a series of 'Classical revivals' which seem intended, consciously or intuitively, to recapture something of the confident humanism and harmony of forces which the style developed in the Periclean era embodies. The Classical Greeks managed to put Archaic art almost completely behind them, but the post-Classical Greeks (and their followers) were never quite able to forget their Classical past.

NOTES

[1] The poems referred to are numbered in Diehl's *Anthologia Lyrica Graeca* as follows: Archilochos, no. 74; Solon, no. 1; Semonides, no. 1; Mimnermos, no. 1; Simonides, no. 6.

[2] A *polis* (plural *poleis*) was in size like a city but in its political independence like a state, and is hence often translated as 'city-state.'

[3] The reconstruction of the pediments are based on A. Furtwängler's thorough analysis of the fragments in *Aegina, Das Heiligtum der Aphaia* (Munich 1906). Many of the details which enhance the effect of Furtwängler's models and drawings are of necessity hypothetical.

Art and Experience in Ancient Greece

Both pediments have recently been re-established, using only the ancient fragments and omitting the well-known restorations of Thorwaldsen, in the rebuilt Glyptothek in Munich. Without the Thorwaldsen additions they make a much more austere impression, but no fundamental alterations in Furtwängler's pattern of reconstruction appear to have been made.

[4] A number of the details of the story vary. I follow here the version of Apollodoros *Bibliotheca* II. 4–8.

[5] Pausanias literally says 'an image of Zeus' (v. 10. 6), implying perhaps that we are to interpret the figure as a 'statue of a statue.' The same may also be true for the central figure of the west pediment.

[6] Pausanias does not actually identify the figure as Apollo, and a few scholars have challenged this interpretation, preferring to interpret the central figure as Peirithoös or as the young Zeus. But the identification as Apollo is almost certainly correct. There are cuttings in the figure's left hand which seem to have been intended for an archer's bow, one of Apollo's typical attributes. Pausanias, working from notes and attempting to harmonize information given to him by a variety of guides with his own memory, seems occasionally, and understandably, to have been guilty of errors of omission or misinterpretation. A summary, with bibliography, of the various suggestions about the 'Apollo' is given in G. Becatti *Il Maestro di Olimpia* (Florence 1943).

[7] This clause of the oath is preserved by Diodorus XI. 29. 3 and Lycurgus *Against Leocrates* 81. As a matter of conscience it should be pointed out that the authenticity of the oath, as well as the Peace with Persia, was questioned by the ancient historian Theopompos, and modern historians, after years of controversy, are still divided on the point.

[8] Personifications were not a completely new phenomenon in Greek art at this time, but their number, diversity, popularity, and complexity all show an increase in the fourth century. For a survey of personifications in Greek art from the Archaic period onward see L. Deubner, s.v. 'Personifikationen,' in W. H. Roscher *Ausführliches Lexicon der Griechischen und Römischen Mythologie* (Leipzig 1902–9) cols. 2110–45.

5. THE PARTHENON

Bernard Ashmole

INTRODUCTION

Bernard Ashmole's *Architect and Sculptor in Classical Greece* (The Wrightsman Lectures), concentrating on three important monuments —the Temple of Zeus at Olympia, the Athenian Parthenon, and the Tomb of Mausolus at Halicarnassus—offers valuable information on the process of building a temple, providing sculpture for it, and financing the project. Throughout, there are memorable passages dealing with the subjects and styles of the sculpture, and one section in particular—a characterization of the Early Classical style at Olympia— has been cited by an eminent scholar as "worth learning by heart." In selecting certain portions of Ashmole's two lectures on the Parthenon, the editor has endeavored to retain, even in the abridged form here, some sense of continuity respecting the building process itself, as well as the author's fine analysis of form and content in the cella frieze.

Bernard Ashmole was co-author, with J. D. Beazley, of a long-respected survey of Greek art: *Greek Sculpture and Painting to the End of the Hellenistic Period*, rev. ed. (1966), originally the chapters on Greek art in the *Cambridge Ancient History*. Works dealing with temple architecture and sculpture that should be mentioned here are: Adolf Furtwängler and others, *Aegina* (1906); Walter Hege and Gerhart Rodenwaldt, *Olympia* (1936); Bernard Ashmole and Nicholas Yalouris, *Olympia: The Sculptures of the Temple of Zeus* (1967); Marie-Louis Säflund, *East Pediment of the Temple of Zeus at Olympia: A Reconstruction and Interpretation of Its Composition* (1970); Rhys Carpenter, *The Architects of the Parthenon* (1970), in which the author theorizes that the Parthenon as we see it today is an enlarged rebuilding of a temple already partially complete; J. J. Coulton,

Ancient Greek Architects at Work: Problems of Structure and Design (1977); Evelyn B. Harrison, "Athena and Athens in the East Pediment of the Parthenon," *American Journal of Archaeology*, LXXI, 1 (1967), 27–58; and an excellent pictorial survey, Martin Robertson and Alison Frantz, *The Parthenon Frieze* (1975). On the removal of the Parthenon marbles, now in the British Museum, see A. H. Smith, "Lord Elgin and His Collection," *Journal of Hellenic Studies*, XXXVI (1916), 163–372; and Jacob Rothenberg, *Descensus Ad Terram: The Acquisition and Reception of the Elgin Marbles* (1977).

The selection that follows is reprinted from Bernard Ashmole, *Architect and Sculptor in Classical Greece* (1972), with the permission of the publisher, New York University Press. Copyright © New York University Press, 1972.

The decision to build [the Parthenon], and the way in which it was financed, have been discussed not only in modern times but in antiquity; in the pages of Thucydides we have one or two almost contemporary references to the project, and the old controversies still echo in Plutarch, where there is an elaborate account of the whole policy of Pericles and the motives underlying it. Plutarch was writing about A.D. 100, five and a half centuries after the event. Of course he had access to earlier sources, but we cannot be certain how far he embroidered them, or indeed how far they had already been embroidered: certainly some passages look as if some orator or other had tampered with them, so exquisitely balanced are they and so highly coloured.

All the same, the main lines of the story to be inferred from Thucydides and Plutarch can hardly be in doubt: they are these.[1] On the defeat of the Persians in 479, there was a general agreement among the Greek cities which had suffered destruction, that they would not rebuild the temples destroyed by the Persians, but leave them as memorials of barbarian sacrilege. Very little building seems to have been done for thirty years, with two notable exceptions, the Hall of Mysteries at Eleusis, for the obvious reason that the Mysteries had to go on and that this was the only place in which they could be enacted; the other the temple of Zeus at Olympia, where too the circumstances were exceptional. Elsewhere little was built. But in armaments there was great activity, and a naval league was formed among the Ionian cities and other maritime states, with Athens at its head, and its centre at Delos. The prime purpose of the league was to maintain a navy at sea as a defence against Persia; but because it was difficult for some of the smaller members of the league to supply even one ship, and inconvenient for some of the larger ones to have many of their citizens permanently afloat, a contribution in money was permitted instead, and the league thus had two classes of members, one of whom supplied ships, the other money. Athens assessed the contributions, and Athenian treasurers administered them, although the money itself was kept on Delos. This Delian League Athens gradually transformed into an Athenian Empire by subjugating any members who attempted to secede; and in 454 she transferred the treasury to Athens.

This was the situation when the great building programmes of Pericles began, and it was with the treasure of the Delian League that they were financed. The Parthenon was part only of a far larger scheme, which included the Propylaea, the Odeon, which was a covered concert-hall, yet another Hall of the Mysteries at Eleusis, and the Long Walls between Athens and Piraeus. . . .

It was in 450 that the proposal by Pericles to use the 5,000 talents of accumulated tribute for the building of the Parthenon was carried. Commissioners were appointed to keep account of the expenditure, and to inscribe each year, on a marble slab, the total sum, and how it had been spent. Fragments of this slab have survived, and the information they give us is of great interest.[2] Their first year's account was not until 447, which suggests a good deal of preliminary planning, clearing of the site and organizing the supply of materials before building started. The accounts run for fifteen years, and the year 432 is almost certainly the last. In addition to the commissioners, someone had to be in charge of the whole work, and we are lucky to know from Plutarch who it was. It was Pheidias, and Plutarch says 'he controlled and directed everything.' For the Parthenon, two architects were appointed, Iktinos, who seems to have been the main designer, what we should call the architect; and second, Callicrates [or Kallikrates], who must have been a master-builder, because we know that he built part of the Long Walls to the Piraeus and other fortifications.

What did the architects find when they surveyed the Acropolis before beginning work? They found, on the site afterwards used for the Parthenon, the remains of a temple which had been half-finished when the Persians burnt it thirty years before—the extremely massive substructures, and a number of unfinished columns and column-drums, mostly spoiled by the burning of the scaffolding round them. Much of this material could be re-used, but mainly where it could not be seen: the column-drums were not of suitable size, and even the substructure was of the rather narrow proportions common in archaic temples; Iktinos needed a broader and slightly shorter foundation. Accordingly he used almost all of the other foundations except at the east end, and where he needed the extra breadth, he obtained it by wisely extending the foundations to the north, away from the dangerous made-up southern slope.

. . . The Parthenon, as it was later called, was not pure Doric, but had certain Ionic elements, and it was to make up for what it lacked in size[3] by its material, solid white marble throughout, without stucco; by the refinement of its proportions and details; and by the richness of its decoration.

Let us go back for a moment, put ourselves in the place of Pheidias as director of the whole project and see what his problems were. He must have discussed them with Iktinos the architect and Callicrates the master-builder, since architectural, structural and sculptural matters were all involved, and a whole army of sculptors, masons and other craftsmen had to be assembled and organized, no doubt from all over the Greek world.

They must have discussed the present condition of the site, how the platform could be broadened to take the broader plan that Iktinos proposed, and how far the earlier foundations could be utilized. They must have discussed the supply of material and, after having decided, if practicable, to build entirely in marble, they must have surveyed the quarries of Mount Pentelicus in order to judge whether there was in fact a sufficient supply of sound, pure white marble in blocks large enough for a building of this size; and they must have organized a special system of transport from those quarries which they did eventually decide to use. About a third of the way up the mountain there is a vast cavern from which it is believed that most of the marble for the Parthenon came; and by the time the temple was complete no less than twenty-two thousand tons of marble had been quarried, brought down from Mount Pentelicus, transported ten miles, on carts drawn by teams of oxen, to Athens, and then hauled up the difficult slope on to the Acropolis. Each block, as we know from the terms of a later contract that has survived, had to pass three tests on delivery: it had to be of uniform colour, free from natural flaws, and free from accidental damage.[4]

Within the quarry, the mechanical means were simple but effective—levers, rollers and wedges. Down the mountainside special paved slipways were built, on which the blocks were lowered on sledges, again controlled by simple means, and not without accidents, as is shown by blocks that have been abandoned. Once down the mountain the usual problem of cartage arose, inevitable when, before the invention of roller- or ball-bearings, great weight was concentrated on the axle of a vehicle. These, however, are at the moment outside our scope.[5]

Pheidias and his colleagues must have discussed the time-schedule of the work on the temple very carefully, since the five major elements in it had to be accurately co-ordinated on the Acropolis itself, where space for workshops, for building materials, and for all the litter of a construction-site, was none too plentiful.

These five major elements were, one, the construction of the temple; two, three and four, the various kinds of sculpture on it, namely, metopes, frieze and pediments; and five, the great gold and ivory statue of Athena Parthenos inside it.

If the unfinished temple at Segesta is a trustworthy guide, the external colonnade would be erected first. The joints between drum and drum had to be perfect, but the flutes were not cut until later, in several finely calculated phases. The nucleus of the temple itself, that is, the walls forming the two rooms back to back, one facing east for the cult-statue, the other a treasury facing west; with porticoes at each end, must have been erected either at the same time as or immediately after the columns, because all these were necessary to support the immensely heavy marble roof, as were the four Ionic columns in the western chamber, and also the rows of super-imposed internal columns, which eventually served as a frame for the cult-statue in the eastern.

Of the sculptures,[6] the metopes were the most urgent, since these had to be inserted as the building went up, and before the roof was on. They could not be moved or changed once the entablature was in place above them, and it is doubtful if much work on them was possible once they were in position. Conversely, they could not go in before the building was ready for them: this seems to have been not before 442, when there is an item in the accounts which suggests that the column-capitals were now in place: after that, when the architrave was on, the builder would be ready to accept the metopes. This implies that the metopes were carved on the ground between 447 and 442. If any were not ready by 442, they would have to be built in as blanks and carved on the building, however awkward that might be. The metopes themselves—or such as have survived—would agree well with the supposition that here was a raw and not too well co-ordinated team of sculptors, some of the highest, some of mediocre ability: and that there were miscalculations, corrections and breakages, as if there had been something of a scramble to finish them in time.

Next was the frieze. . . .

Finally the pediments. There was no special urgency about these, except that, consisting as they did of nearly fifty figures, all over life-size and some colossal, they involved an enormous amount of carving. Their carving, however, need not in any way interfere with the building, and the figures could not anyhow be hoisted into position until after the structure was finished.

Pheidias himself must have been preoccupied by the cult-statue, for this was of over-riding importance, and since we know that it was dedicated in 438, a dozen years from the inception of the whole scheme, he must have started on it immediately, making sketches and models, calculating the mechanism of the armature that supported it, and planning its exact setting within the temple, because this would have to be decided almost at once in close consultation with the architect. Then there was the supply of material. Gold presents few problems, provided you can get enough of it, and the Athenians now probably obtained theirs from Ionia and Thrace; but the ivory must have needed negotiation for a supply sufficient in quantity and suitable in quality. This came probably from Africa by way of Egypt, the ancient trade-route down the Nile.

The model for the head of the statue, perhaps made of wood, must almost certainly have been of full scale, in order that the plates of ivory could be fitted together: they could not be joined to one another without support; and it may well be that this wooden backing remained as part of the statue. A limited amount of softening and bending of ivory is possible, but the basis of the whole technique is that no elephant has a tusk more than six inches in diameter, so we have to imagine a face about seven feet high with a skin pieced together from a number of comparatively small strips of ivory.

The whole colossal statue, standing on a base about twenty-six feet wide and thirteen deep, was constructed on a great armature of timber, the central shaft of which went down through the base deep into the pavement, as we can see from the aperture to receive it that still remains.[7] We know that this wooden framework was the regular system with these great gold and ivory statues, from an irreverent remark by the satirist Lucian, who speaks of the families of rats disporting themselves in the hollow interior.[8] The gold, the ivory and the other materials for various inlays on the statue were precious, and had in the meantime to be kept in some secure place. . . .

When Greek archaeologists excavated the Acropolis between 1885 and 1891 it was found that some of the blocks intended for column-drums and for other parts of the temple which was being built on the site at the time of the Persian invasion, had been brought together to the south side and laid in such a way as to form the walls of a building. They were convenient to lay, since they already had their upper and lower beds cut flat; but the structure was evidently made for temporary use only, because the blocks were of irregular shapes and sizes. It would be a fair guess that a building of this massive construction was one in which precious materials were to be handled. . . . It is wise to take precautions when you have a million dollars' worth of solid gold to look after: I think we can assume that this strange building on the Acropolis at Athens, conveniently placed within a few yards of the Parthenon, must have been the workshop in which the Athena Parthenos was made.

As soon as there are locked doors there is malicious gossip. This is not peculiar to our own day, and the tone is familiar. 'Pericles was taking women into the workshops on the Acropolis, on the pretence of showing them the works of art': 'Pheidias was stealing the gold.' Even the usual disgruntled employee, one named Menon, was found to play the informer. Fortunately Pericles had foreseen some such trouble, and had advised Pheidias to make the gold of the statue, plates about a millimetre thick, removable, so that it could be weighed. The charges were refuted; but the story shows that the statue under the gold was really a statue, not just a framework; and when Lachares, tyrant of Athens in 296 B.C., stripped the gold from it in order to pay his troops, what he left must still have looked complete enough to do duty as a cult-statue.[9]

Now for the sculptures made for the decoration of the building;

and first the metopes. There was no suitable place for carving in the quarries on the mountain, and since a regular system of carting the blocks of marble had been devised, it was probably decided to bring them all the way to Athens in the rough state. Because they could hardly be carved in position, although the finishing touches and some of the colour may have been applied then, we have to assume that they were made in workshops, not necessarily substantial structures, either on the Acropolis itself or somewhere near.

The decision to fill all the ninety-two metopes of the outer colonnade with sculpture was a curious one. With the example of Olympia fresh in mind, you would have thought the advantage was obvious of not bringing two sets of high relief, metopes and pediments, into direct competition of scale and subject with one another. And the Parthenon was anyhow less well suited to this form of decoration than Olympia, because in the Parthenon the metopes are not only more distant from the eye, they are also smaller, about four feet instead of about five feet square, so that the figures are well under life-size instead of being, as at Olympia, almost the size of life. At Olympia, too, the sculptors of the metopes were careful to keep the main lines of their designs simple and the masses bold, partly by omitting finely carved detail and relying on paint instead.

Whether rightly or wrongly, the ninety-two sculptured metopes were decided upon, and it seems that, in order to counteract the disadvantages of their small scale and their distance from the eye, instructions must have been given to make the figures as large as possible and to make them project as boldly as possible from the background. Even among the few that have survived, the results are very mixed, as one would expect with a new and large team of sculptors of varying ability.

There are some obvious differences between one metope and another, both in style and in subject. One which has often been pointed out is the contrast between two metopes on the south side, each showing a fight between a Lapith and a centaur. One centaur has a completely human face with so mild and sensible an expression that it could easily be a portrait of one of the sculptor's friends; the other is so grotesque both in its strongly stylized forms and in its savage expression as to make one think that it is taken direct from some dramatic mask.

From the technical point of view the metopes are of two kinds: one kind has a band of marble left projecting at the bottom to form a ground line, and to give support to the figures: the other kind is without it. The base-line seems an elementary precaution which would make the carving both easier and safer, but it was perhaps abandoned when it was realized that by neutralizing a strip at the bottom it diminished the space available for carving. Or the master-designers may have had different opinions on how metopes should be carved, and instructed their teams of carvers accordingly. . . .

In 438 the great gold and ivory statue of Athena Parthenos was dedicated, and in that same year comes the first record, on the inscribed slab, of payments to sculptors for carving the pediments. The slab is fragmentary, and we are almost, but not quite, certain that it is the first payment. Although the structure of the building must have been complete—if only for reasons of security—when the statue was dedicated, both pediments were empty.

The last payments for loading marble at the quarries for transport to Athens were made in 434, and the record on the inscribed slab ended in 432. In any case nothing much could have been done after the outbreak of the Peloponnesian War, within a year. So it looks as if nearly fifty statues in the pediments, all over life-size, were carved, painted and placed in position in five or six years. No wonder people were astonished, as Plutarch says in a striking sentence of five words μάλιστα θαυμάσιον ἦν τὸ τάχος 'Most wonderful was the speed.'

Even if the carving of the pediments did not begin until 438, there must have been much preliminary planning and model-making. Master-designs for the complete compositions of both pediments must have been prepared, and at a fairly early stage the individual figures must have been designed in some detail, for . . . the exact sizes had to be determined so that perfect marble blocks of the exact measurements could be quarried.

As the statues were finished, they were presumably painted and then put into store somewhere on the south or south-east of the Parthenon. Or were they hoisted one by one into the pediments? This must have been a very awkward process, however and whenever it was done, and there is evidence, from the severe cutting away of the backs of some of the statues, that something was found to be wrong at the last moment—either that some would not go in at all, or that they would not fit in the exact position that had been intended.[10]

I have suggested that the filling of the metopes with sculpture was an error of judgment, and one might say the same of the pediments. If so, it was due to the failure to recognize that a large Greek temple is in effect simply a small one made larger, and that to enlarge a building with sculpture on it creates difficulties of scale and, above a certain size, insoluble problems of visibility. Such a failure seems incredible, in view of the amazing skill and intellectual power that went into the making of the Parthenon: but powerful intellects are not immune from elementary blunders. What justification is there for the carving of so much exquisite detail and then for making much of it invisible by skying it more than fifty feet up, and set tight against the back wall of a pediment? When the figures were in place, on the average only about a third of the total surface of each was visible from the ground. It might be replied that these were made for the honour of the goddess, that artists gladly gave of their best to glorify Athena and Athens; that a sculptor cannot work except by conceiving his statue as a fully three-dimensional object; and that there is satisfaction in doing a thing as well as it can be done, even if no one sees it. All these arguments are valid. Yet artists are seldom quite indifferent to the praise of an enlightened public, and we may suspect that a sculptor, as he put the finishing touches to the back of a statue on which he had spent years of work and which he believed was now to be hidden for ever from human eyes, must, in his heart of hearts, have thought it a very great pity. Nevertheless, there is not the slightest trace of anything slipshod, or careless, or sketchy, on any of the pedimental figures that have survived, and the error of judgment, if it was an error, has produced some of the greatest sculpture the world possesses. . . .

Two or three thoughts soon occur to one when comparing these pediments (so far we can judge them in their shattered state) with those of Olympia. The first is that there is here much more movement in depth. Despite some remarkable and even revolutionary experiments at Olympia in modelling the individual figures in three dimensions, the general effect of each pediment is two-dimensional. The pattern reads as a flat composition, and gains practically nothing, except a certain solidity, from being in the round. The east pediment at Olympia makes its effect by a balance of separate comparatively simple shapes: the west is more flowing, but still in essence a flat pattern. In both this is largely because the figures either face the front or look sideways: there is very little three-quartering.

In the Parthenon, on the contrary, there is a deliberate attempt to give the impression that the events are taking place connectedly in space—I do not mean in the heavens, but in three dimensions—and there is a rhythm of figures turning and half-turning towards or away from the centre. The effect is enhanced by parts of the sculptures projecting over the edge of the pediment, as if they were moving freely, unaware of the architectural frame. They are in fact no longer sculptures decorating architecture, but a group of living creatures enclosed accidentally in an architectural container, and spilling over a little at the edges. . . .

A second thought that strikes one about the pediments of the Parthenon is their comparative failure to solve the problem of varying scales within the pediment. This does not matter so much where the beings represented are not of the same class. For instance, at Olympia, the mind readily tolerates the difference of scale between the human beings and the single divinity in the centre: but in the Parthenon there is a manifest difference of scale between one divinity and another, and this discrepancy is the more incongruous the more realistic the sculptures are.[11] And in the west pediment there is really rather a clutter of beings of assorted sizes, including a number of children. Did anyone, even in antiquity, remember who they all were?

A third impression is the greater diversity of styles in the pediments of the Parthenon than in those of Olympia, as if a number of eminent sculptors, each with a strong individuality, had been invited to make their own contribution. Here, however, we must be careful to distinguish between differences that are differences of style and those that are differences of subject. There is for example in the east pediment an obvious contrast between the solidity and sobriety of Demeter and Persephone and the luxurious indolence of the reclining woman on the other side of the pediment (Fig. 15). True, there is a difference of style, but there is also a difference of subject, which very much enhances the contrast. Anyhow, little of all these subtleties could be seen from the ground.

What was essayed tentatively at Olympia is here a primary

15. TOP: Demeter and Persephone, from the east pediment, Parthenon, Athens, c. 438–432 B.C., Pentelic marble (The British Museum, London)
BOTTOM: Dione and Aphrodite (?), from the east pediment, Parthenon, Athens, c. 438–432 B.C., Pentelic marble (The British Museum, London)

assumption—that the forms of the body and drapery are intended to express both the nature of the beings represented and their state of mind. . . .

Take that splendid figure of Iris from the west pediment: only about half of it is left, but it is instinct with life in every square inch that survives (Fig. 16). This is not simply a study of thin drapery over a well-developed body: this is the spirit of the air, and the motive that runs through the whole of the body and drapery is speed—in the resilience of the body, in the tension of the legs, and in the clothing, forced into a series of ripples on the right thigh, pressed flat against the body itself, and fluttering away at the edges as the air streams through it: every single fold bespeaks the action of the wind. Its subtleties will repay unlimited study.

These words of Plutarch about the works of the Periclean age are often quoted, but they seem to me as profoundly true as when he first wrote them: 'They were created in a short time for all time. Each one was at once antique in its beauty, but in its vigour fresh and newly-cut even today. Such is the bloom of youth upon

16. Iris, from the west pediment, Parthenon, Athens, c. 438–432 B.C., Pentelic marble (The British Museum, London)

them, that they look always untouched by time, as if they were suffused with unfailing life, and a spirit that cannot grow old.'

An ancient Greek stranger coming for the first time to the Acropolis at Athens and looking up at the sculptural decoration of the Parthenon might well have been excused for believing that its architect had taken leave of his senses. The metopes were so small and distant that the figures looked like puppets—good and bad were hardly distinguishable—whilst the pedimental figures were at least fifty feet away, and two-thirds totally invisible. When he came closer, his original impression would have been strengthened by his discovery of where the frieze was hidden, nearly forty feet from the floor and at an angle of vision so sharp that it was difficult to distinguish the main actions, and impossible to see details.[12] The light too was unfavourable, since it was all reflected up, much diffused, from the pavements, columns and walls.

The decision to have an Ionic frieze, and to have it here, was an extraordinary one, and induces the uneasy feeling that, like the decision to fill all the ninety-two metopes of the outer colonnade with sculpture, it was dictated by a kind of artistic *hubris*, a determination to load every available space with decoration, and to show what unlimited money could do. For a perfect use of the Ionic frieze we have to look at the little Siphnian treasury at Delphi.[13] It was only twelve feet from the eye, at which height, in the Greek atmosphere, every exquisite detail could be appreciated, and it was framed above and below by massive decorated mouldings, which made it part of the architecture. The Parthenon, however, was a hybrid, and hybrids are apt to exhibit strange features. It was not a pure Doric building nor was its plan quite normal: it had two rooms—one, with its door facing east, containing the cult image, the gold and ivory Athena Parthenos; the other facing west, not connected with the first, and designed to be a treasury. The roof of this treasury is thought to have been supported by four Ionic columns placed in a square near the middle of the room. Whether there was further Ionic detail inside the Parthenon we cannot say, but round the outside of this complex of two rooms, and of the portico at each end, ran the continuous Ionic frieze of marble, about three feet three inches high and five hundred and twenty-five feet long—in all about one thousand seven hundred square feet of carving.

The designer chose a single subject, even if a complicated one, for the whole run of the frieze, and the subject he chose was appropriate, the people of Athens honouring their own goddess. . . . Until quite recently the subject has generally been identified as the Panathenaic Procession, but of late this has been strongly challenged. For the moment, we can agree that it is a procession of some kind.

The frieze was, as usual, fully coloured, but almost all traces have now disappeared: the background was probably deep blue, the bodies of the men were brown, the women's paler, the eyes were painted in: horses, armour, clothing and hair were in strong decorative colours. In addition, objects such as spears, sceptres, reins and the fittings of armour and harness, where they were not shown by painting or carving, were added in bronze. The drill-holes for these attachments still remain, and they often serve to make clear exactly what was going on—an action such as controlling a restive animal can look strangely weak and meaningless when the taut rope or rein, having been of bronze, has completely disappeared.

For the sketch lay-out of the whole frieze, all four sides of it, I assume a single designer, even if some modifications were made by his colleagues afterwards. I assume also a considerable team of sculptors, consisting of a master-sculptor, who was probably the designer himself, a small number, say three or four, of able pupils or colleagues, sculptors in their own right; and perhaps also some carvers, not original artists, but capable of following instructions for roughing out the main areas of the design and, under supervision, of copying the models, if there were any.

The main lines of the design could have been in the form of drawings on a fairly small scale, say on whitened boards, which before the common use of parchment or papyrus seems to have been a regular method. In individual slabs, however, the complication of the successive receding planes within the relief is often so subtle that it seems to demand something more elaborate and more self-explanatory than a flat drawing, something in three dimensions—a model, in short—if it was to be carved by anyone but the master-sculptor himself or a very able pupil. . . .

When the slab is looked at from the end, it can be seen that the designer, trying to do what he can to counteract the steep angle of vision, has arranged that the carving shall be deeper at the top, and shall gradually diminish in depth towards the bottom of the slab. Deep is a relative term, since the greatest depth of any part of the frieze is not more than two-and-a-quarter inches, and within that compass all the richly modelled effects are achieved: it is hardly possible to believe one's eyes. The principle of increasing the depth towards the top is systematically applied throughout the frieze. This was no easy matter, and it must have been the result of a general and quite precise instruction to the whole band of carvers on the frieze how to go about it: an instruction which could only have been transmitted from the master-designer through his expert assistants, who understood the principle, could apply it themselves when carving, could explain it to others less expert and could supervise them in applying it.

The visitor arriving on the Acropolis through the Propylaea, the only public approach, saw the Parthenon first from a point slightly north of west; but the west end was the back of the building, and the normal way of reaching the front was to walk along the north side.[14] Thus the visitor would first see the west frieze, so far as this was visible behind the colonnade, and would then pass along the long north side round to the east front, and would be likely to look at the south frieze separately. That is what the designer evidently calculated: he has divided the procession into two streams: one starts at the south-west corner, passes northwards along the west side to the north-west corner, round on to the north side, along the north side and round on to the east. The other stream starts also at the south-west corner, but it is heading directly east: it passes along the south side and round on to the east front from the other direction. The elements of the procession, almost identical in each branch of it, are these: horsemen at the rear, chariots in front of them, and in front of them those on foot—elders, musicians and young men bearing ritual vessels and driving victims to the sacrifices. On the east front the two branches of the procession converge, and the head of each consists of women being received by officials. In the centre of the frieze, over the main entrance to the temple, a sacred garment is being handled, and on each side of it is seated a group of the Olympian gods. So far as the general design is concerned, the most important action occurs, naturally, in the middle of the east frieze, over the main doorway: over the west doorway the central slab bears an unusual subject, which we shall consider in a moment. On the long sides of the building, where there were no entrances, the frieze runs continuously, without central focus.

We start with the west frieze, as the normal visitor would. A fairly quiet, upright figure at the south end: he is straightening a cloak, which falls in vertical folds and thus provides a strong perpendicular note at the corner, where the architecture calls for it. The whole scene is one of preparation, horsemen forming up for the procession. Some are not yet mounted but are preparing to mount: one is lacing up a boot, another fastening a cloak more securely, another putting a headstall on a horse, another adjusting the reins. The horses already mounted are still restive, stamping and frisking about in the way that a fresh horse is apt to do if it is reined in before it really gets going. These little tricks of behaviour are acutely observed and recorded, and made to enhance the general effect of things getting under way. There is a rhythm of standing, moving, checking, which opens out at the north end with a couple of horsemen starting to canter. This gradually increasing forward movement is punctuated not only by single figures standing still, or even facing in the opposite direction, but also by what might be called panel-pictures, that is, self-contained compositions designed to fill a single slab. . . .

On the central slab,[15] over the western doorway, is a striking scene, a man restraining a lively, excited horse that is trying to break away. Could this possibly have an allegorical reference to the art of government? Pericles, who at this very moment was struggling to maintain his precarious control of the Athenian demos, may well have seen some such vision as this in his dreams.

The most northerly slab of the west frieze, with two horsemen just breaking into a canter, points the way to a new phase, the full cavalcade. New but not disconnected, for the leader looks back and raises his left arm: the look, the gesture and the turn of the body serve to carry the eye and the mind back over all the scenes we have just been looking at. . . .

. . . If you study the cavalcade in its whole length you will find that it is not a steady surge forward, but a rhythmic progress in which some of the horses trot, some are cantering, but most are prancing. This reflects exactly what happens when restive horses are constantly being reined in.

Nowhere is the artificiality of art more evident than in the representation of horses in movement. The still camera rarely or never catches a horse in a pose that would be acceptable to an artist, and a moving picture, run slowly, shows the reason—such poses hardly exist. The eye of the artist, however, makes a selection from the movements he sees and re-combines them into what, for him, is an animal moving in a credible fashion. On the friezes of the Parthenon these movements are recomposed into such a convincing picture that one cannot believe there is any tampering with nature.

There was another way in which some adjustment of nature was necessary, and that is in the matter of relative sizes. The riding-horses in the procession are shown as ponies. They may, it is true, have been small, but they can hardly have been quite so small in relation to their riders as this. The designer had to change the scale for two reasons: one, that the men should not be dwarfed by the size of their horses when they were dismounted: and second, that there should be room for the riders, when mounted, between the horse's back and the top of the slab. The problem was solved, and as with other problems in the frieze—and in life—when they are solved one soon forgets that they ever existed. . . .

There was a new problem when it came to the chariots. Greek chariot-horses were commonly of a different build from riding-horses—larger, and longer in the barrel. This meant that on the frieze they had to be reduced even more than the riding-horses in order to preserve their proportions, and the charioteer had to be reduced too, in order that he could be accommodated at the top of the relief. . . .

In front of the chariots came the procession on foot. . . . The rear of this procession consists of the thallophori, the old men who carried little branches of olive in honour of the goddess and of her great gift to Athens, the olive-tree. . . .

In front of the old men were musicians, now much destroyed, and in front of them again the boys carrying water-jars. . . .

We now overtake the victims. The horned sheep appear only on the north frieze. I cannot recall ever having seen such stately animals: they must have been deliberately enlarged by the designer in order to maintain the focus of interest fairly high on the slab. We then reach the larger victims, the heifers. It is noteworthy that both here and in the corresponding place on the south frieze it is the middle of the file of heifers that is giving trouble, resisting and trying to break loose; and this may well be intended to suggest the difficulty the drivers had in inducing their charges to mount the rocky ascent on the west of the Acropolis. The loss of the ropes, which were made separately in bronze, often impairs both the meaning of the action and strength of the composition. The leading heifers have calmed down, and the designer presents us with a contrast, now becoming familiar, between the great smooth flank of the animal, in its comfortably-fitting natural hide, and the artificial exterior surface of the human being, the cloak, with its loose but harmonious series of folds. It is in this unhurried, unsensational revelation of the beauties of the commonplace that the classical artist excels. . . .

We now go back to the south-west corner and glance at the procession which moves eastwards up the south side. Its make-up is much the same as the procession on the north, except that there are no sheep and no boys with water-pots, and everyone moves from left to right instead of from right to left, as if the spectator were looking at the procession from the other side of the street. The general impression one gets from the south frieze, so far as its very fragmentary condition allows one to judge, is of a certain unevenness of quality: it seems to contain some of the weakest and some of the noblest work of all the friezes. My own guess is that there may have been some hurry to complete it. Being on the least important or anyhow the least urgent side, because it was the side out of sight when one first came up on to the Acropolis and the area round it was covered with workshops, it may have lagged behind the others. Then someone gave orders that it must be finished and finished quickly, perhaps in time for some particular celebration of the Panathenaea, perhaps even because the war was looming up. Working at high speed, poorer sculptors may lose their nerve, but the fine sculptors may be stirred to display another facet of their talent. There is an inspired touch—almost that of an impressionist painter—about one of the chariots at full speed (Fig. 17) and Ruskin's appreciation of it has never been bettered: 'The projection,' he says, 'of the heads of the four horses, one behind the other, is certainly not more, altogether, than three-quarters of an inch from the flat ground, and the one in front does not in reality project more than the one behind it, yet, by mere drawing, you see the sculptor has got them to appear to recede in due order, and by the soft rounding of the flesh surfaces and modulation of the veins he has taken away all look of flatness from

17. Chariot at full speed, from the south frieze, Parthenon, Athens, *c.* 440
B.C., Marble, Height 43″ (The British Museum, London)

the necks. He has drawn the eyes and nostrils with dark incisions, careful as the finest touches of a painter's pencil: and
then, at last, when he comes to the manes he has let fly hand and
chisel with their full force, and where a base workman (above
all, if he had modelled the thing in clay first), would have lost
himself in laborious imitation of hair, the Greek has struck the
tresses out with angular incisions, deep driven, every one in
appointed place and deliberate curve, yet flowing so free under
his noble hand that you cannot alter, without harm, the bending
of any single ridge, nor contract nor extend a part of them.'

 . . . The quarries on Pentelicus seem to have produced blocks
of about four feet long without much difficulty. The slabs of the
west frieze are of this size, and the north and south friezes each
consist of forty-one of these four-foot blocks with half-a-dozen
rather long ones at the ends. The east frieze, however, differs from
the other three friezes. It was composed, not of a series of small
blocks of almost uniform size, but of five exceptionally large blocks
about three times the normal size, with one small one at one end.
The central block is a magnificent piece of marble nearly fifteen

feet long: there can be little doubt that it was quarried to measure, to take the design consisting of the central ceremony with the two main pairs of gods, Zeus and Hera, Athena and Hephaestus, on each side of it. . . .

. . . Both the procession on the north and that on the south are alike converging on to the east front, and when they turn the corners on to the east we are at once in a different atmosphere. It is like a sudden hush. There have been no women in the procession so far. Now they are all women. They stand waiting, silent, and their quiet poses and soft, heavy, voluminous drapery serve as a foil to the speed and clatter of the horses and chariots below, and the slower movement of those on foot who are climbing up the slope to the Acropolis.

. . . In the centre is the culminating event of the procession, whatever it may be, but certainly concerned with a sacred garment, and on either side of this scene two groups of deities who seem to be turning their backs on it. The gods are conceived as being exactly like human beings and are depicted with an affectionate sympathy for the peculiarities of human character. Here again the designer was faced with a problem of scale, and he solved it so skilfully by making the gods seated and by keeping the heads of all the figures level—a principle followed throughout the frieze. . . .

Until quite lately it has generally been assumed that the gods were seated in a semi-circle on the Acropolis itself, invisibly present at Athena's special festival. Professor Fehl, however, has pointed to certain narrow rough projections under the feet of some of them and has claimed that they are rocks.[16] The gods, he thinks, are seated on the rocky summit of Mount Olympus, engaged in Olympian conversation, and displaying a not too passionate interest in what is going on below.

Another new suggestion relates to the central group between the deities (Fig. 18). This is usually interpreted as the handing over of the sacred peplos, woven every four years by specially chosen maidens, the arrhephoroi, for the adornment of a primitive image of Athena in another temple on the Acropolis. The women at the head of the procession who stand empty-handed are thought to be the arrhephoroi, the man who is handling the peplos the archon Basileus, who had inherited the religious functions of the ancient kings of Athens, and the boy a carefully selected boy of high family who typified the city's youth, and the city's hope for the future. The woman would be the priestess of Athena, directing a girl, one of a pair, each of whom carries on her head a stool on which is a cushion or folded cloth. It is thought that they are setting out the stools in the Theoxenia, a symbolic invitation to the gods to be present at the festival. This explanation, though possible, is not entirely satisfactory, and it is a little strange, first that the interest of the scene is divided between the two actions of folding up the peplos, with no suggestion of what is to be done with it next, and the Theoxenia: and second that the main incident, that concerning the peplos, should be off-centre.

Miss Kardara has advanced a new theory, making the boy on the right the principal actor.[17] He is, she thinks, Erichthonios, son of Hephaestus and the earth goddess Ge, and foster-child of Athena. Erichthonios is usually identified with Erechtheus, and his position next to Athena and Hephaestus on the frieze would hint at that relationship. He would be initiating, as the literary tradition affirms he did, the whole ritual of the peplos, and hand-

18. Central group, from the east frieze, Parthenon, Athens, *c.* 440 B.C., Marble, Height approximately 43″ (The British Museum, London)

ing over the archetypal peplos with its woven design of gods and giants, as a model for all subsequent peploi to imitate, to Kekrops, the first king of Athens. For the artistic type of the child wearing this rather unusual and rather old-fashioned dress Miss Kardara cites a parallel on a cup, found on the Acropolis, where Erichthonios, with Athena beside him, is tasting a libation.[18] The boy on the frieze would then be Erichthonios-Erechtheus, the man Kekrops, the woman the goddess Ge, the girls two daughters of Kekrops, whilst the stools are being set out to receive Erichthonios and his mother Ge among the gods.

In detail there are several difficulties about this theory, but on general grounds it has much to recommend it. It would certainly be more satisfactory if the friezes represented a unique occasion, the original institution of the ritual of the peplos, rather than just any celebration of it. And the preponderance of horses and chariots in the procession would be explained by the fact that it was Erechtheus who taught the Athenians to bring horses under control, and invented the chariot. The theory would also explain the absence of the Panathenaic ship, moving on rollers, on the mast of which the peplos was carried in the procession: if the peplos was being handed out instead of handed in, the vehicle would be unnecessary.

More recently still, Mr. Ross Holloway accepts the identification of the boy as Erichthonios-Erechtheus, but takes a different view of what is being done with the peplos, and of the general purpose of the procession.[19] He thinks that, just as the Parthenon was a restoration of its predecessor on the same spot, the procession is a restoration—'a triumphant renewal,' to use his words—of the dedications on the archaic Acropolis, which had perished in the Persian sack. The peplos is a token replacement of the old peploi which had been destroyed, the riders stand for the statues of riders, the animals are substitutes for the statues of animals once dedicated on the Acropolis: even the water-pots, which would be of metal, represent the wealth of smaller votives of the archaic age. I do not find this concept an easy one to digest, but it is worth thinking about, and one of its merits is that it does account for the absence from this procession of four elements which we know from literature to have formed part of the Panathenaic procession, namely the Panathenaic ship, the hoplites in full armour, the women basket-carriers and the women water-carriers.

The Parthenon

Whatever the occasion was, whether the original institution of the ceremony of the peplos or a subsequent celebration of it, the designer has solved most ingeniously the problem of depicting it. . . .

. . . This is not just a procession—whether the Panathenaic or another—frozen into marble at a particular moment in its progress. There is no unity of time, because events which happened in succession are shown as happening simultaneously. There is no unity of place, for they happen in widely separated places in Athens, and on Olympus as well as in Athens. Yet although there is no static unity there is a dynamic unity. . . . In the Parthenon the spectator, walking along the frieze, as we have done, and as a visitor normally would, from the back to the front, himself supplies the unifying factor. He sees one by one all the elements that compose the procession, just as if he were himself taking part. He can share in spirit the preparations—the awkward moments of persuading one's horse to behave and of getting on to it; the gradual speeding-up—and as he moves up the long sides of the temple he finds that he is among the horsemen in full career. He then leaves the horses and chariots behind in the lower city, and accompanies those on foot who are making their way up to the Acropolis; and when he arrives in front of the temple, he finds that he is still not too late to witness the culminating ceremony.

NOTES

[1] For an excellent brief discussion see R. Meiggs, *The political implications of the Parthenon*, Suppt. to *Greece and Rome*, vol. 10 (1963). An entirely new aspect of this problem has now been opened up by Rhys Carpenter in *The Architects of the Parthenon* (Pelican Books 1970). He advances with clarity and force a theory that the Parthenon as we see it today is 'a rebuilding, on enlarged scale, of an already partially completed temple by a different architect . . . the later building incorporating the earlier one by re-using much of its material.' He believes that under the auspices of Cimon, employing Callicrates as architect, the outer colonnade had already been completed, and even some of the metopes now on the Parthenon had been carved for this earlier temple; but that in 448, when Pericles assumed power after Cimon's death in 450, a new and more ambitious plan was conceived. Iktinos was appointed as architect to replace Callicrates and he dismantled and used in different positions the columns of the Cimonian temple. . . .

[2] W. B. Dinsmoor, *A.J.A.* 17 (1913), pp. 53–80, and 25 (1921), pp. 233–47.

[3] Small is a relative term: it was larger than the temple of Zeus at Olympia but not so large as the Ionic temples of Samos and Ephesus or some of the Doric

temples of Sicily. In Athens itself, the vast Peisistratid temple of Zeus Olympios, which might be regarded as a rival of the Samian and Ephesian temples, is believed by Dinsmoor to have been started as a Doric building [*Architect. of Anc. Greece* (1950), p. 91]; it ended six hundred years later as Corinthian.

[4] R. Martin, *Manuel* I, p. 190.

[5] On quarrying in general and the mechanical devices available see R. Martin, *Manuel* I, ch. 2.

[6] The monumental publications by F. Brommer, *Die Skulpturen der Parthenon-Giebel* (1963) and *Die Metopen des Parthenon* (1967), contain a vast quantity of information on every aspect of the sculptures.

[7] For the structure of the Parthenos see G. P. Stevens, *Hesperia* 24 (1955), pp. 240–76; for its subsequent history W. B. Dinsmoor, *A.J.A.* 38 (1934), pp. 93–106.

[8] Lucian, *Zeus Tragodos* 8.

[9] Plutarch, *Pericles* XXXI: cf. Thucydides II, 13. Albizzati, *J.H.S.* 36 (1916), p. 399 calculated the thickness of the gold as one millimetre, Dinsmoor [*A.J.A.* 38 (1934), pp. 93–106] as three-quarters of a millimetre, and suggested that after the plates were stolen by Lachares gold-leaf was later substituted.

[10] See Corbett, *Sculpture of the Parthenon*, p. 30.

[11] Evelyn Harrison's thorough study of the east pediment in *A.J.A.* 71 (1967), pp. 27–58, shows that the relative scale of each figure is determined by its status. This curiously primitive concept (tolerable in the simple contrast between god and man on votive reliefs) is here disguised, and just saved from absurdity, partly by the designer's skilful manipulation, partly because the remains are so fragmentary.

[12] See, however, R. Stillwell, *Hesperia* 38 (1969), pp. 231–41, an important study of these problems.

[13] De la Coste-Messelière, *Au musée de Delphes*, Pt. II, pp. 237 ff.; Lullies-Hirmer, *Greek Sculpture*, plates 44–51, p. 43f.

[14] See G. P. Stevens, *Hesperia*, Suppt. III (1940).

[15] Not quite central; and this weakens the argument.

[16] *Journal of Warburg and Courtauld Institutes* 24 (1961), pp. 1 ff.

[17] *Eph. Arch.* 1960 (1963), pp. 185–202; *id.* 1961 (1964), pp. 61–158.

[18] *Charisterion (A. K. Orlandos)* 2 (1964), pp. 22–4.

[19] R. Holloway, *Art Bulletin* 48 (1966), p. 223; Chr. Kardara, *Eph. Arch.* 1961 2 (1964), pp. 61–158.

6. THE AESTHETICS OF GREEK ARCHITECTURE

Rhys Carpenter

INTRODUCTION

When it was first published in 1921, *The Esthetic Basis of Greek Art*, from which this selection is taken, was cited by one eminent reviewer as possibly the best study in English on the aesthetics of Greek art. Revised in 1959, it continues to occupy an attractive place in the literature. Its author's interest in the psychology of visual perception has often led him into controversial regions, but always he guides the reader to fresh—and delightful—insights into ancient art.

The standard books in English on Greek architecture are W. B. Dinsmoor, *The Architecture of Ancient Greece*, 3rd ed., rev. (1950, 1973); D. S. Robertson, *Greek and Roman Architecture*, 2nd ed. (1943, 1954, 1969); and A. W. Lawrence, *Greek Architecture*, 3rd ed. (1973). See also J. A. Bungaard, *Mnesicles, a Greek Architect at Work* (1957); H. Berve, G. Gruben, and M. Hirmer, *Greek Temples, Theatres, and Shrines* (1962); Robert L. Scranton, *Greek Architecture* (1962); Rhys Carpenter, *The Architects of the Parthenon* (1970), a stimulating study especially interesting for its reconstruction of the career of Kallikrates. Also of interest are R. E. Wycherley, *How the Greeks Built Cities*, 2nd ed. (1969, 1976); H. A. Thompson and R. E. Wycherley, *The Agora of Athens* (1972); J. J. Coulton, *The Architectural Development of the Greek Stoa* (1977), and by the same author, *Ancient Greek Architects at Work: Problems of Structure and Design* (1977); Philip P. Betancourt, *The Aeolic Style in Architecture* (1977); and for a good survey of Hellenistic architecture, T. B. L. Webster, *The Art of Greece: The Age of Hellenism* (1966). A recent and controversial study of the meaning of Aegean and Greek architecture is the eloquent work by Vincent J. Scully, *The Earth, the Temple, and the Gods*, 2nd ed. (1969). One should read, in conjunction with it, the review of the first edition by Homer A. Thompson in *The Art Bulletin*, XLV, 3 (1963), to fix the outlines of the controversy. A fascinating study, which had some influence on Scully, is C. A. Doxiadis, *Architectural Space in Ancient Greece* (1972), translated from the German original of 1937.

The selection that follows is reprinted from Chapter IV in Rhys Carpenter, *The Esthetic Basis of Greek Art* (1959), with the permission of the publisher, Indiana University Press.

I must presuppose that the history and achievements of Greek architecture are sufficiently familiar to the reader. He will know, for example, that the dominant form or theme is the colonnaded temple; that this is built with wall, column, and horizontal beam; and that the structural elements are the square-hewn, close-fitting, mortarless ashlar block, and the various members of two distinct and characteristic "Orders," the Doric and the Ionic, to the latter of which is allied a sub-Order, the Corinthian, scarcely differing from the Ionic save in the form of its capital (Fig. 19). He will know, further, that there are temple remains dating from the sixth century B.C. and remarkable for their vigor and simplicity; that in the fifth century were achieved the refined and powerful buildings on the Athenian acropolis, in which the Doric Order reached its formal perfection and the Ionic its first flowering on Attic soil; and that in the two succeeding centuries the Ionic style was perfected by Pythius and Hermogenes and their respective schools, on the west shores of Asia Minor in such notable exemplars as the Mausoleum, the Athena temple at Priene, the Artemis temples at Ephesus and at Magnesia on the Meander, and the long-travailled but never-complete giant temple of Didymean Apollo.

I must also assume that most of the technical vocabulary of the architect will convey its legitimate meaning to the reader, and that he has already noticed the obvious and salient virtues or limitations of the Greek style.

Thus he will know that it is a current precept that Greek buildings always express their purpose and the mechanics of their construction. A temple-plan is self-explanatory; its elevation never misleads us with any pretence—although it must be granted that it rather effectually disguises the building's interior conformation by spreading a flatly aligned colonnade in front of it. The entablature is not carved or molded to produce a merely decorative façade: the epistyle has horizontal stressings to show its function; we may guess that ceiling beams bed behind the frieze; the cornice is unashamedly a watershed; the pediment occurs of necessity because a sloping roof can end in no simpler or more obvious manner. The acroteria are the only structural nonessentials—and I am not altogether sure

113

that these may not have been survivals of weights to hold down the roof, like the stones on Swiss chalets, or the interlacing of rafters.

We can scarcely acquit the Greek architects of having followed a third popular modern precept by making their architecture express its material, since they not merely painted their marble, but in the members of the two Orders carved forms (such as triglyphs, dentils, guttae, regulae) which were clearly imitative presentations of timber construction. Yet they exploited the good qualities of their building material, by giving their marble walls that lustrous finish which still endures upon them, and by carving designs whose sharpness of line and shadow-free shallows emphasized those beauties which reside more in fine marble than in any other stone. On the other hand, they could not tolerate rustication or ruggedness (except for fortification walls and similar uses) but covered their coarser materials with a stucco of powdered marble which effectively gave the lie to its native qualities. That they sheathed exposed timber with terracotta or bronze cannot be instanced against them, since it was done not so much to disguise the material as to protect and preserve the wood.

There is a fourth precept to which good architecture is generally supposed to conform. It must express (it is said) the mentality and civilization of its builders—as though whatever man consciously makes could fail to be eloquent of himself! Even a Moorish tower upon a Renaissance palace built for the servants' hall of an American millionaire's countryplace is eloquent of its age and culture. Eclecticism is as much a style as any other—and as significant of its attendant civilization. The skyline of Fifth Avenue is very eloquent of the perturbed and composite culture that made it and enjoys it. But it is intended to assert by this particular precept, that the spiritual qualities of an age should somehow be deducible from the buildings which it produces; and it is clearly true of Greek architecture that it is ordered and logical, that it harmonizes part with part, and parts with whole, and that, to a most remarkable degree, it is unfantastic and, in all its elements and proportions, always implies a human use or service, and a mortal eye and a rational mind to observe and approve it (Fig. 20).

There are no structural irrelevancies in Greek building, such as columns which are not the true supports of their superstructures, or façades which merely mask with decorative additions the dispar-

| | Greek Doric | | Ionic | | Corinthian |

| Greek Doric | Ionic | Corinthian |

Key:

A. Entablature	D. Frieze	G. Shaft	1. Guttae	4. Abacus	7. Fluting
B. Column	E. Architrave	H. Base	2. Metope	5. Echinus	8. Dentils
C. Cornice	F. Capital	I. Plinth	3. Triglyph	6. Volute	9. Fascia

19. Three Greek orders (Reprinted by permission of Penguin Books, Ltd., from John Fleming, Hugh Honour, and Nikolaus Pevsner: *The Penguin Dictionary of Architecture* [1966], Fig. 64. *Order,* p. 206. Copyright © John Fleming, Hugh Honour, Nikolaus Pevsner, 1966)

20. Parthenon, view from the northwest, with corner of Propylaea at right, 448–432 B.C. (Propylaea, 437–432 B.C.) (Acropolis, Athens; Martin Hürlimann)

ate structure behind them. But though there are no structural irrelevancies, neither is there much structural inventiveness or ambition. The Greek temple is, in its intent, a one-story affair. The superposed colonnades in its interior were forced on the builder by the physical necessity of supporting the roofbeams and the aesthetic impossibility of doing so by means of a single story of columns (since these would have to be taller and so more massive than those of the exterior order). The two-story colonnade with ground floor and gallery, thus produced, was often employed to line marketplaces and open squares, but seems not to have incited builders to attempt a third or fourth stage of columns. The tower-like superposition of the Orders was reserved for Roman façades and the restless Renaissance to achieve. The stoa, thus limited by custom to two stages, was further restrained in its height by the characteristically Greek consideration that a column more than 12 feet high would seem out of proportion to the human beings for whose service and convenience it was intended. Here, as so often in things Greek, it seemed that "man is of all things the measure." The temples, being houses of gods or at least their images, were not cribbed and cabined by these demands of human proportion: their single story of columns (you would imagine) could swell to any height. But here another proportion stepped in to check their rise toward the colossal: the distance from column to column always bore some sort of established relation to the height of the shafts, and columns could not be too widely spaced lest they could no longer be safely bridged with horizontal beams of stone. The Greeks were timid engineers:[1] a 15-foot air-span gave them pause, and the lintel of Diana's temple at Ephesus was a gigantic achievement. And so when they strove toward the colossal in height, their columns were allowed but barely sixty feet.[2] Except for such exceptional forms as the lighthouse of Alexandria and the Mausoleum of Halicarnassus, how many Greek buildings (like the Zeus temple at Girgenti) overpassed a height of one hundred feet? The theaters, to be sure, stretched up till their topmost rows might be more than this distance above the dancers' circle; but the seats were all bedded safely on the sloping hillside. For the Greeks before the Roman era, no hillside—no theater. Nothing is more surprising than to sketch the elevation of one of the great French Gothic cathedrals and to the same scale superpose upon it the façade of any of the greater Greek temples. Where the two buildings chance to agree in width, as do the Parthenon and the cathedral of Chartres, it is all the more astonishing to see the Gothic pushing its nave to twice the Greek temple's height before ever it begins to stretch its tower and spires toward the sky.

Nor were plans varied or complex or ambitious.[3] The temple was the god's house and the depository for his possessions. What then should a god do with more than two rooms? When the cult-statue was housed and the dedications and sacred treasures were safely sheltered, nothing remained to do. A surrounding colonnade to accommodate the god's worshippers, perhaps; but nothing more. The altar, if only because of its smoke and fire, was in the open air and escaped housing. A peribolos wall, marking out the god's acreage, often shut in indiscriminately temple, altar, and *ex voto* dedications. The Greek architect had no idea of the mysterious in setting or approach; a few chthonian shrines in caverns is all that can be cited. Nor did it occur to him that his god might house, dark and inaccessible, beyond great walls and many rooms, approached through courtyard and hallway and stair, as the gods of the Pharaohs lived in the penetralia of Karnak or Luxor. Nor were there kings to dwell in magnificent palaces. Even a sixth century tyrant was a man among men. Pisistratus might take the Acropolis for his house, and Dionysius might have his dwelling on Ortygia; but these were fortresses, not palaces. Even the princes of Hellenistic Pergamon have only a paltry bit of the great hillslope for their private places. The "palace" of Pericles? There was none. And the great fifth century Athens, which was responsible for the masterpieces of the Acropolis, was only "a poorly laid-out town"[4] of small mud-brick houses and crooked narrow streets. The greatness of Greek architecture is certainly not domestic, but lies in temples and public buildings of the *polis*. Yet how monotonous are the plans of the Greek temples! and although their settings are often wonderful—on the windy sunrise cape of Sunium, among the waste grey folds of Arcadian Bassae, under the shining frown of the Delphic cliffs—how much reliance is placed on Nature and how little does Art contribute! Delphi is as idly and irrelevantly marshalled as the accretions of a cemetery; Delos is an architectural pepperpot; Olympia is unconsidered and fortuitous; the Athenian acropolis—a crown of splendor upon a head of tangled hair—owes much of its effectiveness to the lofty, clear-shining aloofness of its site. Neither in the planning of the individual building nor in its relation to other buildings does the Greek architect show invention or artistic imagination. I do not feel confident that he even considered this latter relation until the fourth century: the symmetry *à peu près* in the arrangement of the buildings on the Acropolis may be very subtle—or very haphazard.

Mnesicles' unfulfilled design for the Propylaea, the town-plan of Halicarnassus and perhaps Rhodes, the carven giants against the gigantic masses of the Zeus temple of Acragas, the Erechtheum plan with its imperfect reaching-out toward a freer form[5]—a list of six or seven such items seems to exhaust the instances of original and powerful departures from the lucid but easy perfection of an established tradition. Two "Orders" and a variant—only that to show for the activity of centuries! Two entablatures and three kinds of capital—is that fecundity? is that inspiration? Is it then so hard for the human brain to invent, so impossible for it to create, that one of the most intelligent and aesthetically most sensitive of races should have only this to show? They are very fine of their kind, these Orders and these temple-, colonnade, tholos-, and theater-forms; but under what limitations and abnegation of originality was their perfection wrought! And how could so many generations of active architects remain content to copy and recopy from the same meager repertory, as though there were no other way to build, no other plans or forms, nor even any other moldings to be imagined, and as though to alter a proportion or to refine a subsidiary outline were achievement enough for any master?

How can we explain such absence of individual invention and artistic variety? Only by referring it to a deep-seated prejudice of the Greek mind. . . .

The impression that the Greek architects were merely seeking the right form, not striving to be original or emotionally expressive, occurs insistently. The proportions of the Doric Order change rapidly but consistently during the sixth and fifth centuries B.C. With the attainment of the right form in the Athenian Propylaea the process of development is almost entirely arrested. Later, the decidence of the Order from favor for temple-construction and the obvious need of a lightened entablature in the use of this Order for colonnades, entirely altered the ratios: the form was no longer right, an altered use had modified it. The profile of the Doric capital changes greatly during the sixth and fifth centuries; but after the time of the Propylaea the only important change is the slight straightening of the top of the echinus which makes the capital so much easier to cut—and entirely robs it of beauty. When the architects no longer appreciate rightness of form, the Practical and the Labor-saving are allowed to announce their wishes.

Until Hellenistic times there was only one important innovation among architectural forms—the Corinthian capital—and that was produced under logical pressure because of the inadequacy of the existing forms. The Ionic capital posed an insoluble problem at the point where a colonnade changed direction (as at the corner of a temple), while the Doric capital could not be extricated from its use with the Doric entablature whose triglyph was a tyrannous nuisance with its interference in the free spacing of columns. Moreover neither the Doric nor the Ionic capital strictly satisfied the logical requirements for the right form. The capital's function is to take the entablature weight and transmit it to the column-shaft. As an intermediary its shape should be consonant with those which it serves: it should be rectangular above and circular below in its cross section, and in the intervening part it must perform without effort the transition from rectangle to circle. The Ionic capital does not meet these requirements; the Doric lacks the transition; but the Corinthian will withstand the most rigorous criticism. It is a marvellous metamorphosis of a circle into a rectangle by a conventional device of leaves tied around a shaft.

The development of the Ionic column-base from the crude and unfelt forms of the Samian Heraion to the Attic or the fourth-century Asia Minor types is a coherent and gradual process. Contemplating it, we have the impression of beholding in operation that which the metaphysicians call a Final Cause, as though it were not each term in the series which occasioned the next, but the ultimate and perfect form like a magnet exerting its attraction through all the attempts of all the earlier builders. Compare, in particular, the Ionic bases of the Propylaea, of the east porch of the Erechtheum, and the north porch of the same building: the last form lies in the first, and progress is as unhesitant as though the path were known and the goal sighted in advance. Equally impressive is the abrupt cessation of experiments and changes as soon as the right form has been attained. The profile of the north porch bases recurs some eighty years later on the monument of Lysicrates, almost unmodified, and the form seems to have imposed itself upon the ancient builders almost as authoritatively as upon their modern imitators. The

119

Corinthian capital has much the same history; its form, once reached, undergoes little further change until late Hellenistic times.

This explanation for the extraordinary tyranny of the canonic form is manifestly inapplicable to all the elements of the Orders. The shape of a triglyph or mutule could not be deduced from the necessities of a roofed two-room shrine in trabeated stone or from any other intellectual formula or requirement. One could derive the column logically, but not its diminution; the capital, but not its profile; the architrave and perhaps the frieze, but not their scheme of decoration; the cornice, but not its profile. With the substitution of stone for timber in early times (for however much one may differ as to the detail of this timber prototype, it is impossible to refuse credence to it in some form or other) the structural justification for the appearance and pattern of regula, guttae, triglyph, mutule, fasciae, and dentils is their pretence of representing in conventionalized form the beam ends, planks, cleats, and even the nail-heads of timber-work transmuted into stone. Once established, these conventions survived through universal recognition of their artistic usefulness for articulating a structure which otherwise would possess little intelligible appearance. However inappropriate to limestone or marble for their material embodiment, and however irrelevant to the structural demands of squared and fitted blocks of stone, they supplied a recognizable norm for imparting to an assemblage of walls, ceilings, roofs, rooms, and corridors a unified, coherent, and shapely appearance—in short, they transformed mere masonry into a stoa or a temple. Precisely because strict architectural logic made no demand for the presence of most of the elements which composed the Orders and could not dictate to them either their shape or size or surface pattern, they escaped criticism, censure, or attack. They had come into existence in the early days of Greek architectural thinking and thereafter persisted in their own right as established species—much as there might be no discoverable inherent necessity for owls or weasels, but there they were, and each had its distinctive and established form. . . .

It is an impressive discovery when the human mind first catches glimpse of the eternal supersensuous laws ruling the seemingly casual appearances of the world of sense. This moment came to the Greeks early in their career in the course of Pythagorean and other geometric investigations. In musical theory its appearance was most striking. Sounds—those intangible and invisible occurrences, seemingly unruled by anything but a fortuitous concordance among themselves—suddenly admitted their allegiance to the tyranny of geometry and number. The consonance of two notes was shown to depend on the presence of a simple integral numerical ratio between the lengths of the strings which produced them. Beauty and ugliness of sound were but functions of Number and ratio, and therefore founded on something measurable, something intelligible. Everywhere, order showed its control within the universe—in the paths of the stars, in the structure of material things—and everywhere, order seemed to be traceable to the influence of Number. If the right and wrong in something seemingly so elusive and unmeasurable as musical tone was based on Number, was it not even more probable that a similar geometric or arithmetic basis should determine right and wrong in the appearance of seen objects, which were material things, measurable and directly amenable to geometric notions? Nature is orderly. The forms for which she strives are strikingly symmetrical and numerically rational. The accidents of matter obscure and confuse the simple geometry of her intentions; but if we compare enough specimens of any species, we can eliminate the individual accidents and construct the true form. Here then is a cardinal assumption of Greek aesthetic practice—that there is a true form for every class of objects and that such a true form is characterized by its geometric simplicity, by the commensurability of its component members. For if its parts be not simply commensurable, then complex and therefore less perfect numbers will enter and take the place of the more perfect ones which might have been employed. Commensurability of parts, συμμετρία, is consequently a test of rightness of form, and it behooves the architect to work by the aid of its precepts.

The generative ratio of the Doric Order was fixed as 2 to 1 in the earliest times of which we have knowledge. In the round building whose architrave was discovered in the foundations of the Sikyonian treasury at Delphi this ratio was apparently not followed: in Hellenistic times the entablature (because so diminished in height) is frequently poly-triglyphal. But between these limits of time, the ratio of 2 to 1 served for what may be termed the generative formula of the Order in its horizontal extension. To every normal column span we find (enumerating the elements as they lie one above the other)

1 column,
2 regulae,
2 triglyphs + 2 metopes,
4 mutules,
4 lion's-heads,
(8 rows of cover-tiles?)

so that an ordinary Doric colonnade beats out a rhythm of full-notes in the columns, half and quarter notes in the entablature, and (frequently) eighth notes on the sloping roof, and even sixteenth notes in the floral ornamentation of the sima between the lion's-head water-spouts. In the Zeus temple at Olympia the measurements in ancient feet show how thoroughly and coherently the ratio was applied: the width of the roof-tile is taken as two feet, twice this measure gives us the width of a mutule with its *via* as well as the distance from lion's-head to lion's-head on the roof gutter, twice this latter measure gives the width of a triglyph with its metope, as well as the length of an abacus block, twice this measure gives the width from column center to column center, which is also the length of an epistyle block, and twice this last measure gives the height of a column. Finally, if the central acroterion of Nike was life-size, the total height stylobate to peak of gable-figure may very probably have equalled twice this last measurement. And so with $2 \times 2 \times 2 \times 2 \times 2 \ (\times 2?)$ the exterior of the temple is built up, and the tacit assumption seems to be that the eye, contemplating these forms, will be rhythmically affected by the simple numerical ratios inherent in them.

A more sophisticated employment of numerical ratio occurs in the colonnaded portico which the late fourth century architect Philon added to the Hall of Mysteries at Eleusis. There—as building inscriptions state and existing fragments of the architectural elements confirm—the columns' lower diameter was set at six feet while the open floor-space between the columns was set at nine feet; half of the former dimension was assigned to the triglyph width, half of the latter to the metope width; and half of this last measure was given to the overhang of the cornice over the frieze.

The giant columns of Persepolis clearly betray Greek influence, and not least in their careful observation of numerical symmetry. The two fore-parts of bulls which carry the rafters are supported by a four-sided theme, each side of which has four scrolls or volutes (each decorated with sixteen-petalled rosettes) into which a four-filleted band has been wound; this in turn is supported by a capital whose upper portion shows eight, while its lower portion shows sixteen, floral divisions; below, a shaft with forty-eight flutings is supported on a base whose petal forms number twenty-four.

There can of course be no doubt of the conscious use of this simplest of all numerical ratios as a generative formula in the Doric Order, but it should not be imagined that all the measurements therefore will be found to be mathematically exact—all equal or double or quadruple—in the ancient Doric temples. In the Sicilian temples[6] especially there occur the greatest irregularities in the spacing of the columns and the size of the various members. Much of this may be attributed to indifferent workmanship, since the eye really exacts only very general approximations to the mathematically correct in architectural ratios. But in the classic instance of the Parthenon it is a very difficult thesis to maintain that the irregularities are attributable to mason's errors or the architect's indifference to exactness. Rather it appears that the builders deliberately sought to temper the mathematically correct by slight departures from the "true" measurements, even carrying this ideal so far that they left no straight line straight nor any spacing equal.[7] We cannot fail to recall the practice of the sculptors contemporary to the Periclean architects, and particularly that reputedly Polyclitan saying concerning the "many numbers" which *"almost"* give perfection. The so-called "refinements" of Periclean architecture, the slight deviations from perfect regularity and symmetry, are not optical corrections for untrue illusions,[8] but are added in order to give life to the rigid mathematical correctness of the standard norm; they are departures from the "many numbers," out of which arises perfection. Certainly it is a very surprising thing that the Parthenon measurements cannot be reduced to feet and dactyls according to any common scale. A foot of .2957 meters will do fairly well; a foot of .3362 meters will apply with nearly equal success; but neither these nor any other unitary lengths will fit all the measurements, because they are integrally incommensurable. We can only conclude that the builders of the Parthenon (whether by intelligent imitation or by intuitive artistic taste) had applied to architecture the same secret of beauty which governs natural forms—the tempering of geometric accuracy by minute deviations in the interest of irregularity. I need only refer to the extraordinary mathematical precision which underlies natural forms in the vegetable and animal worlds[9] and to the patent observation that in any given individual of the species the precision of the underlying form is always tempered by the irregularities attendant upon the chance elements of environment and growth, and add that we are apt to find the actual slightly irregularized flower or shell more real, more "living," and more artistically moving than the cold geometrical perfection of the underlying form. The form only lives when it is irregularized in matter. In architecture the forms are man-devised; but if they are harmonized with mathematical precision and then irregularized in their material presentation, they will acquire a status analogous to that of a living thing in nature. . . .

I have dwelt a good deal on this numerical aspect of Greek architecture not only because it is philosophically interesting in its own right, but also because of certain remarkable implications which it involves. Out of Number come commensurability of lengths and surfaces and, by repetition, architectural beat and rhythm. But all these in Greek architecture are only effective upon the spectator if the matter in which they are embodied is seen as in one and the same plane.

The rhythm of a Doric colonnade with its measured recurrence of columns moving past, while the triglyphs double and the cornice and roof quadruple the same steady beat—all this is effective, indeed exists for the beholder, only if all these elements are felt to be on a single surface or area or plane. Theirs is an art of related lines and surfaces, not of solids. . . .

Instead of true depth, Greek architecture gives us successive and usually parallel planes. The stoa or colonnade presents the front plane of the exterior order, the middle plane of the columns which support the roof-beam, and the rear plane of the wall at the back. There is no sense of depth or enclosed space. Rather, the true depth has been converted into a succession of nearly flat and wholly disconnected surfaces—precisely as in Archaic Greek relief sculpture. Even the roof, thanks to the straight mounting lines of the cover-tiles, joins in the vertical planes. The human beings moving in this colonnade appear to the exterior spectator like bas-relief on the rear plane.

With the temple it is, of course, the same. On the long sides there are two parallel planes, that of the colonnade and that of the naos wall; on the short sides there are three planes, that of the exterior colonnade, that of the vestibule colonnade and that of the rear wall of the vestibule (with or without its doorway with door or hanging). More complicated vistas in agora or temenos only add other planes. In glimpses across angles of colonnaded squares, or through corners of dipteral temples, the masses are all presented at intervals so that the eye sees a series of superimposed surfaces sharply divided by an intervening break of perfectly indeterminate extent. It should be added that the Greek atmosphere encourages this impression by eating up the air's appearance of solidity, so that space loses its density and surfaces seem directly superimposed. . . .

And so there follows the most remarkable property of all in Greek architecture. Since its appearances all lie in parallel or perpendicular planes, it can only *define or bound solid space, and cannot enclose it.*

Just as there is no true depth to a Greek colonnade, but only the specious depth of Greek sculptured relief, so there is no sense of space shut in and contained in anything that the Greek builders made. Even the temple-interiors offered only more colonnades and walls in parallel planes, topped by a flat ceiling which was only another plane at right angles. Such a procedure bounds space, defines it; but though mechanically it contains space because it shuts it off, it is powerless to impart any such feeling to the human mind. Whereas a vault closes down upon space and makes space sensible, a panel ceiling merely ties the walls. In the terms of relief-carving, it acts like the straight edge or step between successive planes.

That these temple interiors were but half-lighted is perhaps an indication that artistically they were but half-felt or half-considered. They were but the space enclosed by the inner faces of the walls; they were the inside of the treasure-chest, serving to shut in the gold and the sacred heirlooms; and just as the outside of a chest has the craftsman's favor and gets the carving and gilding, so it was the exterior aspect of these enclosing walls which appealed to the ancient builder.

No doubt this is somewhat fanciful, and there exists a better reason for the opinion that interiors were the least successful aspect of Greek architecture. For it is of the utmost importance to note that Greek architecture had almost no need (of a direct practical kind) for trying to shut space in. Greek life was out-of-doors. The houses were mere sleeping-cells about a central patio, the theaters were unroofed gathering-places of the people upon the hillside; the marketplaces were open; even the shops were mere storehouses from which goods for the day's trade could be brought out to be spread in the open bazaar; the colonnades were but casual out-of-door shelters from wind and rain and sun; the schools were out-of-door palaestrae; the hospitals were colonnades in the sacred precinct of Aesclepius. Only the temples and the council-rooms so much as put the problem of enclosing airspace with encompassing masonry. Before the late Hellenistic age, domestic architecture hardly existed. It is not remarkable, therefore, that the architects devoted themselves wholly to external appearances or that, given the Greek conditions of atmosphere and light, they learned, as no other race has done, the secret of surface and line, but got no farther in the aesthetics of their art than the expression of support in vertical parallel planes.

We may assert, therefore, that the Greek architects had no comprehension of the artistic handling of space in interiors. That vast preoccupation of Gothic and modern designers was to them a book unopened. If a paradox is permissible, their only interior compositions were out-of-doors, where the roof was the blue sky. In town-square and temple-precinct they composed spatial complexities; but the picture is always made of overlapping surfaces moving across one another as the spectator moves. The intervening depths are lost, just as they were lost for the ridges and gulleys and forests of their own beloved mountains which still today show like flat bas-reliefs against the Grecian sky. . . .

Upon this two-dimensional character of its visual presentation Greek architecture based its artistic effects. Since support in the immediate vertical plane was all that such an art could present to the eye, all expression of weight sustained and held aloft must appear in the arrangement of lines and surfaces in the frontal plane of the Order. The entablature presses flat upon the columns and therefore can tolerate only horizontal or vertical lines in its decoration, since in this way the heavy uncomprising mass can be made directly intelligible. Our eyes follow the horizontal lines and our emotions instinctively interpret such lines in terms of mass in a state of rest. We have experienced just such a sweep of line in looking at the horizon of plains or of the ocean: it is the line of things outspread, heavy and immovable and enduring, held by gravity, but in no danger of falling. The columns express in their contour successful but not effortless resistance to this downward pressure, which weighs squarely and heavily upon them until they bulge with the pressure. Here presumably is the psychology of entasis: it is the visible yielding to compression until a stable condition of resistance is reached. It establishes an analogy with human muscular effort and presents it directly to our emotional sensibility.

NOTES

[1] *The Greeks were timid engineers.* Consider the elaborate precautions taken with the central span of the Propylaea (W. B. Dinsmoor in *American Journal of Archaelogy*, [1910], pp. 145 ff). By applying the modern engineering formulae given in Kidder's *Architect's and Builder's Pocketbook*, I find that these precautions were superfluous.

[2] *These columns were . . . but barely sixty feet.* Cf. Athens, Olympieum; Miletos, Didymeum; Ephesos, "fifth" or Hellenistic temple of Artemis.

[3] Contrast the rich inventions of plan in late Roman times (Montano, *Scielti di varii tempietti antichi,* and *Raccolta di tempii,* etc.).

[4] πόλις κακῶς ερρυμοτομημένη Dicaearchos I. 1.12.

[5] I do not accept Dörpfeld's suggestion of an original symmetrical plan doubled on a north-south axis.

[6] Cf. Koldewey and Puchstein, *die griechischen Tempel in Unteritalien und Sicilien.*

[7] *. . . they left no straight line straight.* The material for the study of this question is to be found in Penrose, *Principles of Athenian Architecture* and Goodyear, *Greek Refinements.*

[8] *. . . not optical corrections.* Goodyear has abundantly proved this point in the book referred to in the previous note.

[9] Cf. T. A. Cook, *The Curves of Life;* d'Arcy Thompson, *Growth and Form;* A. H. Church, *Relation of Phyllotaxis to Mechanical Laws;* and the two (very popularly written) books by S. Colman and C. A. Coan, *Nature's Harmonic Unity* and *Proportional Form.*

7. HELLENISTIC ART

George M. A. Hanfmann

INTRODUCTION

George M. A. Hanfmann's article "Hellenistic Art" was written in conjunction with Ernst Kitzinger's "Hellenistic Heritage of Byzantine Art," papers presented at an exploratory symposium on the Hellenistic origins of Byzantine civilization held at Dumbarton Oaks in May 1962. Quite apart from its original purpose of providing background for Professor Kitzinger's discussion of Hellenistic elements in Byzantine art, the selection that follows can stand alone as an excellent introduction to Hellenistic art, its thematic range, and stylistic variety; and, as the reader will soon discover, it is not without considerable relevance to developments in Roman art.

The standard work in English on Hellenistic sculpture is Margarete Bieber, *The Sculpture of the Hellenistic Age,* rev. ed. (1961). Chapter II of Gisela M. A. Richter's *Three Critical Periods in Greek Sculpture* (1951) surveys the various trends of the last third of the fourth century B.C. which saw the formation of Hellenistic (as distinct from Hellenic) art. Another work on the fourth century B.C. is B. Brown, *Anticlassicism in Greek Sculpture of the Fourth Century B.C.* (1973). T. B. L. Webster, *The Art of Greece: The Age of Hellenism* (1966) is a good survey. E. Schmidt, *The Great Altar of Pergamon* (1962) and D. Thimme, "The Masters of the Pergamon Gigantomachy," *The American Journal of Archaeology,* L (1946) examine a key monument of Hellenistic art. Other aspects of Hellenistic art, further emphasizing its international character, are discussed in W. A. Lawrence, "Rhodes and Hellenistic Sculpture," *Annual of the British School at Athens,*

129

XXVI (1923–25), and by the same author, "Greek Sculpture in Ptolemaic Egypt," *Journal of Egyptian Archaeology*, XI (1925). Other works are Margarete Bieber, *Laocoön: The Influence of the Group Since Its Rediscovery*, 2nd ed. (1967); Peter H. von Blanckenhagen, "Narration in Hellenistic and Roman Art," *American Journal of Archaeology*, LXI (1957), 78–83; and Christine Havelock, *Hellenistic Art* (1971), a survey. With respect to painting, the reader should also consult the bibliographical suggestions in the introduction for the selection by Otto J. Brendel on the frieze in the Pompeiian Villa of the Mysteries (p. 173).

The selection that follows is reprinted from George M. A. Hanfmann, "Hellenistic Art," *Dumbarton Oaks Papers*, XVII (1963), pp. 83–94, by permission of the author. Several passages, footnotes, and illustrations have been omitted in this reprint. Footnotes and illustrations have been renumbered.

FACTORS LIMITING A COMPARISON OF
HELLENISTIC AND BYZANTINE ART.
ESSENTIAL TRAITS OF HELLENISTIC ART

In an attempt to make the vast subject manageable, Professor Kitzinger and I have agreed to limit our discussion to certain major themes. I shall try to combine this attempt to seek out what was and what was not of interest to Byzantine artists with some intimation of what I conceive to be some of the essential traits of Hellenistic art. Thus we may hope to avoid an undue displacement of emphasis. Nevertheless, some of the major limitations of this procedure must be indicated. To make any useful comparisons with Byzantine art, we must emphasize pictorial media; yet the basic intuition of Hellenistic art was still plastic, and the plastic, three-dimensional human figure held the center of the stage. Then again, the focal themes of Byzantine art are the Sacred Image and the Sacred Cycles of the Old and New Testament. Neither the cult image nor the mythological, biographical cycle are the most expressive vehicles of Hellenistic creativity. Its full grandeur and splendor revealed itself in divinely hallowed, sacral but not sacred, atmosphere of heroic myth, and, on a more comprehensive scale, in complexes in which nature, architecture, sculpture, and probably painting were united for the sake of the total effect in a new sense of an immediate (as against the Classic distanced) nature-given reality. The Victory of Samothrace (Fig. 21) sweeping down from a mountain to alight on a "real" ship over the real water of a fountain pool, the Gauls of the great Attalid dedication fighting their defiant battle against the backdrop of the grand vistas of the eagle eyrie of Pergamon, and the Eros, asleep on his "real" rock, these seem to me to represent the essence of Hellenistic achievement.[1] If we look for their common denominator, it is vitality, *vis vitalis*, heroic or idyllic, manifesting itself within the framework of the vast diversity of nature, which is the true hero of Hellenistic art.

21. Nike of Samothrace, Hellenistic, c. 200–190 B.C., Marble, 8' High (The Louvre, Paris; Marburg-Art Reference Bureau)

EROTICISM

Eroticism pervades Hellenistic art. If any divine powers other than Tyche enjoyed universal and popular interest, it was Eros, Aphrodite, and Dionysus. Hellenistic poetry played countless variations on the theme of the mischievous god of love, sometimes baby, sometimes a small boy, who hits indiscriminately with his arrows, burns lovers with his torch, and is in turn punished, his bow broken, his wings clipped.[2]

A world of infantile fantasies transforms myth and daily life, as when erotes play at adult work.[3] Starting from the theme *omnia vincit Amor,* the erotic invasion of myth brings before us erotes who take away the armor of the god of war and the club of the strongest of mortals, Heracles.[4] In myth after myth, heroic couples are turned into sentimental lovers.[5] . . .

There is frank and joyous love-play, especially among satyrs and maenads, now interpreted as nature's children;[6] but in much of Hellenistic art we sense an overtone of sophisticated perversion. It is the only art which has openly glorified the hermaphrodite.[7] . . .

Hellenistic Art

HUMOR AND LAUGHTER

From Archaic times on, the burlesque, the fantastic exaggeration, the parody was the great vehicle of Greek humor. It is the essence of the gusty, lusty, riproaring laughter of the Old Comedy. In the Late Classical age, this tradition lived on in the Phlyax.[8] Hellenistic humor is first and foremost an extension of this theatrical humor into the reality of daily life. In an amazing outburst of caricature, Hellenistic artists portrayed slaves, dwarfs, misshapen people, and barbarians as real-life cousins of the fantastically ugly and ridiculous people of theatrical comedy. These grotesques combine the traditional satyric approach of the comedy with keen observation, replace the stylized exaggeration of the masks with nature's quirks, and bring the new naturalistic and scientific approach to bear upon the traditional types and situations. This humor is not always good-natured. The Hellenistic world thought funny what we may consider cruel and brutal.

Laughter and smile, on the other hand, were glorified as expressions of an uninhibited, desirable natural state best embodied in Dionysiac beings and children. Laughter as an expression of ebullient vitality achieved a positive value which was not, however, permitted to invade the traditional solemnity of heroic myth—except in little byplays involving satyrs or erotes.[9]

GENRE

With the grotesques, we have already touched upon one kind of Hellenistic genre. Let us consider briefly some examples of other types. Despite their intensive observation of "low life" the "Street Musicians" by Dioscurides of Samos are conceived in the spirit of the satyric grotesque.[10] The brilliantly painted "Woman and Shepherd" on the other hand, have been conjectured to represent a mythological scene from the Wanderings of Demeter.[11] Daily life or humanized myth?—that this question can arise is characteristic of the Hellenistic age. Certainly humanization of myth was progressing in the arts. This desire to make the divine tangible, detailed, and concrete need not lead to lack of belief. Thus it has been said of Dionysus that while the divine child becomes ever more sacred, its representations become ever more human.[12]

The theme of mother and child, on which Professor Kitzinger will touch in his paper, discloses something of the Hellenistic approach to humanization of myth and, at the same time, reveals some interesting traits of the attitude of the artists toward the theme of motherhood. There is genuine human appeal in such pictures as that of Danae nursing little Perseus[13] after she and her baby have been rescued from their floating box by the two fishermen, who look on with astonishment and sympathy; but the picture is not primarily a symbol of tender relation between Mother and Child. Rather it is a humanized visualization of a certain incident important for the mythological story. That nursing mothers are often figures of the Dionysiac thiasos, that tender scenes of women fondling babies show not mothers but benevolent nymphs, that Eros and Aphrodite are the son and mother most frequently shown, that scenes of tenderness sometimes turn out to be erotic—as in the baby cupid sitting in Psyche's lap[14]—all of this suggests that motherhood as such was not being glorified. Indeed, in a recent study on Birth and Childhood of Divine Children[15] J. Laager has concluded that in the Olympian mythology the mother-child relationship tends to fade into the background in favor of a male protector of the child—a Hermes, a Silenus. Hellenistic art impartially humanizes and sentimentalizes both—the mother as well as the male protector.

ENLARGEMENT OF THE PHYSICAL WORLD: LANDSCAPES AND ARCHITECTURAL SETTINGS

One of the most striking creations of Hellenistic art are the so-called "sacral-idyllic landscapes" which lie in a border land between genre and myth. Here the mythical and sacral overtones are an integral part of the vision of an idyllic land of shepherds and wanderers, not the real shepherds and wanderers but the shepherds of the Theocritean idylls. Sometimes this idyllic land is shown for its own sake.[16] Sometimes it forms the setting for a mythological narration such as Odysseus' wanderings through the countryside, the portrayal of which became fashionable in Late Hellenistic Rome. The very sketchiness of the pictorial technique enhances the dream-like quality which is still ideal in a thoroughly Greek—but not in a Classical—way. What is missing here from the point of view of genre is not naturalistic observation but the direct, factual statement such as we encounter in untutored Roman folk art and in the Vienna Genesis where camels behave like real camels, sturdy and mean, in contrast to the evanescent vision of a camel as seen in the Yellow Frieze of the House of Livia.

The "sacral-idyllic" landscapes bring us to the problem of Hellenistic landscape in general. No subject is more controversial. This discussion must center on the famous Odyssey landscapes, certainly the most highly developed renderings of landscape which have come down to us from antiquity. P. H. von Blanckenhagen has argued that these pictures are derived from an earlier frieze-like Hellenistic painting which was not interrupted by columns or pilasters; the Yellow Frieze in the House of Livia and some other "sacral-idyllic" landscapes have been cited in support of this view.[17]

These putative Early Hellenistic landscapes remain phantoms. We must, I believe, accept this astonishing performance for what it is—a monument of the Hellenistic landscape painting in its latest, Roman phase. The most significant aspect of the Odyssey pictures is the sense of pantheistic vastness of nature, a nature which achieves importance equal, if not superior to the myth. This nature still receives its final animation from men; but the heroic mood is now nature's, not man's. The perennial life of the universe will go on, even when the Odyssey has ended.

In their comprehensive scope and sweep, the Odyssey landscapes are unique; but something of the same marriage of myth and nature in a poetic mode occurs in the various "sacral-idyllic" or "idyllic-mythological" paintings. In literature a similar chord, struck first in the descriptions of the Isles of the Blest, echoes in the "Blessed Landscapes" of Hellenistic romances.[18] In the celebrated picture of Paris on Mount Ida the theme is "an ideal shepherd in hallowed solitude of the mountains," not the hero or the villain of the tragedy of Troy. It is this overtone of ideality of a dreamland as remote as Paradise which seems to have inspired Byzantine artists in Ravenna to adopt such a "Landscape with Shepherd" for the portrayal of the Good Shepherd;[19] but as may be readily seen by the Roman rendering of the subject in Hadrian's Villa, the Christian mosaicists drew their inspiration not from the pantheistic interpretations of Hellenism, with their small figures and large, panoramic landscape, but from the simplified "middle-scale" interpretations of the Roman period.[20]

In other Late Hellenistic representations, the ideality of the framework is less obvious and the specific character of the setting is elaborated, with some borrowings from the cartographic tradition. Civilized urban life is made part of this picture of the *oikoumene* when the so-called "city formula"[21] is added to panoramic vistas of sea and rock. Here again, in varying degree, the setting is more prominent than the action. The fall of Icarus is only an incident in the continuous life cycle of man and nature (Fig. 22).[22]

Potentially, this kind of animated landscape was adaptable to historic narration. In the Jonah scene of the Paris Psalter (Fig. 23), the artist seems to have been strongly impressed by the vision of an ancient "city by the sea" (Fig. 22). Indeed, the miraculous delivery from the belly of the whale becomes almost incidental. There are other striking resemblances; the little boat with the spectators here turned into boatmen who throw a sacklike Jonah overboard, the upward thrusts of gesturing hands transformed from astonished comment into pious urgency of prayer, the lofty place of the luminous divinity in the upper regions of the picture—in one Helios, in the other the hand of God in sunlike orb. Here, for once, one feels that a Hellenistic model may have been the immediate source.[23]

We can recall here only briefly the great variety of other Hellenistic experiments in suggesting spatial, physical setting. What we know of Greek geometry and optics confirms the ancient tradition that architectural drawing applied to theater backgrounds was the primary vehicle for the only consistent optic constructions which ancient painting had achieved. We are fortunate in having a Tarentine vase of the Late Classical period a reflection of an early stage in this process.[24] Its final phase is seen in such pictures as that of Iphigeneia on Tauris set against a magnificently Baroque stage background in the house of Pinarius Cerialis.[25] Other solutions show cities climbing up mountains, and bird's-eye views of cities (Fig. 24), intimate close-ups of civilized nature in Roman villas, and rising rocks peopled with heroic, monumental figures as in the Orpheus painting from Pompeii—which is rather strikingly related in its composition to the rendering of Moses on Sinai in the Paris and Vatican Psalters. This experimentation also comprises architectural backgrounds for narrative friezes such as are shown in scenes from the Iliad on the jug from Bernay and in the stucco frieze from Casa del Criptoportico in Pompeii.

Enlargement of the physical world was thus, in the main, a

22. Pompeii, House of Amandus, Wall Painting, *Fall of Icarus*, First Century A.D.

Hellenistic achievement.[26] It remains to point out its obvious limitations. Despite their knowledge of axial perspective, Hellenistic painters never managed to detach this geometric construction from the representations of architecture and to apply it consistently to nature-made elements of landscape. The relation of landscape and figures remains in a kind of labile flux which enhances the sense

23. Paris Psalter, *Jonah, c.* 900 A.D. (Bibliothèque Nationale, Paris, after H. Omont, Fac-similés des miniatures des manuscrits grecs de la Bibliothèque Nationale, 1902, pl. 12)

24. Pompeii, House of the Little Fountain, Wall Painting, *View of Imaginary Town and Landscape*

of unreality. It is the unity of coloristic treatment, the dynamic play of highlights, and the sustained harmony of moods that holds this world together.

ILLUSIONISM

"Illusionism" is a term often used to describe the great advance made by the Hellenistic painters in conveying the impression of a world rich with color, spread out in space, and enlivened with light and shade. The term is not unambiguous—ever since Plato antiquity had felt that there is involved in pictorial representation on a two-dimensional surface an element of illusion in the sense of delusion and deceit, of showing what is not. On the whole, Hellenistic art took a positive attitude toward this deceit. To ancient critics, the pictorial achievements of what we would term Late Classical and Early Hellenistic painting were nothing short of miraculous. To understand their enthusiasm, we must not forget that these were discoveries made for the first time in the history of mankind. A Late Hellenistic theorist, whose views are preserved by Pliny (XXXV:29), states that painting at long last differentiated itself from other arts, discovered light and shade, explored hue, value, and gradations as well as contrasts of colors, and then added something described as *splendor* and specifically said to be different from light (*splendor, alius hic quam lumen*). This is usually translated as "glow"; what it appears to mean is the general heightening of optical effect attained by the use of highlights as well as by coloristic devices.

From our vantage point of Post-Impressionism and highly developed color photography, the achievements of Hellenistic painters seem curiously incomplete. Yet, even in the provincial reflection by Pompeian wall painters, such is the somnambulistic certainty in the evocative handling of the brush that a critic of the rank of a J. Burckhardt felt himself "seduced into impieties toward the Renaissance" by the brilliance and brio of the ancient Campanians. In their best work, the new pictorial means are utilized to endow the human body, by color and highlight, with a pulsating life and a juicy opulence which sculpture cannot attain.

"If there are any first-rate paintings in Pompeii, they are these," says a sensitive critic of this famous picture of Heracles and Omphale (Fig. 25), part of a triptych or trilogy celebrating the power of Dionysus. The picture is quite certainly by one of the best Pompeian painters of the Fourth Style. It is equally certainly a close rendering of a Hellenistic composition of the third century B.C. At the very least it is a testimonial for the ability of painters in the Late Hellenistic-Early Roman phase of illusionism to create an effect of rich coloristic contrasts modelled in broad strokes and enhanced by generalized light. . . .

Ancient painters never accomplished what Correggio and Rembrandt were to achieve—the visualization of vaporous atmosphere and the completely unified rendering of chiaroscuro. That they attempted night scenes at all was a revolutionary venture. What they did manage to convey with their strange and inconsistent flashing white lights is the drama of the night. The picture of the Trojan horse[27] with its ghostly little silhouettes and vague masses of people is perhaps the most far-reaching attempt of antiquity to dissolve its usually plastic figures; and in the moving rendering of Priam guarding the body of Hector, the dark quiet of the night is used to enhance the mood of the sad vigil.[28]

25. Pompeian Wall Painting, Detail: Head of Omphale, First Century A.D. (Museo Nazionale, Naples)

That landscape and still life emerge as independent if subsidiary themes is characteristic of the interpenetration of the scientific interest in nature and the vitalistic attitude of Hellenistic painters. The sunlit solitude of heroic mountains was perhaps never more charmingly evoked than in the picture of the shepherd and ram; the very sketchiness of the landscape, the insubstantiality of the figures in the background emphasize its poetic unreality.[29]

To find that close-up segments of nature were considered subjects valid in their own right is even more remarkable in an art which was still anthropomorphic in essence. Hellenistic painting interprets still life not as *nature-morte* but as nature alive with a pantheistic life of which the carriers are light and color. Thus in a typical Pompeian "still life"[30] the glass, with its miraculous property of responding to light, is even more alive than the animate bird. This truly is "glow and shimmer."

Such Hellenistic splendor, however, is always a heightening of the natural, not a quest for the radiance of the supernatural. Hellenistic monarchs were noted for luxury and the kings of Pergamon had a monopoly on gold-woven textiles, *Attalicae vestes*. Gold was used to depict gold objects and to increase effects of ornamental details; but to my knowledge neither gold nor silver was ever used to produce the effect of unearthly light, not even in representations

140

of the halo which in Pompeian paintings was already used as a symbol of divine effulgence.[31]

EMOTION

The Classical art of Greece had inaugurated a new approach to the portrayal of emotion which was made possible by the discovery of organic art and the resultant ability to establish a convincing relation between the soul and the body. Following up this breakthrough in many directions, Hellenistic artists enormously enlarged the scope and diversity of emotional situations which art might portray. Their precise observation of physical appearances and their careful studies of the relation between somatic and psychological factors enabled them to diversify the portrayal of emotions to an extent which, at first glance, appears infinite. Relaxed sleep[32] and blazing breathlessness[33] are as much within the power of Hellenistic artists as are the skillfully graduated responses in the crowd of spectators commenting on the expiring Minotaur.[34] Nevertheless, within and underneath this seemingly realistic precision, there is always present a typical element, a belief that the general transcends the specific. Apart from the province of the grotesque, Hellenism continues to uphold the Classical belief in the beauty of man—only the human body is now fleshly and sensuously rather than neutrally and ideally beautiful. The heroic gesture still dominates, even when the emotional situation calls for brutality, suffering, and anguish (Laocoön, Sacrifice of Iphigeneia),[35] subjects the ancient critics would describe as scenes of pathos, *pathe, animi perturbationes.*

For Byzantine art, the treatment of the scenes of death, grief, and lament is of particular significance; and for this reason, it may be relevant to end this discussion with some Hellenistic interpretations of the same theme. Following the precedent set by Classical art, the great majority of sepulchral monuments was concerned not with scenes of grief and lament but with perpetuation of the memory of life.[36] The exception—and this is of interest for Byzantine art—are memorials of women who died in childbirth, as did Hediste, commemorated on the Hellenistic stele from Pagasai.[37] It is not impossible that such funerary scenes influenced the portrayals of death and burial in mythological illustrations; in an Ilias cycle, the corpse of Patroclus swathed in a shroud seems to echo the prostrate forms of dying women—and to anticipate curiously scenes of both death and nativity in Early Christian art.[38] From literary sources we learn that the pathetic contrast of an infant and a dead or dying mother was emphatically presented in famous Hellenistic paintings and sculptures.[39] This, however, is only an extension of that theatrical spirit of pathetic tragedy which Hellenism introduced into such legends as the myth of Pyramus and Thisbe. In general, the heroic and mythical sphere interprets death in the spirit of life defiantly ebbing away or as transition to eternal sleep.[40] This grandiose, pathetic tradition is in Roman art transformed into scenes made urgent and drastic to the point of grief-torn ugliness; and it is from this less formalized, "drastic" tradition that some of the Early Christian artists may have drawn their inspiration.[41]

One type of mythological situation, however, did evoke a more "internalized," subdued, and moving interpretation. On an Etruscan urn from Volterra,[42] there is preserved the reflection of a great Hellenistic composition showing the dead and broken but still beautiful Patroclus being lifted from the chariot. Compassion and pity speak eloquently in the group of Patroclus and the two warriors who gently lower the body of the fallen hero. A comparison with Byzantine representations of the Descent from the Cross, as for instance with the fresco of Nerezi,[43] underlines both the common denominator in the motif and the difference in the treatment—the quietly beautiful, subdued, in a sense objective, approach in the Hellenistic work, which excludes the spectator from immediate participation, and the poignantly expressive but also symbolically demonstrative power of the Byzantine masterpiece.

EPILOGUE

In these perfunctory remarks I have sought to indicate something of the range of Hellenistic art which made it such a treasure house for the Romans and the Byzantines. Elaborating and enlarging the anthropomorphic art created by the artists of Classical Greece, Hellenistic art extended the potential of the Classical tradition by searching observation of the variety and diversity of human types and experience. Going beyond the Classic, Hellenistic artists discovered for the ancient world the largeness of nature and the possibility of envisaging a universe in which humanity is but a small part of a larger order. To this expanded cosmos, Hellenism added the new dimensions of textured local color, of light and shade, of splendor designed to heighten the feeling of life. Hellenistic art is a world of realistic unrealities—its major concerns are the defiant heroism of mythical and semi-mythical supermen, the sensuous and sentimental delights of love, the dream of a children's world where children play with gods and heroes; of grotesques uglier but also more exuberant than life; and—perhaps most comprehensively—the image of a sacral-idyllic world of pantheistic landscapes peopled with simple folk, whose worship of their rustic gods is uncorrupted by philosophic doubt, and whose peaceful, natural existence knows neither ambition nor strife. Religion in Hellenistic art is diffused and dispersed through all phases of existence, its myth is an afterglow which, like poetry, serves to elevate man's view of his past and his present. With all this yearning for the Golden Age of innocence and for escape to bucolic nature, the general tenor of Hellenistic art is life-affirming; even death is sleep, not decay. The hedonistic view of *KTO KHRO* parades its skeletons to encourage the spectator to live, not to die.[44] In contrast to Byzantine art, Hellenistic art is entirely and enthusiastically of this world, *huius mundi*, with all the good and evil this might imply for devout Christians.

This Hellenistic art, authentically Greek in essence,[45] was doomed even without the Roman conquest—artistically, by the limits set to any naturalistic cycle; psychologically, by the lack of any powerful religious impetus; biologically, by its enormous geographical expansion from India to Spain, with the resultant thinning out of its carriers and the increasing erosive impact of the native attitudes and traditions. Its Roman heirs understood much of it, but not that *élan vital* which was the unifying idea of Hellenistic creativity. In the three centuries when the Roman Empire prospered (A.D. 100–400) and held sway over men's thoughts, the entire vision of life and the world changed from the heroic superman to the *civis Romanus;* and he in turn was transformed into a citizen of the City of God, as the *interpretatio Romana* of Hellenistic heritage was succeeded by *interpretatio Christiana.* Yet Hellenistic art "dying died not." To assess the share of Hellenistic elements in the medieval image of the Classical world and to trace the persistence of Hellenistic art as a latent force which, especially in the Eastern part of the former Roman Empire, could stimulate creative revivals, is a task which presents fascinating challenges to students of Byzantine art and culture.

NOTES

[1] Gauls: as proposed by A. Schober, *RM*, 51 (1936), pp. 104 ff., and *Die Kunst von Pergamon* (1951), pp. 46, 54, pls. 20 f., 80. Bieber, pp. 108 ff., Figs. 281–283, 424–427. Sleeping Eros: Bieber, p. 145, Figs. 616–618. G. M. A. Richter, *AJA*, 47 (1943), pp. 365 ff., Figs. 1 ff. R. Martin rightly notes that the "monumental urbanism" of Pergamon, which is of one piece with the Pergamene style in sculpture, works toward the heightening of nature rather than against nature, *L'urbanisme dans la Grece antique* (1956), chap. 3.

[2] On poetry, F. Lasserre, *La figure d'Eros dans la poésie grecque* (1946), pp. 150 ff. A. Furtwängler, in Roscher, *Myth. Lex.* (1884), Vol. 1:1, pp. 1365 ff., and *Antike Gemmen* (1900), III, pp. 167 f., 280 f.

[3] Best known from the amorini paintings of the Casa dei Vettii, Herrmann-Bruckmann, *Denkmäler der Malerei*, pls. 22 ff., 35. Their Hellenistic character is discussed in detail by F. Matz, *Ein römisches Meisterwerk* (1958), pp. 169 ff., pl. 36. Cf. those shown in Delos, Curtius, p. 78, Fig. 45.

[4] Although the purpose is different, much material has been collected by F. Matz, *op. cit.*, pp. 62 ff., which also includes amorini with thunderbolt of Zeus, trident of Poseidon, and quiver of Apollo. Amorini and Ares, Curtius, pl. 1., Matz, pl. 7b.

[5] As in groups of Ares and Aphrodite, Perseus and Andromeda, Dionysus and Ariadne, Curtius, Figs. 149 f., pl. 1. E. Simon, *Jahrbuch d. k. d. arch. Inst.*, 76 (1961), pp. 130 f., Fig. 15. L. Richardson, *Mem. of the Amer. Acad. in Rome*, 23 (1955), pl. 20.

[6] Alinari 28 080. Museo Comunale, Antiquarium. Bieber, p. 147, Fig. 627.

[7] Sleeping hermaphrodite, Louvre. Cf. Vigneau, *TEL: Encyclopédie photographique*, III, p. 231; B and C. J. Charbonneaux, *La sculpture du Louvre*, (1936), pl. 45 f.; Bieber, pp. 146 f., Figs. 623, 625 ff., and p. 124, Fig. 492.

[8] Ample illustrations in M. Bieber, *The History of the Greek and Roman Theater*, 2nd ed. (1961), chaps. 3, 7, 8, 10.

[9] Cf. H. Kenner, *Weinen und Lachen in der griechischen Kunst* (Oesterreich: Akademie der Wissenschaften, Philosophisch-Historische Klasse, *Sitzungsberichte* 234:2 [1960]), p. 89, Fig. 21. Kenner, pp. 93 f., emphasizes the rarity of laughing figures and concludes that only satyrs, centaurs, comedy masks, and children— non-human, or not-yet-human beings—were permitted to display laughing faces because an ideal of emotional restraint dominated Greek art. This does not quite do justice to the situation in the Hellenistic age.

[10] Curtius, pp. 337 ff., pl. 9, considers it a theatrical scene. Fig. 14 is after E. Pfuhl, *Malerei und Zeichnung der Griechen*, 3, Fig. 684.

[11] Richardson, *MAAR*, 23 (1955), p. 126, pl. 23:2, "Io Painter." Cf. Curtius, p. 316, Fig. 181.

[12] By M. Seiger in her report on Birth and Childhood of a God in Hellenistic Art.

[13] Richardson, pl. 49:1, "Iphigeneia Painter."

[14] A. S. Arvanitopoulos, *Athenische Mitteilungen*, 37 (1912), pp. 76 ff., pls. 2–3. H. Fuhrmann, *JdI*, 65–66 (1951), pp. 103 ff. L. Leschi, *MonPiot*, 35 (1936), pp. 139 ff. A. Maiuri, *La Casa del Menandro* (1932), pp. 335 ff. Morgoulieff, *Monuments antiques representant les scènes d'accouchement* (1893), and the literature quoted by J. Laager, cf. note 39. For the bathing scene, much discussed since the discovery of the Baalbek mosaic, there are not only Hellenistic but even Archaic forerunners. Cf. M. Lawrence, *De Artibus Opuscula XL: Essays in Honor of Erwin Panofsky* (1961), I, pp. 323–334, II, Fig. 13. K. Weitzmann, *Ancient Book Illumination* (1959), pp. 55 ff., Figs. 62 ff., Achilles. E. Simon, *JdI*, 76 (1961), pp. 160 f., Figs. 32, 34 f. For a typical Dionysiac "mother" who is actually a nymph, cf. the Farnesina painting, Curtius, Figs. 64 f.

[15] J. Laager, *Geburt und Kindheit des Gottes in der griechischen Mythologie* (1957).

[16] Yellow frieze, House of Livia, after P. Marconi, *La pittura dei Romani* (1929), Fig. 78. Cf. *Monumenti della pittura antica scoperti in Italia*, Sez. III: III, pl. 7 (color plate). The most recent, sensitive appreciation of "idyllic" landscapes is at hand in P. H. von Blanckenhagen and Chr. Alexander's *The Paintings from Boscotrecase*, *RM*, Suppl. 6 (1962). Von Blanckenhagen's evaluation, pp. 60 f., agrees so closely with mine that it is perhaps relevant to observe that neither of us had an opportunity to consult the work of the other.

[17] Rizzo, *Le pittura ellenistico-romana* (1929), pl. 163. P. H. von Blanckenhagen, *AJA*, 61 (1957), pp. 79 f. K. Schefold, *AM*, 71 (1956), pp. 211 ff.

[18] M. Hadas, *Hellenistic Culture* (1959), chap. 16, "Blessed Landscapes and Havens," pp. 212 ff.

[19] Curtius, Fig. 208. Ravenna: C. R. Morey, *Early Christian Art* (1942), pp. 158 f., Fig. 168 (Galla Placidia).

[20] E. Pfuhl, *Malerei und Zeichnung*, 3, Fig. 695. Color plate in S. Aurigemma, *Villa Adriana* (1961), p. 169, pl. 18.

[21] F. M. Biebel, *Gerasa* (ed. by C. H. Kraeling) (1938), pp. 341–351, pls. 67b, c; 68 a, b; 75a, 86 ff.

[22] Fig. 9 after Alinari 39 387. P. H. von Blanckenhagen, *AJA*, 61 (1957), p. 82, pl. 32, Fig. 11.

[23] Fig. 10 after H. Omont, *Fac-similés des miniatures et des manuscrits grecs de la Bibliothèque Nationale* (1902), p. 9, pl. 12, MS graec. 139, fol. 431. For the motif of figures emerging from the door, cf. Curtius, p. 250, Fig. 145. and K. Weitzmann, *Ancient Book Illumination* (1959), p. 61, pl. 31, Fig. 69.

[24] H. Bulle, "Eine Skenographie" 94. *Winckelmannsprogramm Berlin* (1934), pl. 2. M. Bieber, *History of the Greek and Roman Theater*, 2nd ed. (1961), p. 68, Fig. 266.

[25] Pinarius Cerialis: Bieber, *op. cit.*, p. 231, Fig. 774.

[26] For the situation in Classical Greek art, cf. G. M. A. Hanfmann, *AJA*, 61 (1957), pp. 75 ff.

[27] Made famous as an example of illusionism by F. Wickhoff, *Roman Art* (1900), pp. 149 f., pl. 12.

[28] House of C. Decimus Octavius Quartio. Spinazzola, *Pompeii*, 2 (1953), Fig. 1049.

[29] Alinari 39 135, Curtius, Fig. 213. Color: B. Maiuri, *Museo Nazionale di Napoli* (1957), p. 108.

[30] From Herculaneum. B. Maiuri, *op. cit.*, p. 134.

[31] On the use of gold, cf. E. Pfuhl, *Malerei und Zeichnung*, 2 (1923), pp. 582, 586, 591, 710, 712. For early empire, cf. A. Boëthius, *The Golden House of Nero* (1960), pp. 102 f., 112. Halo: cf. G. M. A. Hanfmann, *AJA*, 43 (1939), pp. 234 f.

[32] Sleeping Eros, n. 1 . . . Metropolitan Museum, New York, neg. 131094, cf. Bieber, p. 145, Figs. 616–618.

[33] Jockey from the sea near Cape Artemision, E. Buschor, *Vom Sinn der griechischen Standbilder* (1942), pl. 25. Cf. Bieber, p. 151, Fig. 645.

[34] B. Maiuri, *Museo Nazionale di Napoli* (1957), pl. 95, cf. L. Richardson, *MAAR*, 23 (1955), p. 121, pls. 21 f., "Dioscuri Painter." Curtius, pp. 213 f., Fig. 126, thought, probably rightly, that the spectator group goes back to a Late Hellenistic version derived from the same Late Classical original as the superior painting from the Basilica of Herculaneum . . . ; Curtius, Figs. 7 f.

[35] Laocoön in new reconstruction, after F. Magi, *Il ripristino del Laocoonte*, Pontif. Accademia Romana di Archeologia, *Memorie*, 9 (1960), pl. 41. Sacrifice of Iphigeneia, . . . Curtius, pp. 290 ff., pl. 5. Richardson, *MAAR*, 23 (1955), p. 148, pl. 47 : 1, "Iphigeneia Painter." The "beautiful" concept may have been modified to some extent by psychological associations of the kind indicated by references to color of skin and hair as reflections of character in Pseudo-Aristotelian *Physiognomica* and Pollux's catalogue of masks.

[36] For the Classical tradition, cf. K. Friis Johansen, *The Attic Grave-Reliefs of the Classical Period* (1951).

[37] Hediste: Pfuhl, *Malerei und Zeichnung* (1923), pp. 902 f., 907, Fig. 748.

[38] The corpse of Patroclus: House of C. Decimus Octavius Quartio, Spinazzola, *Pompeii*, 2, Figs. 1030, 1032 f. Cf. K. Weitzmann, *The Fresco Cycle of S. Maria di Castelseprio* (1951), pls. 5, 27, Nativity; pls. 3, 29, Joseph's dream; P. Buberl, *Illuminierte Handschriften in Wien* (1937), pl. 34 : 27, death of Isaac; pl. 44 : 48, death of Jacob.

[39] Aristeides of Thebes, painter, Pliny, XXXV : 98, "a mother lying wounded to death in the sack of a city; she appears conscious that her babe is creeping towards her breast." The picture was taken by Alexander the Great to Pella. Epigonus, Pergamene sculptor, Pliny, XXXIV : 88, "infant piteously caressing its dead mother."

[40] . . . Head of giant from copies of "Small Attalid Dedications," German Archaeological Institute, Rome, 36. 1150. Bieber, Figs. 434 f. Sleep—Bieber, Figs. 425, 432.

[41] Meleager sarcophagus Louvre-Borghese. Cf. A. Paoletti, *Materiali archeologici nelle chiese dell' Umbria, Sarcofago con il mito di Meleagro* (1961), pp. 44 ff., where other examples of drastic, "ugly" scenes of grief on Meleager sarcophagi are reproduced. I owe the reference to C. C. Vermeule. On the increase of drastic, desperate grief in rendering of mourners in Roman art, cf. H. Kenner, *Weinen und Lachen* (1960), pp. 57 f. For Early Christian art, cf. Vienna Genesis, Buberl, *Illuminierte Handschriften* . . . (Wien, 1937), pl. 33 : 26, death of Deborah.

[42] Photograph, Soprintendenza Antichità, Firenze, no. 5463, Cf. D. Levi, *Rivista del R. Istituto di Archeologia e Storia dell'Arte*, 4 (1932–3), pp. 7 ff., pl. 2b.

[43] P. Muratoff, *La peinture Byzantine* (1928), pl. 153. UNESCO, *Yugoslavia: Mediaeval Frescoes* (1955), pl. 9.

[44] K. Schefold, *Die Bildnisse der antiken Dichter, Redner, und Denker*, (1943),

Hellenistic Art

pp. 166 f., 216 (goblets from Boscoreale) with references. Photograph, M. Chuzeville. This side shows Zenon (left) pointing at Epicure, who is taking a cake from the table. The scene is inscribed: *to telos hedone*, "pleasure is the [highest] end."

[45] I do not wish for a moment to deny the historic significance and aesthetic potential of forms developed in Egypt, Syria, Mesopotamia, and India through fusion of Hellenistic with native elements, but the center of gravity, the artistic leadership remained in a small area—essentially the Greek islands and the Greek cities in the coastal areas of Asia Minor, with a wider "secondary" zone taking in Athens, Sikyon, Tarentum, Syracuse, Antioch, and Alexandria.

8. ROMAN ARCHITECTURE

William L. MacDonald

INTRODUCTION

During the course of the first and second centuries A.D. a new vaulted architecture, predominantly secular in function, developed in the Mediterranean world. In all parts of the Empire it became a testimony of the Roman presence. Unlike the architecture of the Greeks, this Roman style emphasized enclosure, the interior hollow, thus providing a principle from which later centuries would continue to draw precedent.

William L. MacDonald's volume on Roman architecture, concentrating on four monuments, the Pantheon, the markets of Trajan, and the palaces of Nero and Domitian, is a detailed study of the major forms that define the Imperial architecture. The portions selected for this anthology discuss the materials and methods of construction as well as general characteristics of this new architecture of Imperial Rome.

Other works on Roman architecture are W. J. Anderson and R. P. Spiers, *The Architecture of Greece and Rome*, 2 vols., rev. by Thomas Ashby (1927), G. T. Rivoira, *Roman Architecture*, translated by G. McN. Rushforth (1930); A. Boëthius and J. B. Ward-Perkins, *Etruscan and Roman Architecture* (1970); J. B. Ward-Perkins, *Roman Architecture* (1977); Axel Boëthius, *Etruscan and Early Roman Architecture* (1979); Marion E. Blake and Doris T. Bishop, *Roman Construction in Italy From Nerva Through the Antonines* (1973). There are also, among works on individual monuments and special themes, Axel Boëthius, *The Golden House of Nero* (1960); Richard Brilliant, *The Arch of Septimius Severus in the Roman Forum* (1967); William L. MacDonald, *The Pantheon: Design, Meaning, and Progeny* (1976); E. Baldwin Smith, *Architectural Symbolism of Imperial Rome and the Middle Ages* (1956); and, on the relationship between Roman and Early Christian architecture, see J. B. Ward-Perkins, "The Italian Element in Late Roman and Early Medieval Architecture," *Proceedings of the British Academy*, XXXIII (1947), 163 ff.; and by the same author, "Constantine and the Origins of the Christian Basilica," *Papers of the British School in Rome*, XXII (1954), 69 ff.

Footnotes in the selections that follow cite, in abbreviated form, the following works:

AJA   *American Journal of Archaeology*
Atti   *Atti del . . . congresso* (sometimes *convegno*) *nazionale di storia dell' architettura.*
BC   *Bulletino della commissione archeologica communale di Roma.*
Blake 1   M.E. Blake, *Ancient Roman Construction in Italy from the Prehistoric Period to Augustus* (1947).
Blake 2   M.E. Blake, *Roman Construction in Italy from Tiberius through the Flavians* (1959).
BollCentro   *Bolletino del centro di studi per la storia dell' architettura.*
CIL   *Corpus Inscriptionum Latinarium.*
Durm   J. Durm, *Die Baukunst der Etrusker. Die Baukunst der Römer*, 2nd ed. (1905).
EncIt   *Enciclopedia Italiana.*
ESAR   *Economic Survey of Ancient Rome*, ed. T. Frank, 6 vols. (1933–40), reprinted in 1959.
Meiggs   R. Meiggs, *Roman Ostia* (1960).
Middleton   J.H. Middleton, *The Remains of Ancient Rome* (1892).
NS   *Notizie degli scavi di antichità*
Rostovtzeff   M.I. Rostovtzeff, *Social and Economic History of the Roman Empire*, 2nd ed., 2 Vols. (1957).

ECONOMY OF CONSTRUCTION

Architecture properly includes the art of building, and to omit it would be to suggest a division of knowledge and responsibility that Roman imperial architects would not have recognized. Labor, materials, and methods of building were efficiently organized in an economy of construction second only to principles of design in the formation of the new architecture. Roman attitudes toward making, assembling, and using materials produced the orderly rhythms of preparation and construction essential to success in large buildings of brick and concrete. The great architects had at their disposal ready trains of supply and assembly that reached from the distant clay pits and quarries to the tops of their towering scaffolds, where brick and aggregate, by reversing the processes of nature, were bound by mortar into rock-like structure. . . .

The labor force formed the base of this economy. Unskilled workmen were enrolled or impressed in gangs, and craftsmen and semiskilled workers were organized according to their specialties into corporations or guilds (neither term is very satisfactory; what had begun as mutual assistance associations and funeral colleges were increasingly regulated by the government as the *étatisation* of society deepened).[1] Statius, enthusiastically describing Domitian's new road across the Volturno marshes into Naples, gives a glimpse of Roman divisions of labor and orderly method.

> The first work was to prepare furrows and mark out the borders of the road, and to hollow out the ground with deep excavation; then to fill up the excavated trench with other material, and to make foundations ready for the road's arched bridge, lest the soil give way and a treacherous bed provide an unstable base for the heavily loaded stones; then to bind it with blocks, set close on either side, and with frequent wedges. How many gangs are at work together! Some cut down the forest and strip the mountain sides, some shape beams and boulders with iron tools; others [cement] the stones together . . . others work to dry up the pools and [dig canals] to lead the minor streams far away. These men could cut the Athos peninsula.[2]

. . . There was even a *collegium subrutorum* or guild of demolition experts.[3] During the period under discussion, labor of all kinds seems to have been plentiful in Rome.[4] The proportion of freemen to slaves is not known; we have no document such as the building contract for the north porch of the Erechtheum in Athens, which records that out of a hundred and seven men at work at least forty-two were metics (registered aliens) and twenty were slaves (all of the latter were masons or carpenters).[5] Whatever their status Roman laborers and craftsmen were bonded firmly in groups to which their individualities were largely submerged, just as the small units of materials they put into position were essential but standardized parts of a coherent structural whole. This shaping of manpower and knowledge into a system both orderly and flexible explains certain characteristics of the new architecture. The imperial architect could command a large and well-organized labor force, and with its help he gave monumentality to his ideas and permanence to his buildings.

MATERIALS

In all vaulted buildings of imperial date, with the exception of some provincial work in cut stone, materials were used in a consistent way. Small individual structural elements were combined with mortar to obtain, after the fabric had dried out and cured, structurally continuous and enduring solids. Piers, walls, and vaults were made of concrete, and brick facing was used on piers and non-foundation walls. Wood and stone were as important in erecting buildings as lime, sand, and brick, and a fair amount of metal was used, though not in structural members. These materials will be considered in an approximately ascending order of their significance.

The extensive use of metal in ancient architecture is sometimes overlooked. In addition to decorative elements such as bronze capitals, rosettes, and cornices, metalworkers and foundrymen made doors, conduits, pipes, and a wide variety of fittings and hardware.[6] Metal roof tiles, of the kind used on the Basilica Ulpia and the Pantheon, were not uncommon. Within the structural fabric of ancient stone buildings massive iron clamps, often secured in lead, were frequently used.[7] The timbers of the roof of the Pantheon porch may have been encased in metal, and there were probably other instances of protecting wooden members with metal sheathing. For hanging ceilings of cement and tile, Vitruvius prescribes the use of large iron bars, hung from iron hooks in the beams above, to carry the suspended weight.[8] In the piers and walls of Roman vaulted buildings a great deal of iron and bronze was used, in the form of cramps and plugs, to insure a permanent bond between marble facing, setting beds of cement, and the brick-faced structure proper. . . .

The various colors of Roman bricks and decorative terra-cottas are important. By using different kinds of clay and by varying the length of firing, colors were deliberately produced for visual purposes. Contrasts of color were common. At Ostia, for example, external pilasters of dark red and capitals and moldings of yellow, all of terra-cotta, appear in Trajanic and Hadrianic tombs and buildings. At Isola Sacra, near Ostia, there are many examples of multicolored decorative terra-cotta inserts in external walls. If these details were meant to be stuccoed over, it is difficult to understand why pieces of various colors were produced and then carefully assembled in architectural and decorative patterns. It is apparent that at least some terra-cotta exterior surfaces were meant to be seen.

In and near Rome, and in those parts of the provinces where suitable materials were available, terra-cotta manufacture became an industry. Huge quantities were made by coordinating the several production processes, a high degree of standardization was achieved, and stocks were laid up in excess and in ignorance of requirements. The standard tile and brick sizes and the fixed shapes and sizes of terra-cotta fittings and parts facilitated planning and helped architects and builders to increase the efficiency of construction. Layout and dimensioning were simplified. The extensive interchangeability of terra-cotta parts, so obvious today, was a radical innovation. They were fully utilized in the economy of building, to the extent that each brick was put to more than one use during construction.

Metal, wood, stone, and terra-cotta were all used, temporarily or permanently, in connection with mortar. The word is used here to indicate all materials of mixed composition that were in a semi-fluid state at the time of actual use in construction: the mortar for brickwork, the mix in which aggregates were placed to make concrete, and the various types of aggregate-free cements such as *opus signinum,* a mortar containing both crushed brick and pozzolana that was used to line structures carrying or containing water and to protect the exteriors of vaults.[9] Plasters and stuccoes, being non-structural, belong in another category. They were used chiefly for facings, interior moldings, and decorative reliefs.

In Roman times mortar was already of great antiquity. Greek mortars were famous for their strength and quality. Before developing concrete the Romans had used mortars for many purposes, for example to level courses of stones not cut and finished precisely.[10] By the second century B.C. the properties of mortar were quite fully understood and the development of true concrete construction was well underway. When in the next century kiln-fired brick began to replace unfired brick, and pozzolana came into regular use, mortar became an essential material. The lengthy modern discussions of the various types of Roman wall facings are somewhat misleading, for mortar is the most important structural material in Roman non-trabeated architecture. Facings changed, and the changes give some indication of date, but the facings are not the walls themselves.

Vitruvius says that in making mortar, sea sand should be avoided. Good sands, he adds, crackle when rubbed and do not stain white cloth.[11] Lime, after burning, should be set aside to age.[12] By his day the Romans had mastered the use of pozzolana, which they added to the dry mix in lieu of part of the sand. Pozzolana is a friable volcanic material, found in thick beds of chunks and gravel-sized pieces in Latium and Campania and easily reduced to usable form.[13] It often has a distinct reddish or yellowish hue and has the property of forming hydraulic silicates in combination with lime, quartz sand, and water. The importance of pozzolana can be exaggerated, for some large Roman concrete buildings were built without it, but mortar made with it will set readily underwater, an advantage Roman engineers made good use of. The architects and builders of the high empire must have been convinced that pozzolana improved their concrete, for it was used in all the buildings described above and is rarely absent from high imperial construction in Rome and its environs.

Making mortars and using them in the building processes was in effect a process of dehydration—the burning of lime—and subsequent hydration. Because water could be added to the granular substances at the convenience of the builders, the construction of walls and vaults was much facilitated. The amorphous, dry ingredients could be easily measured and divided into manageable quantities. No highly skilled labor was required. The amounts of mortar needed for use during a given period of time could be readily calculated, and the consecutive steps of preparation and use suited Roman habits of orderly procedure. Mortar gave the architect the basis for structural materials that could be cast in a variety of architectural shapes, and its importance lies in its inherent potential of form. Doubtless there was a long period of trial and experiment. By the early first century the basic problems had been mastered and sound knowledge accumulated empirically. The ruin of part of old Rome in the summer of 64 provided the first city-wide opportunity for the use of mortar, which for nearly three centuries thereafter was the essential substance of vaulted architecture in the capital.

The ultimate synthetic product of Roman experiments with mortars, aggregates, and structural problems was the durable concrete of imperial times. . . . Basically it was a material for casting on a monumental scale. When correctly made and poured it could provide structurally continuous solids from foundations up to the crowns of vaults. The necessity of repeating bearing surfaces was much reduced. Ideally speaking, seamless and jointless structures were made possible. Architects and builders were largely freed from the necessity of thinking and planning in terms of beams and isolated bearing points, and could concentrate upon less fragmented structural and visual forms. Inevitably this led to an architecture more modeled than assembled, and it helps to explain the proliferation of curves in both plans and sections from the middle of the first century onward.

In the economy of vaulted design, shapeless raw materials were transposed into building solids by inverting natural processes.[14] Sand, lime, and pozzolana were made into rock, and clay was baked almost as hard as stone. But the small scale of the individual bricks, and the timing of bringing together the ingredients of mortar, meant that the new materials were pliant and flexible. They were the chief structural resources the great architects of the period had in mind when designing, the equivalent of stone for the Greek masters and steel and reinforced concrete for architects today.

In the use of materials two essential features stand out. One is organization, the result of applying administrative talent to problems of reliable procurement and methodical sequences of construction. Order and system were brought into complex situations involving the mutual adjustment of many variables and the fairly efficient deployment of thousands of men. The Romans learned much about such things from their predecessors, but the mastery of the economy of vaulted construction was peculiarly their own. From this point of view the method of erecting the Palace of Domitian or the Pantheon was as characteristic of Roman civilization as the law or the army. The second and more significant point concerns the inherent connection between the nature of the materials and the space-geometry of the buildings. Roman builders did not subtract from materials to obtain form, as a stonecutter does when he fashions a squared block or a cornice, but added materials together, binding them freely with mortar and building up steadily around and over a space to give it definition. It was in this sense that bricks and concrete were flexible, occupying and forming with ready adaptability the volumetric boundaries conceived by the architect.

METHODS

The building process was largely derived from the nature of the materials, which, because the fabric had to dry out and cure, were unfinished at the moment of use. In order to obtain secure and stable buildings, construction had to proceed according to rhythms of work determined by the setting time of the mortar. The speed with which a portion of newly made structure reached sufficient bearing strength was the key factor both in planning construction and in actual building. Brick-faced walls and piers were built, without shuttering, a horizontal layer at a time, and as soon as a layer could bear enough weight the process was repeated and the building rose another few feet. For both stability and efficiency, timing was all.

In order to obtain better siting or footings the Romans were willing to alter natural contours extensively. Valleys were filled and hills were cut back. By Flavian times it was normal practice to place important buildings on level vaulted terraces or deep concrete mats.[15] Long experience with roads, aqueducts, bridges, ports, and other massive utilitarian works provided a sound knowledge of sinking foundations for stable arcuate and vaulted construction. Foundations tended to be deep and extremely substantial. The Esquiline Wing of the Domus Aurea stands upon a vast, thick sheet of concrete, poured in part at least over preexisting houses. This increased the elevation of the building on the hillside and gave it a substantial base. Rabirius, to obtain his two desired floor levels, filled depressions, cut the Palatine rock back where necessary, and extended his upper platform to the desired limits on lofty vaulted substructures. Again, earlier buildings were filled in or their structure utilized.[16] The vertical staging of Trajan's Markets is composed of vaulted terraces that rise as much as four stories above the slope of the Quirinal. The Pantheon rotunda and drum stand upon a massive ring of concrete. Because of these precautions, evidence of settlement in these buildings is rare. They were quite well prepared to meet the threat of outside forces such as earthquake, subsidence, or extraordinary wind pressure.

The care taken in monumental building to obtain firm footings and to distribute loads fairly evenly is also evident in the supports for bearing walls. The normal practice was to excavate to a depth of two or more meters—foundation walls five and six meters deep are not unknown—and then pour the concrete wall between wooden shutterings. Many of these walls can be examined today. Some have been exposed to the weather for many years, but the negative forms of the shuttering posts (usually placed on the wall side) and of the boards as well are sometimes so clear that the grain of the rough-sawn wood can still be read.

Foundation walls were rarely faced. Once the concrete had cured sufficiently the shuttering was removed and the brick-faced wall was begun above ground level. It is not likely that shuttering, properly shored, was much used to help support faced walls, although a contrary opinion has been held.[17] The use of shuttering against brick-facing would have been difficult. First, the brick wall would have to be built up to a sufficient height to take advantage of vertical timbers long enough to give support to a considerable number of horizontal shutters. Short vertical timbers, supporting only a few boards, would not have kept the wall true. If high shuttering were put up first, the bricks would have had to be laid from the inside, a very unlikely procedure even for thick walls. Since the brick-facing is always very shallow, a mere skin a brick or half-brick deep on the surface of the concrete, it would have become increasingly unstable as it rose without its intended concrete core, and extremely difficult to keep true even if erected from inside up against the shuttering boards. Finally, the risk would be run of having the lower courses of mason's mortar stiffen too much before the concrete was poured in, preventing the two mortars, which were applied separately, from setting together properly.

The only woodwork that seems to have been required for building brick-faced walls was the scaffolding for the masons and the ladder and ramp systems needed for bringing up bricks, mortar, and aggregate. Since the brick-facings did not function structurally once the mortar had hardened, and since shuttering was impractical, speed of erection and accuracy of construction were functions of the stiffening and drying rate of mortar. The unrestored portions of the walls of such buildings as the Markets and the Pantheon, being absolutely uniform, give no indication of the levels at which construction may have been temporarily halted for drying, for the assembly of new scaffolding, or for the end of the working day. If the mixing of mortar and its delivery to the masons, and to the mouth of the wall, were timed so that it would start to stiffen shortly after it was put in place, then perhaps both of the brick skins and the concrete core could all go up more or less together. The operation could then continue for some distance before it was necessary to halt and allow the wall to gain enough strength to carry an additional load safely and without risking distortion.

The vertical distance between halts that might be accomplished under these circumstances cannot be calculated because the most important variables are unknown. It is likely that the mortars stiffened rapidly. The rows of putlog holes for the horizontal members of the scaffolding indicate that about twenty to twenty-five rows of bricks were laid from a given level. The so-called bonding courses, discussed below, may possibly mark the end of a day's work. What is more important is that true and stable walls and piers could be built accurately by this leap-frog method. Concrete was poured between low, thin retaining walls of brick, and as soon as it set sufficiently to bear the load of the next layer, the process was repeated. Nice adjustments in timing and the supply of materials were required if the labor force was to be used with efficiency. The best masons and practical builders alone could not make the system work, for the details as well as the broad outlines of the planning had to be completed in advance. In practice this probably meant that everyone knew their job from long experience. Even so the Roman genius for order and system lay behind all the day-to-day work.

The facing bricks, from Nero's time onward, were usually sawn or broken into triangles before they were used.[18] Laying and jointing, especially in the principal Trajanic and Hadrianic monuments, can only be characterized as nearly perfect. Yet much of this meticulous work was not intended to be seen. Presumably it cannot have been done to protect the concrete, for foundation walls were usually left unfaced and many of them, little damaged by nature, still support their original loads. Also, inside walls as well as peripheral walls were faced. The facing did not provide a sufficiently rough surface for stucco or cement to adhere to satisfactorily, and the hardness of the bricks and the pozzolana mortar made it difficult to attach anything to the wall at all. Yet the bricks were necessary. They formed temporary, low formwork while the wall was going up in stages. At the lower levels this could have been done more easily and economically with shuttering properly shored. But the higher the wall went the more difficult this would have become and, above a certain height, it would have been all but impossible. Walls fifteen and twenty meters high were built, and for these heights no shoring or other form of counterpressure could have been readily provided. Also, the triangular bricks exposed rough and somewhat porous surfaces for marriage with the mortar of the interior concrete core, for by laying the bricks in simple bond a pocketed interior wall of irregular points was produced. In this sense bricks were used simply as another form of aggregate. Since they were evenly dressed on the outside, the task of keeping the wall in alignment was facilitated.

Early Roman experiments with concrete evolved from the use of relatively uncompacted rubble fills placed between ashlar or other types of stone walls. Facing materials grew thinner and progressively less structural, and cores became increasingly able to bear heavier loads. This evolution intersected the discovery of pozzolana mortars and, later, the quantity production of high-quality kiln-fired brick; the builders of the imperial age made the most out of combining tradition and invention. The multiplicity of functions assigned to brick-facing, which in some cases included a purely aesthetic and visual role, is typical of the economy of vaulted design. The reciprocities established among materials and their functions both during and after actual construction were ingenious. Orderly procedures are necessary to all successful monumental construction, but the Romans mass-produced building materials and investigated their efficient and appropriate uses to a greater degree than any pre-industrial people. The ancient Latin principle of order, the instinctive habit of trying to put men and things in their proper places of service, lay behind this. . . .

Once the formwork of a vault was in position the actual construction was relatively simple. Mortar and aggregate were raised to the pouring level and put into position.[19] Usually the extrados was given a coat of waterproof pozzolana cement, though terra-cotta tiles were sometimes laid directly upon the concrete, and the huge Pantheon vault was finished with a thin covering of brick. If an oculus was required a stout wheel-form was built. This was positioned horizontally at the open crown of the vault, and rings of bricks, set vertically, were laid around its circumference. The last pours of concrete then brought the fabric of the vault up to this brickwork, and construction was complete. After a period of drying and curing the formwork could be dismantled and the structure given over to the decorators and marbleworkers.

STRUCTURAL FEATURES

Roman engineering was empirical, based upon deductions made from observation and experience. Not all of these deductions can be reached today by studying the buildings, and important data for the analysis of vaulted-style structure and statics are missing. The drying times and curing rates of the mortars, crucial factors in obtaining stability and in the economy of construction as well, are unknown. The true physical composition and precise structural nature of the concrete itself is uncertain.[20] Yet the basic structural principle is clear: stability depended not upon pressure or friction, as in unmortared arches or vaults of cut stone, but upon something very different, the cohesion and homogeneity of the cured concrete mass.[21]

This principle and its application explain many features of vaulted-style construction.[22] The concrete cores, invisible once the buildings were finished, were in theory continuous bearing solids. Vaults were cast by pouring down upon wooden forms in order to fill up the volumes and obtain the surfaces the forms described, and this was done without any thought of voussoirs or other discrete internal divisions of structure. These vaults were physically continuous with their piers and walls, for there were no intervening bearing surfaces. But in practice the problems raised by giving shape and support to the initially formless concrete led to methods of construction that made the finished fabric structurally less simple than theory indicated. In addition, the procedures followed by the builders often caused the ideal continuity of the fabric, inherent in the basic principle, to be interrupted. By using brick to give shape to the concrete walls and piers until they hardened to bearing strength, certain secondary structural problems were introduced. At the beginning these bricks functioned as shuttering, but as the mortar cured they became an inseparable part of the structure, preserving the concrete core within a thin, weatherproof crust to which new outer finishes could be applied when needed. . . .

Although concrete did most of the work, bricks were essential both to construction and structure proper, and in thin walls the facings are probably as important structurally as the concrete. In monumental buildings the facings were falsework, weatherproofing, and structure all in one, and their various infixed devices were developed to solve the problems inherent in constructing permanent formwork, inseparably bonded to the main structure, at great scale. . . .

In a sense a structure grew out of itself because of the relationships among facings, cores, and compression devices (paradoxically, the bulkiness of vaulted designs was the result of a rather clever and economical way of building). The system helped in answering quite readily and efficiently the need for great quantities of construction. The way buildings were put up assisted in making the act of architecture a social one, no inconsiderable achievement and until then unknown in the ancient world. The Romans were able to build functional, permanent structures of many types by means of one architectural technology. Partly because of this, great buildings for public use became commonplace, and architecture of some consequence was brought into daily life and to ordinary towns far more than in the past. In this the economy of construction was an essential force. Its simplicity and method, synchronized to the needs and purposes of an age of cities, facilitated planning and realizing public building programs. Because of these things, and because of what the buildings inspired in later generations, the economy of imperial construction is a significant part of the history of architecture.

Behind it lay the attitudes and talents of the new architects. The predetermined order and timing of events meant that they had to direct large groups of men and insure that they did their work without appreciable error. Each of these workmen, like each brick in the walls they made, performed as a soldier under orders. The economy of the new architecture derived maximum efficiency and utility from each element in relation to its neighbors, an expression of an inherent Latin trait. The unknown military tribune, who at the battle of Cynoscephalae in 197 B.C. "judged on the spur of the moment what ought to be done" and detached twenty maniples with which he broke the phalanx of Philip V, expressed the same trait.[23] He had the training to give him judgment, and the materials of his contribution to Flaminius' victory were prepared to respond in an orderly way to his decision. Under difficult conditions he was able to move two thousand infantry quickly, efficiently, and successfully. So it was also with imperial architects, their materials and men.

THE NEW ARCHITECTURE

What the palaces, the Markets, and the Pantheon show above all else is the maturity of the concept of monumental interior space. The strength and dynamism of imperial civilization were so great that the need for a suitable architecture could not be denied. The Romans, always building, quite naturally sought for forms that would express this ecumenical experience. Vaults were not in any way new when Severus, Rabirius, and their contemporaries gave architecture a fresh beginning with their great buildings. Yet they fashioned the new style with vaulted spaces, and in the last analysis it is the meaning and effects of these spaces that more than anything else give the style its identification and individuality. In Timgad as in Tralles, at Baia as at Bosra, the Roman stewardship of all antiquity and the imperial hope for one inclusive society—coerced or free—were proclaimed by an architecture of splendid interior spaces.

Rome itself was the nexus where many strains of design and technology were gathered together. There, seen in the light of imperial social and political aims, these strains were adapted and reworked as the new style evolved. The forms and effects of this architecture served the capital and the provinces alike until during the fourth and fifth centuries they were gradually translated into the artistic languages of the early middle ages. In this way Roman concepts of interior space lived on in both East and West. The palaces, Markets, and Pantheon alone cannot carry the whole burden of this complicated story, but they record accurately its first and in many ways most creative chapter and vividly mark the stylistic and emotional distance between the new architecture and that of the past. The inherent value of these buildings as examples is magnified by the long life, after the dissolution of imperial authority in the West, of their architectural principles and the associations evoked by their forms.

CHARACTERISTICS OF DESIGN

The transcendent characteristic of the new architecture was its space-shaping, space-bordering quality (Fig. 26). Whatever the decor, however integrated the trabeation, this quality predominated. Its omnipresent, generative force was the circular curve, occasionally modulated to polygonal shape, upon which progressive architects based their volumetric and spatial creations and with which they resolved and fixed their axes and vistas. The curve gave them the radial focus that more than anything else established the viewer's relationship to their designs. Not only the major vaulted spaces, but their entrances, openings, niches, and decor were evolved from a preoccupation—almost an obsession—with the embracing and focusing qualities of circular lines and surfaces. The indispensable curve gave Roman vaulted architecture its overwhelming sense of place, and its use in three dimensions as the boundary of architectural space is the quintessential feature of the style. Although the formal structure of the style was geometric, a number of shapes were used together in every building. Even the Pantheon, the most unitary of Roman monumental designs, is composed of triangles, a prismatic block, a cylinder, a hemisphere, and apsidal recesses. The imperial architect, unlike a designer such as Ledoux, was not attracted by basic, unadorned geometric shapes standing alone as buildings. Shapes in combination interested him, shapes arranged significantly and harmonically as to scale and meaning, and articulated by an elaborate but consistent system of decoration and well thought-out lighting.

26. Trajan's Forum and Markets, Rome, Early Second Century A.D. (Reprinted from William L. MacDonald, *Architecture of the Roman Empire*, I [1965], Yale University Press, by permission of the author)

Figure A (Eric Spencer after William L. MacDonald
Forum of Trajan and surroundings, plan.
Stone construction throughout Forum, except libraries (E), which were of brick, perhaps for absorption of humidity. Roofs of wood and tiles.

Key:
A. Monumental entrance to Forum of Trajan
B. Equestrian statue of Trajan
C. Basilica Ulpia
D. Column of Trajan
E. Libraries (brick structures)
F. Temple of Trajan
G. Hemicycles, Forum of Trajan
H. Vaulted hall (aula Traiana) in market area
J. Via Biberatica (main street of the markets)
K. Stairs and southeast extension of hemicycle street, originally connecting the
   Forum with the city region to the east
L. Corner of Forum of Augustus
M. Perimeter wall of Caesar's Forum

Figure B (Eric Spencer after B. M. Boyle)
Trajan's Markets. Isometric drawing of remains. Concrete construction
with brick facings.
Key: Same as Figure A

Although in this way Roman design "became absolutely emancipated from precedent, and was pursued as research into the possibilities of form and combination,"[24] the ancient principle of symmetry was not abandoned. Few vaulted-style buildings erected before Hadrian's death in 138 depart to any considerable extent from a basic, underlying frame of mirror or bilateral symmetry. The geometric interior volumes were themselves symmetrical, and were combined symmetrically in plan. Eccentricity of plan and therefore of elevation was extremely rare. Dominant axes and balanced silhouettes, and the almost complete lack of any noncircular curves, explain as much as the solidity of their construction the impression of strength and permanence these buildings give. The stability implied by simple geometric forms was exploited to the full, both through the persistent revelation of their inherent symmetry and by combining them, as for example when a semidomed apse was placed at the end of a barrel-vaulted room. This hyper-symmetry, this unwillingness ever to admit any ambiguity of axis, was so positive a force that even the external axes leading to the entrances of monumental buildings were defined by courtyards or other axially parallel features. By such means even open spaces could be given a certain feeling of interiorness. Unlike the projected axes of Greek monumental architecture, which frequently passed unhindered out across the natural landscape, the center lines of Roman buildings tended to be stopped and fixed by architectural solids nearby—an apse, a nymphaeum, even a gate would do (in a space of centralized plan, another major axis was self-contained within the building itself). Embracing, curved shapes were used to catch and cup the central lines of architectural force as the basin of a fountain catches its jet of water. Against a vertical half-cylinder capped by a shell-form or semidome the movement of an axis was both marked and resolved. The parallel side walls or other bordering features of a central axis, whether of a single space or a large composition of many elements, were almost always exactly alike. As in the atrium house the path along a controlling axis might be interrupted, but this rarely diluted its visual and directive power. The deviations introduced were only temporary, for no real choice of routes was offered and the compelling symmetry of the design was unaffected. . . .

An environment of controlling forms preempted attention and rigorously limited freedom of movement, characteristics inherited from the past. For centuries the open sacred precinct, with its altar and its looming cult building beyond, had given form and direction to the most fundamental rituals of Roman life. The early imperial fora, with their elevated marble temples dominating elongated enclosures, expressed the same principles in more sophisticated fashion. In the vaulted style the evolution of this traditional directionalism and focus was brought to its logical conclusion. One was now either guided toward a focal concavity or brought into an axially terminal space, a large and well-lighted architectural volume from which the natural world was excluded, where enveloping and radially focused surfaces suggested permanence, stability, and security.

IMPERIAL CIVILIZATION AND ARCHITECTURE

. . . The vaulted style was infused with the same hortatory quality found in official statuary and reliefs, upon coins, and in the panegyrical literature. This insistent rhetoric of Roman state art reflects the sharp paternalism upon which the coherence and preservation of society was thought to depend. In the buildings this quality is evident in the way the senses were instructed by axis, symmetry, and the properties of concavity. These characteristics of design and sensory instruction also reflected the balance and order, the almost choreographic clarity, of Roman ritual and liturgy. In these ways the vaulted style was a mimesis of the state, a metaphor in tangible form upon its traditions and its claims to all-embracing sovereignty. Naturally it arose in Rome, the center of these traditions and claims, where after Nero's time it was used to create an *urbs pro maiestate imperii ornata.*[25]

All of the great vaulted buildings were charged with the property of expressing unity. Encouragement to individualism was missing because choice was missing. Vaulted architecture was no more permissive than the state itself. Axis, symmetry, and the terminal feature or volume kept everyone *en face* in fact or in mind with the focal, symbolic shape; there were no true alternatives. Roman architecture might be defined as a body of law in masonry, governing human responses by didactic forms whose expressive force was intended to be recognized or apprehended immediately by the sensory faculties. Grace and elegance were sacrificed to this drive to persuade one and all to conform, and this could explain the preoccupation with the primary geometric shapes so readily yielded by the economy of imperial construction. The age of truly personal expression in architecture lay in the future, for the architecture of Rome, like that of Egypt and Greece, spoke of a particular way of life and the institutions it fostered rather than of the independent opportunity and taste of any single individual.

The nature of imperial society was also expressed in the very orderly way in which diverse human and natural resources were directed toward the end in view. The success of the solution to these essentially logistical problems is evident in the ability of the Romans, during the first and second centuries, to erect large numbers of buildings simultaneously without straining either their knowledge or their economy of construction. Their capacity to move almost as one man toward a desired goal was exploited in an atmosphere of bureaucratic expansion and increasing state regulation, but this made possible that supple manipulation and control of each unit of action and substance that insured the continuity of the necessary rhythms of construction. Bricks and aggregate were deployed through the buildings like maniples and centuries of infantry in the sense that each anonymous unit obeyed the commands of the architect and was dependent upon the proper functioning of exactly similar units assembled in a strictly disciplined order. The hundred foremen, each directing a gang of a hundred men, who are said to have supervised the construction of Hagia Sophia, were the inheritors in Justinian's age of Roman working methods.[26]

The government influenced the new architecture in other practical ways. It largely controlled finances, could focus talent and labor upon architectural objectives if and when it chose, and concerned itself with building codes and schedules of maintenance. Apparently a fair proportion of architects and builders were trained during military service, and many were kept on the government rolls either in the army or in the civil service to be posted to various locations around the Empire as the need arose. The guilds, at first only supervised by the government, were gradually absorbed into its ever expanding, infinitely graded hierarchy. The government was in a position to orchestrate the architectural resources of the whole realm. Sparse as the written evidence is, it suggests that this was done for architecture as for law, the administration, and the army.

That the emperors and their governments used the vaulted style as an instrument of propaganda can hardly be doubted. All official architecture was used in this way. The proliferation in the provinces of large baths based upon first- and early second-century designs in Rome is the most obvious case, but many other vaulted building types were used in the provinces, such as markets, warehouses, amphitheaters, and municipal nymphaea. Districts and towns in Italy were embellished with an apparent generosity that the emperors surely regarded as a sound investment in the future of the state. Though the financial resources of the Empire were primitively managed there was always money for building after the armies and the supply of Rome had been provided for. The doors of the treasuries were open to provincial governments as well. Astute provincial officials and citizens knew how to take advantage of the government's predisposition to build.[27] The pax romana kept communications open, allowing the style to spread and change as it was conditioned, in both Rome and the provinces, by non-Latin concepts.

What happened in Rome and many imperial cities during the years 54 to 138 is very much like what is happening in industrial countries today. Even making necessary allowances for the profound technological changes of the last two centuries, the Roman experience of architecture and building in the High Empire was more like our own than that of any other age. Both periods are marked by a drive to surpass the old led by men who want the new. Both are concerned with the visual as well as the social condition of the municipality. Today, when imitation Georgian and nondescript buildings are razed by the block and replaced by innumerable variations on the rectilinear silhouette, something of what happened in Rome, Ostia, Leptis Magna, Pergamon, or a hundred other cities of the Empire is taking place. Even the smallest town was given some architectural token to represent the imperial peace. In general the Romans built more slowly and more permanently than we, but they had the same compulsion to make their cities conform, in their public buildings at least, to the modern age. And the modern age was the new imperial order, which uprooted hundreds, sometimes thousands, of families to make way for new housing and municipal buildings.

Unlike the Egyptians and the Greeks, the Romans of the Empire built most of their major buildings for the social commonwealth. The importance of the temple, from the architectural point of view, was challenged by the attention given to secular buildings. Since imperial society and the state were shaped in the same image, the new vaulted architecture was essentially social in nature. The concept that Roman architecture is basically utilitarian, so popular for so long, is correct with respect to its emphasis upon social utility. What the Romans wanted were places where they might either act upon or debate and consider the very real and never entirely solved problems that arise among men. Roman architecture is the tangible shape of an innermost Roman trait—the desire for the adjustment of one thing with another. For the Romans this adjustment had to take place in a prescribed place ordered in such a way as to facilitate the means adopted. Because the Romans persisted in interpreting this need, the skyline and visual register of central Rome changed ceaselessly for more than two hundred years and the ancient cities of earlier societies, in many cases already extremely rich architecturally, were rebuilt or enlarged with Roman designs. In less ancient lands miniature Romes sprang up. London and Dougga, Ostia and Dura, whatever their rank in the multinational fabric of Roman imperial civilization, all make this clear: neither earlier styles nor traditional forms could alone express and house what Rome hoped to accomplish.

Western Europe and the lands around the Mediterranean still brim with architectural documents of these intentions. The principles of this architecture, for centuries an effective instrument of Roman culture, were not lost when the political framework of ancient society collapsed. They survived the transition to the early middle ages, and together with Roman literature and law have continued ever since to give inspiration and instruction. And Roman architecture has never ceased to be relevant to the study of the nature and meaning of architectural form, for it was an expressive and powerful art, defining a critically important experience of Mediterranean and Western man.

Roman Architecture

NOTES

[1] Rostovtzeff, *1*, 379–92, 462; Meiggs, p. 319; cf. *ESAR*, *5*, 246–52. The fundamental work on the guilds is J. P. Waltzing, *Étude historique sur les corporations professionnelles chez les Romains*, 4 Vols. (Louvain, 1895–1900).

[2] *Silvae* 4.3.40–58.

[3] The *collegium subrutorum* appears in *CIL* 6.940. Cf. Meiggs, pp. 311–36, esp. p. 319.

[4] *ESAR*, *5*, 234–36.

[5] R. H. Randall, Jr., "The Erectheum Workmen," *AJA*, *57* (1953), 199–210.

[6] See for example Durm, pp. 344–352; *Oxford History of Technology*, *2* (1956), 236, 419; F. Kretzschmer, *Bilddokumente römischer Technik* (Düsseldorf, 1958), pp. 53–58; R. Calza and E. Nash, *Ostia* (Florence, 1959), Fig. 80.

[7] Vitruvius 2.8.4; cf. 1.5.3. See also Middleton, *1*, 40; W. B. Dinsmoor, *The Architecture of Ancient Greece* (London, 1950), pp. 104–05, 174; Blake, *2*, 90, 92, 93.

[8] 5.10.3; cf. Middleton 2, 119–20.

[9] Roman mortars are discussed in detail by Blake, *1*, Chap. 9.

[10] Blake, *1*, 145.

[11] 2.4.1. For Roman screening of sand, see N. Davey, *A History of Building Materials* (London, 1961), p. 127.

[12] 7.2.2. The flare kiln used for burning limestone today is almost exactly like the kiln described by Cato, *On Agriculture* 38.

[13] Vitruvius, 2.6; Strabo, 5.4; A. Maffei, *Enclt* s.v. "Pozzolana"; L. Crema, "La volta nell' architettura romana," *L'Ingegnere*, *16* (1942), 941; Blake, *1*, 42–43.

[14] Vitruvius is at some pains to explain the properties of lime and pozzolana in 2.5.2 and 2.6; for the place of such subjects in his scheme of architecture, see F. E. Brown, "Vitruvius and the Liberal Art of Architecture," *Bucknell Review*, *11.4* (1963), 105.

[15] G. Lugli, "Nuove forme dall' architettura romana nell' età dei Flavi," *Atti*, *3*, 95–102, discusses this among other innovations of Flavian times.

[16] Lugli, *Roma*, pp. 493–508; A. Bartoli, "Scavi del Palatino (Domus Augustana)," *NS* (1929), 26. Very recently an immense concrete foundation of imperial date, 11 m. high, has been found; it is saw-toothed in plan (cf. Vitruvius, 6.8.7).

[17] Middleton, *1*, 57–58; cf. Blake, *1*, 294.

[18] Blake, *2*, 162–63, gives a good summary of this development; cf. Lugli, *Tecnica*, *1*, 584.

[19] These materials were carried up in baskets. The wheelbarrow, which was in use in China in the third century, did not appear in the West until many centuries later; J. Needham, *Science and Civilization in China* (Cambridge, 1954), *1*, 118; *Oxford History of Technology*, *2* (1956), 642. For cranes, etc., see Vitruvius, 10.2; Kretzschmer (above, n. 6), pp. 23–26; J. Rougé, "Ad ciconias nixas," *Revue des études anciennes*, *59* (1957), 320–328 (a study of *CIL* 6.1785, concluding that the inscription refers to a guild of crane operators; I owe this reference to the courtesy of Professor Lionel Casson); A. G. Drachmann, *The Mechanical Technology of Greek and Roman Antiquity* (Copenhagen, 1963), pp. 142–48, 199. For

the huge construction crane, operated by a treadmill, that appears on a relief from the tomb of the Haterii, see A. F. Burstall, *A History of Mechanical Engineering* (London, 1963), p. 88; cf. F. Castagnoli, "Gli edifici rappresentati in un relievo del sepolcro degli Haterii," *BC*, 69 (1941), 59–69.

[20] For the technical literature, see above, n. 13. On the drying rate of mortars see Vitruvius, 2.4.2; Frontinus, *Aqueducts* 123; Ward Perkins, *The Great Palace of the Byzantine Emperors, Second Report*, ed. D. T. Rice (Edinburgh, 1958), p. 79; cf. *AJA*, 65 (1961), 328; Blake, *1*, 316, 352; Fitchen, *Construction of Gothic Cathedrals* (Oxford, 1961), pp. 262–265. I have never seen anything resembling an expansion joint, even in the largest structures. There is no evidence as to whether the concrete was ever compacted after being tipped into the brick or wood forms, but cf. Vitruvius, 7.1.3. The question of the monolithic character of Roman imperial concrete is much debated. In general it appears that small thick vaults can properly be spoken of as monoliths, but large and relatively thin vaults probably cannot; see Ward Perkins, p. 80; cf. Fitchen, pp. 64–65 and citations.

[21] In the strictest terms these buildings are not entirely in compression, for there is a certain amount of beam and tie action within them.

[22] Among them the "hanging" quality of certain vaults which have partly fallen, for example in the Large Baths of Hadrian's Villa (S. Aurigemma, *Villa Adriana* [Rome, 1961], pp. 90–95), and the large flat slabs of concrete flooring that just may have been used to span small distances but which are more probably the layered pieces of floors of upper stories which have separated from the vault concrete. These slabs can be seen for example at Hadrian's Villa in the three-apsed hall by the Poikele, and in the lower level of the Domus Augustana; cf. Vitruvius, 7.1.3. See also Middleton, *1*, 64, 70–72, *2*, 121, 245.

[23] Polybius, 18.26.1–5.

[24] W. R. Lethaby, *Architecture, an Introduction to the History and Theory of the Art of Building*, 3rd ed. (Oxford, 1955), p. 94, Cf. G. Lugli, "Nuove forme dall' architettura romana nell' età dei Flavi." *Atti, 3,* 101–02 . . . L. Crema, *Significato della architettura romana . . .* (Rome, 1959; = *BollCentro, 15*), pp. 14–22.

[25] The phrase is from Suetonius, *Augustus* 28.3.

[26] A. Banduri, *Imperium orientale, sive antiquitates Constantinopolitanae*, in the *Corpus Byzantinae Historiae, 25.1* (Paris, 1711), 69.

[27] See R. MacMullen, "Roman Imperial Building in the Provinces," *Harvard Studies in Classical Philology*, 54 (1959), 209–210.

9. THE GREAT FRIEZE IN THE VILLA OF THE MYSTERIES

Otto J. Brendel

INTRODUCTION

Elsewhere among his many publications on Roman art, the late Otto J. Brendel called attention to the dangers of overinterpretation when dealing with allegorical art, which by its "cryptic," evocative nature alone invites excess and fancy. These dangers are augmented by the fact that the exercise of fancy—or imagination—is one of the tools the scholar must employ when analyzing allegorical art in order to penetrate from the visible data to the invisible idea that lies behind the visible and obvious. This selection is an ideal example of the careful deciphering of a puzzle: the meaning of one of the most important of ancient paintings. One follows Brendel's methodical analysis, as clue after clue falls into place, as one might the reasoning of a master detective. Yet, even as a web of meaning begins to gather, the author consistently draws the reader back to the reality of elusive content, of relevant factors that still await final clarification. The student of art history can learn much from a study of this selection as a demonstration of the scholar's methodology, and, to this end, the editor urges the reader whose appetite may have been aroused to seek the fuller account in Otto J. Brendel, *The Visible Idea* (1980), wherein the original German version (1966) has been translated by Maria Brendel. M. I. Rostovtzeff, *Mystic Italy* (1927), pp. 40–55, contains an earlier and briefer discussion of this frieze. Also of interest are Cyril Bailey, *Phases in the Religion of Ancient Rome* (1932) and John Ferguson, *The Religions of the Roman Empire* (1970).

Another work by Otto J. Brendel, invaluable to the student of Roman art, is his "Prolegomena to a Book on Roman Art" which first appeared in *Memoirs of the American Academy in Rome*, XXI (1953). The first part of this essay was included in the first edition of these *Readings in Art History* (1969) and the full essay has been reissued in an expanded version together with an additional selection, "Roman Art in Modern Perspective," under the title *Prolegomena to the Study of Roman Art* (1979).

On Roman painting, apart from general works like Amedeo Maiuri, *Roman Painting* (1953) and G. C. Picard, *Roman Painting* (1970), there are several studies which the reader may wish to consult: Phyllis W. Lehmann, *Roman Wall Paintings from Boscoreale* (1953); Martin Robertson, "The Boscoreale Figure-Paintings," *Journal of Roman Studies*, XLV (1955), 58–67; H. G. Beyen, "The Wall-decoration of the Cubiculum of the Villa of P. Fannius Synistor near Boscoreale in its Relation to Ancient Stage-painting," *Mnemosyne*, 4th Ser., X (1957), 147–53; P. H. von Blanckenhagen, "The Odyssey Frieze," *Mitteilungen des deutschen archäologischen Instituts, Römische Abteilung*, LXX (1963), 100–46; C. M. Dawson, *Romano-Campanian Mythological Landscape-painting* (1944); M. M. Gabriel, *Masters of Campanian Painting* (1952); W. J. T. Peters, *Landscape in Romano-Campanian Mural Painting* (1963); A. M. G. Little, *Roman Perspective Painting and the Ancient Stage* (1971); and John White, *Perspective in Ancient Drawing and Painting* (1956).

On Roman art in general, there are the two volumes by R. B. Bandinelli, *Rome: The Center of Power. 500 B.C. to A.D. 200* (1970) and *Rome: The Late Empire. Roman Art. A.D. 200–400* (1971); Richard Brilliant, *Roman Art from the Republic to Constantine* (1974); Donald Strong, *Roman Art* (1976); John Ward-Perkins, *Roman Art* (1977); and Bernard Andreae, *The Art of Rome* (1977).

The selection that follows is reprinted from Otto J. Brendel, *The Visible Idea* (1980), with the permission of the publisher, Decatur House Press Ltd., Washington, D.C. Translated by Maria Brendel.

The Villa of the Mysteries, located outside the city walls of Pompeii toward the northwest, takes its name from the great frieze that covers the walls of an "oecus," a kind of lounge. This frieze is doubtless the most important ancient painting still in existence; it is also one of the most enigmatic.*

The astonishing series of twenty-nine life-sized figures (Figs. 27–30), lined up before a strictly rhythmical, painted wall architecture of the so-called Second Roman-Campanian Style, poses more questions than can as yet be answered. For more than sixty years discussion has been going on concerning the artistic origin, the purpose, and especially the meaning of these magnificent paintings. Nevertheless—and despite all previous attempts and partial successes, attained mainly through research of recent years —the pictorial world of the frieze appears more puzzling than ever. . . . There are still too many questions about details which must be answered. . . .

. . . R. Herbig successfully demonstrated some time ago that the walls of the room, as well as the arrangement of the windows and doors, had the same appearance when the painters of the frieze started their work as they have today. The frieze has not been damaged by later rebuildings. It was planned for the architectural conditions that have remained to this day. . . . Furthermore, it seems that the painted architecture preceded the frieze. The figures hardly take it into account, and the perspective socle had to be added in order to provide a base for them. When, at a later date, a portico was constructed as a roofed outside gallery around the building, the already existing large south window was taken into consideration by widening the position of the portico columns so that the light coming in from the terrace would not be diminished. The frieze was to remain clearly visible. In any case, the room was well provided with daylight and was easily accessible. Nothing in the architectural design points at a secret to be guarded.[1]

27. Pompeii, Villa of the Mysteries, Mural, long left wall, c. 50 B.C. (Alinari/
Editorial Photocolor Archives)

28. Pompeii, Villa of the Mysteries, Mural, rear wall, c. 50 B.C. (Alinari/
Editorial Photocolor Archives)

29. Pompeii, Villa of the Mysteries, Mural, detail of the corner group of the right wall, *c.* 50 B.C. (Alinari/Editorial Photocolor Archives)

THE LEFT LONG WALL

We shall now turn to the figures. A young woman has just entered. Perhaps we should assume that she passed through the same little door used by today's visitor. In any case, her still lingering step indicates the direction of the frieze. Our eyes follow hers. The entering woman is certainly an important person, perhaps an initiate. . . .

. . . Into what kind of company does the veiled lady really enter? To this question is tied a very simple methodical considera- tion which is by no means new but which seems to me not always sufficiently noted. I am thinking of the following, obvious fact. The persons who move side by side in this frieze do not all belong to the same sphere of reality. Some of them apparently stand on our side of human reality, the normal one, as it were. They might do things or find themselves in situations which we do not immediately understand because they are unfamiliar to us. Nevertheless, it is clear that in their strange conduct and unusual behavior, they neither do nor indicate anything which under similar circumstances could not be done or experienced by other human beings. They are inhabitants of the realm of our common human reality. The woman who has just entered belongs with them. In contrast, however, there are other beings who are not depicted as less real, but who nonetheless are not of the same nature. They are part of an otherworldly reality, fictitious, mytho-

30. Pompeii, Villa of the Mysteries, Mural, details of the right wall, c. 50 B.C. (Alinari/Editorial Photocolor Archives)

logical, or poetic. Silens and satyrs, even the gods in the center of the back wall, are not real in the same sense as the human beings in the frieze are. Only in art, which itself is invention, can the representatives of these two worlds meet so easily, without reservations. . . .

The wistful lady who has just entered is certainly a real person. . . . The path she is about to take leads past several more or less clearly separated groups. The first, apparently not noticed by the veiled woman, is comprised of a seated woman and a boy reading. It has long been known that the reading itself signifies a religious act, one for which there is other evidence.[2] At the moment nothing new can be added to what has been established. It might be relevant, however, to recall that we do not know what the boy is reading. A prayer, a sacred text—these and other possibilities remain open. A sacred formula into which the name of the arriving person is inserted must also be considered; we know from inscriptions the great importance that was attributed to personal names in the mysteries.[3] Be that as it may, the point is that the group is involved in an entrance rite, an *introitus*. That much is obvious from its position within the whole composition. In the course of the frieze it represents a preparatory and probably a subordinate episode.

Then follows the sacrificial rite, if one can call it so. The young girl with the silver platter is probably part of it, although she is separated from the main action by a small space. The mantle wound around her hip is significant. . . . Acolytes, male and female, often wear it in sacrificial scenes on Dionysiac monuments. Thus the girl so dressed is one of the assistants. . . . The sacrificial group then, consists of four persons. Three are apparently acolytes. Only one, the seated woman who wears a beautiful headdress and a cloak knotted on the left shoulder (the *palladium quadratum*), carries out the ritual attended by the others. She functions as priestess. Unfortunately, not much can be seen of the sacrifice. Even less can be explained. The scene of the ritual is an offering table. The objects that the acolyte carries in on the silver platter are difficult to make out, though they might be loaves of bread. In any case, the sacrifice is not a blood offering. A servant girl who is bending over . . . is the only member of the group who is not adorned with an olive wreath. It is significant that the priestess is seated, for sitting during the sacrifice is not the rule. . . . The fact that the principal person turns her back to the observer adds to the mystery of the undertaking. . . . Apparently there is no known Bacchic ritual which completely corresponds to this act, nor do other mysteries offer precise parallels.[4]

. . . Up to this point we have dealt with actions and actors belonging to the world of human reality. But if one advances only one step, one enters a different world. The border of our side of reality is then overstepped. Directly behind, though turned away from the group that performs the sacrifice, stands the singing silen.

The transition into the mythical world happens abruptly . . . . Silenus's right leg overlaps a considerable portion of the acolyte with the pitcher who stands next to him. Although they are not equally real, both figures move within the same real space. The acolyte stands somewhat in the background, while the silen, broadly drawn, is distinctly a foreground figure. He is almost naked, and no longer a youth. His cloak slips down from his hip. He has propped his nine-stringed lyre on a stone pillar, as was customary in a musical performance.[5] . . . His pose is that of a singer who, thrusting forward, follows the power of his own voice while his body swings back and forth to the rhythm of the music. . . . Our silen is a kind of magic singer, his snub-nosed face and bald head, framed by an olive wreath and sparse gray hair, lifted toward heaven—ecstatic. . . . Intoxicated he is, although hardly from wine. The wise silen here becomes an artist. Rare insight and the magic of music are consolidated into words and sounds in his song. In the context of the frieze, this figure represents the first allusion to the Dionysiac sphere of *enthusiasmos*, the first modality of Bacchic madness, the μανία of the sage, of the singer, of art.[6]

The scenes change very fast. Alongside the silen, a small rock rises from the ground like a stage set-piece, in the middle of the room, as it were. . . . In front of the rock stands a small goat, while on it sits a young female creature who nurses a kid. Her companion holds a syrinx. For the explanation of this group, earlier research may be cited.[7] The three following points may be made in summary. These creatures with pointed ears . . . belong to the family of satyrs, and therefore they are fictional characters, members of the bizarre court of Bacchus. Secondly, they form a self-contained group. Silenus does not notice them nor they him. . . . It remains doubtful whether any meaningful relationship exists between the silen and the satyr children. Both represent Dionysiac elements, but each acts independently. . . . In addition, the question arises whether in the two forms of music before us a contrast is not being deliberately shown between the noble lyre and the rustic syrinx; in other words, between the sublime style of inspired song and the simple manner of a pastoral tune. The miracle of inspiration belongs to a higher level, to that of Silenus.[8]

With this, however, ends the Bacchic following. We are not granted much time for meditation because suddenly a human being, with a sharp outcry, as it were, bursts into the mythical idyl. This time it is a much disturbed real person, a fleeing girl.

THE FLEEING GIRL

She is clearly a foreground figure. Her right leg already covers part of the pastoral group while she, striding out, seems to run obliquely from her left toward the edge of the painted platform. . . . She is the last figure on the left long side of the frieze; looking back, her glance is directed toward the corner of the short rear wall. . . .

It is generally assumed that the girl is running away frightened and terrified. Even the face with the half-opened mouth seems to express alarm. There can be little doubt about the interpretation since the iconography of this action of fear is well known; it can be traced back to the art of classical Greece. Pulling a cloak, or even the upper part of the peplos, over the head is a first reaction when a woman is afraid or feels pursued—as if such a delicate garment could hide or protect her when no other refuge offers itself.[9] The problem of this figure lies therefore not in her pose, which is easily explained, but in the question why is the girl frightened, from what does she flee?

So far, this question has been answered mainly in two different ways. In the first, the girl is afraid of the unveiling of the phallus which is under way at the opposite end of the rear wall;[10] or, in the second, she is frightened by the beating scene, represented in the same corner of the rear wall and continuing on the adjacent long wall on the other side of the room.[11] Both these answers share the disadvantage that they accept a much larger space between the effect represented and its cause—a space filled with other painted scenes—than would be natural for such a representation. . . .

THE LIKNON SCENE

Some considerations of a more general nature have to be added here regarding the unveiling scene at the right end of the rear wall. The group does not only puzzle the modern observer, since the *pentimenti*, more numerous here than elsewhere, show that even the ancient painter faced difficulties.[12] Moreover, the upper part of the group unfortunately has been destroyed. Nevertheless, it can be stated that it consisted of three women, one kneeling in the foreground and two others standing behind her. One of these, approaching from the left, carries an offering plate. She and the kneeling girl turn their backs on the divine couple, which could easily mean that the girls are unaware of the gods, that only the viewer can perceive them, whereas they remain invisible to the persons who are represented.[13] The kneeling girl wears the previously mentioned cloak that is knotted around the hips. A torch rests on her left shoulder indicating that the ceremony takes place at night. She leans forward toward the liknon which, as usual, is represented as a longish basket with a border that rises gradually backward in a curved line. With the right hand she grasps the purple cloth that covers the erect object in the basket. Her left hand is raised slightly above this object, most likely in order to lift the cloth. The unveiling is under way but has not yet taken place. The covered object can hardly be anything but the phallus symbol—to be expected in this setting—in spite of its uncommon, straight upper line. It has indeed always been explained this way. After all, in representation of Bacchic rites—and this scene is one—liknon and phallus belong together.[14]

. . . There can be no doubt that they are part of the Bacchic sphere of symbols, although this is by no means self-evident. In its practical use, the liknon is a winnowing basket, and therefore an implement that serves in Demeter's or Ceres' cultivation of the fields, but not in the cultivation of vines. In fact, the cult of Dionysos Liknites, in which the agricultural corn shovel was connected with Dionysus not only by its myth but also literally by its descriptive name was earlier affiliated with an ancient cult of the earth goddess.[15] Originally bread and wine belonged to separate religious practices, just as different agricultural conditions underlie their cultivation. This fact has always been remembered, even in their common cult.

The question about the meaning of the phallus symbol probably must be asked in a similar way. In an agrarian cult it is not difficult to understand the male symbol as a necessary prerequisite of, or supplement to, female fertility personified by a maternal earth goddess. Actually it seems that in classical times it was mainly associated as a ritual symbol with feminine religions, either in cults that were dedicated to an earth or grain goddess, such as the Eleusinian Demeter, or in sacred rites that were, according to their statutes, performed by women, such as the rituals of the Attic Thesmophorai.[16] In both cases we have reasons to assume that objects in the form of a phallus were part of the ritual. . . . How bread and wine came together in that sphere is still uncertain. Dionysus himself is not a phallic god in all his numerous pictorial representations as was, for instance, Pan or Hermes. On the other hand, he was surrounded from early times by the phallus-happy satyrs and the thyrsos-wielding maenads who made up his mythical attendants. In this context, however, something else should be remembered. Maenads and satyrs, though they are both Dionysiac creatures, by no means always appear as good friends. Just the opposite is true. As is well known, there are numerous representations of maenads who successfully resist the obtrusive satyrs in a rather straightforward way. They disapprove of phallic conduct, or rather misconduct,[17] and on the whole show a dislike for the masculine. Hence Pentheus and Orpheus became the enemies and victims of the frenzied women. Regarding the assessment of phallic symbols in the religion of Dionysus, we must always take into account that in this circle the phallus image can assume an unfriendly connotation, that is to say, a recollection of an original antagonism between the sexes or, more accurately, the female's hostility toward the male. . . .

OTTO J. BRENDEL

ONCE AGAIN: THE FLEEING GIRL

To deny to the liknon scene of the Pompeian frieze the character of a cult ritual will not be possible. This interpretation is supported by the fact that the women who participate in it are identified as human beings—and not as mythical personages—by their costume and demeanor. Not much has yet been gained from the preceding considerations toward an explanation of the fleeing girl at the opposite corner. . . .

. . . The question—of what is the fleeing girl afraid?—remains unanswered. At this point it is best to look for the answers nearest at hand. . . .

Actually the fleeing girl finds herself in a situation which also could daunt others. She is clearly the only human being among the strange phantoms of mythology who, however, still seem to be so real. All the same, she pays attention neither to the singing Silenus nor to his neighbors, the unnatural shepherds. She looks back rather to the group with the mask which is next to her on the rear wall. . . . Her gesture indicates fear mixed with surprise. Thus, there is every indication that the fleeing girl and the group with the mask form a whole with regard to content. On this point I agree with Matz, who not long ago discussed the group with the mask in detail.[18]

. . . Three figures are arranged on three planes from the background directly toward the onlooker. At the very back a young satyr bends forward so that the mask which he holds up with his right hand appears above and even a little in front of the seated Silenus; the mask's beard slightly overlaps his furrowed forehead, which this time is wreathed with ivy. He himself holds a silver vessel with both hands, and the central figure, again a young fellow with pointed ears, bends so deeply into it that one perceives more of his head than of his face. The drinking vessel too is seen from underneath, foreshortened. Silenus, however, does not pay any attention to his action. His face is turned away, and his rolling eyes seem to follow the fleeing girl on the other side.

. . . Actually, two actions are taking place simultaneously. A mask is being held up and exhibited as if it were a symbol with a meaning of its own. One must assume, however, that the youthful satyr has just taken the mask off Silenus. Thus, the unmasking

184

equals an unveiling and corresponds to the unveiling of the phallus symbol on the other side of the group of gods. The arrangement of the pictorial parts on the rear wall is axial and symmetric also with regard to its content. The mask, while it strikes terror, still resembles the comparatively mild face of Silenus. I believe we know the name of the mask. It is Akratos, the daemon of the unmixed wine which, mysteriously murmuring, ferments in new casks until they are opened in the spring. The daemon too is alarming.[19] Thus, a reason supported by ancient sources is given here for the fear of the fleeing girl. It seems to me, therefore, that the best answer to the question of why the girl is behaving as she does is indicated by the monument itself, namely, that she is afraid of the daemonic mask and at the same time amazed by the double play, the two-faced nature of Silenus. Looking back she recognizes him, is frightened, and flees. It is possible or, rather, likely that this double play between mask and reality includes still other meanings which we have not yet discovered, but let us not speculate on them. In any case, here the viewer learns to know, guided by the wise Silenus, the second side of Dionysiac ecstasy: after the *enthusiasmos* of music, the magic of wine.

Another problem arises from the second action, the offering of the drinking vessel. Does it represent an oracular scene or simply the consumption of the offered drink?[20] The question is outside the immediate range of my investigation and cannot be decided by mere inspection. An oracle or prophecy from a reflection in the wine—just as in modern times from coffee grounds—was ancient practice. The evidence goes back to the early classical period.[21] But who can declare with certainty whether the young satyr gazes or drinks? A possibility must definitely be reserved for the latter. The vessel itself, a silver skyphos, resembles the traditional *akratophoron*.[22] But no matter what is happening here, wine is the main agent. While Silenus offers the cup, the mask hangs above him, like a sign board not to be overlooked. Is an invitation conveyed by the glance of his large eyes over toward the corner? Does a call come forth from his open lips? Does the girl withdraw from these?

THE FLAGELLATION

The flagellation group, next to the liknon scene at the far right end of the rear wall and overlapping the adjoining corner of the southern side wall, represents the strangest episode of the entire frieze, the winged, striking woman is its most bizarre figure. Her bizarre character, however, is more make-believe than real. The ancient tradition from which she originated and to which she belongs can be clearly shown.

. . . Obviously, she is a daemonic being, indeed a spirit of darkness equipped with large dark wings like the night.[23] She lifts a switch with her right hand, ready to strike. The upper part of her body is naked, and a short garment is draped around her hips but does not seem to be knotted. In addition, she wears high boots. Suggestions for naming the strange figure have been made, but all raise serious doubts. . . .

. . . The striking figure is certainly a daemon, not a goddess. At the time the frieze of the mysteries was probably produced, the second quarter of the first century B.C., such figures of daemons had long been a part of art in Italy. Late Etruscan monuments, especially funerary urns, show them in an abundance of variations, and some of those examples come quite close to the winged figure in dress as well as conduct.[24] But these Etruscan pictorial fantasies themselves go back to the early beginnings of Greek art in South Italy, namely, to the wealth of images on painted Apulian and Tarentine vases. The Artemis-like costume, the wings, and the weird, often underworldly, meaning are already found together there. It is important that these dark beings sometimes have their names inscribed on the vases, or that they appear in mythical contexts from which the intended name can be deduced with great likelihood, even if the inscribed name is missing. . . . Among the female daemons of this Graeco-Italic pictorial world is one whose character seems to me eminently well suited for the activity of the winged figure on the frieze and for the context in which she appears. I am speaking of the daemon Lyssa.

This figure is properly a psychological personification, first in myth and then especially in Euripidean drama. Madness and indomitable passions are her doing. One might say that she represents this madness in person, and consequently at the same time its incomprehensible and therefore daemonic origin. Beyond this general description, she has been accepted, at least since Euripides, as a Dionysiac daemon. She rouses Dionysiac madness, the whirling passion of maenads or the blinding frenzy with which the god of wine strikes his victims. . . . The means she uses are a blow or sting, a *kentron* or whip. She goads or whips up passions, just as the modern metaphor puts it. Thus, she does exactly what the winged figure on the frieze, shown in an attire that still resembles the named, older representations, sets out to do. The conceptual and iconographical concordances are so close that I do not hesitate to use the name Lyssa for this figure as well. No other personification or daemon we know matches so closely the lashing, winged figure of the frieze, and none is so much at home in the world of the Bacchic imagination. Thus, we might conclude that Lyssa is at work here too. The blow she is ready to strike—she herself in a swift, almost dancing pose—is aimed at the half-naked girl who kneels next to her at the beginning of the south long wall.

THE MAENADS

The stance which the painter has given his winged figure is indeed noteworthy. The torsion of the upper half of the body is certainly grounded on the powerful swinging of the right arm and is a strong emotional action. . . . The impression is that of a volatile apparition barely touching the ground. Half floating, her wings seem to carry her more than her feet. . . . This but transitory step, demanding continuous movement, looks like the pose of a dancer. The naked dancer on the other side of the flagellation group performs almost the same step, seen from the back. Thus, Lyssa herself is introduced as a maenadic character. While she whips, she imparts her nature to her victim.

. . . The maenads' dance is ecstatic but at the same time it is believed to have a relieving and calming effect. . . .[25] The blow dealt by the winged person cannot be interpreted as punishment or judgment. Its meaning might be an initiation or a transformation of a natural human being into the spiritual state of a maenad. Thereby the still missing third Dionysiac mystery, ecstacy through dance, would have been attained.

This explanation implies that the four women at the southeast corner are natural, not mythical characters. This was never doubted with respect to the two dressed figures, as well as to the one kneeling who rests her head on the lap of the fully dressed, seated woman. But then the dancing girl who is shown from the back cannot be meant, in this context, as a mythical figure, since the four figures together form one of those closed groups so characteristic for the style of the frieze. . . . It is indeed the very task of Lyssa to excite in natural otherwise normal people the kind of passion which alienates a human being from himself. This was exactly her role in Greek drama and Apulian vase paintings.[26] She herself is a conceptional abstraction, her beating or whipping is to be understood allegorically, not as reality, for actually she strikes a blow at the mind not at the body.

It is not so easy to discover the additional relations and actions which unite the four women who are placed as a group opposite the striking figure. The kneeling girl seems to expect the impending blow in this position. She is almost naked, her only garment is a purple cloak which reveals her as it loosely slips away; her long hair is untied and hangs dishevelled around her face, as if she had already become a maenad. . . .

The seated woman in this ritual can obviously be called a helper and is probably a friendly character. But she will not ward off the blow. On the contrary, while she looks up at the already present (or awaited?) daemon, she holds the young girl's head on her knees with her left hand and with her right clears her back, so it seems, of the long tresses. Her part is to instruct and to prepare, for she evidently knows what has to happen. . . . The painter has generally made a point, in this group, of delineating all clothing as loosely tied, not closely knotted. Thus, the hair of the kneeling girl is also let down, not bound. Are we to recognize the liberating power of Liber in the freely falling costumes? Another acolyte, approaching from the right, fully dressed in a purple garment, brings the thyrsos. Is it her own or is it to be handed over to the kneeling girl as the badge of honor for a maenad? The dancer in the foreground, with her arms uplifted and her hands holding *crotala*, is, however, certainly a maenad figure. Her only garment is a narrow, gold-colored veil which flutters from her shoulder. And yet her dance is strikingly quiet, we could almost call it formal. The Bacchic ecstasy here lacks all wildness. It seems to be more trance than frenzy.

The Great Frieze in the Villa of the Mysteries

We are confronted here with another problem that has been repeatedly discussed in the past. Are we to regard the frieze as a continuous whole, a sequence of interrelated actions, or, on the contrary, as a paratactic series of unconnected Dionysiac and ritual recollections indifferent to each other in their meaning? . . . Its accentuated center, the group of the gods, interrupts any natural chronological order of the events which we might assume to exist. Neither are there any portrait likenesses which, for instance, might enable us to recognize the same person in different situations.[27] Even Silenus, who certainly occurs twice, appears in each case with a different physiognomy. But all this does not imply that no meaning at all can be found in the sequence of the episodes. There still remains the possibility that the entering young woman, the fleeing girl, and the initiate of the flagellation group stand for the same person in the proper sense of a continuous representation, or that the same three figures depict three different stages of a consistent action in a continuous story. Both solutions are possible. But then we also have to ask whether the kneeling girl and the naked dancer in the flagellation group are two different persons or whether, in the manner of Roman "continuous narration," they rather depict the same person twice, in different moments of a coherent event which follow hard upon each other. It might be difficult to prove that either of the two alternatives is correct, yet it appears to me that the second is not less likely than the first. Assuming this to be true, the situation represented could possibly be translated into words in the following way. The initiate expects Lyssa's blow; once struck she is transformed. She is now *the* maenad. Otherwise one would have to say that she is merely one of the maenads belonging to the throng.

THE BRIDAL SCENES

The large window on the south wall is next to the group with the maenad. Beyond the window the bridal scenes begin. They continue past the southwest corner to the wide door on the west wall and on its other side to the corner of the north wall. The so-called *Domina* occupies the narrow space between the west door and the northwest corner (Fig. 30). With her the frieze comes to an end. . . . The *Domina* . . . directs her glance toward the near end of the opposite south wall. She does not pay any attention at all to the veiled figure on the other side and does not even seem to be aware of her presence. The lack of contact between these two corner figures not only points out the beginning and the end of the frieze but also the direction we have to follow in "reading" it.

By describing the last pictures of the frieze as bridal scenes, this investigation returns to the basic observations which Bieber made years ago. An essentially different interpretation is hardly possible. The bridal scenes represent a closed sequence that consists of two related pictures: the dressing of the bride, and the waiting bride on the *kline*. Both themes derive from an old pictorial tradition which originated in classical art.[28] . . . The selection of the themes proper, that is, of the situations represented, was Greek. The preparatory nature of the two moments likewise recalls their Greek origin; the actual wedding is not represented but only the preceding dressing of the bride and her waiting. On the other hand, we find Roman elements in details, especially in the underlying conceptions of customs and costume.

Among these details belongs, for example, the bride's coiffure, if, as I assume, Bieber's suggestion is correct. In the dressing scene her hair is being separated into strands. This corresponds with the manner of arranging from six different strands the complicated coiffure which the ritual of a Roman wedding, *confarreatio*, prescribed.[29] The symbolic details of this scene still await explanation. The hairdresser, whose task is obvious, is assisted by two half-grown, winged Erotes, the presence of whom in women's rooms stems from a Greek tradition, as do their occupations. . . . The little Eros on the left holds up to the bride a mirror which does not have its usual round form but is, strangely enough, rectangular. Nevertheless, its purpose cannot be doubted: it shows a reflection. Behind the bride on the west wall stands the other winged little boy. Leaning his right arm on a pillar, he lifts his face and supports it with his right hand. With rapt attention he watches the dressing scene round the corner in front of him. His pose and mood belong to Pothos who represents the intense longing for love.[30] The mirror and his glance, both directed toward the same object, complement each other. . . .

Concerning the details of the next picture, the waiting bride

. . . the furniture on which she is sitting is without doubt a *kline* on high feet, which here can signify only the bridal bed.[31] The noble lady who presents herself to us as its owner rests her hand on the head of the bed. . . . The face of the *Domina* is uncovered, the veil falls backward. She too looks thoughtful but her cloak is luxurious and colorful, the ring on her hand is visible, and the *tabellae*, the marriage contract, lie next to her.[32] . . . The pictorial schema tends to bring to light the girl's new rank . . . as a member of a social class with special obligations and privileges. Her festive clothing, the *praetexta* garments which are her new possession, demonstrates this. She has already risen to that peculiarly Roman privileged level of feminine society at which she will spend the rest of her life. That is to say, legally she is no longer considered *virgo* but as *matrona*.

THE FRIEZE AS A WHOLE

All this has little to do with Bacchic rites and ideas. The connection between the bridal pictures and the other episodes of the frieze is not immediately clear. . . . We are definitely confronted with a problem which has so far defied all efforts made to solve it, but that is not reason enough to deny altogether that the bridal scenes belong to the frieze in content as well as in composition.[33] There is no authentic evidence in the painting itself to indicate a separation into two independent parts—unless one wants to interpret the interruptions which the room's architecture imposed on the painter as a mode of division. But in that case the dressing scene would have to be separated from the picture of the waiting bride and that would be most unlikely. The opposite assumption of an inner harmony of the whole frieze holds a greater probability. The argument can be strengthened by considering this harmony as a continuous narration, such as we have described it here. The dressing scene follows the maenad group and can be understood, in a certain sense, as its logical sequence. The progressive undressing of the main figure in the preceding groups is then completed with the naked dancer in the maenad group. The new investiture can now take place as a further step to a new level of meaning. The dancing girl actually looks toward the next scene, that is, away from her present surroundings. This play of glances points to continuity; thus, the maenad group no longer qualifies as the end of a composition. Very little more than what the painting itself intimates is known about the special "theology of dress" which might be preserved in the progressive changes and transformations of the costume.[34]

Thus, the main problem of the entire frieze is still hidden behind all the questions concerning details. How can the various pictures of the frieze of the mysteries be associated as an easily understood whole? In what way do the bridal scenes, for instance, belong to the Bacchic occurrences which above all give the frieze its characteristic quality? This last question, in my opinion, has not yet been answered in a satisfactory manner, and I doubt that the time for it has come. Dionysus was not originally an appropriate patron or model for the matrimonial institution.[35] There are, however, relatively early references to wedding pictures, perhaps used only as metaphors, which occur at least since classical times in the Dionysiac iconography,[36] but their relation to the actual social conditions of the time, that is, to real weddings, so far remains obscure. The so-called wedding of Dionysus and the Basilinna was a single Athenian cult episode.[37] Dionysiac consecrations, if they occurred at all in the fifth century B.C., normally promised everything else but matrimonial order, as we know from Euripides. Moreover, ancient weddings were virtually civil acts, not consecrations. How does all this fit together? . . .

. . . Two conclusions immediately emerge in retrospect. The first one is a matter of a simple statistical fact. If we consider again the difference established at the beginning between real and fictitious characters among the persons in the frieze, we arrive at a clear and important result. The figures who recognizably represent real persons are all women. Not a single male can be found among them, as a matter of fact, with the exception of the reading boy. All the male figures of the frieze, the sileni as well as the satyrs, represent fictitious characters. All those who carry out cult acts are real persons, always women, with the exception again of the boy whose reading is being supervised by a woman. The observation confirms the generally accepted opinion that the scenes depicted allude to actual rites and to the ideas and mythical narratives present in them. Moreover, it leads to the conclusion that the represented actions must be attributed to a women's cult, that means a cult which was exclusively performed by women and which most likely, was only accessible to women. So far as the monument, as the only evidence, justifies an opinion, it must be assumed that no male participants were tolerated in these religious exercises.

A second conclusion concerns the obvious lack of consistency in the meaning of the represented situations. An analysis in this respect shows that we are dealing with three parts. Their diversity is expressed also in the entire arrangement of the frieze. Actions prescribed by the cult form the first part. Neither mythical nor allegorical elements interfere with their reality, which must be interpreted literally. It might be difficult for just this reason to recognize the specific meaning of these actions. Perhaps they are Dionysiac in character, but there is no need to explain them on that basis, even though it remains likely that a mystery rite is being performed. The unmistakably Dionysiac part of the frieze starts only with the singing Silenus and extends without interruption to the dancing maenad. Next come the bridal scenes, the third part of the composition. Here again, Dionysiac allusions cannot be detected. As so often on Roman monuments, the arrangement then is clearly in three parts. The Dionysiac part occupies a cardinal place since it not only covers the entire rear wall but spreads, as with two outstretched arms, to the adjoining long walls, requiring approximately an additional third of each. From all this, we may infer therefore that the cult and the rites demonstrated by the frieze were originally not homogeneous. They were not all Dionysiac in the same way.

THE GROUP OF THE GODS

From a formal as well as a thematic analysis of the frieze it becomes apparent that the east short wall is its principal part. Here, between the group with the mask and the unveiling of the liknon we find Dionysus himself, the *deus praesens*, united with Ariadne in mutual embrace. . . . The destruction of the upper part of the representation is a great loss for us, for the group is beautifully painted and differs considerably from the rest of the frieze not only in the size of the figures but also in style. To start with the content, Dionysus sits on a slightly lower bench next to Ariadne. The preserved remains of the painting suggest that she was a powerful figure, matron-like in appearance rather than maidenly. Leaning decidedly backward, Dionysus clasps her with both his arms while she holds him in hers. With his left arm on Ariadne's thigh, he reposes in her lap. The situation . . . can be understood as a thematic, though not a formal, parallel to the kneeling girl who under quite different circumstances buries her head in the lap of her protectress. A prototypical relationship is indicated here; it should not be overlooked even though it cannot be fully explained.

But the ecstasy is over within the group of the gods, and a state of tranquility has been reached. With the unused thyrsos beside him, Dionysus has slipped back to repose. The shoe, dropped carelessly, seems conspicuous to the onlooker, but it does not necessarily signify more than an accompanying detail, a mute and eloquent testimony to the calm after the storm.[38] Dionysus looks up to Ariadne and although we cannot tell any more whether she returned the amorous glance, it is most likely she did. The group's *ethos*—to use the ancient technical term—was clearly romantic, . . . the transport of love with a happy ending. Once more one comes across a parallel rich in associations. This time it is the exchange of glances between Dionysus and the exalted bride which is echoed by the gods of love in the dressing scene. The god, so it seems, is connected with those who belong to him in many ways, by experience and by fate.

Other peculiarities of this representation belong to the compositional structure of the work, though they should remain part of the question of content as well. Actually, it is wrong to talk about a group of gods here since Ariadne is, strictly speaking, no deity. Only Dionysus is a god. Nevertheless, the group has been placed in the frieze facing the beholder like a cult image. It comes forward out of the background in a frontal-rectangular way like the nearby group with the mask, but not as abruptly. The diagonal position of Dionysus reveals the Hellenistic origin of the formal invention. It has often been pointed out—and with justification—that the fact that Ariadne occupies a higher place constitutes an anomaly.[39] Moreover, the middle axis of the wall, or rather of the entire room, coincides almost exactly with the middle axis of the enthroned Ariadne. Thus, she is in every way the central figure and therefore the main deity of the frieze. Dionysus rests by her side, looking up to her. . . . There is every indication then that the group of gods in the frieze of the mysteries represents a very special and independent variation of the Dionysus myth, in fact a new interpretation of the myth with the roles of the participants reversed. The god has become the *paredros* of the beloved whom he exalted and she is the reigning goddess. As Curtius has already seen, the idea was probably not Greek, but it does belong to the world of Hellenized mother goddesses in Asia Minor.[40] We now understand that the women dedicated to this cult over which the mythical couple presided cannot have been indifferent to the new and unusual interpretation of the mythical pair, an interpretation which differed so widely from that of classical antiquity.

THE CULT: A CONJECTURE

The group of Dionysus and Ariadne was not an unknown work, and is the only part of the frieze to which we have unmistakable reminiscences in other, very different kinds of monuments. A cameo in the Kunsthistorisches Museum in Vienna, as well as a Domitianic coin of the city of Smyrna, render the same group.[41] It is most unlikely that even a single one of these rather summary repetitions goes back to the Pompeian painting. As so often happens in Roman art, we are dealing with reproductions of an older *opus nobile*, and the group on the frieze can be only a link in the same chain of replicas. Thus, in all probability, it is itself a copy after a Hellenistic painting, the original of which would have to be placed in the late fourth or early third century B.C. Evidently it was a work of high quality, an unusually brilliant and impressive invention. . . .

An attempt to make a further statement about this lost original would be sheer hypothesis. If, nevertheless, this essay closes with such a conjecture, it does so only because the ancient tradition offers a reference of great interest for the problems under discussion. The catalogues of Pliny in fact contain a title which is immediately conclusive for the group of the frieze of the mysteries, and thus for the probable prototype as well. The picture in question, representing Dionysus and Ariadne, is by Aristeides of Thebes, an early Hellenistic painter whose work could be seen in the motherland and in Asia Minor.[42] The couple could have been portrayed in various ways, and nothing states that the group by

Aristeides looked exactly like the one we are seeking. Pliny, however, mentions an additional fact. Aristeides' painting "formerly" was to be seen in the temple of Ceres in Rome. "Formerly" probably refers to the fire of the year 31 B.C. which badly damaged the temple. The painting might have been destroyed or else it was taken to another place.[43] In any event, it is interesting that a famous painting with this title was in the temple of Ceres in Rome just at the same time when the Pompeian frieze was painted.

The temple of Ceres at the foot of the Aventine, probably under today's Bocca della Verita, was a very ancient and special place. The history of its foundation connects it with the revolution which established the Roman republic. On the advice of the Sibylline Books, the cult was regulated in 493 B.C. according to the Campanian pattern. From this time dates the official name, the temple of Ceres, Liber, and Libera. Since Dionysus and Ariadne could be meant by the last two names—at least since Hellenistic times —Aristeides' picture was indeed in the right place.[44]

In spite of the relatively rich sources for its history, our idea of the religion which the temple represented is not as clear as one would wish.[45] Ceres, like the Greek Demeter, was by her nature a goddess of women. Grain, seed, and harvest, the fruits of the fields, were her concern. An assimilation with Demeter suggested itself and was carried out early; and with Demeter came her Greek mythology, the legend of the kidnapped daughter, and possibly also a new ritual. In the early first century B.C., the period which concerns us here, the connection with Campania is well attested. Even some of the temple's personnel were called from there.[46] But that does not mean that the cult did not maintain a certain local character, for the temple of Ceres had been declared a sanctuary of the plebs and thus served a segment of the population classified as such only in Rome. The part taken by the town's matrons at the temple's calendar feasts was based on similar social principles and likewise had a local characteristic, a Roman feature.

Women's cults existed in Greece too, especially in the service of Demeter. The Attic Thesmophorai are an obvious example.[47] Nowhere, however, were these institutions so frequent as in Rome. Their membership was firmly organized there in a corporate manner, the basis for which is found not only in the Etruscan-Roman family structure, which granted a relatively large measure of authority to married women, at least inside their home, but also in the sacral order of the state, which could not spare any of its members for multiple tasks. The ruling women of the great families, patrician as well as plebeian in origin, formed in this sacral range a social class with privileges and obligations inside and outside the home. It was for the common interest that these obligations were met regularly. The performance itself lay in the hands of authorized women.[48]

A short survey of these conditions at the end of the Republican period yields two peculiar results. The majority of those cults which were regularly practiced by the matrons are addressed to ancient native deities, often of an obscure significance but endowed with functions proper to the female sphere of influence, such as the Fortunae, Mater Matuta, Bona Dea.[49] In this sphere Ceres is the object of a cult having more than Roman-Latin standing. Secondly, all these cults share a high degree of social exclusiveness. The positions, as well as access to them, are limited, even if in different ways. The matrons themselves are recruited from the leading class of society. The exclusion of men is even more significant, especially in the secret rituals of Bona Dea and in the temple of Ceres. Here then a principle which was to protect an easily vulnerable ritual comes into being, a principle that the maenads of Dionysus had enacted only in a mythical form. The women entrusted with this ritual meet as a closed society. During the ceremony which lasts one night, they are suspended from the institutions of male society. The office they were charged with did not even tolerate male presence.

CERES, LIBER, AND LIBERA

The following questions concerning the great frieze in the Villa of the Mysteries arise from the circumstances just mentioned. According to common iconography, the frieze definitely does not represent a mythical bacchanal, and whether or not it follows any coherent iconography at all remains uncertain. As we stated above, the frieze consists of three sections, the first of which represents cult scenes to be viewed as real. The main part contains mythical detail and, in addition, such symbolic acts like the flagellation scene as can expound the opinions and expectations of a real cult group. Real persons, for instance, the fleeing girl, participate in these episodes. Whether the acts themselves should be judged as actual happenings must remain to be seen. It is at least doubtful whether the kneeling victim of the flagellation really received a blow from the hand of a human being whose place in the painting is taken by the winged daemon. One might ask as well whether the nakedness of the dancing girl is to be understood as real—which would be possible—or only as a symbolic attribute belonging to the world of maenads. Nevertheless, it is certain that the main part of the frieze deals with Dionysiac ideas. Into these Dionysiac elements, mythical or symbolic, a cult scene, the unveiling of the phallus in the liknon, has been inserted, the reality of which we have no reason to doubt. Thus, in the main part of the frieze we are dealing with a mixed iconography which contains fictitious as well as real images, traditional as well as iconographically unusual ones. The third part, however, with the dressing of the bride and the bride waiting on the bridal bed, follows a consistent and traditional iconography of wedding scenes with some realistic additions and alterations taking into consideration specifically Roman views. On the whole, the iconography of the frieze shows a conspicuous lack of homogeneity. This fact supports the assumption that the frieze was created for a special purpose or for the purpose of a special cult community. It is rich in original inventions.

For the reason just mentioned, it is worthwhile to pursue the allusion to a possible connection with the cult in the Roman temple of Ceres. At least the reference indicates an area of historical reality where a cult group like the proposed sodality of the frieze could find a place among existing institutions, that is to say, among the women's cults of the Roman matrons. Not many of the known Roman city cults can be considered for our question as not all of them were suitable for export. Outside Rome the Italic Bacchanalia ought to be given attention first, Campania having been one of their original provinces. In the beginning, they too were esoteric women's cults, but their exclusiveness was no longer maintained after the senatorial edict of 186 B.C.[50] Possibly the frieze includes reminiscences of several of their original observances, but as a whole, the frieze refers to something else and its secret lies in its very lack of homogeneity.

For this reason I shall return once more to the assumption that there is a connection between the frieze of the mysteries and the cult in the Roman temple of Ceres. The cult was most fashionable. The fact that many *Augustae* attached great importance to being portrayed as priestesses of Ceres can be partly explained by the social prestige of her Roman temple. Although it was generally referred to as the temple of Ceres, we must not forget that the goddess shared this place of worship with two equally famous partners. The painting by Aristeides, which Pliny mentioned and which might have been copied in the frieze of the mysteries, reminds us of this fact. It is difficult to imagine how this partnership affected the practical cult since the temple's calendar feasts all refer to the name of Ceres. This does not mean that the other partners were neglected; rather, several cults were superimposed upon each other, a phenomenon which must have occurred at a much earlier time. In classical Greece too Demeter was sometimes associated with Dionysus, and a unification of the cults of Dionysus and the queen of the underworld, Kore-Persephone, probably took place in Greek South Italy.[51] Old religions, however, do not cancel each other out, nor do they really merge, but one of them could be superimposed on another. In this process the original ideas, sentiments, and symbols are maintained though new legends spring from them. . . .

The ancient sources about the cults of the temple of Ceres are rather scarce, but they report extraordinarily interesting details. The calendar of feasts listed three main holidays, one of them a yearly mystery ritual, the *sacrum anniversarium Cereris*. This was a nocturnal ceremony after the Greek pattern, a παννυχίς: *pervigilia Cereris*. Its date has not been transmitted precisely, but it may have been a movable feast; a date in midsummer around harvest time is likely.[52] It was certainly a secret rite executed by women. Men were denied access. A similarly transmitted and perhaps mimetic act concerning the rape of Kore, the *Orci nuptiae*, is generally associated with this mystery, but not for good reason in spite of the fact that the recovery of the raped daughter played a part, though not necessarily in the form of a performance of a cult drama. Even if such a performance belonged to the rites of the *pervigilium*, it would not have required the entire night. There must have been enough time for other celebrations which are now unknown to us. These could have easily included additional and more clandestine thesmophoric ceremonies.[53]

That the nocturnal ceremony in the temple of Ceres included special meanings is clear from the known taboos established for that night. The membership is of importance: women only, and among them *matronae* as well as *virgines*. The words *pater* and *filia* were forbidden. While the latter prohibition might be interpreted as a gesture of respect for the bereaved mother, the former cannot be explained by the same argument.[54] . . . Moreover, Liber Pater must have been affected by the sacral prohibition, even though he was a partner in the cult. Whatever the reasons, the effect of the taboos remained the same and was not accidental. We could call it a verbal supplement to the ritual exclusion of men, that is, the ritual denial of paternal power in the family of women for the duration of one night.

In addition, there are two more prohibitions. The word "wine" was not to be pronounced. A similar prohibition prevailed in the nocturnal ceremony of the Bona Dea which is comparable in some respects.[55] But in the temple of Ceres, Liber, and Libera, this taboo is even more conspicuous. We cannot escape the assumption that it also was directed against Liber Pater, the co-partner whose power is restricted for the duration of the mystery in still another way—by simply not being mentioned. Secondly, before the start of the ceremony, the members had to observe a period of sexual continence which lasted at least nine hours and more likely, nine days. This too probably can be viewed as a thesmophoric arrangement.[56]

The conflicting aims within a merged cult dedicated to an official triad of gods can be of special interest here. They are the noticeable scars left by a superimposition of cults or by an early syncretism.[57] The contradictions can undoubtedly shed light on the comparable inconsistency of the iconography as well as of the content in the large frieze in the Villa of the Mysteries at Pompeii. The frieze itself forms a triad, a kind of colossal triptych, as we stated above. Here too tensions appear between the members of the triad, although the three parts that constitute the frieze cannot be named as accurately as the triad of the temple of Ceres. Therefore, it is not plausible that the frieze describes the cult of the temple of Ceres. . . . Nevertheless, there are significant similarities between the ritual of the Roman Ceres performed by the matrons and the women's cult in the frieze of the mysteries.

To begin with the dissimilarities, the main part of the Pompeian frieze is clearly a Bacchic representation, perhaps even an illustration of a Bacchic mystery. Music, wine, and dance are its three mystical aspects. That the group of gods, which perhaps could be seen in the temple of Ceres as well, hints at something else, was recognized long ago. The oneness of love is split into a duality in which the god does not hold the highest position. The goddess occupies a higher throne. Thus, the ruling deity is, at least in this place, a woman. In this lies the cause of a tension which, in a similar way, has also arisen in the triad of the temple of Ceres. This tension is superhuman; its place is in the realm of the gods.

From now on the similarities become more distinct. . . . We have to consider for instance that two important cult symbols in the frieze are not accepted. The girl flees from Akratos. Then Lyssa, about to administer the blow which will stir the maenad to her own unique passion, turns away from the unveiling of the phallus, in defense, as it were. It looks as if she wanted to say, not now, not here. . . . A parallel exists in the nocturnal ceremony of Ceres where the women are not allowed to pronounce the word "wine" and where sexual continence before the ceremony—hence rejection of the male—is strictly required. . . . We may not claim complete certainty, but the religious conditions of both lines of behavior, as well as ancient reports, support the likely conclusion that in the two cases the underlying purpose of the cult was the same. Even if the other members of the triad, Liber and Libera, were not mentioned in the mystery of Ceres in Rome and only Bacchus and Ariadne were visible on the frieze in Pompeii, the rites, whether depicted or as in Rome only performed, had a similar effect. Both produced in a symbolic way the detachment of the participating women from the patriarchal family unit. In the mystery of Ceres this is accomplished by the ritual independence of the matrons and in the retinue of Bacchus by the maenad who evades marriage as a result of a mystic initiation. . . .

Our attempt at explanation must halt here, at least for the time being, for many details are still missing. The statue of the empress Livia stood in the garden of the villa. Was there a relationship between her likeness, which after all could not be found in every garden in Pompeii, and the esoteric women's club which perhaps still met there during her lifetime?[58] And on a much lover level, one finds on the walls of the same villa the exasperated epigram of a frustrated lover, *Ceres mea*, which M. Della Corte has published with such perception.[59] Is all this mere accident? The bridal scenes especially have not yet been properly placed in the structure of the whole. A final remark should therefore be added in regard to this last question which has always been one of the main problems of the frieze.

The answer to the question is not made easier by the analysis expounded here. In it the world of maenads and of the family appear as separate institutions. Even the transformation into a maenad as it is represented in the frieze has an institutional meaning in that the new member of the society of initiates is furnished with the thyrsos, invested, so to speak.[60] There seem to be only contrasts between the maenad and the declared bride. No link exists. They belong to separate worlds and transitions are unthinkable.

Nevertheless, not transitions but parallels between these antagonistic characters become visible in the same analysis. Both represent social lines of conduct, effected by rites in the case of the maenad, sanctioned by rites in the case of the bride. The bride too submits to ceremonies, although not to initiations in the strict sense of the word. By virtue of these ceremonies she acquires a new position within a hierarchy regulated according to religion and social status. Even in this, her very own place, she is within the domain of the triad Ceres, Liber, and Libera. She is then subject to the law of Ceres.

Does a real wedding actually take place here? . . . The bridegroom is missing. The question deserves serious consideration in a monument such as the frieze of the mysteries which seems to exclude men on principle. Moreover, thesmophoric secret rituals may have been maturity rites in origin. . . . In the frieze in Pompeii the Bacchic element prevails. But the initiation—or initiations—into an exclusive cult was obviously also meant here, perhaps, even in preparation for a wedding. . . . It is not impossible that the bridal scenes were to point out the contrast to the Bacchic world of maenads. . . . The continuity of the themes then would be expressed in the interrelated contrasts rather than in the progress of the action. Thus, the action would have to include all contrasts, from the maenads experiencing only themselves to matrimonial union as the goal and highest degree of fulfillment.

To consider that the *ordo matronarum* received a new member with every appropriate wedding seems to me especially important since this fact establishes a parallel to the Bacchic cult actions that precede the bridal scenes.[61] Our approach shows that many of the rites and actions under scrutiny can be interpreted in multiple ways. In a certain sense, they are all "rites de passage" designed to transfer human beings from one station in life to another. Wedding rites are intended to detach the bride from her original family and to admit her to a new one. Mystical initiations transfer human beings into a new religious frame of mind and, at the same time, award them a new and higher religious degree. Then, initiation and admission become the same, and in this sense—aside from other possible interpretations—mystical initiations and weddings are indeed comparable. If the word initiation is really valid for the frieze, then it means, among other things, admission to a new social class in the form of a cult association whose full members held the rank of matron and which traditionally emphasized the sacral autonomy of the women's society. Normally, the young girl becomes a matron by marriage; through the mysteries she gains a religious position. From this point of view a similarity between the maenad and the bride of the frieze exists, notwithstanding all the contrasts. They can be considered as equals, all the more since the word matron seems to have been used also as an independent title unrestrained by factual marriage.[62] As long as the transition from maenad to matron in the frieze of the mysteries cannot be differently and more convincingly supported by ancient evidence, it seems advisable to consider also the analogical data which may have connected these seemingly contradictory forms of life.

In spite of everything, . . . another solution could still be found, that is, an interpretation demonstrating a direct development from the maenads to the bridal scenes. I would like to recall here . . . the episode of Amata in Vergil's *Aeneid*. There the girl Lavinia, before she can become a bride, is abducted into the woods by a swarm of Latinian maenads and offered by her own mother to the lord of the Bacchic turmoil. J. Gagé has pointed out the possibility that this idea may easily go back to a cult practice that once existed. For the present it is only an

OTTO J. BRENDEL

hypothesis, but if this or a similar suggestion holds, the result would indeed be a sequence of events which corresponds exactly to the pictorial order of the frieze. At least in Vergil's story the identification with the maenads would be equal to what we would have to recognize in the frieze: a preparatory experience, followed by the wedding.[63] The question about the meaning of the bridal scenes and their place in relation to the whole can now be asked in the following manner. Do we have to view the allusions to wedding and marriage as the result of the preceding actions, that is, as their goal and end, or is it rather the opposite? Is the position of a matron the prerequisite for admission into the cult group and participation in its mysteries? For the time being, I would like to leave the question unanswered, exactly because both answers are possible. In both interpretations the frieze is closely drawn together as a whole; if there are any joints, they are not immediately visible. Thus, let us look once more at the *Domina* who concludes the frieze. The young woman in the dressing scene preceding her is definitely a bride. Perhaps both are the same person. In any case the *Domina* waiting on the *kline* is *nova nupta* and therefore already a matron; however, the place and particular moment might suggest that she is principally a titular matron.

NOTES

* It would not be possible to cite the entire literature, which has been accumulating since 1910, regarding every detail of the frieze that will be discussed in the following essay. In most cases this would have meant a repetition of well-known opinions. Instead, we are fortunate enough to be able to refer to two recent papers containing critical summaries of earlier research; these constitute the basis for further investigation. The first includes a brief annotated bibliography, chronologically arranged, almost up to the year of its publication: R. Herbig, *Neue Beobachtungen am Fries der Mysterien-Villa in Pompeji* (1958) bibliography 70ff (hereafter: Herbig *Beobachtungen*). The second is F. Matz's Διονυσιαχὴ Τελετή, *AbhMainz* (1963), which includes publications after 1957 (hereafter: Matz, *Telete*). For earlier literature, see these two papers.

Special attention should be given to two inquiries which have proved to be basic for the discussion of the entire frieze: M. Bieber, *Jdl* 43 (1928) 298ff. and L. Curtius, *Die Wandmalerei Pompejis* (1929) 343ff. Note also that in the same year J. Toynbee in *JRS* 19 (1929) 67ff proposed an interpretation with results very similar to those of Bieber. In order to relieve the footnotes of superfluous repetitions, current dictionaries, like W. H. Roscher, *MythLex* and *RE*, are cited only for special reasons. For the present subject, see especially the following articles in *RE*: XIII 1,

The Great Frieze in the Villa of the Mysteries

538ff., s.v. "Liknon" (W. Kroll 1926); XVI 2, esp. 1290ff., s.v. "Mysterien" (O. Kern 1935); XIX 2, esp. 1701ff., 1712ff., s.v. "Phallos" (H. Herter 1938).

It is not necessary to mention in every case whether or not the author agrees with the opinions of others.

[1] Herbig, *Beobachtungen* 10ff.

[2] Herbig, *Beobachtungen* 33f., 74; also see infra n. 3.

[3] A. Vogliano and F. Cumont, *AJA* 37 (1933) 215ff., inscription from Tusculum.

[4] The action being performed here certainly cannot be explained with the formula "to take and to replace" of the Eleusinian mysteries. These involve very different ideas and symbols; see now M. Mehauden, *Le Sécret Central de l'Initiation aux Mystères d'Eleusis*, ed. C. J. Bleeker (1965) 67ff., with bibliography.

[5] Examples in E. Winternitz, *MittKhInstFlorenz* II (1965) 277ff., esp. 279.

[6] Music inspires *enthusiasmos*; it is the means, not the consequence, of divine frenzy, and in this respect comparable to wine: Aristotle, *Pol.* VIII. 5. 16; 7. 4.

[7] Herbig, *Beobachtungen* 30ff. He, like Bieber, *Jdl* 43 (1928) 304, calls the girl "Paniske." The representation is unique, although it plays with traditional conceptions: maenads suckle kids in Euripides, *Bacchae* 700. On an Etruscan tombstone from Tarquinia (London, Brit. Mus. D 22), a Bacchic initiate, perhaps a priestess, offers a drink from her kantharos to a fawn: F. Messerschmidt, *SteMat* 5 (1928) 26, pl. 4.

[8] The unfavorable rating of the flute started in classical times, after the middle of the fifth century B.C. The sources seem to have been primarily Athenian intellectuals and performing musicians (Melanippos), as well as advocates of a new "ethical" music theory: Plato, *Rep.* III.399.C–D. Here we can but note the long aftereffect of this classical opposition between a "higher" and a "lower" kind of music in neo-Platonic theory and, branching out from there, in Renaissance philosophy. In Roman pastoral poetry the reed pipe is *agrestis*: Vergil, *Ecl.* VI.8. On the other hand, we must remember that the various types of flute, especially the aulos, were generally considered as instruments of Dionysiac music, in contrast to the Apollonian cithara. In this respect too, the lyre-playing Silenus is a remarkable but still problematic figure. For the recently discovered Cybele from Bogazköy whose little companions play the aulos as well as a stringed instrument, see K. Bittel in *Antike Plastik* II (1963) 7ff., esp. 20f.

[9] Examples in Herbig, *Beobachtungen* figs. 35, 36; Matz, *Telete* 22f. The expressive motive of a female figure grasping her mantle as a sign of fright can already be found in early classical painting; cf. the frightened Gaia on the Tityos cup by the Penthesilea Painter in Munich: G. Neumann, *Gesten und Gebärden in der Griechischen Kunst* (1965) 41, figs. 18, 178, n. 127.

[10] Bieber, *Jdl* 43 (1928) 304; similarly, *idem, The Review of Religion* 2 (1937) 8: "The horror is not only injected by the huge symbol, but by the sinister winged figure. . . ." Likewise, Herbig, *Beobachtungen* 29.

[11] Especially Curtius, *Wandmalerei Pompejis* 363.

[12] R. Herbig, *AA* (1925) 262ff.; cf. *Beobachtungen* 15, 37, n. 1.

[13] Invisibility: A. Pease, *HSCP* 53 (1942) 1ff.

[14] Matz, *Telete* 16ff. Neither is the content of the liknon equally clear in all representations nor is it necessarily always the same. The liknon can contain other objects or it can be empty. See also infra n. 51.

[15] The liknon is the cradle of Dionysos Liknites. The child lies in it. The

celebration of the Thyiades on Parnassus and the cult in Delphi are connected with the pre-Apollonian religion, probably the old local cult of the earth goddess. M. P. Nilsson, *The Dionysiac Mysteries of the Hellenistic and Roman Age* (1957) 21ff. (hereafter: *Dionysiac Mysteries*), derives the liknon from the cult of Priapus. In doing so, he emphasizes the originally foreign nature of the liknon in the Dionysiac arsenal, although the derivation from Priapus can hardly explain the situation; cf. F. Matz, *Gnomon* 32 (1960) 534ff. An early example of the connection of liknon, phallus, and Dionysus appears on an Apulian crater in Trieste: E. Simon, *Jdl* 76 (1961) 171, fig. 37. Earth goddess and liknon of the child Dionysus: M. P. Nilsson, *Geschichte der griechischen Religion* I (1941) 546f.; idem, *Dionysiac Mysteries* 38ff.

[16] Phallic rites and symbols in the cult of Demeter: *RE* XIX 2, 1712ff., s.v. "Phallos"; see also infra n. 57.

[17] Many monuments from early classical times on show the frequently represented maenads resisting satyrs: Nilsson, *Dionysiac Mysteries* 567f.; M. E. Edwards, *JHS* 80 (1960) 78f., with older literature. Cf. esp. A. Rapp, *RömMitt* 27 (1872) 695f. concerning the maenads' hostility to men and marriage. In the early sixth century it was still different; on monuments of this time satyrs and their nymphs—who hardly differ from the maenads—get on much better together. Cf. the erotic scene on the Phineus cup in Würzburg: E. Langlotz, *Griechische Vasen im M. von Wagner-Museum* (1932) 23ff.

[18] Matz, *Telete* 31f.

[19] Akratos: main evidence, Paus. 1.2. 5. Interesting material in E. Gerhard, *Schmückung der Helena* 4BWPr (1845) 10. Thus, Akratos was a daemon, represented as a mask, connected with Dionysus but not identical. The name points to the still unmixed new wine; for the religious significance of the new wine, see Nilsson, *Griechische Religion* I 554f., 564, with reference to the feasts of the Anthesteria, Choes, and Pithoigiai. Consequently, the daemon Akratos must be understood as the personification of the new wine. Cf. also the Akratos mask on a round cist, the prop for a Roman statue of standing Dionysus (Rome, Vatican Museums): G. Lippold, *Vat. Kat.* III, *Gall. dei Candelabri*, no. 29. Akratos seems to be especially linked to the mask god of Choes. After all, Dionysos Akratophoros in Phigaleia, according to the description in Paus. VIII.39. 5, must have been quite similar to the mask idol on the so-called Lenaia vases. The mask of Akratos had the features of Silenus: South Italian vase from Lipari, with inscription, now in Glasgow, *JHS* 7 (1886) 55, fig. 2, pl. 62. In Athens Akratos was the patron of the Dionysiac *technites*, that is, the artists and particularly the musicians: E. Maass, *Jdl* 2 (1890) 102ff. The little tomb sanctuary on an Apulian vase, decorated with mask and kantharos, might be related to this conception: *CVA Lecce* (2) pl. 33, 34; the dead perhaps belonged to a sodality of Akratos. The bearded mask in a liknon worshipped by women on a libation vessel should be related, however, to Dionysus himself: G. van Hoorn, *Choes and Anthesteria* (Amsterdam, 1951) no. 271, fig. 38. Cf. also Nilsson, *Dionysiac Mysteries* 28ff., 98, fig. 24: the mask excites fear.

[20] Details in Matz, *Telete* 30ff.

[21] Aeschylus: χάτοπτρον εἰδους χαλχός ἐοῖ, οἶνος δὲ νοῦ, Frag. 670 (ed. H. J. Mette). Anakreon: J. Bergk, *Anacreontea* 60, *Poetae Lyrici Graeci* III² (1914) 33 J.

[22] DarSag, s.v. "Akratophorum." Vessels of this form appear repeatedly on

monuments, but to my knowledge the examples have not been collected. It is interesting that such a vessel occurs on the Munich black-figure vase which Nilsson related to the Attic feast of Choes, the Anthesteria vase in Munich, *SBMünchen* (1930) Abh. 4, fig. I; this is how I would actually like to explain the "jug" which the standing woman on the right holds in her hand. A vessel of the same kind, only larger, is handed to the standing maenad on the left in a Pompeian painting representing the triumphal procession of the child Dionysus: Curtius, *Wandmalerei Pompejis* 298f., fig. 172; from the house of M. Lucretius Fronto, counterpart to *ibid.* 297, fig. 171.

23 The night has black wings: Aristophanes, *Aves* 695. Cf. *Mnemosyne* 7 (1939) 169.

24 Numerous examples, esp. on Volterran ash urns: e.g., C. Laviosa, *Scultura Tardo-Etrusca di Volterra* (1964) 41, pl. 12; 69, pl. 33; 167, pl. 106. R. Herbig, *Götter und Dämonen der Etrusker* (1965) pl. 28, 2 (goddesses of death).

25 Euripides, *Bacchae* 862f.: the Dionysiac ecstasy means rescue and protection.

26 The Latin counterpart of the Greek Lyssa is of special interest here, the description of Alecto and her influence on the unfortunate queen Amata: Vergil, *Aen.* VII.378ff. The fury Alecto is also a daughter of the Night with dark wings, *ibid.* 331. She turns Amata into a raging maenad, driven round like a top by the whip of playing boys, *ibid.* 405f.: *"dant animos plagae."*

27 Most interpreters agree on that. For different opinions, cf. Simon, *Jdl* 76 (1961) 126, 169.

28 Bieber, *Jdl* 43 (1928) 313f. More recently, B. Schweitzer, *Mythische Hochzeiten, SBHeidelberg* (1961) Abh. 6.

29 M. Bieber, *The Review of Religion* 2 (1937) 9.

30 Herbig, *Beobachtungen* 38; Pothos: W. Müller, *Jdl* 58 (1943) 154ff.

31 Herbig, *Beobachtungen* 39. The *kline,* with only one third of its actual length shown, occurs on an onos from Eretria: M. Bieber, *Jdl* 42 (1927) 315, fig. 12.

32 Ring on fourth finger of the left hand signifies bride or wedding: evidence in Bieber, *Jdl* 43 (1928) 312, n. 5. On the wedding contract, see *ibid.* 329. Along with Herbig (*Beobachtungen* 39), I identify it with the *tabellae*—closed diptychon —on the *kline* next to the waiting woman. Herbig's suggestion that she does not represent the bride but the mother contradicts all ancient wedding pictures known to us; moreover, the accumulation of the wedding symbols around her, including the bridal bed, make it unlikely that the waiting figure is not the legitimate owner of these things. The yellow veil, here with a purple seam, also belongs to the bride according to Roman custom: A. Crowfoot, *BSA* 37 (1936/37) 40, n. 6.

33 Curtius, *Wandmalerei Pompejis* 361f. Also Nilsson, *Dionysiac Mysteries* 66ff., esp. 74.

34 Change of clothes for symbolic purposes in later mystery religions, especially of Isis: *RE* XVI 2, 1929f., s.v. "Mysterien."

35 The Athenian month *Gamelion,* in which the Dionysiac feast of Lenaia fell, was named for the institutional protectress of marriage, Hera Gamelia. It cannot be generally designated as a wedding month. Neither can any communal weddings in this month be cited nor were there any initiations of brides. M. P. Nilsson, "Wedding Rites in Ancient Greece, Opuscula Selecta" III (1960) 243f. Connections with Dionysus arise from the season. The wine which was pressed out in early fall could be considered as fully fermented in February: Plutarch, *Q. Conv.* III.7. 1.

The Dionysiac festivals of the Anthesteria follow a little later (supra n. 19). Not much can be stated with certainty about the Lenaia themselves: Nilsson, "Griechische Religion" I 551, 559, n. 2.

36 M. Bieber, "Eros and Dionysus on Kerch Vases," Hesperia Suppl. 8 (1949) 31ff. For the New York libation pitcher and its explanation, see "Procession Personified" in this volume, 1–6: the "sacred wedding" at first was a ritual. Still, vase paintings of the fourth century B.C. show a tendency to attribute to it a more human, sentimental interpretation. These pictures, however, are allegories which are only vaguely related to reality. The meeting of Dionysus and Ariadne at this period sometimes resembles a human love story and marriage; this is hardly applicable to the original character of the myth: E. Simon, AntK 6 (1963) 11ff.; also E. Metzger, Recherches sur l'Imagerie Athénienne (1965) 62ff. Cf. also Nilsson, Dionysiac Mysteries 66ff.; and infra n. 37.

37 The Basilinna thereby represented the city of Athens on account of her position (ὑπὲρ τῆς πόλεως; Demosthenes, Against Neaera LIX.72–73, ed. W. Rennie). The cause of the Boeotian Daidala is comparable, Paus. IX.3: wedding of the city heroine Plataia with Zeus. There the "bride" was a wooden doll (Daidalon), which at the end was burned on Mt. Kithairon. The yearly wedding with Dionysus was a concern of the city, a state act, not unlike that other more famous ceremony: "Wenn der Doge von Venedig/ Mit dem Meere sich vermählt." The office of the Archon Basileus was the place assigned for it, which suggests that even at its beginning the cult was located in the royal dwelling. As to the ritual itself, the sources state only that it was secret. A procession corresponding to a wedding procession probably took place according to the monuments, but this is not documented in writing. Only this connection justifies occasional depictions of the Basilinna on vase paintings, especially in the wedding performed by children on the small pitcher in New York: L. Deubner, Attische Feste (1932) 104, pl. II, 2–4. Cf. Metzger, (supra n. 36) 63, n. 4.

Participation of the Archon Basileus is neither documented nor likely: E. Simon, AntK 6 (1963) 12, and n. 38. Regarding the meaning of sacred weddings generally, cf. Nilsson, Griechische Religion I 110ff., 554f.

38 Herbig, Beobachtungen 22; Curtius, Wandmalerei Pompejis 356.

39 Esp. Curtius, ibid. 367ff. Early Hellenistic dating of the prototype: F. Matz, AA (1944) 94ff. See also infra n. 42.

40 Curtius, Wandmalerei Pompejis 367: originally a matriarchal cult which survived in a paternalistic society. The practice is there related to the Greek Artemis.

41 For illustrations: Bieber, Jdl 43 (1928) 301; Curtius, Wandmalerei Pompejis 369; Simon, Jdl 76 (1961) 133, fig. 15. In addition, highly comparable terracottas from Myrina: R. Lullies, MdI I (1948) 51; Herbig, Beobachtungen figs. 31, 32.

42 Aristeides of Thebes: Pliny, Nat. Hist. XXXV.24. 100; VII.126; Strabo VIII.381; summary: W. Sauer in Thieme-Becker, s.v. The Dionysus picture was probably painted for Corinth. It survived the destruction by Mummius in 146 B.C. but was subsequently sold to Attalus III of Pergamon. From there it came to Rome, probably after 133 B.C.

43 The fact that the Dionysus picture by Aristeides was in Rome, at least for a while, increases the probability that copies of it could have been made and circulated in Italy. The original could be seen easily and was accessible to the public.

The Great Frieze in the Villa of the Mysteries

[44] For the history of the Roman temple of Ceres and related questions, see: H. Le Bonniec, *Le Culte de Cérès à Rome* (1958) 254ff.; Liber identical with Dionysus-Bacchus; *ibid.* 308ff.; Libera-Ariadne: Ovid, *Fasti* III.511ff. Contradictions in the ancient interpretations of the triad Ceres, Liber, Libera: Le Bonniec, *op. cit.* 305f.

[45] Cult and feasts of the triad: *ibid.* 277ff. We must remember that Liber belongs originally to Libera and that therefore the triad must read: Ceres and the couple Liber-Libera, *ibid.* 294.

[46] *Ibid.* 396ff.

[47] Meetings of women in the cult of a triad consisting of Demeter, Kore, Dionysus: the Nymphon in Phlius, Paus, II.11. 3. The same applies to the Attic Haloa. An initiation by a priestess is also mentioned among their ceremonies: Bieber, *Jdl* 43 (1928) 315, n. 2. Literary evidence for a connection between Dionysus and Demeter is more frequent in Rome than in Greece: Le Bonniec, *op. cit.* 298. Thesmophoria: Nilsson, *Griechische Religion* I 109; Deubner, *Attische Feste* 50ff. The late Hellenistic fragments of a frieze that is now partly in Athens and partly in Würzburg could also be of interest here. Perhaps they represent a thesmophoria procession from Asia Minor, possibly from Halicarnassus, third quarter of the second century, H. Möbius, *AM* 77 (1962) 282ff.

[48] Regarding these institutions here and in the following: J. Gagé, *Matronalia* (*Ed. Latomus* LX, 1963) esp. Ch. II, 100ff.

[49] Fortunae: *ibid.* 12ff; cf. also Brendel, *AJA* 64 (1960) 41ff. Mater Matuta: Gagé, *op. cit.* 159. Bona Dea: *ibid.* 137.

[50] Main source is Livy XXXIX.8ff. Mitigating modifications are mentioned on the bronze tablet from Tiriolo: O. Elia, *RömMitt* 69 (1962) 124f., nn. 19, 20. The Senate's objection is directed on principle against the participation of men; this seems to have been the chief reason for the prohibition: Cicero, *De Leg.* II.35–37. Moreover, Nilsson, *Dionysiac Mysteries* 14ff.

[51] Matz, *Telete* 33f. Locrian reliefs: E. Langlotz, *Ancient Greek Sculpture in South Italy and Sicily*, no. 71ff. (with literature); K. Schauenburg, *Jdl* 68 (1953) 38ff. Underworld connections of the bearded Dionysus on late classical, Hellenistic, and Roman monuments: A. Bruhl, *Liber Pater* (1953) 309ff. The important volute crater in the Museo Archeologico in Ferrara, attributed to the Polygnotos Painter and discovered in 1923 at Spina, should be mentioned here too. Best illustrations in S. Aurigemma, *La Necropoli di Spina in Valle Trebbia* I 1 (1960) 48ff., pls. 19–30; earlier literature, *ibid.* and P. E. Arias, *ArchCl* 10 (1958) 21ff. Dionysus and a companion are enthroned in a cult building in order to receive a festival procession which approaches from the right and seems to move around the whole vessel; both deities hold a scepter and libation cups similar to those of the enthroned deities of the Locrian relief. There can hardly be any doubt that it is Dionysus who is represented, but the supposition that he takes the place of Hades as god of the netherworld remains quite uncertain. His crowned *paɣedros* is without name. Her identification as Chloe is based on an erroneous reading: Arias, *op. cit.* 21ff. She lets a small lion play on her shoulder and left arm as if it were a domestic cat. This might be a maenadic element; she is the princess of the thiasos, in this case most likely Ariadne. The procession is led by a white-haired priestess who carries a veiled liknon on her head; behind her, a flute-playing girl, then two orgiastic dancers and two aulists; underneath, children and two men. The women, however,

are in the majority. The liknon appears here for the first time in a Bacchic ritual; the vase is to be dated around 440 B.C. Unfortunately, nothing can be said about the contents of the liknon because it is covered with a cloth. Next to the priestess is a sacrificial altar with logs. We must assume that the contents of the liknon were designed as the sacrifice on this altar. A definite feast is certainly meant. In contrast to the Locrian reliefs where Hades, Persephone, and Dionysus are clearly recognizable in a close cult relationship, nothing points to relations to underworld deities.

52 The *sacrum* is first documented for the year 216 B.C. It was obviously a Hellenistic reorganization from among the Roman cults, Le Bonniec, *op. cit.* 400ff., and thus different from the older Cerealia. The celebration was supervised by Greek priestesses, called probably from Campania, *ibid.* 396ff. These enjoyed high social prestige, *ibid.* 399.

53 *Orci nuptiae:* Le Bonniec, *op. cit.* 438ff. Discovery of Proserpina: *ibid.* 412ff. Even so, the tendency of the entire celebration was not Eleusinian, as far as we know. Only the exclusiveness of the ritual, the categorical limitation to female participants, gives it a thesmophoric character. In this too I follow Le Bonniec, *ibid.* 420f.

54 Servius in *Aen.* IV.58. Cf. Le Bonniec, *op. cit.* 421; Gagé, *Matronalia* 143f.

55 Gagé, *Matronalia* 139, n. 2. Wine was permitted in this celebration but it was not to be mentioned; it was circumscribed with other words, the vessel containing the wine called *mellarium*, the contents called milk: Macrobius, *Sat.* I.12. 25. Also in Greece Demeter generally maintains a reserved attitude toward the Dionysiac drink; for instance, she refuses wine in her sorrow: *Hom. Hymn. Demeter* 206f. The refusal of food and drink is certainly a general and natural expression of mourning. From this it does not necessarily follow that the denial of certain food and beverages cannot also assume special meanings. Demeter's refusal of wine complies with the restriction to the *nephalia*—libations excluding wine—in the cult. Both in themselves presume by definition an opposition to the god of wine.

56 Detailed discussion of the sources, Le Bonniec, *op. cit.* 404ff. It is possible but not certain that in this preparatory period of abstinence the consumption of bread was prohibited. That could be understood as ritual imitation of the Eleusinian myth. The myth itself represents an agrarian logic: the "mourning" field lacks fruits, the bread is not there. The sources, however, are hardly sufficient to make the abstention from bread for the Roman *castum Cereris* more than probable at best.

57 Deubner has similarly concluded that in the procession of the Attic, so-called rustic Dionysia, basket and phallus represented an older religious phase upon which were superimposed the Dionysiac symbols of wine amphora and vine: *Attische Feste* 136. The lack of homogeneity in the cults in the Roman temple of Ceres has rightly been emphasized by Le Bonniec: the mysteries of the *anniversarium* with their thesmophoric character refer only to Ceres and the recovered daughter. Liber and Libera are not considered, they are not mentioned. The complete triad of deities did not participate at any celebration of mysteries: Le Bonniec, *op. cit.* 438.

58 A. Maiuri, *La Villa dei Misteri* (1931) I 223ff., figs. 93–98.

59 M. Della Corte, *RendNap* 24/25 (1949/50) 101ff.

60 Thus the thyrsos is ready for the Dionysus child as proof of his later power. Zeus—the father—holds it in his left hand on the crater by the Altamura Painter while with his right he supports the boy who stands on his knee; certainly he holds it not as his own attribute but in order to hand it over to the child later, or perhaps

to the assisting nymphs: H. Fuhrmann, *Jdl* 65/66 (1950/51) 118ff.

[61] Gagé, *Matronalia* 126ff.; for the Roman characteristics of this institution, *ibid.* 100ff.

[62] *Ibid.* 224; until now only late evidence: Isid. Sev., *Origines* I.573.

[63] Gagé, *Matronalia* 235ff.; 238 with reference to the old celebration of the Liberalia in Lavinium.

10. ORIGINS OF CHRISTIAN ICONOGRAPHY

André Grabar

INTRODUCTION

Continuity and renewal are fundamental forces affecting the history of art, just as they affect human society generally. On the side of continuity, linking era to era, is the inertia of tradition, a handing over of knowledge and customs from generation to generation. Although tradition is a conservative force, it is not impervious to change, as shifts in the social, psychological, and physical environments make their demands upon it. The result is a renewal or refreshment of continuity through change. Iconography—that aspect of art history which deals with the subject matter and meaning of a work of art—is largely on the side of tradition, yet it is constantly undergoing those transformations that adapt it to new conditions. This process of continuity and renewal is nowhere better exemplified than in the development of Christian iconography, wherein a new religious movement found images expressive of its ideas and rituals, and found them chiefly in existing types to which a new context and sometimes altered meanings were applied.

This selection from André Grabar's *Christian Iconography: A Study of Its Origins* vividly traces developments that join images in the art of a new faith to the non-Christian world from which it emerged. For further information on the subject, the reader is referred to the introduction accompanying the selection by Emile Mâle on medieval iconography (p. 327). The reader may wish to consult, in relation to the following selection, P. V. C. Baur, "The Paintings in the Christian

Chapel," *The Excavations at Dura-Europus Conducted by Yale University and the French Academy of Inscriptions and Letters: Preliminary Report of the Fifth Season of Work, October 1931–March 1932,* edited by M. I. Rostovtzeff (1934) and C. H. Kraeling, the Final Report of this study, Vol. VIII, Part 1: *The Synagogue,* edited by A. R. Bellinger and others (1956). A good survey of this subject is Ann Perkins, *The Art of Dura-Europus* (1973). There is also M. I. Rostovtzeff, *Dura-Europus and Its Art* (1938).

Since this selection points out relationships between Jewish and Christian iconography, the reader may also wish to consult the important study by E. R. Goodenough, *Jewish Symbols in the Graeco-Roman Period,* 12 vols. (1953–65). A good survey of Christian art in its infancy is André Grabar, *The Beginnings of Christian Art,* tr. by Stuart Gilbert and James Emmons (1967).

From its beginnings Christian imagery found expression entirely, almost uniquely, in the general language of the visual arts and with the techniques of imagery commonly practiced within the Roman Empire from the second to the fourth century. . . . An incalculable number of features, inseparable from the Greco-Roman imagery of the Empire, passed into the Christian iconographic language just as naturally and inevitably as words, expressions, and syntactical or metrical constructions of the first centuries of our era—of Aramaean, Greek, or Latin—passed into the language of Christian theologians.

Christian iconography, it is true, came into being only about two centuries after the foundation of Christianity, when the religion had been defined and propagated by means of the word. But, except for the difference in time, the use commonly made of means of expression and diffusion by the Christian authors or by the Christian image-makers of late antiquity was the same: they expressed themselves in the language—visual or verbal—that was used around them.

This is only natural. But it means, a priori, that, with regard to Christian imagery, the great majority of its distinguishing features were neither created nor invented by the makers of the first Christian images. Almost everything in their work was dictated by the models they followed; and it was actually because of this that the new, Christian images they created were understandable to their contemporaries, and therefore effectively achieved the ends intended. . . .

Except for a few themes peculiar to itself, Paleo-Christian iconography has no terms of its own. . . .

THE FIRST STEPS

The earliest Christian images appeared somewhere about the year 200. This means that during roughly a century and a half the

Christians did without any figurative representations of a religious character. It almost seems a pity, since this rejection of images— never proclaimed *expressis verbis* by the theologians—leaves us without archaeological testimony as to the spiritual state and reigning disputes of the Christian communities before the year 200. We date the oldest Christian paintings of the catacombs to about 200, and the oldest representational sculptures on Christian sarcophagi to the first third of the third century, even though we know that this chronology is rather insecure, since it does not rest on dated written documents. In fact, a number of topographical, stylistic, and iconographic features indicate that the earliest subterranean mausoleums in Rome, those of Domitilla, Calixtus (crypt of Lucina), Priscilla, etc., are close in date and generally slightly later than the year 200. The first funerary frescoes of Naples and Nola are more or less contemporary with those in Rome. The first sarcophagi with Christian subjects, those of Rome and Provence, belong to about 230; and the mural paintings of the chapel (baptistery) unearthed in the little Roman garrison town of Dura-Europos, on the middle Euphrates, on the Persian frontier, are also of about 230. It is from these monuments that we will take our first examples of Christian images. . . .

Let us consider some examples of painting in the Roman catacombs, choosing them from among the earliest. What one notices first in these funerary hypogea is that the ceilings, and sometimes the walls, are divided into compartments by a pattern of straight and curving lines. This framework of decorative lines is aesthetically predominant in the paintings of the catacombs and is very characteristic of that art which, in the midst of the cemetery, tended to gaiety.

Some of the figures, generally very small (they were to become larger only in the fourth century), are no less attractive; this funerary art goes beyond the fears and sorrows of death and puts on an air of gladness. The little figures isolated in the centers of their delicately framed fields represent orants or Good Shepherds whose decorative effect seems more important to the painters than the meaning, for they use them as motifs that they alternate within their designs. The figures are, however, allegories of the soul of the pious believer and of Christ as the shepherd. . . . But the catacomb painters have not deviated from a pleasing manner, and all of the figures show the imprint of this attitude. In the same agreeable tone they paint a Daniel in the lions' den, a resurrection of Lazarus, Noah in the ark, or the Adoration of the Magi: the protagonists are young and graceful, with elegant gestures and noble mien. And it is rare to find one of these paintings that does not reproduce a conventional scheme. . . .

This art is an easygoing one, indifferent to detail, to the individual expression of the figure, to the precise traits of a face. One finds uncompleted architecture, and surprising negligence in Biblical images of a narrative character. But these paintings of the catacombs are not meant to represent events—they only suggest them. It is enough to indicate one or two salient features, in order to designate a specific person, event, or object. . . . In other words, the paintings are schematic—that is, they are image-signs, which appeal above all to the intellect and which imply more than they actually show. . . . It is imperative that the sign be unequivocally decipherable. We know, of course, that the frequent use of any sign in a certain context permits surprising abbreviations. One may cite the famous paintings in the crypt of Lucina which show a fish that serves as a support for a small basket filled with white ring-shaped objects. The Christians who went there knew how to decipher such a painting: communion.

And they knew, too, that the image of the fisherman alluded to Christ and to the apostles, fishermen of souls. But in some cases the brevity is certainly excessive, as when, for example, a scene that represents a meal of some kind has no detail that would distinguish between the Multiplication of the Loaves, the Miracle of Cana, the Last Supper, or the repast in paradise beyond the tomb. Those who planned the mural paintings in the catacombs were probably not entirely averse to a certain ambiguity in their image-signs, since the Multiplication of the Loaves, for example, was regarded as a symbol of the agapae of paradise or a figuration of the Last Supper. . . .

. . . The image-signs that fill the Paleo–Christian catacombs and sarcophagi are of two kinds with respect to their semantic value. A limited number of iconographic signs represent the two major sacraments of the Christian Church, baptism and communion. The majority of the others serve as references to or citations of divine intervention for the salvation or preservation of certain believers: the preservation of Noah, during the Deluge; the deliverance of Isaac, when Abraham would have sacrificed his son;

the deliverance of Daniel from the lions or the three Hebrews from the furnace; or, from gospel narratives, Lazarus restored to life by Jesus or the paralytic cured, shown carrying his bed.

When these highly schematized scenes are painted in the catacombs or carved on sarcophagi, their presence next to the body of the dead has the same meaning as the prayer of the burial office called the *commendatio animae*: they enumerate the precedents for divine intervention for one of the faithful, and express the desire that God may exercise the same benignity toward the person who is now dead: God, save him, as you saved Daniel, Noah, etc. . . . Prayers of this kind, which seem to have served mostly for individual worship and even for magical invocations, probably go back to Jewish versions. It is even possible that the image-signs of some of these Biblical salvations or deliverances were first created by the Jews for their own use. Jewish examples of deliverance—Abraham, from sacrifice of his son Isaac; Noah; and Daniel—are known. But whether the Christians knew, at the beginning, image-signs of Jewish making or only Jewish prayers with the formula: Save me as you have saved Noah, etc., the great proportion of veterotestamentary salvations in the catacombs and on the sarcophagi, but especially in the catacombs, makes it very probable that there was some initial Jewish contribution. . . .

The psychological intent is slightly different when, instead of the precedents for salvation, one of the sacraments is represented —baptism or communion. . . . Here, obviously, there can be no question about Hebraic influences, nor about the formula: Save me as you have saved others. These images, found only in sepulchral art, serve to point out that the deceased was a Christian by representing the two sacraments. It is no longer only the intervention of God but participation in the sacraments of the Church which assures the salvation of the dead.

The Christian imagery of allusive signs employed, astutely enough, only a very limited number of figures, and this saved it from confusion. Nevertheless, it is surprising, if we think of pagan usage at the time, and of funerary art in the Middle Ages, to see how small a place is devoted to Christ in the earliest Christian art or to symbols that would stand for Christ. This applies to Paleo-Christian art before the edicts of tolerance (A.D. 313). At this early time, the Saviour appeared only in the guise of various allegorical images, which had remarkably few individual traits. There was chiefly the Good Shepherd carrying a lamb, which signified that the shepherd, an allegory for Jesus, saves the lamb, an allegory for the Christian soul. The image-makers made no attempt to be more specific. Like the ceilings of the catacombs, the façades of certain sarcophagi line up three Good Shepherds; and these may have, indifferently, the features of an adolescent or a bearded man of ripe age. Without going into examples that show how the image of St. Peter was influenced by these allegorical images of Christ, it can be said that as a general rule these allegorical images were relatively abstract, on principle; for in pagan Roman art . . . the figure of the shepherd carrying the lamb was a symbol of philanthropy—*humanitas.* . . .

Christ as the Good Shepherd has a counterpart in the deceased as orant. This is evident in the earliest catacombs and on the façades of Paleo-Christian sarcophagi. The pagan symbolism of the Romans had used the same orant to signify *pietas*; thus, here again, Christian art began by representing abstractions not only to designate Christ but also to characterize the ordinary Christian. . . . A second allegorical figure for Christ (or his forerunner Job), the philosopher, . . . occurs as early as the Good Shepherd. This allegory, unlike the Good Shepherd, was afterward quickly forgotten, and this is why it is more difficult for us to recognize an allegorical representation of Christ in the figure of the philosopher on the Christian sarcophagi. But modern exegesis leaves no doubt that the bearded man with the nude or seminude torso in an exomis tunic, shown seated on a stool, often reading a book, is certainly Christ as the true philosopher. . . .

In the oldest catacombs, images of salvation taken from the Old Testament predominate; there are, however, a few instances of the Christ-Thaumaturge, particularly in the representation of the resurrection of Lazarus. But the catacombs and the sarcophagus reliefs of the fourth century freely multiply instances of the miracles of Jesus. What seems to have happened is that the image-makers and their clients grew increasingly conscious of the idea of a more personal image of Jesus, this individualization developing through his thaumaturgical works. However, before multiplying the miracles of Jesus, the early image-makers often reproduced a single scene of his infancy, the Adoration of the Magi. . . . The image of the Adoration of the Magi replaces the whole

Christological cycle. It is the iconographic sign that indicates the principal argument in favor of the salvation of each believer: the fact of the Saviour's Incarnation and his work on earth.

. . . Christians at . . . the period of their first iconographic efforts perhaps used images to express theological ideas. They were close to this when they represented the two principal sacraments of the Church, baptism and communion, in their funerary art at Rome. . . . Images of the sacraments, whether purely symbolic (fish and bread) or descriptive (scenes of the baptism of an anonymous neophyte and of meals taken in common) or Biblical, with allusions to the sacraments (the baptism of Christ, the Multiplication of the Loaves, the Last Supper), contain also in germinal form an affirmation of dogma.

The same thing is true of other Biblical scenes that we have classed among the images which, besides the sacraments, define the religion of the deceased; for example, Adam and Eve with the serpent, and the Epiphany (the Adoration of the Magi). For these evidently contain another affirmation of essential Christian dogmas, original sin and redemption.

Having pointed out these incursions that the first Christian iconography made into the area of dogma, we should stress the fact that the number of images of this kind, and the number of dogmatic themes that they referred to, was extremely limited in comparison with allegorical figures and representations of salvation. This is particularly true for the catacombs. The sarcophagi of the fourth century attempt more in the way of the iconography of dogma. . . .

. . . Early Christian art in its Eastern branch furnishes one remarkable case, unique at the period, of a cycle of mural paintings in which both the subjects and their arrangement proclaim their dogmatic character. These are the mural paintings of a small baptistery of about 230, one of the group of rooms set apart for the Christian cult in a private house in the town of Dura-Europos.

Discovered shortly after World War I, the portion of the baptistery that remains was removed to the Yale University Art Gallery, where, with its frescoes, it has been reconstructed. The date of this building and its paintings cannot be disputed, and thus we know, thanks to the Dura baptistery, that from the reign of Severus the Christians had cult buildings in Roman cities, even though their religion was unlawful, and that they had at their command a relatively rich religious iconography. It is not known whether the existence of such buildings was peculiar to the eastern provinces of the Empire, but there is no reason to assume that it was. We know that places of Christian worship, along with everything in them, were totally destroyed everywhere during the persecutions of the third century and the beginning of the fourth. It is pure chance that saved some portions of the baptistery of Dura; the building was buried deliberately, about 256, by the defenders of the fortified Roman town, on the eve of a Parthian attack, to reinforce the adjacent city walls; the burial, intended to be temporary, became permanent when the Parthians took the town in 256, and the building was not rebuilt.

The iconographic program of the baptistery of Dura is not necessarily one that was peculiar to the Semitic Christians of northern Syria. But whatever its place of origin, it is distinguished from the iconographic ensembles of the catacombs by the relationship that it establishes between its subjects and their arrangement on the walls, with certain subjects manifestly taking priority over others. The hierarchy established by the location of the images is emphasized by differences in proportions and in techniques. Thus the scene of Adam and Eve, which in the catacombs may be placed anywhere among the salvations and without any topographical relationship to the Good Shepherd, is treated differently in the baptistery of Dura. The most central spot in the room, the niche of the *chevet* (behind the font), is reserved for two images, Adam and Eve and the Good Shepherd with His Flock. In other words, images representing the essential dogmas of original sin and redemption are made central by their location; and furthermore, for obvious reasons, it is the image of redemption, in the form of the Good Shepherd and His Flock, that predominates. While the image of original sin takes up only a corner of the niche, at the bottom, the idyllic image of salvation stretches over the rest of the wall.

All the walls of the baptistery were covered with paintings, and as less than half of them remain it is impossible to know the scope of the entire iconographic program. Perhaps it is chance that, in the extant part, evangelical scenes predominate (four to one), whereas in the earliest catacombs of Rome and the Campagna, it is clearly the Old Testament that is pre-eminent. But at Dura the remaining fragments testify that the images were intended to celebrate the baptismal rite: the Samaritan woman at the well and the miracle of Christ walking on the water evoke the theme of water essential to the office of baptism. We are also shown the victory of David over Goliath, the healing of the paralytic, and, naturally, the Resurrection of Christ (the theme being translated iconographically by the scene of the holy women at the tomb).

On this point a comparison is permissible with the catacomb paintings, which surely owe their numerous images of salvation to the office for the burial of the dead. The idea that inspired the Jewish and Christian prayers, as well as the Paleo-Christian liturgical offices which followed them, produced similar results in the catacombs of Rome and in the third-century baptistery at Dura. In praying for the dead or for the neophyte, the Christians constantly went back to evocations of salvation or deliverance and, consequently, to the idea of an appeal to divine power (at Dura: the victory of David over Goliath; the miracle of St. Peter, whom Jesus saves from drowning; the miracle of the paralytic cured). This is the reason for the use, both in the catacombs and in the baptistery, of images whose religious import is identical. As for the Resurrection of Christ, essential to the offices of both baptism and burial, though images of it are still wanting in the catacombs, they are frequent and important on the sarcophagi from the fourth century on. On this point also, therefore, the practices of the image-makers of about 230 at Dura and of the third and fourth centuries in the West are fairly closely allied. One might even suggest that in the place reserved for the mystery of Christian initiation, just as in the burial grounds, the images were intended to do more than recall events of the past: they were intended in some sense to perpetuate the intervention of God, as seen in these instances, for the benefit of the neophytes, just as the sacraments did.

. . . The painters who worked at Dura must have had an iconographic repertory that did not entirely correspond to that available to their Roman counterparts. And if we observe the interpretation of the gospel scenes, we have the same impression of a tradition that is certainly quite close, but distinct: the miracle of the paralytic is presented in two successive episodes (before and after the cure). These scenes, as well as the scene of St. Peter drawn from the waters of the lake, are treated in a more descriptive manner than the salvations of the catacombs. . . . Finally, two different styles are used for the images in the nave, depending upon their location: those on the upper part of the walls (the miracles) are rapidly sketched on a white ground with small figures that are drawn rather than painted; those on the socle (the Resurrection can be identified) have monumental proportions and present large figures completely painted and worked into a solemn and majestic rhythm. These differences in the translation of subjects according to their position on the walls were inherited by the Christian painters of Dura from their pagan predecessors, perhaps from the mural painters of the eastern provinces of Europe, to judge from some examples of frescoes of a similar kind (of the third and fourth centuries) at Kerch, once the Greek colony of Panticapaeum, on the Black Sea. They have the same graphic sketches on a white ground at the top of the walls and sometimes the same monumental figures on the socle.

So far as we can judge from what remains of the baptistery of Dura, it reveals primarily the fact, unsuspected before this discovery, that rooms devoted to the celebration of the Christian cult and decorated with iconographic paintings existed almost a century before the edicts of tolerance. The style of these mural paintings and the manner of adapting figurative painting to the walls prove that their authors followed usages known from earlier pagan examples in the eastern provinces of the Empire. But the painters of the baptistery of Dura followed a system in the choice and distribution of the Christian subjects that they represented, and this surely implies that there existed in the region of Dura slightly earlier Christian antecedents (perhaps coinciding in date with the earliest Christian paintings in the catacombs of Rome). The Roman catacomb paintings resemble the Dura frescoes in a general way, as much as contemporary works created within the Greco-Roman world resemble each other. But the relationship, as we have said, is not very close, since Dura's tendency is toward more descriptive figurations, while the Roman catacombs long held to image-signs that were as abbreviated as possible. But at Naples and Nola the Christian frescoes of the same period were more descriptive, closer to the type of Dura. Furthermore, the painters of Dura were entirely indifferent to the decorative effects which the Roman painters never lost from view. . . .

The iconography of the funerary cycles of the third century at

223

Rome and in Provence and that of the baptismal cycle at Dura are related, as we have said, by their common religious theme: the power of God which assures the salvation of true believers. In both cases, the Good Shepherd (taken from the Gospels) is depicted, and stories of salvation drawn from the Scriptures are also evoked, forming a counterpart to the prayers of the services. It would seem that in both cases the iconography says the same thing, or nearly the same; and, in spite of the difference in the offices which inspired the iconography, the images correspond to the respective offices. All of which means that the inspiration of the first Christian art is liturgical, and belongs exclusively to those offices which concern the individual rather than the entire community: the services of baptism and the burial of the dead.

. . . Christianity was not alone in providing itself with an iconography in the first half of the third century. If it is surprising enough to find Christianity creating a religious figurative art after being for two centuries a religion without images, it is still more astonishing to see a shift in the same direction among the Jews. Many centuries had passed, between Moses and Septimus Severus, during which the Jews rejected any figuration of a sacred character and even any image of living beings. But now, in the first half of the third century—that is, at the same time as the earliest Christian figurations—there appear, one after another, creations of Jewish religious iconography. The first Jewish experiments are similar in character to the Christian: there are the symbolic reliefs of the synagogues of Capernaum in Galilee, followed by other analogous but later examples; the coins of Apamea, in Phrygia, struck by the Jewish community of that city and showing a scene of Noah and his wife praying before the ark which they have just left; and finally, before 243, the great cycle of religious frescoes on the walls of the synagogue of Dura, this same Dura where we saw the frescoes of the Christian baptistery.

Whatever the degree of relationship between the two iconographies, Jewish and Christian, may have been, and the causes of the interdependence of their images, the historian of Christian iconography is faced with the question: Why did the two traditionally aniconic religions, which existed side by side within the Empire, equip themselves with a religious art at the same period? In spite of all that separated them, these Jewish and Christian communities, though enemies, were far from being impervious to influences from one another. There are a thousand proofs of this. We know especially to what extent Christian liturgy, in its beginnings, was inspired by the liturgy of the synagogue in its form and content (aside from its sacraments). Moreover, the synchronism of the appearance of sacred iconography among both Jews and Christians would be most easily explained if it were admitted that these occurrences had the same origin. If this were true, the coincidence of the dates of the earliest Christian images at Rome and at Dura would not depend upon some decision of a Christian authority, but would reflect a movement in favor of religious iconography which affected Jews and Christians alike. . . .

. . . The synagogue at Dura resembles the Christian catacombs and sarcophagi of Rome. . . . However, in contrast to the great majority of the Christian scriptural images of the third century, which are abbreviated and summary, those of the synagogue at Dura are treated as large framed pictures which describe in much detail the scene represented. And there is another essential difference: the iconographic ensemble of the Dura synagogue is unfolded on the walls of a room used for the daily liturgical ceremonies of the religious community—an enterprise which has no Christian counterpart until long after the Peace of the Church. It should not be forgotten that at the beginning of the third century the Jewish faith was authorized in the Empire, whereas the Christian religion was not, and would become legal only under Constantine.

Still more important is the difference in the significance of this image cycle, compared with the Christian cycles of the third century. As we have said, these were always concerned with the salvation of the individual. But at Dura it is the destiny of the chosen people which is the subject of the ensemble. The choice and arrangement of images show this clearly, and in this respect, too, the Jewish iconography of Dura is in advance of the iconographic programs of the Christian churches by more than a century. Without going into detail, let us recall a small number of scenes which leave no doubt of this. Among the symbolic subjects, the Temple with the Ark and the lion of Judah with Jacob's dual benediction on the tribes of Israel are predominant. Among the narrative scenes, there are: Moses leading the chosen people across the Red Sea; an entire cycle dedicated to the Ark and the Temple, which evokes a chapter in the history of God acting among his people; the story of Esther, the benefactress of her people (here, the triumph of her brother Mordecai); the resurrection of the dead before the eyes of Ezekiel; and finally, in the center of these scenes which have for their anonymous hero the chosen people as a whole, compositions showing David the king anointed by Samuel or David enthroned. Beyond all question the great iconographic program on the walls of the synagogue of Dura is concerned with the religious interests of the whole of Israel; and whether it envisages the past or the Messianic future, its subject is always the destiny of the chosen people.

. . . However, these paintings, so different otherwise from Christian images of the third century, are at one with them in attempting to show, through each of the images, the power of God and the felicity of the faithful (here taken collectively, as the chosen people). Here, too, as for the paintings and funerary reliefs and the frescoes of the baptistery of Dura, one can cite prayers which appeal for salvation in enumerating the past favors of God (Jewish prayers such as Psalm 118). In other words, this iconography has a religious meaning very like that which we have seen in the Christian cycles of the same period, except that the salvation in question concerns the entire people chosen by Yahweh.

We can turn this conclusion around and express it the other way; an iconographic program of this kind signified, for whoever contemplated these frescoes, that the God of the Jews is great and the people who are faithful to him have not ceased to enjoy his blessings through the centuries. God has saved his people from many different calamities, he has raised the dead and blessed Israel since the beginning of time. Here again we find the theme of comfort and assurance of protection and salvation which is the theme of the Christian images of the same period; and if one is concerned with the communal life on earth and the other with the salvation of the individual after death, still all these images, Jewish and Christian, are plainly intended to comfort the beholder, and either to strengthen him in his faith or to lead him into the Christian or the Jewish religion.

These observations may help us to see more clearly the reasons for the simultaneous birth of Christian and Jewish iconography in the Severan period. In both cases, the first imagery of which we have any record asserts salvation through reference to the experience of the past. An art which adopts this program serves to hold the faithful or to bring in new converts. Since one of them, the Jewish, seems much more evolved iconographically, and the other, the Christian, better adapted to impress different ethnic groups and at the same time more sensitive to the appeal of the growing spiritualism of the third century, it is surely the new Jewish iconography which seems to have been created first and the equally new iconography of the Christians afterward. And since each of these religions promises salvation, there is a strong possibility that the first Christian iconography came into being as a response or a counterpart to the concurrent Jewish iconography born a short while before.

Much of this is a hypothesis, which is perhaps destined never to be proved. But, whatever the exact order of their appearance may have been, the Jewish and Christian iconographies began at the same period and probably more or less simultaneously, at diverse points in the Empire, where Jewish and Christian communities lived side by side. . . .

In the early third century the Roman East and Persian Upper Mesopotamia were experiencing a time of exceptional iconographic fermentation, which extended to the art of several different faiths. On the Roman side, we have just mentioned the Christian and the Jewish activity. On the Persian side, between about 240 and 270, a new religion, that of Manes, was spreading its propaganda with the aid of images. Starting at Ctesiphon and moving from there into provinces that bordered the Empire, like the region of Dura, Manes was the first to apply this method, for which the Zoroastrians later reproached him; the method is of particular interest to us, since in late antiquity the Jewish and the Christian missions were accomplished with no recourse to images. Gathering the written testimonies, some contemporary and Manichean, others of later date and sometimes by the hands of enemies of Manes (for example, a Moslem like Firdausi in the *Shah Namah*), we can establish the following subjects for the pictures which Manes showed to his auditors: images of God; images of the Last Judgment showing the judge, the good rewarded, and the evil damned. It is amusing to think that the second occurrence of a mission which sought to impress possible converts through the spectacle of the Last Judgment concerns the Christian mission to England of St. Augustine, four centuries after Manes. We know that Manes' successors added other images to those which Manes used, notably that of the bema or throne, which symbolized his passion and his ascension, as well as the portrait of Manes, which indicated his invisible presence at the head of his church. Placed near the bema (I imagine, on the bema), the portrait of Manes was the object of veneration or of worship. To illustrate this Manichean iconography, there remain only some miniatures, much later in date and showing strong Chinese influence, made for a manuscript written in Turkistan.

As is well known, the mission of Manes, starting from Ctesiphon, spread rapidly (in spite of the persecutions which supervened) to Persia and toward Central Asia and throughout the Roman Empire, even to Africa and Italy. This iconography must have accompanied the installation of Manichean communities everywhere and provoked repercussions. The late Wilhelm Koehler thought that the great and scholarly iconography which was created at Rome at the beginning of the fifth century under the impetus afforded it by Pope Leo the Great was a response to the very effective propaganda of Manicheism in the West.

The arts of the West encountered Manicheism only around the year 400. In the eastern provinces of the Empire and in Persia, similar and equally violent contacts occurred in the second half of the third and in the fourth century. Modern scholars in the field of iconography in Iran (Nyberg, Wikander, Puech) admit that it is to the flowering of Manicheism, with its books of divine revelation, its church, and its propaganda, that we owe the codification of traditional Mazdaism and the organization of the Zoroastrian Church, which became the state church of Persia. Further studies will, I hope, show whether the official art of this state religion, as we see it under the Sassanians, also was a reply to Manichean iconography.

We have no reason to believe that the Manichean mission, with imagery as a propaganda instrument, provoked the Jews and Christians of the Levant, inviting them to abandon their traditional rejection of figurative art. Such a hypothesis would have a very good chance of satisfying everyone and of providing an answer to the question still before us, that is: Admitting that the Christians followed the Jews and that both iconographies originated at the beginning of the third century, why did they do so *then*, rather than earlier or later? The Manichean factor would explain everything, especially since it introduced imagery as propaganda. But—happily for the truth to which this hypothesis would have done a disservice—the dates make this answer impossible: the first Jewish and Christian images occur certainly soon after or even slightly before the year 200, while the earliest Manichean images cannot be earlier than about 240.

The Manichean evidence can, however, be used in two ways. Manes could have been led to invent an imagery for the religion which he founded, and to make it an instrument of propaganda, because the Jews and the Christians, his closest neighbors in the domain of religion, had, both of them, just created one. If this was so, one should expect to find a similarity in the three systems of imagery, particularly (which interests us the most) in the religious value one could see in them and in the uses for which they were designed in the religious life of the three communities. But, in the present state of our knowledge, all that can be asserted is that Manes judged imagery to be capable of expressing ideas and of assisting the propagation of the religion which he had founded and which he preached, beginning in Upper Mesopotamia around the year 240. The imagery that he created was destined for the crowds, and the role that the Last Judgment played in it would confirm this.

The second way of using the Manichean evidence is even more prudent. Without presupposing a link between the creation of Manichean iconography and the slightly older Jewish and Christian iconographies, one would limit oneself to pointing out the purely chronological closeness of the beginnings of all these iconographies. Whatever the order of their appearance, there is no question that they followed one another at short intervals. Three iconographies of three revealed religions appear almost simultaneously, and in each instance some of the earliest of its works of art now known—all directed to the average spectator— are found in the same frontier region between the Roman Empire and Persia, in the area of the upper Euphrates. At the beginning of the third century, religions, sects, confessional and philosophical-religious groups, favored by the Pax Romana, lived freely together in the cities of the Empire, and in the eastern provinces in particular. Roman law and prosperity favored this, as well as the intense agitation within these groups which organized, dissolved, clashed, and tore from each other their not very stable membership. It was also Greco-Roman custom which, in this world more or less won over to Hellenism, favored a recourse to art as a means of expressing and propagating ideas. . . . The more these religions competed with each other, the more the iconographies of which they availed themselves resembled each other, because each expressed itself in terms of the same iconographic language of Greek classicism, their differences being differences only of detail.

The excavations at Dura have provided an excellent material illustration of this state of affairs and particularly of the impressive proximity of several religious iconographies, different from each other but similar in form. One has only to look at the frescoes of the sanctuaries lined up one after another along the walls of Dura: the Christian baptistery has not only the synagogue as a neighbor but also a temple of the Palmyrene gods, a Mithraeum, and the sanctuaries of Atargatis, Artemis Azzanathcona, a Semitic Zeus, another local Artemis, and Adonis. Of different dates, but not very far apart, all the paintings in these sanctuaries existed simultaneously at the time of the destruction of Dura in 243. A few years later, there would have been a Manichean sanctuary, too. . . . The existence of imagery in the practice of some religious groups called forth the creation of other systems of imagery, all of them invented under conditions of competition and expressly for the adherents, either assured or possible, of the respective groups. The religions most firmly aniconic, Judaism and Christianity, did not resist the competition, which made its effects felt eventually in an emphasis on the distinction between the two faiths. In this respect, it is striking that at Dura the Christians gave priority to evangelical themes (whereas at Rome they emphasized motifs of the Old Testament, which they held in common with the Jews). At Dura, Christians and Jews were in competition, and their iconographic repertories underlined what was specific to each of them.

THE ASSIMILATION OF CONTEMPORARY IMAGERY

. . . One branch of late classical iconography furnished a great number of motifs for the first generations of Christian image-makers: this was pastoral imagery, whose principal motifs are the shepherd, his dog, his flock of lambs or goats or, more rarely, his herd of cows, or a rocky landscape with a few decorative trees and sometimes a few rustic buildings. In the Roman period, such visions of pastoral calm were the delight of city dwellers, and in mural decorations in particular they were frequent. Paintings of this kind are preserved in the ruins of the Palatine and also in the elegant ancient stuccoes from a Roman house found at the Farnesina and in a great many frescoes, pavement mosaics, and reliefs going back to the first centuries after Christ. Illustrations for Virgil's works afforded Roman painters opportunity to treat the subject of the shepherd with his flock. And pagan funerary art took it up also, in its turn, and used it often in its evocations of the ideal sojourn in the afterlife. . . . Christian iconography was certainly led to this subject by the Scriptures, which compare Jesus to the Good Shepherd and Christians to the flock that he guards. But the existence of the same subject in pagan sepulchral art made it inevitable that these idyllic pastoral images should frequently be transferred to Christian sarcophagi. Both the pagan and the Christian figurations are very similar, and it is sometimes difficult to distinguish one from the other. Visually, the vocabulary and the sentiment are the same. . . .

. . . It is not that the art of paganism made a contribution that came to form the Christian iconographic language; rather, all of these images show the normal effects of the employment of terms, or motifs, common to a single visual language, a language whose terms were used by all makers of images—sometimes in a new sense.

. . . But beyond this common ground shared by all the imagery of the age, Christian iconography in late antiquity shows more specific relationships to certain special areas of contemporary iconography, exactly as a particular technical language can furnish itself with special terms drawn by preference from a certain definite source (such as the military or erotic expressions in religious language). It is thus that Christian iconography drew largely on the conventional motifs of the repertory that previously had served the official art of the Roman state and on those of the secondary currents that flowed from this art. Many of the preceding observations refer to Christian images before the Peace of the Church under Constantine. The Peace of the Church opened the door to increased activity in the field of Christian iconographic creation. But it seems that this flowering did not follow immediately upon the edicts of tolerance (A.D. 313) and that the first great burst of creation in this domain took one specific direction. Since Christian ideas or forms of devotion could now be freely expressed, one might expect Christian iconography to have developed in all possible directions. But this did not occur. . . .

Except for the Christian subjects in the vault of the ambulatory of S. Costanza in Rome, one can set over against all these iconographic monuments, profane and in part frankly pagan (for instance, the images of the Calendar), only the monogram of Christ, the letters chi and rho combined, that Constantine, after a dream, had placed on the shields of his soldiers and on the Imperial standard, the labarum. But let us note, in passing, that this monogram was the equivalent of a symbolic sign, not a representational image. . . . Having broken with idolatry, Constantine could easily have wished to dissociate representational images from the religion of Christ. Moreover, the Chi-Rho monogram adopted by Constantine was particularly appropriate to serve as a symbol of the religion whose destiny he consciously connected with the country of its founder, Christ, and especially with the city of Jerusalem. It is known how much attention Constantine paid to the Palestinian memorials of the earthly career of Jesus. At this time, at Jerusalem and everywhere in the Holy Land, the Jewish tradition of the symbolic sign was a living one and had its application in the art of the synagogue. But, above all, the unique and important contribution of Constantine to Christian iconography—the adoption of the monogram of Christ for the labarum and for the Imperial army—had a practical and military character.

This example of Imperial intervention interests us in two ways. First, we have here a case of Christian iconographic creation whose origins and initiator are known, as well as its place of invention (Rome) and its date (313: the battle of the Milvian bridge). Iconographically, the invention is hardly remarkable; and we can only regret its lack of distinction. Yet here, for once, both written sources and archaeological evidence are exceptionally explicit on the religious significance of the Christian device adopted by Constantine. The device which he put into circulation was a symbol of Christ—I say intentionally Christ and not the

Christian religion—and, since its use was reserved for the army, including the Emperor, head of the Roman army—and, in particular, for the Emperor's helmet—this symbol had manifestly a prophylactic value. The army placed itself under the protection and the guidance of Him whose monogram it bore. . . . One should add that, like earlier iconography, this symbol also in no way attempted to explain or reflect the dogmas or the high principles of Christianity. The salvation assured by Christ was still there (if not represented, at least implied) as the purpose of the display of this symbol, but with this difference—which anticipates the future of Christian art—that the preservation evoked by the symbol was no longer individual but collective. In the Christian view, collectivity means normally the Church of God's people within it; the formula was introduced after the victory of the Church over the Arian emperors and never disappeared. But in 313 Constantine did not see things with the eyes of the Christian clergy: for him, the collectivity to be protected by the Christian symbol that he had adopted was in fact his army, that is to say, the Empire.

It is extremely significant that the initiative for a Christian iconography of universal import, concerned with essential ideas instead of with the personal anxieties of individuals, comes from the government of the Empire, and follows closely upon its conversion. . . .

. . . It was not before about the year 400 that the higher clergy of the Church became conscious of what they could attempt in the domain of iconography if they directed it and fashioned it so as to bring it closer to the dogma and at the same time to render it more edifying. In Constantine's time, the Christian clergy were not prepared for a task of this kind in view of the Christian art they knew—the narrow and utilitarian art which the Christians had practiced in the third century. The government of the Empire, on the other hand, had by tradition all the range of artists' workshops and the indispensable artisans at its disposal, as well as the habit of an official iconography, to interpret for general consumption the facts and moves of the reigning sovereign. It is not astonishing, then, that the great iconographic flowering had its beginnings in the Imperial palace, before control of Christian iconography gradually passed to the Church.

This first phase was important, for it gave an effective direction to Christian iconographic creation; in fact, during the fourth century and at the beginning of the fifth, at the very end of antiquity, some purely Christian subjects were interpreted with the help of iconographic formulas from palatine art. As we have seen, the earliest Christian iconography frequently employed motifs and formulas in more or less common use in all branches of contemporary art; what happened in the fourth century is similar, but distinct. All the "vocabulary" of a triumphal or Imperial iconographic language was poured into the "dictionary" which served Christian iconography, until then limited and poorly adapted to treat abstract ideas. The future of Christian iconography was profoundly modified, and what was created then has remained fundamental for Christian art. Still today, thanks to this tenacious tradition, most of us lend to the appearance of divine things the features, more or less confused, of forms that go back to the art of the late Empire. Christ sits solemnly on a throne; he makes the sign of benediction; he is surrounded by angels or saints standing on either side; he wears a crown, and crowns the saints, beginning with Mary, who has herself a throne and wears a formal costume with pearls and precious stones, etc. It is Christian art such as it was in the Empire after Constantine that has furnished us all these familiar images. . . .

The mark of Imperial iconography in Christian art is recognizable everywhere and in different ways: appropriation of themes and subjects, borrowings of iconographic details, utilization of more remote models for the creation of analogous images. It is to the theme of the supreme power of God that Imperial art contributed the most, and naturally so, since it was the key theme of all the imagery of the government of the Empire. The official monuments of the late Empire furnished the Christian image-makers with a series of tested models, and they profited from them largely. It is, naturally, through the different applications of the general theme of God's omnipotence—as revealed through Christ —that the influence of Imperial art made itself felt. . . .

11. BYZANTINE MOSAICS

Otto Demus

INTRODUCTION

When Otto Demus published his *Byzantine Mosaic Decoration: Aspects of Monumental Art in Byzantium* (1948), it was noted that this was the first work to examine Byzantine mosaics in close relationship to their architectural context and to the religious outlook they served. Demus concentrates on the Middle Byzantine system of mosaic decoration (i.e., from the end of the ninth to the end of the eleventh century), for it was then, after the termination of the Iconoclastic Controversy which had begun around the second quarter of the eighth century, that Byzantine art and thought seem to have achieved harmonic balance. However, in a section of the book not drawn upon for the following selection, Demus surveys the sources of the Middle Byzantine system, its historical genesis and aftermath, providing the reader who turns to the entire work a good overview of Byzantine art in broader perspective. Of particular interest to the reader of this selection from Demus's study is the explanation of the nature and significance of the icon, its place in the total decorative scheme of the Byzantine church, and the reciprocal relationship between image and viewer.

For further reading on Byzantine art there are D. V. Ainalov's *The Hellenistic Origins of Byzantine Art* (1961), first published in Russian in 1900; Kurt Weitzmann, *Greek Mythology in Byzantine Art* (1951); Ernst Kitzinger, "The Hellenistic Heritage in Byzantine Art," *Dumbarton Oaks Papers*, XVII (1963), 98–115; two works by John Beckwith, *The Art of Constantinople* (1961) and *Early Christian and Byzantine Art*, rev. ed. (1980); two popular, well-illustrated works, André Grabar, *Byzantine Painting* (1953), and David Talbot Rice, *The Art of Byzantium* (1959); Richard Krautheimer, *Early Christian and Byzantine Architecture* (1965); O. M. Dalton, *Byzantine Art and Archaeology*

(1965), a reprint of a work published in 1911, but still useful for its survey of a wide range of Byzantine art forms; Otto Demus, *The Mosaics of Norman Sicily* (1950); Kurt Weitzmann, *The Fresco Cycle of S. Maria di Castelseprio* (1951); L. Ouspensky and V. Lossky, *The Meaning of Icons* (1969); and David and Tamara Talbot Rice, *Icons and Their History.* C. R. Morey's *Early Christian Art,* 2nd ed. (1953), has valuable sections on the art of Ravenna; and Cyril Mango's "Materials for the Study of the Mosaics of St. Sophia at Istanbul," *Dumbarton Oaks Studies,* VIII (1962), is useful for its treatment of the existing mosaics and the publication of documents relating to them. S. K. Kostof's *The Orthodox Baptistry of Ravenna* (1965), a fine monograph on an important monument of Ravennate art, stresses the relationship it bears to the art of Byzantium. The reader may also wish to consult Otto von Simson, *Sacred Fortress: Byzantine Art and Statecraft in Ravenna* (1948) and Guiseppe Bovini, *Ravenna Mosaics* (1956), which is a good, brief account with fine color illustrations. Walter Oakshott, *The Mosaics of Rome from the Third to the Fourteenth Centuries* (1967) is a thorough and well-illustrated treatment of this body of mosaic art. In *The Dome: A Study in the History of Ideas* (1950), Earl Baldwin Smith traces the origins and meaning of this important feature of both Byzantine and Islamic architecture. More recent publications that should be mentioned are Otto Demus, *Byzantine Art and the West* (1970); Anthony Cutler, *Transfigurations: Studies in the Dynamics of Byzantine Iconography* (1975); Cyril Mango, *Byzantine Architecture* (1976); and Ernst Kitzinger, *Byzantine Art in the Making* (1977).

The selection that follows is reprinted from Otto Demus, *Byzantium Mosaic Decoration: Aspects of Monumental Art in Byzantium* (1948), with the permission of the publisher, Routledge & Kegan Paul Ltd., London.

If they are considered as isolated works, Byzantine monumental paintings lose something of their essential value. They were not created as independent pictures. Their relation to each other, to their architectural framework and to the beholder must have been a principal concern of their creators. In the case of church decoration—the field in which Byzantine art rose, perhaps, to its greatest heights—the single works are parts of an organic, hardly divisible whole which is built up according to certain fixed principles. In the classical period of middle Byzantine art—that is, from the end of the ninth to the end of the eleventh century—these principles seem to form a fairly consistent whole, in which certain features are permissible and even necessary, while others, considered out of keeping with them, are avoided. This system was not purely a formalistic one; it was the theologian's concern as much as the artist's. But its iconographical and its formal sides are but different aspects of a single underlying principle which might be defined, crudely perhaps, as the establishment of an intimate relationship between the world of the beholder and the world of the image. This relationship was certainly closer in Byzantine than it was in Western mediaeval art. In Byzantium the beholder was not kept at a distance from the image; he entered within its aura of sanctity, and the image, in turn, partook of the space in which he moved. He was not so much a "beholder" as a "participant". While it does not aim at illusion, Byzantine religious art abolishes all clear distinction between the world of reality and the world of appearance.

The complete realization of the formal and iconographic scheme which grew out of this fundamental principle is, however, an ideal or, at least, an optimal case. The nearest approach to this ideal, the classical solution, is embodied in the mosaic decorations of the great monastic churches of the eleventh century. The principles followed in these monuments of Imperial piety and munificence differ widely from those which underlie early Christian and pre-Iconoclast Byzantine, and still more Western mediaeval decorations.

The first thing which strikes the student of middle Byzantine decorative schemes is the comparatively narrow range of their subject-matter. They show a lack of invention and imagination all the more remarkable when we realize that there existed at the same time in Byzantium a powerful current of highly imaginative art which had its source in the naïve imagery of the people. But this current seems to have found expression not so much in monumental painting (save in the provincial hinterland) as in the illustration of popular religious literature, homiletic or allegorical, even of Scriptural books such as the Psalter or liturgical compositions such as the *Akathistos*. In illustrating such texts as these the miniaturists could draw on the store of antique, sub-antique and Oriental imagery which lent itself to an associative elaboration of the written word. No such freedom was either claimed by or permitted to the artists who, as the representatives of official hieratic art, adorned the mosaic-decorated churches of the Byzantine middle ages. The moralistic vein which so greatly influenced the decoration of Western cathedrals, with their didactic and ethical cycles, was likewise entirely outside the Byzantine range. The occupations and labours of the months, for instance, the personified virtues and vices, the allegories of the liberal arts, the expression of eschatological fears and hopes, all that makes up the monumental *speculum universale* of Western decorations,[1] we shall look for in vain inside the magic circle of middle Byzantine mosaic compositions. These latter are to be taken as the Byzantine Church's representation of itself rather than of Greek or Eastern Christianity; as the product of abstract theology rather than of popular piety. There is nothing original, nothing individual, about middle Byzantine decorations if they are considered from the Western point of view, that is, with regard to their contents. The individual pictures do not aim at evoking the emotions of pity, fear or hope; any such appeal would have been felt as all too human, too theatrical, and out of tune with the tenor of religious assurance which pervades the ensembles and leaves no room for spiritual and moral problems. The pictures make their appeal to the beholder not as an individual human being, a soul to be saved, as it were, but as a member of the Church, with his own assigned place in the hierarchical organization. The stress is not laid on the single picture in isolation: that is "common form" to the beholder, since it follows a strict iconographic type, like the suras of the Koran in Islamic decoration, which all the faithful know by heart. The point of interest is rather the combination of the single items of the decoration, their relationship to each other and to the whole. It is in this arrangement that we must look for the unique achievement of middle Byzantine decoration. The single pictures were more or less standardized by tradition; the ever-new problem for the theologian and for the artist was the building up of the scheme as a whole. This is true not only of the content of the pictures, but also of their visual qualities. . . . A majestic singleness of purpose runs right through the Byzantine schemes. Their authors seem to have had as their main aim to represent the central formula of Byzantine theology, the Christological dogma, together with its implications in the organization and the ritual of the Byzantine Church. There are no pictures which have not some relation to this central dogma: representations of Christ in His various aspects, of the Virgin, of Angels, Prophets, Apostles and Saints arranged in a hierarchical order which also includes temporal rulers as Christ's vicegerents on earth. Historical cycles and subjects from the Old and the New Testaments, or from apocryphal and legendary writings, are inserted in this hierarchical system not so much for their independent narrative value as for their importance as testimonies to the truth of the central dogma.

THE THEORY OF THE ICON

Every single picture, indeed, is conceived in this sense, and middle Byzantine pictorial art as a whole draws its *raison d'être* from a doctrine which developed in connection with Christological dogma. This doctrine was evolved during the Iconoclastic controversy of the eighth and ninth centuries.[2] The relation between the prototype and its image, argued Theodore of Studium and John of Damascus, is analogous to that between God the Father and Christ His Son. The Prototype, in accordance with Neoplatonic ideas, is thought of as producing its image of necessity, as a shadow is cast by a material object, in the same way as the Father produces the Son and the whole hierarchy of the invisible and the visible world. Thus the world itself becomes an uninterrupted series of "images" which includes in descending order from Christ, the image of God, the *Proorismoi* (the Neoplatonic "ideas"), man, symbolic objects and, finally, the images of the painter, all emanating of necessity from their various prototypes and through them from the Archetype, God. This process of emanation imparts to the image something of the sanctity of the archetype: the image, although differing from its prototype κατ' οὐσίαν (according to its essence), is nevertheless identical with it καθ' ὑπόστασιν (according to its meaning), and the worship accorded to the image (προσκύνησις τιμητική) is passed on through the image to its prototype.

The Christological theme, however, dominated the doctrinal basis of Byzantine theory regarding images not only *per analogiam* but also in a more direct manner. One of the arguments against pictures and statues put forward by the Iconoclasts had been that any representation of Christ was impossible, since every representation (περιγραφή) must either depict Him as a mere Man, thereby denying His Godhead and falling into the anathematized error of Nestorius; or with His two natures, divine and human, intermingled (χύσις), thus following the heresy of Eutyches. The charge of heresy, however, was returned by the Iconodules, who maintained not only that it was possible to represent Christ without falling into heresy, but that denial of this possibility was itself a heresy. Christ would not have manifested Himself in human form if that form were indeed unfit to receive and express the Divine nature. To deny that He could be represented in the form He took in His Incarnation was to doubt the Incarnation itself and with it the redeeming power of the Passion. The Incarnation could not be considered complete, or Christ's human nature genuine, if He were not capable of being depicted in the form of man. The fact that a picture of Christ can be painted furnishes a proof of the reality and completeness of His Incarnation.[3] A painted representation of Christ is as truly a symbolic reproduction of the Incarnation as the Holy Liturgy is a reproduction of the Passion. The latter presupposes the former, and the artist who conceives and creates an image conforming to certain rules is exercising a function similar to that of the priest.

Three main ideas of paramount importance for the whole subsequent history of Byzantine art emerge from this reasoning on the doctrine of images. First, the picture, if created in the "right manner", is a magical counterpart of the prototype, and has a magical identity with it; second, the representation of a holy person is worthy of veneration; thirdly, every image has its place in a continuous hierarchy.

To achieve its magical identity with the prototype, the image must possess "similarity" (ταυτότης τῆς ὁμοιώσεως). It must depict the characteristic features of a holy person or a sacred event in accordance with authentic sources. The sources were either images of supernatural origin (ἀχειροποίητα), contemporary portraits or descriptions, or, in the case of scenic representations, the Holy Scriptures. The outcome was a kind of abstract verism, governed by a sacred iconography which laid down, enforced and preserved certain rules. In the case of representations of holy persons, this verism made for portraiture in the sense of attaching distinguishing features to a general scheme of the human face and form; in that of scenic representations, for plausibility in the rendering of an action or a situation. If this was done according to the rules the "magical identity" was established, and the beholder found himself face to face with the holy persons or the sacred events themselves through the medium of the image. He was confronted with the prototypes, he conversed with the holy persons, and himself entered the holy places, Bethlehem, Jerusalem or Golgotha.

The second idea, that of the venerability of the icons, follows logically from that of magical identity.[4] The image is not a world by itself; it is related to the beholder, and its magical identity with the prototype exists only for and through him. It is this that distinguishes the icon from the idol. To establish the relation with the beholder, to be fit to receive his veneration, the picture must be visible, comprehensible, easy to recognize and to interpret. Single figures must be identified either by unmistakable attributes or by an inscription. So that they may receive their due veneration from the beholder they must face him, that is, they must be represented in frontal attitude; only so do they converse fully with the beholder (**Fig. 31**). In a scenic image, which likewise must be characterized by an inscription (to fix its ὑπόστασις or meaning, which in this case is not a person but an event), everything must be clear for the beholder to perceive. Details must not detract from the main theme; the principal figure must occupy the most conspicuous place; meaning, direction and result of the action must be plainly shown; actors and counter-actors must be separated into clear-cut groups. The compositional scheme which best answers these demands is the symmetrical arrangement, which at the same time is in itself the "sacred form" *par excellence*.

Frontality, however, cannot always be achieved in scenic representations: its rigid observance by all the participants in a scene would make the rendering of an event or an action all but impossible. No active relationship between the figures could be established

31. Virgin and Child with Saints, main apse, Torcello, Cathedral. Mosaic, Late 12th Century (Alinari-Art Reference Bureau)

under such a limitation, and the law of plausibility, the demand for authenticity, would thus be violated. This was indeed a dilemma for an art which did not know or at any rate recognize pictorial space. Apart from spatial illusionism, the most natural way of rendering an active relation between two or more figures on a flat surface would have been to represent them in strict profile. The figures would then have faced each other, their looks and gestures would have seemed to reach their aims. But this would have severed their relation with the beholder.[5] The attempt was indeed made in such scenes as the Annunciation, the Baptism, the Transfiguration, the Entry into Jerusalem, the Crucifixion, the Doubting of Thomas and the Ascension— scenes in which action counts for less than the representation of glorified existence—to depict at least the main figures in frontal attitudes. But in other scenes, where action is the main theme, this was impossible. For such cases, and for almost all the secondary figures in scenic representations, Byzantine art made use of a compromise between the attitude appropriate to action, the profile, and the attitude appropriate to sacred representation, the full face. The three-quarter view, combining both attitudes, was introduced; and this even became the dominant mode of projection in Byzantine art. Its ambivalent character allows of either interpretation; within the picture as a profile, in relation to the beholder as a frontal view.

In this system there is hardly any place for the strict profile; a figure so represented has no contact with the beholder. It is regarded as averted, and thus does not share in the veneration accorded to the image. Consequently, in the hierarchical art of icon painting, this aspect is used only for figures which represent evil forces, such as Satan at the Temptation, Judas at the Last Supper and the Betrayal. From the point of view of form, the face drawn in strict profile is for the Byzantine artist only half a face showing, as it does, only a single eye. It is drawn exactly like a face in three-quarter view in which the half-averted side has been suppressed. This method of constructing a profile gives the face a curious quality of incompleteness. Formally, something is missing—just as the otherwise indispensable relation to the beholder is left out as regards the meaning. But the evil figures must not receive the venerating gaze of the beholder, and they themselves must not seem to be looking at him: iconographic theory and popular fear of the "evil eye" go hand in hand. Outside the strictest school of Byzantine iconography the pure profile is also, though seldom, used for secondary figures. Full back views do not occur at all in the classical period of middle Byzantine art; for to the Byzantine beholder such figures would not be "present" at all.

As a result, the whole scale of turning is toned down in classical Byzantine art. It is as if the figures were somehow chained to the beholder; as if they were forced as much as is compatible with their actions into frontal positions. The generally lowered key gives, on the other hand, a heightened importance to the slightest deviations from strict frontality. The eye, expecting frontal attitudes, registers deviations in posture and glance much more strongly than it would if frontality were the exception, as it is in Western art. The projection used in scenic images is, from the formal aspect, a qualified *en face* rather than a real three-quarter view.

But even this three-quarter view, apparently, did not seem to the Byzantine artist an entirely satisfactory solution. The gestures and gaze of the figures still miss their aims: they do not meet within the picture, half-way between figures engaged in intercourse, but in an imaginary point of focus outside, that is, in front of it. There is a dead angle between the actors in a scene, an angle which is not quite bridged even by oblique glances. The action takes on a stiff frozen air. To remedy this, to give plausibility and fluency to the representation, two correctives were applied, at first separately, in two different realms of Byzantine art, but from the twelfth century onwards more or less indiscriminately. On flat surfaces, especially in miniatures, ivories, and the like, movements and gestures were intensified in order to bridge the gap between the figures as the actors in the scene. In a field of art which made use of neither pictorial space nor psychological differentiation, gestures and movements could be intensified only, so to speak, from outside, by a heightening of tempo. Intensity of action was preferably conveyed by locomotion. The figures run towards each other with outstretched hands and flying garments. . . . There is a definite tendency in this method of rendering action to point forward in time, to make the result of the action apparent together with the action itself, and so not only to connect the figures of one picture among themselves, but also to establish a relation between the successive pictures of a narrative cycle.

This remedy, however, satisfactory and fertile as it was in illustrative pictures of small size, was hardly applicable to monumental paintings on the grand scale. The violent movements would have seemed too undignified, the whirling forms too contorted and complicated. Another means was therefore needed by the Byzantine decorators to bridge the dead angle and save the threatened coherence. The solution they found was as simple as it was ingenious. They placed their pictures in niches, on curved surfaces. These curved or angular surfaces achieve what an even, flat surface could not: the figures which on a flat ground were only half-turned towards each other could not face each other fully without having to give up their dignified frontality or semi-frontality. Painted on opposite sides of curved or angular niches, they are actually facing each other in real space, and converse with each other across that physical space which is now, as it were, included in the picture. The curvature in the real space supplies what was lacking in the coherence of the image (Fig. 32).

The firm position of the painted figures in physical space makes spatial symbols in the picture itself unnecessary. No illusion is needed in pictures which enclose real space, and no setting is required to clarify the position of the figures. The whole of the

32. Annunciation, Church of the Dormition, Daphni Mosaic in squinch, *c.* 1100 (Alinari-Art Reference Bureau)

spatial receptacles (such the pictures really are) can be devoted to the figures themselves and to such motives as are required from the iconographic point of view. Restrained gestures and movements are sufficient to establish the necessary contact. A large part of the golden ground can be left empty, surrounding the figures with an aura of sanctity. This golden ground in middle Byzantine mosaics is not a symbol of unlimited space; it need not be pushed back, as it were, in order to leave sufficient space for the figures to act. They move and gesticulate across the physical space which opens up in front of the golden walls. The shape and the confines of this physical space are not dissolved, but rather stressed and clarified, by the solid coating of gold. The setting of the gold is close and firm, producing a metallic surface whose high lights and shades bring out the plastic shape of the niche.

There is no need, in this formal system, for the figures engaged in intercourse of whatever kind to approach close to each other. On the contrary, they had to be placed at some distance apart in order that they might be brought opposite each other by the curving of the ground. The resulting distances and empty spaces are filled with a tension, an air of expectancy, which makes the event depicted even more dramatic in the classical sense than violent action and gesticulation, or a closely knit grouping, could have made it. The *cæsuræ* contribute also to the legibility, to the plausibility of the image. The main figure is clearly discernible, because comparatively isolated, and presents itself unmistakably as the main object of veneration.

But the venerability of the icon did not affect its composition alone; it also influenced the choice of material. Controversy about the "matter" (ὕλη) of the images played a large part in the Icono-clastic struggle. It was but natural that, to counter the arguments of the Iconoclasts regarding the incongruity of representing the Divine in common and cheap material, the Iconodules should have chosen the most precious material for this purpose. Mosaic, with its gemlike character and its profusion of gold, must have appeared, together with enamel, as the substance most worthy of becoming the vehicle of divine ideas. It is partly for this reason that mosaic played so important a part in the evolution of post-Iconoclastic painting, and indeed actually dominated it. It allowed of pure and radiant colours whose substance had gone through the purifying element of fire and which seemed most apt to represent the unearthly splendour of the divine prototypes.

ARCHITECTURAL AND TECHNICAL CONDITIONS

These prototypes themselves, to the Byzantine mind, stand to each other in a hierarchic relation, and so their images must express this relationship. They must occupy their due place in a hierarchy of values in which the image of the All-Ruler occupies the central and most elevated position. Clearly, a hierarchical system of images based on the principles which governed the Byzantine Church's own organization could be fully expressed only through an architectural framework that furnished a hierarchy of receptacles within which the pictures could be arranged. A purely narrative sequence of pictures, in the Western sense, or a didactic scheme could be displayed on almost any surface in almost any arrangement. Whether it was used to decorate portals, façades, interior walls or stained-glass windows did not greatly matter. But a Byzantine programme always needed a special framework, namely that in which it had grown up, and which it was developed to suit. This framework was the classical type of middle Byzantine ecclesiastical architecture, the cross-in-square church with a central cupola.[6]

The shaping of this architectural type was a lengthy process, and the final solution was arrived at by several concurring paths. The essential idea seems to have been conceived as early as the sixth century. Architects with widely different traditional backgrounds approached the problem from different sides. . . . There is evidence of a conscious search for a final solution in accord with the liturgical needs and the æsthetic ideals of the time. Local differentiations gave way before the quest for this ideal type; and, when finally elaborated, it was never abandoned, and remained the basis of the whole of the subsequent development. Even changes of scale did not greatly affect the dominant idea. The final type, fully evolved by the end of the ninth century, was something strangely perfect, something which, from the liturgical and from the formal points of view, could hardly be improved upon.[7] This high perfection might have resulted in sterility, had not the central architectural idea been flexible enough to leave room for variation.

The plan was, in short, that of a cruciform space formed by the vaulted superstructure of transepts arranged crosswise and crowned in the centre by a higher cupola. The angles between the arms of the cross are filled in with lower vaulted units, producing a full square in the ground-plan but preserving the cross-shaped space in the superstructure. Three apses are joined to the square on the east and an entrance hall (sometimes two) stands before it on the west. . . . The cupola always dominates the impression. Even the modern beholder directs to it his first glance. From the cupola his eye gradually descends to the horizontal views.

This process of successive apperception from the cupola downwards is in complete accord with the æsthetic character of Byzantine architecture: a Byzantine building does not embody the structural energies of growth, as Gothic architecture does, or those of massive weight, as so often in Romanesque buildings, or yet the idea of perfect equilibrium of forces, like the Greek temple. Byzantine architecture is essentially a "hanging" architecture; its vaults depend from above without any weight of their own. The columns are conceived æsthetically, not as supporting elements, but as descending tentacles or hanging roots. They lack all that would make them appear to support an appropriate weight: they have no entasis, no crenellations, no fluting, no socles; neither does the shape of the capitals suggest the function of support. This impression is not confined to the modern beholder: it is quite clearly formulated in contemporary Byzantine *ekphraseis*.[8] The architectonic conception of a building developing downwards is in complete accord with the hierarchical way of thought manifested in every sphere of Byzantine life, from the political to the religious, as it is to be met with in the hierarchic conception of the series of images descending from the supreme archetype.

The cross-in-square system of vaults is indeed the ideal receptacle for a hierarchical system of icons. Each single icon receives its fitting place according to its degree of sanctity or importance. . . .

THE ICON IN SPACE

. . . To describe these mosaics, encased in cupolas, apsides, squinches, pendentives, vaults and niches, as flat, or two-dimensional, would be inappropriate. True, there is no space behind the "picture-plane" of these mosaics. But there is space, the physical space enclosed by the niche, in front; and this space is included in the picture. The image is not separated from the beholder by the "imaginary glass pane" of the picture plane behind which an illusionistic picture begins: it opens into the real space in front, where the beholder lives and moves. His space and the space in which the holy persons exist and act are identical, just as the icon itself is magically identical with the holy person or the sacred event. The Byzantine church itself is the "picture-space" of the icons. It is the ideal iconostasis; it is itself, as a whole, an icon giving reality to the conception of the divine world order. Only in this medium which is common to the holy persons and to the beholder can the latter feel that he is himself witnessing the holy events and conversing with the holy persons. He is not cut off from them; he is bodily enclosed in the grand icon of the church; he is surrounded by the congregation of the saints and takes part in the events he sees. . . .

If, however, the icons were to exist in, and to share, a space which is normally the domain of the beholder, it was more than ever necessary to place them in individual receptacles—in spatial units which are, as it were, excrescences of the general space. Moreover, since the images are not links in a continuous chain of narrative, they must not flow into one another: they must be clearly separated and each must occupy its own place in the same manner as the events and persons they represent occupy distinct places in the hierarchical system. The formal means to this end is the separate framing of each single receptacle. The single units are set off either by their characteristic shapes as spatial units, especially in the upper parts of the building, or, in the lower parts, by being embedded separately in the quiet colour foil of the marble linings. This marble entablature with its grey, brown, reddish or green hues covers practically all the vertical surfaces of the walls in middle Byzantine mosaic churches, leaving for the mosaics only niches in which they are placed like jewels in a quiet setting. Nothing is more alien to the monumental mosaic decorations of these churches in the central area than the almost indiscriminate covering of the walls with mosaic pictures which is found in the twelfth century in Sicily, Venice and other colonial outposts of Byzantine art. In Byzantium itself the mosaics never lose the quality of precious stones in an ample setting. The icons never cease to be individually framed spatial units; their connection with one another is established not by crowded contiguity on the surface but by an intricate system of relations in space.

THE IDEAL ICONOGRAPHIC SCHEME OF THE CROSS-IN-SQUARE CHURCH

These relations were governed, in the classical period of the tenth and eleventh centuries, by formal and theological principles. . . . We can distinguish three systems of interpretation which are found interlinked in every Byzantine scheme of decoration of the leading, centralized type.

The Byzantine church is, first, an image of the Kosmos, symbolizing heaven, paradise (or the Holy Land) and the terrestrial world in an ordered hierarchy, descending from the sphere of the cupolas, which represent heaven, to the earthly zone of the lower parts. The higher a picture is placed in the architectural framework, the more sacred it is held to be. The second interpretation is more specifically topographical. The building is conceived as the image of (and so as magically identical with) the places sanctified by Christ's earthly life. This affords the possibility of very detailed topographical hermeneutics, by means of which every part of the church is identified with some place in the Holy Land.[9] The faithful who gaze at the cycle of images can make a symbolic pilgrimage to the Holy Land by simply contemplating the images in their local church. This, perhaps, is the reason why actual pilgrimages to Palestine played so unimportant a part in Byzantine religious life, and why there was so little response to the idea of the Crusades anywhere in the Byzantine empire. It may also account for the fact that we do not find in Byzantium reproductions of individual Palestinian shrines, those reproductions of the Holy Sepulchre, for instance, which played so important a part in Western architecture and devotional life. . . .

The third kind of symbolical interpretation was based on the Calendar of the Christian year.[10] From this point of view, the church is an "image" of the festival cycle as laid down in the liturgy, and the icons are arranged in accordance with the liturgical sequence of the ecclesiastical festivals. Even the portraits of the saints follow to some extent their grouping in the Calendar, and the arrangement of larger narrative cycles is frequently guided by the order of the Pericopes, especially as regards the scenes connected with Easter. Thus the images are arranged in a magic cycle. The relationship between the individual scenes has regard not to the "historical" time of the simple narrative but to the "symbolic" time of the liturgical cycle. This cycle is a closed one, repeating itself every year, during which, at the time of the corresponding festival, each image in turn comes to the front for the purpose of veneration, to step back again into its place for the rest of the year when its magic moment has passed. The profound contrast between this conception of time and that implicit in Western decorative schemes is obvious: in the latter a series of scenes illustrates an historical sequence of events, with its beginning and end clearly marked and with a definite direction parallel with the unrolling of the story. In the strict arrangement of Byzantine decorations the time element is symbolical; it is inter-linked with the topographical symbolism of the building, and therefore closely connected with the spatial element. The flow of time is converted into an ever-recurring circle moving round a static centre. These two conceptions of time correspond to the two dominant architectural types: the Western to the basilican type,[11] with its rhythmic movement from entrance to apse, from beginning to end; the Byzantine to the domed centralized building which has no strongly emphasized direction, and in which the movement has no aim, being simply a circular motion round the centre.

All three Byzantine systems of interpretation, the hierarchical cosmic, the topographical and the liturgico-chronological, are so closely accommodated to the dominant architectural type of the cross-in-square church that they must, in fact, have been elaborated for such a building. Only within this framework could a scheme devised after these principles be satisfactorily placed. Every attempt, therefore, to adapt such a programme to other types of architecture must have met with great difficulties, and must consequently have resulted in a weakening of the original concepts, as can actually be seen in the provinces.

THE THREE ZONES

The most obvious articulation to be observed in a middle Byzantine mosaic decoration is that which corresponds to the tripartition into heaven, paradise or Holy Land, and terrestrial world. Three zones[12] can be clearly distinguished: first, the cupolas and high vaults, including the conch of the apse; second, the squinches, pendentives and upper parts of the vaults; and thirdly, the lower or secondary vaults and the lower parts of the walls. These three zones are, in most cases, separated by plastic *cosmetes*—narrow bands of carved stone or stucco which run round the whole edifice.

The uppermost zone, the celestial sphere of the microcosm of the church, contains only representations of the holiest persons (Christ, the Virgin, Angels) and of scenes which are imagined as taking place in heaven or in which heaven is either the source or the aim of the action depicted. Byzantine art from the ninth to the end of the eleventh century made use of only three schemes of cupola decoration: the Ascension, the Descent of the Holy Ghost, and the Glory of the *Pantocrator*, the All-Ruler. This peculiarity distinguishes the strict scheme of the Middle Ages from early Byzantine as well as from Italo-Byzantine decoration. In the five cupolas of the Justinianic church of the Apostles in Constantinople,[13] for instance, there had been five different representations, each forming part of the narrative cycle which filled the whole church. After the Iconoclastic controversy, however, and in connection with the subsequent emergence of the symbolic interpretation of the church building, the cupolas were strictly set apart from the narrative cycle. From the ninth century onwards they contained only representations in which the narrative character had been displaced entirely by the dogmatic content. The three themes above-mentioned dominated Byzantine cupola decorations after the Iconoclastic controversy to such an extent that others were scarcely thinkable; even the small cupolas of entrance halls were decorated with them. . . .

The second of the three zones of the Byzantine church is dedicated to the Life of Christ, to the pictures of the festival cycle. It

251

harbours the monumental calendar of the Christological festivals and is the magical counterpart of the Holy Land. The cycle of feasts was gradually developed by selection from an ample narrative series of New Testament scenes. It is very probable that the decorations which immediately followed the re-establishment of icon worship did not include any festival icons in the naos. But the austere ideal of the early post-Iconoclastic period was relaxed in the course of the tenth and eleventh centuries. . . . The growth of the festival cycle can also be followed in contemporary ecclesiastical literature: there the number rises from seven to ten, twelve, sixteen and even eighteen pictures, the full development being reached from the twelfth century onwards.[14] The classical cycle of the eleventh century comprised, at least in theory, twelve feasts, the *Dodekaeorta:* Annunciation, Nativity, Presentation in the Temple, Baptism, Transfiguration, Raising of Lazarus, Entry into Jerusalem, Crucifixion, Anastasis (Descent into Hades), Ascension, Pentecost and Koimesis (Death of the Virgin). To this series were frequently added, in pictorial cycles, a few images which elaborated the story of Christ's Passion, namely the Last Supper, the Washing of the Apostles' Feet, the Betrayal of Judas, the Descent from the Cross and the Appearance to Thomas. Other developments were attached to the story of Christ's infancy (the story of His parents, the Adoration of the Magi, the Flight into Egypt, etc.) and to that of His teaching (the cycle of the miracles and parables). . . .

The third and lowest zone of centralized decorations does not contain any scenic images: single figures alone make up the "Choir of Apostles and Martyrs, Prophets and Patriarchs who fill the naos with their holy icons".[15] These figures are distributed in accordance with two iconographical principles which intersect each other: one that of rank and function, the other that of calendrical sequence. It is the former of these which predominates. Sainted priests and patriarchs are placed in or near the main apse, in a hierarchical order which descends from the Patriarchs of the Old Testament, by way of the Prophets and the Doctors of the first centuries of Christianity, down to the humble priests of the Eastern Church. The Martyrs fill the naos, arranged in several groups: the holy Moneyless Healers (the Anargyroi) next to the sanctuaries, the sacred Warriors on the pillars and the arches of the central cupola, and the rest mostly in the transept, distributed in groups according to the dates of their festivals in the liturgical calendar. The third category comprises the holy Monks, who are placed in the western part of the church, guarding the entrance of the narthex and the naos. Holy women and canonized emperors are depicted in the narthex. But this order is by no means rigid; it allows of variation according to the dedication of the particular church and to its architectonic type. . . . An eternal and holy presence is manifest in the paintings of the highest zone, to the suppression of all narrative and transient elements. There, the timeless dogma is offered to the contemplation of the beholder . . . a sacred world, beyond time and causality, admitting the beholder not only to the vision but to the magical presence of the Holy. In the middle zone the timeless and the historical elements are combined in accordance with the peculiar character of the festival icon, which simultaneously depicts an historical event and marks a station in the ever-revolving cycle of the holy year. . . . Isolated as holy icons and, at the same time, related to their neighbours as parts of the evangelical cycle, the paintings in the second zone are half picture and half spatial reality, half actual scene and half timeless representation. But in the lowest stratum of the church, in the third zone, are found neither narrative scenes nor dogmatic representations. The guiding thought in this part of the decoration—the communion of All Saints in the Church—is realized only in the sum of all the single figures. They are parts of a vast image whose frame is provided by the building of the church as a whole.

NOTES

[1] J. Sauer, *Die Symbolik des Kirchengebäudes und seiner Ausstattung in der Auffassung des Mittelalters*, Freiburg i. B., 1902.

[2] For a summary of this doctrinal controversy, see K. Schwarzlose, *Der Bilderstreit, ein Kampf der griechischen Kirche um ihre Eigenart und Freiheit*, Gotha, 1890; L. Bréhier, *La querelle des images*, Paris, 1904; N. Melioransky, "Filosofskaya storona ikonoborchestva", *Voprosy Filosofii*, etc. II, 1907, p. 149 ff; L. Duchesne, "L'iconographie byzantine dans un document grec du IXe s.", *Roma e Oriente*, vol. V, 1912–1913, pp. 222 ff., 273 ff., 349 ff.; A. v. Harnack, *Dogmengeschichte*, Tübingen, 1922, p. 275 ff.; G. A. Ostrogorski, "La doctrine des saintes icones et le dogme christologique" (Russian), *Seminarium Kondakovianum*, I, Prague, 1927, p. 35 ff.; *Idem*, "Die erkenntnistheoretischen Grundlagen des byzantinischen Bilderstreites" (Russian with German résumé), *Ibid.*, II, Prague, 1928, p. 48 ff.; *Idem, Studien zur Geschichte des byzantinischen Bilderstreites*, Breslau, 1929; *Idem*, "Rom und Byzanz in Kampfe um die Bilderverehrung" (Russian with German résumé), *Sem. Kondak.*, VI, Prague, 1933, pp. 73 ff.; E. J. Martin, *History of the*

Iconoclastic Controversy, London, 1930; G. Ladner, "Der Bilderstreit und die Kunstlehren der byzantinischen und abendländischen Theologie", *Zeitschrift für Kirchengeschichte*, III, F., I, vol. 50, 1931, p. 1 ff.; V. Grumel, "Récherches récentes sur l'iconoclasme", *Échos d'Orient*, XXIX, 1930, p. 99 ff.—What follows here is a very simplified summary of the main Christological arguments used in the controversy.

[3] This thought can be traced back to the writings of Germanos, at the end of the seventh century. See Ostrogorski, *La doctrine*, etc., *loc. cit.*, p. 36.

[4] Both ideas, that of magical identity and that of venerability, had become firmly established in one branch of popular religious art in the fifth and sixth centuries, long before the beginning of the Iconoclastic controversy. See K. Holl, "Der Anteil der Styliten am Aufkommen der Bilderverehrung", *Philothesia, P. Kleinert zu seinem 70. Geburtstag*, Berlin, 1907, p. 54 ff. The popular belief was that the spiritual force of the venerated Stylites and their power to aid were immanent in their representations. This seems to have been the origin of the belief in the miracle-working power of images.

[5] The problem is similar to that of representing an action on the stage. But there the solution is rendered easier by the fact that the figures are in motion.

[6] The more recent bibliography on this subject will be found in the article "Kreuzkuppelkirche", by W. Zaloziecky, in Wasmuth's *Lexikon der Baukunst*, and in various papers by N. Brunov (*Byz. Zeitschrift*, 27, 1927, p. 63 ff.; 29, 1929–1930, p. 248; 30, 1930, p. 554 ff., etc.).

[7] Few things, indeed, have kept their form so perfectly and unchangingly as the Byzantine cross-in-square church. An analogy from a different field may illustrate this stationary perfection and completion: the violin, whose shape, once perfected, could not be improved upon. Its form is not affected by its scale, whether simple violin or double-bass, just as the form of the Byzantine church remains the same throughout its whole range, from tiny chapel to vast cathedral.

[8] See, for example, the 18th Homily of Gregory of Nazianzus, and Procopius's description of the Haghia Sophia in Constantinople.

[9] See Simeon of Thessalonike, in Migne, *Patrologia Graeca*, tom. 155, col. 338 ff.

[10] The sources of this interpretation are quoted in G. Millet, *Récherches, sur l'iconographie de l'Évangile*, Paris, 1916, p. 25 ff.

[11] For the Western conception, see the writings of A. Schmarsow, especially his "Kompositionsgesetze in den Reichenauer Wandgemälden", *Rep. für Kunstwiss.*, vol. XXXVII, 1904, p. 261 ff., and *Kompositionsgesetze in der Kunst des Mittelalters*, Leipzig, 1915.

[12] This division of the architectural decoration into horizontal zones is in strict accordance with Byzantine and early Christian, as opposed to antique, cosmography. See D. Ainalov, *Ellenisticheskiya osnovy vizantiyskago iskusstva*, St. Petersburg, 1900; and *Rep. für Kunstwiss.*, XXVI, 1903, p. 36.

[13] A. Heisenberg, *Grabeskirche und Apostelkirche*, II, Leipzig, 1908. The Pantocrator programme of the central cupola was the result of later changes. See N. Malicky, "Remarques sur la date des mosaiques de l'église des Stes Apôtres à Constantinople", *Byzantion*, III, 1926, p. 123 ff. with bibliography.

[14] G. Millet, *Récherches, op. cit.*, p. 16 ff., with texts.

[15] After Photius's description of the Nea of Basil I. See O. Wulff, *Altchristliche und byzantinische Kunst*, II, Potsdam, 1924, p. 551.

12. THE ORIGINS OF THE BAY SYSTEM

Walter Horn

INTRODUCTION

This selection is based on a paper presented by Walter Horn at the 1958 meeting of the Society of Architectural Historians in Washington. Here Professor Horn picks up Strzygowski's intuition that the origins of the bay system in medieval architecture lay in the example of wood construction and supports his thesis with convincing evidence reaching as far back as the Iron Age. This article is a fine example of the disciplined weaving together of documentary and archaeological data in support of a reexamined idea. Yet, as the reader will note in the last two paragraphs, the writer is careful to point out some alternate possibilities, however strongly he may reason against their validity. Students of medieval art and culture should not overlook an unusual publication to which the author of this selection devoted years of intense scholarship: Walter W. Horn and Ernest Born, *The Plan of St. Gall: A Study of the Architecture and Economy of, and Life in a Paradigmatic Carolingian Monastery* (1979), a work impressive both as to the range of its content and the quality of its presentation.

For further reading consult Raymond Richards, *Old Cheshire Churches* (1947); Fred H. Crossley, *Timber Building in England* (1953); J. T. Smith, "Medieval Aisled Halls and Their Derivations," *Archaeological Journal*, CXII (1956); Walter Horn, "Two Timbered Mediaeval Churches of Cheshire: St. James and St. Paul at Marton and St. Oswald at Lower Peover," *The Art Bulletin*, XLIV (1962); Walter Horn, "Great Tithe Barn of Chosley, Berkshire," *Journal of the Society of Architectural Historians*, XXII (1963); Walter Horn and F. W. B. Charles, "Cruck-built Barn of Middle Littleton in Worcestershire, England," *Journal of the Society of Architectural Historians*, XXV (1966); and Walter Horn and Ernest Born, *The Aisled Mediaeval Timber Hall* (1966). For remarks on the significance of this timber "vernacular" architecture, the reader might wish to consult Kenneth J. Conant, *Carolingian and Romanesque Architecture, 800 to 1200*, rev. ed. (1973), 20–42, and footnote 6 for chapter I.

The selection that follows is reprinted from Walter Horn, "On the Origins of the Mediaeval Bay System," *Journal of the Society of Architectural Historians*, XVII (1958), by permission of the author.

Joseph Strzygowski advanced the theory in 1924 that the medieval bay system had its origins in northern wood construction.[1] This idea was neither accepted nor rejected by architectural historians; it simply failed to be acknowledged, as were so many of the ideas promiscuously conceived and propagated by this ingenious but undisciplined mind. Strzygowski's theory was based upon the assumption that a tradition of bay-divided wooden houses existed in the formative phases of the Romanesque, but at that date he could not point his finger to any bay-divided house that antedated the emergence of the principle of bay division in monumental medieval masonry architecture, because the first such house on the Continent had yet to be excavated. Doubtless there are striking similarities between the intensely skeletal churches of the Norman and Frankish Romanesque and certain Scandinavian stave churches, but none of the churches which Strzygowski cited in support of his theory were of a date sufficiently early to support the hypothesis that they might have been a contributing force in the formation of the Romanesque style, nor could Strzygowski demonstrate that any such churches existed in the Continental cradle areas of the Romanesque—not to speak of the fact that the stave churches to which he referred were centralized structures, and therefore not truly analogous in type to the basilican bay-divided churches of the Continent.[2]

There is no doubt, however, that timber churches were a common phenomenon even on the medieval Continent. Not only is there an abundance of documentary references to such structures,[3] but an appreciable number of them survive. Most of these churches have not been properly recorded, however, as nobody has ever gathered this material together. Thus, after some hundred years of intensive architectural research in the course of which we have measured the dimensions of even the smallest stone incorporated into the masonry of every fourth-rate medieval country church, the question of the design and constructional layout of a typical Continental medieval timber church has been almost entirely neglected.

33. Honfleur, Normandy, France. St. Catherine's Original Site, 15th Century (Author's reconstruction based on drawings by M. Jullien)

Of the extant medieval timber churches of Continental Europe, probably the most revealing, historically, is the church of St. Catherine at Honfleur, in Normandy, France.[4] In its present state this church consists of two parallel naves of equal height and two smaller aisles. But in 1946, Monsieur Jullien, an architect of the Monuments Historiques, made the interesting discovery that in its original form the church was a three-aisled structure.[5] M. Jullien observed that the octagonal wooden posts which separate the two naves in the center still today show on their southern faces the complete original set of the mortise holes which formed the springing of the crossbeams and bracing struts of the original aisle. I had occasion in the summer of 1957 to check these observations and found them to be correct in all detail. On the basis of M. Jullien's carefully measured sections and elevations I have prepared the perspective which is shown in Fig. 33. In this, its original form, St. Catherine's stems most likely from the time of the general economic resurgence which followed the eviction of the English from this city in 1450. Some time after completion but still within the course of the fifteenth century, as can be gathered from the profiles of the moldings of the new work (the new work being more complex than the original work but still late Gothic in style), the southern aisle was taken down and replaced by a second nave, an alteration to which the church owes its present shape.

In France, St. Catherine of Honfleur is the oldest surviving building of its kind, but in England the type can be traced back to the fourteenth century, in Germany and Holland to the ninth, in Belgium to the sixth or fifth.

A late medieval church from the hamlet of Paasloo, Province Overyssel, Holland, was brought to my attention by Messrs. Jan Jans and E. Jans in Almelo.[6] The walls of the church are built in brick and date from the beginning of the sixteenth century. But the roof-supporting inner trusses of timber appear to be of an earlier date. The original timbers survived until 1954, when, suffering from a heavy infestation of death-watch beetles, they were completely replaced by modern timbers. The new work, however, is a true copy of the original work. A fifteenth-century church of practically identical construction, again unpublished, stands in the village of Nyeven, Province Drente, Holland. The record, however, becomes truly rich as we move across the Channel into England. In the county of Cheshire alone there are five aisled and bay-divided timber churches, and two of those reach back to the fourteenth century: the church of St. James and St. Paul in Marton and the church of St. Werburgh at Warburton. Two further churches of the same design, but dating from the fifteenth century, are to be seen in Lower Peover and in Holmes Chapel, Cheshire; to these can be added a fifteenth-century church in Mattingly, Hampshire, and a fifteenth-century church in Ribbesford, Worcestershire. The Cheshire churches are reproduced and discussed in Raymond Richards comprehensive volume on *Old Cheshire Churches.*[7] Numerous other churches of a similar construction type outside of Cheshire may have escaped my attention or may only be brought to light in the future, as the two great archaeological surveys of the *Victoria History of the Counties of England* and the *Royal Commission on Historical Monuments* draw toward their completion.

As in the Continental timber churches previously discussed, so in the above-named English churches the space is subdivided into a nave and two aisles by two rows of free-standing, inner uprights, which are framed together crosswise by means of tie beams and lengthwise by means of plates and purlins.

What vast distribution this construction type must have had in the Middle Ages may be gathered from a medieval timber church from Stóry-Nupur in Arnessysla, Iceland, torn down in 1875, but accurately recorded in the form of a scale model now on display in the National Museum at Copenhagen.[8] The exact date of this church unfortunately is not known, but a Norwegian Book of Homilies from the beginning of the twelfth century contains a complete description of a church which suggests that the Stóry-Nupur type of church was a common concern in the north Germanic territories of Scandinavia and the Atlantic islands.[9]

Until very recently no evidence existed that bay-divided timber churches of this type existed on the Continent during the formative phases of the Romanesque, but in 1947 P. Glazema unearthed in the villages of Buggenum and Grubbenvorst, Holland,[10] two Carolingian churches of this type. In 1948–50 their number was increased to four when the Landesmuseum in Bonn excavated in the villages of Breberen and Doveren, not far from the Dutch border, two more Carolingian churches of the same construction type on sites which had been bombed in World War II.[11] In Fig. 34 I am reproducing one of these as reconstructed by P. J. Tholen.[12] The discovery of these structures, which could be attributed to the eighth and ninth centuries by pottery shards and other accessories, brought added credence to the results of an excavation which had been made in the 'twenties in connection with the old episcopal church of Maastricht, Belgium (5th–6th centuries). In the interior of this church the excavators had discovered the remains of two ranges of flat stones, which could only have served as base blocks for two rows of wooden uprights, dividing the church lengthwise into three aisles of equal width. Albert Verbeek, who discussed this church at the Sixth Congress of German Art Historians, held at Essen in 1956,[13] pointed at the similarity of the general layout of Maastricht Cathedral to that of the pre-Carolingian churches of Worms and of St. Albans in Mainz, the roofs of which he also presumes to have been supported by two rows of wooden posts.

Taken by themselves these Carolingian and early medieval timber churches are inconsequential. Their significance lies in the fact that they tell us that the constructional layout of a Carolingian timber church was substantially that of the surviving medieval timber churches just discussed, and—if it is the constructional system of a church like St. Catherine's at Honfleur (Fig. 33) or St. James' and St. Paul's in Marton that we have to think of when we read in Thietmar's chronicle (to name just one of countless references to

34. Breberen (Near Aachen), Germany; Carolingian Timber Church (Reconstruction P. J. Tholen)

medieval timber churches that could be cited in this connection) that Bishop Unro of Verden erected in the town of Verden toward the middle of the tenth century a church in timber, and made this church "superior in scale and quality to all other churches" (*et magnitudine et qualitate caeteras precellentem*)[14]—then Strzygowski's theory of the origin of the medieval bay system in northern wood construction would indeed require reexamination.

True enough, the evidence so far available is meager, and I would hesitate to base my views about the validity of Strzygowski's theory of the origin of the medieval bay system upon the fragile pedigree of medieval timber churches above discussed. The inquiry, fortunately, is greatly simplified by the fact that the construction type with which we are here concerned—and here Strzygowski's guess, it has to be admitted, turned out to be correct—was by no means confined to the building of churches. Church construction was only one phase, and centuries before anybody had thought of applying these construction principles to churches they had been a standard procedure in house and barn construction. In Fig. 35 I show the plan and reconstruction of a prehistoric cattle barn which the Dutch anthropologist Albert Egges van Giffen excavated in 1934–36 in a hamlet called Ezinge, Province Groningen, Holland.[15] It dates from the third century B.C. The details of the roof are not assured but the roof-supporting posts and the braided wattle walls which en-

261

35. Ezinge (Prov. Groningen), Holland; Cattle Barn, 3rd Century (Author's reconstruction, drawn by Walter Schwarz)

closed the house and subdivided the aisles into stalls for cattle were preserved to hip and even to shoulder height, and the braided fodder mats in front of the posts were found in such good condition that they could be stepped upon without sustaining damage. The dampness of the ground in conjunction with the acidity of the wood retained the timbers in an unusually fine state of preservation.

This same site revealed on a lower level an entire settlement of houses of the same design, the varying furnishings of which suggest that we are here confronted with an all-purpose house. Depending on the respective presence or absence of fireplaces or fodder mats, or their combined appearance in one and the same structure, this construction type—without undergoing even the slightest structural alteration—could be used as shelter for humans alone, as shelter for humans and animals combined, as shelter for animals alone, or as shelter for the storage of produce and harvest. The arrangement of the posts leaves no doubt, in my opinion, that these were bay-divided structures, for although none of the actual timbers of the upper parts of these houses are preserved, the posts could not have successfully braced the roof against the lateral thrust of wind and storm had they not been framed together at the top by means of crossbeams and long-beams. Bay division lay in the nature of the materials employed. The reconstruction reproduced in Fig. 35 [is]

262

my own. They do not pretend to be trustworthy in all details and, in fact, having been made some six or seven years ago do not altogether correspond to my present views. Nor do I wish to advance the claim through them that each and every three-aisled Iron Age house that has been excavated so far was bay-divided. But I feel certain that in the Iron Age, bay division was a going concern. In some of the smaller houses, if the uprights were anchored deep enough in the ground the roof might well have been capable of taking the normal thrust of the prevailing winds without having the posts connected crosswise by means of tie beams; but in the larger houses, and especially in such cases where the posts rested on base blocks rather than being sunk into the ground, the uprights must have been connected crosswise as well as lengthwise if the house were to stay up at all.[16]

The Ezinge houses [not reproduced here, but as Figs. 12 and 13 in original article] date from the fourth century B.C. When they were discovered in 1934 they were a relatively rare phenomenon. But between 1934 and 1958 over 200 houses of this construction type have been excavated in Holland, in northern Germany, in Scandinavia, and in England, and today we are able to trace their development, century by century, into the Middle Ages and through the Middle Ages to their modern survival forms.[17] The structural layout of this house-type is well exemplified in a model of a house which Werner Haarnagel excavated in 1949–50 in Wilhelmshaven-Hessens where it could be identified in settlement-horizons of the seventh, eighth, ninth, and tenth centuries;[18] and in excavations conducted in 1951–53 in Emden, the same type was discovered in settlement-horizons of the eleventh, twelfth, and thirteenth centuries.[19] For Holland a closely related house-type had been ascertained as early as 1939 for the period of 700–1000 through an excavation undertaken by van Giffen in the vicinity of the parish of Leens, Province Groningen (Fig. 36).[20]

Medieval architectural history has responded to these discoveries with a peculiar apathy, and our failure to evaluate this material in its proper context has prevented us from tackling one of the major unsolved problems of medieval architectural history—which is, in turn, of greatest importance to the excavators—that of the reconstruction of the guest and service buildings of the Plan of St. Gall.

Apart from the monastic buildings proper, i.e., the church, the claustrum, the noviciate and the infirmary, this plan[21] comprises

36. Leens (Prov. Groningen), Holland; Medieval Timber House, *c.* 700–1000 (Author's reconstruction, drawn by Walter Schwarz)

a host of subsidiary structures, which are as common to secular life as they are indispensable to the economy of a monastic settlement. Under this category come such installations as the granaries, the house of the gardener and his crew, the house of the duck and fowl keeper, the house of the workmen, some six or seven structures which serve as shelter for the livestock and its keepers, the so-called

"Outer School," and the two monastic guest houses: the House for Visitors of Rank and the Hospice of the Paupers. A typological analysis of the guest and service structures of the Plan of St. Gall shows that they are variants of the house type above discussed. As the Iron Age houses of Ezinge and their early medieval descendants of Wilhelmshaven-Hessens and Leens (Fig. 36), so in the guest and service structures of the Plan of St. Gall the principal portion of the house consists of a large rectangular center room which contains the hearth and serves as common living room, while the more private and more specialized functions, such as sleeping and the stabling for the livestock, are relegated to the peripheral aisles and lean-tos.

Thus in the Guest House for Visitors of Rank the center space is used as the common "dining hall" (*domus ad prandendum*), the chambers under the lean-tos as the "bedrooms for the distinguished guests" (*caminatae cum lectis*), the aisles as "servants' quarters" (*cubilia servitorum*) and as "stables for the horses" (*stabula caballo-rum*). By the same token, in the Hospice of the Paupers the center space serves as "living room for the pilgrims and paupers" (*domus peregrinorum et pauperum*), while the outer rooms are used as dormitories (*dormitorium*), as "quarters for the servants" (*servitorum mansiones*), as "storage room" (*camera*), and as "cellar" (*cellerarium*). Likewise in the House for the Country Servants, as well as in all of the buildings which accommodate the livestock and its keepers, viz., the sheepfold, the goat-shed and the pigsty, the large rectangular center space is designated as the "common living room" (*domus familiae, ipsa domus*, etc.), while the outer rooms serve as "sleeping quarters for the attendant servants" and as "stables" (*cubilia custodientium, cubilia opilionum, cubilia pas-torum* and *cavil* or *stabula*). In order to be taken to their stalls the animals had to be led through the common center room. This held true not only for the structures specifically devised for the purpose of housing livestock, but also for buildings of such a highly resi-dential nature as the Guest House for Visitors of Rank, where the horses, likewise, in order to reach their stables had to be guided through the common living room.

In the majority of the guest and service structures of the Plan of St. Gall the center room is surrounded by wings on all four sides, but on some of the smaller houses the aisles are confined to two or three sides only. Two typical examples of this latter kind are the House of the Duck and Fowl Keeper and the House of the Physician, while the Guest House for Visitors of Rank is, of course, a typical example of the more common type. Yet in whatever combination this house-type may appear, it is obvious that we are confronted with an all-purpose structure that served a great variety of functions, separate and combined, without entailing even the slightest changes in its basic structural dispositions: it was used in one case as shelter for humans alone, in another as shelter for humans and animals combined, and in still another as storage space for the harvest.

The only medieval house-type known to have comparable versatility of functions (while at the same time retaining unaltered all of its basic structural dispositions) is the house-type of Ezinge, Leens, and Wilhelmshaven-Hessens. The Plan of St. Gall gives us an idea of the immense distribution which this house-type must have had in Carolingian Europe—in fact, it holds the key to the entire unsolved problem of Carolingian residential and rural architecture, for granaries, cow sheds, pigsties, sheepfolds, houses for workmen, guests, and country servants belonged to a category of buildings which in the Middle Ages were even more common to secular life than they were to a monastic settlement.

If we have been negligent in keeping abreast with the discoveries made during the last two decades by our colleagues in the field of prehistory, we have been even more remiss with our own material. France and England are replete with the remains of the most extraordinary aisled and bay-divided medieval timber structures *which we have not even taken the trouble to record properly.* The oldest surviving aisled and bay-divided timber hall of Europe is the castle hall of Leicester. It dates from around 1150. The historical aspects of this structure have been competently dealt with in a study of Levi Fox,[22] but archaeologically this building is as good as uninvestigated. Reliable plans and sections have never been published and are not even locally available. While of the excavated prehistoric and early medieval houses which I discussed above only the ground or bottom timbers survive, in Leicester Castle the situation is exactly reversed. Most of the supporting frame has disappeared, but the roof is preserved. And here we have the earliest residential timber roof of Europe that is still in a perfect state of preservation—a fact which should be of primary concern to the prehistorians who have not had the good fortune as yet of finding

266

among their excavated house remains sufficient evidence to be certain about the details of reconstruction of the roof system. I am stressing "in a perfect state of preservation" since British archaeologists have recently displayed a tendency to assume that the original twelfth-century roof of the hall of Leicester Castle might have been replaced by a new one sometime in the course of the fourteenth century. This view has been expressed by Mr. C. A. R. Radford,[23] who observed that the tie beam which lies contiguous to the southern gable wall cuts across the cornice of the arches of the Norman windows, and hence could not have been part of the original work. Mr. Radford's observation is correct, but I cannot follow his conclusion. The timber frame of the hall of Leicester Castle, while originally keyed firmly into the gable walls by means of half-beams which rested on masonry brackets, had simply sunk away from its original level early in the nineteenth century, when the wooden Norman pillars were cropped three feet below the meeting point of tie beams and plates, and then shored by modern timbers resting on modern piers of brick. In the summer of 1957 I had an opportunity to study this roof timber by timber. To my own surprise I found it to be original and homogeneous throughout. The frame is out of plumb and has buckled severely, and in places has sunk away from its original position for a distance of almost two feet, but the timbers *are Norman!* And this holds true not only for the tie beams and the rafters and all of their connecting bracing struts, but also for the heavy plates as well as for the headpieces of the supporting piers and their entire complement of bracing struts. The profiles, moldings, and scantling of these timbers are Norman and show none of the refinements and mannerisms of fourteenth-century carpentry work.

On one of the walls of the stairwell which leads to the private court rooms installed on the modern second floor of the hall there is on display a woodcut of a perspective reconstruction of the hall, which was made in 1917 by T. H. Fosbrooke of Leicester (Fig. 37).[24] Save for a few minor details which can be corrected only after the building has been systematically measured (a task which I hope to be able to undertake next summer), this reconstruction is, in my opinion, basically correct. Fosbrooke's woodcut takes us into the interior of a typical medieval castle or manor hall such as must have dotted the European countryside in the twelfth and thirteenth centuries in thousands, if not in hundreds of thousands,

37. Leicester Castle (Leicestershire), England; Interior of Great Hall (Reconstruction by T. H. Fosbrooke)

of specimens. In the homes of those of the highest social and economic level the traditional timber walls were often replaced by masonry, as is the case in Leicester, but in general they were built in timber.[25] As in the guest and service structures of St. Gall and the prehistoric and early medieval houses of Ezinge and Wilhelmshaven-Hessens, so here the hall received its warmth from an open fireplace that burned in the middle of the center aisle. The lord sat at the table on the elevated dais at one of the two narrow ends of the hall, while his retainers took their meals on benches and tables set up along the walls in the aisles of the building. The benches and tables were cleared away after the meal to make room for the bolsters and pillows on which the retainers slept. This is the architectural system of the standard hall not only of the great and powerful lords of the secular order, but also that of the hall of the overlords of the church.

One of the most beautiful feudal halls of England—entirely built in timber—is the palace hall of the Bishop of Hereford. It dates from the same general period as Leicester Hall,[26] is equally well preserved, but has received even less attention from medieval architectural historians than the hall of Leicester Castle.[27] The hall appears to have survived in its original form up to the time of Bishop Bisse (1713–1721), when it was robbed of its spatial unity by the insertion of a number of inner-wall partitions. It was subjected to further disfiguration under Bishop Atley (1868–1896), who subdivided what remaining open space there was into a jumble of separate rooms by the insertion of further cross partitions and the construction of a second story. It is in the masonry of these eighteenth- and nineteenth-century wall partitions and in the space above the plaster ceilings of the rooms installed by Bishops Bisse and Atley that three of the original wooden piers and a substantial portion of the original wooden arcades can still be seen. While only three of the original bays can now be traced, it is possible that the original structure was comprised of five bays. This at least was the view of John Clayton, to whom we owe the first description of the hall.[28]

38. Hereford (Herefordshire), England; Interior of Great Hall (Reconstruction by John Clayton)

John Clayton is the author also of the superb reconstruction reproduced in Fig. 38, which I am publishing here with the kind permission of the Lord Bishop of Hereford and the City Library and Old House Committee of this city.[29] While unreliable in many of its details—especially in the rendering of the roof and the doubtful large transverse arches—this picture nevertheless recreates in an arresting manner the sweeping spatial grandeur of a typical timbered medieval palace hall. The large and remarkable arcades of this structure, however, though entirely hewn in timber, are a design feature that is not natural to wood and which already comes, of course, under the influence of stone construction. The standard type of feudal English hall had the traditional timber system of straight long- and crossbeams, framed together with the aid of diagonal bracing struts, and in this form the three-aisled timbered hall served in the Middle Ages not only as a domestic feudal residence, but also as a barn, as a hospital, and as a market hall —even as a church.

Westminster Palace, the largest feudal hall in Europe, and the hall of the kings of England, is unfortunately not preserved in its original form. Today this hall is covered by a single span, a masterpiece of hammer beam construction, which King Richard II raised at the end of the fourteenth century.[30] But prior to the invention of the arch-braced hammer beam a hall of this enormous width could not have been spanned in single trusses; for that reason there is general agreement among British archaeologists that when this hall was built by William Rufus between 1097 and 1099 its roof must have been supported, like the roofs of the halls of Leicester and Hereford, by two rows of free-standing inner timbers which divided the structure lengthwise into a nave and aisles and crosswise into a sequence of bays.[31] We can make ourselves a convincing picture of what that system must have looked like in its original form by stepping into one of the monumental tithe barns of the great monastic orders, such as the fourteenth-century tithe barn of Great Coxwell in Berkshire.[32] This is, in its essential lines, what the royal hall in the Palace of Westminster must have looked like from the time of William Rufus to that of Richard II when it was the administrative center at which a major portion of the political history of England was forged.

In medieval England hall and barn were structurally interchangeable, and if there were any difference between the two it consisted in the fact that the barns, in general, were considerably larger and infinitely more numerous than the halls. No medieval manor was in need of more than one hall, but every medieval manor needed three to five barns. We are in an excellent position to evaluate the density of distribution of medieval barns, not only because of the help provided by the Plan of St. Gall—which gives us the layout of not less than eight such structures—but also because of the survival of a number of written documents of a related nature. One of the most enlightening documents of this type is a dossier of lease agreements of the twelfth century which records the manorial holdings of the dean and chapter of St. Paul's in London.[33] From this inventory we learn that the chapter of St. Paul's derived its sustenance from a total of thirteen manors which were scattered throughout the counties of Hertfordshire, Essex, and Surrey. The number of barns on each of these manors varied from three to five. Thirteen of these barns are so well described that they can be reconstructed on a drawing board. The canon who took the inventory gives us not only the length and width of each barn but, in many cases, even such details as the height and width of the aisles, the height and width of the nave, the depth of the bays and lean-tos, the height from the floor to the crossbeam, and the distance from the crossbeam to the ridge.

In view of the crucial position which this document occupies in the history of the aisled and bay-divided medieval timber barn, I shall translate from the Latin, as a typical example, the description of one of three barns which the chapter of St. Paul's owned on its manor at Wicham, Essex.

> The third barn, which lies further east, is 49½ feet long, not counting its lean-tos, which have a depth of 22 feet. The height of this barn below the tie beam is 15 feet, and above, between the tie beam and the ridge, it is 9½ feet. The nave is 22½ feet wide, and each of its two aisles is 6½ feet wide and 8 feet high. This barn Ailwinus must render full of summer wheat from the entrance toward the east, and from the entrance toward the west it must be full of oats. The center [bay] opposite the entrance must remain empty. It is 11½ feet wide.

The largest of the barns described in the leases of St. Paul's is a barn in a place called Walton on the manor of Adulvesnasa, Essex. It measured 168 feet in length, 53 feet in width, and 33½ feet in height. Its nave was filled to the ridge with huge stacks of oats and summer wheat, and scattered here and there in the aisles were heaps of barley, the dimensions of which are accurately recorded. This description is a striking tribute to the economic acumen of the landowning corporation which, with these details, made sure that all such goods as a new tenant received on entering the manor were dutifully returned at the termination of the lease.

The lease agreements of St. Paul's range in date from 1114 to 1155.[34] Obviously they establish only a *terminus ante;* they say nothing about the age of the barns. Some of them may have been of relatively recent date. Others may have been centuries old; in fact, may date from any time between the date of inspection and the original land grants in the seventh and eighth centuries.

That barns of this layout and design were as common in the Middle Ages on the Continent as they were in England, we may gather from a glance at Dom Milley's superb engravings of the Abbey of Clairvaux.[35] Published in 1708, these engravings show the settlement substantially in the form it had attained by the close of the twelfth century. In the foreground of the bird's-eye view which shows the monastery from the west, one recognizes two large barns, one lying at right angles, the other parallel to the monastery walls immediately to the right of the entrance. Dom Milley's plan reveals that these were five-and six-aisled structures, and the scale with which the plan is furnished permits us to establish their dimensions as amounting to 90 by 120 feet and to 72 by 168 feet, respectively. Inserted into the edge of Dom Milley's great perspective is a view of one of the outlying granges of Clairvaux, the grange of Ultra Albam. It also contains two barns, one subdivided into five, the other into seven, aisles. The larger of these two barns was 210 feet long and 108 feet wide.

The barns of Clairvaux perished when the monastery was demolished in the wake of the French Revolution. Their loss as historical monuments, however deplorable it may be, is not irreparable, as a considerable number of like-type barns survive, both in France and in England. The earliest of these appears to be the abbey grange of Parçay-Meslay, near Tours in France (Fig. 39), a dependency of the monastery of Marmoutier. Dom Edmond Martène, a learned French Benedictine of the Congregation of St. Maur (1654–1739), who was thoroughly acquainted with the history and the archives of this monastery, lists the abbey grange

39. Parçay-Meslay (Indre-et-Loire), France; Abbey Grange, 1211–1227, Interior (Photo: Philip Spencer)

of Parçay-Meslay as belonging to a group of buildings which were erected by Abbé Hugue de Rochecorbon (1211–1227).[36] The general character of the masonry work of the barn, its profiles and its moldings, is in full accord with this date. This impressive structure has a clear inner length of 170 feet, 6 inches, a clear width of 80 feet, 2 inches, and a height to the bottom of the ridgepiece of 44 feet, 4 inches. Reliable plans and sections have never been published, but are available at the Centre de Recherches of the Monuments Historiques in Paris. Even expert photography does not render justice to this building; it is only by drawing it up that one can capture the cathedral-like appearance of this magnificent frame of timbers which penetrates the space in all directions, dividing it into parts, and at the same time braiding the parts together into an all-embracing coherent whole.

There is some question as to whether the present timbers of the barn of Parçay-Meslay are the original ones. Aymar Verdier, who discussed this building in his *Architecture Civile et Domestique*,[37] reports that Mr. Drouet, who acquired the barn after the French Revolution and saved it from demolition, was of the opinion that the original frame of timber had caught fire during the invasion of the Touraine by the English in 1437. I have no means of judging whether this view was based on any valid historical evidence. But even if the present timbers were proved to date from the fifteenth century, this would have little bearing on the basic argument of this study since we are not concerned here with the changing details of carpentry work, but with the constructional system as a whole —and a sufficient number of other thirteenth-century barns survive to indicate that no noteworthy changes took place between the thirteenth and the fifteenth centuries as far as the principle of bay-division is concerned.

A thirteenth-century barn of considerable size and beauty, the property of the Abbey of Longchamp, stood within the very boundaries of the city of Paris until the middle of the nineteenth century, when it was taken down to make room for the fashionable race tracks in the Bois de Boulogne. The timbers of the barn are gone, but they were carefully recorded before being dismantled.[38] And further north, in the abbey grange of Canteloup (Eure), in Normandy,[39] and in the abbey grange of Ter Doest in Belgium[40] there are two thirteenth-century barns of even larger dimensions, the timbers of which are still standing in an excellent state of preservation.

Vast and impressive as they are, there is nothing about these barns that is unique. Good documentary evidence suggests that by the close of the twelfth century the Abbey of Clairvaux alone possessed, on its respective granges, not less than twenty-six such structures, and the Abbey of Foigny probably as many as twenty-eight.[41] If we assume that the agricultural economy of the average Cistercian monastery required in each case a minimum of between ten and twenty barns—and the latter figure may come closer to the truth than the former—we would have to infer that by the end of the twelfth century, when the total of Cistercian foundations had risen to about 500, there were not less than 5,000 to 10,000 Cistercian barns alone.

Of the hundreds of thousands of such barns that once undoubtedly were scattered over the medieval countryside, some thirty or forty survive, and of them the most beautiful, in my opinion, is the great tithe barn of Harmondsworth in Middlesex, whose timbers are still as fresh today as they were in the thirteenth century when they

40. St. Pierre-sur-Dives (Calvados), France; Market Hall, 13th(?) Century, Exterior from SW (Photo: Philip Spencer)

were hewn and framed together. Harmondsworth barn is mentioned in a list of alien properties seized by the Crown of England from 1288–1386, in an entry which refers to the year 1293–94 (22 Edward I).[42] This barn has the distinction of having been competently described and recorded as early as 1875 by Albert Hartshorne.[43] It is also succinctly dealt with in the volume on Middlesex of the Royal Commission for Historical Monuments in England,[44] where, however, without any substantiating evidence the barn is ascribed (and wrongly, in my opinion) to the fourteenth century. Harmondsworth barn is 191 feet, 10 inches long, 37 feet, 6 inches wide, and 37 feet, 6 inches high. The feeling of grandeur which this structure evokes as one steps over its threshold into its massive forest of rising timbers, can only be compared to that experienced in entering a medieval cathedral. If I speak of this barn as the finest and most beautiful of all surviving medieval barns of England, I am referring not only to its general proportions—the full nobility of which can only be perceived on the spot—but also to a specific muscular and skeletal type of beauty that occurs only on the highest level of barn construction and finds its expression in an unusually sensitive and convincing down and upward scaling of the timbers, as the eye moves from primary to secondary to tertiary member and back again.

By the time the barns of Parçay-Meslay and of Harmondsworth were built a new variety of the type had sprung into existence, the market hall. The most impressive medieval market hall I know of is the hall of the sleepy little country town of St. Pierre-sur-Dives (Calvados), in Normandy, which is here published for the first time (Fig. 40). It is astonishing that this extraordinary structure should never have found its way into any authoritative treatise on medieval architecture. The hall is 225 feet, 6 inches long, 64 feet, 6 inches wide, and 42 feet, 6 inches high, and may go back to the thirteenth century. Unfortunately the hall was shelled in 1944, and its original frame of timber was at that time almost completely destroyed by fire. Under the competent direction of Mr. Jean Merlet, Architect-in-Chief of the Monuments Historiques, the hall was subsequently restored, and this restoration, carried out by a team of carpenters who reproduced the ancient system to its smallest detail, is one of the masterpieces of French conservationism.

Last summer, Philip Spencer and I studied and photographed altogether seven such halls, all of them unpublished. St. Pierre-sur-Dives was the largest, but its timbers are new, and as far as the scantling, the patina, and the texture of the wood are concerned, it is surpassed by a considerably smaller hall in the city of Arpajon (Seine et Oise), some thirty kilometers south of Paris,[45] which dates from the fifteenth century, and is used—even today—for the same purpose for which it was constructed five centuries ago. A hall of approximately the same dimensions, and so identical in the details of its carpentry work that it must be ascribed to the same master, stands in the nearby city of Milly-la-Forêt. It was erected by Admiral de Graville in 1479, and the patent letter of Louis XI, in which the construction of the hall is authorized, is still preserved in the city archives of Milly.[46] In the same general region of the department of Seine-et-Oise there are three more market halls of similar description—one of outstanding beauty in the city of Méréville. While they too will probably have to be dated into the fifteenth century, we have good reason to assume that the thirteenth-century halls of Paris cannot have looked much different.

I should now like to summarize what I have tried to demonstrate so far in the analytical part of this study before turning to my conclusions.

Discoveries made during the last two decades by German, English, Dutch, and Scandinavian excavators, and a roundup of a pitifully neglected—in parts even uncharted—area of medieval research, suggest that there existed in the Middle Ages an aisled and bay-

Rome: St. Paul's

Harmondsworth: Tithe Barn

Speyer: Cathedral

Amiens: Cathedral

41. Space Division in Early Christian and Medieval Architecture (Redrawn by Ernest Born after Construction of William Hill)

divided, all-purpose structure in timber, about the imposing density of distribution of which we have been deplorably misinformed in the past. The existence and general prevalence of this type of structure during the formative phases of Romanesque and Gothic architecture casts new light upon Strzygowski's abortive theory of the origin of the medieval bay-system in wood construction.

The bay system is one of the principal distinguishing features of medieval architecture and is perhaps its most distinguishing single feature. It developed on an architectural organism which by origin was not possessed of this feature, namely, that of the West Roman type of the Early Christian basilica, which, in the wake of a general process of political and cultural Romanization that seized the kingdom of Charlemagne toward the end of the eighth century—as

Richard Krautheimer has so convincingly demonstrated[47]—became a leading Frankish building type and the point of departure for the entire development which followed. This West Roman version of the Early Christian basilica was an aggregate of three or more monolithic spaces, internally undivided and of varying dimensions, which shouldered each other axially and transversely, but never intersected one another (cf. Fig. 41, diagram of St. Paul's). The relative measurements of these spaces were not regulated by any set canon of proportions and thus varied greatly. The Romanesque and the Gothic churches, which developed from this prototype form, on the other hand, are bay-divided churches, i.e., churches in which the total space is subdivided into a multitude of equal or homologous parts by means of an all-pervasive skeleton of shafts and arches which act both as divisive and as connective members (cf. Fig. 41, diagrams of Speyer and Amiens Cathedrals).

These concepts are diametrically opposed to one another, and the development which leads from the former to the latter passed through a series of clearly observable steps which have been described frequently and which I shall now recapitulate very briefly.

The first of these consisted of a general rearrangement of the primary geometrical space relationships of the church. The width of the nave and the transept were made equal, their area of intersection, the crossing unit, thus was fixed into a square, and all of the remaining parts of the church were calculated as a multiple of the crossing square. In Carolingian and Ottonian architecture we witness the gradual crystallization of this principle which reaches its apex in the so-called "square schematism" of the Romanesque—but the essential features of this system were already anticipated in the church of the famous Plan of St. Gall of around the year 820. For seven decades the emergence of this peculiar system of unit relationships has been discussed by leading architectural historians, and yet no one has ever been able to explain it. I suggest that the geometricity of the floor plan of Carolingian and Ottonian churches and the modular lay-out of their volume sequence owe their origin to the fact that these churches were constructed by men, to whom—as long as their collective memory could recall—"to build" had been synonymous with building in multiples of a basic spatial unit value.[48] Geometricity and unit sequence had been for them intrinsic elements of timbered frame construction—a feature that becomes strikingly apparent if one glances at the intensely geometrical layout of the large Iron Age cattle barn of Ezinge, Holland (Fig. 35), or the early medieval houses of the type of Wilhelmshaven-Hessens (Fig. 36).

In Ottonian architecture this steadily increasing trend of calculating the general dimensions of the principal spaces of the church as multiples of a basic unit value gathered added momentum with the introduction of the "alternating support system" which carried into the elevation of the church a rhythm of alternating vertical accents that mirrored in the columnar structure of the wall modular prime relationships which heretofore had been a property of the dimensional organization of the space alone. This was a preliminary to a second decisive step in the development of the medieval bay system which was reached when the geometrical layout of the floor plan found muscular embodiment in a system of rising shafts which were engaged into the masonry walls, and when these shafts were interconnected crosswise and lengthwise by means of arches. As soon as this point was reached the churches could be vaulted, the walls between the rising shafts and arches could be perforated and were progressively transformed into curtain walls—and thus the Early Christian basilica with its aggregate of neighboring monolithic spaces separated by rigid walls had been transformed into that intensely skeletal and bay-divided system of the Romanesque. In church construction as well as in domestic building the totality of the space was now conceived of as a multiple of equal or homologous parts, created by an all-pervasive system of structural members, in function both divisive and connective.

It is very hard for me to believe that the appearance of this concept in stone should not have been connected, developmentally, with the fact that in the territories in which this change took place these principles had been for over a millenium a traditional feature of timbered house construction. In timber this concept is old; in stone it is new. In timber it flows as a logical construction method from the natural properties of the material, and for that reason could be invented on a relatively primitive cultural level. In masonry it ushered in a conflict between style and matter such as could be handled only on a very sophisticated level of civilization, to the extent of leading in its terminal phase—the Gothic—to a complete denial of the natural properties of the stone.

The great architects of the Renaissance, to whom the Gothic was a "monstrous and barbarous" way of building, were fully aware of this dichotomy between material and style in Gothic architecture, as is expressed in no uncertain terms by Giorgio Vasari, who complained that Gothic buildings "have more the appearance of being made in paper than of stone or marble,"[49] as well as by the author of the famous "Report on the Remains of Ancient Rome" (once believed to be Raphael, but now more commonly ascribed to Bramante or Baldassare Peruzzi), who compared the soaring flight of the Gothic piers and arches with the tensile action of the trunks of living trees, and based upon this simile his puzzling theory of the origins of Gothic architecture in the wooden huts of the primitive forebearers of civilized man.[50] In order to obviate any misconceptions as to my own views in this matter, let me point out that I am not subscribing to Raphael's, Bramante's, or Peruzzi's views. The study with which I am here concerned is devoted to an analysis not of the complex phenomenon of the origins of the Gothic, but to the specific problem of the origins of the medieval bay system, a feature which is an integral part of both the Romanesque and the Gothic, without being identical with either.

If, with these qualifications in mind, then, I readvance Strzygowski's ill-conceived idea of the origins of the medieval bay system in northern wood construction, I wish to make it clear that I do not mean to imply that the architectural system of the Romanesque and Gothic emerged mechanically like a chemical formula from the simple historical superimposition or interpenetration of two formerly separate building traditions: that of the Early Christian stone basilica and that of the medieval timber house. Primarily and above all, of course, the architectural systems of the Romanesque and Gothic are the expression of a spiritual experience, and in the Middle Ages, bay division was as much of a cultural phenomenon as it was a principle of architectural composition.

Sometime between the year 1230 and 1236 a leading French scholastic, William from Auvergne, gave the finishing touches to a book which dealt with the structure of the universe (*Liber de Universo*) and aimed at a total integration of the metaphysical concepts prevailing in his time into a rounded metaphysical vision. The universe here is envisaged as a triad of structurally related hierarchies, each a mirror reflection of the other as well as of the system as a whole with its identical subdivisions into triads of triads of ranks, and in each of these triads each subordinate rank corresponds in substance to its equivalent part in every other triad. The architectural plan that underlies this metaphysical scheme displays the most astounding analogies with that of the Gothic bay system. As in the latter, so here the whole "is arranged according to a system of homologous parts, and parts of parts"—if I may be permitted to apply to the *substance* of a metaphysical concept a definition which Panofsky in his brilliant essay on Gothic architecture and scholasticism has coined with regard to the *formal layout* of the scholastic treatise.[51]

In its ultimate analysis, then, I would say the problem of the medieval bay system cannot be separated from the rank division of the feudal order, the ecclesiastical order, and the celestial order, and it is in these areas, of course, that we must search for the primary spiritual forces that brought about the transformation of that sluggish organism of the Early Christian basilica into that highly flexible, highly complex, incredibly sophisticated, but equally emotive, organism of the Gothic cathedral. In order to be expressive of the thinking of that period, architecture required a style in which the whole could be conceived as a multiple of homologous parts, and in order to create such a style the rigid Early Christian basilica had to be converted from a monolithic into a cellular and from a crustacian into a skeletal structure. In facing this task, medieval architects had the signal advantage of being able to draw on a tradition in which bay division and skeletal construction had been for over a millenium a guiding principle of construction for the houses in which they dwelled, the halls from which they ruled and governed their land, the barns in which they sheltered their livestock and harvest, the markets in which they traded their produce and even, to some extent, the churches in which they worshiped.

In submitting this theory I should like to end on a precautionary note. I have stressed the native northern aspect of the medieval bay system because this aspect has been generally neglected. But in strongly underscoring what I feel to be in need of primary emphasis I do not mean to diminish the importance of other factors which also may have had a bearing on this matter. While the bay system in the form in which it is here defined is, in my opinion, a typical medieval feature, its primary constituent part—the bay—was known to the Romans, and the morphology of the vaulted canopies of stone which frame the bays of Speyer Cathedral is, of course, a direct derivative of the Roman groin vault, of which the medieval masons had learned to make use, first in the crypts, then in the aisles, and finally in the naves of their churches. It is an incontrovertible historical fact, however, that the vaulted Roman canopy had not found a place of survival in any of the principal spaces of the large Early Christian basilicas of the western type from which the medieval development took its point of departure. Nevertheless there existed, in the sixth century, two churches in northern Syria which had their nave divided into large bays by means of large transverse arches: the basilica of St. Sergios at Rusafa and the Bissos church at Ruweha.[52] I consider it unlikely that either of these two churches exercised appreciable influence upon the development of the medieval bay system. They lie in territory which early in the seventh century had fallen into the hands of the Arabs and which remained outside the sphere of western accessibility even during the time of the Crusades, not to mention the fact that by the time the earliest Crusade took place, in 1096, the medieval bay system had already found its full embodiment in the Cathedral of Speyer.

Yet even if I should be wrong in this assumption—or if it could be demonstrated that similar or related types were known to medieval masons and architects—it must still be pointed out that in Rusafa and in Ruweha bay division remained confined to the nave of the church and was not extended to the church as a whole. The Rusafa-Ruweha bays actually are large compartments rather than bays, and were created by the simple insertion into the nave of the church of two monumental transverse arches carried by elongated piers, but the masonry of the nave walls—diminished as it may be by arcades of extraordinary width—is not reduced to an analogous system of structural members. It is in the full absorption of mass in structure on the one hand, and in the development of an all-pervasive armature of space-dividing and space-connecting shafts and arches on the other hand, that I see the common denominator of the bay division of the Romanesque and Gothic and the bay division of the timbered halls and houses of transalpine Europe.

NOTES

[1] Josef Strzygowski, "Die Europäische Kunst," *Belvedere*, 26 (1924), pp. 35–55; cf. in particular p. 43. The idea is voiced again in Strzygowski's *Nordischer Heilbringer und Bildende Kunst* (Vienna and Leipzig, 1939), p. 233.

[2] On the derivation of the Scandinavian stave churches from central prototypes see Gerda Boëthius, "Stavkyrkans Ursprung och Utveckling," *Festskrift Johnny Roosval* (Stockholm, 1929), pp. 18–33.

[3] For rapid, if only partial, orientation see the references listed under the terms *ligneus* or *bois* in the indices of the following works: Otto Lehmann-Brockhaus, *Schriftquellen zur Kunstgeschichte des 11. und 12. Jahrhunderts für Deutschland, Lothringen und Italien* (Berlin, 1938); Victor Mortet, *Recueil de textes relatifs à l'histoire de l'architecture en France au Moyen Age, XIe-XIIe siècles* (Paris 1911); Victor Mortet and Paul Deschamps, *Recueil de textes relatifs à l'histoire de l'architecture en France au Moyen Age, XIIe-XIIIe siècles* (Paris, 1929).

[4] St. Catherine's is briefly dealt with by M. de Caumont in *Statistique Monumentale du Calvados* (Paris-Caen, 1862), IV, pp. 323–338, but has never become the subject of a special monograph, which is badly needed.

[5] Monsieur Jullien's observations have not been published but are incorporated into a set of carefully measured drawings which are on file in the Centre de Recherches of the Monument Historiques in Paris. Prints of these I owe to the kindness of Mlles. Bertholier and Bloch of the Monuments Historiques.

[6] . . . [To] Messrs. Jan and E. Jans of Almelo . . . I am indebted for the following historical information conveyed to me by Pastor H. L. Lieve of Paasloo: Permission to build a church at Paasloo was granted in 1336 by the chapter of St. Clement's in Steenwyk, according to a document in the archives of St. Clement's. Judging from foundations which were discovered some three feet inward of the walls of the present church, this building must have been a little smaller than the present church. Until 1486 the church of Paasloo was the principal church of the district. Thereafter it sank into the status of a chapel, and Oldemarkt became the seat of the principal church.

[7] Raymond Richards, *Old Cheshire Churches* (London, 1947). For Marton, cf. pp. 229–231; for Warburton, pp. 339–341; for Lower Peover, pp. 200–204; for Holmes Chapel, pp. 186–190. Most of the churches listed above are also dealt with in Fred H. Crossley, *Timber Building in England* (London-New York, 1951), pp. 32 ff., where one will also find a reproduction of the handsome late medieval timber church of Coppenhall, Cheshire, which was torn down in 1821. For a description and photographic reproductions of the church of Mattingly, cf. *Victoria History of the Counties of England, Hampshire* (London, 1911), IV, pp. 50 ff.; for Ribbesford, *ibid.*, *Worcestershire*, (London, 1924), IV, pp. 312–314.

[8] The church is mentioned in Daniel Brunn, *Fortidsminder og Nutidshjem paa Island* (Copenhagen, 1898), p. 212.

[9] Gamal Norsk Homiliebok, Cod. AM 619, ed. Gustav Ludvig Indrebø, *Norske historiske kjeldeskriftfond, Skifter*, Vol. 54 (Oslo, 1931).

[10] Dr. P. Glazema, "Outheidkundige opgravingen in door de oorlog verwoeste Limburgse Kerken," *Publications de la Société Historique et Archéologique dans le Limbourg*, 84 (1948), pp. 226–232, 252–258.

[11] Kurt Böhner, Peter Joseph Tholen, and Rafael von Uslar, "Ausgrabungen in den Kirchen von Breberen und Doveren," *Bonner Jahrbücher*, Heft 150 (1950), pp. 192–228.

[12] Reproduced after *Werdendes Abendland an Rhein und Ruhr* (Ausstellung in Villa Hügel, Essen, 18 May–15 September, 1956), p. 95, Fig. 9.

[13] Albert Verbeek, "Eine merovingische Kathedrale?", *Kunstchronik*, 9 (1956), 280–281, with plan on p. 280.

[14] Cf. Otto Lehmann-Brockhaus, *Die Kunst des 10. Jahrhunderts im Lichte der Schriftquellen* (Akademische Abhandlungen zur Kulturgeschichte, 3rd series [Strassburg, 1935]), VI, pp. 13 ff. To the incident mentioned above I add here at random two further typical examples. After the destruction of the Cathedral of Hamburg by the Slavs, Bishop Unwanus (who acceded to the episcopal see in 1013) rebuilt the episcopal "church and all of its appendices in timber" (*ecclesiam et diversoria . . . omnia lignea*). (Cf. Otto Lehmann-Brockhaus, *Schriftquellen zur Kunstgeschichte des 11. und 12. Jahrhunderts für Deutschland, Lothringen und Italien* [Berlin, 1938], pp. 108–109.) Even as late as 1184 the Emperor Frederic Barbarossa erected in the triangular plain formed by the confluence of the rivers Rhine and Main "a church of considerable size and a stately palace in timber" (*ecclesiam maximam et palatium de lignis honestissime fieri iusserat*), "together with numerous other structures of varying description for the purpose of celebrating in the most magnificent manner the great feast of Joy" (i.e., the coronation of his son Henry as King of Germany). And the reason for this was "the narrowness of the streets in the city of Mainz and the bad air prevailing there." Cf. *Arnoldi Chronica Slavorum*, ed. Heinrich Pertz (Hannover, 1868), p. 88.

[15] Albert Egges van Giffen, "Der Warf in Ezinge, Prov. Groningen, Holland und seine Westgermanischen Häuser," *Germania*, 20 (1936), pp. 40–47.

[16] This holds true for a three-aisled Iron Age house which was excavated in 1940 on the Aalburg, near Belfort, Luxembourg, and which even antedates the earliest Ezinge houses (cf. Gustav Riek, "Ein Fletthaus aus der Wende ältere-jüngere Hunsrück-Eiffelkultur bei Belfort, Luxemburg," *Germania*, 26 [1942], pp. 26–34). The reconstruction problems of this, as well as many other Iron Age houses are discussed authoritatively by Adelhart Zippelius, in "Das vormittelalterliche dreischiffige Hallenhaus in Mitteleuropa," *Bonner Jahrbücher*, 153 (1953), pp. 13–45.

[17] I am confining myself here to the most summary bibliography. The material excavated in Holland and in Germany is not summarized at any place, so far as I know, and is scattered through a vast array of prehistoric and regional periodicals, many of which are not easily available in this country. Good surveys of the Swedish material are to be found in such works as: John Nihlen and Gerda Boëthius, *Gotländska gårder och byar undre äldre järnaldern.* (Stockholm, 1933); Mårten Stenberger, *Öland under aldre järnaldern* (Stockholm, 1933), and Mårten Stenberger, *Vallhagar, A Migration Period Settlement on Gotland, Sweden* (2 vols.; Copenhagen, 1955). The Norwegian material excavated prior to 1942 is summarized in Sigurd Grieg, "The House in Norwegian Archaeology," *Acta Archaeologica*, 13 (1942), pp. 169–178; for the Danish material excavated prior to 1937 see

The Origins of the Bay System

Gudmund Hatt, "Dwelling Houses in Jutland in the Iron Age," *Antiquity*, 2 (1937), pp. 162–173. For later material cf. Paul Nørlund, *Trelleborg* (Copenhagen, 1948). For Iceland, cf. Mårten Stenberger, *Forntida Gårdar I Island* (Copenhagen, 1943). A royal Anglo-Saxon palace of the seventh century, comprising a total of twenty-five houses, was excavated in the summer of 1956 in Northumbria, England, by Mr. Brian Hope-Taylor. The results of this excavation are in process of being published by the Ministry of Works. The earliest bay-divided timber house known so far was unearthed in the summer of 1954 in a place called Jemgum, near Emden, Germany. It dates from the period of transition from the Bronze Age to the Iron Age (seventh-sixth centuries, B.C.) and is dealt with in Werner Haarnagel, "Die spätbronze-, früheisenzeitliche Gehöftsiedlung Jemgum bei Leer auf dem linken Ufer der Ems," *Die Kunde*, Neue Folge, 8 (1957), pp. 1–43.

[18] Cf. Werner Haarnagel, "Das nordwesteuropäische dreischiffige Hallenhaus und seine Entwicklung im Küstengebiet der Nordsee," *Neues Archiv für Niedersachen*, 4 (1950), pp. 88–89, and, same author, "Die Flachabdeckung der Wurt Hessens am Jadebusen bei Wilhelmshaven und ihr vorläufiges Ergebnis," *Germania*, 29 (1951), pp. 223–225.

[19] Cf. Werner Haarnagel, "Die frühgeschichtliche Handelssiedlung Emden und ihre Entwicklung bis ins Mittelalter," *Friesisches Jahrbuch* (1955), pp. 9–78.

[20] Albert Egges van Giffen, "Een Systematic Onderzoek In Em Der Tuinster Wierden Te Leens," *Jaarsverslag Van Den Vereeniging Voor Terpenonderzoek*, 20–24 (1935–1940), pp. 26–117.

[21] A full-scale, eight-color, offset facsimile reproduction of the Plan of St. Gall was published in 1952 under the auspices of the Historische Verein des Kantons St. Gallen, and can be obtained through the Fehr'sche Buchhandlung in St. Gall, Switzerland. The facsimile was accompanied by a study of Hans Reinhardt, *Der St. Galler Klosterplan* (92. Neujahrsblatt herausgegeben vom Historischen Verein des Kantons St. Gallen [St. Gall, 1952]).

[22] Levi Fox, "Leicester Castle," *Leicester Archaeological Society Transactions*, 21, part 2 (1942–1943), pp. 127–170.

[23] In a footnote of C. A. R. Radford's report on "Oakham Castle," published in *Archaeological Journal*, 112 (1956), pp. 181–184; cf. note 1, p. 183.

[24] Fosbrooke's reconstruction is mentioned by Margaret Wood, "Norman Domestic Architecture," *Archaeological Journal*, 92 (1935), 191. For a copy of this woodcut, which is here published for the first time as far as I know, I am greatly indebted to Mr. Albert Herbert in Leicester.

[25] New light has recently been thrown upon the problem of the aisled medieval timber hall by J. T. Smith in an article entitled "Medieval Aisled Halls and Their Derivatives," *Archaeological Journal*, 112 (1956), 76–93. Mr. Smith has also recently made the interesting discovery that the hall of Stokesay Castle was in its original form a three-aisled structure (cf. J. T. Smith, "Stokesay Castle," *Archaeological Journal*, 113 [1957], pp. 211–214).

[26] The editors of the Royal Commission on Historical Monuments, *Herefordshire* (London, 1931), Vol. 1, where the hall is dealt with on pp. 116–117, date it into "the late 12th century." Margaret Wood in her "Norman Domestic Architecture," *op. cit.*, p. 188, dates the hall "*c.* 1160." The Rev. Francis T. Havergal in *Fasti Herefordenses and other Antiquarian Memorials of Hereford* (Edinburgh, 1869),

p. 136, attributes the hall to Bishop William de Vere (between 1174 and 1199). No record as to the name of the builder of the hall or its date of construction exists, but the Norman character of the work is beyond question.

[27] The hall has never been the subject of a special monograph, which is badly needed.

[28] John Clayton discussed the hall in 1847 in a paper read before the Royal Institute of British Architects. Extracts of this discussion are to be found in *Fasti Herefordenses, op. cit.,* pp. 136–138.

[29] Clayton's reconstruction is mentioned in Wood, "Norman Domestic Architecture," *op. cit.,* p. 188. It was not included in John Clayton's work, *Ancient Timber Edifices of England* (London, 1948). A copy of a woodcut fashioned after Clayton's original drawing is in the Refectory Hall of the Bishop's Palace at Hereford, and the City Library of Hereford has a second one. To the Lord Bishop of Hereford as well as to Miss Penelope Morgan and Mr. F. C. Morgan of the Cathedral Library I wish to express my deepest appreciation for their gracious assistance in my studies at Hereford Palace.

[30] Westminster Hall is dealt with in W. R. Lethaby, "The Palace of Westminster in the Eleventh and Twelfth Centuries," *Archaeologia,* 60 (1906), pp. 131–141, and by the Royal Commission on Historical Monuments, *London (West)* (London, 1925), pp. 121–123. For the roof specifically cf. Herbert Cescinski and Ernest R. Gribble, "Westminster Hall and Its Roof," *Burlington Magazine,* 40 (1922), pp. 76–84.

[31] The belief that Westminster Hall in its original state must have been divided into a nave and aisles by two rows of intermediary supports was first expressed by Sidney Smirke in 1836 ("Remarks on the Architectural History of Westminster Hall," *Archaeologia,* 26 [1836], p. 416). Smirke's opinion is shared by every authoritative student of the subject, including the late Director of Works, Sir Frank Baines, Cf. Lethaby, *op. cit.,* p. 136; Cescinski and Gribble, *op. cit.,* p. 76; Royal Commission on Historical Monuments, *op. cit.,* p. 121, and Geoffrey Webb, *Architecture in Britain, The Middle Ages* (Baltimore and Harmondsworth, 1956), pp. 66 and 67, Fig. 38.

[32] Some good photographs and a cross section of this extraordinary structure have been published by Ralph Tubbs, *The Englishman Builds* (Harmondsworth, 1945), pp. 20–21, but otherwise this barn has not been studied.

[33] Published by William Hale, *The Domesday of St. Paul's of the Year MCCXII . . . and other Original Documents Relating to the Manors and Churches Belonging to the Dean and Chapter of St. Paul's in London, in the Twelfth and Thirteenth Centuries,* printed for the Camden Society (London, 1858). The first to draw attention to this precious document was Sidney Oldall Addy, *The Evolution of the English House* (London, 1898), pp. 67, 129 ff.

[34] For the dates see Hale's introductory notes, *op. cit.,* pp. xc-c.

[35] One complete set of these engravings is now in the Cabinet des Estampes of the Bibliothèque Nationale at Paris (Topographie de la France, Aube, Arondissement Bar-sur-Aube, fol. 27, 28, and 29); a second one is available in the Archives de l'Aube at the city of Troyes (Bibliothèque de Troyes, Carteron 1, Planches 2, 3, and 4). The best reproductions are to be found in Alphonse Roserot, *Dictionnaire*

The Origins of the Bay System

Historique de la Champagne Méridionale (Aube) des Origines à 1790 (Langres, 1942), I, pp. 392 ff.

[36] Dom Edmond Martène, "Histoire de l'Abbaye de Marmoutier" (publié et annoté par M. l'abbé C. Chevalier), *Mémoires de la Société Archéologique de Touraine*, 25 (1875), p. 200.

[37] Aymar Verdier and F. Cattois, *Architecture Civile et Domestique au Moyen Age et à la Renaissance* (Paris, 1864), pp. 27–35.

[38] Cf. Viollet-le-Duc, *Dictionnaire Raisonné de l'Architecture Française du XIe au XVIe siècle* (Paris, 1863), VI, 43, with plan, section, and elevation.

[39] The barn of the abbey grange of Canteloup is summarily described by Phillippe Lemaitre, "Notes sur Quelques Granges Dimiéres du Departement de L'Eure," *Bulletin Monumental*, 15 (1849), pp. 196–197, but plans and sections are not available.

[40] For plan, section, and elevation of this structure (not altogether reliable, however), see Thomas H. King, *The Study-Book of Mediaeval Architecture and Art* (Edinburgh, 1893), II, Fig. 137; there listed under "Lissewegh."

[41] These figures are based on the rough assumption that every grange dependent on the mother settlement required for its agricultural economy a minimum of two barns, like the abbey grange of Clairvaux, and the outlying grange of Ultra Albam. Clairvaux had a total of 12 granges, and six of those had already been established during the lifetime of St. Bernard (d. 1153); Foigny had a total of 14 (cf. Marcel Aubert, *L'Architecture Cistercienne en France* (Paris, 1947), II, pp. 60–161.

[42] This document is to be found on Exchequer, Queen's Remembrancer, *Extents, etc., of Alien Priories*, Bundle 2, No. 1, mem. 1 (Reference E. 106/2/1: date 22 Edw. I) and was quoted, but not without errors, in Hartshorne's article mentioned in note 43.

[43] Albert Hartshorne, "The Great Barn at Harmondsworth," *London and Middlesex Archaeological Society, Transactions*, 4 (1875), pp. 417 ff.

[44] Royal Commission on Historical Monuments in England, *Middlesex*, (London, 1937), pp. 61–62. To Miss Vera Dallas, Secretary of the Royal Commission on Historical Monuments, I should like to express on this occasion my deepest appreciation for the generous assistance and support which she has extended to me over a period of many years in my research on aisled medieval barns and halls in England.

[45] Photographs, plans, and sections of the market hall of Arpajon have never been published, to my knowledge, but are on file in the Centre de Recherches of the Monuments Historiques in Paris.

[46] The hall of Milly is briefly dealt with in a booklet by Georges Lasserre entitled *Les Rues de Milly* (Etampes, 1925), pp. 6 ff. For access to this booklet, a copy of which I could not otherwise have obtained, I am greatly obliged to the Comte de St. Périer of Morignon. The patent letter of Louis XI which authorizes the establishment of the market and the construction of the hall of Milly has also never been published, but an exact transcript of this important document has been transmitted to me by Mr. Raymond Geber, member of the Commission des Antiquités et des Arts de Seine-et-Oise, to whom I am deeply indebted for his

kindness. I should also like to express my gratitude at this point to my friend Peter Harnden of Orgival, who was the first to draw my attention to this extraordinary group of medieval market halls.

[47] Richard Krautheimer, "The Carolingian Revival of Early Christian Architecture," *Art Bulletin*, 24 (1942), pp. 1–38.

[48] I do not contend that this explains the entire problem of geometricity in medieval architecture, since intensely geometrical concepts appear in many other areas of medieval art, especially in the field of book illumination where they cannot be explained as an offspring of an architectural way of thinking. The problem of medieval geometricity hence has still another dimension and can only be solved in its full complexity when it is possible to define the general mental (or metaphysical?) concepts which underlie these other forms of geometricity. But it cannot be denied that in timbered frame construction geometricity and unit sequence have an immediate constructional rationale which will have to be taken into consideration in any future discussion of this problem.

[49] "Et hanno più il modo da parer fatte di carta che di marmi." See Erwin Panofsky, "Das erste Blatt aus dem 'Libro' Giorgio Vasaris; eine Studie über die Beurteilung der Gotik in der italienischen Renaissance, etc.," *Städel-Jahrbuch*, VI (1930), pp. 25–72 . . . (cf. p. 43), translated into English in Panofsky's *Meaning in the Visual Arts* (New York, 1955), pp. 169–235 (cf. p. 189).

[50] Cf. Panofsky, *op. cit.*, *Städel-Jahrbuch*, pp. 39–40. *Meaning in the Visual Arts*, p. 182.

[51] Erwin Panofsky, *Gothic Architecture and Scholasticism* (Latrobe, 1951), p. 45.

[52] For Rusafa and Ruweha see Howard Crosby Butler, *Early Churches in Syria* (Princeton, 1929), pp. 145 ff., 161 ff. [A] reconstruction of St. Sergios basilica at Rusafa [is] reproduced in Friedrich Sarre and Ernst Herzfeld, *Archäologische Reise im Euphrat—und Tigris—Gebiet* (Berlin, 1920), II, 4, Fig. 133.

13. THE ROMANESQUE CHURCH AND ROMANESQUE DECORATION

Henri Focillon

INTRODUCTION

Henri Focillon's life with art began in childhood: his father, Victor Focillon, was an engraver and a friend of such artists as Monet and Rodin. In the method of Henri Focillon there is always the recurring motif of the relation between style and technique which could find no better evocation than his reference to the tools in his father's studio as being "warm with humanity and bright with use." The best introduction to his method is probably his *Vie des Formes,* published in 1934, and available in English translation as *The Life of Forms in Art,* issued shortly before his death in 1943. In this work he defines his concept of the evolution of styles, expressed in a format analogous to organic growth and implying some reproductive potentiality within the forms themselves. The application of this method—and the realization of its flexibility—is apparent in *The Art of the West in the Middle Ages,* in which the development of the forms of art takes place in a medium compounded of the inheritance of past traditions, the influences of the contemporary moment, and the experimental thrust into the future. For another schema treating the evolution of style, one should read George Kubler, *The Shape of Time* (1962).

Other readings are Arthur Kingsley Porter, *Medieval Architecture,* 2 vols. (1912), now available in a reprint (1966); by the same author,

Romanesque Sculpture of the Pilgrimage Roads, 10 vols. (1923), also available in a 1966 reprint; K. J. Conant, *Carolingian and Romanesque Architecture 800–1200*, 4th rev. ed. (1978); George H. Crichton, *Romanesque Sculpture in Italy* (1954); Corrado Ricci, *Romanesque Architecture in Italy* (1925); E. W. Anthony, *Romanesque Frescoes* (1951); A. Grabar and Carl Nordenfalk, *Romanesque Painting* (1958), with numerous colorplates; and Denis Grivot and George Zarnecki, *Gislebertus, Sculptor of Autun* (1961).

Additional works are Joan Evans, *Cluniac Art of the Romanesque Period* (1950); Whitney Stoddard, *Monastery and Cathedral in France* (1966); Peter Lasko, *Ars Sacra, 800–1200* (1972); H. E. Kubach, *Romanesque Architecture* (1975). Howard Saalman, *Medieval Architecture* (1962), is a brief survey, and George Zarnecki, *Romanesque Art* (1971), is a handy, well-illustrated picture book with short text. Otto Demus and Max Hirmer, *Romanesque Mural Painting* (1970), is a beautifully illustrated volume. Meyer Schapiro's *Romanesque Art: Selected Papers* (1977) is a collection of his own articles, published as the first volume in a series of anthologies drawn from his extensive publications. It contains his fine essay "On the Aesthetic Attitude in Romanesque Art" and articles on the sculptures of Souillac and Moissac, among others.

The selection that follows is reprinted from Henri Focillon, *The Art of the West in the Middle Ages*, I, edited and revised by Jean Bony, translated by Donald King (1963). Published by Phaidon Press Ltd., London. Footnotes marked with an asterisk indicate additions by Jean Bony.

The Romanesque Church and Romanesque Decoration

THE ROMANESQUE CHURCH

I

Even the most homogeneous style is defined only by the sequence of its development. As early as the eleventh century, Romanesque architecture had taken on a characteristic form marked by the systematic use of wall-arcades and flat pilasters, but it was simultaneously elaborating, in the course of a long series of experiments, the classic Romanesque forms whose apogee fell in the first third of the twelfth century. Historically significant monuments, ambitious programs, a single conception individually expressed by various regional groups and a beautiful and abundant sculpture dominated by the laws of the architecture—these were the main features of this superb moment of equilibrium, when images of God and of man, wrought from the building stone of the churches, mingled with the strangest fantasies of the human mind. The dreams of the most ancient East were reanimated, and embodied once more in figure-compositions; but the primacy of architecture imposed on them a logic, a profound harmony, which were the authentic expression of the West. This equilibrium, once achieved, was not overthrown by a sudden onset or insidious infiltration of new forms. Its stable principles and balanced clarity had emerged out of the flexible and many-sided researches of the experimental period, and they eventually lapsed again into a period of decline, marked by disorganization, ossification, and forgetfulness of the inherent laws of the style. We shall see that Romanesque art had its Baroque phase—using the word not in the limited sense of the historical period which followed the Renaissance, but as a designation for a state of mind whose recurrent manifestations appear in the lifetime of every style. It may be characterized on the one hand by academic dryness and the mechanical repetition of prototypes or, on the other, by forgetfulness of proper functions, profusion of ornament, and extravagant experiments, which call in question the value of acquired experience and the authority of the fundamental stylistic laws. But these destructive variations, these signs of weariness, incomprehension and forgetfulness, are in some sense a confirmation *a posteriori* (one might say, by *reductio ad absurdum*) of the value of the principles which they distort and deny. They are part of and they demonstrate the vitality of a style. If we were to content ourselves with a mere enumeration of the characteristics of Romanesque architecture and sculpture as if they were invariable data, neglecting the fact that they were in constant development from the late tenth to the early thirteenth century and beyond, we should be unable to appreciate all their aspects, which would often seem contradictory, and we should fail to perceive how those contradictions were harmonized by the hidden links which were forged between them by the evolution of the thought and life of the time.

In the monuments of the last third of the eleventh century and the first third of the twelfth, the Romanesque style is seen at the height of its powers. It was no mere passive expression of its place and time. Romanesque man comprehended himself through Romanesque art. The spirit of a great system of architectural thought was the keynote to which poetry, science, philosophy and language were attuned. Then, as never before, the spirit of form determined the form of the spirit. This stylistic maturity coincided with a historical maturity, which furthered it by the consistency of its aims, the boldness of its policies, the abundance of its resources and the moral force of its institutions, particularly those of urbanism and monasticism. Both the latter are forceful illustrations of the twofold character of the Middle Ages, at once sedentary and nomadic, local and European. Each town acted as a focus and magnet of its surrounding countryside, distilled its qualities, and concentrated in itself the peculiar local traditions and experiences. But at the same time the towns were all linked together by trade, and by the identity of their statutes, brought about by copying each other's charters—a fact of which we shall find remarkable confirmation in the Gothic period and which was not without influence, for example, on Burgundian art. Monasticism favored the interpenetration of localities to an even greater extent. By filiation, it propagated itself over enormous distances, and the monasteries were not only the refuge of exemplary Christians, detached from the life of their time, nor mere centers of meditation and culture, nor yet—in accordance with the spirit of their first foundation, renewed by the Cistercians—agricultural stations set up near a source of water for the purpose of tilling the virgin soil of desert places. For besides being planned, as they had already been in the Carolingian era, on the scale of towns, complete with schools, industrial and artistic workshops, scribes, blacksmiths and masons, they also intervened powerfully in the temporal destinies of the world, they cast a fine-meshed net over all Christendom, they were an organizing force and a focus of action. We should have a very inadequate understanding of the history of the early Middle Ages if we failed to take account of the expansion of Irish monachism. Similarly, in the Romanesque period, the political and moral stature of Cluny was outstanding.[1] It was a monarchy of monks, a monarchy of the spirit, ruled over by the abbot of Cluny, the abbot of abbots, whose moral authority was effective even beyond the organization of which he was head. The greatest of these abbots were both saints and leaders of men. Their community gave the Church several popes, numerous theologians, and a number of those great figures who, like St. Odo and St. Hugh, epitomize, and at the same time transfigure by their virtues, the age in which they live. Cluny, said Émile Mâle, was the greatest phenomenon of the Middle Ages. The modern development of orders vowed to contemplation or charity, and lying rather aside from the main currents of spiritual action (even when one takes into account the revival of institutions more exacting in their demands on the life of the spirit), provide no basis for our understanding of this immense priestly organization and its relations with the kings, emperors and popes, whom it often welcomed and entertained within the walls of its principal house. These great abbots were artists, not after the manner of princes enamored of pomp and architectural splendor, but in a more profound and fundamental way. They loved music so greatly that when they came to decorate their church they caused the capitals of the sanctuary to be carved with figures symbolizing the various modes of plainsong. They loved nobility and dignity of form even as embodied in corruptible flesh, and one of them extolled a predecessor for the perfection of his beauty. These men stand in the foreground of the history of Romanesque art, not indeed as initiators of its morphology and style, for the roots of those lay deeper, but in the capacity of organizers. They it was who chose the sites of its activity, or at least it was they who animated the roads along which stand its most important monuments.

Cluny organized the pilgrimages, and thereby became the moving spirit of that nomadic middle age which rolled in wave after unceasing wave down the roads which led towards Santiago de Compostela and the oratory of San Michele on Monte Gargano.[2] This does not mean—far from it—that Romanesque art is exclusively Cluniac and that its leading features are to be traced back to Cluny itself, nor even that it was strictly dependent on the geography of these far-flung routes. The significance of the pilgrimage roads lay in the fact that they traversed various regions, beckoning always towards foreign horizons and intermingling the sedentary and the travelling populace; while acting as channels for the propagation of artistic types, they also attracted to themselves the forces and traditions of the localities through which they passed and these tended both to swell and to modify the character of the waves of influence. At the stages of the journey they fostered the dissemination of the *chansons de geste*,[3] and in doing so they mingled one aspect of the Middle Ages with another. They magnified local saints into saints venerated throughout the Western world, and by permitting the transmission of images over great distances, they enriched the universal language of iconography. The old Roman roads had been instruments of Roman penetration. The pilgrimage roads had a twofold action. They may have contributed to the unity of Romanesque art, but they also ensured its variety.

II

In embarking on the study of the architecture which took its place in this system it is more than ever necessary that we should bear in mind the basic factors of the art of building.[4] A building is composed of plan, structure, composition of masses, and distribution of effects. The architect is simultaneously and to a greater or less degree geometer, engineer, sculptor and painter—geometer in the interpretation of spatial area through the plan, engineer in the solution of the problem of stability, sculptor in the treatment of volumes, and painter in the handling of materials and light. Each type of talent and each phase of a style lays stress on one particular aspect of the art; the perfect harmony is attained only in the great periods. The importance of the plan is primarily sociological, for it is the diagram, the graphic representation, of the program. The proportional relationships are indicative not only of the spirit of the style but also of the practical needs which the building is called upon to serve; the circlet of chapels radiating from the apse is not simply harmonious form but is necessitated by religious practice, while the curving ambulatory is designed to ensure a free flow of movement. For an eye accustomed to the study of architecture and the realization of the plan in space, the plan will suggest much more, and will even indicate the structural solutions. But one must remember that a building is not simply a matter of fitting a suitable elevation on to a pre-arranged plan, and the similarity of two plans does not necessarily and in every case entail the similarity of the composition of masses. Even though the plan is in some sense the abstract basis of these latter, yet they possess their own essential values, especially in a style which lays stress on the beauty of the masses, as does the Romanesque architecture of the twelfth century. They contribute to the stability of the building (here we are considering not a visual harmony, but actual resistance to thrust) and, arranged in order of size and of greater or less projection, they superimpose on the relationships of plane geometry a system of monumental relationships without which there would be no architecture, but only a diagram drawn out, like a flower-bed, on the ground. It is essential, particularly in Romanesque studies, to make the effort of considering a building as a collection of solids and of gauging the relationships between them. This manner of approach is doubly sound, since in Western architecture, at least in the period under discussion, the exterior masses invariably correspond with the internal distribution of parts and their three-dimensional relationships, so that the plan may be deduced from them, though the converse is not true. The truth of this observation may be demonstrated by a single example: a transept which does not project beyond the aisle-walls is hardly apparent on the plan. Finally the silhouette of a building, that most significant of values, results from the composition of masses.

The problems of structure and equilibrium, which are so important in large, complex, lofty, vaulted buildings such as those of the Romanesque period, arise mainly from the use of a stone covering, but this is not necessarily true in every case, since lofty walls surmounted by a wooden roof also require buttressing, though to a lesser extent, and northern and northeastern France, not to mention other areas, can show examples of this type of structure which are completely faithful to the spirit and style of their time in plan, mass and effects. A building is not carved or hollowed out of a monolith, but *constructed,* that is, composed of separate elements, assembled according to rules in which the architect figures as an interpreter of the force of gravity. The Greeks opposed the action of gravity in the vertical direction only. The medieval masters in most cases had to solve a problem involving oblique components and the counteraction of thrust, and, by an admirable process of reasoning, they progressively specialized each member of the structure according to its function, and devised for it a form which was at once the most suitable and the most expressive of its purpose. It is in this respect that their architecture is most truly an art of logical thought, whereas the Greeks, having adopted once for all the straightforward solution of verticals and horizontals, were thereafter interested only in melodic variations of the proportions.

Besides being an interpreter of gravity the architect is also an interpreter of light, by virtue of the calculation and composition of his effects. This question must not be limited to the problems of lighting, though they in themselves are of capital importance, and we shall see how intimately they were linked with the problems of structure and equilibrium, and how their solutions evolved throughout the Middle Ages in step with the structural solutions. But the study of effects is of wider scope. It concerns the relationships of void and solid, of light and dark, and—perhaps most important—of plain and decorated. Again, a building is not an architect's drawing or a photographic print, it is composed of solid matter. It is obvious that this fact has specific and far-reaching effects on every detail of the treatment. It is of fundamental importance for the structure, since the various kinds of material have their own peculiar qualities and requirements, and these determine the functions which they can perform, the types of masonry for which they can be used, and the extent of the program to which they can be applied. Materials, moreover, have texture and color, and with these they make a pleasing and powerful contribution to the life of architecture, which is not intended merely for technical analysis and dissection but for the delight of the eye. They play their part within the system of relationships which we have just outlined, here stressing the solid, the broad luminous surface, the monumental economy of ornament, and there emphasizing the void, the equivocal effect of light and shade, and the profusion of carving; thus, though the vocabulary of forms may be constant, syntax, language and poetry are constantly recreated.

The elements can be isolated intellectually, but it must not be forgotten that they exist together, and that it is their organic interconnection, not their juxtaposition, which makes the building. We already have some idea of the interdependence of plan and structure, plan and masses, masses and equilibrium, and masses and effects. The architect conceives his building synthetically. Even in the first flash of an idea, his thought includes the diversity of the parts. Admittedly, of course, the genius of a school, a locality or a master may concentrate on one particular aspect. There are builders and there are decorators. But a medieval building is a harmony of living forces which mutually penetrate, amplify, restrain, modify and define each other. The interrelationship of the masses, and the various relationships by which the effects are qualified, are transformed from top to bottom, from pavement to rooftree, and in every dimension of the architecture. Each individual member shares in the life of the organism as a whole. And what is true of the Gothic skeleton of arches and ribs is no less so for the massive Romanesque structure of compact vaults and thick walls, as a more detailed examination will show. We are compelled to deal with the elements one by one, but we must never lose sight of the fact that these elements are all functions of each other. And when we analyze the regional varieties of Romanesque architecture, which testify so strikingly to its historical vigor, we shall find that they owe their individuality not so much to what may perhaps be called their superficial features, or to the treatment of details, as to modifications of the interrelationship of parts. In this respect they constitute dialectal varieties comparable with the various romance idioms.

The program of the Romanesque basilicas was that of an enormous reliquary open to all comers. The monastic church of the time served both monks and pilgrims. It sheltered the bodies of the saints and attracted the devotion of the faithful. Renowned relics, the miracles wrought by them, the pious legends which surrounded them, the cult which exalted their virtues, the enhanced value of prayer uttered beside them—all this intense spiritual fervor created the prosperity of the great abbeys, and at once necessitated and made possible the grandeur of their scale. As in the progress of cities, demand created supply. The plan of the pilgrimage churches is as if drawn by the immense throngs which passed through them, by the order of their going and of their standing still, the places where they stopped and the places where they moved onward. Sometimes a great narthex, a survival of the old church of the catechumens, precedes the church, and serves as its vestibule, though large enough, with its central nave, aisles and upper storey, to form a separate church. The church proper has three, and sometimes five, naves. It was thus enabled to impose order on the multitudes within, by cutting parallel furrows in the moving mass. One or two transepts, with oriented chapels opening off them, form two or four projections on the plan, each one so large that it seems an additional church set at right angles to the first. But they did not interrupt the progress of the pilgrim. They provided the throng with auxiliary entrances and exits, and they formed part of that architectural topography of pilgrimage which permitted of uninterrupted circulation within the building, from the west front to the chapels of the apse and from the chapels of the apse back to the west front. Sometimes, as in Saint-Sernin at Toulouse (Fig. 42), a continuous aisle surrounds the transept arm, extends along the choir, makes the circuit of the apse, and so returns. The long choir favored the development of ceremony. But it was the east end which, in both plan and elevation, in both the establishment of the program and the treatment of the masses, was the vital part of the church. Here are disposed the chapels which sheltered the relics of the saints, in addition to those which in some cases were preserved in the crypt, as in the martyrium of the primitive basilica. The most frequent arrangement is that in which small apses radiate from the ambulatory, a scheme whose earliest examples we have already noted in the second half of the tenth century; this was the best arrangement from the point of view of circulation. But a whole family of churches preserved the orientation of the apses by disposing chapels of diminishing scale in echelon; and this plan was best from the point of view of presentation, the chapels being parallel to one another and opening directly on to choir and transepts. This scheme is known as the Benedictine or Berry plan, though it is not confined to that province. The finest and most characteristic example is perhaps that of Châteaumeillant. But it was the radiating plan which prevailed, and Romanesque art, which had received it from the Carolingian tradition, bequeathed it in due time to its Gothic successor. . . .

42. St. Sernin, Toulouse. Romanesque, *c.* 1080–1120 (Reprinted by permission of Penguin Books Ltd. from Kenneth John Conant, *Carolingian and Romanesque Architecture 800–1200* [1974 paperback edition], p. 159, Fig. 113 [4], Architectural plan for St. Sernin, Toulouse. © Kenneth John Conant, 1959, 1966, 1974)

a. Aerial view, St. Sernin, Toulouse (Reportage Photographique Yan)

ROMANESQUE DECORATION

I

. . . At first sight how remote from us [Romanesque sculpture] seems! Is it possible that this is ours—this strange vision, entwined so mysteriously with the stone and inscribing the walls of the buildings with fancies which are often indecipherable, like the characters of a lost language? Can it be that our conception of man, life and the world is divided by such an abyss from that of our forebears? In Gothic sculpture we recognize ourselves, we find our own kind of humanity; it remains our contemporary, almost our neighbor—much more so than Renaissance sculpture, which was based upon the resuscitation of an earlier age for which we can no longer feel more than an intellectual sympathy and admiration. The endless ranks of images which fill the Gothic cathedrals evoke in us a kind of spiritual kinship, which we freely acknowledge; in many ways even, they are like a vivid recollection of our past life, our own past, and that of our towns, our suburbs and our country-side. We can name the animals and the plants, and the saints with their workingmen's faces who stand in the doorways are of the same race as our own fathers. But wherever we turn, the images of Romanesque art disconcert us by their composition and their sentiment. It is an art abundant in monsters, visions, and enigmatic symbols. It seems at first sight much older than the age which it so faithfully expresses and the architecture to which it so exactly conforms.

Let us study it first as a system of signs before we attempt to interpret it as a system of forms. Every art is language, in two ways—once by its choice of subjects, once by its treatment of them. Iconography floodlights the life of the spirit. It is not a collection of symbols, a vocabulary, or a key; the novelty of M. Mâle's studies[5] consists in the widening of its horizons and the deepening of its perspectives, both historical and moral, to form a broad and detailed panorama of the spiritual life of the past. Romanesque iconography was epic. It bestowed super-human proportions on God-made-man and man-in-the-image-of-God; sometimes even it gave them an appearance divorced from humanity. It surrounded them with a cortège of monsters which entwine them in their coils. To expound and present them to the people it chose, as a terrible warning, the most extraordinary page of the whole Bible. The story of the Last Days, foretold in words of fire by an enthusiast filled with the afflatus of the Jewish Bible, inspired it with majestic terror. The seer roused the visionaries. The faithful entering the church were not welcomed by the evangelic Christ of the thirteenth-century *trumeau*, but compelled to file beneath the tympanum of the Last Judgment as if they themselves were about to hear their sentence from the mouth of the inflexible Judge. At La Lande de Cubzac, the sword of the Word flashes from the lips of the Apocalyptic Christ, who stands beside the symbolic candelabrum, holding in his hand the book sealed with seven seals. In a less strange guise, alone or flanked by two angels who seem to fan the flames of the glory which surrounds Him, it is this same God of the Apocalypse who figures on the old Aragonese tympana, at Perrecy-les-Forges in Burgundy and Mauriac in Auvergne, and who finally, in the second half of the twelfth century, appears again and again in monotonous profusion, accompanied by the tetramorph of Evangelists, above the portals of northern France. But it was particularly in the tympana of Languedoc, in the first half of the century, that the theme was developed with the full amplitude of the epic. Christ the Judge, whose kingdom is founded on the destruction of the universe and the punishment of sinners, emerges from the mystery of the end of time like an apparition suddenly risen before the eyes of His terror-stricken followers. Surrounded by convulsive shapes, He is accompanied by the twenty-four Elders carrying lamps and viols. At Beaulieu there appears behind Him the cross of His sacrifice, and of the redemption of mankind. Even when, as at Vézelay, He is the Christ of Pentecost, charging the Apostles with their mission,[6] He is still a terrible God. The Oriental Potentate of Moissac is Lord of a world from which the Good Shepherd of the catacombs, the Christ of Psamathia, and all those figures of Hellenistic Christianity who still combined divinity with youth and harmonious beauty have passed away. One might believe that the Romanesque Apocalypse trembled still with millenarian terrors, passed on by Beatus' illustrated commentary, which served as its guide through this Divine Comedy in stone. There is a breath of the East in these strange figures, this fearful conception of the Master of Days. Yet the same epic spirit, the same legendary disproportions, the same superhuman quality, are characteristic of the tales of knightly prowess created, at the same time and often at the same places, out of the recollection and imagination of the peoples of the West. The God of the sculptors and the heroes of the poets are ornaments of the same horizon of thought: the visionary theology of Scotus Eriugena, if it did not directly inspire the iconography, helps us at least to understand its intellectual climate. The unity of the period is not founded on a congeries of completely heterogeneous borrowings; unfamiliar elements were welcomed because they responded to a need, and we shall see how they were subsequently elaborated.

The stories of the Gospels and the lives of the saints, and still more the representation of the world, are touched with the same strangeness, and many details betray the remoteness of their origin. Sir Arthur Evans has recently shown that the theme of the Adoration of the Kings goes back to the remotest antiquity,[7] and it should be observed that already on Sumerian monuments it is accompanied by the motif of the guiding star. In Syria, Mesopotamia, Transcaucasia and Egypt the East Christian communities were the heirs of an iconographical tradition built up over thousands of years; they in turn devised new elements and established stereotypes which fixed the images for the future. The three cycles of Nativity, Passion, and Parables, the essential chapters of the iconography of the Gospels, are full of Oriental features, whose history and diffusion can be followed from the throne of Maximian and the ampullae of Monza down to Romanesque times. The Byzantine drama *Christos Paskon*,[8] whose influence is vouched for by numerous manuscripts, spread the knowledge of the *mise en scène* of the Resurrection and the other episodes centered on the Tomb. The prophets of the Coming of Christ were born of the Biblical East and insinuated themselves into still older Oriental forms. Daniel standing between the lions who lick his feet is Gilgamesh, the master of animals in Assyrian art. An Oriental silk at Saint-Maurice d'Agaune in Valais, the national sanctuary of the Burgundians, shows the manner in which these themes were able in the early Middle Ages to penetrate the West and to become invested with a Christian significance, before they made their appearance on Romanesque capitals. Thus we find the Biblical and Gospel figures intimately linked with the oldest images of Asia,[9] and even when they are of more recent origin, they have very often been composed and fixed in the East. Hence the indisputably exotic tonality in the choice and treatment of subjects.

The Romanesque Church and Romanesque Decoration

This quality of Romanesque iconography strikes us still more forcibly when we consider the number and the strangeness of the monsters which inhabit it. Man himself loses his identity and, obedient to the law of metamorphosis by which this universe is constantly created, broken down and recomposed, he also assumes a monstrous guise. Even when probability is respected, the animal life is of bewildering variety. The bestiary of the steppes, which had been diffused by the invasions, and the Asiatic fauna which had filled Visigothic manuscripts such as the Sacramentary of Gellone and now reappeared, often in copies after Arabic ivories, introduced into the churches the menagerie, the "paradise" of the Oriental monarch. But, seized by that hidden power which remolded living creatures to its own needs, and conferred on them a multiple existence more mobile and passionate than life itself, the animals are subdivided, reunited, acquire two heads on one body or two bodies for one head, gripe one another, devour one another, and are again reborn, all in an indecipherable tumultuous *mêlée*. What name can we give, what meaning assign to these fancies, which seem to emanate from the caprice or delirium of a solitary visionary and which yet recur throughout Romanesque art, like the images of some vast collective nightmare? Of what virtues, what sins are they the incarnation? At times we seem on the point of penetrating these symbols, but immediately they flicker away into the monstrous inanity of the compositions.

Such are the general characteristics of this iconography. It is rich in Oriental elements. It is epical and teratological. It gives us the epic of God, the epic of the end of the world, and the epic of chaos. Is there not a singular contradiction between the order of the churches and the tumult of these images, between the rules of an architecture whose strength, stability and logic we have been at pains to demonstrate, and the rules of an iconography between whose transfiguration of God and deformation of His creatures one may scarcely find a middle term, between structures dominated by a conception of plan and masses which is purely Western, and an iconography which derives most of its resources from the East? Only the study of the forms permits us to resolve this apparent contradiction; it will likewise assist us to make a true assessment of influences, and it will also demonstrate the profound harmony of thought between the technique of the Romanesque decorative artist and the intellectual technique of his period.

II

This technique had a twofold character: it was architectural, in that the figures were made to conform to their architectural setting and it was ornamental, in that the figures were drawn and composed in accordance with ornamental schemes. In our brief study of the experiments carried out in the course of the eleventh century we have already caught a glimpse of some of the earliest applications of these principles and of the manner in which they tended—in opposition to the academic forms of antique art and in alliance with the abstract repertory which had become diffused through Europe—to substitute for the verisimilitude of the images their just adaptation to a surrounding frame, and to replace the harmony and proportions of life by the harmony and proportions of an abstract system. The forms of architecture and the forms of life being fixed, what compromise could be established between them? Romanesque architecture did not offer indifferent fields to the decorator, but fields whose shape and function were clearly defined. The genius of the style lay in its association of sculpture with these functions. By adopting once for all the frieze-system, which had flourished in the eleventh century alongside more adventurous lines of research, it would have renounced its fundamental originality. It might also have allowed sculpture to flow indifferently over the wall-surfaces, and assimilated it to those severe and powerful masses in truly monumental beauty: but sculpture in architecture and for architecture demanded a much stricter economy. Where is it found, in a twelfth-century church? On capitals, tympana and archivolts. True, it did not altogether abandon the friezes and the arcades, but its development depended on the more tyrannical constraint exercised by frames which were ill-adapted to receive the image of life. Yet these frames seized upon sculpture, bestowed on it a new passion, imposed on it movement, mimicry and drama. To enter the system of the stone, man was forced to bend forward or lean backward, to stretch or contract his limbs, to become a giant or a dwarf. He preserved his identity at the cost of unbalance and deformation; he remained man, but a man of plastic material, obedient—not to the caprice of an ironical idea—but to the exigencies of a system which comprehended the entire structure.

Romanesque art was to make the church "speak"; space had to be found for an abundant iconography, without disturbing the architectural masses and their functions. It was necessary to set on top of the columns, at the same time avoiding the appearance of meagerness and insignificance, not one or two figures—Christ in Majesty, St. Anne and St. Elizabeth, Adam and Eve—which could easily be disposed axially or confronted, but the more numerous actors of the Nativity, the Flight into Egypt or the Last Supper. We must remember that it was in the Corinthian capital that human figures first began to be inserted; they were abducted from the charms of continuous narrative, the storyteller's dispersal of effects, and wedded to architecture, grouped in a colleret of figures or assigned the role of atlantes. In the course of this treatment the living organism was twisted out of shape and out of proportion, but it gained thereby an unexpected eloquence. Bound by every limb to the block of stone, and bound by the continuity of the movement to its companions, which are a prolongation and multiplication of itself, it gave rise to compact systems from which the removal of a single element would entail the ruin of the massive unity of the whole. The loose narrative of the frieze-style was succeeded by the complex strength of drama, with its concentrated impact, and its mimicry accentuated by the deformation of the actors. This architectural conformity did not operate only within the framework of the Corinthian capital. The cushion capital also, when it accepted figure decoration, submitted it to the same discipline. So too, did the capital formed like a truncated and inverted pyramid; and when the capitals of conjoined or adjacent columns were adorned with a single composition, the bridging of the gap between the two masses produced some unexpected but logical applications of the same principle.

A similar problem, but with rather different data, was set by the decorations of the archivolts. How could the image of man, and, in a more general sense, the image of life, be accommodated within the arch-moldings which curve around the semi-circular tympanum? . . . The decoration of the moldings is sometimes disposed radially, while at other times it follows the curve of the arch. In the former case, each voussoir is treated as a unit and closely contains the figure or ornament which it receives—bearers of offerings following one another in procession up to the keystone and down again on the other side, horses' heads, and ornamental frets worked in the stone as in ivory or ironwork. In the latter case, the figure occupies several voussoirs, bending with the arch; a body may cross the keystone, or the heads of two symmetrical bodies may be confronted there; the living creature becomes an architectural curve and is identified with the molding itself. The whole of southwestern France is rich in these surprising configurations. . . . Human figures sometimes try to escape to some extent from this narrow bondage. Instead of the radial or circumferential position, they take up a tangential one, forming with the curve of the arch an angle which hardly ever varies. The elongated bodies stand erect or bend over within the arch, their bellies slightly prominent, and punctuated by a spot of shadow between the thighs. . . .

The composition of a tympanum is not determined by a vague symmetry. Its elements must be both deployed and concentrated. Its lower and wider part extends to very nearly the same length as the lintel on which its rests. The upper segment narrows rapidly. The two parts are held together by the radii of the arch. A fan-shaped composition would seem to be the most favorable and harmonious solution, but the Romanesque sculptors by no means restricted themselves to that alone. Sometimes they made it more complex by the insertion of a triangular pediment, which is not outlined by projecting moldings, but is visible in the lines of heads which rise toward the central axis (and emphasized, as at Vézelay, by the fiery rays emanating from the hands of Christ), or may be suggested, in less elaborate compositions, by the movement of the mandorla-carrying angels as they bow down before the glory of God. Sometimes they subdivided it so as to obtain, with the help of some curvilinear triangles, a collection of rectangular frames, as at Cahors, and Carennac. Sometimes the composition blossoms like a flower or a palmette, with living figures forming the lobes. It was the special function of the monsters to contort themselves to suit these various schemes, but man also conformed. In accordance with a kind of morphological perspective, which, though equivalent with hierarchic perspective, yet precedes it in the structural and logical order, and is more insistent in its demands, the witnesses and actors of these impressive scenes, the attendants of the throne of heaven, increase in scale in proportion to their nearness to the Deity, who alone occupies the center and towers up to the full height of the tympanum.

. . . Finally, we may mention a class of rectangular panels, decorating *trumeaux* and doorjambs, which reveal to us one of the most curious aspects of this technique. The principle of exact conformity to the frame, strictly applied, results (there are many examples) in creatures of absolutely geometrical shape—the circle-men, like the delightful acrobat on the keystone of the archivolt at Vézelay, above the Zodiac, the lozenge-men, and the rectangle-men. But this last shape, once defined, could never satisfy the manifold demands of the iconography, which required other heroes than these massive witnesses, and especially they were unfitted to share in that restless movement with which Romanesque art is filled. Hence the figure conterminous with its frame was displaced by the figure which touched its frame at the greatest possible number of points. With elbow, shoulder, knee, and heel the body, whose parts are disposed on multiple axes, makes contact with the limits of the enclosing field, and thus describes a whole series of triangles. In this way there was produced a family of figures which, even in their immobility, enliven the firm and ponderous masses of Romanesque architecture with ceaseless movement; this sculpture, though dominated by the laws of a massive equilibrium, presents itself in the guise of a series of experimental studies in motion (Fig. 43). . . . To a superficial observer this interpretation might seem a product of vain ingenuity, and this geometric grid a device to support a preconceived system. But the album of Villard de Honnecourt[10] provides, *a posteriori*, a brilliant confirmation. This Picard master-mason, whose notebook testifies to an insatiable curiosity, fed by wide experience, and foreign travel, resurrected some aspects of the "lost art," whose rules had been forgotten by his contemporaries and of which, after him, there seems to be no trace. By insisting on the interest of what he calls the "art de jométrie" and by divulging the secret of the triangulation of figures, he confirms the historical importance, the authenticity, and the systematic character of the processes which we have analyzed.

Architectural conformity and the use of geometric schemes, even if they are the fundamental characteristics of Romanesque technique, do not in themselves account for all its aspects. This essentially architectural sculpture was devised for particular positions and for frames which determined its arrangement and movement; but it is also ornamental—it established or rather modeled its image of life in accordance with the forms of ornament. The man, the beast and the monster are not only volute, medallion, molding, wall-mass, or function, they are not assembled only in accordance with the broad lines of a geometric scheme; they are also palmette

43. Prophet Isaiah, from abutment of doorway, monastery church of Notre Dame, Souillac. Romanesque, Early 12th Century (Marburg-Art Reference Bureau)

and foliage-scroll. Recent research,[11] the point of departure for which was provided by the juxtaposition of a design composed of ornament in the pure state, and a figure composition in which its main lines are exactly reproduced, as if the sculptor wished to leave beside his work the key to its understanding, has brought to light the prodigious decorative "underpainting" of Romanesque sculpture. Moreover, if we envisage the ornament not as a static vocabulary or a collection of invariable formulae but as a dialectic or multiple development in which each term may be deduced from its predecessor, we find that the dialectic of the figure sculpture reproduces, in its movement and variety, that of the ornament. Three primary motifs—the foliage-scroll, the heart (with or without a palmette), and the motif formed by setting two foliage-scrolls back to back about a central axis—give rise to a large number of ornamental variations whose forms and interrelationships reappear in many of the figure compositions of Romanesque sculpture. If it were merely a question of explaining in this way the symmetries of confronted and addorsed objects, or the genesis of the monsters with two heads or two bodies, this fact would amount to no more than evidence of a very common and widespread habit, though it would still be noteworthy, since it was abandoned by European art after the twelfth century. But in fact there is a complete system, an immense variety of forms which can only be explained by the dialectic of ornament. An inexhaustible vitality, differing from organic life, and of even greater richness and multiplicity, but as highly organized, arises out of, and owes its diversity to, these abstract devices, and modulates its variations according to their variations. Very ancient motifs, such as the sea-siren with the double tail, were also admitted to this realm of forms, not as alien elements arbitrarily inserted or passive recipients of influence, but because they, too, had originated in an ornamental idea, whose shape and aptitude for life they still preserved, and were ready participants in the play of metamorphoses. In the setting within which this process of transformation operates, it links together all the movements, leaving no single gesture unconnected, and ensures that all the parts interlock and interpenetrate, so that each block of ornament in pictorial guise is like a small separate world, close-knit and compact, a law unto itself. The great complex compositions of the tympana are very often the expanded and diversified, yet quite regular, version of an ornamental motif which runs through the whole, controlling and influencing every detail. The epic of the Last Day, the Adoration of the Kings, and all the other stories and visions, adorned the stones of the churches with a mysterious flora, with the characters of a hidden language, by which their own poetic content was enhanced. Thus the study of the technique of Romanesque sculpture has revealed to us a poetry and a psychology. The feeling and subtlety of the dialectical process as applied to these forms runs parallel with the dialectic of pure thought. It is not without significance that both church-decoration and the scholasticism of the period were equally dominated by the philosophy of abstraction, and that both groups of purist logicians were given to the spinning of elegant formal patterns. But whereas the dialectician lost himself in a labyrinth of unprofitable composition, the sculptor, in conjunction with the architect, was creating a new world, extending the limits of man's experience, and giving shape and form to his wildest fantasies.

NOTES

¹ E. Mâle, *L'art français et l'art allemand du moyen âge*, pp. 93–4. Gregory VII, Urban II and Paschal II had been Cluniac monks. On the constitution of Cluny see V. Mortet, *Note sur la date de rédaction des Coutumes de Farfa* (Mâcon, 1911). ° More recently: G. de Valous, *Le monachisme clunisien des origines au XVe siècle* (Ligugé and Paris, 1936); J. Evans, *The Romanesque Architecture of the Order of Cluny* (Cambridge, 1938), and *Cluniac Art of the Romanesque Period* (Cambridge, 1950); to which must be added: Société des amis de Cluny, C. Oursel, ed., *A. Cluny, Congrés scientifique* . . . , 9–11 *juillet* 1949 (Dijon, 1950).

² The *Book of St. James*, a fine copy of which is preserved in the chapter-library at Compostela, was written to assist pilgrims, probably by the monks of Cluny, at some date after 1139. See J. Bédier, *Légendes épiques*, III, p. 75; E. Mâle, *L'art religieux du XIIe siècle en France*, p. 291 and notes 3 and 4. The fourth book of the Compostela Codex was published by Père Fita, Paris, 1882. In addition, see Lavergne, *Les chemins de Saint-Jacques en Gascogne* (Bordeaux 1887) Dufourcet, *Les voies romaines et les chemins de Saint-Jacques*, Congrès archéologique de Dax et Bayonne, 1888; Abbé Daux, *Le pèlerinage de Saint-Jacques de Compostelle* (*Paris* 1898), cited by Mâle, *op. cit.*, p. 289, note, and Ginot, *Les chemins de Saint-Jacques en Poitou* (Poitiers, 1912). The part played by the pilgrimage roads in the history of architecture was first studied by the Abbé Bouillet, the historian of Conques and Sainte-Foy, in Mémoires de la Société des Antiquaires de France, 1892, p. 117. The Via Tolosana linked Provence with Languedoc, and leaving Arles, continued by way of Saint-Gilles du Gard, Toulouse, and the Somport pass. The stages of the Auvergne route were Le Puy, Congues, Moissac. A third route connected Burgundy and Aquitaine, from Vézelay to Saint-Léonard and Perigueux. The fourth and last, leaving Tours, traversed Poitou and Saintonge, and passed by way of Bordeaux to join the two preceding routes at Roncevaux, where they crossed the Pyrenees. Each route was an unbroken chain of sanctuaries. The pilgrimage road from France into Italy, crossing the alps by the Great St. Bernard or Mont Cenis passes, joined the Emilian Way via Modena, then the Cassian Way at Arezzo, reaching Rome by way of Viterbo. Influences travelled back and forth along the roads of St. Michael just as they did along those of St. James. On the relationship between Sant' Antimo in Tuscany and Conques, see J. Vallery-Radot. *Églises romanes*, p. 178, and on that between San Michele of Clusa and Le Puy, id., *ibid.*, pp. 176, 177, and the study by E. de Dienne, Congrès archéologique de Puy, 1904. °The most recent editions of the Guide for the Pilgrims of St. James are by J. Vieillard (Mâcon, 1938), and by W. M. Whitehill (Santiago, 1944). See also P. David, *Études sur le livre de Saint-Jacques*, Bulletin des Études Portugaises, Vols. 10–12, 1946–1948.

³ It is well known that the *chansons de geste*, according to Gaston Paris, are the ultimate fruit of centuries of composition whereas for J. Bédier, *Les légendes épiques*, 2nd ed. (Paris, 1914–21), they arose from the pilgrimages themselves. Note also the observations of G. Cohen, *La civilisation occidentale au moyen âge*, p. 211, where he indicates on the one hand the part played in the poems by geography and the northern abbeys, and on the other the continuity of poetic tradition attested by a ninth-century text such as the *Chanson de Saint-Faron de Meaux.*

° 4 H. Focillon has expressed the same views in *Vie des formes* (Paris, 1934), translated as *The Life of Forms in Art* (New Haven, 1942, and New York, 1948).

5 *L'art religieux du XIIe siècle en France* (Paris, 1924), chaps. I, IV.

° 6 On the iconographic meaning of the Vézelay tympanum, see A. Katzenellenbogen, *The Central Tympanum at Vézelay*, Art Bulletin, 1944, pp. 141–151. . . .

° 7 A. J. Evans, *The Earlier Religion of Greece in the Light of Cretan Discoveries* (London, 1931).

8 See V. Cottas, *Le théâtre à Byzance* (Paris, 1931), and *Le drame Christos Paskon* (Paris, 1931).

° 9 See J. Baltrusaitis, *Art sumérien, art roman* (Paris, 1934).

10 Bibliothèque Nationale, ms. fr. 19, 093. First published by Lassus and Darcel (1858), then by H. Omont in the series of phototype albums issued by the department of manuscripts, and most recently by Hans R. Hahnloser (Vienna, 1935).

11 J. Baltrusaitis, *La stylistique ornementale dans la sculpture romane* (Paris, 1931), chap. 5, VII, p. 273, L'animal (genèse des monstres); VIII, p. 301, Le personnage. The method followed in this remarkable book has revolutionized the subject.

14. THE ICONOGRAPHY OF A ROMANESQUE TYMPANUM AT VÉZELAY

Adolf Katzenellenbogen

INTRODUCTION

This selection examines the arrangement and subject matter of the central tympanum in the narthex of Sainte-Madeleine at Vézelay, and proposes a web of meanings in which the prophecies of Isaiah, the old mission of the Apostles, and the new mission of the crusaders have been harmonically interwoven. A fine example of iconographical analysis, this selection has the added interest of linking the complex program of this tympanum to the historical events of the era and to the guiding genius of the theologian, Peter the Venerable. This tympanum is accorded considerable emphasis from another standpoint—its form and composition—in Meyer Schapiro, *Romanesque Art: Selected Papers* (1977), pp. 265–284.

With respect to the fantastic creatures who appear on this relief, the reader may wish to consult such works at T. H. White (ed. and trans.), *The Book of Beasts, Being a Translation from a Latin Bestiary of the Twelfth Century* (1954), or Ernst and Johanna Lehner, *A Fantastic Bestiary: Beasts and Monsters in Myth and Folklore* (1969).

Among other works by the late Adolf Katzenellenbogen are *Allegories of the Virtues and Vices in Mediaeval Art* (1939); "The Prophets on the West Facade of the Cathedral of Amiens," *Gazette des Beaux-Arts*, S.6, XL (1952); and *The Sculptural Programs of Chartres Cathedral* (1959), which was awarded the Charles Rufus Morey Prize by the College Art Association as the best book in the history of art to be published in 1959.

This selection is reprinted from Adolf Katzenellenbogen, "The Central Tympanum at Vézelay: Its Encyclopedic Meaning and Its Relation to the First Crusade," *The Art Bulletin*, XXVI (1944), by permission of Elisabeth Katzenellenbogen (Mrs. A.).

The central tympanum in the narthex of the Abbey Church of Sainte-Madeleine at Vézelay, which was created between about 1120 and 1132, has proved to be one of the most tempting and brittle iconographical enigmas of medieval art (Fig. 44). Its explanation has been attempted time and again with a wide variety of results.[1] In more recent years the conflicting opinions have been narrowed down to two different interpretations, established by Émile Mâle and Abel Fabre.[2]

Émile Mâle has related the program of the tympanum to the events on the day of Pentecost. He has explained the central scene as the *Descent of the Holy Spirit* with Christ Himself bestowing the rays of heavenly grace on His apostles. The numerous groups of figures surrounding the central scene in the eight compartments of the archivolt and on the lintel represent those nations to whom the apostles will preach the gospel, now that they are endowed with the power to speak in all languages. Monstrous races are among these nations. According to medieval belief, they live at the ends of the earth. In the archivolt some people are characterized as being sick. They are already experiencing the miracle-working of the apostles. On the left side of the lintel, however, the groups who offer their gifts and bring a sacrificial bull still remain faithful to their old erroneous belief, but the word of the Lord will reach them too.

According to Abel Fabre the central scene represents the Mission which Christ gave to His apostles immediately before His Ascension.

The apparent discrepancy between the two interpretations which relate the central scene either to the Pentecost or to the day of Ascension may find a solution if one considers briefly the meaning of the tympanum decorating the western portal of the church at Anzy-le-Duc (*c.* 1125).[3] Here the problem is similar, although less complex. The tympanum represents the *Ascension of Christ,* a favorite theme of Burgundian Romanesque sculpture. The enthroned Christ, whose mandorla is held by two angels, occupies the center of the tympanum, while Mary and the twelve apostles, who are

44. Tympanum: The Mission of the Apostles, Center Portal of Narthex, Ste-Madeleine, Vézelay, 1120–1132 (Marburg-Art Reference Bureau)

the witnesses of the Ascension, are rendered on the lintel. Yet the program of the tympanum is not restricted to this event. It also gives visible form to the prediction of the second coming of Christ which the two Men in White made to the apostles: "This same Jesus, which is taken up from you into heaven, shall so come in like manner as ye have seen Him go into heaven."[4] The second coming of Christ, an event still remote at the time of His Ascension, does not remain just a prediction, but is actually represented. In the archivolt the twenty-four Elders are shown as the witnesses of His coming at the end of time. Thus the tympanum gains a twofold meaning. If Christ is considered in context with the figures on the lintel, He is the Christ of the Ascension, if in context with the Elders of the archivolt, the apocalyptic Christ. Two events are clearly telescoped to make the meaning of the tympanum more comprehensive. The triumphant return of Christ to heaven is merged with His triumphant reappearance to judge mankind.

The fact that different events are telescoped here may justify an analogous interpretation of the more complicated aspects of the Vézelay tympanum. Its main literary source may be found in Acts 1:4–9. Just before He was taken up and received by a cloud, Christ prophesied to His apostles that they would receive the power of the Holy Spirit and be His witnesses unto the uttermost part of the earth. In my opinion, just as at Anzy-le-Duc the theme of the *Ascension of Christ* is expanded by giving visible form to the prediction of His second coming, so at Vézelay the *Ascension of Christ* is supplemented by the sculptural rendering of His predictions. The promise of the giving of the Holy Spirit is represented by the rays emanating from His hands. The reference to the future missionary work of the apostles is illustrated on lintel and archivolt by the representatives of the various nations, some of whom were supposed to live at the edge of the world. Thus the representation of the ascending Christ who leaves His apostles and is received into a cloud is merged with the *Mission of the Apostles* and with the giving of complete and final power through the Holy Spirit in what may be called an encyclopedic representation of the Mission. Such a telescoping might have been suggested by the summarizing sentence (Acts 1:2): "Until the day in which He was taken up, after that He through the Holy Ghost had given commandments unto the apostles whom He had chosen."

This interpretation may also be corroborated by the fact that until the fourth century A.D. the Ascension of Christ was celebrated on the afternoon of the day of Pentecost and that a continuous pictorial tradition represents the two events on the same page of manuscripts or even fuses them in a compositional unity.[5]

It seems to me that a more precise analysis, which is based not only on the text of the New Testament, but considers also certain passages of the Old Testament and the historical situation in the epoch of the crusades, can further clarify the meaning of the tympanum. Not merely a general idea is represented here; a program of an astonishing preciseness, of an encyclopedic complexity and of a crystalline clarity seems to have been translated into visible terms. It must have been conceived by an outstanding theologian.

I shall first try to analyze this program, then to relate it to the historical events at the time of its creation. Finally I shall venture to identify the author of the program.

317

I

The encyclopedic *Mission* on the Vézelay tympanum seems to be strongly influenced by Old Testament prophecies referring to the coming salvation of mankind. It also indicates in a definite manner three specific tasks and the power to perform them, which Christ had given to His apostles:

He had given them the power to save or to condemn (Matt. 18:18; Mark 16:16; John 20:23).

He had sent them out into the world to preach the gospel to all the nations (Matt. 28:19), or, as St. Mark says, to every creature (16:15), so that they would be His witnesses unto the uttermost part of the earth (Acts 1:8).

He had given them the command and the power to heal the sick and to drive out devils (Matt. 10:1, 8; Mark 16:17, 18; Luke 9:1).

The task of saving or condemning is indicated in the central scene and in the four lower compartments of the archivolt. The task of preaching the gospel to all the nations is represented on the lintel. The task of healing the sick and of driving out devils is indicated in the four upper compartments of the archivolt. First I shall analyze the central scene, then the lintel and the archivolt.

In the central scene the apostles at Christ's right, the side where, in the Last Judgment, the blessed appear, are shown in the process of saving mankind. The apostle at the extreme left takes the lock away from his book. The next one holds his open book on his lap. His neighbor, probably St. John, shows the open book even more emphatically before his chest, before his heart. St. Peter, next to Christ, holds the key which will open paradise to the blessed. There is an increase in the size of the apostles toward the mighty, towering central figure of Christ. And to this increase in size corresponds a gradual increase in the intensity of the gestures and attributes of salvation. On the left side of Christ, however, the apostles have their books closed, thus indicating that they can condemn. St. Jerome expressed the same idea when he wrote that the apostles reveal the Savior to those who believe, but hide Him from those who do not believe.[6] This conception is also reflected in the clouds which flank the upper side of Christ's mandorla. On His right they are calm. On His left they look like thunderclouds.

The central scene, the final empowering of the apostles by Christ Himself, radiates into the subordinated scenes of the lintel and archivolt, where many of the small figures point with ecstatic gestures toward the center.

The apostles must preach the gospel to every creature. They must convert mankind. This task is represented on the lintel. From both sides approach groups of people engaged in vehement discussions. The procession coming from the right is received by St. Peter, the dispensator, with the keys of the heavenly kingdom, and St. Paul, the teacher of the gentiles. They are the princes of the apostles, also the traditional patrons of the abbey.[7]

At the extreme left the procession begins with a group of barefoot men mostly clad in short tunics and armed with bows and arrows. The next group brings offerings, a bowl full of fruit, a special cake, a fish, an object which is now partially destroyed, probably a box with incense, and a pail with wine or milk in it. Near the center of sacrificial scene is represented, obviously influenced by some classical prototype.[8] A sacrificial bull stands there among priests and helpers of the sacrifice.

At the right side, a soldier clad in mail and armed with a shield hands his sword with its point down to the apostles. He leads a group of other soldiers and men, who have not taken sufficient time to arm themselves, so eager are they to rush toward salvation. There is a pygmy, an inhabitant of Africa, who mounts a horse from a ladder.[9] Close to him at the left stands another pygmy, now partly destroyed, to whom a man of normal size talks in an emphatic manner. The procession is still extremely dramatic at the end, where two family groups gesticulate violently. The group at the very right has a monstrous appearance. It belongs to the fabulous race of the Panotii, the people with large ears. Classical and medieval writers report that they live in India or on some island far in the north.[10]

How are we to explain these two processions? Immediately before His Ascension Christ tells His apostles that they shall be His witnesses unto the uttermost part of the earth (Acts 1:8). The gospel according to St. Mark (16:15) relates that Christ gives His apostles the command to preach the gospel to every creature. These passages suggest in a general manner the idea of representing various and even monstrous peoples as the object of the missionary work of the apostles. Yet they say nothing about a frantic procession, where people admonish and push each other. It is rather the prophecies of the Old Testament which foretell, and in an emphatic manner, the effect of the coming salvation on mankind. Isaiah has described this in great detail. We know that these prophecies were quoted again and again early in the twelfth century.

Isaiah predicts that nations from afar will come that they may be saved: "Behold, these shall come from far, and, lo, these from the north and from the sea, and these from the land in the east" (49:12).[11] He speaks not only of the known peoples, but of the unknown peoples, too: "Behold, thou shalt call a nation that thou knowest not, and nations that knew not thee shall run unto thee" (55:5). Among these unknown peoples the Middle Ages include the pygmies and the Panotii. Even those of unusual appearance, like the man, the woman, and the child with large ears, would be saved. . . .

On the right side of the lintel the people are clearly more bewildered than on the left. Some, as we have seen, are talking vehemently. No better description of their attitudes and gestures could be given than that one provided by another prophecy of Isaiah: "The ends of the earth were afraid, drew near and came. They will help everyone his neighbor, and everyone will say to his brother: 'Be of good courage'" (41:5, 6).

Thus Isaiah's prophecies seem to be translated on the lintel out of dramatic pictorial language into dramatic relief sculpture. And another passage seems to have exerted an even more direct influence. This is the famous crowning prophecy in the last chapter, where the Lord says: "And I will set a sign among them, and I will send those of them that are saved to the nations in the sea, to Africa and Lydia that draw the bow, to Italy and Greece, to the isles afar off, to those that have not heard of me, neither have seen my glory; and they shall declare my glory among the gentiles" (66:19). This passage was interpreted by medieval theologians as the sending out of the apostles to all these nations[12] which, it seems, are represented on the lintel. . . .

The meaning of the lintel is even more complex. Not only do the peoples mentioned by Isaiah seem to be represented here, but they stand at the same time for different classes of humanity. We see the hunters with bow and arrow, the peasants and the fishermen, who bring the fruits of the soil, of the trees, and of the water. We see the priests, the soldiers, and the savage races. These different classes of humanity are arranged in a hierarchical order. The lowest classes form the ends of the two processions, at the extreme left the hunters, at the extreme right the savages. The highest classes, the priests and the soldiers, are accorded the favored places at the heads of the processions.

The other tasks of the apostles are represented in the eight compartments of the archivolt. Here groups of people, who by their appearance and costumes represent different races, discuss in a passionate manner the mission of the apostles and the power which Christ bestowed upon them. Some of them have again a monstrous appearance. There are the sick who will be healed by the apostles, and those whose souls will be saved by them. Specific examples illustrate the tasks of the apostles. The four upper compartments, which show different examples of physically and mentally defective people, are a kind of an encyclopedia of these defects which the sculptor renders in extremely dramatic terms. With feverish gestures some of these sick people express their hopes of being healed. They point toward the central scene, as if the realization of these hopes were now at hand. . . .

The program of the archivolt stresses the idea that the grace about to be accorded to the gentiles descends upon them by degrees. The two compartments at the top show people laboring under the severest permanent physical defects. In the next two transient or minor ailments are shown. These defects and ailments can only be cured by the working of miracles. The following pair of compartments refers to those who can be saved by conversion, while in the lowest pair the effects of grace are already apparent. In a similar manner the groups on the lintel are arranged in graduated symmetry from the ends toward the center. What is true of iconography also applies to form: the idea of gradation is expressed in the very scale of all the sculptured figures. Largest of all is Christ in the center. His size stresses His all-pervading power. By their smaller size the apostles are characterized as His helpers. Still smaller, and therefore least important, are the peoples at the periphery. They are only the objects of the work of salvation which Christ performs through His apostles.

The violent gestures of the little figures show how the grace of the Holy Spirit radiates immediately throughout the world. The *Mission of the Apostles* has a world shaking, cosmic aspect. This cosmic aspect is further enlarged by the outer archivolt, which comprises the twelve signs of the zodiac and little scenes portraying the occupations of the twelve months.[13] Christ is not only the ruler over space, over all the races of the world, but also over time, over the cycle of the year and its activities. . . .

II

The central tympanum at Vézelay was created between the first and the second crusades, in an epoch which gave a new impulse to religious feeling and broadened the outlook of medieval thinkers. It was created in Burgundy, in the center of France, at a place which played a prominent role in the history of the crusades.

In 1095, on the eve of the first crusade, Urban II, the Cluniac Pope of French descent, had planned, according to William of Tyre,[14] to hold a council either in Vézelay or in Le Puy, but decided in favor of Clermont. There he called upon clerics and laymen to rescue the Christians of the East, to liberate by a pilgrimage in arms Jerusalem and the Oriental churches which had been overrun by the Moslems and were suffering so miserably. That was about thirty years before the tympanum was created. About fifteen years after its completion it was in Vézelay that St. Bernard preached the second crusade in 1146 and Louis VII, the king of France, took up the cross. Again it was from Vézelay that, in 1190, Richard Coeur de Lion and Philip Augustus, the French king, started for the third crusade. . . .

The canonical Acts of the Apostles and apocryphal acts report how the twelve apostles had, each in his allotted region, conquered the world for the Christian faith. They had established the Church unto the ends of the world. But later, with the coming of the Arabs, infidels had gradually overrun many parts of the world: all of Asia and Africa, and even parts of Europe.

In 1095, at the end of the Council of Clermont, Pope Urban II addressed the assembly. His speech, as different writers relate it in different versions, sounds like the proclaiming of a new mission which set a twofold task to the clerics and one to the laymen. The clerics alone were urged to persuade men of all ranks to take up the fight against the Moslems. According to Fulcher of Chartres, the Pope said: "Qua de re supplici prece hortor, non ego, sed Dominus, ut cunctis cuiuslibet ordinis tam equitibus quam peditibus, tam divitibus quam pauperibus, edicto frequenti vos, Christi praecones, suadeatis, ut ad id genus nequam de regionibus nostrorum exterminandum tempestive Christicolis opitulari satagant."[15] But both clerics and laymen were called upon to reconquer the lost parts of the world for the Christian faith and to liberate Jerusalem, the navel of the earth, and the Lord's Sepulcher. . . . What had been achieved by the apostles had to be achieved again, at the end of the eleventh century. The clerics were urged to preach the crusade in their districts, and they were sent out, together with the laymen, to reconquer the lost parts of the world which once had been conquered by the apostles. Thus the choice of the subject to be represented in the tympanum just at this time seems to bear a deeper meaning. The encyclopedic *Mission of the Apostles* prefigures the new mission of the crusaders. . . .

We have seen that the prophecy in the last chapter of Isaiah was very likely the main literary source of the lintel. Medieval writers believed that it had been fulfilled by the apostles, but it seemed to be fulfilled again in the first crusade. This is the opinion of Peter the Venerable. Once the prior of Vézelay, he had become abbot of Cluny in 1122. In his sermon *In laudem sepulcri Domini* he quotes this very prophecy which, he believes, came true again, when the crusaders liberated the Holy Sepulcher from the rule of the infidels and "purified with their holy swords the place and habitation of heavenly purity." [16] This idea has its counterpart on the lintel where the foremost soldier on the right, who may be considered as a prototype of the crusading knights, presents his sword to the apostles that it may be made holy.

Some other very characteristic elements in the program of the tympanum seem to reflect quite closely ideas which the abbot of Cluny has expressed in his writings. We have seen that the prophecies of Isaiah may have played a paramount part in the conception of the program. It is this same prophet whom Peter the Venerable likes to quote as his primary witness. He invokes him as "eximie prophetarum" or "maxime prophetarum."[17] "Audite divinum prophetam," he says in his sermon on the Holy Sepulcher, "immo praecipuum in prophetis ad vos ante multa saecula propheticum oculum convertentem." [18]

Shortly after quoting the prophecy of the last chapter of Isaiah, Peter the Venerable gives a list of miracles. He mentions first the giving of sight to the blind, then the restoring of hearing to the deaf and of speech to the dumb.[19] These are the three organic defects, which are represented in the same sequence in the topmost compartment at the left. . . .

Since so many ideas which are expressed in the tympanum can be found in the writings of Peter the Venerable, may we not draw the conclusion that he may have worked out the program to be sculptured in the narthex at Vézelay? Peter the Venerable was a great theologian who took a keen interest in the liberation of the Holy Land. The Abbey of Vézelay was closely affiliated with Cluny and Peter had once been its prior. All this may speak in favor of his authorship. He might even have conceived the program while he was still there, although the actual sculpturing of the tympana was done during his abbotship at Cluny. In any case, the deep and complex meaning of the central tympanum betrays ideas of a great theologian. According to his program, prophecies of the Old Testament, their fulfillment by the *Mission of the Apostles* and their refulfillment by the new mission of the crusaders are interwoven here into a grandiose, cosmic, encyclopedic and at the same time beautifully dramatic unity.

NOTES

NOTE: This article grew out of a lecture given in April, 1943, at The Pierpont Morgan Library, New York.

[1] See, for instance, G. Sanoner, "Portail de l'abbaye de Vézelay," *Revue de l'art chrétien*, LIV (1904), pp. 448 ff.; L. Eugene Lefevre, "Le symbolisme du tympan de Vézelay," *ibid.*, LVI (1906), pp. 253 ff.; Paul Mayeur, "Le tympan de l'église abbatiale de Vézelay," *ibid.*, LVIII (1908), pp. 103 ff.; Paul Mayeur, "Les scènes secondaires du tympan de Vézelay," *ibid.*, LIX (1909), pp. 326 ff.

[2] Émile Mâle, *L'art religieux du XII siècle en France* (Paris, 1922), pp. 326 ff.; Abel Fabre, "L'iconographie de la Pentecôte," *Gazette des Beaux-Arts, 65° année* (1923), II, pp. 33 ff. See also A. Kingsley Porter, "Spain or Toulouse? and Other Questions," ART BULLETIN, VII (1924–25), p. 20.

[3] A. Kingsley Porter, *Romanesque Sculpture of the Pilgrimage Roads* (Boston, 1923), Figs. 96, 97. Conant has recently reinterpreted in a similar manner the tympanum which once decorated the great portal at Cluny. See Kenneth John Conant, "The Third Church at Cluny," *Medieval Studies in Memory of A. Kingsley Porter*, II (Cambridge, 1939), pp. 335, 336.

[4] Acts I: II.

[5] The two events are represented on the same page, for instance, in the Carolingian Bible of S. Paolo fuori le mura, fol. 292v (Amédée Boinet, *La miniature carolingienne* [Paris, 1913], pl. CXXVIII). See also the Golden Gospel Book from

Echternach, late tenth century (Gotha, Landesbibliothek, Ms. 1.19, fol. 112v; Albert Boeckler, *Das goldene Evangelienbuch Heinrichs III* [Berlin, 1933], Fig. 173). Both events are merged in a miniature of a Gospel Book from Seitenstetten of the early thirteenth century (Pierpont Morgan Library, Ms. 808, fol. 24; *Catalogue of the Renowned Collection of Western Manuscripts the Property of A. Chester Beatty*, II [London, 1933], pl. 18). In some eleventh-century illustrations of the *Ascension of Christ* rays emanate from the clouds on which Christ stands. See Ernest T. Dewald, "The Iconography of the Ascension," *American Journal of Archaeology*, XIX (1915), pp. 277 ff.; Figs. 19, 20.

[6] *Commentaria in Isaiam*, lib. III, cap. 6 (*Patrologia Latina*, 24, col. 96).

[7] See Hugo of Poitiers, *Historia Vizeliacensis Monasterii*, lib. III (*Patrologia Latina*, 194, col. 1605): "Ecclesia Vizeliacensis ab inclito Gerardo comite nobiliter fundata, nobilius ab eodem attitulata beatorum Petri et Pauli apostolorum nomini ascripta, juri assignata, regimini credita, protectioni commissa." Cf. also the beginning of a privilege granted by Pope Leo IX in 1050: "Leo episcopus, servus servorum Dei, Gaufrido abbati Vizeliacensis coenobii, quod est in honore Domini nostri Jesu Christi et veneratione ejusdem genitricis et beatorum apostolorum Petri et Pauli et beatae Mariae Magdalenae, ejusque successoribus in perpetuum" (*Patrologia Latina*, 143, col. 642).

[8] See Jean Adhémar, *Influences antiques dans l'art du moyen âge français, Studies of the Warburg Institute*, no. 7 (London, 1939), pp. 177 ff.

[9] Pliny, *Natural History*, VI. 35. 188, ed. H. Rackham, II (London and Cambridge, 1942), p. 478. They are also mentioned as inhabitants of India.

[10] Pliny, *op. cit.*, IV. 13, 95; VII. 2. 30, ed. Rackham, II, pp. 192, 526; C. Julius Solinus, *Collectanea Rerum Memorabilium*, XIX. 8, ed. Th. Mommsen (Berlin, 1895), pp. 93, 94; Isidore of Seville, *Etymologiae*, XI. 3. 19, ed. W. M. Lindsay, Oxford.

[11] Cf. also Isaiah 2:2–4; Jeremiah 16:19; Zechariah 8:20–23.

[12] St. Jerome, *Commentaria in Isaiam*, lib. XVIII, cap. 66 (*Patrologia Latina*, 24, cols. 692 ff.); Isidore of Seville, *De Fide Catholica*, lib. I, cap. 55 (*ibid.*, 83, cols. 493, 494); Haymo of Halberstadt, *Commentaria in Isaiam*, lib. III, cap. 66 (*ibid.*, 116, col. 1082); Hugo of St. Victor, *Sermo de quibuslibet Apostolis* (*ibid.*, 177, cols. 1039 ff.).

[13] The chronological cycle consists of twenty-six medallions, comprising the twelve signs of the zodiac, the twelve labors of the months, and two extra medallions, i.e., the third from below on either side. Four additional medallions, which do not refer to the cycle of the year, form the topmost arc of the semicircle.

The two extra medallions which are inserted in the cycle of the year represent at the left, a man warming himself at a fire and another taking off his garment, at the right, a bearded man carrying a wrapped woman on his shoulders. These four figures may personify the four seasons. The four medallions at the top show an eagle, a dog (?), a man and a siren. One might think that three elements are symbolized by them, air by the eagle, earth by dog and man, and water by the siren. May one even go a step farther and see fire symbolized by the adjoining sign of the lion? Such groups of cosmological significance already frame late antique Mithraic reliefs, thereby stressing the power of the pagan god. On the relief of the *Birth of Mithras* from Trier, for instance, the zodiac and the four winds are grouped around the new-born god, while symbols of the four elements are represented in the crowning gable. See Fritz Saxl, *Mithras* (Berlin, 1931), Fig. 199.

[14] *Historia Rerum in Partibus Transmarinis Gestarum,* lib. i, cap. 14 (*Patrologia Latina,* 201, col. 231).

[15] "Wherefore, I exhort with earnest prayer—not I, but God—that, as heralds of Christ, you urge men by frequent exhortation, men of all ranks, knights as well as foot-soldiers, rich as well as poor, to hasten to exterminate this vile race from the lands of your brethren, and to aid the Christians in time" (August C. Krey, *The First Crusade* [Princeton and London, 1921], p. 29). I am greatly indebted to the Princeton University Press for the kind permission to quote this and other translations from Krey's book. For the original text, see *Fulcheri Carnotensis Historia Hierosolymitana,* lib. i, cap. 3, ed. Heinrich Hagenmeyer (Heidelberg, 1913), pp. 134, 135.

Cf. also the command, as reported by Balderic, Archbishop of Dol, in his *Historia Hierosolymitana,* lib. i, cap. 4: "Et conversus ad episcopos: 'Vos,' inquit, 'fratres et coepiscopi, vos consacerdotes et cohaeredes Christi, per ecclesias vobis commissas id ipsum annuntiate, et viam in Jerusalem toto ore viriliter praedicate. Confessis peccatorum suorum ignominiam, securi de Christo celerem paciscimini veniam'" (*Recueil des historiens des croisades, Historiens occidentaux,* iv, [Paris, 1879], p. 15).

[16] *Patrologia Latina,* 189, col. 985.

[17] *Tractatus adversus Judaeorum inveteratam duritiem,* cap. 1 (*ibid.,* col. 509); cap. 5 (*ibid.,* col. 608).

[18] "Listen to the divine prophet, yes indeed to the foremost among the prophets, who has turned his prophetical eye towards you many ages ago." For the original text, *see ibid.,* col. 982.

[19] *Ibid.,* col. 986.

15. MEDIEVAL

ICONOGRAPHY

Emile Mâle

INTRODUCTION

Since its publication in 1898, Emile Mâle's *L'Art Religieux du XIIIe Siècle en France* has enjoyed an important place in the literature dealing with the iconography of medieval art. The English translation of 1913 (available in paperback as *The Gothic Image*) is the source for the selection in this anthology. In this work the imagery of Gothic cathedral decoration is related to the theological literature of the Middle Ages, particularly to the *Speculum* of Vincent of Beauvais, which supplies the framework for Mâle's study. Since Mâle is primarily concerned with the meaning of the images in Gothic decoration, one should read in conjunction with it Erwin Panofsky's *Gothic Architecture and Scholasticism* (1951), which emphasizes the role played by the diffusion of a scholastic "mental habit" in establishing relationships between scholastic thought and Gothic architecture.

For the iconography of Christian art there are a number of works in English. The numerous volumes by Anna B. Jameson are still valuable references: *The History of Our Lord*, 4th ed., 2 vols. (1881); *Sacred and Legendary Art*, 2 vols. (1911); *Legends of the Monastic Orders* (1911); *Legends of the Madonna* (1911). Other studies are Adolphe Didron, *Christian Iconography*, trans. by E. G. Millington, 2 vols. (1896), and Maurice Drake, *Saints and Their Emblems* (1916). For the iconography of the Renaissance there is Erwin Panofsky's brilliant *Studies in Iconology* (1939), of which the introductory chapter is an excellent orientation to the whole subject of meaning in a work of art.

It is also available in a paperbound edition. For mythological themes in art, there are such works as E. Panofsky and F. Saxl, "Classical Mythology in Medieval Art," *Metropolitan Museum Studies*, IV, 2 (1933); Kurt Weitzmann, *Greek Mythology in Byzantine Art* (1951); and Jean Seznec, *The Survival of the Pagan Gods* (1953). André Grabar, *Christian Iconography: A Study of Its Origins* (1968), deals with Christian images of late antiquity and their origins in the visual arts, especially useful for the metamorphosis from pagan to Christian content. Joan Evans, *Monastic Iconography in France from the Renaissance to the Revolution* (1970), examines the later history of this area of iconography, and Gertrud Schiller, *Iconography of Christian Art*, 2 vols. (1971–72), deals with the iconography relating to Christ. While not, strictly speaking, an iconographical study—for its range is much broader than that—G. B. Ladner's *Ad Imaginem Dei: The Image of Man in Medieval Art* (1965) is a stimulating study of developments.

The selection that follows is reprinted from Emile Mâle, *The Gothic Image: Religious Art in the Thirteenth Century* (1913). Translated by Dora Nussey. Published in the United States by E. P. Dutton & Co., Inc., and reprinted with their permission.

GENERAL CHARACTERISTICS OF
MEDIEVAL ICONOGRAPHY

The Middle Ages had a passion for order. They organized art as they had organized dogma, secular learning and society. The artistic representation of sacred subjects was a science governed by fixed laws which could not be broken at the dictates of individual imagination. It cannot be questioned that this theology of art, if one may so put it, was soon reduced to a body of doctrine, for from very early times the craftsmen are seen submitting to it from one end of Europe to the other. This science was transmitted by the Church to the lay sculptors and painters of the thirteenth century who religiously guarded the sacred traditions, so that, even in the centuries in which it was most vigorous, medieval art retained the hieratic grandeur of primitive art.

These are the general principles which it concerns us to state at the outset as briefly as possible.

I

The art of the Middle Ages is first and foremost a sacred writing of which every artist must learn the characters. He must know that the circular nimbus placed vertically behind the head serves to express sanctity, while the nimbus impressed with a cross is the sign of divinity which he will always use in portraying any of the three Persons of the Trinity.[1] He will learn that the aureole (i.e. light which emanates from the whole figure and surrounds the body as a nimbus) expresses eternal bliss, and belongs to the three Persons of the Trinity, to the Virgin, and to the souls of the Blessed. He must know that representations of God the Father, God the Son, the angels and the apostles should have the feet bare, while there would be real impropriety in representing the Virgin and the saints with bare feet. In such matters a mistake would have ranked almost as heresy. Other accepted symbols enabled the medieval artist to express the invisible, to represent that which would otherwise be beyond the domain of art. A hand emerging from the clouds, making the gesture of benediction with thumb and two fingers raised, and surrounded by a cruciform nimbus, was recognized as the sign of divine intervention, the emblem of providence. Little figures of nude and sexless children, ranged side by side in the folds of Abraham's mantle, signified the eternal rest of the life to come.

There are also accepted signs for objects of the visible world which the artist must learn. Lines which are concentric and sinuous represent the sky, those which are horizontal and undulating represent water. A tree, that is to say a stalk surmounted with two or three leaves, indicates that the scene takes place on the earth; a tower pierced by a doorway is a town, while if an angel watch on the battlements it is the heavenly Jerusalem.[2] Thus we have a veritable hieroglyphic[3] in which art and writing blend, showing the same spirit of order and abstraction that there is in heraldic art with its alphabet, rules and symbolism. . . .

II

The second characteristic of medieval iconography is obedience to the rules of a kind of sacred mathematics. Position, grouping, symmetry and number are of extraordinary importance.

To begin with, the whole church is oriented from the rising to the setting sun, a custom dating back to primitive Christian days for it is found even in the *Apostolical Constitutions*. In the thirteenth century Gulielmus Durandus cites this as a rule without exception:—"The foundations must be disposed in such a manner that the head of the church lies exactly to the east, that is to the part of the sky in which the sun rises at the equinox." And, as a matter of fact, from the eleventh to the sixteenth century it is difficult to find a badly oriented church. Like other traditions of medieval art the rule fell into neglect toward the time of the Council of Trent, the Jesuits being the first to violate it.

Each cardinal point has its significance in churches oriented in this way. The north, region of cold and darkness, is usually consecrated to the Old Testament, and the south, bathed in warm sunlight is devoted to the New, though there are many exceptions to the rule.[4] The western façade—where the setting sun lights up the great scene of the evening of the world's history—is almost invariably reserved for a representation of the Last Judgment. The medieval doctors, with their curiously bad etymology, connected *occidens* with the verb *occidere,* and the west became for them the region of death.

After orientation it was relative position which most engrossed the artist, here again at one with the theologian. In early times certain passages in the Bible led to the belief that the right hand was the place of honor. Is it not written, for example, in the Psalms: "Adstitit regina a dextris tuis in vestitu deaurato?" In the *Shepherd* of Hermas which belongs to primitive Christian literature, the right is the place given to those who are marked out for honor. In the account of the third vision it is said that the Church caused Hermas to be seated on a bench at her side. When he would have seated himself to her right she signed to him to pass to the left, because the right is reserved for those who have suffered in the name of God. The medieval theologians in their turn laid great stress on the dignity of the right hand place, and the artists did not fail to conform to so well-established a doctrine. When, for example, the Savior is represented in the midst of His apostles, St. Peter—first in dignity—occupies a place to the right of the Master.[5] In the same way in the scene of the Crucifixion or in that of the Last Judgment, the Virgin is to the right, St. John to the left.

Again, the higher place was considered more honorable than the lower, and from this some curious compositions resulted. Of these the most striking is that of the figure of Christ in Majesty supported by the four beasts of the Apocalypse. The four beasts, symbols of the evangelists as we shall show later, were placed according to the excellence of their natures—man, eagle, lion and ox. When it was a question of disposing them in a tympanum, the dignity conferred by the higher and that conferred by the right hand place had to be taken into consideration. The following arrangement was the one generally adopted. The winged man was placed at the top of the composition and to the right of Christ, the eagle at the top to the left, the lion at the bottom to the right, the ox at the bottom to the left[6] (Fig. 45). . . .

But no disposition met with more favor than that controlled by symmetry. Symmetry was regarded as the expression of a mysterious inner harmony. Craftsmen opposed the twelve patriarchs and twelve prophets of the Ancient Law to the twelve apostles of the New,

331

45. Tympanum: Christ as Judge and Ruler of the Universe with Symbols of Evangelists, Central Portal, West Façade, Chartres Cathedral, *c.* 1150 (Marburg-Art Reference Bureau)

and the four major prophets to the four evangelists. A window in the south transept at Chartres shows—with audacious symbolism—the four prophets Isaiah, Ezekiel, Daniel and Jeremiah bearing on their shoulders the four evangelists, St. Matthew, St. John, St. Mark, St. Luke. In this way the artists would tell us that although the evangelists rest upon the prophets, yet from their spiritual vantage-ground they have a wider outlook. The four and twenty elders of the Apocalypse frequently correspond to the twelve prophets and the twelve apostles. . . .

Schemes of this kind presuppose a reasoned belief in the virtue of numbers, and in fact the Middle Ages never doubted that numbers were endowed with some occult power. This doctrine came from the Fathers of the Church, who inherited it from those Neoplatonic schools in which the genius of Pythagoras had lived again. It is evident that St. Augustine considered numbers as thoughts of God. In many passages he lays it down that each number has its divine significance. "The Divine Wisdom is reflected in the numbers impressed on all things." [7] The construction of the physical and moral worlds alike is based on eternal numbers. We feel that the charm of the dance lies in rhythm, that is in number; but we must go further, beauty is itself a cadence, harmonious number. [8] The science of numbers, then, is the science of the universe, and from numbers we learn its secret. Therefore the numbers met with in the Bible should be considered with reverent attention, for they are sacred and full of mystery. [9] He who can read them enters into the divine plan. . . .

A few examples will give some idea of the method. From St. Augustine onward all theologians interpreted the meaning of the number twelve after the same fashion. Twelve is the number of the universal Church, and it was for profound reasons that Jesus willed the number of His apostles should be twelve. Now twelve is the product of three by four. Three, which is the number of the Trinity and by consequence of the soul made in the image of the Trinity, connotes all spiritual things. Four, the number of the elements, is the symbol of material things—the body and the world—which result from combinations of the four elements. [10] To multiply three by four is in the mystic sense to infuse matter with spirit, to proclaim the truths of the faith to the world, to establish the universal Church of which the apostles are the symbol. [11]

Computations of this kind were often more than ingenious, and at times reached real grandeur. The number seven, regarded by the Fathers as mysterious above all others, intoxicated the medieval mystic. It was observed first of all that seven—composed of four, the number of the body, and of three, the number of the soul—is preeminently the number of humanity, and expresses the union of man's double nature. All that relates to him is ordered in series of sevens. Human life is divided into seven ages with each of which is associated the practice of one of the seven virtues. The grace necessary for the practice of these seven virtues is gained by addressing to God the seven petitions of the Paternoster. The seven sacraments sustain man in the exercise of the seven virtues, and guard him from falling into the seven deadly sins. [12] The number seven thus expresses the harmony of man's nature, but it also expresses the harmonious relation of man to the universe. The seven planets govern human destiny, for each of the seven ages is under the influence of one of them. Thus seven invisible threads connect man with the scheme of the universe. [13] . . .

III

The third characteristic of medieval art lies in this, that it is a symbolic code. From the days of the catacombs Christian art has spoken in figures, showing men one thing and inviting them to see in it the figure of another. The artist, as the doctors might have put it, must imitate God who under the letter of Scripture hid profound meaning, and who willed that nature too should hold lessons for man.

In medieval art there are then intentions a knowledge of which is necessary to any real understanding of the subject. When for example in scenes of the Last Judgment we see the Wise and Foolish Virgins to the right and left hand of Christ, we should thereby understand that they symbolize the elect and the lost. Upon this all the commentators on the New Testament are agreed, and they explain it by stating that the five Foolish Virgins typify the desires of the five senses, and the five Wise Virgins the five forms of the contemplative life. To take another example, it is not as rivers that the four rivers of Paradise—the Gihon, Phison, Tigris, and Euphrates—are represented pouring water from their urns towards the four points of the compass, but as symbols of the evangelists who flooded the world with their teaching like four beneficent streams.

An Old Testament personage in the porch of a cathedral is but a type, an adumbration of Christ, the Virgin, or the future Church. At Chartres the form of Melchizedek, priest and king, bearing the bread and wine to Abraham, should remind men of another priest and king who offered bread and wine to His disciples. At Laon Gideon calling down rain from heaven on to the fleece he had laid on the earth, reminds men that the Virgin Mother was this symbolic fleece on whom fell the dew from on high.

A detail of apparent insignificance may hide symbolic meaning. In a window at Bourges the lion near to the tomb from which the risen Christ comes forth is a type of the Resurrection. It was generally believed in the Middle Ages that for three days after birth the cubs of the lioness gave no sign of life, but that on the third day the lion came and with his breath restored them to life. And so the apparent death of the lion represents the sojourn of Jesus in the tomb, and its birth was an image of the Resurrection.

In the art of the Middle Ages, as we see, everything depicted is informed by a quickening spirit.

Such a conception of art implies a profoundly idealistic view of the scheme of the universe, and the conviction that both history and nature must be regarded as vast symbols. We shall see later that this undoubtedly was the view of the medieval mind. Further, it should be remembered that such ideas were not the property of the great thirteenth century doctors alone, but were shared by the mass of the people to whom they had permeated through the teaching of the Church. The symbolism of the church services familiarized the faithful with the symbolism of art. Christian liturgy like Christian art is endless symbolism, both are manifestations of the same genius. . . .

From what has been said it is evident that medieval art was before all things a symbolic art, in which form is used merely as the vehicle of spiritual meaning.[14]

Such are the general characteristics of the iconography of the Middle Ages. Art was at once a script, a calculus and a symbolic code. The result was a deep and perfect harmony. There is something musical in the grouping of the statues in the cathedral porches, and in truth all the elements of music are present. Are there not here conventional signs grouped according to the law of numbers, and is there not something of the indefinite quality of music in the infinite symbolism dimly discerned behind the outward forms? The genius of the Middle Ages, so long misunderstood, was a harmonious genius. Dante's Paradiso and the porches at Chartres are symphonies. To thirteenth century art more truly perhaps than to any other might be given the title of "frozen music."

METHOD USED IN THE STUDY OF
MEDIEVAL ICONOGRAPHY

THE MIRRORS OF VINCENT OF BEAUVAIS

The thirteenth century was the century of encyclopedias. At no other period have so many works appeared bearing the titles of *Summa, Speculum* or *Imago Mundi*. It was in this century that Thomas Aquinas coordinated the whole body of Christian doctrine, Jacobus de Voragine collected the most famous legends of the saints,

Gulielmus Durandus epitomized all previous writers on the liturgy, and Vincent of Beauvais attempted to embrace universal knowledge. Christianity came to full consciousness of its own genius, and the conception of the universe which had been elaborated by previous centuries received complete expression. It was believed to be possible to raise the final edifice of human knowledge, and in the universities which had recently been founded throughout Europe—above all the young university of Paris—the work was carried on with enthusiasm.

While the doctors were constructing the intellectual edifice which was to shelter the whole of Christendom, the cathedral of stone was rising as its visible counterpart. It too in its fashion was a *Speculum*, a *Summa*, an *Imago Mundi* into which the Middle Age put all its most cherished convictions. These great churches are the most perfect known expression in art of the mind of an epoch. We shall attempt to show that in them a whole dogmatic scheme found expression in concrete form.

The difficulty lies in grouping in logical sequence the innumerable works of art which the churches offer for our study. Surely we have hardly the right to dispose of the matter according to some arbitrary scheme which appears to us harmonious. It is necessary to discard modern habits of mind. If we impose our categories on medieval thought we run every risk of error, and for that reason we borrow our method of exposition from the Middle Age itself. The four books of Vincent of Beauvais's *Mirror* furnish us with the framework for the four divisions of our study of thirteenth century art.

If Aquinas was the most powerful thinker of the Middle Ages, Vincent of Beauvais was certainly the most comprehensive. He might well be called an epitome of the knowledge of his day. A prodigious worker, he passed his life like the elder Pliny in reading and making extracts. He was called "librorum helluo," the devourer of books. St. Louis threw open to him the fine library containing virtually all the books procurable in the thirteenth century, and at times came to visit him at the abbey of Royaumont, where he loved to hear him talk of the wonders of the universe.

It was probably toward the middle of the century that Vincent of Beauvais published the great *Mirror*, the *Speculum majus*, which to his contemporaries seemed the supreme effort of human learning. Even today one cannot but admire so stupendous a work.[15]

His learning was immense, yet it did not overwhelm him. The order which he adopted was the most imposing which the Middle Age could conceive—the very plan of God as it appears in the Scriptures. Vincent of Beauvais's work is divided into four parts—the Mirror of Nature, the Mirror of Instruction, the Mirror of Morals[16] and the Mirror of History.

In the Mirror of Nature are reflected all natural phenomena in the order in which they were created by God. The Days of Creation mark the different chapters of this great encyclopedia of nature. The four elements, the minerals, vegetables and animals are successively enumerated and described. All the truth and the error which had been transmitted by antiquity to the Middle Ages are found there. But it is naturally on the work of the sixth day—the creation of man—that Vincent of Beauvais dwells at greatest length, for man is the center of the universe and for him all things were made.

The Mirror of Instruction opens with the story of the Fall, the recital of the drama which explains the riddle of the universe. Man has fallen, and only through a Redeemer can he hope for salvation. Yet in his own strength he can begin to raise himself, and through knowledge to prepare for grace. There is in knowledge a quickening power, and to each of the seven Arts corresponds one of the seven Gifts of the Spirit. After expounding this large and humane doctrine Vincent of Beauvais passes in review all the different branches of knowledge; even the mechanical arts are included, for by the labor of his hands man begins the work of his redemption.

The Mirror of Morals is closely connected with the Mirror of Instruction, for the end of life is not to know but to act, and knowledge is but a means to virtue. Out of this springs a learned classification of the virtues and vices, in which the method, divisions and often the very expressions of Aquinas are found—for the *Speculum morale* is the *Summa* in abridged form.

The last division is the Mirror of History. We have studied human nature in the abstract, and we now turn to man himself, watching his progress under the eye of God. He invents arts and sciences, he struggles and suffers, choosing sometimes vice, sometimes virtue in the great battle of the soul which is the sum of the world's history. It is hardly necessary to observe that for Vincent of Beauvais, as for Augustine, Orosius, Gregory of Tours and all the historians of the Middle Ages, true history is the history of the Church, the City of God, which begins with Abel the first just man. There is a chosen people and their history is the pillar of fire which lightens the darkness. The history of the pagan world is deserving of study only with reference to the other; it has merely value as a synchronism. It is true that Vincent of Beauvais did not scorn to tell of the revolution of empires, and even delighted in speaking of pagan philosophers, scholars and poets, but such subjects are really incidental. The dominant thought of his book—the idea which gives it unity—is the unbroken line of saints of the Old and New Testaments. Through them and them alone the history of the world becomes coherent.

Thus was conceived this Encyclopedia of the thirteenth century. In it the riddle of the universe finds solution. The plan is so comprehensive that the Middle Ages could conceive of nothing which it did not include, and until the Renaissance the following centuries found nothing to add to it.

Such a book is the surest guide that we can choose for our study of the great leading ideas which lay behind the art of the thirteenth century. Striking analogies are noticeable, for example, between the general economy of the *Speculum Majus* and the plan followed in the porches of the cathedral of Chartres. As was first pointed out by Didron in the authoritative introduction to his *Histoire de Dieu*, the innumerable figures which decorate the porches may well be grouped under the four heads of nature, instruction, morals, and history. We do not know whether that great decorative scheme was directly inspired by Vincent of Beauvais's book with which it was almost contemporaneous, but it is obvious that the arrangement of the *Speculum Majus* belonged not to him but to the Middle Ages as a whole. It was the form which the thirteenth century imposed on all ordered thought. The same genius disposed the chapters of the *Mirror* and the sculpture of the cathedral. It is then legitimate to seek in the one the meaning of the other.

We shall therefore adopt the four great divisions of Vincent of Beauvais's work, and shall try to read the four books of the *Mirror* in the façades of the cathedrals. We shall find them all four represented, and shall decipher them in the order in which the encyclopedist presents them. Each detail will in this way find its place, and the harmony of the whole will appear.

THE MIRROR OF NATURE

. . . The Mirror of Nature is carved in brief on the façades of most of the French cathedrals. We find it at Chartres, at Laon, at Auxerre, Bourges and Lyons, treated in a restrained and conventional way. At Chartres a lion, a sheep, a goat and a heifer stand for the animal world, a fig tree and three plants of indeterminate character represent the vegetable kingdom; there is an element of greatness in this summing up of the universe in some five or six bas-reliefs. Some naïve details are full of charm. In the representation at Laon the Creator sits in deep reflection before dividing the darkness from the light, and counts on His fingers the number of days needed to finish His work. Later in the series, when His task is accomplished, He sits down to rest like a good workman at the end of a well-spent day, and leaning on His staff He falls asleep.

One might well feel that these few typical forms were inadequate representations of the wealth of the universe, and might accuse the thirteenth-century craftsmen of timidity and want of power, did the animal and vegetable worlds really occupy no further place in the cathedral scheme. But a glance upward shows us vines, raspberries heavy with fruit and long trails of the wild rose clinging to the archivolts, birds singing among the oak leaves or perching on the pillars. Beasts from far-off lands side by side with homely creatures of the countryside—lions, elephants and camels, squirrels, hens and rabbits—enliven the basement of the porch, while monsters securely fastened by their heavy stone wings bark fiercely at us from above. How little do these old masters with their unequalled, if naïve love of nature deserve the reproach of lack of power or invention. Their cathedrals are all life and movement. The Church to them was the ark to which every creature was made welcome, and then—as if the works of God were not sufficient for them—they invented a whole world more of terrible beings, creatures so real that they surely must have lived in the childhood of the world. . . .

There are few cases in which it is permissible to assign symbolic meaning to animal forms, but they are of such a kind that through literary references one may reach sure conclusions.

The four beasts surrounding the figure of Christ in Glory, found in the porch of so many churches, form the first class of representations in which the symbolic meaning cannot be mistaken. The motif of the four creatures—the man,[17] the eagle, the lion and the ox—so frequent in the Romanesque period, became more rare in the thirteenth century though not entirely discarded. The four creatures are seen, for example, on the Porte du Jugement of Notre Dame at Paris. It is true they no longer have the breadth, the heraldic boldness which is so striking at Moissac, and they no longer fill the tympanum but hide humbly in the lower portion of the doorway.

From earliest Christian times the man, the eagle, the lion and the ox, first seen in Ezekiel's vision by the river Chebar and later by St. John round the throne of God, were accepted symbols of the four evangelists.

. . . The emblem of St. Matthew is the man, because his gospel begins with the genealogical table of the ancestors of Jesus according to the flesh. The lion designates St. Mark, for in the opening verses of his gospel he speaks of the voice crying in the wilderness. The ox—the sacrificial animal—symbolizes St. Luke, whose gospel opens with the sacrifice offered by Zacharias. The eagle—an echo of the natural history of the Bestiaries—who alone of created things was reputed to gaze straight into the light of the sun, is the emblem of St. John, who from the first transports men to the very heart of divinity. Again, these same creatures are symbols of Christ, for in them may be seen four great mysteries in the life of the Savior. The man recalls the Incarnation, and reminds men that the Son of God became man. The ox, victim of the Old Law, calls to remembrance the Passion—the Redeemer's sacrifice of His life for mankind. The lion, which in the fabled science of the Bestiaries sleeps with open eyes, is the symbol of the Resurrection, for therein, says the lectionary, is a figure of Jesus in the tomb. "For the Redeemer in virtue of His humanity appeared to sink into the sleep of death, but in virtue of His divinity He was living and watching." Lastly, the eagle is a figure of the Ascension. Christ rose to Heaven as the eagle rises to the clouds. Summing up its teaching in a precise formula, the lectionary lays it down that Christ was man in His birth, ox in His death, lion in His Resurrection, eagle in His Ascension.[18]

But the four creatures have yet a third meaning, and express the virtues necessary for salvation. Each Christian on his way to divine perfection must be at once man, ox, lion and eagle. He must be man because man is a reasonable animal, and he who treads the path of reason alone deserves that name. He must be ox because the ox is the sacrificial victim, and the true Christian by renouncing worldly pleasures sacrifices himself. He must be lion because the lion is the most courageous of beasts, and the good man having renounced all worldly things fears nothing, for of him it is written, "The righteous are bold as a lion." And he must be eagle because the eagle flies in the heights looking straight into the sun, type of the Christian who with direct gaze contemplates the things of eternity.

This is the Church's teaching on the four creatures, but only one of these interpretations, that likening the apocalyptic beasts to the evangelists, survived medieval times. The others shared the fate of all the old mystical theology, and at the Reformation fell into oblivion. But Protestants themselves remained faithful to tradition on the first point, and in the seventeenth century Rembrandt painted his sublime St. Matthew of the Louvre listening with all his soul to the words of an angel who, deep in shadow, whispers to him of eternal things. . . .

THE MIRROR OF INSTRUCTION

The world has come into being. The work of God is finished and perfect, but the harmony is destroyed for man has misused his liberty. Sin has brought misery into the world, and henceforth mankind is like the wretched Adam and Eve who at the top of Notre Dame at Paris seem to shiver in the mist and the rain.[19]

The Church proclaims through her art that fallen humanity can only be restored through the grace of God and the sacrifice of Christ, but that man must merit grace and must take his part in the work of redemption. In the preface to his *Speculum doctrinale* Vincent of Beauvais expresses the conviction—"Ipsa restitutio sive restauratio per doctrinam efficitur" and, as the sequel shows, by "doctrina," he understands work of every kind, even the humblest. The Middle Age was not only the age of contemplation, it was also the age of work accepted and conceived not as servitude but as enfranchisement. Manual labor—in substance we quote Vincent of Beauvais—delivers man from the necessities to which since the Fall his body is subject, while instruction delivers him from the ignorance which has weighed down his soul.[20] And so in the cathedrals, where all medieval thought took visible shape, knowledge and manual labor are given a place of equal honor. In the church where kings, barons and bishops fill so modest a place we find representations of almost every craft. At Chartres and Bourges, for example, in the windows given by the guilds, the lower part shows the donors with the badges of their trade—trowel, hammer, wool-carding comb, baker's shovel and butcher's knife.[21] In those days no incongruity was felt in placing these pictures of daily life side by side with scenes from the legends of the saints. The dignity and sanctity of labor were expressed in this way. . . .

But it was to the primeval work of tilling the soil, the task which God Himself imposed on Adam, that the Church seems to have given the foremost place. In several French cathedrals the cycle of the year's work is carved round the orders of the arch or on the basement of the porch.[22] A sign of the zodiac accompanies each scene of harvest, tillage or vintage. Here are really "The Works and Days."

The custom of decorating the churches with calendars in stone was well-established in primitive Christian times, for we know that the pavements of early basilicas were sometimes engraved with symbolic figures of the seasons. The mosaic from a church at Tyre given to the Louvre by the Renan mission represents scenes of the hunt and vintage accompanied by figures of the months.[23] This work is classical in character, and probably came from some thermæ or villa. The Church did not scruple to borrow pagan forms, and to hallow them by reading into them a Christian meaning. The sequence of the months became a reminder not only of the cycle of labor, but also of the cycle of the Christian year—the round of prayers and festivals.

The Romanesque churches, whose pavements were so often decorated with the signs of the zodiac, show how faithfully the traditions of earlier centuries were preserved. . . .

At Chartres[25] and Paris[26] the signs of the zodiac and the rural scenes which accompany them were disposed so as to follow the course of the sun. The signs of the months mount like the sun from January to June and descend from June to December. . . .

From manual labor man rises to instruction which by dissipating error enables him in some measure to raise himself after the Fall. The Seven Arts (the Trivium and the Quadrivium) open out seven paths of human activity. On the one side are grammar, rhetoric, dialectic, on the other arithmetic, geometry, astronomy and music.

Above the Liberal Arts stands Philosophy, the mother of them all. Philosophy and the Arts contain all the knowledge possible for man to acquire apart from revelation.[27]

The artists of the thirteenth century, intent upon embracing the whole domain of human activity, did not fail to include on the façades of their cathedrals the eight Muses of the Middle Ages. These queenly figures—youthful and serious—were never denizens of this world; they live enthroned above it like the Ideas of which Goethe speaks. . . .

The cathedral teaches that work of any kind demands respect. Another lesson she would teach men is to expect neither riches from manual labor nor fame from learning. Work and knowledge are the instruments of man's inner perfection, and the things which his activities gain for him are of a material and fleeting nature.

In the cathedral at Amiens a curious figure embodies this moral truth. There is in the upper part of the south porch a kind of half-wheel round which seventeen small figures are arranged. Eight of them seem to be carried up with the wheel, and eight others descend with it. At the top a man is seated, his head crowned and a scepter in his hand, motionless while all around him moves. Is this, as Didron tried to prove, an allegory of the different ages of man?[28] We do not think so. The figures descending so abruptly with the wheel are dressed in rags, and have bare feet or shoes through which their toes appear. This surely must convince one with Jourdain and Duval that this symbolic half-circle is not the wheel of Life, but the wheel of Fortune.[29] A miniature in an Italian manuscript of the fourteenth century supports this interpretation.[30] Near to the figure which seems to mount the wheel is written "regnabo," near to that enthroned at the summit "regno," near to those descending on the other side "regnavi" and "sum sine regno." The subject is certainly power, riches, glory, pomps and vanities of the world, and the wheel expresses the instability of these things. . . .

THE MIRROR OF MORALS

Nature, knowledge, virtue—that is the order in the *Speculum majus*. It will be remembered that these are the three worlds of Pascal, the world of material things, the world of mind and the world of love. The unity of Christian thought is so marked that one finds it unchanged through the centuries. Virtue is higher than knowledge or art, said the Middle Ages, it is man's goal. But curiously enough the artists have sometimes placed the highest in the lowliest position. At Paris and Amiens the twelve pensive maidens who symbolize the virtues are not enthroned above the doorway with the angels and the blessed, but are placed at the level of men's eyes so that in passing to and fro they may learn to know them well. Age after age, worn by the rubbing of countless hands, covered with the dust from countless feet, they stand indeed one with the life around them. . . .

Apparently it was Tertullian who first represented the Virtues as warrior-maidens struggling with the Vices in the arena. "See," says he, "wantonness overthrown by chastity, perfidy killed by honesty, cruelty thrown down by pity, pride conquered by humility; these are the games in which we Christians receive our crowns."[31] . . . He was the first to give naïve expression to the profound teaching that Christianity had not brought peace to the world but a sword, and that the soul had become a battlefield. In its ignorance of the true nature of man the ancient world tried to establish a harmony which is not of this world, for so long as man lives will the conflict between his two natures exist. The drama which to the ancients was the struggle of man with Fate is in reality a conflict raging within the soul.

The idea of an inner battle, or Psychomachia, does not indeed belong to Tertullian since it is one of the fundamental ideas of Christianity, but to his imagination is due its concrete embodiment. . . .

From the twelfth century onward the theologians, and after them the artists, began to see the opposition of the virtues and the vices under new aspects. Honorius of Autun, one of the perennial sources of inspiration for medieval art, conceives virtue as a ladder which links earth to heaven.[32] He interprets the vision of Jacob in a moral sense. Each of the fifteen rungs of the ladder is a virtue, and he gives their names—patientia, benignitas, pietas, simplicitas, humilitas, contemptus mundi, paupertas voluntaria, pax, bonitas, spirituale gaudium, sufferentia, fides, spes, longanimitas and perseverantia. . . .

About the same time another metaphor appeared. The theologians of the twelfth and thirteenth centuries who studied the connection between virtues and vices with such diligence, frequently compared them to two vigorous trees. Hugh of St. Victor, one of the first to present this new idea in fully developed form, gives a name to each branch of the two trees.[33] One is the tree of the old Adam and has pride as its root and main stem. From the trunk spring seven great boughs, envy, vainglory, anger, sadness, avarice, intemperance, luxury. In its turn each bough divides into secondary branches. For example, from sadness grow fear and despair. The second tree is the tree of the new Adam with humility for its trunk, and the three theological and the four cardinal virtues as its seven main branches. Each virtue is subdivided in its turn. From faith grow the shoots of chastity and obedience, from hope come patience and joy, from charity concord, liberality, peace and mercy. The first of these trees was planted by Adam and the second by Christ, it is for man to choose between them. One of the most famous of thirteenth-century books, the *Somme le Roi* written in French for Philip the Bold by Brother Laurent, his Dominican confessor, presents Hugh of St. Victor's idea under new forms. The author begins by showing the two trees of good and of evil, but with a deeper knowledge of human nature he gives love, that is charity, as the root of the first tree, and desire, that is egoism, as the root of the second. Thus all the vices spring from love of self, as all the virtues from forgetfulness of self.

THE MIRROR OF HISTORY

So far the subject of our study has been man in the abstract—man with his virtues and his vices, with the arts and sciences invented by his genius. We now turn to the study of humanity living and acting. We have reached history.

The cathedral recounts the history of the world after a plan which is in entire agreement with the scheme developed by Vincent of Beauvais. At Chartres, as in the *Speculum historiale,* the story of humanity is virtually reduced to the history of the elect people of God. The Old and the New Testament and the Acts of the Saints furnish the subject matter, for they contain all that it is necessary for man to know of those who lived before him. They are the three acts in the story of the world, and there can be but three. The course of the drama was ordained by God Himself. The Old Testament shows humanity awaiting the Law, the New Testament shows the Law incarnate, and the Acts of the Saints shows man's endeavor to conform to the Law. . . .

345

But since the Council of Trent the Church has chosen to attach herself to the literal meaning of the Old Testament, leaving the symbolic method in the background. And so it has come about that the exegesis based on symbolism of which the Fathers made constant if not exclusive use, is today generally ignored. For this reason it seems useful briefly to set forth a body of doctrine which so often found expression in art.

God who sees all things under the aspect of eternity willed that the Old and New Testaments should form a complete and harmonious whole; the Old is but an adumbration of the New. To use medieval language, that which the Gospel shows men in the light of the sun, the Old Testament showed them in the uncertain light of the moon and stars. In the Old Testament truth is veiled, but the death of Christ rent that mystic veil and that is why we are told in the Gospel that the veil of the Temple was rent in twain at the time of the Crucifixion. Thus it is only in relation to the New Testament that the Old Testament has significance, and the Synagogue who persists in expounding it for its own merits is blindfold.

This doctrine, always held by the Church, is taught in the Gospels by the Savior Himself, "As Moses lifted up the serpent in the wilderness, even so must the son of man be lifted up," [34] and again, "Even as Jonah was three days and three nights in the belly of the whale, so shall the Son of man be three days and three nights in the depths of the earth." [35] . . .

An immense popular literature relating to the Bible arose in the East. These legends have a very different character according as they refer to the Old or the New Testament. The traditions relating to the Old Testament, which first claim our attention, are full of marvels, and introduce us to a fairy world as strange as that of the *Thousand and one Nights*. The rabbis with their commentaries and the Arabs with their stories created a new Bible, all dream and phantasy;[36] amendment and expansion of the sacred text occur in every line. . . .

Such stories bear the mark of their origin. In the burning deserts of the East the imagination seems to have something of the nature of that light which creates the unreal world of mirage.

All of these marvellous stories were not known to the Middle Ages, though some travelled as far as the West and were accepted by the commentators. Some of them were inserted by Peter

Comestor in the *Historia Scolastica* and by Vincent of Beauvais in the *Speculum historiale.*

At times the artists drew inspiration from them. . . .

No figure in the New Testament owes more to legend than that of the Virgin. The Gospel account in which she rarely appears, and still more rarely speaks, soon seemed inadequate to men who would know of her family, her childhood, the circumstances of her marriage, her latter years and her death. And so there arose in primitive times the apocryphal stories which charmed the Middle Ages. The figure of the Virgin is seen against a background of legend, as in the pictures of the old German masters she is seen against a hedge of roses. . . .

The cult of the Virgin which grew up in the twelfth century developed in the thirteenth. The bells of Christendom began to ring the Angelus, the Office of the Virgin was recited daily, and the finest cathedrals arose under her patronage. Christian thought, meditating through the centuries on the mystery of a virgin chosen of God, anticipated the dogma of the Immaculate Conception, and as early as the twelfth century the mystical church of Lyons celebrated that festival. The monks ever thinking of the Virgin in their solitude extolled her perfections, and more than one of them deserved the title of Doctor Marianus, which was given to Duns Scotus. The new orders, Franciscans and Dominicans, true knights of the Virgin, spread her cult among the people. . . .

The history of the Christian world is presented in the cathedrals as it is in Vincent of Beauvais's *Speculum historiale,* where periods are reckoned not by the deeds of emperors and kings but by the lives of saints. The windows and statuary of the churches proclaim that since the coming of Christ the really great men are the doctors, confessors and martyrs. Conquerors who filled the world with their fame appear in the humblest of attitudes; tiny figures smaller than children, they kneel at the feet of the saints.

We know from the *Speculum historiale* that such was the medieval conception of history. Nothing could be more surprising than the scheme of the great work from which so many generations of men—and the kings themselves—learned history. At the beginning of each chapter Vincent of Beauvais mentions the emperors of the East and of Germany and the kings of France, and devotes a few lines to their battles and their treaties. He then reaches his subject, the story of the saints who were contemporaries of these kings and

347

emperors. His heroes are abbots, anchorites, young shepherdesses, beggars. The translation of relics, the founding of some monastery, the healing of a demoniac, the retreat of a hermit to the desert, are to him the most important facts in the history of the world. . . .

In the eyes of the thirteenth century the real history of the world was the story of the city of God. It is necessary to bear in mind such a conception of history in order to understand the innumerable legends of saints which are painted or carved in the cathedral of Chartres, where each window or bas-relief is like a chapter from the *Speculum majus.* In this reading of history the enormous number of images of saints which decorate the churches find at least partial explanation. . . .

The cathedral is as we have seen the city of God. In it the righteous, and all who from the beginning of the world have worked at the building of the holy city have their place. But those who are descended, as St. Augustine has it, not from Abel but from Cain, are not found there whatever the part they may have played in life. There is no place for Alexander or for Caesar.

The Christian kings themselves are rarely seen there. The honor was not given to all, but was reserved for those who were preeminent as workers for the kingdom of God—for Clovis, Charlemagne and St. Louis. And so profane history when it does appear in thirteenth-century glass may in a sense also bear the name of sacred history. . . .

CONCLUSION

In one of the chapters of *Notre Dame de Paris,* that book in which rare rays of light break through the darkness, Victor Hugo says: "In the Middle Ages men had no great thought that they did not write down in stone." What the poet grasped with the intuition of genius we have labored to demonstrate.

Victor Hugo was right. The cathedral is a book. It is at Chartres, where each Mirror finds its place, that this encyclopedic character of medieval art is most evident. The cathedral of Chartres is medieval thought in visible form, with no essential element lacking. Its ten thousand figures in glass or in stonework form a whole unequalled in Europe.

It may be that other great French cathedrals were originally as complete as Chartres still is, but time has dealt more harshly with them. Yet nowhere else appears so coherent an effort to embrace the whole of the universe. Either intentionally or because the loss of neighboring work has destroyed the balance, each of the other great cathedrals seems designed to place in relief some one truth or doctrine; a diversity which is not without its charm. One chapter for instance is developed at Amiens, another at Bourges.

Amiens is the messianic, prophetic cathedral. The prophets of the façade stand like sentinels before the buttresses and brood over the future. All in this solemn work speaks of the near advent of a savior.

Notre Dame at Paris is the church of the Virgin, and four out of six portals are dedicated to her. She occupies the center of two of the great rose-windows, and round her are grouped the saints of the Old Testament or the rhythmical sequence of the works of the months and the figures of the virtues. She is the center of all things. Never weary, the centuries sang her praises turn by turn, the twelfth century in the Porte Sainte-Anne, the thirteenth in the Porte de la Vierge, and the fourteenth in the bas-reliefs on the north side. Nowhere was she more beloved.

Laon is the cathedral of learning. Knowledge is there placed in the forefront, and the Liberal Arts accompanied by Philosophy are sculptured on the façade and painted in one of the rose-windows. The Scriptures are presented in their most mystical form, and the truths of the New Testament are veiled under the symbolism of the Old. Famous doctors, one feels, must have lived beneath her shadow. She has indeed something of their austerity of aspect.

Reims is the national cathedral. Others are catholic, she alone is French. The baptism of Clovis fills the angle of the gable, and the kings of France occupy the windows of the nave. The façade is so rich that on a coronation day it needs no further decoration, for tapestries of stone hang in the porches. She is ever ready to receive kings.

Bourges celebrates the virtues of the saints. The windows illustrate the *Golden Legend.* Round the altar the life and death of apostles, confessors and martyrs form a radiant crown.

The doorway at Lyons recounts the wonders of creation. Sens unfolds the immensity of the world and the diversity of the works of God. Rouen is like a rich book of Hours in which the center

349

of the page is filled with figures of God, the Virgin and the saints, while fancy runs riot in the margin.

Though in each cathedral one chapter of the Mirror is, as we see, developed by preference, it is seldom that the others are not at least indicated, thus suggesting the desire to give encyclopedic teaching. Aware of the power of art over childlike and humble souls, the medieval Church tried through sculpture and stained glass to instill into the faithful the full range of her teaching. For the immense crowd of the unlettered, the multitude which had neither psalter nor missal and whose only book was the church, it was necessary to give concrete form to abstract thought. In the twelfth and thirteenth centuries, doctrine was embodied both in the drama of the liturgy and in the statues in the porch. By its marvelous inner force Christian thought created its own medium. Here again Victor Hugo saw clearly. The cathedral was the people's book of stone rendered gradually valueless by the coming of the printed book. "The Gothic sun," he says, "set behind the colossal press at Maintz."

At the end of the sixteenth century Christianity had lost its plastic power, and had become solely an inward force.

NOTES

[1] It is not our object, as we have said, to write the history of the nimbus nor of the other attributes passed in review in this chapter. The greater number date back to remote antiquity, and some (like the nimbus) to pagan times. The question has been fully treated by Didron, *Hist. de Dieu*, pp. 25–170.

[2] All these symbols are constantly used in glasspainting.

[3] The word hieroglyphic does not seem too strong if one remembers that the evangelists were sometimes represented in the form of men with the head of the ox, the eagle and the lion (see capital in the cloister at Moissac). Here medieval art joins that of ancient Egypt, and is perhaps even derived from it through the Christian art of Alexandria.

[4] It was scrupulously observed at Chartres. The heroes of the Old Covenant are sculptured in the north porch, those of the New in the south porch. In Notre Dame at Paris the great rose-window to the north is devoted to the Old Testament, that to the south to the New. At Reims the rose-window to the north (mutilated) again shows scenes from the Old Testament (the Creation, Adam, Cain, Abel, &c.), that to the south (restored in the sixteenth century, but doubtless on the old model) is filled with figures of Christ and the apostles. It is curious that the rule is still observed in the fifteenth century. At St. Ouen at Rouen and at St. Serge at Angers

the windows to the north portray the prophets, those to the south the apostles. The practice was also known to the East. In the monastery of Salamis the Old Testament is to the left, that is to the north, and the New to the right, the south. See Didron and Durand, *Iconographie chrétienne. Traduction du manuscrit byzantin du Mont Athos* (Paris, 1845), 8vo, p. xi. On the symbolism of the north and south see especially G. Durand, *Ration.*, lib. IV., cap. xxiii., xxiv.; and Rabanus Maurus, *De Universo*, ix., *Prol.* "auster sancta Ecclesia est fidei calore accensa."

[5] There are a few exceptions to prove the rule. In the great porch at Amiens, for example, St. Paul is to the right of Christ and St. Peter to the left. This arrangement takes us back to primitive Christian art. In early times St. Paul was placed to the right and St. Peter to the left of Christ to mark the substitution of the Gentile for the Jew. This is the reason given even in the twelfth century by Peter Damian in a treatise he wrote on representations of the two chief apostles (*Patrol.*, cxlv.). St. Paul, he said, placed the hosts of the Gentiles on the right hand of God. And he adds, St. Paul was of the tribe of Benjamin, and Benjamin means "son of the right hand." The old doctrine is perpetuated in the papal bull, where St. Paul is seen to the right and St. Peter to the left of the Cross.

[6] Old porch at Chartres.

[7] St. Augustine, *De libero arbitrio*, lib. II., cap. xvi. *Patrol.*, Vol. xxxii, col. 1263.

[8] *Id., ibid.*

[9] St. Augustine, *Quaest.* in *Heptateuch.; Patrol.*, Vol. xxxvi.–xxxvii., col. 589; see also St. Augustine's treatise *De Musica*, chapter "De numeris spiritualibus et æternis," vi. xii., *Patrol.*, Vol. xxxii., col. 1181.

[10] St. Augustine, *In Psalm.*, vi.; *Patrol.*, Vol. xxxvi.–xxxvii., col. 91. "Numerus ternarius ad animum pertinent, quaternarius ad corpus," and Hugh of St. Victor, *Patrol.*, Vol. clxxv., col. 22.

[11] On the number twelve see Rabanus Maurus, *De Universo*, xviii. 3; *Patrol.*, Vol. cxi., "Item duodecim ad omnium sanctorum pertinent sacramentum, qui, ex quatuor mundi partibus per fidem Trinitatis electi, unam ex se faciunt ecclesiam"; and Hugh of St. Victor, *De scripturis et script. sacris, Patrol.*, Vol. clxxv., col. 22.

[12] On the number seven see Hugh of St. Victor, *Exposit. in Abdiam, Patrol.*, Vol. clxxv., col. 400 *sq.*

[13] Subtle and learned Italy connected the planets with the seven ages of man on the capitals of the Ducal Palace at Venice, and in the frescoes in the Eremitani at Padua. *Annales archéol.*, t. xvi. pp. 66, 197, 297.

[14] A question which has given rise to lengthy controversy in medieval archaeology is that of the deviation of the axis of churches, so frequently noticed in the choir. Is such an irregularity due to chance, to necessities of a material order, or has it a symbolic intention? Was it not done in remembrance that Christ, of whom the church is an image, inclined His head when He died on the Cross? Viollet-le-Duc does not commit himself, though recognizing that such an idea would be in harmony with all that we know of the genius of the Middle Ages (*Dictionn. raisonné de l'architect.*, article *Axe*). For my part I was long disposed to interpret the deviation of the axis in a mystical sense. The notable memoir that M. de Lasteyrie devoted to this question, (*Mém. de l'Acad. des Inscript. et Belles-Lettres*, Vol. xxxvii. (1905), has convinced me that this deviation could have no symbolic meaning. When not due to the necessities of the site, it resulted from

an error in measurement, and always corresponds to a break in the work of building. The precise examples given by M. de Lasteyrie must surely remove all doubt. M. Anthyme Saint-Paul, so long one of the champions of symbolic interpretation, almost immediately on the publication of the *Mémoire* signified his adhesion to M. Lasteyrie's theory *Bullet. monum.* (1906). This symbolism discarded, what remains of the ingenious deductions of Mme. Félicie d'Ayzac who had tried to show that the small door in the side of Notre Dame at Paris, the *porte rouge*, was the figure of the wound made by the lance in the right side of Jesus, *Revue de l'art chrétien* (1860 and 1861)? Symbolism has too large a place in medieval art to leave room for the fancies of modern interpreters.

[15] *Speculum majus,* Douai (1624), 4 Vols., folio. This is the reprint made by the Jesuits. We shall constantly refer to this edition.

[16] Vincent of Beauvais had not time to write the *Mirror of Morals,* and the work that bears that title dates from the beginning of the fourteenth century. (See *Histoire littér. de la France,* Vol. xviii. p. 449.) But it is evident that the *Speculum morale* was part of his original plan, and that is all that concerns us here.

[17] The first is not an angel, as is often stated, but a man. It will be seen that he expressly symbolizes human nature.

[18] The miniaturists gave artistic form to this symbolism. Near to the man (St. Matthew) they sometimes represented the Nativity, near to the ox the Crucifixion, near to the lion the Resurrection, and near to the eagle the Ascension. Examples of this practice are known from the tenth century (*Evangeliarium* of the Emperor Otto *Bull. Monum.* [1877], p. 220), down to the fourteenth (Bibl. Mazarine, MSS. 167, f. 1, *Postilla* of Nicolas de Lyra).

[19] The statues of Adam and Eve are modern, but are reproductions of the originals.

[20] *Speculum doctrinale,* I. ix. The same idea is developed by Honorius of Autun in his *De animae exsilio et patria, Patrol.,* clxxii., col. 1241. The idea is this: the soul's exile is ignorance, the native land is wisdom, the Liberal Arts are so many cities on the road which leads there.

[21] At Chartres there are as many as nineteen craft guilds. See Bulteau, *Monogr. de la cath. de Chartres,* i. p. 127.

[22] *E.g.* Senlis (west porch); Semur (north porch); Chartres (old porch, north porch, window in choir); Reims (west porch, mutilated series); Amiens (west porch); Notre Dame at Paris (west porch and rose-window to the west); Rampillon (Seine-et-Marne) (west porch). The rose-window in Notre Dame at Paris as reproduced in Lenoir's *Statistique monumentale de Paris,* Vol. ii., Pl. XIX., is the outcome of several restorations, but the original state is given by Lasteyrie, *Hist. de la peint. sur verre,* p. 141. Didron thought to recognize a third Zodiac at Notre Dame at Paris—west façade, left doorway, trumeau. I do not share his view. The artist did not set out to represent the labors of the months, but to make a sort of thermometer. At the bottom there is a man warming himself before a good fire, higher up a man looking for wood, then a man taking a walk but still wearing a cloak, then a curious figure with two heads and two bodies, one body clothed, the other nude, evidently an expression of the sudden variations of temperature in spring. Then one sees a figure clothed only in breeches, and lastly an entirely nude figure. On the other side of the trumeau there is a ladder of the ages of man.

[23] Reproduced in the *Ann. arch.*, Vol. xxiv.

[24] See the pavements in the church at Tournus, in Saint Rémi at Reims (now removed), in Saint-Bertin at Saint-Omer, and in the church at Aosta. Suger, faithful to tradition, had the works of the twelve months executed in mosaic on the façade of St. Denis (see fragment in the Musée de Cluny).

[25] The archivolts of the north porch.

[26] West façade, Portail de la Vierge; pillars.

[27] Augustine, treatise, *De ordine*, ii. 12. *Patrol.*, xxxii., col. 1011.

[28] Didron, *Iconographie chrétienne. Guide de la peinture du Mont-Athos*, p. 408, note. This theme of the ages of man is not unknown in French medieval iconography. I believe they are to be seen at Notre Dame at Paris (west front, left porch, to the right on the trumeau). There are six ages beginning with adolescence ("infantia" is missing).

[29] Jourdain and Duval, *Le Portail Saint-Honoré ou de la Vierge dorée à la cathédrale d'Amiens* (Amiens, 1844), 8vo.

[30] The miniature was published by G. de Saint-Laurent, *Guide de l'art chrétien*, iii. p. 346.

[31] Tertullian, *De Spectaculis*, xxix. On this subject see Puech, *Prudence* (Paris, 1888), 8 vo, p. 246.

[32] Honorius of Autun, *Scala coeli minor*, col. 869; *Spec. Eccles.*, col. 869; *Patrol.*, clxxii. He did not invent the metaphor, but took it from St. Joannes Climacus.

[33] Hugh of St. Victor, *De fructibus carnis et spiritus. Patrol.*, clxxvi., col. 997.

[34] St. John 3:14.

[35] St. Matthew 12:40.

[36] The Jewish and Arabic traditions relating to the chief persons of the Old Testament are collected in Migne's *Dictionnaire des apocryphes*, 2 Vols., 4to (1858).

16. THE BYZANTINE CONTRIBUTION TO WESTERN ART OF THE TWELFTH AND THIRTEENTH CENTURIES

Ernst Kitzinger

INTRODUCTION

The old stereotype of a static—even stagnant—Byzantine tradition has been effectively overturned by the scholarship in this area over the past thirty-five years. Not only was Byzantine art a continually developing tradition, it was not insulated from the West and, indeed, time and again made significant contributions to the art of western Europe. The major breakthrough in this view of Byzantine art occurred at the inauguration of the Dumbarton Oaks Center for Byzantine Studies, in Wilhelm Koehler's paper "Byzantine Art in the West," published in *Dumbarton Oaks Papers*, I (1941), 61 ff. (*Dumbarton Oaks Papers* are essential to the study of Byzantine art, and the student should consult this series for other titles relevant to this aspect of Byzantine art and to the general field of Byzantine studies.) The line of investigation inaugurated by Koehler's pioneer paper has been carried on by other scholars like Ernst Kitzinger, one of whose articles is reprinted here, and by Otto Demus, whose *Byzantine Art and the West* (1970) is one of the most recent contributions. For further reading on this subject, there are Ernst Kitzinger, "Byzantium and the West in the Second Half of the Twelfth Century: Problems of Stylistic Relationship," *Gesta*, IX, 2 (1970), 49–56; by the same author, "Norman Sicily as a Source of Byzantine Influence on Western Art in the Twelfth Century," in *Byzantine Art—An European Art: Lectures*, Athens (1966). In the same volume are contributions by D. Talbot Rice ("Britain and the Byzantine World in the Middle Ages"), W. F. Volbach ("Byzanz und sein Einfluss auf Deutschland und Italien"), and S. Runciman ("Byzantine Art and Western Mediaeval Taste"), among others. There are also Kurt Weitzmann, "Various Aspects of Byzantine Influence on the Latin Countries from the Sixth to the Twelfth Century," *Dumbarton Oaks Papers*, XX (1966), 3 ff.; and by the same author, his important study of a North Italian ensemble of around 700 A.D., *The Fresco Cycle of S. Maria di Castelseprio* (1951). The reader may wish to compare this last-mentioned work with Meyer Schapiro's remarks on these frescoes in his *Late Antique, Early Christian and Medieval Art: Selected Papers* (1979), pp. 67–142, which reprints two earlier publications by Schapiro: "The Frescoes of Castelseprio," *Art Bulletin*, XXXIV, 2 (June 1952), 147–163; and "Notes on Castelseprio," *Art Bulletin*, XXXIX, 4 (December 1957), 292–299.

The selection that follows is reprinted from Ernst Kitzinger, "The Byzantine Contribution to Western Art of the Twelfth and Thirteenth Centuries," *Dumbarton Oaks Papers*, XX (1966), 25–47, with the permission of the author.

The two centuries from A.D. 1100 to 1300 witnessed the greatest achievements in the history of Western mediaeval art, namely, the creation of Gothic cathedral art in the North and a new birth of painting in Italy. During this same two hundred years' span Western Europe was brought into the closest contact it ever had with the art of the Greek East, the art of Byzantium. The question is whether there is any causal connection between these two sets of facts, and, if so, what that connection is.[1]

The question was answered in essentially negative terms by the originators of modern art historical inquiry, Lorenzo Ghiberti in the fifteenth century and Giorgio Vasari in the sixteenth. Solely concerned, of course, with Italy, they blamed the *maniera greca* for everything that was wrong with painting in that country before the genius of Giotto ushered in a new era.[2] . . .

Since the days of Ghiberti and Vasari, and more particularly during the last hundred years, a good deal of study has been devoted to Byzantine art. Along with this exploratory work has come a thorough-going reappraisal of the role of Byzantium vis-à-vis the art of the West. To stay within the Italian domain for the moment, a school of thought has developed which credits Byzantium with a constructive and positive contribution to the dramatic evolution of painting in that country, particularly in the thirteenth century.[3] Yet, the assessment of Byzantium's role remains ambiguous. As recently as 1948 Roberto Longhi, one of Italy's most brilliant art historians, published a now famous article in which—so far as the value of the Byzantine contribution is concerned—Vasari's case is in effect restated.[4] The *maniera greca* was a blight, the Greeks were the "sterilizers" of Dugento painting, the triumphs of Giotto and Duccio were achieved in the teeth of, rather than with the help of, this alien intrusion. While Longhi's article displays a startling lack of comprehension of Byzantine art and its history, Victor Lazareff, one of the foremost living authorities in that field, with excellent credentials also as a student of Italian art, likewise takes a rather negative view of Byzantium's over-all role in relation to the latter.[5] Thus the issue remains very much alive in our own day; indeed, so far as Italy is concerned, the negative appraisals of the Byzantine contribution have, on balance, won out over the positive.

Study of mediaeval art in the transalpine countries is, of course, of much more recent origin. Born of the historical and aesthetic concepts of Romanticism, it tended from the outset to put a positive evaluation on whatever Byzantine influences and affinities were observed, and this positive attitude has remained characteristic of much of the research in that field. But even in the North examples of the "Vasarian" approach are not lacking. . . .

The point at issue, then, is not whether Byzantine influences are present in Western art of the twelfth and thirteenth centuries—on this the proponents of Byzantium and its detractors are on the whole agreed—but the evaluation of its role. Was Byzantium essentially a retarding, chilling, and obstructing element in Western art or was it a positive, life-giving, and constructive one?

Before going further, I should make it clear that my observations will be confined to the pictorial arts on which the whole debate has been traditionally focussed. Architecture, which of course constitutes an essential part of the total Western achievement during the period in question, had its own distinct development, to which the Byzantine contribution is at best elusive and indirect.[6] Our topic is the role of Byzantium vis-à-vis the emergent Gothic in Northern sculpture and painting, on the one hand, and vis-à-vis the new birth of painting in Italy, on the other.

The conflicting assessments of this role are due in large part to uncertainties about Byzantine art itself. Here again it is useful to go back to Vasari whose concept of that art was of extreme simplicity. To him the *maniera greca* meant monotonous and repetitious representations of saints, tinted rather than painted (i.e., drawn with lines and primary colors rather than modeled in the round), standing on the tips of their toes, with eyes staring and hands open. Moreover, it meant a totally static art, entirely determined by usages and traditions handed on from one painter to another, generation after generation, without any attempt at change or improvement, and thus wholly lacking in development.[7] This is Vasari's "image" of Byzantine art, and in spite of all the attention—and in great part sympathetic attention—given to this art in more recent times, this image (like the image which, two centuries after Vasari, Edward

Gibbon drew of the Byzantine state and Byzantine civilization as a whole) is still very much with us, witness the modern art historians whom I quoted. Vasari's concept refused to die for the same reason, no doubt, that Gibbon's will not die, namely, that it is partly true. Monotonous rows of saints with staring eyes and open hands are not hard to find in Byzantine art. It is also true that such representations recur without essential change through many hundreds of years, so that one may well speak of virtual stagnation, especially if one uses as a yardstick the pace of development, say, in the Italian Renaissance, or in our own time. But, of course, there is another side to Byzantine art, a side perpetually nourished and reinvigorated by Byzantium's Greco-Roman heritage, thanks to which figures may appear in lively action, in three-dimensional corporeality, and in spatial settings. Frescoes such as those of Castelseprio and Sopoćani, and miniatures such as those of the Joshua Roll or the Paris Nicander Manuscript (B.N., suppl. gr. 247) are just as "Byzantine" as Vasari's rows of saints, and it is on works displaying to a greater or lesser degree this antique heritage that the proponents of a positive role of Byzantine art vis-à-vis the West have most often drawn. In one sense, however, the proponents have tended to agree with Vasari. They, too, have often treated Byzantine art as essentially static, witness the fact that the examples with which they have illustrated Byzantine influences have at times been chosen rather indiscriminately from different centuries. Yet, one of the achievements of modern scholarship has been an increasingly clear understanding of the development that took place within Byzantine art through the long centuries of its existence. While this development has not as wide a range as that of Western art, while the swings of the pendulum are, as it were, less great, the evolutionary pattern is nevertheless real and organic. To be aware of this, to take the measure of where Byzantine art itself stood at the time the intensive contacts with the West began and how it progressed from this point on is a first prerequisite for a proper appraisal of the East-West relationship.

The mosaics of Daphni (see Fig. 32), the most representative monument of Byzantine pictorial art remaining to us of the period about A.D. 1100, provide a logical starting point for such a survey, which in the circumstances must necessarily be brief and somewhat oversimplified. The Daphni style embodies a rare synthesis, a moment of extraordinary equilibrium between the two antithetic elements always present in Byzantine art, the "classical" and the "abstract." Figures stand out clearly, almost starkly, against large areas of empty ground and are structured firmly by means of a rather simple and schematic system of lines, which also stands out very clearly, particularly in the draperies, and recurs time and again in more or less identical and stereotyped patterns. But, in spite of these abstract settings and linear "armatures," figures are organic and three-dimensional. This is due partly to subtle and skillful modeling within the linear framework, but chiefly to a bold use of contrasts of light and dark, whereby the figures acquire a great deal of relief and a solid bodily presence.

Of the two elements so nicely balanced here—the organic and the linear—it is the latter which wins out more and more in Byzantine art in the course of the twelfth century. In the votive panel of the Emperor John II Comnenus in the south gallery of St. Sophia, a mosaic of about 1120, the "painterly" elements of the Daphni style have already been largely eliminated (Fig. 46). Every feature—eyes, nose, mouth, hands—is so fully and clearly defined by neat and emphatic lines and all shading is so smooth and regular that, instead of solid flesh, we seem to behold a brittle, sharp-edged mask of fine porcelain. This calligraphic, linear quality remains dominant in Byzantine painting throughout the twelfth century. The head of St. Panteleimon from the frescoes at Nerezi in Macedonia, dated 1164, is indeed a direct descendent of the heads of the mosaic panel of John II, with the pattern of lines refined almost to the point of preciousness. But Nerezi, in its famous cycle of Gospel scenes, also illustrates a further step, namely, an increasing complexity of these linear patterns (Fig. 47). In the draperies these begin to form all manner of zigzags, curls, and eddies, which, though not really motivated by the action of the body underneath, do impart to the figures a new liveliness, a nervous intensity. And this agitation is not confined to draperies; it seizes the entire figure, as well as the scenic setting, so that the whole composition begins to heave and swirl. What we see here is, in fact, the beginning of that "dynamic" phase which was to dominate Byzantine art in the last decades of the twelfth century. It is only rather recently that this phase has come to be recognized as a major and distinctive phenomenon in the main stream of the Byzantine stylistic evolution.[8] As we shall see, to be aware of this phase is of considerable importance for a correct understanding of what happens in the West during the same period.

46. Empress Irene (detail), from mosaic panel of the Virgin and Child between Emperor John II Comnenus and Empress Irene, South Gallery, Hagia Sophia, Istanbul, Byzantine, *c.* 1118 (The Byzantine Institute, Dumbarton Oaks)

When paintings such as those of Nerezi first became known they were called "neo-hellenistic," because of the evident fact that there is in them a new intensity of gesture and facial expression, a new emotional power and human empathy.[9] But in the purely formal sense the term is misleading because these paintings remain essentially within the linear tradition of the first half of the century. There is no return here either to the "painterly" devices or to the solidity and monumentality (or, for that matter, to the classic nobility and poise) of the human form which we found at Daphni. Certainly the highly sophisticated interplay of agitated linear patterns adds to the emotional power of these figures, and to do so may well have been the original purpose of the new dynamism. But it soon becomes an

47. Lamentation of Christ, Wall Painting, Naos, Church of St. Panteleimon, Nerezi, *c.* 1164 (Josephine Powell)

end in itself, divorced from all inner motivation, and what may at first have seemed to have the makings of a powerful Byzantine baroque ends up, in the 1190's, in a strange sort of mannerism (Fig. 48). Looking back from this point to the mosaics of Daphni, one must certainly grant that there was in Byzantine art of the twelfth century a stylistic development of considerable magnitude.

What is true of the twelfth century applies even more to the thirteenth. In the whole history of Byzantine art this is one of the most crucial centuries and one of the most obscure. At one time it was considered simply a hiatus. Art in Constantinople was thought to have gone into a decline in the latter half of the twelfth century and to have come to a virtual standstill during the period of the occupation of the city by the Crusaders (1204–1261).[10] The new flowering under the Palaeologan dynasty in the early fourteenth century was thought to have been due to new impulses from Italy.[11] Today this view is no longer tenable. We still lack, and probably always shall, a coherent series of monumental mosaics and paintings from the capital itself with which to bridge the gap between the late twelfth and the early fourteenth century. But in miniature painting a continuity of production has been conclusively demonstrated.[12] And the more we have learned of mural paintings in some of the Byzantine "successor states," notably Serbia, Bulgaria, and Trebizond, the more we have come to realize that the monuments in these areas reflect a common tradition, a single, organic development. It may well be that Constantinople was the main generative center of this development throughout.

48. Angel of the Annunciation, Wall Painting from bema arch, Church of St. George, Kurbinovo, *c.* 1191 (Josephine Powell)

Having already made use of mural paintings in the Balkans as representatives of some stylistic phases in the twelfth century, I shall draw on the great Serbian fresco decorations of the thirteenth century to illustrate the major evolutionary trends in Byzantine art of that period. Except in certain provincial backwaters[13] the phase of excessive, mannerist agitation was at an end by A.D. 1200. In its place (and, one is tempted to assume, by way of a reaction) there now appear a new simplicity and calm monumentality both of form and expression.[14] The change is strikingly apparent in wall paintings of the Church of the Virgin at Studenica, dated A.D. 1208–1209. This new concentration on the essential structure and integrity of the human form and on the power of its simple presence is the basis of the entire subsequent development. At first the monumental effects are still achieved with the linear means inherited from the twelfth century. But—and this is the essence of the stylistic evolution in the thirteenth century—increasingly this linear frame is filled with volume and weight. Monumentality, at first achieved mainly through great, sweeping lines, becomes more and more a matter of solid modeling and heavy mass and is vastly enhanced in the process. The

363

frescoes of Mileševo show how far this evolution had progressed by about 1235; those of Sopoćani, another thirty years later represent its peak (Fig. 49). It is still possible here to detect in many figures the old linear framework underlying the design, particularly of the draperies. But certain passages—thighs, elbows, heads above all— are modelled so conspicuously as to appear to be thrust forward from the picture plane. What is more important, these thrusts are not isolated; they are centrally motivated and controlled by a powerful body which thus appears endowed with an autonomous inner force, rhythm, and weight, such as it had not possessed at any time since classical antiquity. It is by their own power that these figures seem to bulge out from the wall. It is their own volume also which appears to create space around and depth behind them, so that the traditional and conventional "stage props," the mountains, buildings, and pieces of furniture likewise curve and bulge—but inward *into* the picture, thus creating a "cave space" for the figures to breathe and act in. This "volume style" has long been known from the mosaics of the Kariye Djami, its outstanding representative in Constantinople itself. Actually, in this great and miraculously well-preserved ensemble dating from the first decades of the fourteenth century the style already appears slightly prettified, mannered, and overcharged with conscious classical reminiscences. The heroic age of the "volume style" was the 1260's and 1270's, the period immediately following the Greek reconquest of Constantinople under the Palaeologan dynasty.[15] It hardly needs emphasizing that the remarkable—and still imperfectly understood—stylistic evolution leading up to this climax is one to which Vasari's description of the *maniera greca* is almost entirely irrelevant.

Before trying to determine what bearing all this has on the art of the West we must consider two preliminary questions. The first is whether, in focussing on the stylistic aspects of Byzantine art, we have not from the start narrowed down the issue too much. Are there not other aspects—Byzantium's preeminence in certain crafts and techniques, for instance, or its highly developed religious and imperial iconography—which loom just as large, or larger, in the total picture? Our other preliminary question—and a very basic one—is what actual knowledge of Byzantine art the West can be shown or presumed to have had in the period which concerns us.

As to the first of these two questions, the artistic relationship

49. Patriarch, Wall Painting, Naos, Church of the Holy Trinity, Sopoćani, c. 1258–1264 (The Byzantine Institute, Dumbarton Oaks)

between East and West does, of course, have other aspects aside from the stylistic one. There are, for one thing, certain *media* which became prominent in Western art during the twelfth and thirteenth centuries and which were wholly or largely imported from Byzantium. One such medium is wall mosaic, a forgotten art in the West until it was revived in the latter half of the eleventh century under Byzantine tutelage;[16] another is panel painting, which we are apt to think of as a typically Western art form until we pause to consider how much its central role in the history of Western art owes to the impact of the Byzantine icon on Italian Dugento painting;[17] a third medium which should be mentioned here is stained glass, an art form which until recently was considered quite exclusively Western, but which in the light of some new finds in Istanbul may turn out also to have received an initial stimulus from Byzantium, though the Greeks never developed the aesthetic potential of this medium as it was developed in the Gothic cathedral.[18]

Then there is the Byzantine canon of *iconographic themes and types,* which all along had exerted great and authoritative influence in the West; this, too, was heavily drawn upon in certain contexts, in the "imperially" oriented art of Sicily and Venice, for instance;[19] in the illumination of luxury manuscripts in England and France about and after 1200,[20] and in thirteenth-century panel painting in Tuscany.[21]

Finally, mention must be made of the West's perennial fascination with the splendor and luxuriousness of the Byzantine *sumptuary arts,* a fascination powerfully stimulated during this period through reliquaries and other precious objects brought back by the Crusaders, and particularly through the mass of Byzantine objects d'art which came to the West after the sack of Constantinople in 1204. In certain types, especially of devotional and liturgical objects and utensils, this influence is clearly discernible.[22]

Yet, for our purposes, I feel justified in concentrating on the strictly stylistic aspect. In an over-all assessment of the role and meaning of Byzantine influences in Western art in the twelfth and thirteenth centuries style undoubtedly is the crucial issue.[23]

Turning now to the question of the actual means of transmission whereby Byzantine art became known in the West, the first point to be made is that opportunities for contact were, of course, plentiful in the age of the Crusades. I have just now referred to the objects d'art brought back in large quantities by the Crusaders themselves. Merchants and diplomats also added to this traffic. The two Byzantine reliquaries enshrined in the Morgan Library Triptych, for instance, probably were brought to the Monastery of Stavelot by its great Abbot Wibald, who travelled to Constantinople twice on diplomatic missions.[24] Other contacts were established not through travellers but through commissions placed in Constantinopolitan workshops by wealthy Western patrons, and it is noteworthy that this practice is well attested as early as the second half of the eleventh century.[25]

Still, when one tries to put together all the solid evidence, the picture remains spotty. What important and representative examples of Byzantine art would a twelfth-century artist, say in France or England, actually have had occasion to see? How many Western artists ever did set eyes on the mosaics of Daphni or of St. Sophia? Even in the case of so massive an exposure to Byzantine art as is generally agreed to underlie the *maniera greca* in thirteenth-century Italy, how much do we know of actual, concrete links?

In trying to give an answer, however summary, to these questions it is necessary to distinguish between the travel of *objects* and the travel of *artists*. So far as the former is concerned, the richest and most consecutive evidence is indeed in the area of the sumptuary arts, especially metalwork. Beginning with the series of bronze doors commissioned in Constantinople by the Pantaleoni and other South Italian magnates since the 1060's,[26] and the great gold and enamel pala ordered in the Byzantine capital soon thereafter by the Venetians for the high altar of San Marco,[27] there was a steady flow of such objects, a flow powerfully reinforced by the Crusaders' quest for relics which also involved the relics' precious containers.[28] But for portable objects in the pictorial media—especially illuminated manuscripts and icons—which are of particular interest in relation to our central problem of stylistic influences, the evidence is far less ample. Thus, it must be borne in mind that few, if any, of the great examples of Byzantine miniature painting preserved in Western libraries today were in the West during the Middle Ages. Most of these manuscripts came to the West during the age of Humanism. Undoubtedly, Byzantine illuminated manuscripts had travelled earlier. One manuscript, now in Vienna, was commissioned in Constantinople for the Church of St. Gereon in Cologne about A.D. 1077.[29] Another, in Paris, apparently came to France with a Constantinopolitan delegation in 1269.[30] There is also the remarkable group of manuscripts with miniatures in a near-Byzantine style, recently identified by Professor Buchthal as products of ateliers in the Crusader States.[31] All these manuscripts are in Western European Libraries, and in the great majority of cases this presumably means that they were brought to the West before the final collapse of Latin rule in 1291. In a few instances there are specific indications to that effect.[32] This, however, is the only major group of manuscripts which one can point to as a possible conveyor of a fairly continuous, if not altogether pure, sampling of Byzantine artistic developments. In the matter of icons the evidence is more meager still. Important as this medium came to be for the West, I know of only one authentically Byzantine icon of the Crusader period which is definitely known to have reached the West within that period, namely, the icon of the Virgin which Frederick Barbarossa gave to the Cathedral of Spoleto in 1185.[33] A number of twelfth- and thirteenth-century mosaic icons—outstanding among works of Byzantine art of those centuries—may have reached Italy (and particularly Sicily) at an early date,[34] but we do not know how early and the same is true of the one and only icon from the Crusaders' ateliers in the Holy Land so far located on Western soil.[35]

One may well wonder whether in the over-all picture the traffic in objects was as important as it is sometimes thought to be. It is true that this traffic, aside from exposing Western artists to samples of more or less contemporary Byzantine art, may also have brought to their attention works of earlier and in some cases perhaps *much* earlier periods; we shall have occasion to refer to the role which Byzantine "antiques" may have played in the Western stylistic development.[36] I strongly suspect, however, that in the final reckoning the migration of artists was of greater moment than the mute challenge of objects.[37] Here mention must be made first of all of the Byzantine mosaicists working in Italy. The first such workshop was established in Montecassino about the year 1070 at the bidding of Abbot Desiderius,[38] and this is, in fact, the only quite reliably documented case of Byzantine artists executing wall mosaics on Western soil during the entire period which we are considering. There is no doubt, however, that further teams of Byzantine mosaicists were imported by Italian patrons (notably the kings of Sicily and the doges of Venice) throughout the twelfth century, and the influx continued, if on a reduced scale, in the thirteenth. Thanks to the activities of these workshops, a major and highly representative branch of Byzantine pictorial art was continuously and through successive phases of its development kept before the eyes of Westerners, and while the influence of the mosaics, particularly in the countries north of the Alps, has sometimes been overrated, it was certainly real and important. What counts here is not only the example of the finished product, but also the opportunity of personal contacts with Greek masters which the mosaic workshops afforded.[39] Occasionally a Greek icon painter also may have found his way to the West.[40] As for Western artists travelling East, we now know, thanks to the recent explorations by Professors Buchthal and Weitzmann, that there were illuminators and panel painters from Italy, France, and other Western countries in the Crusader states.[41] It is possible, or even probable, that some of these artists eventually returned to their homelands.[42] Much scantier, but in many ways more important, evidence is provided by certain fragments of sketchbooks, especially those of Freiburg and Wolfenbuettel. Here we see Western artists in the actual process of noting down motifs from Byzantine models—and very up-to-date models—for subsequent use in their own or their colleagues' work. It is most unlikely that these studies and exercises were done at home solely with the help of some stray objects from the East that happened to have come to hand. In all probability these are travel notes—comparable in this sense to many of the drawings in Villard de Honnecourt's famous and nearly contemporary sketchbook—but travel notes made in a Byzantine, or, at any rate, semi-Byzantine milieu.[43]

So much for the actual contacts, the channels of communication, between Byzantine art and the West. The fact that there is a strong "live" element in this relationship is important, especially when considered in conjunction with our earlier observations concerning the internal development in Byzantine art during the period under discussion. The existence of these live contacts further adds to the image of Byzantine art as a living entity. This is indeed a basic point, essential to a true understanding of our entire problem. The greatest obstacle to a correct assessment of Byzantium's contribution to the art of the West is what may be called the "ice box" concept, the idea that the art of Byzantium was merely a sort of storehouse, an inert receptacle in which a repertory of traditional forms was conveniently and immutably preserved for the West to draw on. In actual fact it was an art still in the process of evolution and still capable of sending forth live impulses and live emissaries. How crucial a point this is will soon become apparent as we turn to the art of the West and consider its relationship to Byzantium in its successive phases.

A major breakthrough in the study of this relationship was accomplished exactly twenty-five years ago by Wilhelm Koehler. In a lecture given at the inauguration of Dumbarton Oaks,[44] Koehler introduced the concept of a great wave of Byzantine stylistic influence which powerfully affected the pictorial arts of Western Europe in the first half of the twelfth century. All of Koehler's specific observations were not new. But there was a three-fold significance to this truly seminal study: it pointed up the essential unity of what had until then been treated as more or less disparate phenomena in various branches of the pictorial arts in Italy, in France, in England, and in Germany; it focussed on style as the crucial area of contact between East and West during this period; and it penetrated beyond the mere definition of stylistic features to an understanding of what motivated Western artists in adopting these features. The epitome of this international style of the first half of the twelfth century is what Koehler called the "damp fold," the soft, clinging drapery which so often is seen enveloping the limbs of painted or carved figures of this period in characteristic curvilinear patterns. When one compares earlier (or contemporary, but conservative) work from the same regions in which this feature does not appear, it becomes apparent that behind this purely formal device lies a new interest in the human form and its organic structure and movement; it signifies, to use Koehler's own words, "a new type of human being." The "damp fold" implies a fully rounded, actively and autonomously functioning body such as the flat, wraith-like creatures of the preceding era—creatures that were, so to speak, bent, twisted, and patterned by an outside force—do not possess. And it is quite evident that the source of the "damp fold"—and of the underlying concept of the human form—was Byzantium.

Koehler was aware that this massive Byzantine influence had its origin in the greatly intensified artistic contacts with the Greek East which were established in the second half of the eleventh century, particularly in Italy.[45] I have referred to some of these contacts, which, be it noted, belong to what would seem to be from a purely historical point of view an unpropitious era, the era just after the great Schism of 1054 and before the First Crusade. The arrival of Byzantine artists and objects in Montecassino, Venice, and elsewhere during this period can be shown to have had stylistic repercussions in the West even before the "damp fold" became the hallmark of an international Western European style.[46] Indeed, that style already embodies a mature and sophisticated stage in the process of Western apprenticeship. The emergence of the "damp fold" and all that it implies may have been, however, not only a matter of the West gradually penetrating closer to the essential formal qualities of Byzantine art. It may have been aided by recent stylistic trends in Byzantium itself; specifically, by the increased linearism which we have found to be characteristic of Byzantine art after 1100, and by the clearer exposure of the body's organic structure inherent in that development. . . . Byzantium may indeed have set, early in the twelfth century, new patterns and new challenges to which the West responded.

This was most certainly true in the second half of the twelfth century. I referred earlier to the "dynamic" style which emerged in Byzantine pictorial art during that period, and I said that this stylistic phase has been recognized only rather recently as a distinct and important one within the Byzantine development itself. The realization of what this phase meant for the West is more recent still. Indeed, its importance is only just beginning to be understood. . . .

On Italian soil the Byzantine dynamic style is represented in pure, or almost pure, form by a number of mosaic and fresco decorations. Foremost among these are the mosaics of Monreale, executed by a team of Greek artists largely, or even entirely, within the decade from 1180 to 1190 (Fig. 50).[47] Reflections of the style can be seen in many places in Austria,[48] in Saxony,[49] in the Rhineland,[50] in France,[51] and in England.[52] English art was particularly deeply touched by this wave and, more than any other, derived from it ways of expressing extremes of emotional agitation.

Yet we must beware lest we go too far. A spirit of more or less intense agitation is an almost universal phenomenon in the pictorial art of Western Europe in the final decades of the twelfth century, and all of this agitation cannot be ascribed to the influence, or, at any rate, the *direct* influence of Byzantium. Byzantium is not a universal key. To illustrate the limits of what it can account for let me refer to one of the great masterpieces produced in the West during this period, the Klosterneuburg Altar of 1181.[53] Its superb series of enamel plaques illustrating events from the Old and New Testaments in typological confrontation is the work of Nicholas of Verdun, the enigmatic genius whose oeuvre is the culminating glory of the great twelfth-century flowering of the goldsmith's art in the Meuse valley and the Rhineland. That there is a good deal of Byzantium in Nicholas' stylistic background there can be no doubt.[54] This Byzantine ingredient, however, is not really the dynamic style, but rather the art of the 1150's and 1160's when that style had not yet come into being. Where Nicholas' basic Byzantine affinities lie can be shown best, not through the finished enamels, but through an unfinished engraving which came to light on the back of one of the plaques in a recent restoration: this plaque, which depicts the Holy Women's visit to the Sepulchre, shows, so to speak, the skeleton of Nicholas' style, and the relationship to Byzantine work of about 1160–1170 is evident.[55] On the basis of such antecedents Nicholas develops his own version of the dynamic style, and while it is impossible to ignore the fact that the date of the Klosterneuburg Altar coincides roughly with the beginning of the work at Monreale the relationship here is not specific. Time and again in studying and analyzing Nicholas' enamels, one is reminded of Byzantine work of

50. Angel (detail), from mosaic of the Expulsion of Adam and Eve from Paradise, Nave, Cathedral, Monreale, before 1183 (Alinari-Art Reference Bureau)

the "dynamic" phase.[56] Yet it is difficult to point to any concrete connections.

Thus, there arises here the problem of *parallelisms* between East and West as distinct from that of direct influences. Of course, the problem can arise only because Byzantine art was a moving stream, not a stagnant pool. It now appears that not only was there a succession of currents branching off from this stream and flowing into the stream of Western art, but, in addition, the two streams shared a common general direction. As a matter of fact, this was true not only in the late twelfth century, but in other periods also.

The Byzantine Contribution to Western Art
of the Twelfth and Thirteenth Centuries

Parallelism, as distinct from, and in addition to, direct influences, may have been a factor of some importance as early as the year one thousand when the Ottonian style was reaching maturity in the West, and Constantinople was distilling from the classical revivals of the "Macedonian renaissance" a mature mediaeval style of its own. Indeed, from that time on, and until about A.D. 1300, one can speak in a very broad sense of a common artistic evolution embracing both East and West and betokening a common cultural framework for all of European Christendom.[57] But in the late twelfth century this phenomenon becomes particularly evident and it will remain so for the ensuing one hundred years. Perhaps one should avoid the slightly mystical concept of a "Zeitstil" and think rather in terms of loose and broad connections, of general impulses which may have gone in either direction. In the particular case of Klosterneuburg there may have been a vague and perhaps indirect stimulus from Byzantium's "dynamic" phase, a stimulus which in the mind of a great artist like Nicholas of Verdun merged and coalesced with others from quite different sources to produce a broadly comparable result.

I have purposely singled out Nicholas of Verdun. He was a dominant figure in a region which played a leading role in Western Europe at the time when the Gothic pictorial style took shape. By focussing a little longer on his oeuvre and sphere of influence I can best illustrate Byzantium's role in that process, a role which after the 1180's and the 1190's becomes more and more elusive. Nicholas' own style undergoes a striking development.[58] Agitation and dynamic power reach a climax in the latter stages of the Klosterneuburg series and in some of the majestic figures of prophets from the Cologne Shrine of the Three Kings which are generally agreed to be his work. But the storm abates in his late work, the Shrine of the Virgin at Tournai dated 1205, and gives way to a calm, quiet serenity. It is a remarkable change, perhaps the most remarkable that can be observed in any one personality in the generally anonymous world of mediaeval art. Nicholas, in his later years, became an exponent of a style which about the year 1200 began to dominate the pictorial arts, not only in his own region of the Meuse, but in northern France and in England as well. Towering figure that he was, he himself undoubtedly had helped to pioneer the new style. The classic calm and lucid serenity which characterizes his work at Tournai had appeared a few years earlier in English and northern French art: in the last of the miniatures of the great Winchester

Bible, for instance; in the Westminster Psalter; and in the Psalter of Queen Ingeborg. It was a broad and broadly-based movement to which terms such as "neo-classicism" and "classical revival" have been aptly applied. It was a prelude to true Gothic rather than Gothic itself.[59]

Now there was, as we have seen, at precisely the same time a return to calm and monumental serenity also in Byzantine art, where this phase played much the same role in relation to subsequent developments that the Meusan, French, and English "neo-classicism" was to play in the evolution of Gothic. But this surely is *only* a case of parallelism, and parallelism of the most general kind. There is no question, no evidence here of a broad and massive wave of influence comparable to the great Byzantine waves that swept the West in the twelfth century.

The sources of this Western "neo-classicism" are varied and complex. The heritage of the West's earlier classical revivals—the Carolingian and Ottonian particularly—undoubtedly played an important part. Indeed, in the Meuse region, which was Nicholas' true home ground, a taste for classical forms was almost endemic. But there is in his style, and in his late work particularly, a closeness to the real antique, an almost Phidian quality which time and again has defied explanation. An acquaintance with such remains of Roman provincial art as may have been visible in northwestern Europe could not by itself account for this quality. On the other hand, I also find it hard to believe that Nicholas travelled to Greece and studied the sculptures of the Parthenon. I would suggest that an important part was played in his development by an encounter, not so much with true antiques, as with works of what has come to be known as the "Byzantinische Antike" of the sixth and seventh centuries, works of the minor arts of the period of Justinian and Heraclius in which there is a very strong classical element. When one places side by side with figures from the Tournai Shrine reliefs from Maximians' Chair, one finds specific similarities in facial types, in stances, in the strange apron-like garments, and in details of drapery design which it would be difficult to match elsewhere. The heads of certain of the prophets of the Cologne Shrine also invite such comparisons. . . .[60]

Thus, there *is* a Byzantine element here, but it is an element stemming from a Byzantine past so remote that in the perspective of the year 1200 it must have seemed like antiquity itself. I have previously suggested that during the Crusades such ancient works may have reached the West in increased numbers, and although examples of Justinianic ivory carving and metalwork had been available all along, interest in this art may have been stimulated by new imports. In this sense the Western "neo-classicism" of A.D. 1200 may owe something to the East-West traffic of the time. . . . But the point is that [it] was an essentially autonomous achievement inspired primarily by works of the distant past and not dependent on, though vaguely parallel to, the exactly contemporary phase in Byzantine art.

This "neo-classicism," however, was the seed bed in which the classical phase of French thirteenth-century cathedral art grew. There are paths leading from Nicholas of Verdun and the Ingeborg Psalter to the sculptures of Laon, Chartres, and Rheims.[61] I cannot follow these steps in any detail. Many scholars believe that the great classical statuary of Rheims could not have come into being had not their creators seen true and large-scale Greek or Roman sculptures.[62] But, if so, they merely broadened and deepened the approach to the antique which Nicholas and his contemporaries had made a generation earlier.

Thus, we can now see what the over-all contribution of Byzantium to the nascent Gothic was. We have moved, step by step, from waves of massive influence to parallelism, and finally to a classical revival which draws on sources altogether independent, at any rate, from contemporary Byzantium. The waves of influence were absorbed only to be transcended, and, in the end, the West achieved its own sovereign approach to classical antiquity.[63] There had been moves in this direction before. The importance of the various "proto-Renaissances" of the twelfth century, especially in Italy and France, should not be minimized.[64] But it was Byzantine art with its continuous and living challenge which had provided the principal schooling for the great and decisive breakthrough in the early thirteenth century. In successive stages it had held before Western eyes an ideal of the human form, first as a coherent and autonomous organism, then as an instrument of intense action and emotion. This was what enabled the West finally to make its own terms with the classical past, and to create its own version of a humanistic art. Ultimately Byzantium's role was that of a midwife, a pace-maker. Though, in this sense, the part it played was crucial, it had little direct influence on mature Gothic art. Once the great independent breakthrough toward the classical had been accomplished in the early thirteenth century, the countries that had been responsible for it—northern France, Flanders, and England primarily—were no longer susceptible to massive stylistic influences from the Greek East. Of the transalpine countries, only Germany experienced a further strong wave of Byzantine stylistic influence in the first half of the thirteenth century, a wave which produced the so-called "Zackenstil"; but this, in European terms, was a cul-de-sac.[65] Otherwise, from here on, so far as northern Europe is concerned, the relationship to Byzantium is mainly a matter of that broad and elusive parallelism of which I spoke earlier. This parallelism, however, continues throughout the great period of "high" Gothic. When one stands in the church at Sopoćani and beholds its fresco decoration with those great statuesque figures seemingly bulging forward from the walls (Fig. 49), and, at the same time, soaring upward with a powerful thrust, one cannot help thinking of the sculptured statues of French and German cathedrals.[66] But what, if any, concrete links this may involve is still a mystery.[67]

I shall be brief on the subject of the new birth of painting in Italy at the end of the thirteenth century. Obviously I could not do justice here to this vast and complex story. I only want to make one point which I consider essential, namely, that in its broad outlines, in its over-all pattern, the evolution in the Italian Dugento repeats that which we have just followed in the north: waves of Byzantine influence lead to an intensive and independent encounter with the antique which, in turn, is the prelude to complete emancipation.[68]

The further waves of Byzantine influence which reach Italy in the thirteenth century are what is commonly known as the *maniera greca*, that controversial phenomenon of which I spoke at the outset. In claiming it as analogous in character and effect to the Byzantine waves of the twelfth century that led to the emergence of Gothic, I have, by implication, declared my view of the matter. The *maniera greca* was not the dead hand of tradition. It reflects a series of live impulses from a living art. These impulses entered the main stream of the Italian development, and far from retarding or interrupting that development played an important, if indirect, part in bringing about its final climax.

This can be shown most readily by focussing on the second half of the Dugento and, more particularly, on the impact made on Italian painting of that period by what was then the latest Byzantine development, namely, the "volume style" of the early Palaeologan period. The influence of this style was immediate and obvious in the Venetian mosaic workshops,[69] but it also made itself felt as early as the 1270's in central Italy,[70] and, above all, in what was to become the heartland of the Italian Renaissance, Tuscany. Some details from the mosaics in the dome of the Florence Baptistery which have sometimes been attributed to the young Cimabue invite direct comparison with Palaeologan work.[71] So do the frescoed Evangelists in the Upper Church at Assisi, which are generally agreed to be a work of Cimabue of the 1280's or early 1290's. If these figures are heavy and corporeal, if, with their obliquely placed furniture, they seem to come forward from the picture plane, if the accompanying architecture appears staged in depth, it is obvious where the principal source for all this lies.[72] In the young Duccio's Ruccellai Madonna, also a work of the 1280's, the same influence may be less immediately identifiable because it has been sublimated, as it were, and tempered with other elements, most obviously in the throne.[73] Shown in the same oblique and depth-creating view as that of the Assisi Evangelists, it has become a fanciful and elegant piece of miniature Gothic architecture. But Duccio's strong and direct indebtedness to contemporary Byzantium becomes evident in comparing the busts on the frame of the Madonna with Byzantine miniatures of the same period,[74] or the head of one of the angels[75] with an angel from Sopoćani.[76] What is even more important here than the purely formal similarities is an ethos of serene, aristocratic humaneness which these figures share. And whatever the complexities of Duccio's development, whatever other ingredients contributed to the further evolution of his style, there is still a strong Palaeologan flavor in his Maestà of 1308, witness a comparison with the almost contemporary work in the Kariye Djami (Figs. 51 and 52).

Clearly, then, the Greek influence involved something more than an endless repetition by unimaginative Italian craftsmen of stale and outworn Byzantine formulae. It was a living challenge emanating from the most recent developments in Constantinople and taken up by leading artists.[77]

Meanwhile, however, there had been another movement of great importance, namely, a return to Italy's own antique heritage. A number of Italian thirteenth-century artists borrowed consciously and systematically from Roman and early Christian art, thus continuing the chain of "proto-renaissances" of the twelfth century. Niccolo Pisano is a famous example. But the most systematic and

51. The Temptations of Christ (detail), from mosaic in outer narthex, Kariye Djami, Istanbul, second decade of the 14th Century (The Byzantine Institute, Dumbarton Oaks)

52. Christ in Gethsemane (detail), from Duccio's *Maestà*, Opera del Duomo, Siena, 1308–1311 (Anderson-Art Reference Bureau)

deliberate effort to revive the ancient native heritage took place in Rome in the last decades of the century, when Cavallini restored the fifth-century wall paintings of San Paolo f.l.m. and Torriti "recreated" in the apse of S. Maria Maggiore an early Christian type of mosaic complete with rich, fleshy acanthus rinceaux and a Nilotic landscape with sporting cupids.[78] What is important here—and to realize it one need only look at the figures of saints in Torriti's mosaic—is that the early Christian element merges and coalesces with a strong influence from the Byzantine "volume style" (Fig. 44).[79] What might otherwise have been a fussy accumulation of antiquarian detail becomes part of a monumental vision in which the grandeur and majesty of the human figure are powerfully proclaimed. And it was from this fusion of Eastern Hellenism and native late antique art, accomplished in Rome in the closing decades of the thirteenth century, that Giotto received decisive impulses. Giotto's new image of man—dignified, autonomous, creating, and completely dominating his spatial environment—owes much to Cavallini and his Roman circle, though it was nurtured also by further borrowings from the antique.[80] Thus, there is indeed a repetition of the chain of evolution that a century before had led from direct Byzantine influence to the "neo-classicism" of Nicholas of Verdun, and, finally, to the classic art of Chartres and Rheims.

Both in Italy and in the Gothic North, the Byzantine contribution was essentially a midwife service. It is not true to say that the Byzantine currents were without a future, let alone that they were merely obstructions. It *is* true to say that in the end the West found salvation elsewhere. Both of the decisive breakthroughs in the history of Western mediaeval art involved intensive and independent study of, and borrowing from, classical and early Christian antiquity. In this sense they were reactions against Byzantium. But they were preceded and, indeed, triggered by intensive waves of Byzantine influence.

It is clear also what accounts for this influence. The spell which Byzantine art held for so long—and in Italy so much longer than in the North—was due to its sustained quest for humane values. The Greek artists who in the twelfth and thirteenth centuries pursued their age-old interest in the human form and proclaimed successively its organic cohesion, its capability of conveying emotions and moods, and, finally, its power to create and dominate space, held out challenges and provided lessons such as the West's own mute relics of antiquity could never have provided by themselves. Italy, for profound historical reasons, was captivated by these values far more strongly than were the transalpine countries. Hence the long duration of her state of apprenticeship—but hence also the thoroughness of the humanistic revolution which followed. Italy after 1300 was far less prone to "mediaeval reactions" than was the Gothic North; she was, in fact, firmly launched on the road to the Renaissance.

My subject was the Byzantine contribution to Western art, not the artistic relationship between East and West in its entirety. Had the latter been my theme more would have had to be said about the limitations to which Byzantine influence always was subject in the West. Whenever one puts side by side with a Byzantine work of art a Western mediaeval one—even, and, indeed, especially, a Western work that cleaves very closely to a Byzantine model—one cannot help being forcibly struck by what are, from the Byzantine point of view, misunderstandings, misreadings, or, at any rate, reinterpretations. The manner and direction of the departure from the Byzantine norm differ depending on the period and on the national background of the Western artists involved. But there are definite trends. There are strictly morphological changes, such as the tendency to replace Byzantium's soft, painterly lines by sharper and more calligraphic ones,[81] or its rather loose and vague correlation of figures and objects in space by some form of constructivism whereby the single elements of a picture become, so to speak, building blocks neatly and often tightly stacked in zones and staged in receding planes.[82] And there are the more subtle psychological changes, the casting-off of emotional restraints, the attempts at increased empathy, the unwonted touches of drastic realism, and the expressionist excesses which in some instances lead to distortion and caricature.[83] All these are Western attitudes of long standing; most of them can be discerned in the Western approach to the art of the Greek East even in the Carolingian period, and some earlier still. They bespeak deep and fundamental differences, differences that reach far beyond the realm of form and have to do with wholly divergent attitudes toward the role and function of religious art, and ultimately toward the entire world of the senses.

Here lies a vast field of further enquiry. It is a fascinating field encompassing as it does the whole problem of the Greek and the Western world in their estrangement as well as in their kinship. But my purpose was a more limited one. It will have been accomplished if I have been able to show that during a crucial period of its artistic development the West received from Byzantium vital help in finding itself.

NOTES

[Asterisks indicate references to Vol. XX of *Dumbarton Oaks Papers* (1966)]

[1] The problem is part, or rather the core, of the Byzantine Question, which has occupied historians of mediaeval art for more than one hundred years. See Ch. Diehl, *Manuel d'art byzantin*, 2nd ed., II (Paris, 1926), p. 712 ff.

[2] On *maniera greca*, see, in general, E. Panofsky, *Renaissance and Renascences in Western Art* (Stockholm, 1960), pp. 24 f., 34.

[3] See especially P. Toesca, *Storia dell'arte italiana*, I (Turin, 1927), p. 918 ff.; P. Muratoff, *La peinture byzantine* (Paris, 1928), p. 132 ff.; R. Oertel, *Die Frühzeit der italienischen Malerei* (Stuttgart, 1953), pp. 38, 57, and *passim;* also G. Millet, "L'art des Balkans et l'Italie au XIIIe siècle," *Atti del V congresso internazionale di studi bizantini*, II (= *Studi bizantini e neoellenici*, VI [Rome, 1940]), p. 272 ff., where, however, a rather sharp distinction is drawn between the art of the Balkans and the art of Byzantium proper. Millet's ideas are developed further in a recent book by R. Valland, eloquently entitled *Aquilée et les origines byzantines de la Renaissance* (Paris, 1963).

[4] R. Longhi, "Giudizio sul Duecento," *Proporzioni*, 2 (1948), p. 5 ff., especially pp. 9 f., 21 f., 24 ff. See also F. Bologna, *La pittura italiana delle origini* (Rome, 1962), a book based on Longhi's premises.

[5] V. N. Lazareff, "An Unknown Monument of Florentine Dugento Painting and some General Problems Concerning the History of Italian Art in the Thirteenth Century" (in Russian), *Ezhegodnik Instituta Istorii Iskussto* (1956; published in 1957), p. 383 ff., especially p. 427 ff. While Lazareff explicitly rejects Longhi's extreme position (p. 437), essentially he considers the *maniera greca* of the thirteenth century as a foreign interlude antithetic to what he regards as the main line of development of a national Italian art.

[6] H. Sedlmayr, *Die Entstehung der Kathedrale* (Zurich, 1950), pp. 198 ff., 346 f.

[7] G. Vasari, *Le vite de' più eccellenti pittori scultori ed architettori*, ed. by G. Milanesi, I (Florence, 1878), pp. 242 f., 250 f.

[8] O. Demus, *The Mosaics of Norman Sicily* (London, 1949), p. 417 ff.; E. Kitzinger, *The Mosaics of Monreale* (Palermo, 1960), p. 75 ff.; K. Weitzmann, "Eine spätkomnenische Verkündigungsikone des Sinai und die zweite byzantinische Welle des 12. Jahrhunderts," *Festschrift für Herbert von Einem* (Berlin, 1965), p. 299 ff.

[9] Muratoff, *op. cit.*, p. 127.

[10] N. Kondakoff, *Histoire de l'art byzantin considéré principalement dans les miniatures*, II (Paris, 1891), p. 166 ff.

[11] The principal proponent of this thesis was D. V. Ainalov; for references, see O. Demus, "Die Entstehung des Paläologenstils in der Malerei," *Berichte zum XI. Internationalen Byzantinisten-Kongress München 1958*, IV, 2 (Munich, 1958), p. 33 f., note 141; p. 36, note 158.

[12] K. Weitzmann, "Constantinopolitan Book Illumination in the Period of the Latin Conquest," *Gazette des Beaux-Arts*, 6th ser., 25 (1944), p. 193 ff.

[13] O. Demus, "Studien zur byzantinischen Buchmalerei des 13. Jahrhunderts," *Jahrbuch der österreichischen byzantinischen Gesellschaft*, 9 (1960), p. 77 ff., especially p. 86 ff.

[14] Demus, *op. cit.* (*supra*, note 11), p. 25 ff.

[15] *Ibid.*, p. 29 f.

[16] See *infra*, p. 36.°

[17] Lazareff, *op. cit.* (*supra*, note 5), p. 428 ff., especially p. 436; H. Hager, *Die Anfänge des italienischen Altarbildes* (Munich, 1962), *passim*.

[18] A. H. S. Megaw, "Notes on Recent Work of the Byzantine Institute in Istanbul," *Dumbarton Oaks Papers*, 17 (1963), p. 333 ff., esp. p. 349 ff.

[19] The most obvious examples in these two centers are provided by mosaic decorations; see, in general, O. Demus, *Byzantine Mosaic Decoration* (London, 1947), p. 63 ff.

[20] H. Buchthal, *Miniature Painting in the Latin Kingdom of Jerusalem* (Oxford, 1957), p. 56.

[21] Cf. note 17, *supra*.

[22] A. Grabar, "Orfèvrerie mosane—orfèvrerie byzantine," in: *L'art mosan*, ed. by P. Francastel (Paris, 1953), p. 119 ff.; *idem*, "Le reliquaire byzantin de la cathédrale d'Aix-la-Chapelle," *Forschungen zur Kunstgeschichte und christlichen Archäologie*, III: *Karolingische und Ottonische Kunst* (Wiesbaden, 1957), p. 282 ff. (Grabar, however, fails to mention the key witness for the adoption in the West of the Byzantine type of utensil symbolizing the Heavenly Jerusalem, namely, Theophilus' chapters on censers: *Theophilus De Diversis Artibus*, ed. by C. R. Dodwell [London-Edinburgh-Paris-Melbourne-Toronto-New York, 1961], p. 111 ff.). R. Rückert, "Zur Form der byzantinischen Reliquiare," *Münchner Jahrbuch der Bildenden Kunst*, 3rd ser., 8 (1957), p. 7 ff. A. Frolow, *Les reliquaires de la vraie croix* (Paris, 1965), pp. 105 ff., 126 ff. and *passim*.

[23] For evidence that during the period here under consideration the stylistic aspect of Byzantine works of art became for Western artists an object of study and imitation in its own right, quite often dissociated from iconographic meaning, see the two papers by K. Weitzmann in the present volume (especially pp. 20, 76)°; also my remarks on "motif books" on p. 139 ff. of a paper published in Athens (cf. *infra*, note 39).

[24] A. Frolow, *La relique de la vraie croix* (Paris, 1961), p. 335 f.

[25] H. R. Hahnloser, "Magistra latinitas und peritia greca," *Festschrift für Herbert von Einem* (Berlin, 1965), p. 77 ff., esp. p. 79 ff.

[26] *Ibid.*, p. 81.

[27] *Ibid.*, p. 80 ff. Hahnloser questions the traditional date of 1105 for this commission and suggests that work on it may have begun soon after the accession of Alexius I in A.D. 1081 (p. 93). He also suggests that in commissioning works of art in Constantinople the Venetians may have been influenced by South Italian precedents (p. 80).

[28] (Comte Riant), *Exuviae sacrae Constantinopolitanae* (Geneva, 1877–1878). Frolow, *op. cit.* (*supra*, note 24), p. 144 ff. (on relics and reliquaries of the True Cross; see also the interesting graph on p. 111).

The Byzantine Contribution to Western Art
of the Twelfth and Thirteenth Centuries

[29] Vienna, Nationalbibliothek, MS Theol. gr. 336. See P. Buberl and H. Gerstinger, *Die byzantinischen Handschriften*, 2 = *Beschreibendes Verzeichnis der illuminierten Handschriften in Oesterreich*, N. S. IV, 2 (Leipzig, 1938), p. 35 ff. I am grateful to Prof. H. Buchthal for drawing my attention to this manuscript.

[30] Paris, Bibliothèque Nationale, MS Coislin gr. 200. See *Byzance et la France médiévale* (exhibition catalog, Paris, Bibl. Nat., 1958), p. 30 f.

[31] Buchthal, *op. cit. (supra,* note 20).

[32] *Ibid.,* pp. 41, 66 f., 92 note 2.

[33] S. G. Mercati, "Sulla Santissima Icone nel duomo di Spoleto," *Spoletium,* 3 (1956), p. 3 ff.

[34] V. Lazareff, "Early Italo-Byzantine Painting in Sicily," *The Burlington Magazine*, 63 (1933), p. 279 (icons in Palermo and Berlin). There is reason to believe that the mosaic icon of the Transfiguration in the Louvre (E. Coche de la Ferté, *L'antiquité chrétienne au Musée du Louvre* [Paris, 1958], p. 71) also was in Sicily before it came to Paris; the evidence for this is in the papers of the architect L. Dufourny (Paris, Bibl. Nat., Cabinet des Estampes, Ub 236, vol. VII).

[35] See K. Weitzmann's paper on Crusader icons in the present volume (p. 75 and fig. 52).°

[36] *Infra*, p. 41 f.°

[37] As long ago as 1893, E. Muentz wrote: ". . . l'influence byzantine . . . s'exerça pour le moins autant par l'action personnelle des artistes fixés en Italie principalement, que par l'importation des oeuvres d'art." ("Les artistes byzantins dans l'Europe latine," *Revue de l'art chrétien*, 36 [1893], p. 182 ff.). Muentz' study, supplemented for Italy by A. L. Frothingham (in *American Journal of Archaeology*, 9 [1894], p. 32 ff.), was based on literary and epigraphic evidence. I do not know of any systematic modern re-examination of that evidence.

[38] Leo of Ostia, *Chronicon Casinense*, III, 27 (Migne, PL, 173, col. 748).

[39] I have discussed the background and the impact of the Byzantine mosaicists working in Italy in the twelfth and thirteenth centuries in another paper read at the Dumbarton Oaks symposium of 1965; also, with special reference to the Sicilian workshops, in a lecture given in Athens in 1964 ("Norman Sicily as a Source of Byzantine Influence on Western Art in the Twelfth Century," *Byzantine Art—An European Art:* Lectures Given on the Occasion of the Ninth Exhibition of the Council of Europe [Athens, 1966], p. 121 ff.).

[40] The icons discussed by Lazareff in his paper "Duccio and Thirteenth-Century Greek Ikons" (*Burlington Magazine*, 59 [1931], p. 154 ff.) are probably too late in date to prove this point for the period before A.D. 1300. See the paper by J. Stubblebine in the present volume (p. 101). On the other hand, Professor Stubblebine has suggested that the two icons from Calahorra in the National Gallery in Washington may have been painted by Greek artists on Italian soil (*ibid.,* note 38).

[41] Buchthal, *op. cit.*, p. xxxiii and *passim;* K. Weitzmann, "Icon Painting in the Crusader Kingdom" (in the present volume, p. 49 ff.).°

[42] Weitzmann, *ibid.*, p. 75.°

[43] *Ibid.*, pp. 76, 79 ff.° See also my paper published in Athens (*supra*, note 39), especially, p. 139 ff.

[44] "Byzantine Art in the West," *Dumbarton Oaks Papers*, 1 (1941), p. 61 ff.

[45] *Ibid.*, p. 79.

[46] Cf., e.g., the wall paintings of the baptistery of Concordia Sagittaria, which reflect the style of the mosaics of the main portal of San Marco in Venice, mosaics which in turn are closely dependent on those of Hosios Lukas (see the exhibition catalog *Pitture murali nel Veneto e tecnica dell'affresco* [Venice, 1960], p. 36 f. and pl. 3. I owe this reference to Professor O. Demus.).

[47] For references, see *supra*, note 8.

[48] The pen drawing of the seated Christ in Vienna MS 953 (from Salzburg), which generally has been attributed to the period about or soon after 1150 (see H. J. Hermann, *Die deutschen romanischen Handschriften = Beschreibendes Verzeichnis der illuminierten Handschriften in Oesterreich*, N. S., II [Leipzig, 1926], p. 138 ff. and fig. 84), in my opinion cannot be earlier than the mosaics of Monreale.

[49] Weitzmann, *op. cit.* (*supra*, note 8), p. 309 ff.

[50] Demus, *op. cit.* (*supra*, note 8), p. 445 ff.; also my paper published in Athens (*supra*, note 39), especially, pp. 131 f., 135 f.; and K. Weitzmann's paper quoted *supra*, note 41, p. 23 f.

[51] J. Porcher, *L'enluminure française* (Paris, 1959), pl. 36 and p. 38.

[52] Demus, *op. cit.* (*supra*, note 8), p. 450 f.; also my paper published in Athens (*supra*, note 39), especially, p. 136 ff.

[53] Fl. Röhrig, *Der Verduner Altar*, 2nd ed. (Vienna, 1955).

[54] For general discussions of Nicholas' background, in which many influences converge, see H. Swarzenski, *Monuments of Romanesque Art* (Chicago, 1954), p. 29 ff.; Röhrig, *op. cit.*, p. 30 ff.; H. Schnitzler in *Der Meister des Dreikönigenschreins* (exhibition catalog, Cologne, 1964), p. 7 ff.

[55] O. Demus, "Neue Funde an den Emails des Nikolaus von Verdun in Klosterneuburg," *Oesterreichische Zeitschrift für Denkmalpflege*, 5 (1951), p. 13 ff., esp. p. 16 ff. and fig. 26. Röhrig, *op. cit.*, fig. 53.

[56] H. Schnitzler, *Rheinische Schatzkammer: Die Romanik* (Düsseldorf, 1959), p. 9. What H. Swarzenski once called "the enigmatically early date" of the Klosterneuburg Altar ("Zwei Zeichnungen der Martinslegende aus Tournai," *Adolph Goldschmidt zu seinem siebenzigsten Geburtstag* [Berlin, 1935], p. 40) certainly appears less puzzling when seen in this light.

[57] See in general M. Gigante, "Antico, bizantino e medioevo," *La Parola del Passato*, 96 (May-June 1964), p. 194 ff., esp. p. 212.

[58] Schnitzler, *op. cit.* (*supra*, note 54), p. 9 ff.

[59] O. Homburger, "Zur Stilbestimmung der figürlichen Kunst Deutschlands und des westlichen Europas im Zeitraum zwischen 1190 und 1250," *Formositas Romanica: Beiträge zur Erforschung der romanischen Kunst Joseph Gantner zugeeignet* (Frauenfeld, 1958), p. 29 ff. O. Pächt, "A Cycle of English Frescoes in Spain," *Burlington Magazine*, 103 (1961), p. 166 ff., esp. p. 171. L. Grodecki, "Problèmes de la peinture en Champagne pendant la seconde moitié du douzième siècle," *Romanesque and Gothic Art = Studies in Western Art: Acts of the Twentieth International Congress of the History of Art*, I (Princeton, 1963), p. 129 ff., esp. p. 140 f.

[60] These stylistic connections seem to me more specific than those with more recent products of Byzantine metalwork, such as the silver reliefs from Tekali and Bochorma (H. Schnitzler, *op. cit.* [*supra*, note 54], p. 10 and figs. on pp. 7, 57).

The Byzantine Contribution to Western Art
of the Twelfth and Thirteenth Centuries

Works of the minor arts of the *early* Byzantine period were cited long ago by Wilhelm Vöge to account for the classicizing strain in early Gothic art ("Ueber die Bamberger Domsculpturen," *Repertorium für Kunstwissenschaft*, 22 (1899), p. 94 ff., esp. p. 97 ff.; *ibid.*, 24 (1901), p. 195 ff., esp. p. 196 f.). Influences from works of Byzantine art of the tenth and subsequent centuries should not, however, be ruled out altogether (see *infra*).

[61] W. Sauerländer, "Beiträge zue Geschichte der 'frühgotischen' Skulptur," *Zeitschrift für Kunstgeschichte*, 19 (1956), p. 1 ff., esp. p. 2 (importance of Meusan metalwork; for earlier literature on this subject, see the references in note 5), p. 15 with note 56 (relationship of Laon to Nicholas of Verdun), p. 21 ff. (relationship of Chartres to Laon); see also *idem*, "Die Marienkrönungsportale von Senlis und Mantes," *Wallraf-Richartz-Jahrbuch*, 20 (1958), p. 115 ff., especially p. 135 (importance of English illuminated manuscripts). H. Reinhardt, *La cathédrale de Reims* (Paris, 1963), p. 145 ff.

[62] Reinhardt, *ibid.*, p. 148 f.

[63] See the excellent formulation by O. Demus apropos of Nicholas of Verdun: "Er dürfte der erste nordische Meister gewesen sein, der durch die Oberflächenschicht des italobyzantinischen Stilhabitus zu den antiken Grundlagen der Form durchsteiß und damit der langdauernden Lehrzeit der nordischen Kunst bei der byzantinischen ein Ende machte" (*op. cit.* [*supra*, note 55], p. 18).

[64] Panofsky, *op. cit.* (*supra*, note 2), p. 55 ff.

[65] H. Swarzenski, *Die lateinischen illuminierten Handschriften des XIII. Jahrhunderts in den Ländern an Rhein, Main und Donau* (Berlin, 1936), p. 8; O. Demus, *op. cit.* (*supra*, note 13), p. 88. The "Zackenstil" is not simply a lingering reflection of the Byzantine "dynamic" wave of the late twelfth century, but was formed on the basis of quite up-to-date Byzantine models; see Weitzmann, *op. cit.* (*supra*, note 12).

[66] This was my experience when visiting Sopoćani in 1953. I was happy to find during the preparations for the 1965 symposium at Dumbarton Oaks that my friend Professor Otto Demus had independently come to the same conclusion. In the lecture on wall paintings which he gave at the Symposium, Professor Demus made striking comparisons between figures from Sopoćani and statues from Naumburg Cathedral which are of virtually the same date.

[67] A. Frolow has recently suggested a direct influence of Byzantine paintings and mosaics to account, or to help account, for the characteristic sweeping curve of Gothic statues ("L'origine des personnages hanchés dans l'art gothique," *Revue archéologique* [1965], I, p. 65 ff.). But, if there was such an influence in the thirteenth century—as distinct from, and in addition to, a development growing from seeds sown during the period of the West's own "neoclassicism" about A.D. 1200—that influence was absorbed and transposed in the freest and most sovereign manner. The gradual and essentially autonomous emergence of the motif in French early thirteenth-century sculpture has been beautifully described by W. Vöge ("Vom gotischen Schwung und den plastischen Schulen des 13. Jahrhunderts," *Repertorium für Kunstwissenschaft*, 27 [1904], p. 1 ff., esp. p. 5).

[68] This parallelism between the Northern and the Italian development was noted by Koehler, *op. cit.* (*supra*, note 44), p. 86 f., and Panofsky, *op. cit.* (*supra*, note 2), p. 137.

[69] O. Demus, "The Ciborium Mosaics of Parenzo," *Burlington Magazine,* 87 (1945), p. 238 ff., esp. pl. 1 A and p. 242; *idem, op. cit. (supra,* note 11), p. 39.

[70] Toesca, *op. cit. (supra,* note 3), p. 970 f. (Grottaferrata).

[71] *Ibid.,* p. 1003 and fig. 705. The figures of prophets in the central disk of the vault of the Scarsella, which also derive very obviously from Palaeologan art, have been attributed by O. Demus to Venetian mosaicists who came to Florence after 1301 ("The Tribuna Mosaics of the Florence Baptistery," *Actes du VIe congrès international d'études byzantines,* II [Paris, 1951], p. 101 ff., esp. p. 106 ff.; for illustrations, see *I mosaici del Battistero di Firenze* [a cura della Cassa di Risparmio di Firenze], V [Florence, 1959], pl. 15 ff.

[72] Demus, *op. cit. (supra,* note 11), p. 40 and figs. 18, 32. For Cimabue's work at Assisi and its Byzantine affinities, see also the paper by J. Stubblebine in the present volume (p. 96 f. and figs. 14–17).°

[73] Stubblebine, *ibid.,* p. 99 f. and fig. 22.°

[74] *Ibid.,* p. 99 and figs. 16, 21, 23.° See also V. N. Lazareff, in *Vizantiiskii Vremennik,* 5 (1952), p. 178 ff., esp. fig. 8.

[75] Stubblebine, *op. cit.,* fig. 26.°

[76] V. J. Durié, *Sopoćani* (Belgrade, 1963), pl. 32. For comparisons with Byzantine icons, see Stubblebine, *op. cit.,* figs. 28, 29 and p. 99 f.°

[77] Stubblebine, *ibid.,* p. 100.° For Palaeologan influences on miniature painting in Sicily in the early fourteenth century, see the paper by H. Buchthal in the present volume (p. 103 ff).°

[78] W. Päseler, "Der Rückgriff der römischen Spätdugentomalerei auf die christliche Spätantike," *Beiträge zur Kunst des Mittelalters* (Berlin, 1950), p. 157 ff. Panofsky, *op. cit. (supra,* note 2), p. 137. For Cavallini's work in S. Paolo see J. White, "Cavallini and the Lost Frescoes in S. Paolo," *Journal of the Warburg and Courtauld Institutes,* 19 (1956), p. 84 ff.

[79] P. Toesca, *Pietro Cavallini* (Milan, 1959), p. 6.

[80] Oertel, *op. cit. (supra,* note 3), p. 68. Panofsky, *op. cit. (supra,* note 2), pp. 119, 137, 148, 151 ff. (with further references).

[81] See, e.g., figs. 34, 35; also K. Weitzmann's two papers in the present volume, *passim* (e.g., p. 7 f. and figs. 8–11; p. 66 and fig. 32; p. 69 and fig. 33 f.; p. 81 f. and fig. 66 ff.).°

[82] See, e.g., Stubblebine, *op. cit.,* p. 87 f. and fig. 1 f; p. 92 f. and fig. 11 f; p. 97 and fig. 18.°

[83] See, e.g., fig. 13; also K. Weitzmann's two papers, p. 16 f. and fig. 27; p. 60 and fig. 19; p. 63 f. and fig. 23; p. 64 and fig. 26.°

17. THE GENERAL PROBLEMS

OF THE GOTHIC STYLE

Paul Frankl

INTRODUCTION

This selection from Frankl's posthumously published *Gothic Architecture* (1962) is from the second part of that volume, and it is considered by some to be the most stimulating section. Following a broad survey of the genesis and changing fortunes of the idea of "Gothic," this selection treats the development of a Gothic Style as an "immanent" or internal process within the constructional problems confronting the Gothic builders. In it Frankl stresses the interrelationship of building practices, patronage, function, and symbolism as determinants.

Frankl's earlier work *The Gothic: Literary Sources and Interpretations Through Eight Centuries* is not only a thorough review of the literature on the Gothic, but it examines as well a number of special problems. Erwin Panofsky's *Gothic Architecture and Scholasticism* (1951) is especially valuable in drawing attention to correspondences between the form of medieval scholastic writings and the form of Gothic architecture presuming a pattern of thought common to both. Clarence Ward's *Medieval Church Vaulting* (1915) is still useful and Joan Evans's *Art in Medieval France* (1948) is a fine survey. The second volume of Henri Focillon, *The Art of the West in the Middle Ages* (1963; first published in French, in 1938) treats Gothic art in general. Works dealing with more specific aspects of Gothic art are: Otto von Simson, *The Cathedral of Chartres* (1956), and by the same author, *The Gothic Cathedral: Origins of Gothic Architecture and the Medieval Concept of Order*, 2nd ed. (1974); H. Jantzen, *The High Gothic: The*

Classic Cathedrals of Chartres, Reims, and Amiens (1962); A. Katzenel-lenbogen, *The Sculptural Programs of Chartres Cathedral* (1959, 1964); J. Pope-Hennessy, *Italian Gothic Sculpture* (1955); J. Dupont and C. Gnudi, *Gothic Painting* (1954); Whitney Stoddard, *The West Portals of Saint Denis and Chartres* (1952); L. Grodecki, "The Transept Portals of Chartres Cathedral," *Art Bulletin*, XXXIII (1951), 156–164; James R. Johnson, *The Radiance of Chartres* (1965); *Abbot Suger on the Abbey Church of St. Denis and Its Art Treasures*, translated by Erwin Panofsky (1946); James Ackerman, " 'Ars sine scientia nihil est.' Gothic Theory of Architecture at the Cathedral of Milan," *Art Bulletin*, XXXI (1949), 84–111; George Kubler, "A Late Gothic Computation of Rib-vault Thrusts," *Gazette des Beaux-Arts*, series 6, XXVI (July–December 1944), and other articles on Gothic vaulting in this same issue; and Alan Borg and Robert Mark, "Chartres Cathedral: A Re-interpretation of Its Structure," *Art Bulletin*, LV, 3 (1973), 367–372. *Chartres Cathedral*, edited by Robert Branner (1969), is a handy, well-illustrated paperback anthology of documents and writings on that monument of the Gothic style. Other works are Robert Branner, *Gothic Architecture* (1961); James H. Acland, *Medieval Structure: The Gothic Vault* (1972); W. Sauerländer and M. Hirmer, *Gothic Sculpture in France 1140–1270*, trans. by J. Sondheimer (1973); P. Watson, *Building the Medieval Cathedrals* (1976); Louis Grodecki, *Gothic Architecture* (1977); John Fitchen, *The Construction of Gothic Cathedrals: A Study of Medieval Vault Erection* (1981).

Finally, there is one literary work—Henry Adams's *Mont-Saint-Michel and Chartres* (1904, reprinted many times)—that remains an enduring delight.

1. THE TERM "GOTHIC" AND THE CONCEPT
OF THE GOTHIC STYLE

THE architect who built the choir of St Denis must have spoken to Suger about the *arcus* in the vaults; William of Sens in speaking to the Abbot of Canterbury no doubt used the term *fornices arcuatae,* and Villard de Honnecourt probably spoke to his apprentices of *ogives.* However, no name for the style itself is known to have existed at this time; indeed, it is unlikely that any name did exist, for, in the regions where the Gothic style was born and developed, "building in the Gothic style" was simply called building. In Germany, the chronicler Burckhard von Hall wrote, about 1280, that the church at Wimpfen im Tal, which was begun in 1269, was built *more francigeno.* This name does not describe the style, but simply indicates its origin, which confirms the view that no special name yet existed for the style as a whole.

Petrarch (1304–1374) was in Cologne in 1333 and wrote that he had seen an uncommonly beautiful *templum* there which was unfinished, but which was rightly called the most magnificent in the world (*summum*). In spite of that Petrarch was among the first men, if not the first, to value the age of classical antiquity higher than his own on every count. He did not base this conclusion only on the poor quality of the Latin of his time, compared with that of Cicero and Vergil, and on the low standard of scholarship, compared with that of Plato (of whom he knew little); he also compared the poor quality of the painting and sculpture of this age with the perfect reproductions of natural forms achieved by the Greeks and Romans. Since he regarded himself as a descendant of the Romans, it is in his works that the theory that everything bad came from the "barbarians" was born.

This "Barbarian theory" was adopted by humanistic circles.[1] In his biography of Brunelleschi, Manetti wrote that architecture fell into decadence after the end of the Roman Empire, that the Vandals, the Goths, the Lombards, and the Huns brought their own, un-talented architects with them, that architecture improved slightly for a few years under Charlemagne, and that it then fell into decadence once more until the appearance of Brunelleschi in 1419.

Filarete, who lived from about 1400 to about 1469, had similar ideas on the history of architecture. He wrote, "cursed be the man who introduced 'modern' architecture." By "modern" he meant Gothic, which still appears to have had no name. He continued, "I believe that it can only have been the barbarians who brought it to Italy."

Alberti said that it would be absurd to paint Helen or Iphigenia with Gothic hands—with the hands of old women. In the Italian text, the phrase is *mani vecchizze e gotiche,* but, in the Latin edition, Alberti translated this with the words *seniles et rusticanae.* The word Gothic does not therefore seem, as yet, to have acquired its modern sense. Gothic meant rustic or coarse, like the Goths.

Gradually the word Gothic came to be applied not to barbarians in general, but only to certain specific barbarians. Filarete puts the blame on the *transmontani,* expressly adding, "the Germans and the French." In 1510, in the report of the so-called Pseudo-Raphael, the idea was further narrowed down: he spoke only of the *maniera tedescha.* In this report, too, the theory is first advanced that the Gothic style had its origins in the forests, because the Germans could not cut down trees, but bound together the branches of living trees, thus creating the pointed arch. This theory that the Gothic style was born in the forests of Germany lived on in various forms with unbelievable tenacity, sometimes in a literal form, and sometimes in the form of metaphors.

In 1520, page xv of Cesariano's work is headed, "secundum Germanicam symmetriam."

Vasari contrasted this bad architecture with the classical orders, and wrote: "There is also another manner of architecture which is called the German manner." He completely forgot the real culprits, the French, and went on to say: "This manner was invented by the Goths." In writing of the Palazzo dei Signori at Arezzo, he used the term *maniera de' Goti,* while Palladio reverted to the phrase, *maniera tedesca*—not *gotica.*

In France, however, it was never forgotten that the Gothic style was not born in Germany. Philibert de l'Orme, who lived from 1512 to 1570, called it *la mode Françoise.*

The General Problems of the Gothic Style

In Germany, Sandrart, in his *Teutsche Akademie*, which was published in 1675, revived the Italian theories. He seems to have been familiar with Filarete's manuscript, or at least to have had indirect knowledge of it, for he wrote that, by inventing bad architecture, the Goths "had called down more than a thousand million curses on their heads." Filarete had modestly contented himself with a single curse.[2]

From the history of the name of the Gothic style, it can be seen how muddled the concept was. The Goths, who in 410, under the leadership of Alaric, destroyed Rome, or rather parts of it, were made responsible for all the architecture that was created between 410 and 1419, and, in countries other than Italy, even for works executed up to the time of Vasari—that is, about 1550.

During the eighteenth century, in the course of a slow process of development, a more positive view of the Gothic style was reached, and, with it, the concept of what was Gothic changed. Historians began to distinguish two periods; they gave separate names to different parts of the earlier periods and reserved the term Gothic for the last period alone. The evil reputation of the men who destroyed the good architecture of Rome, however, stuck until the connexion was either forgotten, or was no longer felt. As early as 1840, Kugler said that we no longer think of the Goths when we say "Gothic." Nevertheless, those men who were beginning to feel enthusiasm for the Gothic style tried to find a better name for it, but none of these names, neither *style ogival*, nor Kugler's Germanic style, nor any of the others, found support.

When in the course of the nineteenth century historical knowledge of the birth of the Gothic style, its development, and its spread increased, the Late Gothic style was still regarded as part of the Gothic style. Moreover, the growing study of the essential Gothic elements, beginning with Wetter's book, and the attempts to interpret the essence of the Gothic, which began with the work of Viollet-le-Duc, and have continued to our own day, have neutralized the effects of personal taste and have led to a more intensive analysis of the concept of Gothic style.

The scholarly consideration of the Gothic style began with descriptions of individual buildings and so came to the study of individual members, such as pointed arches, piers, rib-vaults, windows, doorways, roofs, and towers. At the same time a desire grew to understand the essence of the Gothic style which could permeate

391

such divergent features as piers and windows. The Gothic style was said to possess a picturesque quality, a quality of infinity, a vegetal quality, a romantic quality. All these different concepts were first formulated in the eighteenth century and were then considered more closely in the nineteenth and systematically bound into one unified concept.

Some of these concepts were also applicable to sculpture and painting, and the concept of what was Gothic was widened to include, not only architecture, but also the fine arts. After this, the term became more and more extensible, until critics began to speak of Gothic literature and poetry, of Gothic music, of Gothic philosophy and metaphysics, of Gothic civilization, and, finally, of the Gothic man. This process was begun by de Laborde in 1816, when he wrote an introduction on political history to his work on French architecture. In 1843, Schnaase went further; he presented his public with a panorama of medieval civilization. At about the same time, Vitet proposed the theory that the Romanesque style was created by the clergy, whereas the Gothic style was the creation of the laity. Viollet-le-Duc tacitly accepted this theory, but broadened it with a combination of *l'esprit gaulois* and his own theory of functionalism. Succeeding generations accepted this legacy, and *l'esprit gaulois* developed further under the influence of the fantastic racial theories of Gobineau, whose forerunners had appeared as early as the eighteenth century. The study of medieval symbolism can also be traced back to the Romantic period (e.g. to works of Boisserée and later of Ramée), and the background to the history of Gothic civilization grew more and more rich and colourful.

The sceptics, who appeared about 1900, did not perceive the metaphorical driving belt which must be assumed to run between Gothic civilization and Gothic architecture, if one is to accept an explanation of stylistic developments in terms of the many factors which go to make a civilization. It was, of course, obvious that certain architectural traits must be a reflection of the civilization of their time, but it was not known whether these traits should be interpreted as reflections either of social factors or of national ones, or whether perhaps they sprang from a change in the nature of piety. Perhaps it was these factors, and many others besides, which were the roots from which history grew, and which provided the branch of architecture with its sap. Historians spoke of many different roots, but, basically, their search was for the primary root of all these roots, and they gave this title sometimes to one root and sometimes to another.

Nobody can doubt the legitimacy of these studies, but, if one stands in front of an actual building and asks oneself what a certain base of a certain pier, or a certain triforium, or a certain rose-window has to do with scholasticism, chivalry, courtly love, or even the liturgy, not to mention politics and economics, one realizes that all these many theories do not give a sufficient answer: and yet the problem is one which must be faced.

. . . The development of the Gothic style [can be viewed] as an immanent process which took place within building lodges. To clarify the problem, one can call those other factors which penetrated the lodges from outside external factors, and one can exclude them from architectural discussion, in which they would only cause confusion. As soon as one starts to look for the influence of these external factors, however, one realizes that every other branch of human activity followed its own immanent development, just as did the field of architecture. The problem that was so disturbing to nineteenth-century historians can be expressed in a single question. Did all these immanent lines of development run parallel to one another, and, if so, what was the force which produced this parallel course?

2. THE DEVELOPMENT OF THE GOTHIC STYLE SEEN AS AN IMMANENT PROCESS

The improvement of Romanesque groin-vaults came about as a result of a rational consideration of the geometric construction of the arches and the surfaces of the cells; the building technique employed, that is, the centering; their statics, both during and after construction; and also the economic problems which they presented. But all these considerations always went hand in hand with the aim of producing an aesthetically satisfying result. The changes had nothing to do with the Crusades, which began only later, or with the liturgy, or with philosophy. The architects were intent simply upon making necessary improvements. As far as can be reconstructed, this was a process of trial and error which led to the replacement of diagonal, wooden centering arches by the stone *cintre permanent*, that is the rib.

Here, the question must indeed have arisen as to whether the architectural patrons of this time, the clergy, were in agreement with the introduction of this innovation; but this question can be ignored for the moment. The development . . . shows that the rib-vault, in its turn, was further improved by a combination of rational considerations and aesthetic criticism, which resulted in the introduction of pointed arches, first over the four sides of each bay, and finally in the diagonals also. This process, too, was an immanent, or an internal one. Just as master-masons did not determine the form of the liturgy or indulge in metaphysics, so the clergy did not build scaffolding, or draw designs for arches or for the profiles of ribs. These are different spheres, different jobs, requiring special skills, and it need hardly be said that no amount of knowledge of metaphysics can help one to build a rib-vault, and that on the other hand the ability of an architect to build a vault cannot help him to decide whether general concepts are realities or mere names.

However, rib-vaults presented only part of the problem. The real problem was how to achieve conformity throughout a whole church. History shows that the transformation of Romanesque architectural members to conform with the ribs was not achieved overnight. Ribs, being members crossing each other diagonally, demanded that shafts also be turned diagonally. Therefore, the form of bases and capitals had also to be altered. In the case of sexpartite vaults, this meant that the number of shafts had to be increased. The question as to what form piers should take became an urgent one. The steps taken to solve this problem led ultimately to the dissolution of the wall into a grille and the introduction of the new Gothic kind of relief. In this kind of relief, one layer is conceived as projecting in front of another, not as lying behind it, just as ribs are seen to project in front of the cells of a vault rather than cells to lie behind the ribs. The slenderness of the rib set the proportions for slenderer supports, and its structural character seemed to demand the change from Romanesque structure to specifically Gothic structure. The new system allowed an increased emphasis on verticals (Fig. 53), yet left the architect of Sens the possibility of choosing the golden mean, and the architect of the Sainte-Chapelle that of using the fairly moderate proportional ratio of 1 : 2. The tendency to emphasize verticals only governed the work of certain schools and generations. . . .

The real propelling force of the rib lay both in its diagonality, and in its property of dividing each spatial compartment of the church into interdependent, fragmentary spatial units. The tendency to-

53. Amiens Cathedral, interior of nave, view toward apse, French Gothic, begun 1220 (Marburg-Art Reference Bureau)

wards a more and more resolute reshaping of spatial parts and architectural members to conform to the principle of partiality, and the resulting change in the forces of the members . . . must also be considered in discussing the immanence of the development of Gothic architecture. . . .

It must not be supposed that all architectural members became Gothic to the same degree at the same time. Vaults had achieved their classic Gothic form long before bases had undergone the same degree of change. But, in every case, it was the criticism of architects and their imaginative energy which demanded these changes, devised them, and finally realized them. The philosophers, the clergy, the knights, and the kings played no part in the solution of the problems; they were internal problems of the lodges.

Although every good monograph deals with the forms of bases, and distinguishes between the work of architects by the profiles they used, a detailed examination of the history of this one member would not be sufficient to explain the immanent development of the Gothic style.

The changes in the forms of the great circular windows show this development much more clearly. . . . It is easy to recognize the variations and combinations in the forms of circular windows as the result of consistent steps. . . .

. . . Every step which marked some degree of progress in the solving of the problem of filling oculi was conditioned by the demands of the whole church, and was therefore part of the greater progress of the continual increase in the emphasis on partiality: and yet every such step also set its own special problems within the greater overall problem. Every architect was involved in the common task as a follower of his predecessors and, more particularly, of his own teacher, and found in this general task his own personal task, which he fulfilled with his own imaginative powers and his own spiritual energy, according to the nature and the degree of his personal talents.

Within this process, there are those who vary, those who combine, and those who correct, some tending towards increased clarity, others towards increased splendour, yet others to both. There are steps which created something entirely new, like the system of Noyon (or perhaps earlier of the choir at St Denis), the consequences that were drawn from the form of the buttresses and flying buttresses at Chartres, and the form of the tracery at Reims. In our historical consideration we follow the works of all these architects, both the modest ones, like the architect of Senlis, and the men of genius, like the designer of Lincoln, the architects of the English chapter houses and their successors at Ely and Gloucester, Peter Parler, and many others. It is their spiritual achievements which have given us such rich gifts. However, even these men of genius were firmly bound by the whole process of development; for even the great intuitions come only out of hard work. No man who was not a member of one of the lodges could take part in the creative development of the Gothic style, not even Albert the Great, although, according to legend, he is supposed to have done so. To participate, one had to belong to the profession.

The continuity of the development was the product of instruction, and on this subject we are fairly well informed. The more the Gothic style developed, and the more complicated it became, the more impossible it was for a self-educated man to enter the field. From the ranks of the trained masons the most gifted were picked out, after they had completed their compulsory period of journeying, and were made the foremen who constituted the link between the creative architect and his executive craftsmen. Where foremen not only seemed capable of forming this link and controlling the actual labour, but also showed some aptitude for creative design, they were put to work as draughtsmen under the supervision of the architect, until they were finally equipped to carry out their own designs. The reason we have better knowledge of the organization of Late Gothic lodges is that the architects of the earlier period had easier problems to solve and could therefore treat legal and instructional problems more lightly. In the Late Gothic period, proper examinations were held, at which the apprentices had to produce a master-piece.[3] But by whatever process architects were selected from the twelfth century onwards, it is clear that an apprentice was subject to the judgement of the older generation and that he had to be familiar with the ideas of the masters before he could reach the stage at which he himself, when faced with a new problem, could make his own constructive criticism of their work.

This explains the small extent of the steps taken within the lodges, and the interplay of influences, which was the result of the travel of apprentices and of the calling of architects from one place to another. Even in the spread of the style over regions far distant from one another, which was the result of journeys of whole bands of masons, or of educational journeys like that of the German architect who began the church at Wimpfen in 1269 and "had just returned from Paris," continuity was always conditioned by the personal ties which kept architects to lodges. Every architect was, according to his talent and imagination, free to make a leap if he dared, but his spring-board was provided for him, and his work became, in turn, a spring-board for his pupils.

The picture drawn here explains the connexion between the factors of tradition and originality: what we call immanence is founded on both. Younger architects followed existing tracks and continued them, and they were bound to understand the sense of direction set by a strong tradition, because they had to append their innovations organically to what already existed. Only rarely, as in the case of Brunelleschi, did an architect make a radical break with this sense of direction, and even he stood in a current and was the exponent of the ideas of his own social class of humanists. The lodge of S. Maria del Fiore at Florence did not consist so exclusively of masons as did those in other towns. Here there are also laymen, and it was their presence which produced the spiritual atmosphere that enabled Brunelleschi to break with all the traditions of the Gothic style. . . .

The immanence of the development of the Gothic style is no mystery. It would be one if one were to believe that the last Gothic works, such as King Henry VII's Chapel, Annaberg, and the network of flying ribs at Frankfurt, had been in existence in some other sphere outside our world since 1093, waiting for their own realization and, like a magnet, directing the countless little steps in the development towards their own creation. Immanence, on the contrary, operates the other way round. The introduction of the rib-vault proposed a general sense of direction, leading to a goal which could not be foretold, but could only be realized through a strict adherence to this direction. This is not like a search for the North Pole, which already exists, but is a chain of creations, providing a chain of surprises, which culminates in the final surprises of the ultimate Late Gothic style.

This aspect of the immanence of the development is the product of the inner, spiritual labours of the professional workers engaged in the field of architecture. *Immanere* means to stay within. By immanence, we mean that tendency in a course of development which is determined from within the subject of the development. However, as has already been explained, the different immanent processes in different spheres of activity existing within the same cultural environment seem to be subject to another, higher, and all-embracing immanence. It is to these other spheres that we shall turn next.

3. THE MEANING AND THE PURPOSE
OF CHURCH ARCHITECTURE

An architect builds a pulpit as well suited as possible to its purpose; he seeks the most suitable position in the church, raises the level of its floor, and builds steps, a rail, and a sounding-board. The purpose of the pulpit is that sermons shall be preached from it. The sermon, too, has a purpose; it is intended to instruct, to edify, and to confirm belief, but its meaning lies in what is preached. To understand the meaning of a pulpit, it is sufficient to recognize its purpose, but to understand the meaning of a sermon, it is not enough to understand that its purpose is to edify: one must actually understand what is said by the preacher. Purpose is a limited case within the wider concept of meaning.

The same thing is true of an altar. The architect must arrange it to fulfil its purpose, so that Mass can be read and a congregation attend, but the meaning of this arrangement lies within the Mass itself.

Church architecture embraces a number of purposes, which are the products of the various actions of the Christian cult. The overall purpose of a church is to serve the whole cult, but its meaning lies in religious devotion. The meaning embraces the whole gamut of religious ideas and feelings—contemplation, repentance, and the resolution not to sin any more, consolation and hope. The meaning of a church lies in belief, and only the differentiation between all the activities of the cult splits this meaning into a variety of individual functions. To understand the meaning of a Gothic church, one must understand both the meaning of religion and, more especially, the meaning of the Christian religion during the age of Gothic architecture, and the special purposes underlying the church, according to whether one is entering either a cathedral, a monastic church, a parish church, or a chapel of a castle.

Dehio has discussed very fully the changes within the architectural programme of the church while the Gothic style reigned.[4] Some of the innovations which were introduced had their roots in the period of the Romanesque, for instance the building of longer choirs to allow for the larger number of clergy. The lengthening of an existing choir at *Laon* is a specially clear expression of the demands of the clergy about 1205.

A second innovation which influenced architecture was the exhibition of newly acquired relics on altars, and the translation of older relics from crypts to the churches above. Even within the Romanesque style, the Cluniacs of Hirsau and the Cistercians had decided against crypts. At *St Denis* Suger preserved the old crypts because, as consecrated ground, they seemed sacrosanct to him. From the time of the building of *Noyon*, however, crypts were only built where the site demanded it, for instance at *Bourges, Siena,* and *Erfurt*. The building of crypts resulted in choirs lying several steps higher than the naves: with their disappearance, choirs and naves came to lie at the same, or almost the same, level.

399

The clergy needed some kind of barrier to separate them from the laity, in order not to be disturbed at their prayers, which took place seven times a day, and it was from this need that rood-screens and screens dividing choirs from choir aisles developed. In Spain and in England, this tendency was taken a stage further, and the east end of the nave was also reserved for the clergy. These high screens, which sometimes take the form of walls, . . . destroy the open view that was originally intended, and, because of this, many rood-screens in France and Germany were later removed. The exclusion of the congregation was felt to be too aristocratic, and even the clergy probably found this attitude of separation presumptuous. . . . There were Gothic rood-screens in *Notre-Dame* in *Paris,* in the cathedrals at *Reims, Naumburg,* and *Strassburg,* and in many other churches. Moreover, in Paris, the screens between the choir and the choir aisles have been preserved, and one can experience for oneself how exclusive the effect of these insertions is in every sense. Judged stylistically, they are extreme cases of the insertion of one spatial unity into another, and certainly nobody would wish that the one at *Albi* did not exist. However, it can be seen in all these parts of churches whose access was more or less forbidden to the laity, that their purpose, stated barely and soberly, was to express a system of social strata.

The increase in the number of the clergy was one of the reasons for the increase in the number of altars and therefore also of chapels. The rows of chapels round choirs were continued along choir aisles. Dehio noted that the cathedral in *Barcelona* has thirty-one chapels and that the church of S. *Petronio* at *Bologna* was intended to have fifty-eight; and, in an imaginary description of the church of the *Holy Grail,* there are seventy-two. Although this was a church on a central plan and the number is probably connected with some symbolism of numbers (3 times 24), the need for so many chapels must, nevertheless, be understood to be the result of the number of the Knights of the Holy Grail, who must also be regarded as clergy.

The significance of purpose can be seen equally clearly where its action is negative. In parish churches, where there were few priests, and sometimes only one, there was no increase in the number of chapels, and in the churches of the mendicant orders the position of the chapels and the significance of sermons influenced the designs to which they were built.

To these factors must be added the fact that allowances had to be made for processions. We know that the ante-rooms or porches at *Cluny* and *Vézelay* served the purpose of protecting participants in processions from the weather while they were lining up for their entrance into the church. Both these ante-rooms date from the Transitional period, and they had only a few impressive Gothic successors; their function appears to have been transferred to porches and the lower storeys of towers.[5] The arrangement of processions may have been variable, but it is nevertheless legitimate to say that Gothic cathedrals are processional spaces. . . .

However, the form of a building is not determined by purposes only. This is true even if one does not confine oneself to the consideration of subsidiary functions, such as those of altars and pulpits. Even the reciprocal interplay of all the ritual functions embraced within a whole church does not give a clear, unequivocal solution, although the architect must try to achieve the best possible interplay. It is not in this respect that sacred functions can be differentiated from secular ones. The fabrication of tools, weapons, clothes, bridges, means of transport, or signs proceeds, in every case, from a general conception of what is required, and continues with a search for the most suitable materials and forms. The fabrication of a hammer proceeds from a general conception of its purpose and its mechanical principles; this conception is then narrowed by a consideration of the special function which it is to serve—whether it is to be used by a mason or a precision engineer. Finally, however, it must be decided what materials are to be used for the handle and the head and what form they shall take. In other words, function always leaves a "margin of freedom" which cannot be resolved by utilitarian considerations and which is not objectively pre-determined.

So far we have only considered purposes which spring from human activity, but one can also speak of the functions of structural members. It is just as much a matter of course to demand that they should function in a church building as in a secular building. The forms of piers, arches, walls, and vaults are dictated by their own special functions, but even these functions never entirely determine their forms: there always remains a "margin of freedom." A purely utilitarian building is determined by its own special purpose in just the same way as a church, but even here, purpose can never determine form completely. Gothic vaults must be examined in the light of their function; it is important to understand their static principles and the functions of diagonal ribs, ridge-ribs, and tiercer-ons, but, even when these functions have been understood, the question as to why these members have so many different profiles in different churches still remains unanswered, since each profile fulfils the necessary static function, in so far as it exists, equally well.

Although much could be said about the functions of the spatial parts of a church, and about the functions of its architectural members, it need not be said here. It will also be sufficient to say that lighting and the arrangement of windows and lamps primarily serve a practical purpose, but that there is, once again, a "margin of freedom" in the siting of windows and lamps, and in the choice of the dimensions and the shape of windows.

This consideration leads to the question as to what are the tendencies by which the "margin of freedom" is eradicated and a final form reached. In reaching it, the architect appears to be absolutely free; but he is not, for the question of cost always plays a part, either by inhibiting his imaginative powers, or by influencing him to build something of great splendour. The designs for most of the buildings of rich monasteries and dioceses were made with confidence in the charity of future generations, and economic factors, combined with the course of wars, often determined the fate of Gothic buildings. Some, like the cathedrals of Beauvais and Narbonne, have remained unfinished to our day; some, like the cathedrals of Cologne and Prague, were not finished during the Middle Ages; and others, like the façade at Strassburg, were completed in the Middle Ages, but to a changed plan. In every case, the financial administrator had a say in the discussions. However, the economic position only laid down the general framework of how much splendour the architect could allow himself. The actual form to be taken within the "margin of freedom" was not determined by the treasurer, but by the architect. Within the bounds of the conditions laid down, he seems, then, to have been perfectly free—but even this is not quite true.

4. SYMBOLS OF MEANING

In addition to the actual programme of building, there were sometimes also special wishes and demands of a patron to be taken into consideration. Suger wrote that the choir of St Denis was built with twelve supports, to signify the twelve apostles: *duodecim apostolorum exponentes numerum.* He went on to say that the twelve supports in the ambulatory signify the twelve minor prophets. He gave the *tertium comparationis* by quoting St Paul's epistle to the Ephesians 2:19: both believers and churches are built upon the foundations of the apostles and the prophets; both are *habitaculum Dei in Spiritu,* and both therefore signify the same thing. Our text does not say that these piers portray the apostles and the prophets, but that those in the choir indicate (*exponentes*) the number of the apostles, and that those in the ambulatory signify (*significantes*) the number of the prophets. Portrayal would require caryatids. There may be other documentary evidence of cases in which it would be justifiable to say that an architectural member portrays something, but . . . in the case of St Denis, it would be senseless to say that the figure twelve was portrayed, and inexact to say that the apostles and the prophets were portrayed in the figure twelve. The number of the piers indicates the number of the apostles which, in turn, directs the attention of the visitor to the text from St Paul. In this way, it can be understood that the meaning of church architecture as a *habitaculum Dei in Spiritu* came to life in Suger's mind—as it can in anybody's mind who counts the supports and knows the relevant text.

This kind of "representation" is called symbolic. The piers and columns at St Denis are only piers and columns to a visitor—and were even to Suger and his architect. The connexion between the number and its significance was made in Suger's mind; we can understand this process only if we are told of it; and this is true also of many other cases. Often, of course, patrons and architects did not think of any symbolism. At St Denis, Pierre de Montereau added a pair of piers to the end of Suger's series of twelve. The older piers, of course, preserve their symbolism, but there are now fourteen, and the two new ones either represent nothing, or something other than apostles. In countless cases, symbols were fitted to architectural members afterwards, and, since the time of the Romantics, much research has been done into this symbolism. Nowadays, people often find it difficult to understand. For example, Durandus says that the tiles on the roof of a church are the warriors and princes who defend it against the heathens.[6] Of course, one can easily answer that a heathen is unlikely to climb on the roof, and that the tiles protect the church against rain and snow; or one can answer that mosques also have tiles, but that these are not designed as a protection against Christians. What is meant, however, is that, just as the princes protect the Church as an institution, so the tiles protect the church as a building. To examine every one of these countless abstruse likenesses and comparisons from a rational point of view would be to miss the point. None of the men who created these symbols intended his likenesses to be taken literally. To those who claim that any simile limps, one can reply that they should trust to the leg that does not limp. It must be realized, however, that these symbols vary in value, and that some of them are immediately convincing, while others are far-fetched.

Suger was not an architect: he was a theologian and had been educated according to the precepts of his age. From the time that Christian churches were first built, it was the theologians who ordered their construction, even if princes and emperors sometimes decided the programme and gave money for the project. Theologians were thoroughly familiar with the New Testament, which is full of comparisons and symbols. . . . Jesus's metaphors and symbols refer to purely spiritual things which are illuminated by the metaphor, and can often not be expressed better, if at all, in any other terms.

Medieval theologians altered the direction of these comparisons. Jesus had said, "I am the door" (that is, to the Father): they inverted this and said that the door was Jesus. This difference may seem small, but the idea of Jesus remained a spiritual one, and, in this connexion, even the door became an intellectual and spiritual passageway, for the symbolists mentally changed the real doorway into a spiritual one. Whether one takes this difference seriously or not, one must understand the inversion involved if one is to understand the way in which the Gothic clergy regarded churches, and the way in which they educated the laity to grasp this kind of symbolism.

Where symbolism made use of sculpture or painting, the underlying idea was more easily comprehensible. Where a statue of Christ was placed in front of the central pier of a main doorway, and one therefore walked past him into the interior, anyone could understand that here Christ was supposed to be understood as a spiritual door.

. . . Just as every architectural member represents something, so does every spatial part, and so, above all, does the church as a whole. Recent research has been very productive in giving interpretations of Romanesque architecture. Thus, the building of a west as well as an east choir in the same church, as it was done in the Romanesque period, has been shown to derive from the opposition between *sacerdotium* and *imperium*. The emperor, when he personally attended state services, sat in the western choir, and the purpose of building a fixed architectural section of a church to correspond to the choir which was the ceremonial territory of the bishop can be traced to the rivalry between popes and emperors, which dates back to the time of Constantine.[7] However, functions do not always produce symbols: thus, while naves were built for the laity, they do not represent the laity. In the case of a reserved space, the idea may arise that this space represents the person for whom it is reserved. A choir does not necessarily represent God, or the bishop as the representative of God, but this meaning could be introduced, and probably was, where a western choir, as the space reserved for the emperor, was set opposite an eastern choir. There are also other interpretations of spatial parts as symbols representing something, and they can be very fruitful, but they do not yet seem to have been studied with reference to the Gothic style. In the Gothic churches, double choirs disappeared, and this may lead one to conclude that the French kings did not feel the same opposition to the papacy, nor the same rivalry over certain questions of their rights and powers, as the German emperors. However, it is doubtful whether the significance of this disappearance contributes much to the understanding of the Gothic style. . . .

The interpretation of double choirs as representing the split between the Church and the Empire leads to the idea of the indivisible unity of the *Civitas Dei*, and thus to the real meaning of the architecture of a church as a whole—the Christian idea of the kingdom of God. This idea embraces both the eternal, that is the timeless and placeless, existence and omnipotence of God, and his temporary and earthly existence in Man and the works of Man. The building of churches on earth as the seat for religious services is, at the same time, always a symbol of the transcendent kingdom of God. Church architecture may mark the contrast between pope and emperor or between monks and laymen; it may set nuns' galleries in isolation, and so on; but these functional divisions always reflect the differences between certain social strata, or at least strata of responsibilities within the *Civitas Dei*, which remains an immutable idea to which any division is subordinate. The building of churches as houses of God can therefore always be interpreted as a symbol of the *Civitas Dei*, of the *regnum Dei*, both here and in eternity—and this is the sense in which it was interpreted.

A Christian church has this idea in common with every holy place of every other religion. Greek and Roman temples, too, were intended to be places that were not of this world—to be "numinous." Even the flat ceilings and vaults of classical antiquity were characterized, by their decoration with sculpture and painting, to represent the sky.[8] According to ancient beliefs, the sky was a spherical bowl in which, or beyond which, lay a world to come; it was the boundary between the visible and the invisible, though, of course, there is also much on earth that is invisible, especially the ideas of men and their intellectual processes. Man embraces within himself the world to come. "The kingdom of God is within you."[9] Man is the *habitaculum Dei*, but with the essential addition, *in Spiritu*. God dwells in the mind and in the heart: this is his kingdom. If one says that the kingdom of Heaven lies in the heart of Man, then Heaven becomes a symbol; it ceases to be the astronomical sky of classical antiquity or of Copernicus and Kepler, and becomes a symbol of the life to come, which is within Man, who lives continuously in this world and the next at one and the same time.

Symbols are a special kind of concept. The material parts of a church are drawn from nature; they consist of minerals, metals, and woods, and even if, like glass, they are artificially made, their raw material still comes from natural sources. In the building of a church, this aspect is always the main consideration, and Suger showed great concern for the finding of a suitable quarry and of trees of the right length for roof-beams. Even in the preservation of buildings, one is bound to return to this first degree of concepts, for it is physical and chemical aspects which come to the fore when downpours, or a change in the level of the water-table, or lightning, or fire produce material changes.

In a finished church, the materials from which it is built become part of the concept of the church as a whole. The spiritual meaning of the activities which take place in the church, in so far as they have a function, is not a natural product, but a human conception or a combination of human conceptions. All that is material remains as an integrating factor, but the fact that this visible, tangible, and spatial distribution of materials has been created for the purpose of Divine Service means that there is a second degree of concepts. In this second concept of church architecture, which exists within the concept of function, a church is regarded as "suitable" for the sacred activities of religious men. In the formulation of the programme for the building of a church, and in its design, this concept is perpetually alive and active. If the building is suitable for religious services, then the material structure of the church is embraced in the conception of the *habitaculum Dei*—but *in Spiritu.* A "suitable" building thus becomes a "suitable" sacred building; it offers all that the spiritual man demands. . . .

This second degree of concepts is contained within a third degree. . . . God dwells in a church in the same way as he does in the hearts of men. A material structure which is regarded as a building suitable for the holding of religious services becomes an element in the concept of a house of God. The first degree of this concept comprises natural objects; the second comprises the works of Man; but the third embraces the field of symbols. . . .[10]

A church as a whole is a symbol of God—or rather, one symbol of God, for there are many others. Kingship is another symbol: a king possesses the kingdom over which he reigns. The Church is the kingdom of God. The Christian religion is eschatological. The world is temporary; it was created, and, on the Day of Judgement, it will cease to exist. Then the everlasting kingdom of God will come into being, in the form of an eternal heaven and an eternal hell. It is of this kingdom that St John speaks in the book of the Revelation. . . .

One would like to quote the whole book, for it is a continuous chain of symbols; every conception in it contains more than is inherent in the words in which it is expressed. The city, its dimensions, its geometrical form, precious stones, pearls, gold, and glass: all these are symbols, and, in combination, they symbolize the kingdom of heaven after the end of the world. If one sees them as symbols, one can similarly regard any church as a representation of the kingdom of heaven—here and now, or after the end of the world. . . .

With their material substance (this is the first degree, that of natural materials), painting and sculpture can reproduce a natural model, or an inner conception (the second degree, that of representation); but they can also be symbols (and this is the third degree). It increases our understanding when iconography reconstructs the literary or poetic source on which the painter or the sculptor has drawn. . . . Our differentiation between the three degrees of meaning makes it possible to recognize that iconography deals with the mere portrayal of a person, a landscape, an action, etc., that is, with the second degree, and at the same time to investigate whether this meaning itself is a symbol—that is, a symbol of a meaning. Iconography as such remains within the literary, or, in some cases, the poetic sphere of painting or sculpture, that is, it remains within the intellectual content of the fine arts.[11] However, studies of iconography usually move beyond the consideration of symbols of meaning to that of symbols of form.

The difference between these two fields of symbolism is an important one, and leads to the real root of the problem. It has been shown that a Gothic church, like every other church, is a symbol of the kingdom of God; and this symbol remains a literary one. How, then, can a Gothic church be a means to opening the mind to the idea of this kingdom, or of the New Jerusalem, even if the visitor does not know the Apocalypse and has never heard of the idea of the kingdom of God?

5. FORM SYMBOLS

. . . Form itself can become a symbol, co-ordinated with the realm of the symbolism of meaning and expressing the same things by the use of its own means. If we can understand the symbolism of the form of a church, it will tell us more than can a comprehension of the symbolism of its meaning.

Every church is different in form; the form of its space, of its members, and of its light are all different from those in any other church. It consists of different-coloured materials, of light limestone, dark granite, red brick, etc., or it may have had colour added in the form of paint or plaster. Every individual building is a unification of these factors, tending towards a particular style. It is always true to say that a church represents *the* New Jerusalem, but, according to its form or, more especially, to its style, the New Jerusalem may be Byzantine, Carolingian, Romanesque, or Gothic. Within each style, one can further differentiate between its phases and between its local schools. Hagia Sophia and St Mark in Venice represent a different New Jerusalem; so do the church of St Mary-in-Capitol at Cologne and the cathedral at Speyer, Notre-Dame in Paris and the cathedral at Reims, Annaberg and King's College Chapel, Cambridge.

We have . . . taken it for granted that everyone knows not only that every church is a house of God or the new paradise, but also that the form of the house or the garden changed from Romanesque to Early Gothic, High Gothic, and finally Late Gothic. . . .

. . . A man who feels in a Gothic way, and who stylizes himself accordingly, requires, for divine services, not only a building which fulfils its utilitarian purposes and furthermore the function of symbolizing the concept of the house of God, but also a building which, through its Gothic form, symbolizes what that particular man feels.[12]

The question as to how a form devoid of meaning can become a symbol, and thus take on a meaning, can easily be answered: it assumes meaning through our own aesthetic attitude.

Man is born into this world and, from the cradle to the grave, stands in a perpetually changing relationship to it; he is determined by it, and, with tools and other means, works to create his own world out of it. This is a practical attitude towards the world. Only in the course of the development of mankind and of the individual does a second attitude appear, by which the world is seen independently of its usefulness. In the pursuit of scientific knowledge, man does not ask himself whether a circular form can be used to create a wheel, but what a circle is, what it was before the world was created, and what it will be after the end of the world. When man assumes an objective attitude he strives to see beyond himself and to consider the world separately from himself. The aesthetic attitude is the exact opposite of this: here man seeks to draw the world *into himself*. The fact that subjectivity takes a different form in the case of every individual is immaterial, for subjectivity draws on the views of man, in contrast to the scientific exclusion of the human being. This change does not take place in the realm of reason, but in the realm of feeling.

When a Gothic architect built a circular window, his work was bound up with a practical and theoretical attitude: for he had to know how to construct a circle geometrically and how, in practice, to set about building it in stone on a big scale, on a façade, and at a considerable height; but his decision to make the window circular was based on aesthetic grounds. There were many possibilities open to him, and this multiplicity corresponds to the "margin of freedom" mentioned earlier. Economic and practical questions may also have played a part in determining, for instance, whether or not it would have been cheaper to build a rectangular window. Questions of symbolism may have arisen too, for instance as to whether the window was intended to represent a wheel of fortune, or the sun; but the final decision regarding the position of the centre, the length of the radius, and the interior form could only spring from the aesthetic attitude of the architect.

Historians of mechanics say that, originally, fallen trees were used for the transportation of loads; later, circular discs were made by sawing or, more probably, chopping logs, and finally the wheel, with a hub and spokes, was invented. It is impossible to say whether this is what did in fact happen; the wheel, however, was presumably not the product of an aesthetic attitude. A mechanic considers a circular form valuable because it can be rolled; a theorist, as such, assigns no value to anything, but merely defines concepts; but the man who considers a circular form aesthetically, feels the connexion between any point on the circumference and the centre as an inter-relationship, as a contrast between radial movement and concentration, and as a form representing repose. The symbolist moves past objective existence, and can choose a circle as a symbol for the *orbis*, for fortune, for the sun, or for Christ. If he remains within the realm of meaning he creates a symbol of meaning, but even this is based on the aesthetic factor of comparison. Science seeks identities and equations; poetry seeks likenesses and metaphors; but the symbolist of form regards a circle aesthetically, and he chooses a circular form as a symbol of perfection and eternal tranquillity and peace. His symbol is not conventional: it is immediate and compelling.

Science seeks to recognize what things are in terms of themselves: an aesthetic attitude feels what they are in relation to us. A blue ceiling can be cold or warm, according to the temperature, but, to our feeling, it is always cool. It stands at a measurable distance from us, but, for us, it is always far away, even if we climb on to a scaffolding. We thus change the temperature and the distance of an objectively existent colour. Every aesthetic reaction produces an interchange within various fields of the senses—in visibility, warmth, taste, statics, dynamics, and so on. For instance, blue is restful, yellow is pungent; everyone is familiar with these frequently quoted phenomena. The architect lives perpetually in this realm of empathy in which forms are felt. Some decisions can be made without any hesitation, but others can only be made through a careful weighing of whether one form matches others which have already been chosen—whether it creates harmony or disturbs it.

The General Problems of the Gothic Style

A visitor who is susceptible to aesthetic effects can understand the forms chosen by the architect. He may be delighted by them, or he may be passionately opposed to them, but before he feels one or other of these emotions, he must thrust his practical and theoretical ideas to the back of his mind for the moment and consider the work aesthetically. If he cannot do that, he is like a blind man trying to see light. There are people who are unmusical; others have no feeling for architecture and cannot understand the language of stone. Some people understand the language of poetry better than that of architecture. Anyone who has feeling for architecture also possesses a certain degree of understanding of it, and the creative master must possess this understanding in its highest degree. . . .

. . . Every form of vault and pier, of spatial subdivision, of window and doorway, and of tower and roof was directed at the aesthetic understanding of the visitor; every one was a formal symbol, as were density, laxity, movement, rotation, colour, sparkle, roughness, shadow, etc. They say an infinite quantity of things, and one need only be able to see in order to hear what is said tacitly. Beside this symbolism of form, the symbols of meaning pale.

In the symbolism of form, we can see splendour or asceticism, oppression or verve, sterility or elastic vitality, a cheerful enjoyment of life or sombre depression. One says of space that it spreads, it rises, that it is quick or slow in tempo, that it circles, it spirals, or it concentrates. Some historians of art positively luxuriate in the application of their own feelings to architectural interiors, and it is equally possible to project one's feelings into architectural members. Figures cannot do justice to the wealth of the proportions and rhythms at St Germer, although everything there still breathes simplicity, nor to the infinitely more complicated proportions and rhythms of Pirna or Tomar, and even the best description of an aesthetic impression is far surpassed by the original impression. . . . Admittedly, well-chosen words can open the eyes of an unpractised visitor, but perfectly to understand the symbolism of form is like understanding the mime of a great actor.

Besides the three attitudes that we have discussed, which Man can adopt towards the world, there is a fourth. We can regard, recognize, and feel ourselves and the world as standing on a common, metaphysical foundation; and this is the religious attitude, in which the common background is God. During his devotions, a religious man performs a certain mime; he kneels, lowers his head, and folds his hands. This is the visible expression of the fact that he submits, that his hands are inactive, and that his spirit is seeking contemplation. He can pray anywhere, in his own room, even in the open air, but a prayer chamber for the multitude, a church, must aim, through its symbolism of form, to provide a suitable aesthetic framework for the prayers of the many.

One should be wary of anthropomorphic discussions of works of art, but they can sometimes be of more help than a host of words. We can say, for instance, that a church should be practical for the holding of services, and that its meaning can be left to the realm of the imagination. We can simply say, "This must be the house of God," but, in fact, we demand more than this. We want to be able to *see* that it is the house of God. Metaphorically, we demand that a church should itself be devout, that it should praise the Lord day and night, and at all times. This is what church architecture is.

NOTES

[1] On this, and on what follows, see Frankl, *The Gothic*, 299 ff.

[2] For Christopher Wren's theory of the Saracen origin of Gothic, see Frankl, *The Gothic*, 360 ff.

[3] Frankl, *The Gothic*, 110 ff.

[4] Dehio, *K. B.*, II, 24.

[5] Examples are Noyon, Dijon (Notre-Dame), Troyes (St Urbain), and Casamari.

[6] The best and most comprehensive introduction is given in Joseph Sauer, *Symbolik des Kirchengebäudes* (Freiburg i. Br., 1902). On the subject of the figure twelve, see p. 66. There are also much older treatises on numerical symbolism; see Frankl, *The Gothic*, 211 ff.

[7] Günter Bandmann, *Mittelalterliche Architektur als Bedeutungsträger* (Berlin, 1951), 229. His interpretation seems doubtful when applied to places where the emperor could hardly have been expected to worship—for instance, at Maria Laach.

[8] Karl Lehmann, "The Dome of Heaven," *The Art Bulletin*, XXVII (1945), 1–27.

[9] Luke 17: 21: regnum Dei intra vos est.

[10] Unfortunately, mathematicians also call their signs symbols, although they are really only signs. In the terminology of my *System etc.* (Note 181 to Chapter 4), signs like signposts, numbers, and letters have a meaning in the second degree of concepts; signposts or the marks on a scale are cognate with their meaning (direction, distance, etc.), and letters and musical notation are conventions. Signs become symbols when they take on a higher meaning—for instance, a cross is a sign for a meaning of the second degree in mathematics, but if it signifies the Cross of Christ, or Christ himself, it becomes a symbol of the third degree, as do the attributes for the saints.

[11] It should be stressed once more that representational art embraces sculpture and painting, but not architecture. The Italians classified all three arts under the heading *arti del disegno*, but one could also put the art of writing (signum), that is calligraphy, under this heading.

[12] Fundamental for the definition of the concept Art is Willi Drost, "Form als Symbol," *Zeitschrift für Ästhetik und allgemeine Kunstwissenschaft*, XXI (1927), 358.

18. THE CLASSICAL TRADITION IN THE MIDDLE AGES

Erwin Panofsky

INTRODUCTION

Since its first appearance—in embryonic form—as an article in *Kenyon Review* (1944), Erwin Panofsky's *Renaissance and Renascences* has earned its reputation as one of the classics in the literature of art history. Drawing attention to the persistence in western Europe, during the long medieval era, of a classical tradition fostered by the art forms, mythology, history, and ideas of the Greco-Roman past, Panofsky's work has done much to alter and give better balance to our concepts of the art of the Middle Ages, as well as to provide a more informed basis for our assessments of the Renaissance and its relationship to Greco-Roman antiquity.

A section of the second edition of the expanded version of this work, published in 1965, has been selected for this anthology. Here Panofsky surveys, over the broad sweep of the Middle Ages, the various survivals and revivals of a classical tradition in western Europe, isolating the distinctive characteristics of each of these manifestations and accounting for the contexts in which they appeared.

For the reader interested in pursuing the fortunes of the classical tradition in art, the *Journal of the Warburg and Courtauld Institutes* is an invaluable resource. Among works that deal specifically with this tradition are Gilbert Highet, *The Classical Tradition in Western Literature* (1957); Walter Oakeshott, *Classical Inspiration in Medieval Art* (1959); Benjamin Rowland, Jr., *The Classical Tradition in Western Art* (1963); Jean Seznec, *The Survival of the Pagan Gods* (1953); Cornelius Vermeule, *European Art and the Classical Past* (1964); J. Hubert, J. Porcher, and W. F. Volbach, *The Carolingian Renaissance* (1970); and Francis Haskell and Nicholas Penny, *Taste and the Antique: The Lure of Classical Sculpture 1500–1900* (1981). A brief account is in Harold Spencer, *The Image Maker* (1975), pp. 357–463. Other works relating to the classical tradition which may be of interest to the reader of this anthology are Emerson Swift, *Roman Sources of Christian Art* (1951), reprinted in 1970; Fritz Saxl and Erwin Panofsky, "Classical Mythology in Mediaeval Art," *Metropolitan Museum Studies*, IV (1933), 228–280; C. R. Morey, "The Sources of Mediaeval Style," *Art Bulletin*, VII (1924), 35ff.; George Boas, ed., *The Greek Tradition* (1939); Kurt Weitzmann, *Greek Mythology in Byzantine Art* (1951), and by the same author, "The Survival of Mythological Representations in Early Christian and Byzantine Art and Their Impact on Christian Iconography," *Dumbarton Oaks Papers*, XIV (1960), 43–68. The latter is also available in W. Eugene Kleinbauer, *Modern Perspectives in Art History* (1971).

The selection that follows is reprinted from Erwin Panofsky, *Renaissance and Renascenes in Western Art* (1965), with the permission of the publisher, Almqvist & Wiksell, Stockholm.

There was a Renaissance "which started in Italy in the first half of the fourteenth century, extended its classicizing tendencies to the visual arts in the fifteenth, and subsequently left its imprint upon all cultural activities in the rest of Europe". . . . Can qualitative or structural—as opposed to merely quantitative—differences be shown to distinguish not only this Renaissance from earlier, apparently analogous, revivals but also these earlier revivals from each other? And, if so, is it still justifiable to define the latter as "mediaeval" phenomena?

. . . The radical alienation from the Antique that characterizes the high and late phases of what we call the Gothic style . . . did not result from a steady decline of classical traditions. Rather it may be said to mark the lowest point on an undulating curve of alternate estrangements and *rapprochements*. . . .[1]

The first of these *rapprochements* is known as the Carolingian revival or, to use the designation employed in Charlemagne's own circle, the Carolingian *renovatio*.[2] During and after the disruption' of the Western Roman Empire, the interrelated and overlapping processes of barbarization, Orientalization and Christianization had led to an almost total eclipse of classical culture in general and classical art in particular. Oases had been left in regions such as Italy, North Africa, Spain and South Gaul, where we can observe the survival of what has nicely been termed a "sub-antique" style; and in at least two centers we even find what amounts to revivals as opposed to survival. Determined efforts to assimilate Latin models were made in England, which produced, for example, the *Codex Amiatinus* and, in sculpture, the Crosses of Ruthwell or Bewcastle, and where the classical tradition was always to remain a force both more persistent and more self-conscious (either in the sense of purism or in the sense of romanticism) than was the case on the Continent. And a kind of Greek or Early Byzantine revival, apparently caused or at least promoted by the influx of artists fleeing from Arabic conquest or iconoclastic persecution, took place in seventh- and eighth-century Rome, whence it spread, to some extent, to other parts of the peninsula.[3] But precisely those regions which were to form the nucleus of the Carolingian Empire—the northeast of France and the west of Germany—represented, from the classical point of view, a kind of cultural vacuum.

As happens so often in history (suffice it to remember the formation of the Gothic style in the thus far comparatively unproductive Ile-de-France or that of both the High Renaissance and the Early Baroque in Rome, where none of the great masters was either born or trained), it was in this very vacuum that there occurred a conflux and fusion of forces which resulted in a new synthesis: the first crystallization of a specifically Northwest European tradition. And chief among these forces was a deliberate attempt to reclaim the heritage of Rome, "Rome" meaning Julius Caesar and Augustus as well as Constantine the Great. When Charlemagne set out to reform political and ecclesiastical administration, communications and the calendar, art and literature, and—as a basis for all this—script and language (the documents emanating from his own chancellery during the early years of his regime still tend to be very illiterate), his guiding idea was the *renovatio imperii romani.* He had to invite a Briton, Alcuin, as his chief adviser in cultural matters (just as his grandson Charles the Bald had to enlist the help of an Irishman, John the Scot, to obtain a satisfactory translation of Dionysius the Pseudo-Areopagite's Greek); but all these efforts served, to use the contemporary phrase, to bring about an *aurea Roma iterum renovata.*

. . . Today we can read the Latin classics in the original largely because of the enthusiasm and industry of Carolingian scribes.

Nor can it be doubted that the employers and advisers of these scribes learned their lesson well. Their often excellent verses in classical meters fill four fat volumes of the *Monumenta Germaniae Historica,* and their ear became astonishingly sensitive to the refinements of Latin prose. . . .

In art, the "back-to-Rome" movement had to compete with orientalizing tendencies on the one hand and insular influence on the other; for the same British Isles which had been so important as a refuge of the classical tradition in pre-Carolingian times had simultaneously produced that antinaturalistic, "Celto-Germanic" linearism, either violently expressive or rigidly geometrical, which was to counteract and ultimately to triumph over this classical tradition. On the Carolingian continent, however, these opposing forces stimulated rather than weakened the energies of the *renovatio* movement.

Charlemagne's palace chapel in Aix-la-Chappelle is, in a general way, modeled upon the pattern of Justinian's San Vitale at Ravenna; but it received a west front suggested by Roman city gates, and its exterior was enlivened not by oriental blind arcades as in San Vitale but by Corinthian pilasters of self-consciously classical cast. In the porch at Lorsch the polychromatic facing of the walls conforms to pre-Carolingian tradition; but its structural conception—not to mention the capitals of the pilasters, which evince the same classicizing spirit as do those of the palace chapel in Aix—harks back to the Arch of Constantine and, possibly, the Colosseum. The idea of incorporating towers with the basilica, so fundamentally important for the development of high-mediaeval church architecture, originated, it seems, in Asia Minor; but the plan of the basilica itself was revised *romano more*, that is to say, after the fashion of St. Peter's, St. Paul's and St. John in the Lateran. As Richard Krautheimer has shown,[4] Constantinian edifices were, from the Carolingian architects' point of view, no less but perhaps even more "classical" than the Pantheon or the Theater of Marcellus. . . .

In the decorative and representational arts the spirit of "aurea Roma iterum renovata" loomed even larger than in architecture. The Oriental component having been all but neutralized by the beginning of the ninth century, the *modus operandi* of painting, carving and goldsmithery was determined by two powerful influences: that of the British Isles and that of contemporary Italy where, as has been mentioned, the seventh and eighth century saw an artistic efflorescence doomed to be eclipsed by the very movement which it helped to produce in the North.[5] Both these influences, however, were vigorously challenged by a third, that of classical antiquity. Drawing from all the sources that were accessible to them both physically and psychologically, the Carolingian masters resorted to Roman as well as Early Christian and "sub-antique" prototypes, book illuminations as well as reliefs in stone and stucco, ivory carvings as well as cameos and coins; for, as in architecture, no fundamental distinction was made between the pagan and the Christian Antique. But the very intensity and universality of their endeavor enabled them to develop, with surprising speed, a sense of discrimination as to the quality of their "material" and a certain ease and freedom in its exploitation.

In ornamental borders or initials classical motifs—the egg-and-dart pattern, the palmette, the vine *rinceau* and the acanthus—began to reassert themselves against the abstract interlaces and schematized animal patterns of insular and "Merovingian" art; and in the illustrative rendering of figures and things a first determined effort was made to recapture that affirmative attitude toward nature which had been characteristic of classical art. The more progressive masters attempted to do justice to the human body as an organism subject to the laws of anatomy and physiology, to space as a three-dimensional medium—in at least one case a Carolingian illuminator anticipated the Dugento and Trecento in appropriating from an Early Christian model a genuine interior with a reasonably well-foreshortened ceiling[6]—and to light as that which determines the surface appearance of solid bodies. In short, they sought a kind of verisimilitude which had long been absent from the West European scene.

. . . Evangelists . . . in the Vienna "Schatzkammer-Evangeliar," the chief product of what is often called the "Palace School" of Charlemagne (Fig. 54), give an impression so deceptively antique that they have been ascribed to artists from Byzantium; so vigorous is the modeling of the bodies beneath their white draperies, so gracefully are they posed in front of what has been called impressionistic landscapes.[7] The mythological characters that represent the planets and constellations in such *Aratea* manuscripts as the *Codex Vossianus Latinus* 79 in the University Library at Leiden[8] might have stepped out of a Pompeian mural. And the airy landscapes in the Utrecht Psalter of 820–830, organized in depth by undulating mountain ranges, dotted with buildings *all'antica* and feathery, light-dissolved trees, alive with bucolic or ferocious animals and teeming with classical personifications, are reminiscent of the wall paintings and stucco reliefs in Roman villas and palaces.[9]

To mention mythological characters and classical personifications is to hit at what is, from our point of view, perhaps the most important aspect of the Carolingian *renovatio*. Personifications of localities, natural phenomena, human emotions and abstract con-

54. The Evangelist Mark, from the *Coronation Gospels*, Carolingian, *c.* 800–810, Manuscript illumination, Height 12¾″ x 9⅞″ (Kunsthistorisches Museum, Vienna)

cepts as well as such familiar products of classical imagination as Victories, *putti*, Tritons and Nereids had continued to play their role in Early Christian art up to the beginning of the seventh century. Then, however, they had disappeared from the scene, and it was left to the Carolingian artists not only to reinstate this interrupted tradition but also to make fresh excursions into the realm of Graeco-Roman iconography. Book illuminators reproduced . . . innumerable pictures of an unadulteratedly secular character: the miniatures found in scientific treatises on botany, zoology, medicine, or the insignia of Roman public offices; in the *Comedies* of Terence and the *Fables* of Aesop; in calendars and encyclopaedias; and, above all, in those astronomical manuscripts, just mentioned, which more than any other single source served to transmit to posterity the genuine effigies of the pagan gods and heroes that had lent their names to the celestial bodies. Ivory carvers, gem cutters and goldsmiths assimilated classical models of all kinds, thus furnishing further material to the illuminators, while, on the other hand, freely appropriating the latter's designs.

Thus Carolingian art acquired a rich and authentic vocabulary of what I shall henceforth refer to as classical "images": figures (or groups of figures) classical not only in form—this, needless to say, applies to numberless motifs handed down by the Antique to Early Christian art and thus held in readiness for the Carolingian revival—but also in significance. And it is characteristic of the Carolingian *renovatio* that these classical "images," including the *dramatis personae* of the pastoral and the divinities of the pagan pantheon, were given liberty to escape from their original context without abandoning their original nature. In at least one case—and there may have been many more—a Carolingian *ivoirier* decorated the case and handle of a flabellum (a liturgical fan used to keep the flies away from the priest when saying Mass) with scenes from Virgil's *Eclogues* hardly susceptible to an *interpretatio christiana.* Some of the arches that enframe the Canon Tables and Evangelists' portraits in the Gospel Book of Ada, the putative sister of Charlemagne, are adorned with what may be called facsimiles of Roman cameos unchanged in iconography.[10] And according to the most recent investigations it was in the Carolingian period that classical personifications— such as the Sun on his chariot drawn by four horses, the Moon on her chariot drawn by two oxen, the Ocean represented in the guise of the river-god Eridanus, the Earth nursing two infants or reptiles, Atlas or Seismos shaking "the foundations of the earth" —were permitted not only to proliferate in illustrations of the Octateuch and the Psalter (where they had played a rather modest role in Early Christian art) but also to invade the Passion of Christ, where, so far as we know, they had not been tolerated before at all.[11]

This Carolingian revival, virtually ended with the death of Charles the Bald in 877, was followed by eight or nine decades that have been called "as barren as the seventh century." This judgment, chiefly reflecting the art historian's point of view, has lately been challenged. What may be described as the dark age within the "Dark Ages" has justly been credited not only with a number of important agricultural and technical improvements (mutually interrelated with an enormous and necessary increase in population) but also with noteworthy achievements in music and literature. . . .

As far as art is concerned, it remains true that the years from *ca.* 880 to *ca.* 970 amounted only to a "period of incubation"; it is not until the last third—in England about the middle—of the tenth century that we can observe a general resurgence of artistic competence and discipline—a resurgence so marked that it is often spoken of as the "Ottonian Renaissance" with reference to works produced in Germany, and as the "Anglo-Saxon Renaissance" with reference to works produced in England. In spite of such sobriquets, however, this new flowering does not primarily concern us here. It was a revival in all possible senses except in that of a concerted effort to revive the Antique. Imbued with the religious fervor of the Cluniac Reform, it proclaimed a Christocentric spirit profoundly opposed to the universalistic attitude which at the time of Charlemagne and Charles the Bald had tended to bridge the gulfs that separate the "era under Grace" from the "era under the Law," and the latter from the "era before the Law." The literary portrait of an Ottonian emperor could hardly have been patterned, like Charlemagne's in Eginhard's biography, after the model of a Roman Caesar; nor could he have been addressed as "David" by his intimates.

With only relatively few and well-motivated exceptions, the revival of *ca.* 970–1020[12] drew inspiration only from Early Christian, Carolingian and—very important—Byzantine sources. It thus widened and deepened that stream of tradition which carried classical motifs, placed in the service of the Judaeo-Christian faith, from Hellenistic and Roman sources into the sea of mediaeval art; but it did little to add to the volume of this stream by new and direct appropriations from the "pagan" antiquity. As far as classical "images" are concerned, the "Ottonian Renaissance" even tended to deemphasize their importance and to de-classicize (if I may coin this word) their appearance. By and large the art of *L'An Mil* may be said to have been animated, in form as well as content, by a prophetic vision of the high-mediaeval future rather than by a retrospective enthusiasm for the classical past.[13]

After another hundred years, however, when this high-mediaeval future was about to become a reality, when art approached the High Romanesque stage all over Europe and the Early Gothic stage in the Royal Domain of France, we do find a renascence movement in the sense here under discussion; or, to be more exact, two parallel and, in a sense, complementary renascence movements. Both began in the latter part of the eleventh century; both reached their climax in the twelfth and continued into the thirteenth; and both deliberately reverted to classical sources. They differed, however, from one another in place as well as in the direction of interests.

One of these movements is commonly—though somewhat loosely—referred to as the "proto-Renaissance of the twelfth century."[14] In contrast to both the Carolingian *renovatio* and the Ottonian and Anglo-Saxon revivals of about 1000, it was a Mediterranean phenomenon, arising in Southern France, Italy and Spain. Though it drew strength, it seems, from an admixture of latent "Celto-Germanic" tendencies (so that the initial contribution of Burgundy was more vital than that of Provence, that of Lombardy, Apulia and Sicily more vital than that of Tuscany and even Rome), it originated outside the Carolingian territory: in regions where the classical element was, and in a measure still is, an inherent element of civilization; where the spoken language had remained fairly close to Latin; and where monuments of ancient art—were not only plentiful but also, in certain regions at least, of real importance. In further contrast to the two earlier revivals, the "proto-Renaissance of the twelfth century" came into being at a time when—with the beginnings of urbanization on the one hand and the development of organized pilgrimages, not to mention the Crusades, on the other—the importance of local centers of production, mostly monastic, began to be superseded by that of more or less secularized regional schools (it is not until the eleventh century that we speak of the "schools of Auvergne, Normandy or Burgundy" rather than of the "schools of Reims,

Tours or the Reichenau," and not until the middle of the twelfth that we encounter the professional lay architect), and when a determined attempt was made to extend the influence of art to the "common man."

A new emphasis was therefore placed on such forms of expression as could exert that mass appeal the preoccupation with which is so touchingly evident in the writings of Abbot Suger of St.-Denis. The crucifixes, the tombs of the saints, the altars—now beginning to be embellished with retables as well as antependia because it became customary for the officiating priest to take his place in front rather than behind the *mensa*, thus leading the community instead of facing it—grew to a size unheard of before. Wall painting emancipated itself from the influence of book illumination so that, where Ottonian murals tend to look like large miniatures, Romanesque miniatures tend to look like small murals. . . . And wall painting in turn was supplemented, and in the Northern countries gradually eclipsed, by two great art forms virtually absent from the pre-Romanesque scene: figural and narrative glass painting and, above all, major sculpture in stone— an art all but extinct up to the second half of the eleventh century,[15] and the ascendancy of which was to transform the House of God into a richly decorated public monument.

Thus confronted, for the first time since the downfall of the Roman Empire, with the problem of monumentality, the Romanesque artists approached the classical past from a point of view quite different from that of their predecessors. Less omnivorous than the Carolingians and almost reversing the principle of selection established by the Ottonians, the champions of the proto-Renaissance tended to focus their attention upon the actual remnants of pre-Christian antiquity, that is to say, on Roman and Gallo-Roman architecture and architectural ornament, stone sculpture, goldsmith's work, gems and coins.

It was, therefore, almost exclusively in the three-dimensional arts that fresh contacts were made with the Antique—except where the narrative of a painting or book illumination specifically required the presence of a pagan idol, or where a man like Villard de Honnecourt (an architect by profession!) used pen and ink to make a record of some classical object. When the equestrian statue of Marcus Aurelius—generally assumed to represent the first Christian emperor, Constantine, and duplicated in countless Romanesque reliefs and even free-standing monuments—occasionally recurs in a twelfth-century mural, contemporary sculpture can be shown to have served as an intermediary between the painting and the Roman original;[16] it was in the workshop of a great sculptor-goldsmith, Nicolas of Verdun, and not until about 1180, that the rippling and clinging drapery style characteristic of so much classical sculpture from the Parthenon down to Imperial Rome was first transplanted to a two-dimensional medium, enamel; and it was through the influence of the statuary of Paris, Chartres and Reims, and after another thirty or forty years, that it took roots in painting, book illumination and stained glass.[17]

Romanesque architecture not only appropriated a wealth of details hitherto ignored but also produced structures as persuasively classicizing as the façades of St.-Trophîme in Arles (Fig. 55), the Masons' Chapel in St.-Gabriel or the Badia at Fiesole. The masters of Cluny, Autun and Beaune, in addition to patterning their triforia after the fashion of the Porte d'Arroux (the influence of which can still be felt in the blind arcades of the cathedrals of Lyons and Geneva), resumed the Roman techniques of vaulting large, longitudinal units. And in Romanesque sculpture classical influence was, if anything, even more powerful. . . .

It is characteristic of the macroscopic tendencies of this proto-Renaissance sculpture that it was able to liberate, if one may say so, the latent grandeur of models diminutive in size but potentially monumental by virtue of their classical ancestry or provenance. Syrian or Byzantine ivories were thus "monumentalized," for example, in the ambulatory reliefs of St.-Sernin in Toulouse and in the much-debated Bari throne of 1098,[18] and a no less important role was played by the products of classical glyptography.

In the twelfth century—first, it seems, in Norman-ruled Sicily and probably with the aid of artists called in from Byzantium— the ancient art of the *sculptor* regained the status of a living practice in the Western world; and while the few Carolingian and Ottonian artists interested in classical cameos and their less ambitious relatives, classical coins, had been content to imitate them on their original scale (and preferably, we recall, in book illuminations rather than "in the flesh"), their Romanesque successors employed them as models not only, as is no more than natural,

55. St. Trophîme, Façade Portal, Arles, Late 12th century (Photographie Giraudon)

for other cameos and other coins as well as for seals and small metal reliefs,[19] but also, more surprisingly, for large-size sculpture in stone.

. . . It was in the very heart of France—that is to say, outside the orbit of the proto-Renaissance proper—and not until the end of the twelfth century—that is to say, not until the Gothic style was passing . . . from infancy to youth and maturity—that mediaeval art acquired the ability to meet the Antique on equal terms.

Within its original geographical limits and during its initial stages, proto-Renaissance sculpture had selected and interpreted its model in a spirit either too emotional and independent or too dispassionate and imitative to absorb the essential qualities of classical art. Some schools, especially the school of Burgundy and its derivatives, subjected classical composition to a *transposition à la bourguignonne,* as it has nicely been termed, which sacrificed their original character on the altar of expressiveness, all but obscuring it by linearization, elongation and contortion: the figures appear almost dehumanized, their garments, "halfway between toga and contemporary costume, agitated by a violent and arbitrary breeze." Other schools—and this applies especially to those of Provence, the ancient *Provincia Romana*—reproduced the Roman and Gallo-Roman originals with so much attention to decorative detail,[20] drapery motifs, facial types and surface texture that the results came, on occasion, dangerously close to unimaginative duplication. Some of the masks and angels' heads on the façade of St.-Gilles might well be mistaken for Gallo-Roman originals. . . .

What was not as yet perceived, however, and could not be perceived by Romanesque artists, was what must be considered as the essential principle of classical statuary: the interpretation of the human body as an autonomous, quite literally "self-centered" entity, distinguished from the inanimate world by a mobility controlled from within. As long as the sculptor thought of his work as a piece of inorganic and homogeneous matter bulging out into projections, retreating into cavities, incised with sharply defined contours but never losing its homogeneous density, he was unable to represent the living creature as an organism articulated into structurally different parts. To impart to the human figure . . . organic balance and freedom . . . and to treat drapery in such a way that it appears to be independent from, yet functionally related to, the body was possible only when homogeneous matter ("mass") had been replaced by differentiated structure; and this could happen only when proto-Renaissance sculpture came to be practiced within an architectural system based upon what may be called the "principle of axiality."[21] This principle of axiality, which had prevailed in classical art from the sixth century B.C., had ceased to be respected after the disintegration of the Graeco-Roman world. It had been formally abrogated by the Romanesque style, and it was not reinstated—paradoxically yet understandably—until the advent of that style of architecture which we call Gothic.

In architecture, this style required that the mass of wall and vault be concentrated into tubular shafts and ribs . . .; in sculpture, it required that what I once proposed to term a *"relief en cabochon,"* a form conceived as projecting from a plane surface outside itself (regardless of whether this surface is physically present or only implied by the shape of the figure), be converted into a form conceived as centered around an axis within itself. The jamb figure—originally, if one may say so, an overblown relief even if the "ground" of this relief happens to be, in some exceptional cases, a column—developed into a genuine statue attached to a colonnette, these two components resulting from a process which began by attacking the block diagonally rather than frontally or laterally. This new approach led to the crystallization of both the figure and what may be called the "residual mass" into two basically cylindrical units, the statue and the colonette; it continued with the gradual attenuation of this colonette and ended with the latter's disappearance, the figure becoming completely detached and being either placed within a niche or set out against the flat wall in which case the development has come full circle. An analogous process can be observed in the evolution of the archivolt decoration; and figures playing their part in a relief composition move and act before an imaginary backdrop much like actors on the platform of a small theater stage.[22]

This architecturally inspired reaffirmation of axiality—possible, I believe, only in France, the one country which borders both on the Mediterranean and the North Sea—was an accomplished fact by the middle of the twelfth century. And when a new wave of Byzantinism (first noticeable, for obvious reasons, in such "minor arts" as book illumination, ivory carving and metal work but soon extending to monumental sculpture in wood and stone) swept all over Europe some twenty-five or thirty years later,[23] it was in what had been the very heart of the Carolingian empire and was to become the very heart of the High Gothic style, Lorraine, the Ile-de-France and Champagne, that art became capable of isolating what was still Hellenic in the Byzantine style.

With Nicolas of Verdun in the van of the development, the schools of Laon, Senlis, Chartres and Paris reimparted to their figures a serene animation as close to Graeco-Roman *humanitas* as mediaeval art could ever come. Posed in resilient, gyratory, *contrapposto* attitudes, their pliant drapery accentuating rather than concealing well-proportioned bodies, the figures began to move in natural yet rhythmical fashion . . . and to establish psychological contact with one another.

It was thus precisely within an Early Gothic atmosphere that "surface classicism," as it may be called, grew into an "intrinsic classicism" which, needless to say, culminated in the school of Reims. Suffice it to mention the Apostles in the portal of the Last Judgment, particularly the two magnificent figures of Saints Peter and Paul, the head of the former bearing an unmistakable likeness to that of Antoninus Pius[24] . . . and the famous "Man with the Odysseus Head". The even more famous Visitation group (Fig. 56) is so classical in pose, costume and facial types that it

56. The Visitation, from the west portals, center doorway, Reims Cathedral, *c.* 1225–45, Stone, Height, 10'2" (Art Reference Bureau/Bildarchiv Foto Marburg)

430

was long assigned to the sixteenth rather than the thirteenth century.

It is, however, significant that just those figures which are the nearest to classical antiquity in spirit . . . are often the most difficult to derive from any specific model. The most accomplished of these mediaeval sculptors had learned to master the language of classical art to such an extent that they no longer needed to borrow individual phrases or vocables. And we must always envisage the possibility that they were inspired not so much by large-scale stone sculpture as by those graceful Greek and Hellenistic statuettes in bronze or silver, frequently known to us only from their faint echoes in terra-cotta figurines, which often reflect the products of monumental art and found their way as far as Germany.[25]

In France, then, mediaeval art came closest to the Antique when a proto-Renaissance movement born in the Romanesque South was drawn into the orbit of the Gothic style developed in the Royal Domain and Champagne; and we can understand that in Italy a stage was not reached until, conversely, the Gothic style developed in the Royal Domain and Champagne had interpenetrated with, and in a sense transformed, the indigenous proto-Renaissance. In Apulia and Sicily, ruled by Normans and thus particularly exposed to French infiltration, this process bore fruit. . . .

Whatever role a local Roman[26] tradition may have played in the formation of the schools of sculpture, glyptography and die-cutting called into life by Frederick II, and to whatever extent they may have been dominated by his personal leanings, their French affiliation remains evident throughout. That a monarch who thought of himself as a second Augustus, bestowed upon the cities founded by him such names af Augusta, Caesarea and Aquila, and dedicated the church of his winter encampment before Parma (significantly called Victoria) to St. Victor[27] tended to stress the classical element in his artistic enterprises—except, characteristically, for the comparatively few paintings and book illuminations which were produced on his initiative—is not surprising; and it is probable that, if the occasion demanded it, he personally indicated the models to be followed.[28] But in favoring a classicizing mode of expression in art, just as he favored a classicizing mode of thought in legislation, city planning, etc., he exploited and gave fresh impulse to a movement that had been going on for a long time. He promoted the classical style as a matter of imperial policy rather than of "aesthetic" preference, and he never went so far as to exclude other artistic tendencies— indigenous, Byzantine, Saracenic, and, above all, French.[29]

. . . Nicolo Pisano (*ca.* 1205–1280) . . . exemplifies, on the largest possible scale, the very situation that I have tried to describe. Probably born and brought up in Apulia and certainly familiar, from the outset, with the "Frederician" tradition nourished by classical as well as Gothic sources, he acquired the power of synthesizing these two currents on a new level; but he acquired it only in a new political and spiritual environment.

That he made new contacts with the "Gothick North" is demonstrated, apart from more general factors, by such specific if secondary motifs as capitals and tracery patterns; and it is even more significant that he was the first Italian artist, anticipating Giotto and Duccio by several decades, to accept the Gothic innovation of affixing the crucified Christ to the cross by three nails instead of four—an innovation deemed important enough to be denounced by a contemporary prelate who felt that the French sculptors of the early thirteenth century, in order to strengthen the impression of plastic volume and organic movement (that is to say, for purely artistic reasons), had wantonly defied an iconographic tradition observed for nearly a thousand years.[30] But just these modern tendencies, their effectiveness enhanced by a change of scene which transplanted him from a sphere of imperial authoritarianism into one of republican self-government, enabled Nicolo Pisano to become the greatest—and in a sense the last—of mediaeval classicists.

As major Italian poetry, first flowering in the "Sicilian school" under Frederick II, was brought to perfection by the great Florentines from Guido Guinicelli to Dante and Petrarch,[31] so did the South Italian "proto-Renaissance" culminate in the works produced by Nicolo Pisano after his transmigration to Tuscany. Everyone knows that in his Pisa pulpit of *ca.* 1260 he transformed a Dionysus supported by a satyr into aged Simeon witnessing the Presentation of Christ, a nude Hercules into a personification of Christian fortitude (Fig. 57), a Phaedra into the Virgin Mary;[32] and that some five or six years later, in the *Massacre of the Innocents* seen on the Siena pulpit, he borrowed a gesture of grief

57. Nicola Pisano, Fortitude, detail of the pulpit of the Baptistery of the Duomo, Pisa, *c.* 1259–60, Marble, Height approximately *22"* (Alinari/ Editorial Photocolor Archives)

from the same Meleager sarcophagus—in fact, from the same unforgettable figure—that was to inspire the despairing St. John in Giotto's *Lamentation* and one of the mourners in that memorable product of the Verrocchio workshop, the *Death of Francesca Tornabuoni.*[33] It should not be overlooked, however, that Nicolo Pisano, in thus "rediscovering" a collection of Roman monuments always available at Pisa and Florence yet never exploited by any of his predecessors, merely repeated what the masters of Reims had done a generation before.

In short, the acme of mediaeval classicism was reached within the general framework of the Gothic style, much as the acme of seventeenth-century classicism, as represented by Poussin, was reached within the general framework of the Baroque, and that of late eighteenth- and early nineteenth-century classicism, as represented by Flaxman, David or Asmus Carstens, within the general framework of "Romantic sensibility."

NOTES

1 The literature on the revival and survival of classical culture is so extensive that a listing of contributions published in three years (1931–33) fills more than eight hundred pages: *Kulturwissenschaftliche Bibliographie zum Nachleben der Antike, herausgegeben von der Bibliothek Warburg, I, Die Erscheinungen des Jahres 1931*, Leipzig and Berlin, 1934; II (with English title, *A Bibliography of the Survival of the Classics, Edited by the Warburg Institute, The Publications of 1932–1933*), London, 1938; see now F. Heer, "Die 'Renaissance'-Ideologie im frühen Mittelalter," *Mitteilungen des Instituts für Österreichische Geschichtsforschung*, LVII, 1949, p. 23ff. . . . I must confine myself to a few hints: C. R. Morey, "The Sources of Mediaeval Style," *Art Bulletin*, VII, 1924, p. 35ff.; H. Beenken, "Die Mittelstellung der mittelalterlichen Kunst zwischen Antike und Renaissance," *Medieval Studies in Memory of A. Kingsley Porter*, Cambridge (Mass.), 1939, I, p. 47ff.; D. Miner, "The Survival of Antiquity in the Middle Ages," *The Greek Tradition*, G. Boas, ed., Baltimore, 1939, p. 55ff.; . . . In spite of the topographical limitations expressed in its title, the excellent study by J. Adhémar, *Influences antiques dans l'art du moyen âge français; Recherches sur les sources et les thèmes d'inspiration* (Studies of the Warburg Institute, VII), London, 1939, deserves to be counted as a general discussion of the problem. For Byzantine art, see the brilliant summary by K. Weitzmann, "Das klassische Erbe in der Kunst Konstantinopels," *Alte und neue Kunst, Wiener kunstwissenschaftliche Blätter*, III, 1954, p. 41 ff.

2 See P. E. Schramm, *Kaiser, Rom und Renovatio* (Studien der Bibliothek Warburg, XVII), Leipzig and Berlin, 1929. . . .

3 I borrow the term "sub-antique" from the excellent survey by E. Kitzinger, *Early Mediaeval Art in the British Museum*, London, 1940, p. 8ff. . . . For the *Codex Amiatinus*, see E. H. Zimmermann, *Vorkarolingische Minaturen*, Berlin, 1916, Plate 222, Fig. 24; A. Boeckler, *Abendländische Miniaturen bis zum Ausgang der romanischen Zeit*, Berlin and Leipzig, 1930, p. 19f., Plate 12; E. A. Lowe, *Codices Latini Antiquiores*, Oxford, 1934 ff.; III, pp. 8 (No. 299), 43. For pre-Carolingian English art in general, see F. Saxl and R. Wittkower, *British Art and the Mediterranean*, London, New York and Toronto, 1948, p. 14ff. (for the Ruthwell Cross in particular, see F. Saxl, "The Ruthwell Cross," *Journal of the Warburg and Courtauld Institutes*, VI, 1943, p. 17ff.; M. Schapiro, "The Religious Meaning of the Ruthwell Cross," *Art Bulletin*, XXVI, 1944, p. 232ff.). For pre-Carolingian art on the Continent, see W. Holmqvist, *Kunstprobleme der Merowingerzeit* (*Kungl. Vitterhets Historie och Antikvitels Akademiens Handlingar*, XLVII), Stockholm, 1939; *idem*, *Germanic Art in the First Millennium A.D.* (*ibidem*, XC), Stockholm, 1955. Cf. also *Werdendes Abendland am Rhein und Ruhr. Ausstellung in Villa Hügel, Essen, May 18–Sept. 15, 1956*, Essen, 1956. The superb survey of early mediaeval painting by Grabar and Nordenfalk (A. Grabar and C. Nordenfalk, *Early Medieval Painting from the Fourth to the Eleventh Century*, Lausanne, 1957) appeared just in time to be cited but too late to be used for the correction of my errors.

4 R. Krautheimer, "The Carolingian Revival of Early Christian Architecture," *Art Bulletin*, XXIV, 1942, p. 1 ff. For other recent contributions to Carolingian architecture, see the instructive critical bibliography, covering the period from 1928 to 1954, by K. E. Kubach, "Die vorromanische und romanische Baukunst in

434

The Classical Tradition in the Middle Ages

Mitteleuropa," *Zeitschrift für Kunstgeschichte*, XIII, 1951, p. 124ff.; XVII, 1954, p. 157ff. . . .

[5] For the Carolingian revival in the representational arts, see (in addition to the general literature referred to above): R. Hinks, *Carolingian Art*, London, 1935. To be added: E. Patzelt, *Die karolingische Renaissance*, Vienna, 1924; S. Singer, "Karolingische Renaissance," *Germanisch-Romanische Wochenschrift*, XIII, 1925, p. 187ff.; W. Köhler, "An Illustrated Evangelistary of the Ada School and Its Model," *Journal of the Warburg and Courtauld Institutes*, XV, 1952, p. 48ff.; E Rosenthal, "Classical Elements in Carolingian Illustration," *Bibliofilia*, LV, 1953, p. 85 ff. For the Italian—or, if you will, Graeco-Italian—prelude to the Carolingian Renaissance in the North, see M. Schapiro's review of K. Weitzmann's *The Fresco Cycle of S. Maria di Castelseprio* in *Art Bulletin*, XXXIV, 1952, p. 147ff., especially p. 162f.; cf. also D. Tselos, "A Greco-Italian School of Illuminators and Fresco Painters; Its Relations to the Principal Reims Manuscripts and to the Greek Frescoes in Rome and Castelseprio," *Art Bulletin*, XXXVIII, 1956, p. 1ff.; E. Rosenbaum, "The Evangelist Portraits of the Ada School and Their Models", *Art Bulletin*, XXXVIII, 1956, p. 81ff. . . .

[6] Bible of Moutier-Grandval, London, British Museums, MS. Add. 10546, fol. 25v.; Boinet, *La Miniature Carolingienne*, Paris, 1913, Plate XLIV; Kitzinger, *op. cit.*, Plate 20; W. Köhler, *Die karolingischen Miniaturen; Die Schule von Tours*, Berlin, 1930–1933, I, pp. 194ff., 386ff., Pl. 51. Cf. G. J. Kern, "Die Anfänge der zentralperspektivischen Konstruktion in der italienischen Malerei des 14. Jahrhunderts," *Mitteilungen des Kunsthistorischen Institutes in Florenz*, II, 1912, p. 39ff., particularly p. 56f., Fig. 15; E. Panofsky, "Die Perspektive als symbolische Form," *Vorträge der Bibliothek Warburg*, 1924–1925, p. 258ff., particularly p. 311, Fig. 15. . . .

[7] See Boinet, *op. cit.*, Plates LVIII–LIX; Hinks, *op. cit.*, p. 138ff.; Boeckler, *Abendländische Miniaturen*, p. 27ff., Plate 18. The Byzantine origin of the illuminators was cautiously endorsed by A. Goldschmidt, *German Illumination*, Florence and New York, 1921, I, p. 9f., Plates 21, 22. . . .

[8] For this famous manuscript (published by Hugo Grotius, with illustrations engraved by Jacob de Gheyn, as early as 1600), its relatives (particularly British Museums, M.S. Harley 647, perhaps originally owned by Lupus of Ferrières and in certain respects even more "Pompeian" in style than the *Leidensis Vossianus*) and its later derivatives, see J. Thiele, *Antike Himmelsbilder*, Berlin, 1898; F. Saxl, *Verzeichnis astrologischer und mythologischer illustrierter Handschriften des lateinischen Mittelalters in römischen Bibliotheken* (*Sitzungsberichte der Heidelberger Akademie der Wissenschaften*, phil.-hist. Klasse, VI, 1915), pp. xvi ff., 4ff., 103; E. Panofsky and F. Saxl, "Classical Mythology in Mediaeval Art," *Metropolitan Museum Studies*, IV, 2, 1933, pp. 228ff., F. Saxl and H. Meier (H. Bober, ed.) *Catalogue of Astrological and Mythological Illuminated Manuscripts of the Latin Middle Ages*, I, London, 1953, pp. xiii ff. and *passim*; J. Seznec, *op. cit.*, p. 151ff.; H. Swarzenski, *Monuments of Romanesque Art, The Art of Church Treasures in Northwestern Europe*, London, 1954, p. 50, Figs. 156–158; Rosenthal, *op. cit.*, Figs. 1 and 2 (interesting juxtaposition of the Twins in the *Leidensis Vossianus* and a Pompeian Apollo).

[9] For the Utrecht Psalter (reproduced *in toto* by E. T. DeWald, *The Illustrations of the Utrecht Psalter*, Princeton, 1932), see the recent pamphlet . . . by F.

Wormald, *The Utrecht Psalter*, Utrecht, 1953, where the importance of Roman stucco reliefs for the "impressionistic" treatment of the scenery is stressed; for an interesting parallel with other classical reliefs, particularly the *Tabulae Iliacae*, cf. Rosenthal, *op. cit.*, Figs. 12, 13. Yet the main source of inspiration must be sought in late fourth- and early fifth-century book illumination (for a particularly instructive parallel compare the group on fol. 14, identified as an Allegory of the Church in D. Panofsky, "The Textual Basis of the Utrecht Psalter Illustrations," *Art Bulletin*, XXV, 1943, p. 50ff., Fig. 18, with the Theano group in the Milan *Iliad*, illustrated, e.g., in Morey, *Early Christian Art*, Fig. 39). It should be noted, in particular, that a "pictorial" relief composition like the much-debated "Seaport Sarcophagus" in the Vatican (W. Amelung, *Die Sculpturen des Vaticanischen Museums*, Berlin 1903, II, Pl. 5), which in such details as the animated seascape in the foreground and the "Triumphal Arch of Ostia" in the right-hand background amazingly anticipates the Utrecht Psalter (fols. 38v. and 55v.), is hardly imaginable without a painted prototype; that late-antique illumination frequently exhibits an "impressionistic" treatment of accessories, especially the foliage of trees (see, e.g., the Vatican *Virgil* and, above all, the "Quedlinburg *Itala*" in Berlin, H. Degering and A. Boeckler, *Die Quedlinburger Italafragmente*, Berlin 1932); and that the use of pure line drawing as a medium may have been suggested by the Psalter's Early Christian model itself. . . . For medical and botanical manuscripts, e.g., C. J. Singer, *Studies in the History and Method of Science*, Oxford, 1917–1921, and K. Sudhoff, ed., *Archiv für Geschichte der Medizin und der Naturwissenschaften*, Leipzig, 1908–1943; . . . For the *Comedies* of Terence, L. W. Jones and C. R. Morey, *The Miniatures of the Manuscripts of Terence*, Princeton, 1930–1931; for Aesop's *Fables*, A. Goldschmidt, *An Early Manuscript of the Aesop Fables of Avianus and Related Manuscripts*, Princeton, 1947; for the *Chronograph of 354* and its Carolingian copy, the *Codex Luxemburgensis* (now lost but still known to Peiresc), Stern, *op. cit.*, for encyclopaedias, A. M. Amelli, *Miniature sacre e profane dell'anno 1023 illustranti l'Enciclopedia medioevale di Rabano Mauro*, Monte Cassino, 1896 (cf. Panofsky and Saxl, "Classical Mythology in Mediaeval Art," pp. 250, 258, Panofsky, *Studies in Iconology*, p. 76, and Jean Seznec, *The Survival the Pagan Gods* (Bollingen Series, XXXVIII), New York, 1953, p. 166); for the flabellum of Tournus, L. E. A. Eitner, *The Flabellum of Tournus* (*Art Bulletin Supplement*, I), New York, 1944.

10 For simulated classical cameos in manuscripts of the so-called Ada group, see, apart from the St. Luke page in the Ada Gospels itself (Trèves, Stadtbibliothek, MS. 22, illustrated, e.g., in Boinet, *op. cit.*, Plate VIII; Hinks, *op. cit.*, Plate 13; Boeckler, *Abendländische Miniaturen*, Plate 15), the instances reproduced in Boinet, Plates XV, XVII, XIX, XXI–XXIII, and Goldschmidt, *German Illumination*, Plates 33, 38, 40, 43. It should be noted, however, that these cameos tend to be gradually Christianized in later manuscripts belonging to, or deriving from, the same tradition. . . .

11 For classical personifications of nature in the Utrecht Psalter, see DeWald, *op. cit.* (Index), and Wormald, *The Utrecht Psalter*, p. 11, correctly emphasizing the fact that some of them, e.g., the river-gods, were borrowed from the *Aratea* manuscripts referred to above, Note 8; it is interesting that the Stuttgart Psalter, probably executed at about the same time as the Utrecht Psalter (E. T. DeWald, *The Stuttgart Psalter, Biblia Folio 23, Württembergische Landesbiblio-*

thek, Stuttgart, Princeton, 1930), is less rich in personifications of nature but includes such curious pagan motifs as the Celtic god Cernunnus (fol. 16v., here used as an equivalent of Hades). For classical personifications in Carolingian Crucifixions, see A. Goldschmidt, *Die Elfenbeinskulpturen aus der Zeit der karolingischen und sächsichen Kaiser,* I, Berlin, 1914, Figs. 41, 78, 83, 85, 88, 100, 132a, 163a. Occasionally, as in an ivory illustrated in Goldschmidt, Fig. 71a, or in the Sacramentary of St.-Denis, Paris, Bibliothèque Nationale, MS. lat. 1141, fol. 3 (H. Swarzenski, *Monuments of Romanesque Art,* Fig. 9), the personifications of Earth and/or Ocean are also found in representations of the *Majestas Domini.*

[12] For the "Ottonian" and "Anglo-Saxon" Renaissance in art, see H. Jantzen, *Ottonische Kunst,* Munich, n.d. [1947]; H. Focillon, *L'An Mil,* Paris, 1952; Saxl and Wittkower, *British Art and the Mediterranean,* p. 21ff.; O. Homburger, *Die Anfänge der Malerschule von Winchester im X. Jahrhundert,* Leipzig, 1912. For the absence of an "antik-heidnische Wiedergeburtsidee," see Heer, *op. cit.,* p. 80.

The conscious revival of Carolingian models after an interruption of nearly two hundred years has been brilliantly demonstrated in one specific case (the "Gerokodex," Darmstadt, Landesbibliothek, MS. 1948) by W. Köhler, "Die Tradition der Adagruppe und die Anfänge des ottonischen Stiles in der Buchmalerei," *Festschrift zum 60. Geburtstag von Paul Clemen,* Düsseldorf, 1926, p. 255ff.; and in another (here with reference to script and bookmaking), by E. A. Lowe, "The Morgan Golden Gospels, The Date and Origin of the Manuscript," *Studies in Art and Literature for Belle da Costa Greene,* Princeton, 1954, p. 266ff., exposing the Morgan manuscript M. 23 as an Ottonian imitation of a Carolingian original. For other significant instances in various fields, cf. H. Swarzenski, *Romanesque Monuments,* p. 22ff. (copies of the Utrecht Psalter, beginning with the early-eleventh-century manuscript, British Museum, MS. Harley 2506, and the slightly later manuscript, British Museum, MS. Cotton Tib. B. V). Similarly, St. Bernward of Hildesheim employed Carolingian models, both works of sculpture and book illuminations, in his silver crucifix as well as in the famous doors originally destined for St. Michael's (see E. Panofsky, *Die deutsche Plastik des elften bis dreizehnten Jahrhunderts,* Munich, 1924, pp. 73–78, Plates 2–5, Text Ills, XI, *a–c;* A. Goldschmidt, *Die deutschen Bronzetüren des Mittelalters,* Marburg, 1926; H. von Einem, "Zur Hildesheimer Bronzetür," *Jahrbuch der preussischen Kunstsammlungen,* LIX, 1938, p. 3ff.; F. Tschan, *Saint Bernward of Hildesheim,* Notre Dame, Indiana, 1942–1952, especially Vols. II and III; R. Wesenberg, *Bernwardinische Plastik,* Berlin, 1955). His no less famous bronze column, however, unfolding the story of Christ's public life on a continuous spiral, evidently presupposes, in spite of the enormous difference in style and conception (Panofsky, p. 21f.), the impression of the triumphal columns in Rome and thus constitutes one of the exceptional cases of direct classical influence upon Ottonian art. . . .

. . . St. Bernward's column, . . . reflects his personal memories of a visit to Rome in January, 1001—a visit which bore fruit in his own triumph over Archbishop Willigis of Mayence who, exactly six years after St. Bernward's arrival in Rome, was forced to concede to him the long-contested rights to the important convent of Gandersheim. It is, perhaps, not too hazardous to suppose that the unique monument, patterned after the triumphal columns at Rome, commemorates the major success of St. Bernward's administrative career as well as his devotion.

[13] For an important Ottonian artist, possibly active both as a book illuminator

and an ivory carver, whose style so clearly heralds the things to come that he has been called "the founder of the Romanesque style," see the excellent article by C. Nordenfalk, "Der Meister des Registrum Gregorii," *Münchner Jahrbuch der bildenden Kunst*, 3rd Ser., I, 1950, p. 61ff.

[14] For this "proto-Renaissance," see C. H. Haskins, *The Renaissance of the Twelfth Century*; J. Roosval, "Proto-Renaissance at the End of the Twelfth Century," *Essays in Honor of Georg Swarzenski*, Chicago, 1951, p. 39ff.; Toffanin, *op. cit.*, Vol. I. For the proto-Renaissance in France, see particularly R. Hamann, *Südfranzösische Proto-renaissance* (*Deutsche and französische Kunst im Mittelalter*, I), Marburg, 1923; *idem*, *Die Abteikirche von St. Gilles und ihre künstlerische Nachfolge*, Berlin, 1955 (cf. also W. Horn, *Die Fassade von St.-Gilles, eine Untersuchung zur Frage des Antikeneinflusses in der südfranzösischen Kunst des 12. Jahrhunderts*, Hamburg, doctoral diss., 1937); *idem*, "Altchristliches in der südfranzösischen Protorenaissance des 12. Jahrhunderts," *Die Antike*, X, 1934, p. 264ff.; M. Schapiro, "The Romanesque Sculpture of Moissac, Part I," *Art Bulletin*, XIII, 1931, pp. 249ff., 464ff. . . . For the proto-Renaissance in Italy, see G. H. Crichton, *Romanesque Sculpture in Italy*, London, 1954; R. Julian, *L'Eveil de la sculpture en Italie*, Paris, 1945–49; *idem*, *Les Sculpteurs romans de l'Italie septentrionale*, Paris, 1952; R. Salvini, *Wiligelmo e le origini della scultura romanica*, Milan, 1956. For South Italy, see still E. Bertaux, *L'Art dans l'Italie méridionale*, Paris, 1904; M. Wackernagel, *Die Plastik des 11. und 12. Jahrhunderts in Apulien*, Leipzig, 1911; for more recent literature, see C. A. Willemsen, *Apulien*, Leipzig, 1944; C. D. Sheppard, "A Chronology of Romanesque Sculpture in Campania," *Art Bulletin*, XXXII, 1950, p. 319ff. . . . For Venice, where the proto-Renaissance set in at a comparatively late date and was characterized by a particularly marked dependence on Late Antique and Early Christian monuments (at times producing what might be termed real "forgeries") and where sculpture tended to absorb the additional influence of the more developed mosaic, see O. Demus, "A Renascence of Early Christian Art in Thirteenth Century Venice," *Late Classical and Mediaeval Studies in Honor of Albert Mathias Friend, Jr.*, Princeton, 1954, p. 348ff. For Dalmatia, etc., see O. Kutschera-Woborsky, "Das Giovanninorelief des Spalatiner Vorgebirges," *Jahrbuch des kunsthistorischen Instituts* [deutsch-österreichisches Stattsdenkmalamt], XII, 1918, p. 28ff. For a still unrivaled wealth of illustrations covering the whole field of European sculpture in the twelfth century, see A. Kingsley Porter, *Romanesque Sculpture of the Pilgrimage Roads*, Cambridge (Mass.), 1923.

[15] For the rather rare examples of West European stone sculpture produced in Carolingian and Ottonian times . . . see A. Kingsley Porter, "The Tomb of Hincmar and Carolingian Sculpture in France," *Burlington Magazine*, L, 1927, p. 75ff.; H. Focillon, *L'Art des sculptures romanes*, Paris, 1931, especially p. 43ff.; *idem, L'An Mil, passim*; O. Homburger, "Ein Denkmal ottonischer Plastik in Rom mit dem Bildnis Ottos III," *Jahrbuch der preussischen Kunstsammlungen*, LVII, 1936, p. 130ff.; and, most particularly, R. Wesenberg, "Die Fragmente monumentaler Skulpturen von St. Pantaleon in Köln," *Zeitschrift für Kunstwissenschaft*, IX, 1955, p. 1ff.

[16] For Romanesque representations of Constantine reflecting the statue of Marcus Aurelius, see Adhémar, *op. cit.*, p. 207ff., Figs. 60–64; for Villard de Honnecourt, *ibidem*, p. 278ff., Figs. 106–112.

The Classical Tradition in the Middle Ages

[17] For the role of Nicolas of Verdun, see now H. Swarzenski, *Romanesque Monuments*, particularly pp. 29ff., 82 (with further references), Figs. 513–520.

[18] For the reliefs in the ambulatory of St.-Sernin in Tolouse, see Kingsley Porter, *op. cit.*, p. 206ff., Figs. 296–305, 307. For the Bari throne, see *ibidem*, p. 59ff., Figs. 152–155; A. Grabar, "Trônes épiscopaux du XIᵉ et XIIᵉ siècle en Italic méridionale," *Wallraf-Richartz-Jahrbuch*, XVI, 1954, p. 7ff. In my opinion the treatment of the nude in this astonishing monument can be explained only by the influence of Byzantine ivories such as the so-called rosette caskets (see, e.g., A. Goldschmidt and K. Weitzmann, *Die byzantinischen Elfenbeinskulpturen des X.–XIII. Jahrhunderts*, Berlin, 1930–34, I, Figs. 12, 15, 18, 21, 24, 26–33, 35, 38–43, 47–51) and two remarkable plaques, both in the Kaiser Friedrich Museum at Berlin, which show the Entry into Jerusalem and the Death of the Forty Martyrs; for two stone reliefs directly copied after Byzantine rosette caskets (one in Ferrara, the other in Como), see K. Weitzmann, "Abendländische Kopien Byzantinischer Rosettenkästen," *Zeitschrift für Kunstgeschichte*, III, 1934, p. 89ff. It is interesting that the same group of Byzantine ivories continued to interest the South Italian sculptors as late as the thirteenth century, as demonstrated by H. Wentzel, "Die Kamee mit dem ägyptischen Joseph in Leningrad," *Kunstgeschichtliche Studien für Hans Kauffmann*, Berlin, 1956, p. 85ff.

[19] For the appreciation, use and influence of classical gems and the mediaeval revivals of glyptography, see Adhémar, *op. cit.*, p. 106ff.; W. S. Heckscher, "Relics of Pagan Antiquity in Mediaeval Settings," *Journal of the Warburg Institute*, I, 1937–38, p. 204ff.; Déer, "Die Baseler Löwenkamee"; and a long series of articles by H. Wentzel, to whom our discipline owes a great debt for having called attention to a phenomenon largely neglected by earlier historians of mediaeval art. . . .

[20] For the contrast between the imitation of classical models in Provence and Burgundy ("imitation plus intelligente"), see the pertinent remarks in Adhémar, *op. cit.*, pp. 233ff. and 241ff.

[21] See Panofsky, *Die deutsche Plastik*, particularly p. 12ff.

[22] This stylistic difference between Romanesque and Early Gothic sculpture was first formulated by W. Vöge, *Die Anfänge des monumentalen Stiles im Mittelalter; Eine Untersuchung über die erste Blütezeit der französischen Plastik*, Strasbourg, 1894, now more than sixty years old but unsurpassed in fundamental insight. . . . For further discussion of this problem, E. Panofsky, *Early Netherlandish Painting*, p. 13ff., and W. Paatz, *Von den Gattungen und vom Sinn der gotischen Rundfigur* (*Sitzungsberichte der Heidelberger Akademie der Wissenschaften*, phil.-hist. Klasse, III, 1951). For an illuminating account of the encounter between the Gothic and the Romanesque principles in a German workshop of *ca.* 1230–35, see A. Goldschmidt, *Die Skulpturen in Freiberg und Wechselburg*, Berlin, 1924, p. 9ff. For a special problem in this connection, see C. Seymour, "Thirteenth-Century Sculpture at Noyon and the Development of the Gothic Caryatid," *Gazette des Beaux-Arts*, 6th Ser., XXVI, 1944, p. 163ff.

[23] The first to call attention to this new wave of Byzantinism (with special reference to German art) was, so far as I know, A. Goldschmidt, "Die Stilentwicklung der romanischen Skulptur in Sachsen", *Jahrbuch der königlich preussischen Kunstsammlungen*, XXI, 1900, p. 225ff. As far as France is concerned, the phenomenon was especially stressed by W. Vöge, "Ueber die Bamberger

ERWIN PANOFSKY

Domskulpturen," *Repertorium für Kunstwissenschaft*, XXII, 1899, p. 94ff.; XXIV, 1901, pp. 195ff., 255ff.

24 For the Master of Saints Peter and Paul, *see idem*, "Die Bahnbrecher des Naturstudiums." I wish to repeat that the similarity between the St. Peter and Antoninus Pius was called to my attention by Professor Karl Lehmann.

25 For possible sources of the Reims *Visitation*, see Adhémar, *op. cit.*, p. 276ff., and, as far as the hairdress and headdress are concerned, G. Swarzenski, *Nicolo Pisano*, Frankfurt-am-Main, 1926, p. 18, Plate 26; Wentzel's tentative attempt to connect it with classical gems ("Mittelalter und Antike," p. 88, Fig. 22) is limited to the facial type of the Virgin and, even so, does not appear convincing. In regard to pose and drapery treatment, however, full-scale classical statuary has not yielded convincing prototypes either. The closest parallels are found, curiously enough, in certain "Tanagra" statuettes (see, e.g., G. Kleiner, *Tanagrafiguren; Untersuchungen zur hellenistischen Kunst und Geschichte* [*Jahrbuch des deutschen archäologischen Instituts*, Ergänzungsheft, No. 15], Berlin, 1942, Plates 17c, 21a, 24c, 27b,c; G. M. A. Richter, *The Metropolitan Museum of Art, Handbook of the Classical Collection*, New York, 1917, Fig. 88d, f, our Fig. 41). It should, however, be borne in mind, first, that, as recently emphasized in a brief but very important article by D. B. Thompson, to whom I am much indebted in regard to the questions here under discussion ("A Bronze Dancer from Alexandria," *American Journal of Archaeology*, LIV, 1950, p. 371ff., particularly p. 374), small-sized sculpture in clay often reproduces small-sized sculpture in silver or bronze; second, that metal statuettes of high quality—in turn occasionally reflecting "major art"—can be shown, even after the enormous losses caused by theft or recasting, to have found their way as far north as France and Germany in ancient times. . . .

26 The possibility that Rome had a greater influence on the formation of the proto-Renaissance style than is generally assumed has been suggested by Wentzel, "Antiken-Imitationen," particularly p. 59ff. It is certainly remarkable that a base in the cloisters of St. John in the Lateran (produced, however, as late as 1222–1230) faithfully imitates a genuine Egyptian sphinx, apparently appropriated through a Roman intermediary; see Wentzel, *ibidem*, and *Reallexikon zur deutschen Kunstgeschichte*, IV, col. 750ff., Fig. 1.

27 For Frederick II's city foundations, especially Victoria, see E. H. Kantorowicz, *Kaiser Friedrich der Zweite*, 3rd ed., Berlin, 1931, I, p. 598f.; II ("Ergänzungsband"), p. 242. It is no more than an accident—but an illuminating one—that the "Unanimes Antiquitatis Amatores" under Sixtus IV made the same St. Victor their patron saint. . . . The difference would seem to be that Frederick II attempted to press the Antique into the service of his political and cultural aims while "the Sodalitas Litteratorum Sancti Victoris et Sociorum" attempted to place their much-criticized worship of the Antique under the protection of a suitable Catholic saint.

28 For the artistic activities of Frederick II in general, see, in addition to Kantorowicz, *ibidem*, I, p. 479ff.; II, p. 209ff.; Willemsen, *Apulien, passim*; W. Krönig, "Staufische Baukunst in Unteritalien," *Beiträge zur Kunst des Mittelalters* (*Vortäge der ersten deutschen Kunsthistorikertagung auf Schloss Brühl, 1948*), Berlin, 1950, p. 28ff.; and Wentzel, "Antiken-Imitationen," with further references (a typewritten Marburg dissertation of 1922 by E. Holler, *Kaiser Freidrich II und die Antike*, referred to by Wentzel, p. 30, Note 7, was not accessible to me).

29 The classicistic tendency indubitably present—though by no means exclusively

prevailing—in "Frederician" sculpture and glyptography . . . is absent from the miniatures in Frederick's treatise on falconry (A. Wood and F. M. Fyfe, *The Art of Falconry, Being the "De Arte Venandi Cum Avibus" of Frederick II. von. Hohenstaufen*, London, 1943 [2nd ed., Boston, 1955]); nor does it seem to have been evident in the mural which in his palace at Naples (Kantorowicz, *ibidem*, I, p. 215; II, p. 89) once proclaimed the ritual of imperial jurisdiction. This mural is lost, but it would seem that an approximate idea of its style can, after all, be formed on the basis of the *Praeconium Paschale* miniature in the Exultet Roll in the Biblioteca Capitolare at Salerno (Kantorowicz, II, frontispiece; cf. G. B. Ladner, "The 'Portraits' of Emperors in Southern Italian Exultet Rolls," *Speculum*, XVII, 1942, p. 181ff., particularly p. 186. . . .

30 For literature on the "three-nail type," see Panofsky, *Early Netherlandish Painting*, p. 364f. For Giotto's early Crucifix, see Oertel, *Die Frühzeit der italienischen Malerei*, pp. 66 and 219, Notes 120, 122, correctly crediting Nicolo Pisano with the introduction of this Gothic innovation into Italy.

31 See, for example, W. Mönch, *Das Sonett*, Heidelberg, 1954. In this connection it is interesting to note what happened in Tuscany to the "Justice picture" first exemplified by Frederick's mural in his palace at Naples. This authoritarian and, in a sense, bureaucratic pronouncement, where the populace, kowtowing before the enthroned Emperor, was enjoined to direct its complaints to his chancellor, Petrus de Vinea, rather than to himself, was replaced by affirmations of civic liberty, first, in Giotto's lost fresco in the Arte della Lana at Florence where Brutus was glorified as the paradigm of republican justice (S. Morpurgo, "Brutus, 'il buon giudice', nell' Udienza dell'Arte della Lana," *Miscellanea di Storia dell'Arte in onore di Igino Benvenuto Supino*, Florence, 1933, p. 141ff.); and, second, in Ambrogio Lorenzetti's famous allegories in the Palazzo Pubblico at Siena.

32 See G. Swarzenski, *Nicolo Pisano*, Plates 16, 19–21, 26. For later literature on Nicola Pisano, see W. R. Valentiner, "Studies on Nicola Pisano," *Art Quarterly*, XV, 1952, p. 9ff.

33 See A. Bush-Brown, "Giotto: Two Problems in the History of His Style," *Art Bulletin*, XXXIV, 1952, p. 42ff. (cf., however, Panofsky, *Early Netherlandish Painting*, p. 367 . . .).

19. DUCCIO AND GIOTTO

John White

INTRODUCTION

In the fourteenth century, before the Black Death fell upon Italy during the summer of 1348, there was a remarkable flowering of Italian painting. Associated with this brilliant era are the names of the great Florentine master, Giotto, and the Sienese painters Duccio, Simone Martini, and the Lorenzettis, among other worthy artists less well-known. Duccio has been the subject of two recent publications that deserve special mention: James Stubblebine, *Duccio di Buoninsegna and His School* (1979) and John White, *Duccio: Tuscan Art and the Medieval Workshop* (1979). This selection, taken from the latter work, offers the reader discerning comparisons between Duccio and Giotto that bring into focus the distinctive character of each painter's work, particularly with respect to the handling of narrative, while at the same time evoking the larger context of their milieu, the immediate past from which their art stemmed, and the future their work would have as it affected artists of other times and places. Of interest, too, is White's discussion of the general subject of attributions as related to the workshop tradition of the time.

For further consultation, the following titles represent a fair sampling: John White, *Art and Architecture in Italy, 1250–1400* (1966); Raimond van Marle, *The Development of the Italian Schools of Painting*, I–IX (1923–38); Andrew Martindale, *The Rise of the Artist in the Middle Ages and the Early Renaissance* (1972); Erwin Panofsky, *Renaissance and Renascences in Western Art*, 2nd ed. (1965); George H. Edgell, *A History of Sienese Painting* (1932); Enzo Carli, *Sienese Painting* (1956); Richard Offner, *Studies in Florentine Painting, the 14th Century* (1927); George H. and Sylvia R. Crichton, *Nicola Písanu and the Revival of Sculpture in Italy* (1938); John Pope-Hennessy,

Italian Gothic Sculpture, 2nd ed. (1972); Osvald Sirén, *Giotto and Some of His Followers*, 2 vols. (1917); L. Tintori and E. Borsook, *Giotto: The Peruzzi Chapel* (1965); Eugenio Battisti, *Giotto*, trans. by J. Emmons (1960); James Stubblebine, ed., *Giotto: The Arena Chapel Frescoes* (1969); Eve Borsook, *The Mural Painters of Tuscany from Cimabue to Andrea del Sarto* (1960); V. Lazarev, "Duccio and Thirteenth Century Greek Icons," *The Burlington Magazine*, LIX (1931), 154–68; J. H. Stubblebine, "Byzantine Influences in Thirteenth Century Italian Panel Painting," *Dumbarton Oaks Papers*, XX (1966), 87–101, and by the same author, "Byzantine Sources for the Iconography of Duccio's Maestà," *Art Bulletin*, LVII (1975); Ernst Kitzinger, "The Byzantine Contribution to Western Art of the Twelfth and Thirteenth Centuries," *Dumbarton Oaks Papers*, XX (1966), 25–47; John White, "Measurement, Design and Carpentry in Duccio's Maestà," I, II, *Art Bulletin*, LV (1973), 332–66, 547–69, and by the same author, "Giotto's Use of Architecture in 'The Expulsion of Joachim' and the 'Entry into Jerusalem' at Padua," *The Burlington Magazine*, CXV (1973), 439–47.

As with any artist, the only way to an understanding of the true nature of Duccio's achievement is to see his work, and to see it again and again and, above all in his particular case, to go to see the *Maestà* (Fig. 58), dismembered as it is. In the face of that unique experience, the questions of origins and of fame and influence, of what went before and what came after, fall into perspective. Indeed, if the history and the archaeology of the art of the period is to be a help and not a hindrance, it is vital that they should. That these questions can, if misused, become not merely a hindrance but a positive danger, is shown by one of the most worrying phenomena of recent years. This has been the way in which the removal of the fresco from the wall by modern methods, which began as an entirely worthy enterprise, undertaken only when it was essential for the preservation of the work, has shown distinct signs of becoming a self-perpetuating industry. There seems to be an increasing danger that the discovery of the sinopia, which was no more than an incidental, if exciting by-product of the necessary processes of conservation, has become, and will increasingly become, a primary motive for the stripping. If it does, art history will 'advance' at the expense of art.

In less dramatic, intellectual as opposed to physical spheres of operation, the business of attribution, which provides the essential base for any art-historical biography, has long seemed to be getting out of hand as far as thirteenth- and early fourteenth-century Italian painting is concerned. What should be no more than a starting point often appears to have become a goal. It has turned a purposeful activity into a self-perpetuating, purposeless and rather irritating game. In dealing with the great artistic surge which took place in this period, there is no doubt at all that the creative power of the individual, and the social and artistic consequences of that power, should be properly stressed. Whatever the mistakes that have been made or the distortions which have occurred at the hands of individual historians from Vasari on-

58. Duccio di Buoninsegna, *Maestà* (The Passion Scenes), *c.* 1308–11, Museo dell'Opera del Duomo, Siena (Alinari/Editorial Photocolor Archives)

wards, the beginnings of the evolution from artisan to artist and the growth of conscious interest in development and change are crucial factors in the history of the times. The other side of this particular coin is that the emphasis on workshop methods, on the nature of artistic cooperation and on the physical processes and sequences of operation involved in the making of material objects, which has been among the major preoccupations of a number of recent studies, is no less important. The transformation in our understanding and appreciation of the finished *Maestà*, which arguably should result from a better understanding of the means by which it was created, has consequences reaching far beyond the *Maestà* itself or the handful of surrounding works which can, with reason, be associated with it. The implications are as great

446

for Nicola Pisano's Siena pulpit as they are for Lorenzo Maitani's Orvieto sculptures. They extend to Giotto's Padua, as well as to the Bardi and Peruzzi Chapels and to Assisi. In a peculiarly acute form they raise the whole question of what is meant in this or any other period by the attribution of a given work to a given artist.

. . . From Giotto onwards genuine signatures have been placed, for various reasons, sometimes good and sometimes less so, upon works for which the signatories were only in part or even not at all responsible in terms of manufacture. The process of attribution should invariably include, if not begin with, the accumulation of every scrap of evidence from signatures and documents, from first and secondhand accounts; but in the end the problem of stylistic likeness cannot be avoided. Often . . . it is the only thing there is to go on. When, in addition, what is known of workshop methods has been taken into account, it is no surprise to find works sloshing back and forth from name to name like flotsam on the tide.

The excesses of the seemingly unending game of attribution and reattribution only obscure the real advances which have been made. They do no more than reflect the fact that there are many works for which it is now impossible, in principle, to say with reason any more than that they come from this or that workshop or belong to this or that loosely defined group or should be included in the circle of such and such a master and his shop. To appear to be more precise is to hinder rather than to help. It represents a move away from, rather than towards, the actualities of the world in which the works concerned were made.

There is nothing wrong in talking of Duccio's *Maestà* or Nicola Pisano's Siena pulpit, in the sense that they were the responsible leaders of the groups concerned. The establishment of general criteria of morphology and quality and of detailed characteristics by which to judge the likeness or unlikeness of surrounding works is a perfectly reasonable occupation. On the other hand it is as misleading to give particular panels on the *Maestà* to Ugolino de Siena, who may well have worked on it and in whose later paintings its echoes and reverberations are continuous, both in general and in detail, as it is to ascribe the *Massacre of the Innocents* on the Siena pulpit to Giovanni Pisano, who is known from documents to have almost certainly worked on that.[1] . . .

When the establishment of even an initial core of works is often such a chancy business, it is more than ever essential that the logic and limitations of the attribution process should be understood, and the nature of the problem is nowhere more clearly laid out than it is in Giotto's case. There . . . the initial dilemma is whether to start from the Louvre *Stigmatization*, the Baroncelli *Coronation* and the Bologna polyptych, the three works which are signed upon their frames but which appear to differ considerably from each other both in quality and in style, or whether to use the Arena Chapel, which is both undocumented and unsigned but arguably of higher quality, as the primary artistic touchstone on which other attributions should be based.

For Duccio, the situation . . . is more straightforward, since the *Maestà*, which is both signed and documented, and the *Rucellai Madonna*, which is documented but not signed, are in both scale and quality by far the most important of the surviving works which can reasonably be given to him. . . .

. . . In the later thirteenth century, a new and vital visual language . . . despite the different dialects in which they spoke, was common to all the leading central Italian artists of the period. The Pisani, Cavallini, Cimabue, the Isaac Master and the Master of the St. Francis Cycle were all of them primarily concerned with bringing the sacred narratives and personages more vividly and immediately alive before the eyes of the faithful. They were no less concerned to bring out the significance and symbolic meanings of their subjects to the full. It is therefore no surprise that Duccio and Giotto were both of them leaders in exploring the consequences and the possibilities inherent in the fundamental fact that visual narratives, unlike their written or their spoken counterparts, are not confined to rigid, linear sequencing. As Leonardo, in a later period, never tired of pointing out, the picture, as distinct from music, is eternally and completely present.[2] It is always open to perception in its entirety. It is true that visual perception and information gathering are scanning processes and that, despite the almost incredible speeds which are habitual in the human animal, it does take time. The difference is that whereas in music speed and direction in scanning are externally controlled, and in reading the direction is controlled and the speed is subject to relatively severe restrictions, in art the entire process is under the control of the observer and the sequencing is infinitely variable. The imposition of a certain order on this potentially anarchic situation, whilst at the same time taking advantage of the freedoms it presents, is one of the principle functions of the artist. In every representational design there is a conscious or unconscious tendency to set up major compositional pathways and the outcome is one of the most intriguing aspects of the work of all the artists mentioned. Each one of them emerges as being vitally concerned with the creation of new methods of control at the same time as the visual complexity and informational content of their narrative compositions are steadily increasing.

In Duccio's case, the chances of survival have meant that the process can only be studied within the contracted time-span and physically compressed compass of the painting of the *Maestà*. In that of Giotto, the selfsame process, so clearly visible on the walls of the Arena Chapel, is steadily continued in the Bardi and Peruzzi

Chapels. It is, however, primarily in the *Maestà* and in the Arena Chapel that the processes of control and the exploitation of alternative pathways, not merely within individual narrative incidents or designs, but within the narrative and compositional structure as a whole, can be appreciated. Though what they have to say is often very different, what is striking is the extent to which they speak the same language. What is also very seldom stressed is the extent to which Duccio is the more adventurous in some respects.

Giotto analyses. He simplifies and concentrates. Within each individual design he goes for clarity of presentation. In the Paduan cycle as a whole he eschews the pattern of the printed text, in which the three tiers on each wall would be read from left to right and top to bottom, like successive lines upon a page. Because his narrative is concentrated on the exegesis of the Gospels and of the immediately preceding apocryphal stories, he also avoids the typological, New Testament against Old Testament opposition of wall and wall, which is reminiscent of the opposition of the pages in an open book. In so doing, he departs from the principles established in the two-tier designs of the great Roman basilicas of old St Peter's and of S. Paolo fuori le Mura and their progeny. On the other hand, he does respect the straight line continuity of the written word in the ordering of his scenes and simply wraps his narrative in one, unbroken linear progression round the walls. What is more, he accepts, indeed exploits, the traditional constraint and discipline of placing every scene within a standard sized container. Because each episode in the Gospels is presented in a closed and concentrated composition, each contains its own particular climax, with the corollary that the narrative as a whole has none. The *Crucifixion* is in no way emphasized. It is not enlarged in any way or even set in the centre of a wall. Whether in the individual scene or in the narrative sequence, Giotto willingly imposes and accepts restraints in order to achieve his fundamental purposes. This is not to say that the Arena Chapel has no climax, for that lies in the great *Last Judgment* looming over the observer as he leaves.

Duccio, faced by the very different formal problem, not of a three-, but of a six-layered narrative pattern on a single surface, and of forty-three, instead of eighteen, separate episodes, pulls out all the stops. He moves about as far as it is possible to move, and certainly as far as any artist ever did move in the next six hundred years, away from the visual layout characteristic of the written text. . . . His narrative begins at the bottom instead of at the top. Typically, his introduction in the front predella is a straight-line sequence, and the same straightforward pattern holds good for the rear predella. Then he purposefully breaks the rule of symmetry by doubling the size of the *Entry*. This is quite unlike the casual asymmetries to be found in certain early art forms and in much provincial art, either because of a lack of preplanning or because of a desire that every subdivision should be directly, if relatively haphazardly, scaled to its own particular, localized, compositional needs. The immediate effect of Duccio's action is to break down the dominance of the horizontal layering. It straight away, in visual terms, serves notice that the vertical coupling within each of the two principal subdivisions of the main body is as important as the lateral, left to right progression and, indeed, is more important than any straight-line horizontal movement. This enables him to escape the linear narrative at certain points in the story and to suggest the simultaneity of happenings in different places which is central to the actuality of events as they occur. The unique zig-zagging progress through the subsequent narratives is no less bold in its departure from the relative monotony of the written line and from traditional pictorial sequences.

Then again, not only is the *Crucifixion* set upon the central axis and, as in the nave of old St Peter's, enormously enlarged in relation to the preceding and succeeding episodes, but the crucified figure of Christ himself is given very special emphasis. This is achieved by grouping all the flying angels in the narrow zone above the cross-tree, so that for the only time upon the whole rear face of the altarpiece, a vast blank area of gold is left to isolate and emphasize the central figure. In contrast to the patterns adopted by Giovanni Pisano or by Giotto, the absolute separation of the figure groups works to the same end by leaving the whole of the vertical of Christ's cross completely visible. The effect is even further accentuated by the curving slope of heads on either side. This means that there is no encouragement, as there is in Cimabue's *Crucifixion* at Assisi, for the eye to spark across the gap.

Finally, . . . Duccio uses a chronological break or contradiction at the centre of both sequences of pinnacle panels, as well as a change of scale, to confirm his great central axis. As a result, the horizontal layering is held in balance, the central core of subject-matter and of symbolism is accentuated and the importance of the alternative, significant pathways through the overall design is stressed. The opening horizontal sequences of the *Last Supper*, the *Leave Taking* and the *Agony in the Garden*, with above them the *Washing of the Feet*, the *Judas Taking the Bribe* and the *Betrayal*, or the closing horizontal of the *Entombment*, the *Maries at the Tomb* and the *Apparition on the Road to Emmaus*, become readily apparent as significant alternatives to the regular zig-zag progress of the story.

Within the more rigidly restricted patterns of the Arena Chapel, Giotto exploits the possibilities of the alternative pathway in a strictly analogous fashion. Vertical correspondences in form and content are created wherever possible. The process reaches its climax on the left wall, in the four scenes of the *Feast at Cana* and the *Raising of Lazarus* in the middle register, and the *Lamentation* and the *Noli Me Tangere* immediately beneath them (Fig. 59).

Firstly, the *Feast at Cana*, as a prefiguration of the sacrifice of the mass and of the cross, is significantly juxtaposed with the mourning over the dead sacrificial victim which takes place immediately below. Secondly, the *Raising of Lazarus* is a prefiguration of the *Noli Me Tangere* with its implicit resurrection theme. Finally the *Raising*, with its implicit story of death, of a three days' sojourn in the tomb and of eventual resurrection, is also in itself a summary of the essential content of the two lower scenes taken together. The downward continuation of the diagonal rock slope of the *Raising of Lazarus* in the even more dramatic diagonal of rock in the *Lamentation* below it and to the left, makes the point in the most emphatic of visual terms. The process is completed by the way in which, when once the lower register is reached, what now becomes the rising rockslope of the *Lamentation* as one moves from left to right along the wall, finds its exact continuation in the downslope of the rock in the succeeding scene. . . .

Giotto's *Lamentation* and his *Noli Me Tangere* are also especially important in that they provide perhaps the clearest exposition of another aspect of the newly developing common visual language. As soon as an apparent three dimensionality

59. Giotto di Bondone, clockwise from upper left: *Feast at Cana, Raising of Lazarus, Noli me Tangere, Lamentation, c.* 1304–13, Fresco, Arena Chapel, Padua (Alinari/Editorial Photocolor Archives)

becomes a serious intention in the figurative arts, the problem of maintaining two-dimensional coherence in the composition, of linking foreground figures to their land- or townscape backgrounds or surroundings in a satisfactory manner, takes on quite a new significance. . . .

In the Paduan *Noli Me Tangere* . . . dramatic power gives way to subtle, finger-tip control. There the trees, of which the trunks alone survive, immediately to the right of the left-hand angel, formerly possessed their bushy tops. They were therefore much more emphatic in their compositional effect. Indeed, they played a vital role in what is actually a double scene. As the observer moves along the wall and comes upon the composition from the left, the down-sweep of the rock slope and the angel's outstretched arm point on towards the second angel and, beyond him, to the figure of Christ himself. Then the trees provide a visual stop, a partial pause. They draw attention down towards the tomb and in so doing they ensure that the all-important fact of its emptiness, with its essential proof of resurrection, is neither missed nor easily passed over. To this same end the line of rock is brought to a still more sudden stop in the angel's shoulder and the vertical of his left wing. Nevertheless, the figure of Christ on the far right remains the most important element in the entire design. Therefore the angel's other wing slopes downwards in a sweeping curve that runs on till it blends into the contour of the rock, reiterating and accelerating the more jagged, introductory rock form on the left. Finally, this curving, swift descent is brought to a sudden halt by the solid, vertical cliff form of the figure of Christ. It is typical of Giotto that, as Christ looks back and gestures to the Magdalen, ensuring that the human and the spiritual relationship between the two is given its due weight, his outstretched thumb and finger tips appear, as lightly as a feather, to caress the background hillside. Simultaneously, the angle of the rock slope changes to accommodate and cup the gesture. The coincidence is exact and the intention clear and, in the light of many similar effects in the Arena Chapel, clearly conscious.

Exactly the same principles are used by Giovanni Pisano in the scenes of the *Nativity* and the *Adoration of the Magi*, which were carved for the Pisa pulpit within a year or two either way of the painting of Giotto's fresco.[3] Indeed, in the *Adoration* the parallel is exact. There, a flying angel's wing again becomes, by an exact coincidence of form, the rock on which the leading wise man kneels. The draperies of his kneeling leg then merge into the cloak of the third king. Finally, the angel's pointing hand runs on into the circling rock form of the cave with just that same ambiguous cunning as the pointing finger of the serving maid in the *First Denial* on the *Maestà* runs on into the balustrade that leads the eye towards the upper chamber where Christ stands.

Here, although the Pisa pulpit was still about two years from completion when work began on the *Maestà*, the priority almost certainly lies with Giovanni Pisano, whom Duccio must have known extremely well from the sculptor's twelve-year sojourn in the city as Capomaestro of the Opera del Duomo. Certainly, there is no question that exactly the same visual and compositional principles are again at work in Duccio's *Christ in Limbo*. Not only does the curving top line of one fallen gate of hell run on into the rock wall of the hell-mouth, whilst the other closes off its lower margin, but it is precisely at the junction of these two continuous forms that Christ's hand firmly grasps the wrist of Abraham to haul him to his heaven.

This use of a light-dark contrast with the background to accentuate a gesture is a constant feature of the *Maestà*. In the *Washing of the Feet*, Christ's hand grasps St. Peter's foot exactly at the point where wall and floor and the black margin of the doorway meet. What is more, Christ's other hand touches the contrasted vertical where the black doorway opening ends and the green wall begins, exactly as it does in the scene of *Christ Taking Leave of the Apostles*. . . .

At Padua, Giotto uses similar methods time and again to emphasize a gesture, although he is more catholic in his use of the device than Duccio, who tends to confine such accents to the central action of a scene. The *Birth of the Virgin*, the *Presentation of the Rods*, the *Marriage of the Virgin*, the *Presentation* and the *Teaching in the Temple*, and the *Expulsion of the Moneychangers*, all provide examples. . . .

In landscape terms, the hollowing of the rock to silhouette the hands of Christ in the *Agony in the Garden* or the way in which the mountain crag, cradled behind the Magdalen's upraised arms in the *Lamentation*, seems to weigh like sorrow on her back, are analogous to the hollowing of rock that forms an upright cradle for the saddened Joachim or to the way in which the rock cleft turns the shepherd's staff into a crook in Giotto's *Joachim Returning to the Sheepfold*. There, the use of trees is no less notable. First, at the point of entry on the left, there is the introductory form used as a counterpoise for Joachim's bowed head and shoulders. Then there is the smaller tree that helps to bridge the gap of sadness and of inturned loneliness that lies between him and the questioning, uncertain shepherds. Finally, there is the larger tree which, in the context of the composition as a whole, provides the shepherds with a necessary accent overhead. The analogy with Duccio's use of trees in the *Agony* and the *Betrayal* could hardly be more precise. Indeed, just as the one dead tree in the Arena Chapel shows all nature mourning the dead Saviour in the *Lamentation*, so the dead thorn in the *Entry* on the *Maestà*, which is again unique in the whole cycle, is . . . a portent of Christ's Passion.

In some respects it is the difference in scale which stops us instantaneously appreciating the degree to which the fresco and the panel painter share a common aim. In another field, the wide screen drama in the cinema at first seems very different when transposed in otherwise unaltered form onto a two foot television tube. Nevertheless, it is enough to set the dead Son cradled in his mother's arms in Giotto's *Lamentation* up against a detail of the *Deposition* on the *Maestà* to sense the depth and intensity of feeling that is shared between them. The urgency with which the Virgin reaches up to take her Son once more into her arms; the tension of her drapery against the limpness of the hand that still seems to caress the shoulder that it clutched so happily in childhood; the crimson of the nail-wound set against the dark blue of her cloak; the way her hand comes up to cup his bearded face; mother and child are cheek to cheek as they so often were, and as they still so often are upon a host of altarpieces. The well remembered image is made new; its burden of humanity unforgettably increased. And it is one of many.

Giovanni Pisano, Giotto, Duccio: it is not so much the detail of the flow of influence or the search for evidence of direct borrowings back and forth, as the existence of a common tongue that is substantially to remain in use for centuries, that is important. This commonality is not confined to the major aspects of its syntax and its grammar, which must quickly have become familiar to artists and to audiences alike all over central Italy. It also reaches to the still experimental frontiers of the new language. . . .

Another feature common to both artists . . . is their exploration of the further possibilities of the observation of the unity of place. Both were concerned in their own way to extend its realistic implications beyond mere repetition of identical backgrounds or surroundings. Giotto's most striking innovation occurs in the *Presentation of the Virgin*, in which he rotates the sanctuary-temple of the *Expulsion of Joachim* in order to give the effect of walking round it and seeing it from another point of view. His prototype was probably provided by such sanctuary enclosures as that in S. Clemente, and the analogy with the effects obtained by walking round such structures is quite striking. Though each of Giotto's compositions tends to be a severely closed and centralized design, he extends a variation of the same idea to landscape. It is clearly his intention to suggest that walking past the peak on the right of *Joachim Returning to the Sheepfold* will bring it once more into view, seen from a slightly different angle, on the left of *Joachim's Sacrifice.*

In some ways Giotto's focus on a single action leads him to great caution in his handling of architecture. Whilst he was quite prepared to use the frame to cut a fraction from the roof or side of a building, the radical suggestion of vertical and lateral continuity in Duccio's *Presentation* on the *Maestà* lay quite outside his range of compositional interest. The continuation of the same extensive structure in a subsequent scene, as in Duccio's extension of the temple cloisters of the *Presentation* into the courtyard of the *Teaching in the Temple,* is a development of the idea of architectural unity and continuity which was, by the same token, clearly contrary to Giotto's principles of design. Nevertheless, the very fact that it is in the context of the temple and its representation that both are at their most adventurous, leads on to interesting speculations as to the degree of contact that there may have been between them during the early years of the century. Certainly if they did learn from each other it was at a fundamental level, since they each of them had very different things to say in the new visual language which they were forming.

Duccio, in particular, was far more ready to experiment with open-ended compositions. The sense of entering on the left, of curving up and round and disappearing into an extensive city, which is apparent in Duccio's *Entry into Jerusalem,* is unparalleled in Giotto's work. . . .

Unity of lighting and increasing interest in coherent perspectival structure are other features common to the art of Giotto and of Duccio alike, though they are used in very different ways. For Giotto it is the concentrated study of the actual appearance of the individual object, as you look at it, that has the prime importance. Since all rectangular solids of which more than a single side is visible can only be seen with all their visible surfaces receding, it is on the resulting oblique setting in all its various forms that he increasingly concentrates his attention. Duccio, in contrast, deals not with the focused, concentrated view, but with the multiplicity of things, and since in its early stages of development the oblique construction was inimical to the coordination of large numbers of different structures within a single composition, he avoids it. In this respect he is conservative and keeps his feet well planted on the solid ground of Byzantine and Italo-Byzantine precedent. In this one aspect of perspective structure Duccio stands more firmly than does Giotto in the direct line that leads to the Renaissance and to Brunelleschian and Albertian Artificial Perspective. One of the essential characteristics of the latter system is that all planes parallel to the picture surface should retain their undistorted form. The rectangle remains a rectangle, and as in the foreshortened frontal system which is used consistently by Duccio, only the surfaces receding at an angle to the picture plane are drawn in as being foreshortened.[4] . . .

Because of the particular qualities of their own achievement and of the subsequent nature of what has been seen as the mainstream of central Italian art in the fifteenth and the early sixtenth centuries, there is no doubt whatsoever that the direct influence of Giotto and the Pisani on men such as Masaccio and Donatello or Michelangelo and Raphael completely overshadows any conceivable firsthand contribution that Duccio may have made. But even in this context he must not be totally ignored. The *Maestà* is certainly the first stride on the path that leads to the development of the *Sacra Conversazione*, which, by any standards, ranks among the major themes in the history of Early and High Renaissance art. Whatever the fine detail of the format of Masaccio's own dismembered Pisa polyptych may have been, the altarpiece must certainly have been instantly recognizable as lying in the direct line of descent from Duccio's epoch-making early fourteenth-century innovations.[5]

There is every reason to think that the multi-storey polyptych to which Duccio and his immediate successors, Simone Martini, Pietro Lorenzetti and Meo da Siena, gave definitive form in the first and early second decades of the fourteenth century, was essentially a Sienese development. . . . The structural pattern, which Duccio appears to have created, runs on through this major work of the 1320s, with which Masaccio must have been thoroughly familiar, and through Bernardo Daddi's S. Pancrazio altarpiece of the 'thirties, to Taddeo Gaddi's altarpiece of 1353 for S. Giovanni Fuorcivitas in Pistoia and Giovanni del Biondo's Rinuccini altarpiece of 1379, also in S. Croce.[6] Such altarpieces follow on in an unbroken line throughout the whole of the trecento and, with Lorenzo Monaco and Masaccio, continue well into the fifteenth century. Elsewhere, all over Gothic Italy from end to end, the progeny of the Sienese multi-storied altarpiece remains the dominant form for major works. Again, such altarpieces flow in a continuous line past such diverse figures as Piero della Francesca and Carlo Crivelli into the final years of the fifteenth century.

What is more, no other Italian artist apart from Duccio had such seminal influence through his own work and the work of his close circle and immediate followers on the artists and the arts of France and of the Franco-Flemish borderlands. His role is vital from the time of Jean Pucelle in the late 1320s to 1340s to that of the full flowering of the art of the International Gothic with the de Limbourgs in the early years of the fifteenth century.

For Jean Pucelle, whose atelier dominated Parisian illumination during the whole of the second quarter of the fourteenth century, Duccio's *Maestà* proved, without a doubt, to be the climactic experience of the trip which he appears to have made to Italy at some time in the 1320s.[7] . . . The *Maestà* was the work that opened his eyes to a new world and presented it to him in a form which he was immediately able to grasp and make his own. It showed him fresh pictorial patterns and a new way to approach the real, three-dimensional world. . . .

The debt which Duccio owed to northern art was more than amply repaid, not merely through Pucelle, but through Duccio's inspiration, both direct and indirect, of the most important of the great illuminators of the late fourteenth and early fifteenth centuries. Men such as Jacquemart de Hesdin and the Master of the Parement de Narbonne, whose fainting Virgin in the *Crucifixion* reflects the Crawford and Balcarres pattern, and, above all, Pol de Limbourg, owe him much. Even if the debt in Pol de Limbourg's *Carrying of the Cross* is not in fact to a lost version of the theme by Duccio himself, as might well be the case, the impact of Duccio's *Entry into Jerusalem* on both Simone Martini's and Pietro Lorenzetti's evocations of the *Carrying* would be hard to overstress.[8] In spite of the change of format and the elaboration of the detail, Pietro's version, in particular, is virtually Duccio's *Entry* in reverse. The really important thing is not that the de Limbourg's *Carrying of the Cross* is founded on direct experience of Sienese painting at its source. What is at stake is the whole handling of crowds and of the multifarious detail of the natural world; its animation, its variety, and its confusion, its bustle and its energy; all the things which play a vital role in innumerable other compositions of the International Gothic period and which eventually flow back to Florence in such works as Gentile da Fabriano's *Adoration of the Magi* of 1423. These are the aspects of reality which Duccio represents.

Duccio's vision of the world and of the function of the painter in portraying it was very different, and no less important in these respects, from that of Giotto. If, in such seminal designs as Duccio's *Entry into Jerusalem*, the figures are not wholly solid and the road is still tip-tilted, it is nonetheless an evocation of a hilltop city and a happy and excited crowd that lies as far outside the range of Giotto's interest and ability as Giotto's grand pictorial equations lie beyond his own. Without his pioneering work and the foundations which he laid, the advent of Ambrogio Lorenzetti's town- and landscape of *Good Government* in the Palazzo Pubblico in Siena is inconceivable in its present form.[9] It is a sobering thought that it required the passage of a full two and a quarter centuries before any European artist was able to find the means to travel further than Ambrogio. This single fact alone gives some idea of the significance of the creative surge of Sienese art in the first half of the fourteenth century. It gives an indication of what died in the Black Death and never could be subsequently resurrected in a steadily declining city. The path leads not to man and nature or to man in front of nature, but to man in nature, as a natural part of it. It leads to . . . the modern concepts of the fundamental unity of the whole of nature.

NOTES

[1] For attributions to Ugolino on the *Maestà*, see J. H. Stubblebine, "Duccio and his Collborators on the Cathedral Maestà," *Art Bulletin*, LV, 1973, pp. 196–98 and for the Siena pulpit documents, see E. Carli, *Il pulpito di Siena* (Bergamo, 1943), pp. 41–3.

[2] See I. A. Richter, *Paragone* (London, New York, Toronto, 1949), sections 25–7, pp. 59–64 and section 35, pp. 78–80.

[3] The relative position depends on where the Arena Chapel frescoes are placed within the possible time range between 1304 and 1312–13. The *Noli Me Tangere* belongs to the latter phases of Giotto's work. The pulpit was begun in September

1302. Work seems to have gone ahead rapidly, at least at the start, and the *Adoration* is one of the earlier reliefs. We do not know at what stage the work on the narratives was carried out and it may, of course, have been well before the terminal date December 1310. The latter is sometimes quoted as 1312, but this is caused by a confusion, firstly in translating Pisan dating into modern terms, and secondly in reading the inscription put up by Burgundio di Tado, the Operaio, in the year following the completion of the pulpit.

4 See J. White, *The Birth and Rebirth of Pictorial Space* (London, 1967), pp. 82–3, for discussion of Duccio's use of the foreshortened frontal construction, and p. 27, Fig. 1, for a diagrammatic illustration of the relationship to Artificial Perspective.

5 See C. Gardner von Teuffel, "Masaccio and the Pisa Altar-piece: a New Approach," *Jahrbuch der Berliner Museum*, 19, 1977, pp. 23–68.

6 For Ugolino, see G. Coor-Achenbach, "Contributions to the Study of Ugolino di Nerio's Art," *Art Bulletin*, XXXVII, 1955, pp. 153–65, and M. Davies, *The Earlier Italian Schools* (London, 1951), pp. 249–56. For Daddi, see R. Offner and K. Steinweg, *A Corpus of Florentine Painting* (Berlin and New York, 1930–   ), Section III, Vol. III, p. 54, Pl. XIV, Section III, Vol. III, pp. 23–4, Pl. V, and B. Berenson, *Italian Pictures of the Renaissance: Florentine School* (London, 1962), Vol. I, Pl. 129. For del Biondo, see Offner, *op. cit.*, Section IV, Vol. V, pp. 77–83, Pl. XX.

7 See K. Morand, *Jean Pucelle* (Oxford, 1972), pp. 6 ff.

8 See J. Longnon, R. Cazelles, and M. Meiss, *Les Très Riches Heures du Duc de Berry* (London, 1969), Pl. 111, f. 47r.

9 See J. White, *op. cit.*, pp. 93–9, and *Art and Architecture in Italy 1250–1400* (Harmondsworth, 1966), pp. 251–56.

20. PAINTING IN

FLORENCE AND SIENA

AFTER THE BLACK DEATH

Millard Meiss

INTRODUCTION

Painting in Florence and Siena After the Black Death examines the emphatic shift of style and mood in Tuscan painting around the middle of the fourteenth century in the context of a series of social and economic setbacks climaxed by the dreadful circumstances of the Black Death. Meiss contends that these disastrous events influenced the character of the art, turning it away from the gentle Franciscan-inspired painting of the earlier decades of the century, exemplified by Giotto and his followers. The new art, pessimistic and guilt-ridden, became more Dominican in tone and appealed to the conservative taste of a new population drawn largely from provincial backgrounds. In linking together the experiences of a society and the temper of its art, Meiss has developed a fascinating—and penetrating—study of some of the determinants involved in changes of style. The range of this work is such that it must be considered essential not only to students of the history of art, but to students of cultural history generally.

Other works that examine art in its social context—from a Marxist point of view—are George Plekhanov, *Art and Society* (1937) and Frederick Antal, *Florentine Painting and Its Social Background* (1948). Francis Klingender, *Art and the Industrial Revolution* (1947) deals with questions regarding the relationship between developments in

British art and the impact of industrialization. A general history of this type is Arnold Hauser's *Social History of Art* (1951). In conjunction with the selection that follows, one might read the reviews in *The Journal of Aesthetics and Art Criticism*, XI, 4 (1953), and *The Art Bulletin*, XXXIV, 4 (1952). A good, well-illustrated survey of the painting of this era is Robert Oertel, *Early Italian Painting to 1400* (1968). The reader may also wish to consult the bibliographical suggestions in the introductions for the selections by Panofsky and White (pp. 415 and 443).

INTRODUCTION

In one of his *Trecento novelle,* written around 1390 toward the end of his life, Franco Sacchetti relates the following incident: "In the city of Florence, which has always been rich in talented men, there were once certain painters and other masters who were at a place outside the city called San Miniato al Monte for some painting and other work that had to be done in the church; after they had had a meal with the abbot and were well wined and dined, they began to converse; and among other questions, this was posed by one of them called Orcagna, who was head master of the noble oratory of Our Lady of Orto San Michele: 'Who was the greatest master of painting that we have had, who other than Giotto?' Some replied Cimabue, some Stefano, some Bernardo [Daddi], others Buffalmacco, and some named one master, and others another. Taddeo Gaddi, who was one of the company, said: 'Certainly there have been plenty of skillful painters, and they have painted in a manner that is impossible for human hand to equal; but this art has grown and continues to grow worse day by day.'"[1]

The story, which has come down to us incomplete, then takes a jocular turn in the remarks of the sculptor Alberto di Arnaldo. He belittles the opinions of the others, saying that excellent painters, the equals of Giotto, were working at that very moment—the Florentine women, whose skill in cosmetics corrects the defects of the greatest painter of them all, God.

The proposals for Giotto's nearest rival have an authentic ring, and it is generally agreed, though we cannot be certain, that the story reflects a conversation at a gathering at S. Miniato in the late 'fifties.[2] We know all the artists present and those mentioned in the discussion—one group, Taddeo Gaddi, Orcagna, Bernardo Daddi, Cimabue, Alberto di Arnaldo by their works, another, Stefano and Buffalmacco (the St. Cecilia Master?), by reputation. We should expect the assembled masters to accept the preeminence of Giotto without question. And as for the choices expressed by the group, they are remarkable, so far as we can judge, only for the omission of Maso, surely Giotto's greatest follower, and perhaps Nardo. Taddeo Gaddi himself was not proposed, possibly because he was present; nor Orcagna, who was both present and the proponent of the question. Quite surprising, however, at least on first consideration, is the statement of Taddeo Gaddi. For it goes beyond an acceptance of the superiority of Giotto, already dead some twenty-three years, to assert a continuous decline of the art into the present moment.[3]

Though laments about the state of contemporary art are common enough in history, precisely in the fourteenth and fifteenth centuries they were exceedingly rare. Taddeo's pessimistic opinion is thus exceptional in its time, and it is all the more remarkable because of the occasion on which it was expressed. For it was spoken in the very presence of Orcagna, certainly the greatest Florentine Trecento painter after Giotto, excepting only Maso di Banco. And it ignores the stature not only of Orcagna but of his brother Nardo and of Andrea Bonaiuti, who were inferior to Maso but no less gifted than any of the other masters of the earlier part of the century, Bernardo Daddi and Taddeo Gaddi himself included.

The significance of this extraordinary judgment may be grasped, I believe, if we consider the historical position and the taste of its author. Taddeo Gaddi was the most devoted pupil of Giotto. He had worked with him, according to Cennino Cennini, for twenty-four years, and in the later 'fifties he was the only veteran of Giotto's circle still alive. His insights and his taste were those of an earlier time, and the utter failure to recognize the greatness of Orcagna, if we may trust Sacchetti, suggests an important truth—the profound difference of the art of this painter and his contemporaries from that of Giotto and his successors in the earlier part of the century.

This difference implies not only that people with a taste formed in the earlier Trecento might fail to understand Orcagna, but also that some members of Orcagna's generation might feel less enthusiastic than their elders about Giotto. Possibly we may find an intimation of this in a rather cryptic comment of a writer of the time. In the great chorus of approval of the painting of Giotto that begins with Dante and Riccobaldo and extends into the fifteenth century there was only one discordant note. It was introduced by a writer just a few years younger than Orcagna, Benvenuto da Imola. Though

Benvenuto was not Florentine, he lived for a time in Florence[4] and he was quite familiar with Florentine critical and historical thought. In his commentary on the *Divine Comedy*, which he wrote c. 1376, he upheld the reputation and the superiority of Giotto, but qualified it with what, in the light of earlier and later opinion, amounts to heresy. "Giotto," he said, "still holds the field because no one subtler than he has yet appeared, even though at times he made great errors in his paintings, as I have heard from men of outstanding talent in such matters."[5]

These are serious charges against the man who had been widely hailed as the founder of modern painting and the greatest master since the Greeks. They have been ignored by almost all later historians, and recently one scholar has attempted to dispel them by attributing their meaning exclusively to their context. Benvenuto's statement occurs in the course of his discussion of Dante's famous passage on the transitory nature of fame. The poet says that the renown of Oderisio the miniaturist was short-lived because he was immediately succeeded by Franco, just as Cimabue was eclipsed by Giotto.

> O vana gloria dell'umane posse,
> Com' poco verde in su la cima dura,
> Se non è giunta dall'etadi grosse!
> Credette Cimabue nella pittura
> Tener lo campo, ed ora ha Giotto il grido,
> Sì che la fama di colui è oscura.[6]

It has been suggested that Benvenuto's reference to the great errors of Giotto was simply contrived *ad hoc*, to extend to this painter also Dante's thought about the brevity of fame.[7] But neither the verses themselves nor Benvenuto's comments permit this interpretation. Dante was concerned first of all with reputation and renown, not with problems of criticism and value. Benvenuto himself understood this, devoting most of his commentary on the passage to a discussion of Dante's condition for the loss of fame. The glory of Plato, he says, was dimmed by Aristotle. But since Aristotle was not followed by a philosopher equally as subtle, his reputation survived to the present day.[8] Virgil enjoyed a similar good fortune, for similar reasons, while Cimabue was unlucky enough to find himself not "in aetatibus grossis" but "subtilioribus." Giotto on the other hand, Benvenuto says, *had* no equally subtle successor. Benvenuto would have been inconsistent then if he had supposed a necessary decline in Giotto's reputation; and if he himself had for some personal reason felt called upon to detract from it, would he not have written simply and vaguely that nowadays "some people are no longer unqualified in their praise" rather than the careful statement "he made great errors, as I have heard from outstanding critics"? It seems indeed quite probable that Benvenuto's comment was not provoked by Dante's text alone, but reflected current criticism of Giotto's pictorial style.[9]

Whatever the real meaning of Benvenuto's remarks, a certain kind of adverse criticism of the work of Giotto and his followers was certainly common at this time in the paintings themselves. Every one of the younger masters after 1345–1350 rejected, at least in part, Giotto's most easily imitable accomplishment, linear perspective. None attempted to rival the equilibrium in his art between form and space, or his supple figures moving freely in a measured, easily traversible, receptive world. And which of these masters subscribed without equivocation to his conception of the divine immanent in an exalted and profoundly moral humanity? In all these respects Maso di Banco, of whose activity we do not hear after the early 'forties, was Giotto's last follower. It is striking that the influence of this major master was not dominant in the late 'forties and 'fifties. He had no real succession among the younger painters, who turned unanimously to Orcagna and Nardo.[10]

All of this is indicative of an important change in style and in taste around the middle of the fourteenth century. Variety and change there was of course in the preceding years, too, however dominant the figure of Giotto. The space with which he had surrounded his figures was extended and deepened, the environment made more specific and more familiar. In the hands of Taddeo Gaddi his massive forms became ponderous and rather assertive, in Bernardo Daddi refined and lyric. Maso introduced a marvelous subtlety of color, and gave to the ambience of the figures a wholly new intensity of form and meaning. Other painters, the S. Cecilia Master, Pacino, Jacopo del Casentino, the Biadaiolo Master, whose work has been defined in recent years chiefly by Richard Offner,[11] heeded Giotto's example relatively little, seeking an effect of greater animation and spontaneity, and a more fluid mode of expression. They avoided the grave and the monumental. Unlike Giotto and

Taddeo and Maso they were more effective in smaller works —tabernacles, miniatures, little histories in altarpieces—than in fresco. The departures of the mid-century from Giottesque style, however, are not connected with differences of scale or technique or the conditions of exhibition: they appear in large murals as well as in retables, tabernacles, and miniatures. And whereas some of the masters of the earlier part of the century are un-Giottesque, most of the later ones are, in a sense, anti-Giottesque.

There were similar changes in Siena, too, around the middle of the century. The great styles that succeeded one another during the preceding fifty years—those of Duccio, Simone Martini, Pietro and Ambrogio Lorenzetti—show despite their diversity many related qualities and a certain community of purpose. They constitute a rather orderly development, the younger painter in each instance developing one or another aspect of the older master's style. Around 1350 this continuity seems interrupted. Though the influence of the earlier tradition persists, many of its fundamental elements were rejected, and others were combined in a new and wholly different way. These transformations occurred despite the fact that only one of the painters active at this time, Barna, approximated in stature the great masters of the preceding years. He belonged to an earlier generation, however, and with all his originality he remained in many ways more fully within the tradition of the first half of the century. The younger painters, Bartolo di Fredi, Luca di Tommè, Andrea Vanni, were all less gifted, but they created distinctive forms nevertheless, very similar to one another and related to those of contemporary Florence without being dependent upon them.

Previous accounts of Sienese painting of this period have been devoted less to the analysis of its distinctive character than to its dependence upon the art of the earlier part of the century.[12] It has always, furthermore, been studied separately from Florentine. And when these studies have been part of a comprehensive account of Italian painting, they have emphasized the differences between the two schools rather than the similarities, although they have pointed to the influence upon the Florentines of the earlier art of Simone Martini and the Lorenzetti.[13] Without minimizing these differences, our present purpose is to consider those aspects of the form and content of the two schools that are related.

These similarities between the painting of the two towns are interesting in the light of the remarkably similar circumstances surrounding their appearance. Though the history of the two city-states had corresponded in many ways from the late twelfth century onward, the resemblances between them were especially numerous just before and after the middle of the fourteenth century. During this brief period, both the Sienese and Florentines lived through a series of deeply disturbing events, which provoked in each a social, moral, and cultural crisis. For what light it may throw on the similarities of their painting, therefore, we shall consider the history of the two people together—their common experience of economic failure, pestilence and social conflict, their fear, their sense of guilt, and the varieties of their religious response.

THE TWO CITIES AT MID-CENTURY

For both Florence and Siena the first forty years of the fourteenth century had been generally years of great prosperity and of political stability. Already at the beginning of this period the two cities had risen to European prominence as centers of finance and manufacture. Just before 1300 the contest between the rising middle class and the long-established noble landholders had ended in a victory for the former. The middle class acquired complete control of the state. Though many noble families, particularly in Florence, had entered trade or banking and had merged to a great extent with the business groups, they were, like all the members of their class, excluded from communal offices.

As in other late medieval towns, Florentine and Sienese society was organized for political and economic purposes in a series of guilds. Citizenship depended upon membership in one of them. The thousands of workers in the chief industry, the manufacture or refinement of woolen cloth, were forbidden to form or to join guilds, and they thus had no political rights whatever. The guilds of the great merchants, bankers, industrialists, and professional men (jurists and physicians) formed the Greater Guilds, or *Arti Maggiori*. The shopkeepers and artisans were members of the more numerous *Arti Minori*. The state, which shortly before 1300 had assumed the form of a bourgeois republic, was actually administered by a wealthy oligarchy centered within the *Maggiori*. Their rule, as well as the guild structure which supported it, lasted in both cities for about half a century.

Painting in Florence and Siena after the Black Death

The great entrepreneurs were engaged in production for foreign more than for local consumption, and with their large accumulation of capital they financed the Papacy as well as many princes throughout Europe. Seeking wider markets in their own regions, they pursued a policy of local "imperialism." During their rule almost all of Tuscany was brought under the domination of one or another of the two cities. As long as the oligarchy succeeded in maintaining a high level of prosperity, it was not seriously challenged in either Florence or Siena.

Though political power was thus highly concentrated, the form of the state reflected a libertarian ideal. The oligarchy sought to maintain the approval of the entire middle class, which believed it had the right to determine the policy of the government, and at times of crisis, as in Florence in 1343, exercised it. The republican principle, which implied the evolution of a nonhierarchical, more horizontal social order, was apparent also in other forms of association—in the guilds, for instance, with their elected captains. It was apparent also, within the sphere of religion, in the confraternities. These societies, formed by laymen for purposes of worship and mutual aid, grew rapidly from the late thirteenth century on. Their members, though subject to canon law, lived in the world without taking vows or adhering to a fixed rule. They were drawn from all classes; priests and friars were admitted too, but they had no special rights or privileges. The fraternities were governed, and their religious services conducted, by lay rectors elected for short periods of time. On the altar of the chapel that each of these societies possessed there stood almost invariably a retable that was the visible center of the cult. There the members assembled periodically, singing hymns to the Virgin before her painted image. No phenomenon of town life was more expressive of its democratic and lay tendencies, and none impinged more directly upon the art of painting.

As in other advanced European centers, but nowhere more than in Florence and Siena, the new competitive economy fostered (as well as it implied) independent individual inquiry and action in all fields of endeavor, and it stimulated a greater measure of individual self-consciousness. The middle class, concerned with the techniques of manufacture and the kinds of calculation required by production and banking on an unprecedented scale, developed increasingly empirical, inductive, and quantitative modes of thought. The burghers emphasized family and civic responsibilities and they val-

60. Giotto, Meeting of Joachim and Anna, Fresco, 1305–6 (Scrovegni [Arena] Chapel, Padua)

ued circumspection, moderation, and, above all, industriousness.[14] Though they remained deeply pious, they believed with increasing assurance that they could enjoy themselves in this world without jeopardizing their chances in the next. Their optimism seemed to be confirmed by the prosperity and the comparative peace of the first forty years of the century.

The arts flowered as at few other moments in history. The painters and sculptors, developing a more naturalistic style, created an image of an orderly world, substantial, extended, traversable. They endowed the people in it with a new range of intellectual and emotional awareness, and great moral strength. The realm of human values was immeasurably enlarged, the relation of man to man becoming as important as the relation of man to God. It is no accident that the most memorable episodes in the Arena Chapel include the return of Joachim to his sheep, his meeting with Anna at the Golden Gate (Fig. 60), and the lament over the dead body of Christ. These are scenes that had held only a subordinate meaning in earlier Christian art or had only recently been represented at all. In the early Trecento cycle they seem more congenial to the painter and more deeply felt than the episodes involving the pro-phetic and the symbolical (Last Supper), or the supernatural (Wedding at Cana, Ascension, Pentecost—the last executed by an assis-tant). Giotto's human sympathy and insight reach an astonishing profundity in the wonderful soldier standing at the left in the Massacre of the Innocents, a wholly unprecedented figure who, though traditionally on the side of brutality and evil, now withdraws in anguish from the bloody work of his men.

THE ECONOMIC CRISIS

From about 1340 on, the whole of Florentine and Sienese society was shaken by a series of increasingly disastrous events. The per-sistent and costly attempt of Florence to add Lucca to its domain was frustrated in 1341 by the capture of that city by the Pisans. The expansion of Milan under the Visconti began to present a serious threat,[15] and the burden of meeting this, together with the failure of the English branches of two of the largest Florentine banks, provoked an economic and then a political crisis. In 1343 the great house of the Peruzzi declared bankruptcy, and it was followed by the Accaiuoli, the Bardi (1345) and almost every other bank and mercantile company in Florence.[16] Many of the Sienese houses were brought down also. Throughout the cities workshops and stores closed because commissions were lacking and funds were not avail-able for the purchase of materials or the payment of wages.[17] The crash plunged the towns into an unprecedented depression. Long after it had passed it continued to weigh upon the spirit of enter-prise, engendering a more cautious and conservative attitude. For many years, fear of comparable loss tended to divert investment from trade and manufacture to farms and land. The merchant and chron-icler Giovanni Villani, who himself suffered severe reverses and who was even thrown into the Stinche for inability to pay his debts, re-ported that by 1346 the Florentine companies had lost around 1,700,000 florins. No such calamity, he said, had ever overtaken the commune.[18] He wrote this judgment on the eve of a far greater one, in which he lost not his fortune but his life.

POLITICAL AND SOCIAL CHANGE

The ruling merchants and bankers in Florence tried to meet the mounting crisis by the usual method of the Italian communes in time of distress—transference of municipal authority to a dictator. In 1342 the Duke of Athens was called to Florence and given supreme power in the state. But this expedient, which in many other cities had resulted in the permanent loss of republican government, proved unsatisfactory to all sections of the Florentine middle class. Rallying to the cry of liberty, they united to expel the Duke in 1343. The republic was restored, but with new provisions that curtailed the power of the great merchants, industrialists, and bankers who had controlled the state almost uninterruptedly since the end of the thirteenth century. Weakened by the failure in the Lucchese war, the financial collapse, and the necessity of relying upon other groups to expel the *signore* whom they had installed, they were obliged to admit to the priorate representatives of sections of the middle class that had not previously had a voice in its councils. . . .

If the smaller entrepreneurs and the professional men, the *mezzani* of the Greater Guilds, were actually dominant in the government of Florence from 1343 to 1378, this era was not quite so "democratic" as many historians have maintained.[19] But in any event the oligarchy was overthrown, the new priorate was more widely representative, and the lower middle class did acquire a share in the regime. There were, moreover, corresponding readjustments of power within the guilds themselves, so that the consequences of the revolution were felt through Florentine society.[20] The rise to power of the *mezzani* and the necessity for the political recognition of the lower middle class shattered the confidence of the very wealthy, which had already been shaken by the crash. They and all those in the city who depended upon, or sympathized with, the old oligarchy bitterly opposed the new government. In 1345 Giovanni Villani ridiculed the rulers of Florence as "artisans and manual workers and simpletons."[21]

In Siena during these years there was a corresponding series of revolutions, though they occurred at different intervals of time and on the whole the swing to the left extended farther than in Florence.[22] . . .

Painting in Florence and Siena after the Black Death

During the years of lower middle class participation and ascendancy, several Sienese painters—Andrea Vanni, Bartolo di Fredi, Luca di Tommè, Giacomo di Mino—were active in the political parties and in the government, occupying a variety of offices and serving as municipal envoys.

THE BLACK DEATH

During the 'forties, just after the fall of the oligarchy in Florence and several years before it was overthrown in Siena, both cities suffered seriously from lack of grain.[23] The bankruptcies reduced the financial resources of the cities and weakened the influence of the great Florentine houses of the Accaiuoli and the Bardi in Naples, so that normal imports from that region were not forthcoming.[24] On top of this, crops failed throughout Tuscany in 1346, and they were badly damaged in 1347 by exceptionally heavy hailstorms. Weakened and terrified by these deprivations, which they attributed to divine displeasure, the Florentines and Sienese attempted to appease God. They engaged in collective prayer and public displays of repentance. Giovanni Villani tells of great processions, in one of which, continuing for three days, he marched himself.[25] These had scarcely disbanded when an unimaginable catastrophe struck both towns.

Suddenly during the summer months of 1348 more than half the inhabitants of Florence and Siena died of the bubonic plague.[26] By September only some 45,000 of the 90,000 people within the walls of Florence were still living; Siena was reduced from around 42,000 to 15,000.[27] Never before or since has any calamity taken so great a proportion of human life. The plague struck again in 1363 and once more in 1374, though it carried off far fewer people than in the terrible months of 1348.[28]

The survivors were stunned. The Sienese chronicler Agnolo di Tura tells of burying his five children with his own hands. "No one wept for the dead," he says, "because every one expected death himself."[29] All of Florence, according to Boccaccio, was a sepulcher. At the beginning of the Decameron he wrote: ". . . they dug for each graveyard a huge trench, in which they laid the corpses as they arrived by hundreds at a time, piling them up tier upon tier as merchandise is stowed in a ship . . ."—sights not unfamiliar to modern eyes. For years the witnesses were haunted by memories of bodies stacked high in the streets and the unforgettable stench of flesh putrefying in the hot summer sun. Those fortunate few who were able to escape these horrible scenes by fleeing to isolated places were, like Petrarch, overwhelmed by the loss of family and friends.

The momentous nature of the experience is suggested by the words of Matteo Villani as he undertook after a few years to continue the chronicle of his dead brother:

> The author of the chronicle called the Chronicle of Giovanni Villani, citizen of Florence and a man to whom I was closely tied by blood and by affection, having rendered his soul to God in the plague, I decided, after many grave misfortunes and with a greater awareness of the dire state of mankind than the period of its prosperity had revealed to me, to make a beginning with our varied and calamitous material at this juncture, as at a time of renewal of the world. . . . Having to commence our treatise by recounting the extermination of mankind . . . my mind is stupefied as it approaches the task of recording the sentence that divine justice mercifully delivered upon men, who deserve, because they have been corrupted by sin, a last judgment.[30]

Though the rate of mortality was doubtless somewhat greater among the poor, about half of the upper classes succumbed. Agnolo di Tura's comments about Siena are significant: four of the nine members of the oligarchic priorate died, together with two of the four officers of the Biccherna, the podestà, and the capitano di guerra.[31] The painters were not spared. The plague carried off Bernardo Daddi, the most active and influential master in Florence, and perhaps also his associate whom Offner has called the "Assistant of Daddi."[32] It is generally assumed that the disappearance of all references around this time to Ambrogio and Pietro Lorenzetti signifies their death in the epidemic.[33] Undoubtedly a great many minor painters suffered a similar fate. This sudden removal at one stroke of the two great Sienese masters and of Daddi along with numerous lesser painters produced a more than ordinary interruption in pictorial tradition. It gave to the surviving masters, especially the younger ones, a sudden, exceptional independence and a special freedom for the development of new styles.

476

ECONOMIC AND SOCIAL
CONSEQUENCES OF THE PLAGUE

In the immediate wake of the Black Death we hear of an unparalleled abundance of food and goods, and of a wild, irresponsible
life of pleasure. Agnolo di Tura writes that in Siena "everyone
tended to enjoy eating and drinking, hunting, hawking, and gam-
ing,"[34] and Matteo Villani laments similar behavior in Florence:
"Those few sensible people who remained alive expected many
things, all of which, by reason of the corruption of sin, failed to
occur among mankind and actually followed marvelously in the
contrary direction. They believed that those whom God's grace had
reserved for life, having beheld the extermination of their neighbors,
and having heard the same tidings from all the nations of the world,
would become better men, humble, virtuous, and Catholic; that they
would guard themselves from iniquity and sins; and would be full
of love and charity for one another. But no sooner had the plague
ceased than we saw the contrary; for since men were few, and since
by hereditary sucession they abounded in earthly goods, they forgot
the past as though it had never been and gave themselves up to
a more shameful and disordered life than they had led before. . . .
And the common people (*popolo minuto*), both men and women,
by reason of the abundance and superfluity that they found, would
no longer work at their accustomed trades; they wanted the dearest
and most delicate foods for their sustenance; and they married at
their will, while children and common women clad themselves in
all the fair and costly garments of the illustrious ladies who had
died."[35]

This extraordinary condition of plenty did not, of course, last very
long. For most people the frenzied search for immediate gratifica-
tion, characteristic of the survivors of calamities, was likewise
short-lived. Throughout the subsequent decades, however, we continue to hear of an exceptional indifference to accepted patterns
of behavior and to institutional regulations, especially among the
mendicant friars. It seems, as we shall see, that the plague tended
to promote an unconventional, irresponsible, or self-indulgent life,
on the one hand, and a more intense piety or religious excitement,

on the other. Villani tells us, in his very next sentences, of the more lasting consequences of the epidemic:

"Men thought that, through the death of so many people, there would be abundance of all produce of the land; yet, on the contrary, by reason of men's ingratitude, everything came to unwonted scarcity and remained long thus; . . . most commodities were more costly, by twice or more, than before the plague. And the price of labor, and the products of every trade and craft, rose in disorderly fashion beyond the double. Lawsuits and disputes and quarrels and riots arose everywhere among citizens in every land, by reason of legacies and successions; . . . Wars and divers scandals arose throughout the world, contrary to men's expectation."[36]

Conditions were similar in Siena. Prices rose to unprecedented levels.[37] The economy of both Florence and Siena was further disrupted during these years by the defection of almost all the dependent towns within the little empire of each city. These towns seized as an opportunity for revolt the fall of the powerful Florentine oligarchy in 1343, and the Sienese in 1355. The two cities, greatly weakened, and governed by groups that pursued a less aggressive foreign policy, made little attempt to win them back.

The small towns and the countryside around the two cities were not decimated so severely by the epidemic, but the people in these regions felt the consequences of it in another way. Several armies of mercenaries of the sort that all the large states had come to employ in the fourteenth century took advantage of the weakness of the cities. Sometimes in connivance with the great enemy of the north, the Duke of Milan, they invaded, or threatened to invade, the territory of Florence and Siena. These large marauding bands— the companies of the Conte Lando, of John Hawkwood, and of Fra Moriale, the Company of the Hat and the Company of St. George— hovered in the neighborhood throughout the 'fifties and 'sixties, a continual threat to the peace of the *contado* and a serious drain on the already shrunken communal treasuries. Florence, the stronger of the two cities, was less troubled by them. Siena paid out huge ransoms,[38] in twenty years some 275,000 florins, but even then its lands were pillaged and the people on the farms and in the villages lived in constant terror. For them the story of Job, an old paradigm of trial and affliction, acquired a specially poignant meaning. Not only did Job suffer from a disease whose outward symptoms were like those of the plague; his cattle were driven off and his children killed. It is not surprising that his history, rarely if ever represented in earlier Tuscan panels and frescoes, should now have been portrayed several times. . . .

The ravages of the merchant companies accelerated a great wave of immigration from the smaller towns and farms into the cities that had been initiated by the Black Death. Most of the newcomers were recruits for the woolen industry, who were attracted by relatively high wages. But the mortality offered exceptional opportunities also for notaries, jurists, physicians, and craftsmen. In both Florence and Siena the laws controlling immigration were relaxed, and special privileges, a rapid grant of citizenship, or exemption from taxes were offered to badly needed artisans or professional men, such as physicians.[39] . . .

In addition to bringing into the city great numbers of people from the surrounding towns and country, the Black Death affected the character of Florentine society in still another way. Through irregular inheritance and other exceptional circumstances, a class of *nouveaux riches* arose in the town and also in decimated Siena.[40] Their wealth was accentuated by the impoverishment of many of the older families, such as the Bardi and the Peruzzi, who had lost their fortunes in the financial collapse. In both cities, too, many tradesmen and artisans were enriched to a degree unusual for the *popolo minuto*. Scaramella sees as one of the major conflicts of the time the struggle between the old families and this *gente nuova*.[41] Outcries against both foreigners and the newly rich, never lacking in the two cities, increased in volume and violence. Antagonism to "the aliens and the ignorant" coalesced with antagonism to the new municipal regime; the government, it was said, had been captured by them. . . .

THE EFFECT UPON CULTURE AND ART

The painting of the third quarter of the century, more religious in a traditional sense, more ecclesiastical, and more akin to the art of an earlier time, may reflect these profound social changes in Florence and Siena, or rather the taste and the quality of piety that they brought into prominence. For these *homines novi*, the immigrants, the newly rich and the newly powerful, had not on the whole been closely identified with the growth of the new culture in the first half of the fourteenth century. They adhered to more traditional patterns of thought and feeling, and it may well be that their ideal of a religious art was still the art of the later thirteenth century—an art that was still visible almost everywhere in the cities, and even more in the churches of the *contado*. At other times, less educated, provincial people have clung to an art that had been supplanted for as long as fifty years, and we are given hints that this was so around the middle of the fourteenth century. Writing in 1361 in his will about a Madonna by the "outstanding" painter Giotto, Petrarch says that though its beauty is a source of wonder to the masters of the art, the ignorant do not understand it.[42] Boccaccio wrote that, as a poet and a student of classical antiquity, he was regarded as a sorcerer in the town of Certaldo.[43] Elsewhere he attacked the noisy adversaries of poetry (primarily ancient poetry) who, ignorant of its character and its true meaning, constantly opposed religion to it.[44] There is no reason to suppose that these ready "theologians" or the friars and other groups whom he excoriates for similar reasons were any less antagonistic to certain aspects of the more advanced style of the Trecento in the figure arts. We cannot expect them to have proved anything but hostile to Ambrogio Lorenzetti's fascination with ancient sculpture. One of the known objects of his fascination, a newly discovered statue by Lysippus, was broken into bits by frightened members of the Sienese public. It may be that these same groups were unsympathetic also to the assimilation of ancient forms in the work of Ambrogio or Cavallini or Nicola Pisano. We cannot then suppose them to have been much more friendly to all those dispositions and qualities of the new style that lie behind such assimilations—in other words, to the essence of the new style itself. Because known comments on painting and sculpture in the fourteenth century are few, and limited mostly to scholars, writers, and the artists themselves, such attitudes are difficult to ascertain. It is notable, however, that Fra Simone Fidati seems to disapprove, by implication at least, the warm relationship between man and wife in paintings such as Giotto's. And in the *Meditations on the Life of Christ*, oddly enough in the very treatise that exercised so great an influence on painting, we find the old antagonism to the arts themselves reasserted. Except for their employment in the cult, they are, the Franciscan writer says, stimulants of a "concupiscenza degli occhi."[45]

Whether or not conservative tastes of this sort were felt by the painters at the moment of decisive change and innovation around the middle of the century, their wider diffusion and their prevalence among people who had acquired wealth and influence as patrons at least broadened the acceptance of the new styles and helped to maintain them. A painting such as Giovanni del Biondo's St. John the Evangelist trampling on Avarice, Pride, and Vainglory (Fig. 61)[46] may thus have struck an immediate response because of its older symbolic pattern and the austere frontality of its chief figure. The panel was doubtless widely approved for its subject, too, particularly the representation of the conquest of avarice. At this time avarice was, as we have mentioned, associated especially with the unlimited desire for profit and accumulation that had already

61. Giovanni del Biondo, *St. John the Evangelist,* c. 1370 (Uffizi, Florence)

Detail of above

become characteristic of early capitalism. Neither this motive nor the new economic system had been accepted by a considerable part of society. They were often opposed, it seems safe to assume, by the same people who were conservative in other spheres also, particularly religion and the arts. These people clung to the medieval belief in a just price and the limitation of wealth to the amounts needed for a livelihood by persons in the several stations of life.[47] Their antagonism to the new system and its values was certainly more assured after the bankruptcies and other events of the 'forties. Segre states that in 1354 twenty-one Florentine bankers were fined for usury, and in tracing the fluctuating policy of Florence on the lending of money at interest, he implies a greater opposition to loans in the second half of the fourteenth century.[48] At this time many people undoubtedly took a special pleasure in the sight of a defeated Avarice sprawled on the ground and ignominiously trodden underfoot.

Though the *gente nuova* was doubtless pleased by this portrayal of the triumph of St. John, it is questionable whether any of them played a leading part in the selection of the painter or the determination of the subject. The work was actually commissioned, as we have seen, by the *Arte della Seta,* one of the seven greater Florentine guilds. Though within it, as in all the other guilds, there were during this period certain shifts of responsibility and power, it was still dominated by established merchants and industrial entrepreneurs.[49] These were, in fact, the chief patrons of painting at the time, just as they had been earlier in the century. It was the Tornaquinci who commissioned the frescoes by Orcagna in the choir of S. M. Novella, the Strozzi who employed Orcagna and Nardo for the altarpiece and murals of their chapel, one of the Guidalotti who provided the funds for the frescoes in the Spanish Chapel, though they were executed after his death. But, these wealthy patricians were deeply affected, too, by the events of the 'forties and 'fifties. They had never freed themselves of doubt as to the legitimacy of their occupation. The Church had not explicitly sanctioned either their activities or their profits, and "manifest" usury it strongly condemned. The distinctions between usury of this kind and permissible interest, while precise, were very fine, and in advanced age merchants and bankers quite commonly sought to quiet their conscience and assure their salvation by making regular provision for corporate charity and by a voluntary restitution of wealth that they judged was improperly acquired. As the most eminent living student of Floretine economic history has written: "Reading the last wills of the members of the Company of the Bardi . . . there becomes evident and dramatic the contrast between the practical life of these bold and tenacious men, the builders of immense fortunes, and their terror of eternal punishment for having accumulated wealth by rather unscrupulous methods."[50]

The guilt of the entrepreneurs and bankers was greatly quickened around the middle of the century. The bankruptcies and the depression struck just as hard at their conscience as at their purse. The loss of exclusive control of the state and the terror of the Black Death seemed further punishments for dubious practices. Giovanni Villani attributed the failure of the companies of the Bardi and the Peruzzi, in the second of which he himself had invested money before he joined the Buonaccorsi, to the "avarizia di guadagnare," and his strictures imply a condemnation not so much of poor judgment in this single instance as of all financial practices that involve great risks. Since few large ventures of the time could be undertaken without such risks, Villani comes close to turning his back on capitalism itself, and he had earlier signified that moneylending was a disreputable occupation.[51]

In the wake of the disasters of the 'forties and 'fifties, then, the established wealthy families of Florence very probably welcomed a less worldly and less humanistic art than that of the earlier years of the century. Their own position seriously threatened, they felt sustained by the assertion in art of the authority of the Church and the representation of a stable, enduring hierarchy. Their taste would have tended to converge, then, with that of the *gente nuova*, who emerged from circles that still clung to a pre-Giottesque art in which very similar qualities inhered.

All sections of the middle class were, in any event, clearly united in their desire for a more intensely religious art. It was not only great merchants such as Giovanni Colombini, with their own special reasons for remorse, who vilified and abandoned their former mode of life. Masses of people, interpreting the calamities as punishments of their worldliness and their sin, were stirred by repentance and religious yearning. Some of them joined groups that cultivated mystical experiences or an extreme asceticism; many more sought salvation through the traditional methods offered by the Church. Several painters—Orcagna, Luca di Tommè, Andrea da Firenze—

were, as we have seen, moved to a greater piety or a mystical rapture. Others who were less deeply stirred saw fit nevertheless, as the craftsmen of images for the cult, to adopt many of the new values and the new artistic forms, though in a more conventional way. For the painting of the time this religious excitement, and the conflict of values which it entailed, was a crucial cultural event. . . .

GUILT, PENANCE, AND RELIGIOUS
RAPTURE

The years following the Black Death were the most gloomy in the history of Florence and Siena, and perhaps of all Europe. The writing of the period, like the painting, was pervaded by a profound pessimism and sometimes a renunciation of life.[52] "Seldom in the course of the Middle Ages has so much been written," Hans Baron has said recently, "concerning the 'miseria' of human beings and human life."[53] Though religious thought throughout the Middle Ages had dwelt on the brevity of life and the certainty of death, no age was more acutely aware of it than this. It was preached from the pulpits, most vividly by Jacopo Passavanti, and set forth in paintings, both altarpieces and murals (Fig. 62). . . .

The majority of the people expressed their devotion within the traditional patterns established by the Church. In Florence they were inspired chiefly by the great Dominican preacher, Jacopo Passavanti. Passavanti, who was born in Florence at the beginning of the century, became a preacher at S. M. Novella in 1340 after a period of study and teaching in Paris and Rome. From the late 'forties on he was in charge of maintenance and construction, and from 1354 to his death in 1357 he served as prior.[54] During this period the new church was completed, the Spanish Chapel was built, and funds were received for its frescoes. Orcagna, furthermore, painted the altarpiece of the Strozzi Chapel and Nardo its walls, and the former may also have undertaken the mural cycle in the choir. Much of this activity was due to Passavanti's influence, and all of it was under his supervision. The existence of iconographic similarities between the paintings in the Strozzi and Spanish Chapels is therefore not surprising, even though the latter were not executed until some years after his death.

62. Francesco Traini, *The Triumph of Death*, Fresco, *c.* 1325–50 (Camposanto, Pisa; Alinari-Art Reference Bureau)

Passavanti's thought has been preserved in a treatise called "Lo Specchio di Vera Penitenza."[55] In it he brought together in a systematic way ideas expressed in his sermons, especially those delivered in 1354. They center on the necessity, or rather the urgency, of penitence, for which he accumulates evidence among the writers of the past, and which he makes vivid for his contemporaries by numerous "esempi," brief but highly colored images or stories interspersed through his more formal discourse. His thought and his mood are closely related to contemporary painting. Man appears a perpetual sinner, hovering in the shadow of death and judgment. His only hope lies in penitence, a mordant contrition that continually torments the spirit. Recalling the common experiences of 1348, Passavanti describes for his audience the frightful decay of human flesh, more odorous, he insists, than that of putrefying dogs or asses.[56] He tells of skeptics who, uttering words of doubt, were struck by lightning and immediately reduced to ashes.[57] He follows them to hell, lingering with their tortures and listening for their anguished shrieks, as though he were under the spell of Orcagna's fresco in S. Croce, where the faces of the damned are torn by the claws and teeth of wildly sadistic devils. Passavanti tries to convey by calculation the incalculable endlessness of their doom. "One day," he says "a French nobleman wondered if the damned in hell would be freed after a thousand years, and his reason told him no; he wondered again if after a hundred thousand years, if after a million years, if after as many thousands of years as there

485

are drops of water in the sea, and once again his reason told him no." [58]

To Passavanti sin is a demonic power and life a relentless struggle against it, grimly maintained because of fear of something worse. And in many paintings of the time, devils, the embodiments of guilt, become more prominent, more aggressive and more vengeful, attacking the lost souls in Orcagna's Hell, menacing the patriarchs in Andrea's Limbo [59] [Andrea da Firenze, in Spanish Chapel, S.M. Novella, Florence], and the unrepentant thief in Barna's Crucifixion, the most intense image of guilt and fear in the art of the fourteenth century [Collegiata, S. Gimignano]. In the fresco of Limbo one devil munches ecstatically on a human head, and in Orcagna's Hell a group of them lacerate the faces and bodies of their victims. For Giotto, on the other hand, hell is a place more of disorder than of excruciating pain [in *Last Judgment*, Arena Chapel, Padua]. The damned and all the devils except Satan are reduced in scale. Hell is more remote and less substantial than heaven. Indeed Giotto's outlook, serene and assured, differs from that of these later masters in much the same way as Giotto's Dominican contemporary Domenico Cavalca (*c.* 1270–1342) differs from Jacopo Passavanti. Of these two preachers De Sanctis wrote: "Cavalca's muse is love, and his material is Paradise, of which we get a foretaste in that spirit of charity and gentleness which gives his prose so much softness and color. But Passavanti's muse is terror, and his material is vice and hell, pictured less from their grotesque and mythological sides than in their human aspects, as in remorse and the cry of conscience. . . ." [60] Can we avoid thinking of Giotto and Orcagna?

NOTES

[1] Sachetti, *Novella* 136.

[2] Orcagna was capomaestro of Or S. Michele from 1355 to 1359, and both Taddeo Gaddi and Alberto di Arnaldo were in Florence at that time (see J. von Schlosser, *Quellenbuch für Kunstgeschichte*, XLVIII [Vienna, 1896], p. 349).

[3] The story has been mentioned by previous writers simply as evidence of the pessimism, the "Epigonengefühl," of all the artists present. See J. V. Schlosser, in *Kunstgeschichtliches Jahrbuch der K. K. Zentralkommission*, IV, 1910, p. 126; P. Toesca, *Florentine Painting of the Trecento* (New York, n.d.), p. 50 (the translation in part incorrect); W. R. Valentiner, in the *Art Quarterly*, XII, 1949, p. 48 (Taddeo's reply incorrectly read).

[4] From 1357 to 1360 and in 1373–1374 (see P. Toynbee, *Dante Studies* [London, 1902], pp. 218–222).

[5] *Comentum super Dantis Aldigherii Comoediam,* ed. (Florence, 1887), III, p. 313.

[6] "O empty glory of human powers! How short the time its green endures at its peak, if it be not overtaken by crude ages! Cimabue thought to hold the field in painting, and now Giotto has the cry, so that the fame of the former is obscured." (*Purgatorio,* XI, 91–95.)

[7] R. Salvini, *Giotto* (Rome, 1938), p. iii.

A later Dante commentator, perhaps under the influence of Benvenuto, also imputed errors to Giotto, but in architecture, where they are far less significant. The Anonimo, writing about 1395, says that he made two errors in the Campanile, of which he was aware and which led him to die of a broken heart. . . . (see Milanesi in Vasari, I, p. 371). Schlosser, *op. cit.,* p. 124, refers to changes in the design made by Giotto's successors as a possible source of the Anonimo's fable.

[8] *Commentum cit.,* p. 311.

[9] It is true that eulogies of Giotto were not lacking around this time. Petrarch spoke admiringly of him in a letter, and in his will of 1361 he referred to the praise of the "magistri artis" as Benvenuto had of the "ingenii." But Petrarch, living far from Florence, may not have been in close touch with the growth of Florentine opinion on the arts. Boccaccio's famous statement in the Decameron was written in 1350–1352, thus at the very beginning of a profound change of taste in Florence. (For the passages in Petrarch and Boccaccio, see Salvini, *op. cit.,* pp. 4–5.)

[10] This statement seems to me essentially correct even though some elements of Maso's style were assimilated by two or three younger masters, among them the author of the frescoes of the Nativity and Crucifixion in the Chiostrino of S. M. Novella (Van Marle, *The Development of the Italian Schools of Painting* [The Hague, 1924], III, Fig. 241), and Orcagna himself.

[11] *Studies in Florentine Painting* (New York, 1927), pp. 3–42, and *Corpus of Florentine Painting* (New York, Sec. III, Vols. I, 1931, and II, 1930).

[12] See for instance C. Weigelt, *Sienese Painting of the Trecento* (New York, 1930), pp. 56–57.

[13] Resemblances between Florentine painting of the period and Bartolo di Fredi have already been observed, however, by G. Gombosi (*Spinello Aretino* [Budapest, 1926], p. 14) and F. Antal (*Florentine Painting and its Social Background* [London, 1947], p. 205). But I cannot agree with Antal's belief that Giovanni del Biondo and several contemporary Florentine painters were influenced by Fredi.

[14] See, for instance, a collection of middle class precepts such as that of Paolo di Messer Pace, *Il libro di buoni costumi,* ed. by S. Morpurgo (Florence, 1921). For burgher modes of thought, see also the comments below on the Villani chronicles (note 17 . . .).

[15] The growth of the power of Milan weighed so heavily upon the minds of the Florentines that a large part of Matteo Villani's chronicle from 1351 on (book II) is devoted to it. For the consequences of the Milanese threat see H. Baron, in *Annual Report of the American Historical Association for 1942* (Washington, 1944), pp. 123–138.

[16] See A. Sapori, *La crisi delle compagnie mercantili dei Bardi e dei Peruzzi*

(Florence, 1926); also A. Doren, *Italienische Wirtschaftsgeschichte* (Jena, 1934), pp. 464 ff.

[17] Sapori, *op. cit.,* p. 140.

[18] "Maggiore ruina e sconfitta che nulla che mai avesse il nostro comune" (book xii, chap. 55). Villani was a *socius* of the Buonaccorsi Company.

[19] This government, furthermore, suppressed as firmly as the oligarchic one preceding it the *sottoposti* of the woolen guilds, who comprised the great majority of the working population of Florence (see G. Capponi, *Storia della Repubblica di Firenze* [Florence, i, 1875], p. 245).

[20] See, for instance, the changes within the guild of the physicians and apothecaries to which the painters belonged, described by R. Ciasca, *L'arte dei medici e speziali* (Florence, 1927), pp. 86 ff., and A. Doren, *Entwicklung und Organization der florentiner Zünfte* (Leipzig, 1897), pp. 51–59.

During these years the painters acquired greater independence and influence within the guild, but this was in part the consequence of special factors, chiefly the greater public esteem won by this craft during the course of the fourteenth century. The painters entered the guild in 1314 as dependents of the *membrum* of the apothecaries, classified simply as men who buy, sell, and work colors. In the guild lists of the 'forties or 'fifties painters of panels and frescoes are called *dipintori,* and differentiated from painters of chests and furniture. Not long afterward the *dipintori* became dependents of the physicians, the only professional group in the guild. Finally, in 1378 the group of painters was authorized to form an independent *membrum* because, as the record states, "aveva conseguito una grande importanza nella vita dello stato, ed appariva già maturo per la vita dello stato" (Ciasca, *op. cit.,* p. 131).

[21] "Signori artefici e gente manovali e idioti" (book xii, chap. 43). In 1340, before the revolution, Villani had advocated a government representative of all classes (book xi, chap. 118).

[22] See G. Luchaire, *Documenti per la storia dei rivolgimenti politici del comune di Siena dal 1354 al 1369* (Lyons, 1906); P. L. Sbaragli, "I mercanti di mezzana gente al potere in Siena," in *Bullettino senese di storia patria,* viii, 1947, pp. 35 ff.; F. Schevill, *Siena* (London, 1909), pp. 213–228; L. Douglas, *A History of Siena* (New York, 1902), pp. 149 ff.

[23] See N. Rodolico, *Il popolo minuto* (Bologna, 1899), p. 51.

[24] See Doren, *Italienische Wirtschaftsgeschichte,* p. 391.

[25] Book xi, chap. 21.

[26] In a previous epidemic, during the spring of 1340, 15,000 Florentines died, according to Giovanni Villani (book xi, chap. 114).

[27] These estimates of Doren (*op. cit.,* pp. 634–635) are conservative. Others suppose a higher rate of mortality. N. Rodolico, *La democrazia fiorentina nel suo tramonto* (Bologna, 1905), pp. 7, 32, 35, gives an overall figure for Florence in 1347 of 120,000; after the plague 25,000 to 30,000, a death rate of four-fifths. Boccaccio in the Decameron said that 100,000 Florentines died, and the Chronicle of Stefani puts the figure at 96,000. Matteo Villani gives a general death rate of three-fifths (see note 30).

Agnolo di Tura seems to say that 80,000 Sienese died, leaving only 10,000 alive (*Rerum Italicarum scriptores,* xv, part vi, ed. by A. Lisini and F. Iacometti, Bologna, 1932, p. 555) and an anonymous chronicler (*ibid.,* p. 148) asserts that the "grande morìa" carried off three-fourths of the people. A. Lisini, commenting on this statement (*ibid.*, p. 148 note 2), says that if three-fourths did not die, at least a half did. Lisini estimates as many as 70,000 people in Siena before the plague. Commenting on Siena, Matteo Villani (book ɪ, chap. 4) says "non pareva che fusse persona."

[28] See for Siena, W. Heywood, *"Ensamples" of Fra Filippo* (Siena, 1901), pp. 80 ff., and for Florence, F. T. Perrens, *Histoire de Florence* (Paris, 1888–90), ɪᴠ, pp. 379 ff. The plague of course became endemic, reappearing in 1400, 1411, 1424, and thereafter, but with a greatly diminished rate of mortality.

[29] *Rerum Italicarum scriptores*, xv, part 6, pp. 555–556.

[30] Book ɪ, end of chap. 1 and beginning of chap. 2.

The entire passage is interesting for its careful, precise account of the spread of the plague through Italy and Europe. Villani is assiduous in the collection of facts and opinions but cautious in accepting them, and he frequently records them with skepticism or with contrary argument. Thus he tells about the reports of a great fire in Asia, and the belief that the plague originated in areas ravaged by it, but adds, "ma questo non possiamo accertare." To the assertion of the astrologers that the plague resulted from the conjunction of three superior planets in the sign of Aquarius, he replies that a similar conjunction had occurred in the past without producing such dire results. He is quick to calculate, and to propose laws and principles: on the basis of reports from many countries, he says that the pestilence may be said usually to last five months in a given region. It normally carried away three out of every five persons.

[31] Agnolo di Tura, *op. cit.*, p. 555–556. One hundred and thirteen of the friars in S. M. Novella in Florence died (C. di Pierro, in *Giornale storico della letteratura italiana*, xʟᴠɪɪ, 1906, p. 14), and in Avignon nine cardinals and seventy prelates, despite the great fires which were maintained in the papal palace to purify the air (P. Schaff, *History of the Christian Church*, (New York, 1910), ᴠ, part 2, p. 100).

[32] *Corpus*, sec. ɪɪɪ, vol. ᴠ, p. 119.

[33] Their names are lacking not only in all documents, but in the list of the best Sienese painters compiled around 1349 for the *operaii* of S. Giovanni, Pistoia (C. von Fabriczy, *Repertorium für Kunstwissenschaft*, xxɪɪɪ, 1900, pp. 496–497).

[34] Agnolo di Tura, *op. cit.*, p. 560.

[35] Book ɪ, chap. 4. A translation of the entire chapter—upon which the above is based—may be found in G. C. Coulton, *The Black Death* (London, 1929), pp. 66–67.

[36] Book ɪ, chap. 5.

[37] Chronicle of Neri di Donato, *Rerum Italicarum scriptores*, xv, pp. 633–636. On the inflation throughout Europe after the Black Death see J. W. Thompson, in *American Journal of Sociology*, xxᴠɪ, 1920–21, p. 565, and Kovalevsky in *Zeitschrift für Sozial- und Wirtschaftsgeschichte*, ɪɪɪ, 1895, pp. 406–423.

[38] Twenty thousand florins, for instance, to Lando in 1356 (see Neri di Donato, *op. cit.*, p. 585). On the merchant companies and Florence, see especially Perrens, *op. cit.*, ɪᴠ, pp. 424, 457–470.

[39] See R. Ciasca, *op. cit.*, p. 291. Despite these inducements the number of physicians did not increase as rapidly as the shopkeepers and tradesmen in the same guild (*ibid.*, p. 117). For immigration into Florence see also N. Rodolico, *I ciompi*, pp. 40–42, and *idem, Democrazia fiorentina*, pp. 36 ff. For Siena, see Kovalevsky, *op. cit.*, p. 421 and L. Douglas, *op. cit.*, pp. 155–156. All these writers comment

only very briefly on the immigration. The entire phenomenon, and its consequences for contemporary society and culture, has not hitherto been given ade-
quate attention.

[40] Agnolo di Tura (*op. cit.*, p. 560) wrote that "tutti li denari erano venuti a le
mani di gente nuova." See also Matteo Villani (book III, chap. 56); Perrens,
op. cit., IV, p. 391.

[41] *Op. cit.*, p. 34. Through Scaramella does not observe it, all references that he
cites to the *homines novi* are from the period after the plague (Matteo and Filippo
Villani, Giovanni di Paolo Morelli, etc.).

[42] ". . . tabulam meam sive iconam beatae Virginis Mariae . . . cuius pulchri-
tudinem ignorantes non intelligunt, magistri autem artis stupent." See R. Salvini,
Giotto (*Bibliografia*) (Rome, 1938), p. 5.

[43] H. Hauvette, *Boccace* (Paris, 1914), p. 464.

[44] See books XIV and XV of the *Genealogia degli dei*, trans. by C. G. Osgood,
Boccaccio on Poetry (Princeton, 1930).

[45] *Meditations*, chap. XII (see the edition of the Italian text by A. Levasti,
Florence, 1931, pp. 46–47): "Cotali cose [i.e. lavorìo curioso, bello, . . . delicato]
sono concupiscenza degli occhi, lo quale vizio è uno de' tre peccati, ai quali tutti
gli altri si riducono." The author condemns works of craft and of art also because
they waste time, promote vanity, and are contrary to poverty.

The passage in the *Meditations* is based on ideas about the *concupiscentia
oculorum* expressed by St. John (First Epistle, 2:16) and developed by St. Augustine (*Confessions*, book X, esp. chap. 34), after whom they became part of the
medieval tradition. The latter speaks of the "attractions" that men, with the aid
of the arts, have added to paintings and other things.

[46] The association of these vices with St. John is probably connected with the
passage from this saint cited in the previous note and later interpretations of it.

[47] See Paolo di Messer Pace da Certaldo, *Il libro di buoni costumi*, ed. by
S. Morpurgo (Florence, 1921), p. CL (Paolo is mentioned in documents from 1347
to 1370). The writer, son of a jurist, recounts the perils of avarice, and then concludes: "Sia temperato in se, e non disiderare più che'l tuo stato richegha."

[48] A. Segre, *Storia del commercio* (Turin, 1923), p. 223.

[49] A. Doren, *Entwicklung und Organization der florentiner Zünfte* (Leipzig,
1897), p. 71, pointed to the greater recognition given at this time to silk weavers
and dyers in a guild that continued to be dominated by silk merchants. See also
idem, Florentiner Zunftwesen (Stuttgart and Berlin, 1908), p. 199.

[50] A. Sapori, in *Archivio storico italiano*, III, 1925, p. 250. On the subject of
voluntary restitution, see B. N. Nelson, in *Tasks of Economic History*, supplement VII, 1947, to the *Journal of Economic History*. Even in the fifteenth century,
Cosimo dei Medici sought the advice of Pope Eugene IV on the restitution of
money that he confessed had been illegitimately gotten.

[51] Book VII, chap. 147.

[52] See, for instance, the beginning of Sacchetti's *Trecento novelle:* "Considerando
al presente tempo, ed alla condizione dell' umana vita, la quale con pestilenziose
infirmità, e con oscure morti, è spesso vicitata; e veggendo quante rovine, con
quante guerre civili e campestre in esse dimorano; e pensando quante populi e
famiglie per questo son venute in povero ed infelice stato, e con quanto amaro

sudore conviene che comportino la miseria, là dove sentono la lor vita esser trascorsa; e ancora immaginando, come la gente è vaga d'udire cose nuove, e spezialmente di quelle letture che sono agevoli a intendere, e massimamente quando danno conforto, per lo quale tra molti dolori si mescolini alcune risa; . . ." (Franco Sacchetti, *Proemio del Trecento novelle*).

[53] *Speculum*, xiii, 1938, p. 12. Baron discusses the diffusion of stoicism and the ideal of poverty in the period following the epidemic.

For the preoccupation with death, see A. M. Campbell, *The Black Death and Men of Learning* (New York, 1931), pp. 172 ff.

[54] C. di Pierro, "Contributo alla biografia di Fra Jacopo Passavanti," *Giornale storico della letteratura italiana*, xlvii, 1906, pp. 1–24.

[55] Ed. by M. Lenardon (Florence, 1925). See also N. Sapegno, *Storia letteraria d'Italia, Il trecento* (Milan, 1942), pp. 505–510; A Levasti, *I mistici del duecento e del trecento* (Rome, 1935), pp. 64 ff.; A. Monteverdi, "Gli esempi di Jacopo Passavanti," *Giornale storico della letteratura italiana*, lxi, 1913, pp. 266 ff., and lxiii, 1914, pp. 240 ff.

[56] *Specchio, cit.*, pp. 307–308.

[57] See A. Monteverdi, *op. cit.*, 1914, pp. 249, 287. The monastery of S. M. Novella itself was struck by lightning several times during the priorate of Passavanti. In 1358 the choir was hit and the frescoes of Orcagna damaged (see Matteo Villani, book viii, chap. 46).

[58] Monteverdi, *op. cit.*, 1913, p. 305.

[59] Antal, *op. cit.*, p. 202, has pointed to the prominence of the devils in this scene, connecting them with "popular taste."

[60] F. De Sanctis, *History of Italian Literature,* trans. by J. Redfern (New York, 1931), i, p. 123.

Index

Page numbers of illustrations appear in boldface.

Accaiuoli family, 473
Acropolis, 44, 74, 90, 92, 101, 106, 107–110
Adulvesnasa, Essex, barn at, 271–272
Aeschylus, 37–38, 60, 64–67, 73
Aesop, 422
Agnolo di Tura, 475, 476, 477
Aix-la-Chappelle, 419
akratophoron, 185
Akratos, 185, 201
mask of, 184–185
Alaric, 391
Albert the Great, 396
Alberti, Leone Battista, 390
Alberto di Arnaldo, 465
Alcamenes, 44
Alexander the Great, 16, 78
Alexandria, 79, 116
Amenemhat III, 11, 16
Amiens Cathedral
bays of, **277**, 278
interior of nave, 394, **395**
Andrea da Firenze, 483, 486
"Anglo-Saxon Renaissance," 423, 424
Antioch, 79
Anzy-le-Duc, 317
Aphaia, temple of, at Aegina, 60
Apollo, 67
Aquinas, St. Thomas, 335, 337
architecture
bay system, 255–288
Byzantine, 246–249
Egyptian, 10, 11–12
Gothic church, 398–402
Greek, 111–127
interior space in, 125–126
numerical aspects of, 120–124
Orders, **115**, 118–123
parallel planes in, 124–125
space division in, **277**
temple plan and, 113–118
Roman, 149–172
building materials of, 152–156
construction process of, 156–160
design characteristics of, 163–167
economy of construction of, 151–162
Imperial, 167–170
"new" architecture, 162–163

pozzolana mortar, 154, 155, 159, 160
structural features of, 160–162
vaulted style of, 107–168
Arena Chapel (Padua), 472–473, 486
Giotto's frescoes in, 472–473, **472**
Aristeides of Thebes, 195
painting of Dionysos and Ariadne, 195–197
Aristophanic comedy, 53
Aristotle, 54, 467
Arnessysla, Iceland, timber church at, 260–261
Arti Maggiori, 470
Arti Minori, 470
Asklepios, 77–78, 81
Assisi, Upper Church, frescoes in, 377
Assurbanipal, 28
Assurnasirpal, palace reliefs of, 25–27
King Assurnasirpal II's Chariots Passing a Fortified City, **27**
Assyrian art, 21–34
naturalism in, 23, 30
palace reliefs, 25–33
draughtsmanship of, 26–27
historical epic in, 25–26, 31–32
human figures in, 27
spatial rendering in, 27–32
religious beliefs and, 24–25
seals, 23–25
secular scenes in, 24
winged monsters in, 24–25
Athena Nike, temple of, 76, 77
Athena Parthenos (statue), 44, 90–92, 94, 99
"Athenian Empire," 88
Atley, Bishop, 269
Augustine, St., 332–333

Bacchic dance, 188–189
See also Dionysiac mysteries and rituals
Balawat, palace gates at, bronze reliefs, 27–28
Bardi family, 473, 479, 483
Barna, 469
Baroque art, 136, 291
Bartolo di Fredi, 469, 475

basilicas, Romanesque, building of, 297–298
Basilica Ulpia, 152
bay system, 255–288
  Carolingian, 260, 261, 266, 278
  Continental churches, 257–261, 263–266
  development of, 277–281
  Gothic architecture and, 279–281
  hall and barn (in England), 266–272
  houses and barns, 261–263
  Iron Age, 263, 279
  Leicester Castle hall, 266–268
  origins of, 255–288
  Plan of St. Gall, 263–266, 272
  space-division, 277–279
Beauvais Cathedral, 402
Benedictine scheme (Berry plan), of church architecture, 298
Bernard, St., 322
Biadaiolo Master, 468
Biondo, Giovanni del, 481
Bishop of Hereford, Palace hall of, 268–270, **269**
Bisse, Bishop, 269
Bissos Church at Ruweha, 282
Black Death, 460, 475–476
  economic and social consequences of, 477–479
  effect of, on culture and art, 479–484
  guilt, penance, religious rapture and, 484–486
Boccaccio, Giovanni, 475, 486
Bonaiuti, Andrea, 466
Bramante, Donato, 280
Breberen, Carolingian timber church at, **261**
Brunelleschi, Filippo, 389, 390, 397, 398
Buffalmacco, 465
Byzantine art, 235–254
  architecture, 235–238
    cross-in-square church plan, 249–251
    compared to Hellenistic art, 131, 141, 143–144
    contribution of, to Western art, 355–386
      channels of transmission, 366–369
      conflicting assessments of, 357–359
      "damp fold" style of, 369–370
      "dynamic" style of, 370–372
      Italian "proto-Renaissances" and, 377–380

      manuscript illumination and, 367
      neo-classicism and, 374–375, 379
      parallelisms between East and West, 372–374, 375
      in twelfth century, 360–362
      use of various media in, 364–366
      "volume style" of, 364, 376–377, 379
    icons, theory of, 239–246
    mosaics, 235–254
      architectural and technical conditions of, 246–248
      frontality in, 241–243
      movement and gestures in, 244–246
      similarity theory of, 240–241
      subject matter of, 238–239
      three zones of, 251–253
"Byzantinische Antike," 374

Carolingian art and architecture, 260, 261, 266, 278, 298, 374
Carolingian revival (renovatio), 417–423
  classical mythology, 420–421
  Latin classics, 418
  ornament, 420
  Palace School of Charlemagne, 420
  Utrecht Psalter, 420
Casentino, Jacopo del, 468
Castelseprio frescoes, 359
catacomb paintings, 216–220
cathedrals
  Amiens, 277, 278, 394, 395
  Beauvais, 402
  Chartres, 396
  Cologne, 402
  Ely, 396
  Gloucester, 396
  Lincoln, 396
  Maastricht, 260
  Narbonne, 402
  Prague, 402
  Speyer, 277, 281, 282
  Spoleto, 367
  Strassburg, 402
  See also styles of architecture
Cavalca, Domenico, 486
Cavallini, Pietro, 379, 480
Cennini, Cennino, 466
centaurs, 66
Central group, from east frieze of the Parthenon, 106, **107**

Ceres, 182, 196–203
  cult at, 197, 199–203
  temple of, at Rome, 196, 200–202
Cesariano, 390
Chariot at full speed, from south frieze of the Parthenon, 104, **105**
Charlemagne, 277, 390, 417, 418, 419, 420
Charles the Bald, 423
Chartres Cathedral
  flying buttresses of, 396
  tympanum, *Christ as Judge and Ruler of the Universe with Symbols of the Evangelists,* 331–332, **332**
Châteaumeillant (church), 298
chiaroscuro, 139
Christos Paskon (Byzantine drama), 302
churches
  bay system, 225–288
  Carolingian, 260, **261**, 266, 278
  cross-in-square, 249–251
  Gothic, 398–402
  Ottonian, 278
  Romanesque, 291–311
  See also cathedrals; names of churches
Church of the Virgin at Studenica, wall paintings in, 363
Cicero, 389
Cimabue, Giovanni, 377, 451, 465, 467
Clairvaux, Abbey of, 272, 274
Classical revivals, 82
Classical tradition, 3, 4, 415–441
  Byzantine art, 426, 428
  Frederich II, 431–432
  Gothic style, 427, 428
  "principle of axiality," 428
  school of Reims (Reims Cathedral), 430, **430**
  sculpture on Reims Cathedral, 430
Classicism and romanticism, 433
Cluny monastery, 293–294
Cologne Cathedral, 402
Colombini, Giovanni, 483
Company of the Hat, 478
Company of St. George, 478
Conte Lando, 478
contrapposte, 430
Corinthian Order, 113, **115,** 119, 305
Correggio (Antonio Allegri), 139
Council of Clermont, 322–323

crotala, 188
Ctesiphon, 228

da Fabriano, Gentile, 460
da Vinci, Leonardo, 449
Daddi, Bernardo, 465, 468, 476
"damp fold" style, 369–370
Dante Alighieri, 335, 418, 419, 432
Daphni, mosaics of, 359–360, 362, 366
"Dark Ages," 423
de Honnecourt, Villard, 307, 389, 425
de Limbourg, Pol, 459
de l'Orme, Philibert, 328
de Siena, Ugolino, 448
Delian League, 71, 87–88
Delphic oracle, 57
Demeter (Ceres), 182, 183, 196
Demeter and Persephone, from east pediment of the Parthenon, 96, **97**
Demetrius, 45
Desiderius, Abbot, 368
Didymean Apollo, temple of, 113
Dionysiac mysteries, 179–182
  enthusiasmos, 180
Dionysiac rituals, 192–193
Dionysos, 78
  See also Dionysus
Dionysos Liknites, 182
Dionysus, 183, 192–199, 432
Dioscurides of Samos, 133
Diskobolus (Myron), 99
Domitian, 151
Domus Aurea, Esquiline Wing, 156–157
Doric Order, 113, **115**
  generative ratio of, 121–123
  proportions of, 118–119
Duccio di Buoninsegna, 357, 377, 421, 432, 443–461
  architectural representations of, 457
  northern Europe and, 459–460
  perspective of, 457–458
  Renaissance and, 458
  Sacra Conversazione and, 458
  Siennese tradition and, 458
Dugento painting, 357, 365, 376
Dura-Europos
  baptistery of, 220–225
  synagogue of, 224–227
  town of, 216
Durandus, Gulielmus, 330, 336

early Byzantine revival, 412–418
eclecticism, 90
Egyptian art, 7–20, 25, 32
  architecture, 10, 11–12
  cubical forms in, 10
  depiction of historical events in, 14
  hieroglyphs, 14
  naturalistic elements in, 9–10, 12
  paintings, 12–15
  reliefs, 12
  religious beliefs and, 17–20
  sculpture, 9, 11–12, 39–40
  style characteristics of, 16–17
  tomb art and architecture, 11–12
  wall paintings, 12–16
    brush-strokes, 13
    subject matter of, 14–16
Eleusis, Hall of Mysteries at, 78, 87, 88, 122
Ely Cathedral, 396
Ephesus, temple of Diana at, 113, 116
eremiai, 69
ēthos, 68, 80
Euripides, 75, 186–187
Eutyches, 240
The Evangelist Mark, 420, **421**
Ezinge, cattle barn, 261–263, **262**

Fallen Warrior, from east pediment of temple of Aphaia, 60–61, **62**
Fallen Warrior, from west pediment of temple of Aphaia, 60–61, **62**
Feast at Cana (Giotto), 452, **453**
Fidati, Fra Simone, 480
Filarete (Antonio di Pietro Averlino), 390, 391
Florence Baptistery, mosaics in dome of, 377
Florentine and Sienese painting, 463–491
  Black Death and, 475–477
    economic and social consequences of, 477–479
    effect of, on culture and art, 479–484
    guilt, penance, religious rapture and, 484–486
  economic crisis of 1340's and, 473
  in mid-fourteenth century, 470–473
  political and social change and, 474–475
  See also names of artists

Foigny, Abbey of, 274
form and content, 4
Fortitude (Pisano), 432, **433**
Forum of Trajan, **164**
Franco, Battista, 467
Fulcher of Chartres, 322–323

Gaddi, Taddeo, 465, 466, 468, 469
Ghiberti, Lorenzo, 357
Giacomo di Mino, 475
Gibbon, Edward, 358–359
Giotto di Bondone, 357, 371, 443–461, 465–466, 467, 468, 480, 486
  architectural representations of, 457
  Arena Chapel frescoes of, 448–450, 452–454, 455–456
  Bardi Chapel frescoes of, 449
  perspective of, 457–458
  Peruzzi Chapel frescoes of, 449
  Renaissance and, 458
Gloucester Cathedral, 396
Gothic style, 258, 277, 298, 357, 358, 365, 375, 387–413
  bay system and, 279–281
  church architecture, 398–402
    altar styles, 399–400
    chapels and ante-rooms, 401
    rood screens, 400
  development of, 393–398
  Late period, 397–398
  symbolism in, 402–412
    doors, 404
    double choirs, 405–406
    of form, 408–412
    of meaning, 402–408
    windows, 334, 396, 409–410
Goths, 390, 391
Greek art
  the absolute and the relative, 73–74
  analysis of forms, 55
  Archaic period, 53–57, 58–70. *See also* Archaic Greek art
  architecture, 111–127
    interior space in, 125–126
    numerical aspects of, 120–124
    Orders, **115**, 118–123
    parallel planes in, 124–125
    space division in, **277**
    temple plan and, 113–118
  Classical style, 70–74
  early Classical style, 58–69
  early Classical "severe" style, 67–68

emotion, 56, 80, 81
fourth century, 78
Hellenistic, 129–147. *See also* Hellen-
    istic art
idealism and abstraction, 81–82
influence of environment on, 38–39,
    40
the irrational, 74
later fifth century, 74–79
order and chaos, 53–57
personification, 82
sculpture, 35–49
    Archaic period, 60–63, 66–67
    architectural uses of, 43–44, 47–48
    chief uses of, 43–49
    commemorative groups of, 44–45
    contour and, 43
    genre art, 48–49
    grave monuments, 45
    human form in, 40, 43, 44–46
    idealism and, 40–42
    proportions of, 42–43
    relief, 43–44
    religion and, 37, 43, 46–48
    sensuousness, 80
    simplification of form in, 42
    the specific and the generic, 55, 81
    subjects represented in, 45–48
    temple pediments, 43, 47–48
Greek drama
    comedy, 53
    tragedy, 63–67
Greek lyric poets, 53–54
Greek philosophy
    anthropocentrism, 73

Hagia Sophia, mosaics, 361
Halicarnassus, Mausoleum of, 116
Harmondsworth barn, 274–275
Hawkwood, John, 478
Hellenistic art, 78–82, 126, 129–147
    assessment of, 142–144
    compared to Byzantine art, 129, 141,
        143–144
    emotion in, 141–142
    eroticism in, 132
    essential traits of, 124
    genre, 133–134
    humor in, 133
    illusionism in, 138–140
    landscapes and architectural settings
        in, 134–140

Henry VII, Chapel of, 398
Hereford Castle, England, interior of
    Great Hall, 268–270, **269**
Hermogenes, 113
Hesiod, 37
hieroglyphs, 14
Holmes Chapel, Cheshire, 259
Holy Trinity, Church of, Sopoćani,
    wall painting, *Patriarch*, **365**
Homer, 37
House of Amandus, wall painting from,
    137
House of the Little Fountain, wall
    painting from, **138**
Hugh, St., 155
Huns, 390
hybris, 63

Iconography
    accepted symbols of, 267–268
    Christian, 213–234
        Abraham and Isaac, 217, 218
        Adam, Eve, and the serpent, 220
        Adoration of the Magi, 217, 218–
            220
        baptism images, 217
        baptistery of Duro-Europos and,
            221–225
        beginnings of, 213–234
        Christ as the Good Shepherd, 216,
            219
        Christ the philosopher, 219
        Christ-Thaumaturge, 219
        communion images, 217, 218
        Constantine and Chi-Rho mono-
            gram, 232
        Daniel, 217, 218
        earliest images of, 215–216
        Hebrews and the furnace, 218
        image of the fisherman, 217
        image-signs, 218
        Jewish sources, question of, 218,
            224–227, 230
        Last Supper, 220
        Lazarus, 217, 218, 219
        Manicheism and, 228
        Noah, 217, 218
        pagan sources of, 231–234
        pastoral imagery, 231
        prayers of salvation, 218
        Roman Imperial sources of, 231–
            234

Iconography (*Continued*)
  sacraments, 220
  shepherd as pagan image of
    humanitas, 219
  controversy of 800–900 A.D., 239–240
  Gothic symbolism, 402–412
    of form, 408–412
    of meaning, 402–408
  Jewish, 218, 224–227, 230
  Manichean (Manes), 227–229
    Last Judgment, 227
    propaganda, 228–229
  Mirror (Vincent of Beauvais), 335–
    348
  position, grouping, symmetry, and
    number, 330–333
  Romanesque, 300–303
    quality of, 303
    tympanum at Vézelay, 313–326
  as symbolic code, 334–335
icons, theory of, 239–246
idealism, in Greek art, 40–42
illusionism, 138–141
Imola, Benvenuto da, 466–468
Ingeborg Psalter, miniatures in, 374,
  375
International Gothic style, 460
introitus, 179
Ionic Order, 113, **115**
  column-base development of, 119,
    120
Iris, from west pediment of the Parthenon, 98, **98**
Irish monachism, 293

John II Comnenus, votive panel of,
  360–361, **361**
Joshua Roll, miniature in, 359

Ka-aper, called "Sheikh-el-Beled,"
  statue of, **10**
Kariye Djami, mosaics of, 364, 377
  The Temptations of Christ (detail),
    378
Kephisodotos, 82
Klosterneuburg, Altar of, 371, 373
Knossos, Cretan palace of, 13
Kore-Persephone, 199
kosmos, 55, 72
kouros (pl. *kouroi*), 58–59, 68
Kouros of Sounion, 39

krater, by Euphronius, 67, **68**
Kritios Boy, 58–60, **60**

L'An Mil, 424
La Lande de Cubzac, 301
Lachares, 92
Lamentation (Giotto), 452, **453**, 455,
  456
Lamentation of Christ, wall painting,
  Church of St. Panteleimon, **362**
landscapes
  in Hellenistic art, 134–138
Languedoc, tympana of churches in,
  301
Laocoön, 141
Lapiths, 66
Latin comedy, 80
Leens, timber house at, 263, **264**
Leicester Castle, Great Hall, 266–268
  reconstruction of, **268**
Liber and Libera, 196, 200, 202
Lincoln Cathedral, 496
Lion Facing Horseman, relief from
  Nineveh, 33
Lombards, 390
Long Walls, 88
Longchamp, Abbey of, 274
Longhi, Roberto, 357
Lorenzetti, Ambrogio, 460, 469, **476**,
  480
Lorenzetti, Pietro, 469, 476
Lorsch, 419
Louis XI, King, 276
Louis VII, King, 322
Luca di Tommè, 469, 475, 483
Lucian, 92
Lysicrates, monument of, 119
Lysippus, 480
Lyssa, 186–189

Maastricht Cathedral, 260
maenads, 183, 197
Maestà (Duccio), 378, 445–446, **446**,
  448–454
  Christ in Gethsemane (detail), **378**
  Giovanni Pisano and, 454
  Order of Passion scenes in, 450–452
Maitani, Lorenzo, 447
"man, measure of all things," 72
maniera greca, 357, 358, 364, 365, 376–
  377
manuscripts, illuminated, 367

Marcus Aurelius, statue of, 425
Martini, Simone, 469
Maso di Banco, 466, 468, 469
Mattingly, Hampshire, church in, 259
Meeting of Joachim and Anna (Giotto), 472–473, **472**
Menander, 79–80
metastasis, 54
Mene-na tomb of, wall painting in, **15**
Méréville, market hall at, 276
Middle Ages
    architecture, bay system, 255–288
    Gothic style, 387–413
    iconography, 327–353
    tympanum at Vézelay, 313–326
    See also Florentine and Sienese painting; names of cathedrals
Milesevo, frescoes of, 363–364
Milesian philosophers, 54–55
Mino, Giacomo di, 475
Mirror (Vincent of Beauvais), 335–338
    background of, 335–338
    of History, 345–348
    of Instruction, 341–343
    of Morals, 343–345
    of Nature, 339–341
Mnesicles, 118
monasticism, 292
Monreale, mosaics of, 371
    Expulsion of Adam and Eve from Paradise, **372**
Montecassino, 368, 370
Montereau, Pierre de, 403
Morgan Library Triptych, 366
Moriale, Fra, 478
mosaics, Byzantine, 235–254
    Annunciation, Church of the Dormition, Daphni, **245**
    architectural and technical conditions, 246–248
    Empress Irene, from mosaic panel of *Virgin and Child between Emperor John II Comnenus and Empress Irene,* Hagia Sophia, **361**
    frontality in, 241–243
    magical identity in, 241
    movement and gestures in, 244–246
    similarity theory of, 240–241
    subject-matter of, 238–239
    theory of icon, 239–246
    three zones of, 251–253

Venetian, 377
Virgin and Child with Saints, Torcello, Cathedral, **242**
Murals of the Villa of the Mysteries, 173–211, **176, 177, 178**
Myron, 69

Narbonne Cathedral, 402
Nardo, 466, 468, 484
naturalism
    in Assyrian relief art, 23, 30
    in Egyptian art, 9, 10, 12
nemesis, 69
Nerezi frescoes, 142, 360–361, **362**
Nero, 159
"New Comedy," 80
Nicholas of Verdun, 371–372, 373–375, 379, 426, 429
Nikai, 76
Nike, from temple of Athena Nike, 76, 77
Nike of Paionios at Olympia, 44
Nike of Samothrace, 131, **132**
Noli me Tangere (Giotto), 452, **453**
Nyeven, Province Drente, Holland, church in, 259

Odeon, 88
Oderisio, 467
Odo, St., 393
Odyssey landscapes, 135
Orcagna (Andrea di Cione), 465, 466, 468, 482, 483, 484, 485, 486
Ottonian art, 278, 373, 374
"Ottonian Renaissance," 423, 424

Pacino, 468
Pagasai stele, 141
painting, 357, 358
    in Florence and Siena, 463–491
        Black Death and, 475–477
        consequences of plague, 472–486
        economic crisis of 1340's and, 473
        in mid-fourteenth century, 470–473
        political and social change and, 474–475
    See also wall painting
Palace of Amenhotep III, at Tell el Amarna, 11
Palace of Domitian, 156
palladium quadratum, 179

Panathenaea, 104
Panathenaic Procession, 100–109
panel painting, 365, 366, 368
Pantaleoni family, 367
Pantheon, 156, 157, 162, 163
Parçay-Meslay, Abbey Grange, 272–274, **273**
Paris Nicander Manuscript, miniatures in, 359
Paris Psalter, miniatures in, **137**
Parler, Peter, 396
Parthenon, 44, 47–48, 85–110, **115**
  as hybrid, 99
  Callicrates and, 88–89
  comparison with the temple of Zeus at Olympia, 95–96
  Doric and Ionic elements of, 88–89
  foundations of, 88–89
  friezes of, 99–109
  Iktinos, 88–89
  metopes, 90
  Mount Pentelicus, 89, 105
  Pheidias and, 88, 90–91
  pediments, 94–99
  records of construction, 88
  sculptors and, 100
  transport of marble, 89, 94
Passavanti, Jacopo, 484, 486
pathos, 68, 80
Peloponnesian War, 71, 77, 78, 94
Pericles, 70–72, 88
  Funeral Oration, 70–72
Persian Wars, 58–63, 70, 87–88
Perrecy-les-Forges, tympana at, 301
Persepolis, columns of, 122–123
Peruzzi, Baldassare, 280
Peruzzi family, 473, 479, 483
Peter the Venerable, 323–324
Petrarch, 389, 432, 476, 480
Phidias, (Pheidias), 44, 48, 88, 90–91
Philip II Augustus, 322
Philon, 122
Pisano, Giovanni, 448, 451, 454, 456, 458
Pisano, Nicola, 377, 432, 447, 448, 458, 480
Plan of St. Gall, 263–266, 271
Plato, 54, 57, 72, 81, 82
Pliny, 139
Plotinus, 42
Plutarch, 87, 98
polis (pl. *poleis*), 56–57, 74

Polyclitus (the Younger), 44
Pompeii, wall paintings from, **137, 138, 140**
Poseidon, **45**
Prague Cathedral, 402
Praxiteles, 81
Priene, Athena temple at, 113
Propylaea, 88
Protagoras, 72
"proto-Renaissance," 424
Pucelle, Jean, 459
Pythagoreans, 54
Pythius, 113

Raising of Lazarus (Giotto), 452, **453**
Ramesside temple reliefs, 16
Raphael Sanzio, 280
religion
  Assyrian art and, 24–25
  Egyptian art and, 17–20
  Greek sculpture and, 37, 43, 46–48
  See also iconography
Rembrandt van Rijn, 139
rhythmos, 55, 69
Riccobaldo, 466
Richard I, King, 322
Richard II, King, 270
Richards, Raymond, 259
Rochecorbon, Abbé Hugue de, 273
Roman art, 149–172
  architecture, 149–172
    building materials of, 152–156
    construction process of, 156–160
    design characteristics of, 163–167
    economy of construction in, 151–162
    Imperial, 167–170
    "new" architecture, 162–163
    pozzolana mortar and, **154, 155,** 159, 160
    structural features of, 160–162
    vaulted style of, 167–168
Romanesque art, 257, 260, 277, 393, 394, 399, 405, 425–428
  church architecture, 289–311
    art of building, 294–299
    Baroque phase of, 291
    Benedictine (or Berry) plan, 398
    conformity and geometric schemes of, 307–308
    creation of, 322
    decoration of, 300–309

iconography of, 300–303
moulding decoration of, 305–306
ornamental motifs in, 308–309
religious feeling and, 322–323
sequence of development of, 291–294
technique (architectural and ornamental), 304–309
sculpture, 315
square schematism of, 278
tympanum at Vézelay, 313–326
    conflicting interpretations of, 315–322
    contribution of Peter the Venerable to, 323–324
Romanticism, 358
Royal Commission on Historical Monuments, 259
Ruccellai Madonna (Duccio), 377
Rufus, William, 270
Ruskin, 104
    on detail of frieze of the Parthenon, 104–105

S. Costanza in Rome, 232
Sacchetti, Franco, 465
Sack of the City of Hamanu in Elam, relief from Nineveh 31
Sacramentary of Gellone, 303
Sacrifice of Iphegenia, 141
St. Catherine's, Church of, at Honfleur, 258–259, **258**, 260
Sainte-Madeleine, Abbey Church, Vézelay, 301, 306, 307, 313–326
    Mission of the Apostles, tympanum, 315–316
St. George, Curbevino, wall painting, *Angel of the Annunciation*, 363
St. Gereon in Cologne, Church of, 267
St. James and St. Paul, church of, at Marton, England, 259, 260
St. John the Evangelist (Biondo), **481**
Saint-Maurice d'Agaune, Valais, 302
St. Panteleimon, Nerezi, wall painting, *Lamentation of Christ*, 362
St. Pierre-sur-Dives, market hall, 275–276, **275**
St. Sergios at Rusafa, basilica of, 282
Saint-Sernin, Toulouse, 298
    aerial view, **299**
    plan, **296**

St.-Trophîme at Arles, 426, **427**
St. Werburgh, church of, at Warburton, England, 259, 260
San Croce, 485
Sandrart, Joachim von, 391
San Michele, oratory of, 293
San Petronio, Bologna, 400
Santa Maria del Fiore, 398
Santa Maria Maggiore, 379
Santa Maria Novella, 482, 484, 486
Santiago de Compostela, 293
satyrs, 183
Scaramella, 479
Scotus Eriugena, 302
sculpture
    Egyptian, 9, 11–12, 39–40
    Greek, 35–49
    Romanesque, 315
seals, Assyrian, 23–35
Segesta, temple at, 90
Sennacherib, reliefs of, 28–30
Serapis, 78
Sesostris III, 15, 16
Sesostris III (Se'n Wosret), fragment of head, **15**
Seti I, reliefs of, at Karnak, 26
Siena. *See* Florentine and Sienese painting
Silenus, 180–181, 184
Siphnian Treasury at Delphi, 99
Skopas, 82
Socrates, 41–42
Sophists, 72
Sophocles, 70, 74–75
sōphrosynē, 57
Sopoćani frescoes, 359, 365, 376, 377
Souillac, monastery church of Notre Dame, sculpture, **308**
Spanish Chapel, S. M. Novella, Florence, 486
Speyer Cathedral, bays of, 277, 281, 282
Spoleto, Cathedral of, 367
"square schematism" of Romanesque architecture, 278
stained glass, 365
Stavelot, Monastery of, 366
Stefano, 465
Strangford Apollo, 58–59, **59**
Strassburg Cathedral, 402
Street Musicians (Dioscurides of Samos), 133

Strozzi Chapel, 484
Strozzi family, 482
Strzygowski, Joseph, 257, 261, 277
Styppax, 48
Suger of St. Denis, Abbot, 425
symbolism, medieval, 392, 402–412
  of church architecture, 398–403
  of form, 408–412
  of meaning, 402–408
symmetria, 55, 69

technē, 73
Tell el Amarna, 11
temple pediments, Greek, 43, 47–48, 94–99
Temptations of Christ, detail, mosaic, Kariye Djami, Istanbul, **378**
Terence, 422
Theophrastus, 79
Thesmorphorai, 183, 196
Thucydides, 87
thyrsos, 188
Tournai Shrine reliefs, 374
Traini, Francesco, 484, 485
Trajan's Forum and Markets, Rome, **164–165**
Triumph of Death, The (Traini), 484, **485**
Tukulti-Ninurta, Assyrian palace of, paintings in, 13

Unro of Verden, Bishop, 261
Urban II, Pope, 322–323

van Beuningen altarpiece, 350
Vandals, 389–390
Vanni, Andrea, 321, 475
Vasari, Giorgio, 280, 357, 358, 359, 364, 390, 391
vaulted architecture, 167–168
Vergil (Virgil), 203, 387, 422, 467
Vézelay. *See* Sainte-Madeleine, Abbey Church, at Vézelay
Victoria History of the Counties of England, 259
Villa of the Mysteries, at Pompeii, 173–211
  bridal scenes, 189–191
  confarreatio, 190
  Dionysiac mysteries, 198
  Dionysus and Ariadne, 193–197

Domina, 189–191, 204
  flagellation scene, 186–189
  kline, 190
  Liknon scene, 182–183
  ordo matronarum, 203
  phallus symbol, 182
  statue of Empress Livia, 201–202
  tabellae, 191
Villani, Giovanni, 473, 474–475, 483
Villani, Matteo, 476, 477, 478
Virgin and Child with Saints, mosaic, Torcello, Cathedral, **242**
The Visitation, Reims Cathedral, **430, 431**
Visconti family, 473
Visigoths, 303
Vitruvius, 153, 154
von Hall, Burckhard, 389
Voragine, Jacobus de 335–336

wall paintings
  Egyptian, 12–16
  Hellenistic, from Pompeii, 134–141
Westminster Palace, 270
Westminster Psalter, miniatures in, 374
Wibald, Abbot, 366
Wilhelmshaven-Hessens, house-type discovered at, 263, 265, 266, 268
William of Auvergne, 280
William of Sens, 389
William of Tyre, 322
Wimpfen, church at, 389, 397
Winchester Bible, miniatures in, 373–374
winged monsters, in Assyrian glyptic art, 24–25
Woman and Shepherd (Hellenistic genre painting), 133

Yellow Frieze in the House of Livia, 135

Zackenstil, 376
Zeitstil, concept of, 373
Zeus, 63, 65–66
  temple of, at Acragas, 118
  temple of, at Girgenti, 116
  temple of, at Olympia, 65–66, 87, 93
Zodiac, representations of, 307, 321
Zoroastrianism, 227, 228
Zoser, limestone statue of, **10**